Young Adult Development at the School-to-Work Transition

EMERGING ADULTHOOD SERIES

Books in the Series

Emerging Adults' Religiousness and Spirituality: Meaning-Making in an Age of Transition
Edited by Carolyn McNarnara Barry and Mona M. Abo-Zena

Flourishing in Emerging Adulthood: Positive Development During the Third Decade of Life
Edited by Laura M. Padilla-Walker and Larry J. Nelson

The Marriage Paradox: Why Emerging Adults Love Marriage Yet Push it Aside
Brian J. Willoughby and Spencer L. James

The Life Story, Domains of Identity, and Personality Development in Emerging Adulthood: Integrating Narrative and Traditional Approaches
Michael W. Pratt and M. Kyle Matsuba

The Romantic Lives of Emerging Adults: Getting From I to We
Varda Konstam

Leaving Care and the Transition to Adulthood: International Contributions to Theory, Research, and Practice
Edited by Varda Mann-Feder and Martin Goyette

Young Adult Development at the School-to-Work Transition: International Pathways and Processes
E. Anne Marshall and Jennifer E. Symonds

Young Adult Development at the School-to-Work Transition

International Pathways and Processes

Edited by

E. Anne Marshall and Jennifer E. Symonds

OXFORD
UNIVERSITY PRESS

OXFORD
UNIVERSITY PRESS

Oxford University Press is a department of the University of Oxford. It furthers the University's objective of excellence in research, scholarship, and education by publishing worldwide. Oxford is a registered trade mark of Oxford University Press in the UK and certain other countries.

Published in the United States of America by Oxford University Press
198 Madison Avenue, New York, NY 10016, United States of America.

Library of Congress Cataloging-in-Publication Data
Names: Marshall, E. Anne, 1951– editor. | Symonds, Jennifer, editor.
Title: Young adult development at the school-to-work transition :
international pathways and processes / E. Anne Marshall and Jennifer E. Symonds, editors.
Description: New York, NY : Oxford University Press, [2021] |
Series: Emerging adulthood series |
Includes bibliographical references and index.
Identifiers: LCCN 2020030384 (print) | LCCN 2020030385 (ebook) |
ISBN 9780190941512 (paperback) | ISBN 9780190941536 (epub) |
ISBN 9780190941543
Subjects: LCSH: School-to-work transition. | Career education. |
Young adults—Employment. | High school graduates—Employment. |
College graduates—Employment. | Adulthood.
Classification: LCC LC1037 .Y676 2021 (print) | LCC LC1037 (ebook) |
DDC 371.2/27—dc23
LC record available at https://lccn.loc.gov/2020030384
LC ebook record available at https://lccn.loc.gov/2020030385

DOI: 10.1093/oso/9780190941512.001.0001

1 3 5 7 9 8 6 4 2

Printed by Marquis, Canada

Contents

SECTION 3: SCHOOL EXPERIENCES

SECTION 4: DIVERSE PATHWAYS—VULNERABLE GROUPS

SECTION 5: DIVERSE PATHWAYS—CULTURAL GROUPS AND GLOBALIZATION

Preface

Jeffrey Jensen Arnett

It is my pleasure to write a preface for this important book. There is perhaps no greater challenge in the lives of young people today than finding a secure and satisfying place in the world of work. This book provides a wide range of well-informed perspectives from diverse countries and cultures. In this preface I will preview three themes addressed in the book: the shift to a knowledge economy, the search for identity-based work in emerging adulthood (ages 18–29), and some positive aspects of current economic changes for the future of emerging adults.

The Challenges of the Knowledge Economy

One key to understanding the challenges facing emerging adults today in making this transition is recognizing the worldwide shift from a manufacturing economy to a "knowledge economy" based on information and technology (Arnett, 2015; Carnevale, Jayasundra, & Cheah, 2013; Hippe & Fouquet, 2018). Because of this shift, there has been a dramatic change over the past half century in the kinds of jobs available. For most of the 20th century, developed countries were dominated by an economy with a vigorous and expanding manufacturing sector that provided abundant, well-paying jobs in sectors such as the textile, automobile, and steel industries. Young men—in those days, it was mostly men who were employed—with no more than a high school education (or even less) could get manufacturing jobs that provided relatively high wages, enough to support a wife and children. It was hard work, but it paid extremely well.

Since that time, however, most high-paying manufacturing jobs have disappeared in developed countries, as companies used new technologies to reduce the number of workers needed and moved their manufacturing sites to countries where they could pay lower wages to their remaining workers. Employment has shifted from a manufacturing base to information and services in the developed countries that are the focus of this book. The best service jobs in the knowledge economy require skills in using information and technology, and tertiary education credentials are widely taken as a signal of these skills (Carnevale et al., 2013).

Consequently, emerging adults who have tertiary education credentials have a huge advantage in employment and income compared to those who do not. In the past 25 years, new jobs available for persons with tertiary education have increased substantially, whereas jobs available to persons with a high school degree or less have fallen steeply. Similarly, from the early 1970s to the present, inflation-adjusted incomes rose substantially more for persons with tertiary education than for those without (Carnevale et al., 2013; National Center for Education Statistics, 2018). In fact, incomes declined steeply for workers with a high school degree or less over this period, and their unemployment rates were much higher than for their peers with college degrees. Consequently, in the early years of the 21st century, emerging adults face a workplace situation that is challenging and in some ways formidable, especially if they lack tertiary education credentials.

There is good news as well. Jobs in the knowledge economy are more cognitively challenging and less physically taxing than jobs in the manufacturing economy, so workers can expect to get better at what they do over the course of their careers, rather than being gradually broken down physically in a grueling manufacturing job. Also, manufacturing jobs favored the greater size and strength of men, whereas the knowledge economy evens the scales between the genders. In fact, all over the world young women are more likely than young men to obtain the tertiary education that is the entry ticket to the best jobs in the knowledge economy (OECD, 2018). This change raises the status and economic power of women and opens the possibility for more gender-equal marriage and parenting arrangements.

The Search for Identity-Based Work

Another important shift, abundantly recognized in the chapters of this book, is the shift in what people seek from work. It is no longer enough simply to make enough money to support yourself and, eventually, a family. Today, the search for work in emerging adulthood focuses on identity questions: "What do I really want to *do*? What am I best at? What do I enjoy the most? How do my abilities and interests fit in with the kinds of opportunities that are available to me?" In asking themselves what kind of work they want to do, emerging adults are also asking themselves what kind of person they are. In the course of emerging adulthood, as they try out various jobs they begin to answer their identity questions; that is, they develop a better sense of who they are and what work suits them best. The ideal today is *identity-based work,* a job that you believe makes the most of your talents and interests and that you look forward to doing each day (Arnett, 2015; Baxter-Magolda & Taylor, 2016).

That is a lot to ask out of work, and it is an elusive goal. For most emerging adults, the reality of their work through their 20s is far from this ideal. Usually the road to a stable, long-term job—satisfying or not—is long, with many brief, low-paying, dreary jobs along the way. In the United States, for the average college graduate it takes 4 years to find a job that will last 5 years or more; for emerging adults who have a high school degree and maybe some college, it takes 10 years; and for those who never even graduated from high school, it takes at least 15 years (U.S. Department of Labor, 2012). The average American holds eight different jobs between the ages of 18 and 29.

Most emerging adults would agree it's better to have a job than not to have a job, but many of the jobs they have in their 20s are far from the ideal of identity-based work. In a national survey I directed in the United States, 59% of 18- to 29-year-olds agreed that "I haven't been able to find the kind of job I really want" (Arnett & Schwab, 2012). Often their jobs in their 20s are part-time work, either because they are also going to school or because that is all they can find. Even for those who obtain a college degree, many of them are underemployed for years afterward, doing work that has no relation to what they learned in school and that may not even require a degree (Lauff & Ingels, 2014). Into their mid-20s many of them are still unsure what they want to do, which makes it difficult to search for identity-based work, and even if they know, they may not be able to find a job in that field.

Eventually nearly all find their way to a stable job, if not to an identity-based job. By their late 20s most college grads have found a job they will hold for at least five years. For those who have less education, it may take until their early 30s, but most of them, too, ultimately find a stable job. However, most governments could do a lot more to develop effective policies to assist emerging adults in navigating the entry to the job market. The Scandinavian countries are widely regarded as being at the forefront in this area, providing individualized plans that offer training to emerging adults and link their training to the skills employers need. These countries, along with Germany and Switzerland, also have a long tradition of apprenticeships that remain effective in preparing new workers and linking them to employers (Hamilton & Hamilton, 2006). But these programs cost money, and in the southern European countries that need such programs most because of their astronomical youth unemployment rates, it is difficult to generate funding for a vast new government program, however valuable it might be for young people and for the country's future.

Amidst the Challenges, Some Good News

This book does an excellent job of delineating the many challenges that face young people and their societies in improving the quality and effectiveness of the transition from school to work. Amidst all the difficulties and problems this transition entails, perhaps it is worth recognizing that young people have a better chance than ever before of finding identity-based work. Prior to about a half century ago, when people married and had their first child in their early 20s, men quickly experienced pressure to find a job that would enable them to support a family, and women experienced pressure to leave the work force to devote themselves to caring for the children and running the household. Now, with the postponement of marriage and parenthood into the late 20s, young people can use their emerging adulthood years to seek out satisfying work without the pressure of family obligations. For young women, the range of possible occupations is suddenly vast, greater than it has been for any generation of women in human history.

However, there are will continue to be many daunting challenges in the work lives of emerging adults. With such high expectations for what work will provide to them, with the expectation that their jobs will serve not only as a source of income but as a source of self-fulfillment and self-expression, some of them are likely to find that the actual job they end up in for the long term falls considerably short of this ideal (Arnett, 2015). Also, the knowledge economy of today requires a high level of education for the best jobs, and emerging adults who lack the abilities or opportunities to pursue tertiary education often find themselves excluded from competition for these jobs and left with only the lowest-paying and least-rewarding service jobs (Krahn, Howard, & Galambos, 2012).

More than ever, education is the great divider in adulthood. Emerging adults with tertiary education credentials generally have the happy prospect of a prosperous and comfortable middle-class adult life. Some emerging adults who do not have tertiary education may prove to have an exceptional gift in music or sports or for running a small business. However, for many emerging adults without tertiary education, adulthood can become a perpetual economic struggle, and they are more likely to fall considerably short of the goal of finding satisfying, well-paying, identity-based work. This book, in assembling esteemed scholars to address many different aspects of the work lives of emerging adults, can help inform better public policies to give more emerging adults a chance at reaching something resembling their dreams.

References

Arnett, J. J. (2015). *Emerging adulthood: The winding road from the late teens through the twenties* (2nd ed.). New York, NY: Oxford University Press.

Arnett, J. J., & Schwab, J. (2012). The Clark University Poll of Emerging Adults: Thriving, struggling, and hopeful. *Clark University.* Retrieved from http://www.clarku.edu/clark-poll-emerging-adults/

Baxter Magolda, M. B., & Taylor, K. (2016). Developing self-authorship in emerging adulthood to navigate college. In J. J. Arnett (Ed.), *The Oxford handbook of emerging adulthood* (pp. 299–315). New York, NY: Oxford University Press.

Carnevale, A. P., Jayasundera, T., & Cheahthe, B. (2013, November). The college advantage: Weathering the economic storm. *Georgetown Public Policy Institute, University Center on Education and the Workforce.* Retrieved from https://cew.georgetown.edu/wp-content/uploads/2014/11/CollegeAdvantage.FullReport.081512.pdf

Hamilton, S., & Hamilton, M. A. (2006). School, work, and emerging adulthood. In J. J. Arnett & J. L. Tanner (Eds.), *Coming of age in the 21st century: The lives and contexts of emerging adults* (pp. 257–277). Washington, DC: American Psychological Association.

Hippe, R., & Fouquet, R. (2018). The knowledge economy in historical perspective. *World Economics, 19*(1), 75–108.

Krahn, H. J., Howard, A. J., & Galambos, N. (2012). Exploring or floundering? The meaning of employment and educational fluctuations in emerging adulthood. *Youth & Society, 44*, 1–22. doi:10.1177/0044118X12459061

Lauff, E., & Ingels, S. J. (2014). Education Longitudinal Study of 2002 (ELS:2002): A first look at 2002 high school sophomores 10 years later (NCES 2014-363). *Center for Education Statistics.* Retrieved from https://nces.ed.gov/pubs2014/2014363.pdf

National Center for Education Statistics. (2018). The condition of education, 2018. Retrieved from https://nces.ed.gov/pubs2018/2018144.pdf

OECD. (2018). Education at a glance 2018: OECD indicators. Retrieved from https://doi.org/10.1787/eag-2018-en

U.S. Department of Labor. (2012). Number of jobs held, labor market activity, and earnings growth among the youngest Baby Boomers: Results from a longitudinal survey summary (Economic news release, Table 1). Retrieved from http://www.bls.gov/news.release/nlsoy.nro.htm

Contributors

Jos Akkermans, PhD
Associate Professor
School of Business and Economics
Vrije Universiteit Amsterdam
Amsterdam, The Netherlands

Jeffrey Jensen Arnett, PhD
Senior Research Scholar
Clark University
Worcester, MA, USA

Chelsea Arsenault, MEd
Doctoral Student
Department of Educational Psychology
University of Alberta
Edmonton, Canada

Nancy Arthur, PhD, RPsych (Alberta, Canada)
Dean of Research
Unisa Business
University of South Australia
Adelaide, Australia

Pieter E. Baay, PhD
Researcher
Education ECBO Utrecht
Utrecht, The Netherlands

Wendi Beamish, PhD
Senior Lecturer
School of Education and Professional Studies
Griffith University
Capalaba, Queensland, Australia

Rowena Blokker, MSc, PhD
Department of Management and Organization
Vrije Universiteit Amsterdam
Amsterdam, The Netherlands

Gawaian Bodkin-Andrews, PhD
Professor
Centre for the Advancement of Indigenous Knowledges
University of Technology Sydney
Sydney, Australia

Corine Buers, MSc
Doctoral Researcher
Utrecht University School of Governance
Utrecht University Utrecht
Utrecht, The Netherlands

Deirdre Curle, PhD
Adjunct Instructor
Department of Educational & Counselling Psychology, and Special Education
University of British Columbia
Vancouver, Canada

Michael Davies, PhD
Program Leader/Associate Professor
Counselling and Human Services
Australian Institute of Professional Counsellors
Auchenflower, Australia

Ans De Vos, PhD
Professor
R&V Department
Antwerp Management School
Antwerpen, Belgium

Christopher DeLuca, PhD
Associate Professor
Faculty of Education
Queen's University
Kingston, Canada

Tiziana Di Palma, PhD
Adjunct Professor
Department of Humanities
University of Naples Federico II
Naples, Italy

Eric Dion, PhD
Full Professor
Éducation et formation spécialisées
Université du Québec à Montréal
Montreal, Canada

José F. Domene, PhD, RPsych
Professor
Werklund School of Education
University of Calgary
Calgary, Canada

Véronique Dupéré, PhD
Associate Professor
Psychoeducation
Université de Montréal
Montreal, Canada

Asmae El Bouhali, MSc, MEd
Department of Educational Psychology
University of British Columbia
Vancouver, Canada

Maurice Gesthuizen, PhD
Assistant Professor
Sociology
Radboud University Nijmegen
Wijchen, The Netherlands

Lorraine Godden, PhD, FHEA
Instructor II
Career Development and Employability
Faculty of Public Affairs
Carleton University
South Frontenac
Ontario, Canada

Tammy J. Halstead, EdD
Director of Alumni Advising and Development
Office of Student and Post-Graduate Development
Franklin & Marshall College
Mountville, PA, USA

Kathryn S. Isdale, PhD, MSc
Honorary Research Fellow
Education and Skills Development Programme
Human Sciences Research Council
Cape Town, South Africa

Sarah M. Johnson, MEd
Counsellor
Counselling Services
University of New Brunswick
Fredericton, Canada

Rachel King, MEd, PhD
Psychologist
Mental Health
Grey Nuns Community Hospital
Edmonton, Canada

Denise Larsen, PhD, RPsych
Professor
Department of Educational Psychology
University of Alberta
Edmonton, Canada

Laurence Lavoie, MSc
École de psychoéducation
Université de Montréal
Ottawa, Canada

Breanna Lawrence, PhD
Assistant Professor
Department of Educational Psychology
Brandon University
Brandon, Canada

Vanessa L. Madrazo, PhD
Director
National Alliance on Mental Illness
South Miami, FL, USA

Jenni Menon Mariano, PhD
Professor
Department of Educational Psychology
University of South Florida
Sarasota, FL, USA

E. Anne Marshall, PhD
Adjunct Professor
Department of Educational Psychology and Leadership Studies
University of Victoria
Victoria, Canada

Sheila Marshall, PhD
Professor
School of Social Work
Division of Adolescent Health & Medicine
University of British Columbia
Vancouver, Canada

Selina McCoy, PhD
Professor
Social Research
Economic and Social Research Institute
Dublin, Ireland

Denis W. Meadows, BEd, MSc, PhD
Adjunct Senior Lecturer
Education and Professional Studies
Griffith University
Brisbane, Australia

Todd Milford, PhD
Associate Professor
Curriculum and Instruction
University of Victoria
Victoria, Canada

Ardita Muja, MSc, PhD
Sociology
Radboud University Nijmegen
Nijmegen, The Netherlands

John Murray, MA
Education and Counselling Psychology, and Special Education
University of British Columbia
New Westminster, Canada
Assistant Professor
Department of Educational Psychology
University of Illinois at Urbana–Champaign
Urbana, IL, USA

Christopher M. Napolitano, PhD
Assistant Professor
Department of Educational Psychology
University of Illinois at Urbana Champaign
Urbana, IL, USA

Oana Negru-Subtirica, PhD
Associate Professor
Department of Psychology
Babeş-Bolyai University
Cluj Napoca, Romania

Filomena Parada, PhD
Researcher
Department of Educational Sciences
University of Helsinki
Helsinki, Portugal

Philip D. Parker, PhD
Professor
Institute for Positive Psychology and Education
Australian Catholic University
West Wollongong, Australia

Natalee Popadiuk, PhD, RPsych
Psychologist
Private Practice
Victoria, Canada

Vijay Reddy, PhD
Distinguished Research Specialist
Inclusive Economic Development Research Programme
Human Sciences Research Council
Glenwood, South Africa

Katariina Salmela-Aro, PhD
Professor
Department of Educational Sciences
University of Helsinki
Helsinki, Finland

Mattijs C. Schipper, BA
Team Manager
Social Sciences
Interim Division
Huxley B.V.
Utrecht, The Netherlands

Laura Aleni Sestito
Professor (Retired)
Department of Humanities
University of Naples Federico II
Naples, Italy

Luigia Simona Sica, PhD
Associate Professor
Department of Humanities
University of Naples Federico II
Naples, Italy

Emer Smyth, PhD
Research Professor
Social Research Division
Economic and Social Research Institute
Dublin, Ireland

Tim Stainton, PhD
Director
Canadian Institute for Inclusion and Citizenship
School of Social Work
University of British Columbia
Delta, Canada

Suzanne L. Stewart, PhD
Professor
Dalla Lana School of Public Health
University of Toronto
Toronto, Canada

Jennifer E. Symonds, PhD
Associate Professor
School of Education
University College Dublin
Dublin, Ireland

Éliane Thouin, MSc, PhD
School of Psychoeducation
University of Montreal
Montreal, Canada

Michelle Trudgett, BA, MPS, EdD
Pro Vice-Chancellor
Aboriginal and Torres Strait Islander Education, Strategy and Consultation
Parramatta South Campus
Lane Cove, Australia

Katja Upadyaya, PhD
Postdoctoral Researcher
Faculty of Educational Sciences
University of Helsinki
Oakland, CA, USA

Beatrice Van der Heijden, PhD
Full Professor of Strategic HRM
Head of Department Strategic HRM
Institute for Management Research
Radboud University
Nijmegen, The Netherlands

Jessie Wall, PhD
Registered Clinical Counsellor
Department of Educational and Counselling Psychology, and Special Education
University of British Columbia
Langley, Canada

Maggie Walter, PhD
Professor
School of Social Science
University of Tasmania
Tinderbox, Australia

Lolita D. Winnaar, BSc, BSc (hon), MPhil, DPhil
Senior Research Specialist
Inclusive Economic Development
Human Sciences Research Council
Pretoria, South Africa

Maarten H. J. Wolbers, PhD
Full Professor
Department of Sociology
Radboud University
Nijmegen, The Netherlands

Dan Woodman, PhD
TR Ashworth Associate Professor
Department of Sociology
School of Social and Political Science
University of Melbourne
Parkville, Australia

Siwei Wu, PhD
Assistant Professor
College of Educational Science
Hengyang Normal University
Markham, Canada

Johanna Wyn, PhD
Redmond Barry Emeritus Distinguished Professor
Melbourne Graduate School of Education
University of Melbourne
Melbourne, Australia

Richard A. Young, EdD
Professor
Department of Educational and Counselling Psychology, and Special Education
University of British Columbia
Vancouver, Canada

Ma Zhu, MA
Graduate Student
Department of Educational and Counselling Psychology, and Special Education
University of British Columbia
New Westminster, Canada

Tia Linda Zuze, PhD
Research Fellow
ReSeP
Stellenbosch University
Johannesburg, South Africa

Introduction and Overview

E. Anne Marshall and Jennifer E. Symonds

School-to-work (STW) pathways and transitions are key developmental processes in young adulthood. Recently, the critical importance of planning and flexibility during this time has been highlighted by the coronavirus pandemic and the resulting social, workplace, and economic upheaval. In this book, we examine the social, cultural, familial, contextual, and personal factors that shape STW transitions. Internationally renowned scholars in the fields of developmental psychology, applied psychology, counseling, and sociology have contributed chapters focusing on theory, research and application related to STW and educational transitions. We also give attention to subgroups who have particular transition issues, including young adults with disabilities and special needs, cultural minorities, international students, and migrants.

While many definitions of the STW transition have been proposed, one offered by Wolbers (2013) describes it as "the period between the end of individuals' enrolment in initial education or training and their stable and secure settlement in the labour market" (p. 167). This transition is identified as a "major developmental task" of young adulthood, meaning that its achievement is seen as a key part of a successful transition to adulthood (Dietrich & Salmela-Aro, 2016, p. 334). Obtaining work after finishing education is a crucial marker of the transition to adulthood and a key step in establishing a work identity (Kim, Lee, Lee, & Lee, 2015); however, the STW transition is just one of several markers of the transition from youth to adulthood, along with leaving the family home, finding a long-term partner, and, for some, becoming a parent (Bradley & Devadson, 2008; Brannen & Nilsen, 2002; Young, Marshall, Valach, & Domene, 2010). Unlike the preceding adolescent life stages that are characterized by relatively similar experiences (e.g., living at home and attending secondary school), there is a great deal of variability in the paths young adults take as they navigate the transition to adulthood (Kuron, Lyons, Schweitzer, & Ng, 2015). The transition is further complicated because these different markers are achieved at different times and in different orders (Thomson et al., 2002).

E. Anne Marshall and Jennifer E. Symonds, *Introduction and Overview* In: *Young Adult Development at the School-to-Work Transition.* E. Anne Marshall and Jennifer E. Symonds, Oxford University Press (2021). © Oxford University Press.
DOI: 10.1093/oso/9780190941512.001.0001

Timing of the School-to-Work Transition

The timing of the STW transition varies considerably throughout the literature, based on factors such as disciplinary definitions, national or geographic context, and what specific subgroups are being studied. Young et al. (2010) associate the transition to adulthood with the end of adolescence, while noting that preparing socially, financially, and legally for adulthood often extends into one's 20s and even 30s. Lehmann (2014) describes the SWT as beginning toward the end of secondary school as young people begin to consider their career options. A recent book by Jeffrey Arnett (2015) that provides multiple perspectives on the transition from STW associates it with the period from age 18 to age 25, known as *emerging adulthood.* In comparing transitions across a number of countries, Pastore (2015) notes that the point at which young people are expected to make decisions about their SWTs varies; with countries such as Germany requiring students to make education track decisions as early as age 10, while other countries incorporate greater flexibility to delay such decisions until later adolescence. Some studies focus on the transition of young people who are going straight from secondary school into the workforce, known as *noncollege-bound youth* (NCBY; Ling & O'Brien, 2013), while others investigate the experience of transitioning to the workforce after a period of postsecondary education (e.g., Kuron et al., 2015).

The Nature of the School-to-Work Transition

The nature of STW transitions has also been described in different ways. Several scholars have observed that transitions are impacted both by internal characteristics and external contextual factors (Kim et al., 2015; Lehmann, 2014). Young et al. (2010) emphasize the importance of balancing consideration of the sociopolitical climate with general understandings of this transition period. Wendlandt and Rochlen (2008) describe the transition process as consisting of three distinct stages: *anticipation*, or the exploratory process before entering into an organization; *adjustment*, as young adults actually begin working for an organization, they orient themselves to the culture of their workplace and establish a reputation as a worker; and finally, *achievement*, where individuals solidify their understanding of themselves in the work environment, which often involves a renegotiation of values. Bradley and Devadson (2008) divide young people's transitions into three patterns: pursuing higher education to secure a more stable and high-status job, working in short-term careers in positions that require lower skill levels, or working in noncareer unskilled labor jobs. Anticipation of transitional phases can be helpful in the planning process, however, Brannen and Nilsen (2002) contend that a standard set of specific and ordered stages is not a realistic way to describe the transition from STW, due to increased variability in the paths young people take to enter the labor market. Moreover, the widespread work-related changes and uncertainty associated with the Covid 19 global pandemic has increased the variability of STW transition opportunities and experiences for young adults (OECD, 2020).

Identity

STW transitions are intermingled with identity development processes. Engagement involves actively pursuing career objectives and building a work identity (Akkermans, Brenninkmeijer, Schaufeli, & Blonk, 2015), although some young adults feel adrift and not ready for long-term work commitments (Marshall & Butler, 2016). Young people consider work as a key piece of their identity; thus, it impacts their overall well-being, particularly if their expectations of success are not met (Marshall & Butler, 2016). Baxter Magolda and Taylor (2016) describe *self-authorship* as the capacity to base decisions on internal factors such as critical thinking, ethical and moral compasses, and mature intercultural relationships; they maintain that this "way of organizing meaning [allows young adults] to mediate external influences and internally define their own beliefs, identities and relationships" (p. 301). Dietrich and Salmela-Aro (2016) note that renegotiation of identity may occur in response to identity conflicts and feedback that does not match with the young adult's view of self. They also caution against equating the length of identity exploration with its quality; lengthy identity rumination and repeated reconsideration are not typically beneficial in the long run.

Influence on Later Career Outcomes

Research shows that while it is normal for the STW transition period to be marked by some degree of uncertainty, the nature of the initial transition period has long-term impacts on future career trajectories (Wolbers, 2013). Dorsett and Lucchino (2014) offer one interpretation of successful transitions as either a smooth move from secondary education to the labor market or a long period of education followed by employment, as compared to unsuccessful transitions involving neither education nor employment for a prolonged period of time. These authors found that 90% of their British sample of young adults experienced a "successful" transition. Likewise, Schoon and Lyons Amos (2016), using British national cohort data, found clusters of young adults who either participated in extended education, had some higher education and then were continuously employed, went straight from education into work, or were excluded from work through unemployment or inactivity. Unfortunately, claims of successful employment outcomes have often been linked somewhat limiting overall national or regional employment and unemployment figures, while factors such as job stability and work quality that also affect success have often been overlooked (Ling & O'Brien, 2013; Quintini & Martin, 2014). In a review of work-readiness programs for unemployed young adults, Symonds and O'Sullivan (2017) identified that program outcomes were predominantly measured using broad brush indicators such as employment and education statistics, rather than refined indicators of transferrable human capital competencies for adaptive career functioning, such as motivation, self-regulation, higher-order thinking skills, social skills, and work engagement.

Factors That Influence the Transition Process

Individual Factors

Diverse factors contributing to a successful or challenging transition from STW have been identified. Feighery (2013) emphasizes the role of *social capital* or the "network of relationships of 'mutual acquaintance and recognition'" (p. 65). Building and maintaining this network is held to be a key career competence for adaptive functioning at the STW transition (Akkermans et al., 2015). Active, directed personal engagement with the activities made available by social structures is also an important individual factor in how young adults manage the transition process (Schoon & Heckhausen, 2019). Dietrich and Salmela-Aro (2016) describe *phase-adequate work engagement*, which is "intentionally engaging in behavior that is appropriate in meeting the demands related to the transition to work life" (p. 335). Along with Akkermans et al. (2015), these authors also speak about *career adaptability*, which involves career concern, control/decision-making, curiosity, and confidence and leads to positive outcomes, including a better chance of meaningful employment after education.

A factor that is increasingly evident in the STW transition literature is the role of chance events in career development; the coronavirus pandemic is a dramatic illustration of this. Kim et al. (2015) note that the ability to transform chance events into learning opportunities is a vital skill for successful transitions; this skill can act as a buffer against the ill effects of negative influences on career trajectories, increasing young adults' resilience in the STW transition. Hirschi (2010) also emphasizes the impact of chance events on young adults' career paths such as unexpected barriers to achieving career objectives or "being at the right place at the right time" (p. 47). Almost two thirds of the adolescents in Hirschi's study perceived chance events as having a strong influence on their upcoming or ongoing transition from compulsory education to the workforce. Chance events often affect the work choices that are available. Some research suggests that young adults who find themselves in a job that they entered as the result of a chance event results in lower job satisfaction; other studies have found no effect or a positive outcome from chance events (Marshall & Butler, 2016).

Relational Factors

Relational context is an important factor—other people directly and indirectly affect transitions to and engagement in work in multiple ways (Domene, et al., 2012). Young people "make meaning by interpreting their experiences and reinterpreting them in light of their interactions with important others and thereby craft a personal narrative that provides life with purpose" (Baxter Magolda & Taylor, 2016, p. 300).

Co-regulation refers to support and collaboration, as well as others' level of involvement (Salmela-Aro, 2009). At the beginning of the STW transition period, parents are typically the most influential. Parental support is related to "career self-efficacy and career identity formation and evaluation" and young people are more satisfied with their transition when parents are involved and supportive (Dietrich & Salmelo-Aro, 2016, p. 340). The closer young adults are to their parents, the more distraught they will be if their parents disapprove of the career choice and the more likely they are to change it (Marshall & Butler, 2016). They need support from their parents but also freedom to make their own choices. Over time, friends and partners become more important, but parents remain influential as well (Dietrich & Salmela-Aro, 2016). Goals can be shared with significant others; for example, in romantic partnerships, goals may relate to the couple or to one specific person but supported by the other. Marshall and Butler (2016) identify that romantic partners are an important consideration, as people have to accommodate their partners' goals and want to support them. This involves balancing time together, negotiating the timing of starting a family, and deciding where to live. Siblings can have an influence on young people's transition (Aaltonen, 2016). They can offer emotional support, informational support, and examples to either follow or avoid. Workplace relationships also have an important role to play in the transition from STW; relationships with supervisors and coworkers have been found to be supportive during the transition process (Marshall & Butler, 2016).

Even as the STW transition is recognized as relational, focus on the transition as an individual pursuit is increasing with time. In Norway, a cohort of men born between 1948 and 1953 described the transition more in relational and sociocultural terms, while a comparative cohort born in 1978 and 1979 painted it more as an individualized decision-making activity (Chelsom Vogt, 2018). Although relational factors are central to the transition, this example shows how the broader structural forces and social webs of individual lives can shift in salience depending on the individual, context, and era.

Recent Changes in School-to-Work Transitions

Considerable scholarly research and writing have focused on recent changes in the STW transition process. Bradley and Devadson (2008) claim that the transition takes longer in these contemporary times due to increased exploration, more participation in higher education, and the difficulty in finding stable long-term employment. They specify that changes in the labor market due to globalization, technology, and the increased participation of women in the workforce over the last 40 years require workers to be increasingly more flexible to adapt to evolving demands. Similarly, Feighery (2013) asserts that today's labor market is different from that of previous generations, making transitions longer and less predictable. Several researchers have identified that more young people are participating in higher education and the average length of time spent in school has increased in response to the demand for skilled workers (Brannen & Nilsen, 2002; Symonds & Hagell, 2011; Wolbers, 2013; Young et al., 2010). Contemporary STW transitions are characterized by variability, lack of certainty, and fast-paced change (Dietrich & Salmela-Aro, 2016). The older generation of workers is not yet ready for retirement, leaving fewer opportunities for jobs, while the increase in postsecondary education attainment causes people to delay entry into the workforce (Marshall & Butler, 2016). Labor force mobility makes investment in employees less necessary, while the *marketizing of education* makes it more important to build social and professional capital to break into the labor force (Feighery, 2013).

A recent overview of the STW transition in emerging adulthood by Marshall and Butler (2016) addresses several of the factors that impact young people's transitions to employment. Globalization and technology are two factors they highlight that significantly affect the STW process. Young adults are heavily impacted by globalization because of the co-occurrence of global events with their life transitions and development (examples include the 2008 global financial crisis and the 2020 coronavirus pandemic). Marshall & Butler provide a relational perspective that acknowledges the crucial impact of significant others on emerging adults' transitions and identify the variety of paths from STW that young people are taking. They also identify patterns and challenges relevant to particular groups, such as Indigenous young adults and immigrants.

Overview of Chapters

The authors in this book are addressing the previously highlighted social, political, economic, and workforce changes that are affecting young adults transitioning to the world of work. The 21 chapters are organized into six sections: personal resources, social resources, school experiences, vulnerable groups, cultural groups/globalization, and the nature of the STW transition as a definable and debatable concept.

The first section on personal resources focuses on young adults' mental attributes that help construct their STW experiences. The chapters center on how young adults actively direct their personal resources to accrue social resources that support their transition through different educational and work activities. Upadyaya Symonds, and Salmela-Aro examine how people's ability to engage in studies or work through self-directed emotional, motivational, and physical action develops across adolescence and young adulthood, through an embedded quantitative case study of Finnish participants. They identify how this development can diffract or intensify at points of educational and occupational transition and connect the development of engagement to personal well-being. Baay, Napolitano, and Schipper query the contribution of preparedness and opportunity in young adults' chance events that impact their STW transition (e.g., being offered a job unexpectedly). They find that in in a Dutch sample young adults create their own serendipity by being better prepared and networked, which appears to encourage "lucky" events to occur and gives young adults more confidence to pursue them. Madrazo and Mariano assess the role and development of *purpose* in life in young adults' career trajectories. They present case studies from the United States, illustrating young adults with a clear sense of purpose and follow these cases into their careers to determine what is done and can be done to support young people to experience a purposeful transition to work. Finally, Akkermans, Blokker, Buers, Van der Heijden, and De Vos introduce key personal career competencies that are adaptive for young adults' employability and discuss the notion of employability in the context of agency and structural factors that shape young adults' careers in modern societies.

The second section considers social resources that support and shape young adults' STW transitions: romantic relationships, parental relationships, economic and social structures, and national policies. Domene and Johnson examine the intersection of romantic relationships and STW transitions, with a focus on the interpersonal negotiation and pursuit of career goals. Two case studies of Canadian young adults illustrate the negotiation of career goals between romantic partners as they transition from university into work. Sica, Sestito, and Di Palma present a conceptualization of parents as co-authors and identity agents in young adults' life and work stories in Italy. They discuss the impact of delayed departure from the family home on young adults' autonomy and parents' role in co-constructing their young adult children's vocational identity, using a narrative approach. Parada critically reviews the patterns and timings of young adult STW transitions in Greece, Italy, Portugal, and Spain, making note of how these available economic and societal structural supports impact broader areas of life functioning. She discusses how the current economic situations in the South of Europe have important implications for the way young adults conceptualize and navigate the STW transition. Finally, Godden and DeLuca present a detailed case study of the STW transition policy in Ontario, Canada, using a person-in-context framework to analyze the impact of policy on individual and systemic factors.

The school experiences section focuses on how education systems contribute to young adults' career trajectories in the diverse cultural contexts of Ireland, South Africa, Canada, and the Netherlands. Smyth and McCoy track young adults' school-leaving destinations in Ireland, identifying the impact of personal factors including gender, social class, and academic attainment on postschool pathways. They enrich our understanding by demonstrating that school climate helps consolidate young adults' habitus of social advantage or disadvantage by further shaping postschool pathways independently of personal factors such as attainment. Isdale and colleagues analyze a longitudinal study of South African youth to find varying patterns of educational progression including continued education, staggered education, and dropout. They examine the role of personal educational expectations and school type to identify how these pathways emerged. Lavoie, Thouin, Dupéré, and Dion critically review the notion of school dropout and explore the types of STW pathways young adults' experience after dropping out of school in Canada. They discuss pathway antecedents, prevention programs for high school dropouts, and promotion programs for helping disadvantaged young adults obtain employment and education. Finally, Muja, Gesthuizen, and Wolbers perform a detailed analysis of the vocational specificity of different education systems in Europe. They introduce a framework of vocational specificity at the levels of the individual, study program, and education system, which helps clarify the extent to which young adults are exposed to vocational education before school-leaving and the relationship between vocational specificity and postschool outcomes.

The fourth section explores the STW transition for vulnerable groups including young adults with intellectual disability, those formerly in care, and those with diverse range of special educational needs. Curle and co-authors highlight the specific transitional needs of young people with intellectual disabilities and their families. They use contextual-action theory to conceptualize the joint construction and strategizing around the STW transition these young people undertake with their families. King, Arsenault, and Larsen call attention to key factors that impact STW transitions of youth aging out of government care. While many barriers exist for these youth, the authors argue that personal and mediated focus on hope can mitigate some of these barriers and lead to more positive transition outcomes. Finally, Milford, Lawrence, Beamish, Davies, and Meadows report on a collaboration between a university and educational district with the purpose of supporting the STW transition for young people with special needs. The authors outline the history and context of Australian STW transitions, present findings from surveys completed by staff and parents, describe capacity building approaches used in the schools, and summarize the initiative's main achievements.

The fifth section looks at STW transitions among different cultural groups. Marshall and Stewart explore the factors that affect Indigenous young adult educational and work transitions. They bring together findings from qualitative research projects in Canada that highlight cultural issues, options, and pathways for these young people. Parker, Bodkin-Andrews, Trudgett, and Walter explore geographic, economic, sociological, cognitive, and noncognitive predictors of downward mobility and university dropout among Indigenous Australian youth. They suggest that structural barriers prevent younger generations from accessing higher education and suggest that Indigenous research paradigms can be the key to unraveling these issues and barriers. Popadiuk and Arthur describe the findings of a qualitative study on international students' STW transitions, with a specific focus on overcoming barriers. The main categories that emerged from this research were the self, relationships, organizations, and society, and these are analyzed from a relational theoretical framework. Last, Negru-Subtirica introduces readers to the trend of early career exploration outside of one's home country. She presents an overview of multiple perspectives on previous research on transnational transitions to work, and a case study of labor migration among Romanian youth. This is followed by discussion of policy implications for facilitating occupational and social integration of migrant youth.

In the sixth section, the nature of the STW transition is presented through two lenses. In the first, Halstead takes an occupational psychology perspective, conceptualizing the STW transition as a metamorphosis, where young adults' pathways through the diverse and altered social context, and experiences of being emerging adults result in new individual psychological and behavioral phenomena. In the second, Wyn and Woodman take a critical sociological perspective, questioning the STW transition as a phase of individually directed development by drawing attention to the social and cultural structures that shape lives in nonlinear ways. They reposition this developmental construct within the broader notion of a new adulthood, moving away from its distinction as an individual phase.

Summary

The STW transition for young, or emerging, adults is a complex process that is impacted by multiple and intersecting factors. The timing of the transition varies greatly, and its co-occurrence with a number of other life transitions makes it challenging to summarize or generalize. While some authors identify ordered stages, others argue this cannot accurately capture the complex and varied experiences of STW transitions. The identity formation that occurs during this period of life both influences and is influenced by the transition process, not least because the process has been shown to have a strong influence on the course of later career development. Much research has been dedicated to the exploration of what helps and hinders young adults as they move from education to the workforce, including the impact of factors such as culture and socioeconomic status, and recommendations have been offered to those wishing to understand and support young adults from particular populations (e.g., Marshall & Butler, 2016; Symonds & O'Sullivan, 2017). Some of the challenges associated with navigating this transition have to do with individual differences and normative developmental factors, while other challenges relate to external contextual factors such as changing economic circumstances, global events, and cultural shifts. The chapters in this book highlight the trends, issues, and actions that researchers, academics, practitioners, and policymakers need to consider to effectively support young adults' transition to work pathways.

References

Aaltonen, S. (2016). "My mother thought upper secondary school was OK, but then my sibling said no": Young people's perceptions of the involvement of parents and siblings in their future choices. *Sociological Research Online*, *21*(1), 1–12.

Akkermans, J., Brenninkmeijer, V., Schaufeli, W. B., & Blonk, R. W. B. (2015). It's all about CareerSKILLS: Effectiveness of a career development intervention for young employees. *Human Resource Management*, *54*(4), 533–551. doi:10.1002/hrm.21633

Arnett, J. (2015). *The Oxford handbook of emerging adulthood.* New York, NY: Oxford University Press.

Baxter Magolda, M. B., & Taylor, K. (2016). Emerging adults and work: A model of phase-adequate engagement. In J. J. Arnett (Ed.), *The Oxford handbook of emerging adulthood* (pp. 299–315). New York, NY: Oxford University Press.

Bradley, H., & Devadason, R. (2008). Fractured transitions: Young adults' pathways into contemporary labour markets. *Sociology*, *42*(1), 119–136.

Brannen, J., & Nilsen, A. (2002). Young people's time perspectives: From youth to adulthood. *Sociology*, *36*(3), 513–537.

Dietrich, J., & Salmela-Aro, K. (2016). Emerging adults and work: A model of phase-adequate engagement. In J. J. Arnett (Ed.), *The Oxford handbook of emerging adulthood* (pp. 316–333). New York, NY: Oxford University Press.

Domene, J. F., Nee, J. J., Cavanaugh, A. K., McLelland, S., Stewart, B. L., Stephenson, M., . . . Young, R. A. (2012). Young adult couples transitioning to work: The intersection of career and relationship. *Journal of Vocational Behavior*, *18*, 17–25. doi:10.1016/j.jvb.2012.03.005.

Dorsett, R., & Lucchino, P. (2014). Explaining patterns in the school-to-work transition: An analysis using optimal matching. *Advances in Life Course Research*, *22*, 1–14.

Feighery, W. G. (2013). Cultural diversity and the school-to-work transition: A relational perspective. In G. Tchibozo (Ed.), *Cultural and social diversity and the transition from education to work* (pp. 55–85). New York, NY: Springer.

Hirschi, A. (2010). The role of chance events in the school-to-work transition: The influence of demographic, personality and career development variables. *Journal of Vocational Behavior*, *77*(1), 39–49.

Kim, B., Lee, B.H., Ha, G., Lee, H. K., & Lee, S. M. (2015). Examining longitudinal relationships between dysfunctional career thoughts and career decision-making self-efficacy in school-to-work transition. *Journal of Career Development*, *42*(6), 511–523.

Kuron, L. K., Lyons, S. T., Schweitzer, L., & Ng, E. S. W. (2015). Millennials' work values: Differences across the school to work transition. *Personnel Review*, *44*(6), 991–1009.

Lehmann, W. (2014). *Choosing to labour: School-work transitions and social class.* Montreal, QC: McGill-Queen's University Press.

Ling, T. J., & O'Brien, K. M. (2013). Connecting the forgotten half: The school-to-work transition noncollege-bound youth. *Journal of Career Development*, *40*(4), 347–367.

Marshall, E. A., & Butler, K. (2016). School-to-work transitions in emerging adulthood. In J. J. Arnett (Ed.), *The Oxford handbook of emerging adulthood* (pp. 316–333). New York, NY: Oxford University Press.

Quintini, G., & Martin, S. (2014). Same same but different: School-to-work transitions in emerging and advanced economies (OECD Social, Employment and Migration Working Papers). Retrieved from https://doi.org/10.1787/1815199X

Salmela-Aro, K. (2009). Personal goals and well-being during critical life transitions: The four C's—Channelling, choice, co-agency and compensation. *Advances in Life Course Research, 14*(1-2), 63–73. doi.org/10.1016/j.alcr.2009.03.003

Schoon, I., & Heckhausen, J. (2019). Conceptualizing individual agency in the transition from school to work: A social-ecological developmental perspective. *Adolescent Research Review, 4*(2), 135–148. doi:10.1007/s40894-019-00111-3

Schoon, I., & Lyons-Amos, M. (2016). Diverse pathways in becoming an adult: The role of structure, agency and context. *Research in Social Stratification and Mobility, 6*(Pt. A), 11–20. doi:10.1016/j.rssm.2016.02.008

Schoon, I., & Mann, A. (2020). School-to-work transitions during coronavirus: Lessons from the 2008 Global Financial Crisis. *OECD Education and Skills Today.* Retrieved from https://oecdedutoday.com/school-work-during-coronavirus-2008-global-financial-crisis/

Symonds, J. E., & Hagell, A. (2011). Adolescents and the organisation of their school time: a review of changes over recent decades in England. *Educational Review, 63*(3), 291–312. doi:10.1080/00131911.2011.560248

Symonds, J., Schoon, I., & Salmela-Aro, K. (2016). Developmental trajectories of emotional disengagement from schoolwork and their longitudinal associations in England. *British Educational Research Journal, 42*(6), 993–1022. doi:10.1002/berj.3243

Symonds, J., & O'Sullivan, C. (2017). Educating young adults to be work-ready in Ireland and the United Kingdom: A review of programmes and outcomes. *Educational Review, 5*(3), 229–263. doi:10.1002/rev3.3099

Thomson, R., Bell, R., Holland, J., Henderson, S., McGrellis, S., & Sharpe, S. (2002). Critical moments: Choice, chance and opportunity in young people's narratives of transition. *Sociology, 36*(2), 335–354.

Vogt, K. C. (2018). From job-seekers to self-searchers: Changing contexts and understandings of school-to-work transitions. *Young, 26*(4 Suppl), 18S–33S.

Wendlandt, N. M., & Rochlen, A. B. (2008). Addressing the college-to-work transition: Implications for university career counsellors. *Journal of Career Development, 35*, 151–65.

Wolbers, M. H. J. (2013). Introduction: Research on school-to-work transitions in Europe. *European Societies, 16*(2), 167–174.

Young, R. A., Marshall, S. K., Valach, L., & Domene, J. (2010). Transition to adulthood: Introduction. In R. A. Young, S. K. Marshall, L. Valach, J. F. Domene, M. D. Graham, & A. Zaidman-Zait (Eds.), *Transition to adulthood* (pp. 1–9). New York, NY: Springer.

SECTION 1
PERSONAL RESOURCES

1

The Development of Study and Work Engagement in Young Adulthood

Katja Upadyaya, Jennifer E. Symonds, and Katariina Salmela-Aro

Introduction

In young adulthood, individuals experience many personal, social, and environmental changes. They also undergo multiple types of transitions in main activity (e.g., the school-to-work transition), romantic relationships, and living arrangements. Because of these rapid and significant shifts, it is important for young adults to maintain their study-and work-related well-being, which includes being engaged in their studies/work (Upadyaya & Salmela-Aro, 2017). During this developmental period, which Arnett (2000) and others have called "emerging adulthood," completing one's studies and starting a career are main developmental tasks, and engagement in studies/work helps young adults move forward with these tasks. However, only a few studies have examined the development of study and work engagement across young adulthood and its embedded educational and work transitions (e.g., Symonds, Schoon, Eccles, & Salmela-Aro, 2019; Upadyaya & Salmela-Aro, 2013a).

Researchers examining how engagement develops across young adulthood have found that while most young adults have high engagement in their studies and later on at work, some young adults experience decreases in engagement or have a stable, low level of engagement across the transition between studying and working (Upadyaya & Salmela-Aro, 2013a). This variety of engagement trajectories might reflect the complex array of personal, social, study, and work-related demands and resources that young adults experience (Demerouti, Bakker, Nachreiner, & Schaufeli, 2001; Salmela-Aro & Upadyaya, 2014). For example, higher self-efficacy (a personal resource) is often associated with higher engagement in studying (Salmela-Aro & Upadyaya, 2014) and working (Bakker & Demerouti, 2008; Xanthopoulou, Bakker, Demerouti, & Schaufeli, 2009), whereas stress and strain can lead to

Katja Upadyaya, Jennifer E. Symonds, and Katariina Salmela-Aro, *The Development of Study and Work Engagement in Young Adulthood* In: *Young Adult Development at the School-to-Work Transition.* E. Anne Marshall and Jennifer E. Symonds, Oxford University Press (2021). © Oxford University Press. DOI: 10.1093/oso/9780190941512.003.0001.

difficulties in studying (Salmela-Aro & Upadyaya, 2014) and working (Bakker, Demerouti, & Schaufeli, 2003; Upadyaya, Vartiainen, & Salmela-Aro, 2016). Further, engagement in studies and work is often positively associated with several adaptive outcomes, such as learning (Salanova, Agut, & Peiro, 2005); adaptation, feelings of connectedness (Furrer & Skinner, 2003; Libbey, 2004); commitment (Hakanen, Bakker, & Schaufeli, 2006); values, goals, participation in classroom activities (Fredricks, Blumenfeld, & Paris, 2004); and psychological well-being (Li & Lerner, 2011).

In the present chapter, we review the diverse pathways of study and work engagement in young adulthood, the role of various personal and environmental demands and resources that might promote or hinder engagement, and the co-development of study/work engagement and well-being. In addition, we use the perspectives of demands and resources (Bakker & Demerouti, 2017; Bakker, Demerouti, De Boer, & Schaufeli, 2003), conservation of resources (Hobfoll, 2001), and person–environment fit theory (Eccles & Roeser, 2009) to interpret the broader pattern of results. We begin by discussing conceptualizations of study/work engagement and then discuss how engagement develops in relation to various personal and environmental resources and demands in the context of study/work. Next, we trace the development of study/work engagement in Finnish young adults, referring to a large sample studied across the past 15 years. In the context of these participants, we demonstrate how engagement co-develops with study/work well-being, discussing the mechanisms of this interaction from the perspectives of spillover, developmental cascades, and demands and resources theories. We conclude by identifying general trends in engagement observed in Finland and elsewhere and suggest implications for practice.

Aspects of Study and Work Engagement

Typically, study/work engagement is conceptualized as a multidimensional construct (Upadyaya & Salmela-Aro, 2013a). Different research traditions use different sets of dimensions, tied to notable researchers, and the apparent utility of those dimensions in the field. In one approach, student engagement is thought to comprise psychological, academic, social, behavioral, cognitive, and affective components (Appleton, Christenson, & Furlong, 2008; Appleton, Christenson, Kim, & Reschly, 2006; Finn & Voelkl, 1993; Fredricks et al., 2004) of which behavior, cognition, and emotion have been investigated the most (Jimerson, Campos, & Greif, 2003). *Psychological* engagement refers to students' sense of belonging, identification with studies, and sense of relatedness, whereas *academic* engagement describes time used on a task, earned credits, and homework completion (Appleton et al., 2008, 2006). *Social* engagement refers to interrelationships between students, peers, and educators (Wang & Hofkens, 2019); collaboration with other students in the classroom (Fredricks et al., 2016); and attendance at different social activities at school/work (Rumberger & Larson, 1998). The *affective* or *emotional* component describes students' interest in study challenges, positive and negative reactions to teachers and classmates, and attitudes toward academic tasks (Appleton et al., 2008; Finn, 1989; Fredricks et al., 2004; Jimerson et al., 2003). The *cognitive* component further describes students' investment in studies and willingness to learn and exert the necessary effort in studying (Appleton et al., 2008; Fredricks et al., 2004; Jimerson et al., 2003). Finally, the *behavioral* component describes one's involvement, being present at classes, and complying with the rules (Appleton et al., 2008; Finn & Voelkl, 1993; Fredricks et al., 2004; Jimerson et al., 2003). These components are used separately or in combination within individual studies and are often positively associated with each other (Fredricks et al., 2004).

Another engagement approach describes study/work engagement in terms of three dimensions: dedication, energy, and absorption (Salanova et al., 2005; Schaufeli, Bakker, & Salanova, 2006). These dimensions position students' and workers' psychological engagement as similar to flow, a state of deep and complete absorption in an activity (Csikszentmihalyi, 1990). However, in the study/work conceptualization, each dimension has a discrete focus (Salmela-Aro & Upadyaya, 2012). Of these three dimensions, *energy* refers to high mental resilience while studying/working, a willingness to invest effort in one's studies/work, and a positive approach toward studies and work (Salmela-Aro & Upadyaya, 2012; Schaufeli, Salanova et al., 2002), representing the combination of volition and motivation. Energy has been described as a central element of study/work engagement, promoting the two other engagement dimensions (i.e., dedication and absorption; Upadyaya & Salmela-Aro, 2015). *Dedication* is characterized by a sense of significance, meaningfulness, enthusiasm, pride, identification, and inspiration (Schaufeli, Salanova et al., 2002), representing a more latent psychological orientation to studying/working that interacts with energy. *Absorption* is characterized by behavioral accomplishments, concentrating, and being happily engrossed in one's studies/work so that time passes quickly (Schaufeli, Salanova et al., 2002). Similar to the five dimension model described earlier, these three dimensions can be researched as separate or conjoined aspects of study/work engagement and correlate highly with each other (see also Seppälä et al., 2009, for construct validity and factor structure).

Recently, researchers have developed a third perspective on engagement, where engagement is conceptualized as a dynamic system of motivation, emotion, and mental and physical action occurring in momentary time (Symonds et al., 2020). These components of engagement continually co-act in mutually influencing and non-linear ways, shaping each other and the engagement system as a whole. For example, for a student to study in a library, they must utilize their motivation and control their mental and physical action to generate engagement in studying. As part of that engagement, they will feel different emotions (e.g., peacefulness or frustration), which can act to help or hinder their mental action. The dynamic system perspective does not prevent researchers from investigating components of engagement separately, but it does draw attention to the importance of seeing the components as inherently interconnected and the nonlinear ways in which they might co-act. Momentary engagement also interacts externally with context and with other aspects of psychology such as attitudes toward learning that build more slowly over momentary time.

In line with the momentary engagement perspective (Symonds et al., 2020), research on engagement occurring across situations has shown that approximately 50% of students' engagement with school is situation specific and that students' emotional and behavioral engagement is sensitive to varying learning situations, domains, and lesson contents (Vasalampi et al., 2016). Thus, students modify their behavior according to the situational factors that surround them and influence their involvement and engagement in the current task. This means that a variety of situational resources (e.g., support from others) and demands (e.g., stress related to completing the task) may shape engagement, and over time, these processes may become more stable and typical to certain students or young adults (e.g., person-related variation in engagement). In sum, engagement in studying and working can be conceptualized as a momentary phenomenon that comprises emotional, cognitive, and behavioral functioning directed toward task involvement. Over time, patterns of engaged behavior are thought to converge into more stable trait-like phenomena, while at the same time, each episode of engagement becomes situation specific.

In the following section, we consider how specific aspects of engagement (drawing broadly from the previously described conceptualizations) manifest across adolescence and young adulthood. Owing to the broad and ambiguous nature of the overall engagement concept, we pay close attention in our review to which aspects of engagement have been measured and how. We are also critically aware of the grain size (Sinatra, Heddy & Lombardi, 2015) at which engagement is measured in relation to time, meaning how engagement is captured as occurring over different time periods, including years, months, weeks, days, and moments. For example, longitudinal measures typically conceptualize engagement in study or work as a latent concept (e.g., "I enjoy working") that represents general attitudes that have developed over longer time periods, whereas situational measures take snapshots of real-time situations (e.g., "I am enjoying the work activity I am doing right now"). This is important because participants' reflections of engagement across, within, and during time are conceptually and empirically different from each other.

Mechanisms of Study and Work Engagement Development in Young Adulthood

In Western societies there are many environmental, personal, and social changes that characterize the school-to-work transition (Marshall & Butler, 2015; also see Akkermans, Blokker, Buers, Van der Heijden, & De Vos, this volume; Domene & Johnson, this volume; Muja, Gesthuizen, & Wolbers, this volume). In the study/work domain, these changes include moving into more selective educational systems such as technical colleges and universities (where subject choice is more differentiated and personalized than during secondary schooling), entering a wide range of occupational sectors with an abundance of entry-level short-term contract jobs, taking on part-time employment to buffer a delayed transition to full-time employment or education, and doing numerous alternative main activities, such as full-time caregiving, taking a gap year, or having longer-term or multiple short-term spells of unemployment (Parker, Thoemmes, Duineveld & Salmela-Aro, 2015; Symonds, Schoon & Salmela-Aro, 2016).

Transfer into each of these main activities brings young adults into contact with a different set of environmental resources and demands that can impact the development of their engagement with studies and work. This process can be understood, even outside of the employment context, using the Job Demands-Resources (JD-R) model (Bakker & Demerouti, 2017; Bakker et al., 2003; Demerouti et al., 2001). Research using this model has shown that key environmental and personal demands and resources tied to the activity context often predict young adults' study-/work-related engagement, which, in turn, is negatively associated with educational/occupational stress and burnout (e.g., exhaustion, cynicism, feelings of inadequacy at work; Salmela-Aro & Upadyaya, 2014).

Demands that can hinder or promote young adult's engagement include those aspects of studying and work that create physical strain and emotional and psychological costs (Demerouti et al., 2001). Study/work demands are not necessarily initially negative; however, demands may turn into stressors when the strain they are causing becomes high and when multiple demands are present simultaneously (Bakker et al., 2003). Contextual study and work demands include, for example, workload and time pressure (Bakker et al., 2003). Psychological demands are those aspects of studies/work that also present challenges in the educational context or workplace such as perceived setbacks to achieving study-related goals (Salmela-Aro & Upadyaya, 2014) and emotional strain (Bakker et al., 2003). Demands are often associated with burnout symptoms, which, in turn, may lead to subsequent health problems and depression (Bakker & Demerouti, 2017). However, resources may help in reducing the negative influence of demands on one's well-being and achievement.

Resources include the aspects of a person or study/work that (a) help in reducing demands and the related costs; (b) help in achieving study/work-related goals; and (c) stimulate personal growth, development, and learning (Bakker & Demerouti, 2017; Demerouti et al., 2001). Psychological resources such as self-efficacy, self-esteem, resilience, and optimism positively predict high subsequent study and/or work engagement (Bakker & Demerouti, 2008; Salmela-Aro & Upaydaya, 2014; Xanthopoulou et al., 2009). Similarly, environmental resources (e.g., social support, opportunities for autonomy) are positively associated with higher stable study/work engagement trajectories (Mäkikangas, Bakker, Aunola, & Demerouti, 2010), which, in turn, are associated with an adaptive transition to higher education/work (Upadyaya & Salmela-Aro, 2013b). Even family-related resources (e.g., parental affect and monitoring), which are outside of the immediate studies/work context, tend to be associated with young people reporting greater engagement over time, across the transition from postsecondary studies to work, whereas young adults with lower levels of family environmental resources exhibit less positive engagement trajectories (Upadyaya & Salmela-Aro, 2013a).

Various personal and study/work related demands and resources evoke different types of processes that further influence young adults' engagement and well-being (Demerouti et al., 2001). For example, high demands that exhaust one's physical and psychological resources may evoke an energetic process of wearing out, which can ultimately lead to burnout followed by health problems (Schaufeli & Bakker, 2004). However, adequate personal and study/work related resources often lead to the development of motivational resources that promote involvement in work activities (Schaufeli & Bakker, 2004). During various transitions in young adults' lives, the combined role of different demands and resources may become pronounced, as young people are making decisions about their further education and career paths. These demands and resources can also interact dynamically, creating complex ways in which they impact specific outcomes (see also Bakker & Demerouti, 2017).

Trajectories of Study/Work Engagement in Young Adulthood in Finland

In this section, we provide empirical examples of how study and work engagement develops in young adulthood, using the case study of Finland. These examples are drawn from the longitudinal Finnish Educational Transitions Study (FinEdu), which followed adolescents and young adults across transitions to postcomprehensive education and, later, into higher education or work. Participants were first surveyed at 16 years of age (initial $N = 804$) and then were surveyed annually or biannually until they were 30 years old. Those participants attended schools in a medium-sized town in central Finland (population = 88,000) where the schooling system is two-tiered, like the rest of the country. In Finland, students transfer from comprehensive secondary school to tracked education (either academic or vocational school) at age 16 or 17 and then move from tracked education around age 19 to 20 into a range of main activities including polytechnic (vocational college), studying for university entrance examinations (although cost-free for all students, university places are limited and highly competitive), university, employment, military service, or taking a gap year.

In the FinEdu study, we can observe how engagement with studies/work developed across the mid-schooling and school-to-work transitions, and throughout young adulthood, using a variety of measures to represent engagement (e.g., energy and absorption in studies/work, attainment values, interest) as a multidimensional construct. First, we observed that average levels of participants' study/work engagement, measured as energy, dedication, and absorption, increased across the transition from secondary education to higher education/work (Upadyaya & Salmela-Aro, 2015). Second, we documented increases in participants' motivation and decreases in their amotivation to study/work across the ages of 15 to 22, measured as attainment value, disinterest, futility, and inertia (Symonds et al., 2019). Neither study found that those trajectories were greatly moderated by gender or social class. Therefore, in both studies, we can see a slow growth of investment in studying/working across a complex set of engagement indicators throughout young adulthood.

In the FinEdu study, engagement growth was impacted by the type of main activity that participants transferred into at the mid-schooling and school-to-work transitions (Symonds et al., 2019). There, positive growth of study/work motivation was greater for participants transferring into vocational school at age 15, whereas those transferring to academic school had a more stable trajectory. These differences align with findings that students following an academic track (e.g., high school education) often experience more exhaustion than students in vocational education (Salmela-Aro, Kiuru, & Nurmi, 2008), which may manifest in a lack of motivational growth. This finding reversed somewhat at the school-to-work transition, where those transferring from vocational school to further study/work showed slower growth in motivation than those transferring from an academic school to a polytechnic or university. Here we could be observing changes in person–environment fit as young adults encountered a new set of environmental resources and demands in the new study or work environment and then, in a process of adapting to that new environment, began to perceive the activity as more or less interesting and appropriate for their career (Eccles et al., 1993; Eccles & Roeser, 2009).

Engagement in the FinEdu sample has also been studied using person-oriented approaches. Instead of focusing on mean level differences, which is common in variable-oriented research (Bergman & Andersson, 2010), researchers used person-oriented statistical models to elicit varying latent trajectories of engagement within the sample. This approach is based on the logic that some people's engagement changes over time, whereas others' engagement levels remain relatively stable (see also Mäkikangas et al., 2010).

In the FinEdu study, person-oriented research revealed that most young adults experienced a high level of study and work engagement across the transition from secondary education to higher education/work (Upadyaya & Salmela-Aro, 2013b). These results hold true even during macrolevel societal changes, such as an economic downturn, thus showing that despite societal hardship, young adults are highly motivated to work and their investment and engagement in work can remain high (De Hauw & De Vos, 2010; Upadyaya & Salmela-Aro, 2016). However, some felt less involved with their subsequent studies or work, with a small portion (5%) of young adults reporting continuously low engagement before and after this transition. Also in this analysis, among some young people, lower levels of engagement increased after the transition to higher education or work (Upadyaya & Salmela-Aro, 2013b), again in line with the notion that the new study or work environment may have provided a better person–environment fit for some young adults (Eccles et al., 1993; Eccles & Roeser, 2009).

In a study of engagement (measured as energy, dedication, and absorption) and burnout (experiences of exhaustion and feelings of inadequacy and cynicism toward study/work), latent profiles of young adults aged 17 to 19 emerged from the data (Tuominen-Soini & Salmela-Aro, 2014). There, the largest group, *engaged* (n = 430; 44%), had higher scores on engagement and moderately low burnout. Next, the *engaged-exhausted* group (n = 276; 28%) were engaged but also had higher levels of exhaustion and inadequacy. There were two smaller groups of *burned-out* (n = 136; 14%) with high burnout and low engagement, and *cynical* (n = 137; 14%) who experienced higher cynicism in studies or work. This study revealed that although most young adults were engaged with study/work, approximately one fourth of the students were simultaneously feeling exhausted with study/work. We explore these overlaps between engagement and other indicators of well-being in more detail next.

Study and Work Engagement and Well-Being in Young Adulthood

Following from our review of research from the FinEdu study, we now discuss the broader literature on how study/work engagement interacts with well-being. In one perspective, study/work engagement and career satisfaction are seen as components of a broader system of study/work well-being (Hakanen & Schaufeli, 2012; Upadyaya & Salmela-Aro, 2013b), whereas life satisfaction reflects context-free happiness and well-being (Lewis, Huebner, Malone, & Valois, 2011). Within this broader system are other components of cognition and action, for example, an individual's study-/work-oriented self-concept. There, study/work engagement and other components of the well-being system interact dynamically, just as the components of study/work engagement co-act dynamically with each other, presenting a set of continually nested systems that create psychological development. Co-actions of study/work engagement and other components of the study/work well-being system are indicated by studies that use correlational methods. For example, previous studies have shown that engagement is positively associated with career and life satisfaction (Hakanen & Schaufeli, 2012; Upadyaya & Salmela-Aro, 2013b), job resources (Mäkikangas et al., 2010), and perceived support from others over time (Green, Hirsch, Suárez-Orozco, & Camic, 2008), and that similar changes occur in these variables over time.

One mechanism of the developmental co-action of engagement and other aspects of study/work well-being is spillover. This is where certain indicators of study/work well-being, such as study/work self-concept, can spill over to other indicators of study/work well-being such as study/work engagement. Similarly, positive gain spirals and developmental cascades occur within the dynamic system of study/work well-being in young adulthood (see also Masten, Desjardins, McCormick, Kuo, & Long, 2010). Considering the integrated development of components of study/work well-being may become especially important in young adulthood, when significant personal and environmental changes occur in young adults' lives, creating novel challenges and disruptions within the study/work well-being system.

Among young adults in the FinEdu study, positive spillover occurred between life satisfaction and engagement (measured as energy, dedication, and absorption; Upadyaya & Salmela-Aro, 2017). There, life satisfaction positively predicted these young adults' subsequent study/work engagement during their tracked education (ages 17–18) and during and after their transition to higher education or work (ages 19–25). Young adults' study/work engagement, in turn, positively predicted young adults' life satisfaction at the latter waves of the school-to-work transition (ages 21–25) but not during tracked education. Thus, the connection between life satisfaction and engagement (measured as energy, dedication, and absorption) intensified in the latter waves of the school-to-work transition, when young adults might have felt better adjusted to their new educational/occupational environments and were probably experiencing higher person--environment fit (Eccles & Roeser, 2009), as these environments were more suited to them in comparison to tracked education.

As a further example of the co-action of study/work engagement and other aspects of the study/work well-being system, quantitative research finds parallel developmental trajectories of these variables when studied individually. For example in Finland, career satisfaction and study/work engagement have been found to develop in similar ways across young adulthood, although the average level of career satisfaction was slightly higher than engagement during secondary education. However, after the transition to higher education/work the level of study/work engagement increased higher than the level of career satisfaction (Upadyaya & Salmela-Aro, 2015b). There, young adults might have found their new career environment more relevant and interesting and, hence, experienced a better fit with their study/job values and goals (see also Sortheix, Dietrich, Chow, & Salmela-Aro, 2013), which manifested as an increase in their posttransition engagement.

However, in a different cultural context, research with young adults in the United Kingdom found that those following an academic track experienced higher anxiety than young adults following a vocational track, probably due to their experiences of higher academic pressure and preparation for university entrance exams (Symonds, Dietrich, Chow, & Salmela-Aro, 2016). Conversely, those transferring from school to full-time work or an apprenticeship reported a decrease in depressive symptoms and an increase in eudaimonia (Symonds et al., 2016). This study gives further indication of how changes in environment can trigger the development of study/work related well-being, possibly through person–environment fit processes. Certainly, more studies are needed to examine the possible fit/misfit between students and high school environment to help researchers and educators better understand how to promote students' mental health and help students manage the pressure they are facing in their studies.

Overall, the findings suggest that the role of life satisfaction and study/work engagement becomes increasingly important in young adulthood when young adults are preparing for adult work roles (Arnett, 2000). Also, well-being at work spills over to general well-being (and vice versa) as a part of developmental cascades (Masten et al., 2010), promoting young adults' adjustment to their adult work roles.

There is also research that finds that young adults' career satisfaction can decline at the school-to-work transition. Career satisfaction is one indicator of study/work well-being; changes in career satisfaction are often reflected in changes in life satisfaction and engagement Erdogan, Bauer, Truxillo, & Mansfield, 2012). Young adults can encounter a high level of study- and work-related demands and a limited number of good jobs (e.g., the jobs offered may be below their expectations or present a low level of challenge), manifesting as a decrease in young adults' career satisfaction (de Jonge et al., 2001; Karatzias, Power, Flemming, Lennan, & Swanson, 2002). Moreover, during secondary education, support from various resources (peers, teachers, parents) is readily available to enhance young people's satisfaction with education and engagement (Rosenfeld, Richman, & Bowen, 2000), whereas after the transition these resources might be limited, as young adults are establishing new social networks. These changes in social support might impact the development of young adults' career satisfaction. Also, beginning new occupational trajectories in young adulthood can mean that young adults have often not accumulated a large number of resources (e.g., networks of colleagues, work experiences, income) which can manifest as increases in burnout symptoms (Maslach, Schaufeli, & Leiter, 2001; Salmela-Aro & Upadyaya, 2018). In summary, study/work engagement co-develops with broader psychological processes, such as study/work well-being and career satisfaction. Depending on the available resources in the new main activity and young adults' ability to accrue resources and adapt in response to environmental demands, this might provoke an increase or decline in their overall well-being during and after the school-to-work transition.

The results of these studies indicate that it is important to consider young adults' general well-being and study/work well-being when researching study/work engagement. According to the conservation of resources theory (Hobfoll, 2001), different gain and loss spirals can exist between resources, study/work engagement, life satisfaction, and educational/occupational stress (see also Hakanen et al., 2008; Hakanen & Schaufeli, 2012). For example, work-related resources (e.g., support from colleagues) and personal resources (e.g., health, self-esteem) are likely to be linked with higher engagement and increases in other similar resources (e.g., optimism, coping with challenges), whereas a lack of work-related and personal resources is likely to be associated with lower engagement, poor coping with challenges, and increases in burnout symptoms (Hobfoll, 2001). In addition, a lack of resources at an earlier time point in development often fosters the loss of future resources (Hobfoll, 2001). For example, students with lower academic performance (when conceptualized as a behavioral resource) and who are not in education, employment, or training are more prone to experience subsequent mental health problems (Symonds et al., 2016). Further, those who have greater resources at an earlier time point are assumed to have more resources available to them later on (Hobfoll, 2001). This might precipitate the spillover of engagement to life satisfaction and other context-specific and context-free characteristics of well-being. General life satisfaction and depressive symptoms, in turn, might incur increases or decreases in study/work burnout and engagement.

Conclusion

In the present chapter we discussed the development of study and work engagement in young adulthood using a resources and demands perspective, reviewed the associations between study/work engagement and well-being, and explored some ways in which these associations can occur developmentally through the processes of spillover and developmental spirals. Together, the reviewed studies show that young adults are typically highly motivated to study or work and their engagement and expectations remain high even during macrolevel societal changes, such as an economic downturns (De Hauw & De Vos, 2010). However, other factors, such as life and career satisfaction can simultaneously decrease, probably due to new challenges young adults face during their transition to adulthood. Concurrent changes in engagement and well-being can also happen during young adults' educational and occupational transitions, probably reflecting their exposure to specific sets of personal and study/work related demands and resources and experience of altered person–environment fit (Eccles et al., 1993; Eccles & Roeser, 2009). Given the complexity of study/work engagement and its interaction with other developmental processes, more research is needed to examine study/work engagement in context and in association with other psychological phenomena (e.g., goals, aspirations, health, resilience, study- and work-related values) that become increasingly important in emerging adulthood.

Accordingly, the school-to-work transition is an optimal time for interventions (e.g., promoting work readiness, utility values, and possible selves) supporting the development of young adults' study/work engagement and associated career and general well-being (Harackiewicz, Rozek, Hulleman, & Hyde, 2012; Symonds & O'Sullivan, 2017; Vinson et al., 2010). For example, some studies have shown that interventions designed to enhance the content of students' possible selves and to promote development of academically focused possible selves help youth to feel more connected with their studies (Oyserman, Terry, & Bybee, 2002). Similar interventions could be developed to enhance young adults' connectedness with their studies and emerging career. Such interventions could help prevent possible decreases in engagement and support emerging adults' overall adjustment to their new study/work environments. In addition, intervention programs designed to promote young adults' work readiness (e.g., teamwork skills, self-efficacy, positive attitude, career motivation) might manifest as increases in work engagement and job satisfaction (Symonds & O'Sullivan, 2017; Walker & Campbell, 2013). Such programs could be designed both for emerging adults in general or according to young adults' more specific career interests and could help young adults stay employed and engaged for longer, helping them avoid demotivating forms of unemployment.

References

Appleton, J. J., Christenson, S. L., & Furlong, M. J. (2008). Student engagement with school: Critical conceptual and methodological issues of the construct. *Psychology in the Schools*, *45*, 369–386. doi:10.1016/j.jsp.2006.04.002

Appleton, J. J., Christenson, S. L., Kim, D., & Reschly, A. L. (2006). Measuring cognitive and psychological engagement: Validation of the Student Engagement Instrument. *Journal of School Psychology*, *44*(5), 427–445. doi:10.1016/j.jsp.2006.04.002

Arnett, J. J. (2000). Emerging adulthood: A theory of development from the late teens through the twenties. *American Psychologist*, *55*(5), 469–480. doi:10.1037/0003-066X.55.5.469

Bakker, A. B., & Demerouti, E. (2008). Towards a model of work engagement. *Career Development International*, *13*(3), 209–223. doi:10.1108/13620430810870476

Bakker, A. B., & Demerouti, E. (2017). Job demands-resources theory: Taking stock and looking forward. *Journal of Occupational Health Psychology, 22*(3), 273–285. doi:10.1037/ocp0000056

Bakker, A. B., Demerouti, E., De Boer, E., & Schaufeli, W. B. (2003). Job demands and job resources as predictors of absence duration and frequency. *Journal of Vocational Behavior, 62*(2), 341–356. doi:10.1016/S0001-8791(02)00030-1

Bakker, A., Demerouti, E., & Schaufeli, W. (2003). Dual processes at work in a call centre: An application of the job demands–resources model. *European Journal of Work and Organizational Psychology, 12*(4), 393–417. doi:10.1080/13594320344000165

Bergman, L. R., & Andersson, H. (2010). The person and the variable in developmental psychology. *Journal of Psychology, 218*(3), 155–165. doi:10.1027/0044-3409/a000025

Csikszentmihalyi, M. (1990). *Flow: The psychology of optimal experience.* New York, NY: Harper and Row.

De Hauw, S., & De Vos, A. (2010). Millennials' career perspective and psychological contract expectations: Does the recession lead to lowered expectations?. *Journal of Business and Psychology, 25*(2), 293–302. doi:10.1007/s10869-010-9162-9

De Jonge, J., Dormann, C., Janssen, P. P., Dollard, M. F., Landeweerd, J. A., & Nijhuis, F. J. (2001). Testing reciprocal relationships between job characteristics and psychological wellbeing: A cross-lagged structural equation model. *Journal of Occupational and Organizational Psychology, 74*(1), 29–46. doi:10.1348/096317901167217

Demerouti, E., Bakker, A., Nachreiner, F. & Schaufeli, W. (2001). The job demands-resources model of burnout. *Journal of Applied Psychology, 86*, 499–512. doi:10.1037/0021-9010.86.3.499

Eccles, J. S., Midgley, C., Wigfield, A., Buchanan, C. M., Reuman, D., Flanagan, C., & Mac Iver, D. (1993). Development during adolescence: The impact of stage-environment fit on young adolescents' experiences in schools and in families. *American Psychologist, 48*(2), 90. doi:10.1037/0003-066X.48.2.90

Eccles, J. S., & Roeser, R. W. (2009). Schools, Academic Motivation, and Stage-Environment Fit. In R. M. Lerner & L. Steinberg (Eds.) *Handbook of adolescent psychology* (3rd ed., pp. 404–434). Hoboken, NJ: Wiley.

Erdogan, B., Bauer, T. N., Truxillo, D. M., & Mansfield, L. R. (2012). Whistle while you work: A review of the life satisfaction literature. *Journal of Management, 38*(4), 1038–1083. doi:10.1177/0149206311429379

Finn, J. D. (1989). Withdrawing from school. *Review of Educational Research, 59*(2), 117–142.

Finn, J. D., & Voelkl, K. E. (1993). School characteristics related to student engagement. *Journal of Negro Education, 62*, 249–268.

Fredricks, J. A., Blumenfeld, P. C., & Paris, A. H. (2004). School engagement: Potential of the concept, state of the evidence. *Review of Educational Research, 74*, 59–109. doi:10.3102/00346543074001059

Fredricks, J. A., Wang, M. T., Linn, J. S., Hofkens, T. L., Sung, H., Parr, A., & Allerton, J. (2016). Using qualitative methods to develop a survey measure of math and science engagement. *Learning and Instruction, 43*, 5–15. doi:10.1016/j.learninstruc.2016.01.009

Furrer, C., & Skinner, E. (2003). Sense of relatedness as a factor in children's academic engagement and performance. *Journal of Educational Psychology, 95*, 148–162. doi:10.1037/0022-0663.95.1.148

Hakanen, J., Bakker, A., & Schaufeli, W. (2006). Burnout and engagement among teachers. *Journal of School Psychology, 43*, 495–513. doi:10.1016/j.jsp.2005.11.001

Hakanen, J. J., Perhoniemi, R., & Toppinen-Tanner, S. (2008). Positive gain spirals at work: From job resources to work engagement, personal initiative and work-unit innovativeness. *Journal of Vocational Behavior, 73*(1), 78–91. doi:10.1016/j.jvb.2008.01.003

Hakanen, J. J., & Schaufeli, W. B. (2012). Do burnout and work engagement predict depressive symptoms and life satisfaction? A three-wave seven-year prospective study. *Journal of Affective Disorders*, *141*(2), 415–424. doi:10.1016/j.jad.2012.02.043

Harackiewicz, J. M., Rozek, C. S., Hulleman, C. S., & Hyde, J. S. (2012). Helping parents to motivate adolescents in mathematics and science: An experimental test of a utility-value intervention. *Psychological Science*, *23*(8), 899–906. doi:10.1177/0956797611435530

Green, G., Rhodes, J., Hirsch, A. H., Suárez-Orozco, C., & Camic, P. M. (2008). Supportive adult relationships and the academic engagement of Latin American immigrant youth. *Journal of School Psychology*, *46*(4), 393–412. doi:10.1016/j.jsp.2007.07.001

Hobfoll, S. E. (2001). The influence of culture, community, and the nested-self in the stress process: advancing conservation of resources theory. *Applied Psychology*, *50*(3), 337–421. doi:10.1111/1464-0597.00062

Jimerson, S. R., Campos, E., & Greif, J. L. (2003). Toward an understanding of definitions and measures of school engagement and related terms. *California School Psychologist*, *8*, 7–27.

Karatzias, A., Power, K. G., Flemming, J., Lennan, F., & Swanson, V. (2002). The role of demographics, personality variables and school stress on predicting school satisfaction/dissatisfaction: Review of the literature and research findings. *Educational Psychology*, *22*(1), 33–50. doi:10.1080/01443410120101233

Lewis, A. D., Huebner, E. S., Malone, P. S., & Valois, R. F. (2011). Life satisfaction and student engagement in adolescents. *Journal of youth and Adolescence*, *40*(3), 249–262. doi:10.1007/s10964-010-9517-6

Li, Y., & Lerner, R. M. (2011). Trajectories of school engagement during adolescence: Implications for grades, depression, delinquency, and substance use. *Developmental Psychology*, *47*, 233–247. doi:10.1037/a0021307

Libbey, H. P. (2004). Measuring student relationships to school: Attachment, bonding, connectedness, and engagement. *Journal of School Health*, *74*, 274–283. doi:10.1111/j.1746-1561.2004.tb08284.x

Mäkikangas, A., Bakker, A. B., Aunola, K., & Demerouti, E. (2010). Job resources and flow at work: Modelling the relationship via latent growth curve and mixture model methodology. *Journal of Occupational and Organizational Psychology*, *83*, 795–814. doi:10.1348/096317909X476333

Marshall, E. A., & Butler, K. (2015). School-to-work transitions in emerging adulthood. In J. J. Arnett (Ed.), *The Oxford handbook of emerging adulthood* (pp. 316–333). New York, NY: Oxford University Press.

Maslach, C., Schaufeli, W. B., & Leiter, M. P. (2001). Job burnout. *Annual Review of Psychology*, *52*(1), 397–422. doi:10.1146/annurev.psych.52.1.397

Masten, A. S., Desjardins, C. D., McCormick, C. M., Kuo, S. I-C., & Long, J. D. (2010). The significance of childhood competence and problems for adult success in work: A developmental cascade analysis. *Development and Psychopathology*, *22*, 679–694. doi:10.1017/S0954579410000362

Oyserman, D., Terry, K., & Bybee, D. (2002). A possible selves intervention to enhance school involvement. *Journal of Adolescence*, *25*, 313–326. doi:10.1006/yjado.474

Parker, P. D., Thoemmes, F., Duineveld, J. J., & Salmela-Aro, K. (2015). I wish I had (not) taken a gap-year? The psychological and attainment outcomes of different post-school pathways. *Developmental Psychology*, *51*(3), 323–333. doi:10.1037/a0038667

Rosenfeld, L. B., Richman, J. M., & Bowen, G. L. (2000). Social support networks and school outcomes: The centrality of the teacher. *Child and Adolescent Social Work Journal*, *17*(3), 205–226. doi:10.1023/A:1007535930286

Rumberger, R. W., & Larson, K. A. (1998). Student mobility and the increased risk of high school dropout. *American Journal of Education*, *107*(1), 1–35. doi:10.1086/444201

Salanova, M., Agut, S., & Peiro, J. M. (2005). Linking organizational resources and work engagement to employee performance and customer loyalty: The mediation of service climate. *Journal of Applied Psychology, 90*, 1217–1227. doi:10.1037/0021-9010.90.6.1217

Salmela-Aro, K., Kiuru, N., & Nurmi, J.-E. (2008). The role of educational track in adolescents' school burnout: A longitudinal study. *British Journal of Educational Psychology, 78, 663–689.* doi:10.1348/000709908X281628

Salmela-Aro, K., & Upadyaya, K. (2012). The Schoolwork Engagement Inventory: Energy, dedication and absorption (EDA). *European Journal of Psychological Assessment, 28*, 60–67. doi:10.1027/1015-5759/a000091

Salmela-Aro, K., & Upadyaya, K. (2014). School burnout and engagement in the context of the demands-resources model. *British Journal of Educational Psychology, 84*, 137–151. doi:10.1111/bjep.12018

Salmela-Aro, K., & Upadyaya, K. (2018). Role of demands-resources in work engagement and burnout in different career stages. *Journal of Vocational Behavior, 108*, 190–200. doi:10.1016/j.jvb.2018.08.002

Schaufeli, W. B., & Bakker, A. B. (2004). Job demands, job resources, and their relationship with burnout and engagement: A multi-sample study. *Journal of Organizational Behavior, 25*(3), 293–315. doi:10.1002/job.248

Schaufeli, W. B., Bakker, A. B., & Salanova, M. (2006). The measurement of work engagement with a short questionnaire: A cross-national study. *Educational and Psychological Measurement, 66*, 701–716. doi:10.1177/0013164405282471

Schaufeli, W. B., Salanova, M., Gonzalez-Roma, V., & Bakker, A. B. (2002). The measurement of engagement and burnout: A two sample confirmatory factor analytic approach. *Journal of Happiness Studies, 3*, 71–92. doi:10.1023/A:1015630930326

Seppälä, P., Mauno, S., Feldt, T., Hakanen, J., Kinnunen, U., Tolvanen, A., & Schaufeli, W. (2009). The construct validity of the Utrecht work engagement scale: Multisample and longitudinal evidence. *Journal of Happiness Studies, 10*, 459–481. doi:10.1007/s10902-008-9100-y

Sinatra, G. M., Heddy, B. C., & Lombardi, D. (2015). The challenges of defining and measuring student engagement in science. *Educational Psychologist, 50*(1), 1–13.

Sortheix, F. M., Dietrich, J., Chow, A., & Salmela-Aro, K. (2013). The role of career values for work engagement during the transition to working life. *Journal of Vocational Behavior, 83*(3), 466–475. doi:doi:10.1016/j.jvb.2013.07.003

Symonds, J., Dietrich, J., Chow, A., & Salmela-Aro, K. (2016). Mental health improves after transition from comprehensive school to vocational education or employment in England: A national cohort study. *Developmental Psychology, 52*(4), 652. doi:10.1037/a0040118

Symonds, J. E., & O'Sullivan, C. (2017). Educating young adults to be work-ready in Ireland and the United Kingdom: A review of programmes and outcomes. *Review of Education, 5*(3), 229–263. doi:10.1002/rev3.3099

Symonds, J., Schoon, I., Eccles, J., & Salmela-Aro, K. (2019). The development of motivation and amotivation to study and work across age-graded transitions in adolescence and young adulthood. *Journal of Youth and Adolescence, 48*(6), 131–1145. doi:10.1007/s10964-019-01003-4.

Symonds, J., Schoon, I., & Salmela-Aro, K. (2016). Developmental trajectories of emotional disengagement from schoolwork and their longitudinal associations in England. *British Educational Research Journal, 42*(6), 993–1022. doi:10.1002/berj.3243

Symonds, J. E., Schreiber, J. B., & Torsney, B. M. (2020). Silver linings and storm clouds: Divergent profiles of momentary engagement emerge in response to the same task. *Journal of Educational Psychology* [Epub ahead of print]. doi::10.31219/osf.io/nh8zk

Tuominen-Soini, H., & Salmela-Aro, K. (2014). Schoolwork engagement and burnout among Finnish high school students and young adults: Profiles, progressions, and educational outcomes. *Developmental Psychology, 50*(3), 649–662. doi:10.1037/a0033898

Upadyaya, K., & Salmela-Aro, K. (2013a). Development of school engagement in association with academic success and well-being in varying social contexts: A review of empirical research. *European Psychologist, 18*, 136–147. doi:10.1027/1016-9040/a000143

Upadyaya, K., & Salmela-Aro, K. (2013b). Engagement with studies and work: Trajectories from post-comprehensive school education to higher education and work. *Emerging Adulthood, 1*, 247–257. doi:10.1177/2167696813484299

Upadyaya, K., & Salmela-Aro, K. (2015). Cross-lagged paths between energy, absorption and dedication during the transition from education to employment. *Journal of Positive Psychology, 10*, 346–358. doi:10.1080/17439760.2014.983958

Upadyaya, K., & Salmela-Aro, K. (2016). Career engagement and life satisfaction during transition from school to work in times of economic downturn in Finland. In A. C. Petersen, S. H. Koller, F. Motti-Stefanidi, & S. Verma (Eds.) *Positive youth development in global contexts of social and economic change*. New York, NY: Routledge.

Upadyaya, K., & Salmela-Aro, K. (2017). Developmental dynamics between young adults' life satisfaction and engagement with studies and work. *Longitudinal and Life Course Studies, 8*, 20–34. doi:10.14301/llcs.v8i1.398

Upadyaya, K., Vartiainen, M., & Salmela-Aro, K. (2016). From servant leadership to work engagement, life satisfaction, and occupational health: Job demands and resources. *Burnout Research, 3*(4), 101–108. doi:10.1016/j.burn.2016.10.001

Vasalampi, K., Muotka, J., Pöysä, S., Lerkkanen, M. K., Poikkeus, A. M., & Nurmi, J. E. (2016). Assessment of students' situation-specific classroom engagement by an InSitu Instrument. *Learning and Individual Differences, 52*, 46–52.

Vinson, D., Nixon, S., Walsh, B., Walker, C., Mitchell, E., & Zaitseva, E. (2010). Investigating the relationship between student engagement and transition. *Active Learning in Higher Education, 11*(2), 131–143. doi:10.1177/1469787410365658

Walker, A., & Campbell, K. (2013). Work readiness of graduate nurses and the impact on job satisfaction, work engagement and intention to remain. *Nurse Education Today, 33*(12), 1490–1495. doi:10.1016/j.nedt.2013.05.008

Wang, M.-T., & Hofkens, T. L. (2019). Beyond classroom academics: A school-wide and multicontextual perspective on student engagement in school. *Adolescent Research Review*. doi:10.1007/s40894-019-00115-z

Xanthopoulou, D., Bakker, A. B., Demerouti, E., & Schaufeli, W. B. (2009). Reciprocal relationships between job resources, personal resources, and work engagement. *Journal of Vocational Behavior, 74*(3), 235–244. doi:10.1016/j.jvb.2008.11.003.

2

It Wasn't Sheer Luck After All

Opportunity and Preparation Predict Chance Events in School-to-Work Transitions

Pieter E. Baay, Christopher M. Napolitano, and Mattijs C. Schipper

Luck is what happens when preparation meets opportunity (Seneca, 4 BC–AD 65)

Receiving a job offer while talking to someone at the gym, seeing a job advertisement while browsing the newspaper for sports news, or meeting a prospective employer at a birthday party; these are examples of events that may contain an element of chance. Chance factors are defined as unplanned, unpredicted events that can potentially affect a person's vocational choices, behaviors, and success (Bandura, 1982; Crites, 1969). Theoretical models on career development emphasize that chance plays a role in careers (Krumboltz, 2009; Pryor & Bright, 2003; Dew, 2009; Cunha, 2005; Denrell, Fang, & Winter, 2003); empirical research corroborates that most people indeed perceive chance to have played a role in their own careers (e.g., Bright, Pryor, & Harpham, 2005; Bright, Pryor, Wilkenfeld, & Earl, 2005; Bright, Pryor, Chan, & Rijanto, 2009; Hirschi, 2010). Clearly, chance events can be considered as potentially important contributors to success in school-to-work transitions.

Individual differences in reports on chance events reveal two distinct patterns. The first is that people differ in their attribution of events, to either internal (e.g., effort) or external (e.g., chance) processes (Heider, 1958; Lefcourt, 1966). External attributors, one could reason, may be more likely to report chance to have influenced their school-to-work transition. However, empirical work has shown that people's locus of control, which indicates their tendency to attribute to internal or external factors, only explains a small portion of individual differences in chance events (Bright, Pryor, & Harpham, 2005; Bright, Pryor, Chan, & Rijanto, 2009; Hirschi, 2010). The second pattern, next to individual differences in the perception of chance events, is the likelihood of experiencing—and even capitalizing on—unexpected opportunities (e.g., Bandura, 1998; Graebner, 2004; Merton & Barber, 2004). Indeed,

Pieter E. Baay, Christopher M. Napolitano, and Mattijs C. Schipper, *It Wasn't Sheer Luck After All* In: *Young Adult Development at the School-to-Work Transition.* E. Anne Marshall and Jennifer E. Symonds, Oxford University Press (2021). © Oxford University Press. DOI: 10.1093/oso/9780190941512.003.0002.

it was Seneca who, centuries ago, postulated that such "luck" requires opportunity and preparation. In the current chapter, we address whether job seekers' opportunity and preparation for chance events helps explain individual differences in the experience and capitalization of chance events.

This balance of chance events, and their effects, being part opportunity and part preparation is further supported by the etymology of the word *serendipity* (see Merton & Barber, 2004). The origins of the word trace back to 1754, when Horace Walpole described to a colleague his ability to find precisely the book he was looking for after simply "dipping" his hand into a bookshelf. Walpole termed the ability to "always (make) discoveries, by chance and sagacity" serendipity, deriving the word from an ancient name for Sri Lanka. Therefore, Walpole's original definition of serendipity involves both opportunity (chance) and preparation (sagacity). This original definition began to shift, as a group of antiquarians and bibliophiles debated how serendipity occurred and how chance events shaped lives.

For instance, in 1880, while Edward Solly wrote in *Notes and Queries* that serendipity was used to "express a particular kind of natural cleverness" (Merton & Barber, 2004, p. 51) involving the "the discovery of things that the finder was not in search of" (p. 52), Andrew Lang described, one year later, that serendipity involved simply "the luck of falling on just the literary document which one wants at the moment" (p. 57). Over time, Lang's notion of serendipity as based in luck and opportunity (rather than preparation) became the common use of the term in the popular lexicon (Merton & Barber, 2004). We believe that viewing chance events as simply chance presents an impoverished view of their role in school-to-work transitions. Thus, a broad aim of this chapter is to reintroduce the role of the individual into the study of chance events, recapturing the richness described by Seneca and Walpole.

Contributions of the current chapter are both theoretical and empirical. First, we review prior theoretical work on individual differences in people's preparation and opportunities for chance events. We also describe process models that suggest that the role of chance events is dependent on different phases—the occurrence, perception, and selection of chance events (e.g., Erdelez, 2004; Lawley & Tompkins, 2008; Makri & Blandford, 2012; Merton & Barber, 2004; Napolitano, 2013). Investigating chance events from a process perspective will allow us to better determine whether individual differences in the experience of chance events relate to opportunity, preparation, or both. Then, we test individual differences in preparation and opportunities for chance events in two empirical studies. In addition to longitudinal self-reported data on the experience of chance events in the school-to-work transition (Study 1), we report on a controlled research design in which all job applicants were exposed to the same ostensible chance events (Study 2). Together, the studies investigate opportunity and preparation differences in self-reported experience as well as observed capitalization of chance events.

The Role of Chance Events in Careers

Various terminologies are employed in the research on chance events. These terms include chance (Roe & Baruch, 1967), happenstance (Miller, 1983; Mitchell, Levin & Krumboltz, 1999), fortuity (Bandura, 1998), synchronicity (Guindon & Hanna, 2002), and, as described earlier, serendipity (Merton & Barber, 2004). Some researchers have focused on the unexpectedness of the event, whereas other researchers have considered how the chance event linked to inner thoughts or individual behavior. The common ground of these terminologies, which are used in chance models like cognitive information processing theory (Sampson, Lenz, Reardon, & Peterson, 1999), chaos theory of careers (Pryor & Bright, 2003), and happenstance learning theory (Krumboltz, 2009), is that chance events are unanticipated and potentially affect a person's vocational choices, behaviors, and success. We draw on all theoretical work that considers such events, but use the term *chance events* to be consistent throughout this chapter.

According to self-reported accounts of careers, chance events are indeed perceived to play a role in career decisions, behaviors, and success. Typically, more than 60% of respondents have reported chance events to influence their careers, whether they were adolescents (Hirschi, 2010), college students (Bright, Pryor, & Harpham, 2005; Bright, Pryor, Wilkenfeld, et al., 2005), adults (Betsworth & Hansen, 1996; Diaz de Chumaceiro, 2004; McDonald, 2010; Roe & Baruch, 1967), nonprofessional workers (Hart, Rayner, & Christensen, 1971; Salomone & Slaney, 1981), scientists (Lerner, Peterson, Silbereisen, & Brooks-Gunn, 2014; Williams et al., 1998), or chief executive officers (Blanco & Golik, 2015). Not only did these studies reveal that people often perceive chance to have played a role in their career; they also found that chance events occurred in different forms (e.g., meeting a person, encountering information, change of context). Importantly, the extent to which people acted upon such chance events also varied, from deliberate lack of change to a change of goals (e.g., internship instead of job) or a change of strategy to achieve those goals (e.g., to follow up on a website link that was advertised at the gym instead of simply browsing the Internet for vacancies). We describe this process further in the next section.

Individual Differences in Chance

Some people may be more likely to experience chance events than others (e.g., Bandura, 1998; Graebner, 2004; Merton & Barber, 2004). Existing process models on chance events help to shed light on the nonrandom component of experiencing and capitalizing on chance events. Such models describe what happens before, during, and after the occurrence of a chance event (e.g., Erdelez, 2004; Lawley & Tompkins, 2008; Makri & Blandford, 2012; Merton & Barber, 2004; Napolitano, 2013). Drawing from these process models, we discuss the three phases that may help explain individual differences in experiencing and capitalizing on chance events: occurrence, perception, and selection. Again, we draw on all theoretical process models, but we use the terms *occurrence*, *perception*, and *selection* herein for reasons of consistency.

Occurrence

A chance event starts with its occurrence (while preparation may have started long before). Although a chance event may often be considered synonymous with a lucky accident (Napolitano, 2013), its occurrence is not always random. Factors that may predict the occurrence of chance events include job seeker's opportunities, personality, and preparation.

With regard to the opportunity to experience chance events, it has been argued that people with larger social networks naturally have more social contacts who can incidentally approach them with information (Granovetter, 1974). Evidence in this direction shows that social networks are beneficial for employment chances even among people who do not search for employment (e.g., Chua, 2014; Lin & Ao, 2008; McDonald & Elder, 2006; McDonald & Day, 2010), possibly due to unanticipated help (Dew, 2009; Lin, 2006). One study considered this explicitly and found that people with larger social networks receive more unsolicited job leads (McDonald, 2010). Hence, the opportunity to experience chance events may be higher among those with a larger social network.

The personality trait *openness to experience* is related to enlarging one's experiences and environments (McCrae, 1996). Creating opportunities for chance events, an open person's curious mind actively searches for new experiences by exploring and browsing, which increases the opportunity to acquire incidental information (Heinström, 2002; Nahl & James, 1996). Personality may also predict the opportunity for chance events to occur in a more passive manner. With regard to interpersonal chance events, people evoke action in others who approach them or share information. This may be more likely to happen to agreeable and extraverted people, who may be more likeable and therefore evoke more positive action in others (Bandura, 1982; Pickering & Gray, 2001). Hence, it is expected that chance events occur more frequently among more agreeable, extraverted, and open job seekers.

People who have prepared for their job search process more intensively have probably mobilized more people and places where information can be obtained (e.g., websites, information markets). Mobilization of other people and contexts can result in unanticipated benefits (Chen, 2005; Pálssdóttir, 2010). For example, if people search for a new job then find the internship they have always dreamed of, this event may contain a chance element for them (i.e., Diaz de Chumaciero, 2004). Also, if employers with a vacancy in their company visit a networking event (e.g., conference) where they see two potential future employees, they seem more likely to offer the vacancy to the well-prepared job seeker. So, even without the job seeker knowing about this vacancy, preparedness may make them more likely to receive the unanticipated offer. Hence, chance events may occur more frequently among people who prepare more intensively for their job search process. It may even be that people's actions enacted years prior coincidentally set the stage for the occurrence of chance events (e.g., having done the same voluntary work as the employer).

In sum, it seems that social contexts, personality, and preparation shape opportunities for the occurrence of chance events (Bandura, 1982; McCay-Peet, 2013). That is, open, well-prepared job seekers with a larger social network seem more likely to encounter something they did not expect. We explore these hypotheses in the empirical portion of this chapter.

Perception

Once a chance event has occurred, a second requirement for it to play a role in careers is that the person notices the event (Dew, 2009; Erdelez & Rioux, 2000). Although some chance events are perceived, others go unnoticed. Process models suggest that personality and preparation predict the perception of chance events (Makri & Blandford, 2012; Napolitano, 2013; see also Pasteur, 1923). For example, openness to experience may help the person be ready for, and recognize, unanticipated events (Pickering & Gray, 2001), as open people may be more flexible during active seeking and more ready to explore unanticipated leads and connect those to their goals (Chen, 2005; Foster & Ford, 2003; McBirnie, 2008).

Preparation may also help people to notice chance events. As mentioned before, chance events are more likely to occur among people who have already engaged in explorative action in the domain of the chance event (e.g., preparatory job search behavior; Pálssdóttir, 2010). In turn, it is easier to perceive events that have a higher probability of occurring (Chen, 2005; Mitroff & Biggs, 2014). For example, job seekers browsing the Internet for vacancies seem more likely to notice an advertisement for a potentially relevant internship abroad compared to people browsing the Internet for a new phone. Thus, job seekers who engage in more preparatory job search behavior will be more likely to perceive job search-related chance events.

Selection

Simply perceiving a chance event does not guarantee its influence on a person's career development. Instead, after perceiving a chance event, a person may need to select it for further investment. This *selection* refers to the action taken after perceiving a chance event. To benefit from a chance event people typically require a change of goals or goal strategies. For example, a new goal needs to be defined if someone initially strived for a new job but then received an unanticipated offer to do an internship, while a new goal strategy is required if someone initially searched through the Internet and is now recommended to call an acquaintance. In some cases, immediate or extensive action is required before the chance event has an impact; in other cases, delayed or little effort is enough. In rare cases, no selection is needed for the event to have an impact (e.g., a co-worker unexpectedly leaving the company). However, active event selection is needed most of the times.

One straightforward predictor of the willingness to take such action is the perceived potential value of the event (e.g., Guindon & Hanna, 2002; Lawley & Tompkins, 2008; Makri & Blandford, 2012). Perceived potential value is higher when people consider the event to potentially contribute to their future success. The event could be valuable because it aligns with someone's goals or because it contributes to identifying a new goal. Yet, not all individuals may value chance events in the same way. Given the need for flexible adjustment of goals and goal strategies, more open and flexible people may be more likely to perceive chance events as valuable (Costa & Crae, 1997; Hirschi, 2010; Krumboltz, 2009). In turn, open people will be more likely to select and capitalize on chance events (Mitchell, Levin, & Krumboltz, 1999; Napolitano, 2013).

Current Research

The aim of the current research is to shed light on the nonrandom component of the experience and capitalization of chance events. First, we describe individual differences in the experience of chance events. Despite theoretical work that predicts individual differences in people's preparation and opportunities for chance events, few empirical studies have addressed this issue empirically (Hirschi, 2010; Napolitano, 2013). This may in part be due to participants' difficulties in conceptualizing and recalling past experiences of chance events (Erdelez, 2004; Pritchard & Smith, 2004). Accordingly, in Study 1 we use longitudinal data on school-to-work transitions, in which emerging adult job seekers report on specific job search-related chance events to predict chance events by indicators of job seekers' opportunities, personality, and preparation.

Second, we describe people's active contribution to the occurrence and effects of chance events. Previous qualitative work has yielded a general understanding of how people can successfully deal with chance events. For example, the occurrence of chance events seems higher among individuals who inform their social network about their wishes and who feel free and flexible to act upon chance events (Blanco & Golik, 2015; McDonald, 201; Williams et al., 1998). However, in part because chance events are difficult to observe (Erdelez, 1999), insight into people's active contribution to the occurrence and effects of chance has remained limited (Napolitano, 2013). Specifically, previous work has not differentiated between the three phases of chance events (i.e., occurrence, perception, and selection). Doing so would provide insight into whether individual differences in the role of chance exist as a result of different exposure, perception, or selection of these events.

Contributing to this understanding, Study 2 employs a controlled design in which applicants were exposed to the same chance events during a job interview process. This way, people's own perception of what constituted a chance event did not play a role. Also, having controlled the occurrence of chance events, Study 2 standardized the setting for people's subsequent perception and selection of the events and then examined these factors in relation to their personality and preparation.

Hypotheses

Figure 2.1 gives an overview of the three chance phases and related constructs that are examined in the current research. Study 1 and Study 2 examine opportunity, personality, and preparation differences in the self-reported experience and observed capitalization of chance events. Study 1 tests to what extent those with better opportunities, certain personality traits, and more job preparation experience more chance events. Study 2 tests to what extent those with certain personality traits and more job preparation experience and capitalize on more chance events.

In Study 1, in which opportunities for chance events may vary, we used the size of the social network as an indicator for opportunities, as social ties can provide (unexpected) information (Granovetter, 1974; Lin, 2006). Hence, we predicted that the larger someone's social network is, the larger the opportunity for chance events. In Study 2, opportunities for chance events were held constant.

With regard to personality, we expected that open, extraverted, and agreeable job seekers would report more chance events. Although empirical evidence for the role of openness to experience is not unequivocal (Heinström, 2002, 2006; Hirschi, 2010; McCay-Peet, 2013; Pálssdóttir, 2010; Williams et al., 1998), prior research has documented open job seekers to report more chance events; they seem more likely to be exposed to, notice, and value

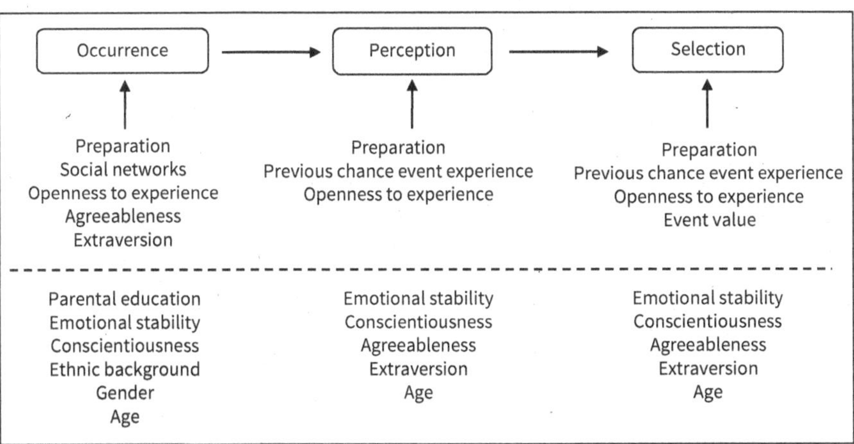

Figure 2.1 Examined relations between job seekers' characteristics and the three phases of chance. The relations between chance phases and constructs above the dotted line are hypothesized relations; constructs below the dotted line are examined for exploratory purposes.

chance events (Costa & Crae, 1997; Heinström, 2002; Nahl & James, 1996; Napolitano, 2013). Agreeable and extraverted job seekers may report more chance events because they evoke a more positive reaction in their social environment, which may lead to more unexpected information (Bandura, 1982). In Study 2, in which exposure to chance events is controlled, no effect of agreeableness and extraversion was expected. The roles of conscientiousness and emotional stability were considered for exploratory purposes, as these traits may predict whether people are receptive to chance events in stressful contexts (e.g., job interview).

We also expected that better-prepared job seekers would report more chance events. This is because prior research has found that those who have prepared for their job search more intensively have mobilized more people and contexts, which may result in unanticipated benefits (Chen, 2005; Pálssdóttir, 2010). Also, being active in the job search domain is proposed to make people more alert to unanticipated situations in that domain (Chen, 2005; Pálssdóttir, 2010).

Study 1

Study 1 examined whether chance events in the school-to-work transition occurred randomly to job seekers or whether they could be predicted from job seeker's social networks, personality, and preparation. Similar to previous empirical work (e.g., Hirschi, 2010), participants reported on what they considered to have been chance events, and no distinction was made between the occurrence, perception, and selection of chance events.

Method

We used data from the School2Work project, which is a longitudinal investigation of the school-to-work transition of vocational education and training graduates in the Netherlands. The project followed students from their final year before graduation until three years later (Baay, van Aken, de Ridder, & van der Lippe, 2014; see Baay, Buers, & Dumhs, 2014, for an extensive description of the project and data collection process). The current study uses the first data collection wave for information about job seekers' personality, preparation, and social networks (administered on average nine months before graduation from the vocational education and training program; September–December 2011). Given that chance events can play a role in the job search process, which already starts before graduation, we assessed chance events both before and after graduation. Chance events before graduation were assessed at the second data collection wave (February–May 2012); chance events after graduation were assessed in the first wave after students had graduated (i.e., depending on graduation date, this could be the second, third [December 2012] or fourth [December 2013] data collection wave).

Students were included in the analyses if they had filled out the questions in the first wave and at least one measure about chance events (before or after graduation). Fourteen participants were excluded because they did not fill out the questionnaire seriously (indicated by a series of 30 neutral answers). Two hundred sixty-four of the remaining job seekers who had filled out the first wave reported on chance events before graduation, and 228, after graduation. In the longitudinal sample, some students participated in the wave reporting on chance events before graduation; others, in a wave reporting on chance events after graduation; and others, in both.

In total, 390 emerging adult job seekers provided information before and/or after graduation about their experience with job search related chance events. Fifty-eight percent of the sample was female, and the sample had an average age of 21.20 years at the first wave (SD = 4.76). Twenty-four percent of participants had at least one parent born abroad, which is the criterion for being considered an ethnic minority in the Netherlands (Statistics Netherlands, 2014). Table 2.1 presents descriptive statistics and bivariate correlations of the Study 1 variables.

Measures

Personality was measured with the Quick Big Five (Vermulst, 2005), which is a shortened version of Goldberg's Big Five questionnaire (Gerris et al., 1998; Goldberg, 1992). The Big Five is a widely used conceptualization of personality and taps into respondents' extraversion (sample item: *talkative*), conscientiousness (*systematic*), agreeableness (*pleasant*), emotional stability (*nervous*; reverse coded), and openness to experience (*exploratory*). All five traits were measured with six items, on which participants indicated whether they agreed this was characteristic of them on a 7-point scale, ranging from 1 (*completely disagree*) to 7 (*completely agree*). Cronbach's alphas are satisfactory for extraversion ($\alpha = 0.86$), conscientiousness ($\alpha = 0.86$), agreeableness ($\alpha = .76$), and emotional stability ($\alpha = 0.80$). Consistent with prior research (e.g., Heinström, 2006; Hirschi, 2010), the reliability for openness to experience was somewhat lower ($\alpha = 0.65$).

Preparation for job searching was assessed with a 4-item index (Blau, 1994) that measured how often participants had performed preparatory job search behavior. Items were as follows: How often in the past six months have

Table 2.1 Descriptive Statistics and Bivariate Correlations of Study 1 Variable

	M	*SD*	5	6	7	8	9	10	11	12	13	14
1. Age	21.20	4.76	0.02	0.18^{***}	0.07	0.04	0.01	−0.06	0.24^{***}	−0.04	0.07	−0.10
2. Ethnic minority	0.24	0.42	0.03	0.15^{**}	0.06	$0.09^{\dagger}$	0.01	0.08	0.25^{***}	0.12^{*}	−0.01	0.09
3. Parental education	5.27	1.91	0.06	-0.20^{***}	0.01	0.04	0.12^{*}	0.05	-0.15^{**}	−0.06	0.11	0.04
4. Female	0.58	0.49	−0.02	0.13^{**}	0.10^{*}	-0.18^{***}	-0.11^{*}	-0.12^{*}	0.20^{***}	−0.03	−0.01	$-0.15^{\dagger}$
5. Extraversion	4.64	1.16		−0.06	0.22^{***}	0.49^{***}	0.17^{**}	0.20^{***}	0.03	0.04	-0.15^{*}	0.11
6. Conscientiousness	4.96	1.06			0.15^{**}	0.00	0.16^{**}	0.03	0.18^{***}	0.08	0.02	0.04
7. Agreeableness	5.76	0.59				0.11^{*}	0.33^{***}	0.07	0.15^{**}	0.07	−0.01	$0.14^{\dagger}$
8. Emotional stability	4.17	1.05					$0.09^{\dagger}$	0.15^{**}	−0.07	0.02	-0.14^{*}	0.10
9. Openness to experience	4.99	0.79						$0.10^{\dagger}$	$0.10^{\dagger}$	$0.11^{\dagger}$	0.03	0.19^{*}
10. Social network size	6.98	2.71							0.11^{*}	0.24^{***}	−0.06	0.10
11. Preparation for job searching	2.01	0.95								0.23^{***}	−0.04	0.05
12. Chance events before graduation	3.76	2.96									0.22^{*}	0.41^{**}
13. Chance events after graduation 0–1	0.65	0.48										1
14. Chance events after graduation 1–4	4.78	3.28										

$^{***}p < 0.001$; $^{**}p < 0.01$; $^{*}p < 0.05$; $^{\dagger}p < 0.10$.

you (1) read information about how to best apply for a job, (2) written down your wishes and talents to prepare for job applying, (3) searched for and read vacancies on the Internet, and (4) searched for and read vacancies in the newspaper or professional journal. Respondents rated the frequency on a 5-point scale from zero (never) to 4 (more than 10 times; $\alpha = 0.83$).

Social network size was assessed with the Position Generator, which maps an individual's social relations through their professions (Lin & Dumin, 1986). Respondents received a list of professions and were asked to indicate whether they know someone with that profession (Lin, 1999). The Position Generator is a typical way to examine people's social network, because it can capture a variety of relations. Instead of focusing on intimate or geographically close social ties, the Position Generator is content-free and, therefore, more representative of someone's social network (Lin, Fu, & Hsung, 2001). For 12 combinations of professions (e.g., janitor, garbage collector, window cleaner), respondents indicated whether they knew anyone with these professions. In line with previous research using this instrument, the sum was used as an indicator for social network size ($\alpha = 0.71$).

The experience of chance events was assessed with a 5-item index, which was composed of types of chance events that people have described in qualitative studies (e.g., McDonald, 2010; Williams et al., 1998). Similar to previous research (e.g., Bright, Pryor, & Harpham, 2005), we did not present a definition of chance events to the respondents. Instead, respondents gave their own assessment of whether certain events happened by chance. Items were as follows: How often, in the last three months, have you (1) received information about vacancies without you asking about it; (2) by mere chance, received information about a vacancy; (3) by mere chance, met people who could help you search for a job; (4) received a job offer without you asking; (5) felt like you got a job by mere chance. Respondents rated the frequency on a 5-point scale from zero (never) to 4 (more than 10 times; $\alpha = 0.73$). Within this sample, the average of the five items was close to a rating of 4 ($M = 3.76$) and indicates that respondents have experienced quite a number of chance events in their job search process before graduation.

The experience of chance events after graduation was completed by people who had found employment as well as by people who were still searching for employment. As this questionnaire was filled out after graduation (i.e., at home), efforts were made to keep the questionnaire concise. To this end, they were first asked whether they had experienced that chance played a role in their job search process. Only if this was true to some degree (i.e., ≥ 5 on a scale of zero to 10) did respondents fill out the 5-item index that was also used for chance events before graduation ($\alpha = 0.79$). Sixty-five percent ($n = 148$) of respondents after graduation had experienced at least some chance in their job search process; among those, they reported to have experienced an average of just under five chance events ($M = 4.78$).

Analyses

Simultaneous multiple regression analyses were performed using SPSS. The two indicators for chance events after graduation (i.e., whether or not they had experienced chance events and the extent to which they experienced chance events) were analyzed in tandem. Outcomes are presented in Table 2.2. Specifically, a two-part model was estimated, which is used for continuous variables with a nonproportionate number of zeroes. This was the case for chance events after graduation, as 29% reported to not have experienced chance. The two-part model estimates the effects of the independent variables on the probability of chance events after graduation being zero versus nonzero (see Table 2.2, column 2) and the effects of the independent variables on the number of chance events after graduation given that this is not zero (see Table 2.2, column 3).

Analyses were controlled for job seekers' gender, age, parents' highest educational level, and whether or not the job seeker was an ethnic minority.

Table 2.2 Prediction of Experiencing Serendipitous Events in the Job Search Process (Study 1).

	Chance Events Before Graduation (0–4)		Chance Events After Graduation (0/>0)		Chance Events After Graduation (1–4)	
	B	*SE*	*B*	*SE*	*B*	*SE*
Age	−0.02*	0.01	0.03	0.04	−0.03**	0.01
Ethnic minority	−0.04	0.11	0.34	0.42	0.07	0.20
Parental education	−0.02	0.02	0.17*	0.08	0.01	0.04
Female	−0.06	0.07	0.01	0.35	−0.26*	0.13
Extraversion	−0.00	0.04	−0.22	0.17	0.03	0.07
Conscientiousness	−0.01	0.04	0.07	0.16	0.12†	0.07
Agreeableness	0.05	0.06	0.01	0.30	0.22†	0.13
Emotional stability	−0.01	0.04	−0.29	0.18	0.12	0.07
Openness to experience	0.04	0.05	0.13	0.22	0.09	0.09
Social network size	0.05***	0.02	−0.05	0.07	0.01	0.02
Preparation for job searching	0.11**	0.04	−0.11	0.19	0.18*	0.08
R^2	.13		.09		.24	

***$P < 0.001$; **$P < 0.01$; *$P < 0.05$; †$P < 0.10$.

Results

The general expectation tested in Study 1 is that chance events in the job search process are not random and that job seeker's opportunity (i.e., through their social networks), Big Five personality, and preparation predict individual differences in chance events. Supporting the position that chance events are not entirely random, the variables in the model explain 13% and 24% of the variance in chance events before and after graduation, respectively.

Table 2.2 presents the regression models that predict the experience of chance events before and after graduation. Older job seekers reported fewer chance events before and after graduation. Ethnic minorities and majorities did not report differences. Those with a higher parental education were more likely to have experienced chance events after graduation. Men, if they had experienced chance after graduation, reported more chance events than women.

In line with the hypothesis that those with better opportunities will experience more chance events, we found that those with a larger social network reported more chance events (before graduation, but not after graduation). Follow-up analyses indicated that both the number of social relations with whom the job seeker had discussed job searching ($\beta = 0.34, t = 4.37, P < 0.001$) as well as the number of social relations whom the job seeker knew but had not discussed job searching with ($\beta = 0.03, t = 2.13, P = 0.034$) predicted chance events before graduation. A test for equality of estimates showed that mobilized social relations had a significantly stronger effect than unmobilized social relations ($\Delta\beta = 0.14, t = 2.13, P = 0.033$). Also, social network size was the strongest predictor of chance events before graduation ($\beta = 0.25$). Given the nonsignificant relation of social network size with chance events after graduation, we found partial support for the hypothesis that social network size predicts chance events.

With regard to personality, it was hypothesized that openness to experience, agreeableness, and extraversion would relate to more chance events. Extraversion and openness to experience were not correlated with the frequency of chance events, while agreeableness was marginally related ($P < 0.10$) to higher levels of chance events after graduation. Exploring the role of the other two Big Five personality traits, we found that emotional stability did not relate to the experience of chance, while conscientiousness related marginally to ($P < 0.10$) to higher levels of chance events after graduation. Given the lack of significant relations, the hypothesis that personality is a predictor of the experience of chance events was not supported.

Those who prepared more intensively for their job search process reported more chance events, both before and after graduation. In fact, preparation for the job search process was the strongest predictor of chance events after graduation (β = 0.23). Hence, the hypothesis that preparedness predicts chance events was supported.

Discussion

The experience of chance events, which is often described as "luck" or "by mere chance" is not random: Several individual factors were significantly associated with the experience of chance events in the school-to-work transition. Two findings stand out in Study 1. First, the experience of chance events seems shaped by opportunity. Both job seekers with a larger social network as well as job seekers whose parents were better educated reported more chance events. This points to the idea that the social environment is important for the occurrence of chance events. The second conclusion is that people can play a role themselves in experiencing chance events. Increased preparation for the job search process was related to experiencing more chance events. Hence, both the social environment as well as the individual can contribute to the experience of chance events.

Although Study 1 provided some insight into the nonrandom distribution of chance events, some questions remain open. First, there is some evidence that people differ in their attribution of events, to either internal (e.g., effort) or external (e.g., chance) processes (Bright, Pryor, & Harpham, 2005; Hirschi, 2010, but for a null finding, see Bright et al., 2009). Hence, we cannot conclude from our correlational study whether certain people (e.g., those who prepared more intensively) were exposed to more chance events or whether they only perceived it as such. Second, even though the role of preparation points to an active component in experiencing chance, it remains unclear whether the active component relates to differences in people's exposure, perception, or selection of chance. Study 2 addressed both questions.

Study 2

The general expectation tested in Study 2 was that the extent to which job applicants perceive and select chance events in a job interview process can be predicted from their personality and job interview preparation. As all applicants were exposed to the same chance events, people's own perception of what constitutes a chance event did not play a role. Also, Study 2 differentiated between the two chance phases of perception and selection (by asking if participants perceived the events and by observing these participants for selection of these events). Applicants' event perception and selection was, again, assumed to be related to their personality and preparation. To examine whether participant reports on previous chance experiences aligned with their behavior in a setting with controlled chance events, we also considered whether a measure of past experience with chance events would predict the perception and selection of chance events in the current study.

Method

Participants. Participants applied for six research assistant positions that involved collecting data in schools. The vacancy was advertised through flyers on the university campus and university websites that present job vacancies for students. The job advertisement contained an e-mail address to which interested students could send their resume and letter of motivation. From a total of 109 applicants, 37 did not meet the initial requirement of currently being enrolled as a student of Utrecht University. Seventy-two applicants were invited for the job interview.

Design. An observational controlled study was conducted to expose applicants to chance events during the job interview process. The manipulated procedure was added to an existing job application process to ensure a realistic setting and produce realistic responses from the participants.

Several precautions were taken to deal with potential ethical issues that would arise from accompanying a job interview with research-related measures and methods. All participants were exposed to the same information to ensure equal chances during the job interview. Also, participants were kept unaware of the study until the job interview was completed. The person conducting the job interviews was not permitted to see any collected data until the vacancies were filled. Each participant was asked permission beforehand to record the job interview, and, afterwards, each participant was informed that the study accompanied the job interview. All participants were given the opportunity to withdraw their data collected for the study. One applicant from the pilot group did so; she was removed from the analyses (and still considered for the vacancies).

The Advisory Committee for the Medical Research Involving Human Subjects Act of the Psychology faculty of Utrecht University provided ethical approval for the study.

Manipulated chance events. The aim of the study was to examine whether applicants would perceive and select chance events in the job interview process. Acknowledging that chance events can occur in different forms, we exposed applicants to three chance events that differed in the required action and presentation form (i.e., a digital, a written, and a verbal chance event).

Event A was a statement in the digital invitation for the job interview. Besides practical information (i.e., date, time, location, name of person doing the interview), the digital invitation included the following sentence: "Should you like to know the exact procedures of the data collection, you can send an e-mail to [research assistant's name + e-mail address] to retrieve last year's protocol." If applicants sent an e-mail, the research assistant sent the protocol and additionally wrote, "Unfortunately, I don't have the questionnaire anymore, but I think another research assistant will still have it. Maybe you would like to see it before you apply? Her e-mail address is [. . .]." The opportunity to obtain the questionnaire was added in the design to be able to differentiate between initial selection (i.e., request protocol) and sustained selection (Napolitano, 2013). Instead of this distinction, we decided to use a different indicator for event selection. Specifically, our reasoning was that this chance event only becomes valuable in the job interview process if the applicant can make a well-informed impression during the job interview by mentioning this information. Hence, selection of the event is indicated by mentioning the protocol or questionnaire in the job interview rather than by requesting the documents (see Measures for details).

Event B was a poster in the waiting room, which each applicant occupied for five minutes before the interview. The waiting room contained several chairs, a table, a bottle of water with some cups and the poster. The poster was ostensibly created by the company *Veni, Vidi, Accepta* (i.e., "I came, I saw, I was hired" in Latin), which offered courses on job applications. Besides a link to a website and contact information, it contained three tips for a job interview. These tips were "Apart from skills that you master, mention at least one skill you could still improve," "Refer explicitly to your resume when you discuss your work experience," and "Convey an interested attitude by asking the interviewer how he got his job." These tips were chosen because it was possible to measure whether people would use these tips in the interview (i.e., selection). For example, if the poster had recommended to give a firm handshake, it would be more difficult to code. Also, the tips were considered strategies that applicants typically would not use by themselves but seemed reasonable to adopt.

Event C was a (verbal) comment made at the end of the job interview. This comment was "It might be interesting for you to know that, next to the vacancies you are currently applying for, [the employer's name] offers a research internship in his department. If you would like to receive more information about this opportunity, you can send him an e-mail." It was mentioned that this opportunity was independent of the research assistant vacancies. As this event was presented in all interviews, we assumed that all applicants would hear (i.e., perceive) the event, so only selection of this event was assessed (see Measures for details).

Procedure

Applicants received an invitation for the job interview and were sent information regarding the job interview via an e-mail. This e-mail included chance event A.

Applicants were asked to report in a room at the campus for the job interview. Upon arrival, a research assistant asked applicants to wait in an adjacent room. The interviewer tracked the time that the applicant was in this room to ensure equal exposure to chance event B (i.e., the poster) for every applicant. After five minutes, the interviewer brought the applicant to a third room, in which the interview took place. During the job interview, which lasted 10 to 15 minutes, chance event C (i.e., the research internship) was presented. After finishing the job interview, applicants were asked to report back to the research assistant and were debriefed. Applicants were then given an informed consent form about the accompanying research, and upon providing consent, participants completed a brief questionnaire. Applicants were reassured that the job interview was real and not set up for data collection. Also, they were reassured that refusing to fill out the questionnaire would not impact the selection process, as the research assistant would not discuss this with the interviewer.

The first five participants were positioned as a pilot to ensure that questions asked during the job interview were structured and contained a minimal amount of variation between interviews. These applicants were still considered for the vacancies. The remaining 67 participants (7 men, 60 women, mean age = 21.14, SD = 1.94) were a good representation of the faculty of social sciences, especially given that the vacancies were mainly advertised among psychology students (i.e., 83% of psychology students are female).

Measures

All measures were conducted after the job interview. Table 2.3 presents descriptive statistics and bivariate correlations of the Study 2 variables.

Like in Study 1, personality was assessed with the Quick Big Five (Vermulst & Gerris, 2005). Items were answered on an agreement scale of 1 (*strongly disagree*) to 5 (*strongly agree*). Internal consistency was satisfactory ($\alpha = 0.86$ for extraversion, $\alpha = 0.88$ for conscientiousness, $\alpha = 0.74$ for agreeableness, $\alpha = 0.72$ for emotional stability, and $\alpha = 0.71$ for openness to experience).

Preparation for the job interview was assessed with the item "How well did you prepare this time for the job interview?" with answer categories ranging from 1 (*not well at all*) to 5 (*very well*).

Previous chance event experience was assessed with an index that had the same items as in Study 1. Because applicants were still in education, we

Table 2.3 Descriptive Statistics and Bivariate Relations of Study 2 Variables

	M	SD	2	3	4	5	6	7	8	9	10
1. Age	21.14	1.94	0.21†	−0.14	0.06	0.07	−0.12	0.02	0.12	−0.18	0.04
2. Extraversion	5.03	0.96		−0.10	−0.04	0.12	0.14	0.06	0.06	−0.12	0.01
3. Conscientiousness	4.97	1.08			0.21†	0.05	−0.04	0.24*	0.02	0.25	0.17
4. Agreeableness	5.87	0.44				0.15	0.12	−0.06	0.15	−0.08	0.20
5. Emotional stability	4.07	0.88					−0.10	0.12	0.10	−0.73	0.15
6. Openness to experience	5.02	0.76						−0.01	0.18	−0.05	−0.05
7. Preparation for job interview	3.40	0.99							−0.12	0.38	0.29*
8. Previous chance event experience	1.23	0.59								−0.55	0.47*
9. Event perception	0.90	0.22									1
10. Event selection	0.41	0.24									1
11. Event value	4.99	0.78									0.81***

Note: Given the nested data (i.e., chance events were nested in job applicants), the relations of independent variables with event perception and selection represent unstandardized bivariate multilevel estimates (βs).

$^{***}P < 0.001$; $^{**}P < 0.01$; $^{*}P < 0.05$; $^{\dagger}P < 0.10$.

excluded the fifth item about job offers and kept four items. Answer categories ranged, again, from zero (*never*) to 4 (*more than 10 times*). Cronbach's alpha was 0.69.

Event perception was assessed by asking applicants "Did you notice that you could send an e-mail to [research assistant's name] to ask for the protocol of the data collection?" and "Did you notice that there was information on the wall with job interview tips in the waiting room before the job interview?" Answer categories were Yes/No. It was assumed that all applicants had heard the suggestion for the research internship (i.e., chance event C), so perception was not assessed for this event. Event value was assessed if applicants had perceived the event. Statements were "[Description event] I considered valuable" with answer categories from 1 (*completely disagree*) to 7 (*completely agree*).

Event selection was assessed based on recorded job interviews and received e-mails. For selection of event A (i.e., protocol and questionnaire through e-mail), three independent raters watched the job interviews and observed whether applicants mentioned that they had read (at least one of) these documents. For selection of event B (i.e., job interview tips on the poster), raters observed whether applicants applied the tips. Only 13 out of 190 excerpts that related to the selection of events A and B were coded differently by the raters, leading to high inter-rater agreement (Cohen's kappa = 0.85–0.87). Disagreements were resolved through discussion. Selection of event C (i.e., comment in interview about research internship) was assessed by whether or not applicants sent an e-mail asking for more information about the internship.

Analyses

Because each applicant was exposed to multiple chance events, we have nested data. The dependent structure of the data was accounted for with multilevel regression analyses in SPSS. For event perception, two events were nested in applicants (event C was perceived by all); for event selection, three events were nested in applicants. Applicant characteristics (i.e., personality, preparation) were estimated on the between-level; event characteristics (i.e., perceived value) were assessed on the within-level.

Results

Perception of chance events was very high, as almost all applicants had seen the note in the e-mail about the protocol (93%) and the tips on the poster in the waiting room (87%). Selection of these chance events was lower: 70% had mentioned the protocol/questionnaire, 43% applied one or multiple tips of the poster, and 10% sent an e-mail about the research internship.

Table 2.4 Prediction of Perception and Selection of Chance Events in the Job Interviewing Process (Study 2)

	Event Perception		Event Selection	
	B	SE	B	SE
Between level				
Age	−0.12	0.11	0.03	0.09
Previous chance event experience	−0.21	0.52	.49*	0.23
Extraversion	0.04	0.30	0.04	0.16
Conscientiousness	0.13	0.24	−0.00	0.15
Agreeableness	0.07	0.50	0.08	0.31
Emotional stability	−0.77*	0.33	.01	0.19
Openness to experience	0.30	0.55	−0.16	0.25
Preparation for job interview	0.43	0.35	0.35*	0.16
Within level				
Event value			0.80***	0.20

***$P < 0.001$; **$P < 0.01$; *$P < 0.05$.

Table 2.4 shows the relations of personality, preparation, and chance event experience with the perception and selection of chance events. For event perception, it was predicted that especially the Big Five personality trait *openness to experience* would be related to higher levels of event perception. However, openness to experience did not correlate with a higher likelihood of event perception. Applicants low in emotional stability were more likely to notice the events they were exposed to. Preparation for the job interview and applicants' experience with chance events were not related to likelihood of event perception.

Selection of the events was not predicted by applicants' personality. However, applicants who had prepared more for the interview were more likely to select chance events. Also, applicants' previous chance event experience was predictive: Those who had experienced more chance events in the past were more likely to select the events they were exposed to in the job interview process. The perceived value of an event predicted selection such that applicants were more likely to select events they considered more valuable.

In the questionnaire, we asked whether applicants had suspected that the job interview process was also part of a research project. Zero applicants indicated "Yes, I knew this beforehand"; 8 out of 67 applicants indicated "Yes, I had a presumption"; the rest (88%) said, "No, I had no idea." Performing the analyses without applicants who had suspected something did not change the results.

As a final exploration, it was examined whether the six applicants who were hired differed from the 62 applicants who were not hired. All hired applicants had seen the note in the e-mail (i.e., event A) and the poster in the waiting room (i.e., event B). Hired applicants were more extraverted ($t = 4.34$, $P = 0.002$) and more likely to have used tips on the poster ($\chi^2[1, n = 67] = 4.68$, $P = 0.031$).

Discussion

When chance events are examined in a controlled setting, individuals' perception and selection of these events is, again, not random. When given the same opportunities to experience and capitalize on chance events, well-prepared individuals were better able to benefit from these chance events. Also, less emotionally stable individuals were more likely to perceive the events. Attesting to the ecological validity of the study, applicants' experience with chance events was predictive of their action upon chance events in the controlled setting. Specifically, those having experienced more chance events in previous job searching were more likely to select the chance events they were exposed to in the job interview process. These findings indicated that individuals may differ in their way of acting upon chance events.

A particular strength of Study 2 was that the operationalization of chance events was controlled by the study design. Reports on chance events in previous research (and in Study 1) were affected by people's own conception of what constitutes a chance event (Bright, Pryor, & Harpham, 2005, 2009; Hirschi, 2010), but the equal event exposure for all applicants in the current research made their own conception of a chance event irrelevant. Further advantages of the design included that the chance events spanned a variety of information channels (i.e., digital, written, and verbal) and that they neither seemed too strange (i.e., to prevent applicants becoming suspicious about the job interview process) nor too straightforward (i.e., to prevent all applicants selecting the events). Also, the perception and selection of the events were reliably measurable. What might be regarded as a disadvantage of the chance events is that applicants might have differed in the extent to which they consider the events valuable. For example, those who applied for the job because they needed the money might have been less attracted by the possibility for an (unpaid) internship. Yet, we considered it realistic to have events that some people considered more valuable than others. We also accounted for this with a measure of event value, which indeed predicted the probability of selecting the event. Together, the events seemed realistic, unanticipated, and potentially valuable in the job interview process. This is further evidenced by the finding that chance event experience outside the job interview process was related to chance capitalization in this process.

General Discussion

The current research found that chance events played an important role in the job search process and that their occurrence, perception, and selection was not random. In the context of school-to-work transitions, Study 1 indicates that labor market entrants might experience more chance events if they are better prepared and if they have a larger social network. Exposing all respondents to the same chance events in Study 2, we found that better prepared job applicants were more likely to select these chance events. Also, those who had experienced more chance events in the past were more likely to capitalize on the chance events they were exposed to in Study 2. Answering the same question with different methods, the studies together present opportunity, preparation, and personality differences in the experience and capitalization of chance events (see also Figure 2.1).

The first conclusion from the current research is that people seemed to have different opportunities to experience chance events. Study 1 showed that job seekers with larger social networks and better-educated parents reported to have experienced more chance events. This replicates previous work (McDonald, 2010), which showed that the unsolicited receipt of job leads was related to social class and network characteristics. Extending these findings, we found that social networks were especially important if social relations had been involved in the job search process but that also unmobilized social relations were predictive of chance events. Hence, our findings corroborate McDonald's (2010) conclusion that chance is structured by the social world.

The second conclusion from our research is that—at least for the sample assessed in this study—it was not opportunity alone that determined whether people experience chance. Well-prepared job seekers in the school-to-work transition were more likely to experience chance events, both before and after graduation (Study 1). Although Study 1 could not present conclusive evidence as to whether well-prepared job seekers were more exposed, more perceptive or more active in capitalizing on chance events, Study 2 shed light on this issue. When all job applicants were exposed to the same number of chance events, well-prepared job applicants were more likely to act upon these chance events. Indeed, as Pasteur (1854) formulated, "chance favors the prepared mind."

With regard to personality, we found some unanticipated results. Openness to experience was theorized to predict exposure, perception, and selection of chance events (Costa & Crae, 1997; Heinström, 2002; Nahl & James, 1996; Napolitano, 2013). Yet, this personality trait did not predict the experience of chance events in the school-to-work transition (Study 1) nor the perception or selection of chance events in the job interview process (Study 2). Previous research on the relation between openness to experience and chance events found mixed support (Heinström, 2002, 2006; Hirschi, 2010; Pálssdóttir, 2010; McCay-Peet, 2013; Williams et al., 1998), which may, in part, be attributable to relatively low reliability of the scale (αs of 0.65 and 0.71 in the current studies, which are comparable to previous studies). Besides its reliability, the exact meaning of this Big Five personality trait is somewhat more vague, and the label has differed from *openness* to *creativity* to *intellect* (John, Naumann, & Soto, 2008). With regard to the current research, it may be that being open is not sufficient to capitalize on chance events. Specifically, it may require intentionality and flexible self-regulatory capacities that can better be assessed from a more behavioral angle; in other words, a person's openness alone may not predict positive outcomes from chance events, but rather it is some combination of openness and selection that transform chance events into sustained sources of positive development (Napolitano, 2013).

We also explored the role of emotional stability in the experience and capitalization of chance events. In Study 2, less emotionally stable (i.e., more neurotic) job applicants were more likely to perceive the chance events they were exposed to. One explanation may be that less emotionally stable individuals experienced higher state anxiety briefly before the job interview, which may result in heightened perception of the environment (Berggren, Blonievsky, & Derakshan, 2013). In the current setting, this alertness was beneficial to identify chance events that may otherwise have gone unnoticed.

Strengths, Limitations, and Suggestions for Future Research

The current paper contributes to previous research on individual differences in chance events in three ways. First, we confirmed theoretical work that predicted individual differences in the opportunities and preparation for chance events (e.g., Bandura, 1982, 1998). Second, we shed light on process models that proposed chance events to consist of different phases (i.e., occurrence, perception, and selection; Erdelez, 2004; Lawley & Tompkins, 2008; Makri & Blandford, 2012; Merton & Barber, 2004; Napolitano, 2013). Indeed, holding occurrence of chance events constant in Study 2, we provided a first indication that these phases can be distinguished. Third, besides reporting longitudinal self-reported data on the experience of chance events, we observed how people capitalized on chance events in an ecologically valid, controlled setting. The critical notion of what people themselves consider as a chance event when reporting on their past experience could not affect the results in this study. Together, the studies illustrated opportunity and preparation differences in self-reported experience as well as observed capitalization of chance events. At a more meta-level, this research illustrated that empirical research on the role of chance events is possible (and, we would argue, may be fruitful), in contrast to earlier researchers who had argued the study of chance events was "fundamentally unresolvable at the data level" (e.g., Krantz, 1998, p. 93).

Future research could improve upon the current research by using more domain-specific measures and by further studying predictors of the chance phases. While the current study used general indicators of personality (i.e., the Big Five), it may be that more specific and behavioral measures can shed additional light on the process of experiencing and capitalizing on chance. In addition to the measures tested in the current research, people's flexibility and self-regulatory skills may be important (Napolitano, 2013). Predictors of the different chance phases may also depend on the type of chance events that are considered. Study 2 focused on informational pieces, which is one important category of chance events. Interpersonal chance events constitute another salient category (McBirnie & Urquhart, 2011), and different factors (e.g., extraversion) may be more important in recognizing and acting upon such chance events (McCay-Peet, 2013). Also, even though the sample of university students in Study 2 was relevant to examine chance events in a job search context, findings may not be generalizable across the life span. Future research is encouraged to examine perception and selection of chance events after exposing participants to a variety of less and more salient chance events. Finally, we note that the results on our Dutch samples should be generalized with considerable caution, as our samples were not representative of broad populations.

Conclusion

The current research found empirical support for Seneca's proposition that luck (i.e., chance) happens when opportunity meets preparation. Specifically, the experience of chance events among emerging adult job seekers in their school-to-work transition was dependent on their social context as well as their preparation for their job search. Also, job applicants who received the opportunity to benefit from chance events did so especially if they had prepared well. In short, in this study, chance was not sheer luck after all.

Acknowledgment

Data for Study 1 are collected as part of the School2Work project, which is embedded in the Coordinating Societal Change focus area of Utrecht University. Financial support for this study was provided by Instituut Gak (#2013-203), although the opinions expressed in this paper are solely those of the authors. We wish to thank the fellow project members—in particular, Lisa Dumhs and Corine Buers—for the collaboration on the School2Work project. We wish to thank Matthijs Nijboer for his helpful insights and practical assistance in designing Study 2.

References

Baay, P. E., Buers, C. C. E., & Dumhs, L. (2014). *School2Work: A longitudinal study of the transition from vocational education and training to the labour market in the Netherlands.* Working paper, Utrecht University. Retrieved from https://www.narcis.nl/publication/RecordID/oai%3Adspace.library.uu.nl%3A1874%2F328202

Baay, P. E., van Aken, M. A. G., van der Lippe, T., & de Ridder, D. T. D. (2014). Personality moderates the links of social identity with work motivation and job-searching. *Frontiers in Psychology, 5*, 1044.

Bandura, A. (1982). Self-efficacy mechanism in human agency. *American Psychologist, 37*, 122–147.

Bandura, A. (1998). Health promotion from the perspective of social cognitive theory. *Psychology and Health, 13*, 623–649.

Berggren, N., Blonievsky, T., & Derakshan, N. (2013). Enhanced visual detection in trait anxiety. *Emotion, 15*, 477–483.

Betsworth, D. G., & Hansen, J. I. C. (1996). The categorization of serendipitous career development events. *Journal of Career Assessment, 4*, 91–98.

Blanco, M. R., & Golik, M. N. (2015). Born under a lucky star? Latin American CEOs' perceptions about their own career development. *International Journal of Human Resource Management, 26*(14), 1865–1888.

Blau, G. (1994). Testing a two-dimensional measure of job search behavior. *Organizational Behavior and Human Decision Processes, 59*, 288–312.

Bright, J. E., Pryor, R. G. L., Chan, E. W. M., & Rijanto, J. (2009). Chance events in career development: Influence, control and multiplicity. *Journal of Vocational Behavior, 75*, 14–25.

Bright, J. E. H., Pryor, R. G. L., & Harpham, L. (2005). The role of chance events in career decision making. *Journal of Vocational Behavior, 66*, 561–576.

Bright, J. E., Pryor, R. G. L., Wilkenfeld, S., & Earl, J. (2005). The role of social context and serendipitous events in career decision making. *International Journal for Educational and Vocational Guidance, 5*, 19–36.

Chen, P. (2005). Understanding career chance. *International Journal for Educational and Vocational Guidance, 5*, 251–270.

Chua, V. (2014). The contingent value of unmobilized social capital in getting a good job. *Sociological Perspectives, 57*, 124–143.

Costa, P. T., & McCrae, R. R. (1997). Personality trait structure as a human universal. *American Psychologist, 52*, 509–516.

Crites, J. O. (1969). *Vocational psychology: The study of vocational behaviour and development.* New York, NY: McGraw-Hill.

Cunha, M. P. E. (2005). *Serendipity: Why some organizations are luckier than others.* FEUNL working paper no. 472. Retrieved from http://ssrn.com/abstract=882782.

Denrell, J., Fang, C., & Winter, S. G. (2003). The economics of strategic opportunity. *Strategic Management Journal, 24*, 977–990.

Dew, N. (2009). Serendipity in entrepreneurship. *Organization Studies, 30*, 735–753.

Diaz de Chumaceiro, C. L. (2004). Serendipity and pseudoserendipity in career paths of successful women: Orchestra conductors. *Creativity Research Journal, 16*(2–3), 345–356.

Erdelez, S. (1999). Information encountering: It's more than just bumping into information. *Bulletin of the American Society for Information Science, 25*, 25–29.

Erdelez, S. (2004). Investigation of information encountering in the controlled research environment. *Information Processing and Management, 40*, 1013–1025.

Erdelez, S., & Rioux, K. (2000). Sharing information encountered for others on the Web. *The New Review of Information Behaviour Research, 1*, 219–233.

Foster, A., & Ford, N. (2003). Serendipity and information seeking: An empirical study. *Journal of Documentation, 59*(3), 321–340.

Gerris, J. R. M., Houtmans, M. J. M., Kwaaitaal-Roosen, E. M. G., Schipper, J. C., Vermulst, A. A., & Janssens, J. M. A. M. (1998). *Parents, adolescents and young adults in Dutch families: A longitudinal study.* Nijmegen: Institute of Family Studies University of Nijmegen.

Goldberg, L. R. (1992). The development of markers of the Big-Five factor structure. *Psychological Assessment, 4*, 26–42.

Graebner, M. E. (2004). Momentum and serendipity: How acquired leaders create value in the integration of technology firms. *Strategic Management Journals, 25*, 751–777.

Granovetter, M. (1974). *Getting a job.* Cambridge, MA: Harvard University Press.

Guindon, M. H., & Hanna, F. J. (2002). Coincidence, happenstance, serendipity, fate, or the hand of God: Case studies in synchronicity. *The Career Development Quarterly, 50*, 195–208.

Hart, D. H., Rayner, K., & Christensen, E. R. (1971). Planning, preparation, and chance in occupational entry. *Journal of Vocational Behavior, 1*, 279–285.

Heider, F. (1958). *The psychology of interpersonal relations.* New York, NY: Wiley, 1958.

Heinström, J. (2002). Fast surfing, broad scanning and deep diving. The influence of personality and study approach on students' information-seeking behavior. *Journal of Documentation, 61*, 228–247.

Heinström, J. (2006). Psychological factors behind incidental information acquisition. *Library & Information Science Research, 28*, 579–594.

Hirschi, A. (2010). The role of chance events in the school-to-work transition: The influence of demographic, personality and career development variables. *Journal of Vocational Behavior, 77*(1), 39–49.

John, O. P., Naumann, L. P., & Soto, C. J. (2008). Paradigm shift to the integrative big five trait taxonomy. In O. P John, R. W. Robins, & L. A. Perwin (Eds.), *Handbook of personality: Theory and research* (3rd ed., pp. 114–158). New York, NY: Guilford.

Krantz, D. L. (1998). Taming chance: Social science and everyday narrative. *Psychological Inquiry, 9*, 87–94.

Krumboltz, J. D. (2009). The happenstance learning theory. *Journal of Career Assessment, 17*(2), 135–154.

Lawley, J., & Tompkins, P. (2008). Maximising serendipity: The art of recognising and fostering potential: A systemic approach to change. Retrieved from https://www.cleanlanguage.co.uk/articles/articles/224/1/Maximising-Serendipity/Page1.html

Lefcourt, H. M. (1966). Internal versus external control of reinforcement: A review. *Psychological Bulletin, 65*, 206–220.

Lerner, R. M., Petersen, A. C., Silbereisen, R. K., & Brooks-Gunn, J. (Eds.). (2014). *The developmental science of adolescence: History through autobiography*. New York, NY: Psychology Press.

Lin, N. (1999). Building a network theory of social capital. *Connections, 22*, 28–51.

Lin, N. (2006). A network theory of social capital. In D. Castiglione, J. van Deth, & G. Wolleb (Eds.), *Handbook on social capital* (pp. 35–78). Oxford, England: Oxford University Press.

Lin, N., & Ao, D. (2008). The invisible hand of social capital: An exploratory study. In N. Lin & B. Erickson (Eds.), *Social capital: An international research program* (pp. 107–132). New York, NY: Oxford University Press.

Lin, N., & Dumin, M. (1986). Access to occupations through social ties. *Social Networks, 8*, 365–385.

Lin, N., Fu, Y. C., & Hsung, R. M. (2001). The position generator: Measurement techniques for investigations of social capital. In N. Lin, K. Cook, & R. S. Burt (Eds.), *Social capital: Theory and research* (pp. 57–81). New York, NY: Aldine de Gruyter.

Makri, S., & Blandford, A. (2012). Coming across information serendipitously – Part 1 A process model. *Journal of Documentation, 68*, 684–705.

McBirnie, A. (2008). Seeking serendipity: The paradox of control. *Aslib Proceedings: New Information Perspectives, 60*, 600–618.

McBirnie, A., & Urquhart, C. (2011). Motifs: dominant interaction patterns in event structures of serendipity. *Information Research, 16*(3). http://InformationR.net/ir/16-3/paper494.html

McCay-Peet, L. (2013). *Investigating work-related serendipity, what influences it, and how it may be facilitated in digital environments*. (Unpublished doctoral Dissertation), Dalhousie University Halifax, Nova Scotia. Retrieved from http://dalspace.library.dal.ca/bitstream/handle/10222/42727/McCay-Peet-Lori-PhD-IDPhD-December-2013.pdf?sequence=5

McCrae, R. R. (1996). Social consequences of experiential openness. *Psychological Bulletin, 120*, 323–337.

McDonald, S. (2010). Right place, right time: serendipity and informal job matching. *Socio-Economic Review, 8*, 307–331.

McDonald, S., & Day, J. C. (2010). Race, gender, and the invisible hand of social capital. *Sociology Compass, 4*, 532–543.

McDonald, S., & Elder, G. H. (2006). When does social capital matter? Non-searching for jobs across the life course. *Social Forces, 85*(1), 521–549.

Merton, R. K., & Barber, E. (2004). *The travels and adventures of serendipity*. Princeton, NJ: Princeton University Press.

Miller, M. J. (1983). The role of happenstance in career choice. *Vocational Guidance Quarterly, 32*, 16–20.

Mitchell, K. E., Levin, S., & Krumboltz, J. D. (1999). Planned happenstance: Constructing unexpected career opportunities. *Journal of Counseling & Development, 77*(2), 115–124.

Mitroff, S. R., & Biggs, A. T. (2014). The ultra-rare-item effect visual search for exceedingly rare items is highly susceptible to error. *Psychological Science, 25*, 284–289.

Nahl, D., & James, L. (1996). Achieving focus, engagement, and acceptance: Three phases of adapting to Internet use. *Electronic Journal of Virtual Culture, 4*(1), 276–286.

Napolitano, C. M. (2013). More than just a simple twist of fate: Serendipitous relations in developmental science. *Human Development*, *56*, 291–318.

Pálsdóttir, Á. (2010). The connection between purposive information seeking and information encountering: A study of Icelanders' health and lifestyle information seeking. *Journal of Documentation*, *66*(2), 224–244.

Pasteur, L. (1923). Inaugural lecture, University of Lille, December 7, 1854. In *The life of Pasteur* (R. L. Devonshire, Trans., p. 76). Garden City, NY: Garden City Publishing.

Pickering, A., & Gray, J. A. (2001). Dopamine, appetitive reinforcement, and the neuropsychology of human learning: An individual differences approach. In A. Eliasz & A. Angleitner (Eds.), *Advances in individual differences research* (pp. 113–149). Lengerich, Germany: Pabst Science.

Pritchard, D., & Smith, M. (2004). The psychology and philosophy of luck. *New ideas in Psychology*, *22*, 1–28.

Pryor, R. G., & Bright, J. E. (2003). Order and chaos: A twenty-first century formulation of careers. *Australian Journal of Psychology*, *55*(2), 121–128.

Roe, A., & Baruch, R. (1967). Occupational changes in the adult years. *Personnel Administration*, *30*, 26–32.

Salomone, P. R., & Slaney, R. B. (1981). The influence of chance and contingency factors on the vocational choice process of nonprofessional workers. *Journal of Vocational Behavior*, *19*, 25–35.

Sampson, J. P., Lenz, J. G., Reardon, R. C., & Peterson, G. W. (1999). A cognitive information processing approach to employment problem solving and decision making. *The Career Development Quarterly*, *48*(1), 3–18.

Statistics Netherlands .(2014). Statline. Retrieved from https://opendata.cbs.nl/statline/#/CBS/en/

Vermulst, A. A., & Gerris, J. R. M. (2005). *QBF: Quick Big Five personality test manual.* Leeuwarden, The Netherlands: LDC.

Williams, E. N., Soeprapto, E., Like, K., Touradji, P., Hess, S., & Hill, C. E. (1998). Perceptions of serendipity: Career paths of prominent academic women in counseling psychology. *Journal of Counseling Psychology*, *45*, 379–389.

3
Purpose and Career Goals
A Qualitative Study

Vanessa L. Madrazo and Jenni Menon Mariano

Introduction

It is no wonder that educators and researchers are deeply interested in helping youth successfully transition to the work world. "Work" is what one is supposed to be engaged in after leaving school. There is an expectation that work should provide a decent livelihood to accomplish adult life tasks, and thus, work is a marker of independence and maturity that is considered to be positive. However, emerging adults may also receive negative cultural messages about work. Consider, for instance, this classic statement: "It's not supposed to be fun—that's why they call it work" (Ryan, 2016, para. 7). Usually, postsecondary education is considered to be the pathway to obtaining work, but for many young people, college may seem out of reach or irrelevant. For others who take the college route to work, the promise that one will get a job and paycheck afterward may be inadequate incentive by itself to pursue this course with enthusiasm. These scenarios may not enable emerging adults to achieve successful or healthy transitions to the work world because they do not consider a global sense of purpose and well-being. Research among college-going emerging adults found that focusing on financial success over prosocial goals undermined well-being and increased substance use (Vansteenkiste, Duriez, Simons, & Soenens, 2006). Having prosocial goals as a college senior predicts greater well-being outcomes in middle adulthood (Hill, Burrow, Brandenberger, Lapsley, & Quaranto, 2010). For those in high school who are just starting to think about careers, intrinsic work goals that are directed toward both benefit of self and benefit of others can predict greater meaning and purpose in life two years later (Yeager, Bundick, & Johnson, 2012). If we are to understand how to promote successful school-to-work transitions for emerging adults, it is important to consider well-being variables such as purpose.

Vanessa L. Madrazo and Jenni Menon Mariano, *Purpose and Career Goals* In: *Young Adult Development at the School-to-Work Transition.* E. Anne Marshall and Jennifer E. Symonds, Oxford University Press (2021). © Oxford University Press.
DOI: 10.1093/oso/9780190941512.003.0003.

In this chapter, we discuss purpose as it pertains to stability and change in career intentions for emerging adults transitioning out of high school and into college or the work world. A currently popular view is that work with purpose, or "on purpose" (Galinsky, 2011), is just what emerging adults are seeking; it represents more than a paycheck and provides individuals with both a sense of personal meaning and clear sense that they are able to contribute in a positive way to the world beyond the self. Hopes and plans for achieving purposeful work—as opposed to nonpurposeful work—may lend significant support to the transition to adulthood. Schwartz, Côté, and Arnett (2005) suggest that emerging adults who feel more responsible for their life's direction are more likely to pursue opportunities for growth that would improve the transition (Burrow & Hill, 2011, p. 1197). The cultivation of a sense of purpose affects positive development during life transitions by protecting against negative mental health outcomes like depression and suicide (Damon 2008; Costello, Erkanli, & Angold, 2006). The search for purpose is associated with increased life satisfaction during emerging adulthood, underscoring the developmental importance of cultivating purpose during school-to-work transitions. During life transitions, a sense of purpose can deter against "drift" while affording a sense of meaning and direction (Damon, 2008).

Interestingly, when researchers have asked young people about what is most important to them, many mention having a good career (e.g., Damon, 2008, pp. 52–53). Yet, although many people find employment after school or college, not all individuals experience a sense of purpose within that work, nor do they necessarily identify clear career pathways that help them live out their purposes over time. The current research study examines what supports, sustains, or hinders a sense of purpose in work over time for emerging adults. We studied profiles of stability in purposeful intentions pertaining to career in six emerging adults selected from a larger sample of participants aged 18 to 24. These individuals were transitioning through school, college, and work in the United States as the country headed into the Great Recession of 2008. Their experiences provide a particular perspective on career-related challenges for the emerging adults of this historical period, as discussed, for example, in Chao & Gardner (2017); we considered the role of purpose in helping these individuals navigate life stage transitions during that time. We first define purpose and purposeful work and then review literature on pathways and processes that may support or hinder purposeful work in emerging adulthood. Next we describe the larger Stanford study, selection of our subsample of six participants, and data analysis. Findings are presented as well as implications, limitations, and suggestions for future research.

Purpose and Purposeful Work

Purpose is an intention to accomplish something that is at once meaningful to the self and benefits some aspect of the world beyond the self (Damon, Menon, & Bronk, 2003). The sources of purpose and contexts in which individuals seek to live out their purpose are diverse (Bronk, 2014; Malin, 2015). When present, however, a distinguishing feature of a strong and clear purpose is that it organizes one's life goals and activities (Kashdan & McKnight, 2009) often around one or more life domains (i.e., work). In this chapter we refer to individuals achieving "purposeful work" or "purposeful work intentions" when they discuss their purpose as primarily centered around and lived through their career. Furthermore, individuals with purposeful work intentions articulate clear future plans and report behaviors around their career goals, as opposed to harboring mere hopes for present or future action (Mariano, Going, Schrock, & Sweeting, 2011).

Pathways and Processes for Achieving Purposeful Work

There is limited research on how emerging adults achieve purpose through their careers (Bronk, 2014, p. 120). Kashdan and McKnight (2009) describe three pathways to a broader sense of purpose that help explain how emerging adults may orient toward work life: proactive, reactive, and social learning pathways. In practice, individuals may be on more than one of these pathways at any given time, but each is conceptually discrete.

On the proactive pathway, purpose emerges gradually through effortful exploration. Purpose unfolds over time for individuals on this pathway, and it arises after deliberate reassessment (Kashdan & McKnight, 2009, pp. 307–309). This view accords with the idea of emerging adulthood as an extended period of identity exploration even after adolescence (Arnett, 2004). For example, it is likely that as individuals explore their career identities they will also explore their purpose in life (Erikson, 1968). Pursuing career goals with effort may also change how emerging adults think about themselves as professionals (Bronk, 2011). Furthermore, Burrow and Hill (2011) found that purpose mediates the association between identity commitment and indices of well-being for emerging adults. In sum, the proactive pathway theory aligns with the conscious personal development work that most emerging adults naturally engage in by virtue of their life stage (e.g., deciding who they are, what they want to accomplish and, on a more mundane level, simply what they are going to do every day) and which usually involves career decisions.

On the second, reactive pathway, transformative life events turn one in the direction of a purpose not previously pursued (Kashdan & McKnight, 2009, p. 309). While on this path, one could already be exploring possibilities for purpose, although this is not typical (Hill, Sumner, & Burrow, 2014). Nevertheless, a sudden event can trigger an epiphany, which accelerates the process (Hill et al., 2014, p. 309). This pathway appears to mostly promote prosocial commitments (Hill et al., 2014). For example, in one case study, a shooting occurred at a young man's high school, which catapulted him over time into a career in political activism (Bronk, 2014). Stories like this are often told after the fact, but they represent salient interpretations by the individual of what happened to help them choose their work. For some emerging adults, burnout through tiring and meaningless work can be stressful enough to trigger purposeful career development. Work may even be of high status and require considerable commitment to training but lacks purpose for the individual. For instance, Galinsky (2011) followed the lives of young social entrepreneurs who had found highly purposeful work. Each had experienced some crisis of meaning in their previous jobs that produced a deep dissatisfaction and triggered a dramatic career change. In sum, the reactive pathway theory explains how some emerging adults are drawn in to work that they find purposeful, often unexpectedly, by life-changing experiences or events.

The third pathway, that of social learning, is supported by purpose research and by research on vicarious learning through observing and interacting with others (Kashdan & McKnight, 2009, pp. 310–311). Having multiple types and sources of social support in one's life (i.e., a network) may be advantageous to purpose development, beginning in the school years (Mariano et al., 2011). More specifically, warm relationships with family members are indicated in research as important for purpose development in young adulthood (e.g., Malin, Reilly, Quinn, & Moran, 2014; Mariano & Vaillant, 2012). Early childhood social learning activities may influence habits and future intentions based on what one has been exposed to, such as when individuals display similar religious, eating, or other habits as their parents (Kashdan & McKnight, 2009) or when the social norms of one's culture influence goal setting and evaluation of success in meeting these goals (e.g., Nurmi, 1991, as discussed in Malin et al., 2014). Peers may be influential too, such as when young adults make new friends in college who expose them to new interests (Malin et al., 2014), and mentors play a role in inspiring the trajectories of young adult purpose exemplars' work (Bronk, 2014). In sum, social learning pathways represent instances where development of purpose was neither proactive nor reactive but rather a result of learning.

Although we need more evidence about purposeful work paths, support exists for three suppositions (Hill et al., 2014). First, engagement with any of the proactive, reactive, or social learning pathways leads to greater well-being because these pathways can all lead to greater purpose. Second, the proactive pathway is the most common among college-aged students studied. Third, individuals can follow more than one pathway to some degree (Hill et al., p. 229). In addition, a person's path may not be unitary or straight: the focus of individuals' purposes may not follow a clear pattern across adolescence and emerging adulthood, such as from self-oriented to other-oriented (Malin et al, 2014), or in relation to career (Malin, 2015). A common theme for many emerging adults is that college is a holding pattern for their purposes and a time when re-evaluation of previous goals takes place (Malin et al., 2014).

Psychological Strategies

A number of psychological and action strategies related to purpose have been observed among emerging adults. In one account, Galinsky (2011) examined strategies pursued by young social entrepreneurs. To find purposeful careers, these individuals went through a deliberate process to identify work that aligned with the social issues that moved them most and engaged their unique talents. They then formulated concrete ways to act—and did so over time. This strategy has subsequently become a purposeful work development program used in colleges and universities (Heart + Head = Hustle; see Galinsky, 2011). The psychological strategies presented in this formulation have a couple of features. First, they emphasize the individual's deliberate and authentic achievement of an alignment between their personal passions, abilities, and preferred action choices. Second, they emphasize a considerable amount of personal reflection. In one study, Bundick (2011) assigned young adult college students to two conditions: one that involved reflective interviews about their purposes in life and one that did not. The group that engaged in the structured reflection reported gains in the goal-directedness component of purpose some months later (Bundick, 2011). Research such as this suggests that pursuing goals just for their own sake is not sufficient to cultivate purpose, but rather it is the reflection on purpose that acts in a self-sustaining fashion to bolster the individual's goal-directed sense of purpose.

Focusing on something greater than one's own immediate concerns is a promising strategy described by several organizational psychologists (Grant,

2008; Grant & Hoffmann, 2011). This strategy has applications in different ways to individuals in different circumstances, such as those in school or college, or those at work doing different jobs. For example, studies show that people report doing even the most repetitive and boring work tasks more effectively, and that they find these tasks more meaningful, when they focus on something beyond themselves (Grant, 2008). People achieve this by thinking about the many ways in which their work can contribute to the greater good. This applied to jobs across population served, social status implied, and monotony of tasks involved (Grant, 2008; Grant & Hoffmann, 2011).

The process by which a greater-than-self focus may lead to purposeful careers is further illumined in research by Yeager et al. (2012). They found that high school students who were motivated to learn for reasons beyond their own self-interest were more likely to persist in their goal to go to college than those with self-oriented motives alone. These self-transcendent motives may play a unique part above and beyond other motives by lending strength to persist in even tedious activities in school or work. Over time, practicing persistence also builds self-regulation skills. These skills not only help one focus on specific career goals at the beginning, but also help one stay the course against obstacles over time.

A nuance of research on beyond-the-self motives is the distinction between intrinsic and extrinsic motivations. Self-determination theorists differentiate between motives to benefit others that are ultimately personally rewarding and those that are supported by feelings of obligation or social pressure (Deci and Ryan, 2008; Grant, 2008). Given the personally agentic and meaningful nature of purpose pertaining to career, intrinsic motivations are more promising for achieving purposeful career goals than those moved by social expectations alone. Overall, research shows that focusing on self-interests for career goals, such as the desire for enjoyment, making money, or doing something interesting, may not have enough motivational power by itself to sustain purposeful engagement in a line of work over time: There has to be a beyond the self-focus to fuel a sense of satisfaction in one's work and allow one to persist over the long haul.

Another mental strategy to achieve purposeful work is making proactive physical and cognitive changes to one's current job, otherwise known as "job crafting" (Wrzesniewski, LoBuglio, Dutton, & Berg, 2013). Through the removal or repositioning of mental boundaries, one redesigns the workplace so as to experience greater purposefulness and satisfaction. For example, one may change the content of the tasks or the time spent on them. One can improve relationships with workmates or those served by changing boundaries or refining communication, or one can change the meaning ascribed to both the tasks and relationships at work. Job crafting is useful for purposeful career development in the school-to-work transition because it shows how individuals have power to determine the quality of their work experience even when they may have foreclosed on a specific job. It underscores that career-oriented purpose development is a dynamic, ongoing process open to refinement and does not stop once a job or career of choice is obtained. Job crafting seems to require that one already be in a workplace that engages one's career goals; however, the strategies may be practiced in other environments as well. Making changes at school or college may act as dress rehearsals for job crafting in future work.

Influence of Career Type and Structure

A focus on something greater than oneself can endow almost any work with a sense of purpose. However, work or career type may also impact purposeful work in the transition to adulthood, possibly due to the structure of training programs or the predictability and stability of the profession itself. Research that examined portions of the larger data set from which the current study is drawn found that young adults pursuing helping professions were able to sustain their purpose better across time than those pursuing creative careers (Malin et al., 2014). Specifically, participants who went in to nursing, medicine, and teaching reported a greater sense of purpose overall in the transition from school to work than did those who pursued journalism, advertising, graphic design, and theater. Loss of purpose in the creative career seekers appears to be explained by abandonment of their initial desire to make a social contribution through their work. Their sense of purpose was further sidelined by the challenge of finding a job after college in a creative field and by the concern for making a living in a challenging and sometimes undefined work domain (Malin et al., 2014). In contrast, it stands to reason that helping professions intrinsically involve motives for benefiting others, whereas this is not always the case with creative professions. Training programs certainly can and very well may encourage all students to connect their chosen course of study with prosocial activity, but this training effect can fall apart on entering some professions if the workplace culture does not continue to support it (Malin et al., 2014).

Influence of Economic Factors

These days, deferral of life transitions to work and family is considered normative for many young adults as economies have moved from industrial to information-based (Tanner, Arnett, & Leis, 2009). Even accepting this reality, there is little research directly linking economic downturns to youths' purpose development during the school-to-work transition. Both negative and positive effects are plausible. For example, in one study researchers used a large population-wide data set collected in the United States over a 30-year period. They discovered that economic challenges experienced by graduates during times of recession have had long-term negative effects on these individual's futures in terms of earning potential, negative behaviors, health, and even mortality into midlife (Schwandt, 2019; Schwandt & von Wachter, 2018). This study does not directly mention psychological factors like purpose, but the authors observed significantly higher risk of death from unhealthy behaviors and drug overdoses over time—so-called deaths of despair—among those who were transitioning from school during recessions. They suggest a "hysteresis" phenomenon (Schwandt, 2019, p. 3), or effects that continue after the original causes (i.e., economic hardship and uncertainty when transitioning to the job market) are removed. Other research argues that good employment rates are a buffer against uncertainty during emerging adulthood and boost a sense of optimism. Crocetti et al. (2015) compared Italian and Japanese youths' views of the emerging adult period and found that Japanese youth living in times of economic stability associated this life stage with a higher sense of possibilities than did their Italian counterparts who were living with high rates of unemployment. Optimism and possibilities appear consistent with a sense of purpose.

In contrast to the negative effect hypothesis, Greenfield's theory of social change and human development posits an inverse relationship between economic downturns and development of purposes that extend beyond the self among young people. A large-scale longitudinal study conducted in the United States found that high schools students' concern for others (i.e., values and behaviors) increased during recession eras (Park, Twenge, & Greenfield, 2014). These recessions may have had a balancing effect wherein long-term trends in youth valuing money and jobs that make lots of money leveled off, to be replaced with greater concern for the collective. Even though purpose was not the subject of this study, a greater concern for others paired with a moderated interest in material work goals appears consistent with purposeful work intentions.

In sum, the studies just reviewed offer two perspectives on how economic factors can impact purpose for emerging adults. This research is descriptive of what may happen at a macro level however and is not about development of purposeful work for any particular individual. A study by Bronk, et al. (2018) indicates how individuals could and do, in fact, successfully deal with economic challenges and still achieve a sense of purpose in their careers. They surveyed and interviewed young adults living in Greece during the Great Recession and found several personal characteristics and strategies about work that may buffer economic pressures. Young people with higher than average purpose scores reported choosing jobs that were personally meaningful and enjoyable and conceptualized work as a source of professional growth and fulfillment. The work narratives of individuals with lower purpose described work as a means of self-sufficiency and "getting by" (p. 7). Furthermore, participants did not in general differ in their understanding of the economic realities they faced. In fact, those with purpose felt that the economy influenced their plans more than did the participants with lower purpose. But those with purpose responded to these realities with a "stick-to-it-iveness" and indication that they needed to persevere more. This study demonstrates how a strong general sense of purpose can transfer over to the development of a purposeful work orientation. The study, in fact, reflects psychological strategies to achieve purposeful work, which are not unlike some of those articulated earlier. However, it is unique in demonstrating how purposeful work intentions interact with economic factors for emerging adults and can help them overcome them.

Based on our review of research and theory, it appears that psychological, structural, and economic factors matter to sustain purpose in one's work as emerging adults transition to the work world. To examine these issues further, we developed the following research questions. What is the definition of purpose and how does it relate to work? How is purpose associated with stability and change in terms of career intentions among emerging adults that are transitioning from school to work? What are the pathways and processes that support of hinder purposeful work in emerging adulthood? We analyzed interview data to identify the supports of purposeful work that emerging adults themselves mention during this transition.

Method

The present study is a secondary analysis of six participants who were purposefully selected from a larger sample ($N = 270$) of interviews collected by researchers at Stanford University that included the second author (see Malin, et al., 2014). The Stanford sample included a cross-section of young people recruited from schools and colleges across the United States (attending 6th grade, 9th grade, 12th grade, and college) and selected for regional and demographic diversity. A subsection of participants ($N = 146$)

was interviewed at two intervals over a two- to three-year period; our sample of six cases was drawn from this subsection. We obtained permission from the Stanford Center on Adolescence and institutional review board approval at Stanford and the University of South Florida for use of the de-identified data.

Interview Measure

The Stanford Youth Purpose Interview (Andrews et al., 2006; Malin, et al., 2008, pp. 196–197) takes approximately 45 minutes to administer, was developed by teams of researchers over time, and has been piloted in previous studies (Malin et al., 2008, p. 189). Participants are asked direct and indirect questions about their most important life goals, including activities related to those goals, as well as goal origins, reasons, supports, obstacles, and future plans. Examples of questions include "If you had to imagine your perfect world, what would that look like?"; "When you refer to your life, what's important about that?"; and "What are you good at?" At the end of the interview, participants are asked whether they think they have a purpose, and what the word *purpose* means to them.

Selection of Six Cases From the Stanford Data

In the primary analysis, Stanford researchers used a coding scheme to reliably assess participants' responses in each interview transcript for the presence of a generalized sense of purpose and other features. More information on the full primary coding process and interrater reliability is reported elsewhere (see Malin et al., 2008; 2014). For the current study, we used several participant characteristics and assigned coding labels derived from the Stanford researchers' analysis to meaningfully narrow the sample.

First, we selected only those interview participants that were in late adolescence and college/post college, therefore eliminating younger participants ($N = 139$ of the original 270).

Second, interview transcripts had to be available for each participant at two time points to enable longitudinal assessment and to observe stability of interviewees' purposeful work intentions. These interviews took place over a two- to three-year period: once in 2005/2006 (Time 1) and again in 2007/2008–2009 (Time 2). These criteria yielded 12 available interviews, representing two cohorts. Cohort 1 was in the last year of high school at

Time 1 and transitioning into college or work at Time 2. Cohort 2 was in college or at work at Time 1 and was in graduate school or at work at Time 2.

Third, to sift further for relevant narratives, we chose transcripts with "category" and "domain" code labels that pertained to career or work. The Stanford researchers had previously assigned category and domain labels identifying what aspects of participants' lives were top of mind when they talked about their purpose. We used these labels as signposts indicating that participants' work intentions were central topics for some participants and that their transcripts were thus likely to yield substantive information for the current analysis. Understandably, organizing the content of an individual's professed purpose into succinct subject areas is inherently tricky because purpose pervades many aspects of one's life—so individuals may speak about their purpose in relation to many parts of their life at one time. Therefore, it was important for participants' work narratives to be substantive so that we could target themes of support for purposeful work intentions rather than for participants' purpose in general.

In an attempt to isolate supports of purposeful work over time, we sought to use only those cases labeled as either "have a good career" (category) and/or "career" (domain) at Time 1 and Time 2. After looking in the data, we found that this rule could be fully applied to Cohort 2 cases at both time points. For the younger Cohort 1, the data yielded career domain and category labels present at either Time 1 or Time 2. Consequently, when applying our selection rules (age, interviews at two time points, and category and domain work/career labels), we isolated our cases to the final six.

Participants

Table 3.1 presents demographic characteristics of the six participants, who are designated by pseudonyms. Participants were from California, ethnically diverse, and 83% female.

Participants were also diverse in how their global sense of purpose changed between Time 1 and Time 2, as reliably assessed by the Stanford researchers using one of four "purpose form" labels. Purpose forms were qualitative assessments of the degree to which participants fulfilled all dimensions for purpose at each time period based on a global reading of the case (i.e., not necessarily centered on participant's career goals). "Nonpurpose" form accounts meant that the interviewee did not mention clear or coherent goals in their life (i.e., they were thus "drifting" without

Table 3.1 Participant Demographics

Cohort	Pseudonym	Sex	Race/ Ethnicity	Age T1	Age T2	Attendance T1	Attendance T2
1	Andre	Male	African American Italian	19	21	High school senior	Working
	Olivia	Female	White	18	20	High school senior	College sophomore
2	Leah	Female	White Jewish	21	23	College senior	Working
	Grace	Female	White	22	24	College senior	Working
	Aiyana	Female	Native American	21	23	College senior	Enrolled in postgraduate course
	Sofia	Female	Hispanic/ Latino	21	23	College junior	College graduate; unemployed

Note: Cohort 1 = School to college/work; Cohort 2 = college/work to work.

any anchor to personal goals or they were "dabbling" in a lot of activities that lacked a central goal structure). "Dreamer" form accounts were those in which participants expressed goals and aspirations directed at self and/ or benefiting others but without clear plans or actions to make them a reality. In the remaining two forms, and using the definition of purpose described earlier by Damon et al. (2003), participants discuss clear goals, actions, and plans that are primarily self-oriented (self-oriented purpose or "self life goal" form) or they have these self-oriented goals, actions, and plans but also profess the desire to have a positive impact on some aspect of the world beyond the self ("beyond the self-purpose" form; see Malin et al., 2008). Consequently, a "beyond the self" purpose form is said to fulfill all aspects of the purpose definition and other forms fulfill partial dimensions. Interestingly, higher percentages of emerging adults were found to fulfill more complete purpose forms than do younger adolescents; however, the progression through these forms has not been found to follow a linear pattern (Malin et al., 2014). We did not use purpose form as a selection criteria for our six cases; however, we report it here because the label informs how these participants experienced purpose in their lives over time and in a global sense—albeit not necessarily related to their work. All our participants evinced self-oriented purpose forms at Time 1. By Time 2, however, two participants showed purpose form growth (from self-oriented to beyond the self), three showed purpose form stability (from self-oriented to self-oriented), and one showed purpose form decline (from self-oriented to self-oriented dream).

Analysis

Analysis of the six cases was completed in several iterations to arrive at reliable findings (Hruschka et al., 2004; Krippendorf, 2004). Steps included developing codes that addressed the research questions, segmenting units in the interview text, establishing inter-coder reliability, and, finally, developing inter-coder agreement on the content and meaning of findings.

Code Development, Reliability, and Agreement

Coders were the authors, both independent scholars with advanced training in research on youth purpose. In the code development stage, a list of codes to address the research question was drafted with definitions and general supporting examples. The authors developed these through first reading the 32 interviews with young adults made available from the larger Stanford sample (see age and interview criteria) and identifying themes pertaining to the research focus. A simple coding scheme with few codes was used (Campbell, Quincy, Osserman, & Pedersen, 2013, p. 15). The first author, who was familiar with the interview protocol, segmented the text into meaningful coding sections. Segments varied from single units, to several paragraphs, to one whole global code for an interview, but each was considered within the context in which they were presented. Second, the authors coded the interviews independently. Code reliability was tested, discrepancies discussed, and problematic codes were refined and modified. In some cases, text segments were modified or new ones were identified. Modified codes were then applied independently to a random selection (25%) of the transcripts again by each coder and final acceptable inter-rater reliability coefficients obtained (Cohen's Kappa = 0.95–1.0). Next, the authors sought to establish agreement on a method for further organization and interpretation of the findings. A memo of each case was independently written by one of the coders who then corroborated and discussed with the other coder. Memos pulled evidence for each code at each time point and developed a descriptive and interpretive story of each case to address the research questions and take into account new insights that may have arisen (see Campbell et al., 2013). Finally, in the code deployment phase, the 12 transcripts (six cases) selected for this study were independently coded by one coder. The same coder wrote memos and the findings section, and the two coders came to a negotiated agreement on the memos and the findings content (Campbell at al., 2013, p. 14). Table 3.2 shows code definitions and examples.

Table 3.2 Sample Code Definitions and Examples

Code Label	Definition	Example
Career goal	Mention of specific or general goals related to work or career (i.e., desire to be successful in a career, job, work; desire to follow a career path, or engage in a specific form of work).	"I'd like to have a job where I can support my family and still have money left over to do some traveling." "I always loved telling stories so I thought about becoming a writer."
Beyond the selfness	Explicitly stated intentions/goals or reasons aimed at impacting others positively in some way (i.e., helping, caring for, teaching others, contributing to others or society).	"I'd say my purpose in life is to help others reach their full potential. It's great when I can impact others in a positive way." "Purpose? Maybe learn from my mistakes and use them to teach others about how to make good choices. My little sister, she's a good kid, but I always remind her to stay focused about school. I don't want her to have to repeat the year like I did."
Supports/ positive influence	Reference to people, processes, or things that are seen by the participant to positively influence or support them in the direction of the career/work. May be psychological, social, or refer to strategies/practices/behaviors used by participant as pertains to the work/career.	"When I'm at school, I feel like my teachers really want me to do well. One teacher stopped me in the hallway to tell me that I did a really good job on my essay. I felt like, wow that's great." "My parents. They're there for me, whenever I need something, like even if it's just to ask advice, I feel that I can always count on them."
Detracts/ Negative Influence	Reference to obstacles—people, processes, or things –seen by the participant to negatively influence or detract progress in the direction away from the career/work. The obstacle can be seen as surmounted or surmountable but can still be assigned this code. May be psychological, social, or refer to strategies or practices used by participant as pertains to the work/career.	"Working sometimes cuts into my time to study for class. Sometimes after going to work, going to school, my time left to actually do the work that is needed for class is really limited." "My friends tease me sometimes. They ask why not just start working? They don't see the importance of going to school. To them it's a waste of time."

Note: Underlined phrases show content that indicates the code.

Findings

Earlier, we defined *purposeful work* or *purposeful work intentions* as aims to benefit some aspect of the world beyond the self, plus a clear association of these aims with career goals. In this section we use the two terms interchangeably. Our first finding is that all six of the emerging adults in our sample were deliberating about their future career at Time 1. This is not surprising considering our case selection process. However, five out of the six cases indicated stability in purposeful work intentions, meaning that they described purposeful work at both Time 1 and Time 2, whereas the sixth case did not describe purposeful work at either time point per se, but rather demonstrated purpose through higher education and family obligations. Our second finding is that among those five participants who described stable purposeful work, we found trends over time pertaining to content, breadth, and change in intentions to make a contribution through their work. Third, a variety of factors were found to support (positive influence) or detract from (negative influence) purposeful work for these individuals, including psychological, social, and behavioral factors, as well as financial factors and time. Among these factors, more positive than negative career-related influences were reported at Time 1 than at Time 2 (see Table 3.2 for definitions). Fourth, there was a fundamental coherence in these emerging adults' career interests between Time 1 and Time 2, yet participants also adopted a dynamic approach to the content and execution of their career goals across time.

Differences in Career Focus Between Stable and Absent Purposeful Work Cases

The majority of our discussion focuses on the five stable cases of purposeful work because they are examples of a successful school-to-work transition by emerging adults. To briefly describe between-group differences, we found that stable (Andre, Olivia, Leah, Grace, and Aiyana) and absent (Sofia) purposeful work cases varied in how the participants viewed their intentions to contribute to the world beyond the self in light of their career goals and their ability to connect good things they were doing to their present work. For instance, the five stable purposeful work cases had a desire to positively benefit someone or something other than self that was both identified as their life purpose and connected to their career goals. In comparison, the one absence of purposeful work case (Sofia) did not link her aims to contribute with her career aspirations. She said she wanted to help others by recycling, donating money to church, and taking care of family members but did not refer to work. When asked about her purpose at Time 1, Sofia stated that she wanted to be a good daughter and have a great job, but these aspirations were unconnected with specific professional goals. Furthermore, at Time 2, Sofia made no connection between positive things she was doing in her life and a career. She stated, "My purpose in life is . . . based on God because—He knows who I am, He knows what my life will be, so He has everything planned for me." This statement is representative of Sofia's narrative, which shows an orientation to being of consequence to something greater than or other than herself and centering her plans in these sources (i.e., being a good daughter in Time 1 and following God's plans for her in Time 2) but which lacks specific and elaborate connection to work. Compare Sofia with the stable purposeful work case of Andre, who demonstrates that the needs of other people are important to inform his purpose and subsequent career goals. For example, Andre mentioned attending City Council meetings to stay informed of environmental regulations so that he could pass the information along to co-workers: This example is representative of the five stable purposeful work cases in that the participant makes an explicit connection of their desire to contribute to career-related tasks and aspirations.

Growth in Purposeful Work Intentions

The five purposeful work participants showed growth over time in beyond-the-self intentions pertaining to work. The trend occurred in all cases, with a progression between Time 1 and Time 2. Growth took the form of expanding the reach of participants' intentions and also specifying and multiplying the targets of their intentions within the workplace. The reach became more broad for some, at first mentioning others who were close to them, but later referencing larger groups of people. For example, Grace mentioned taking care of patients at Time 1, but at Time 2 she talked about making the whole world a better place through a career in medicine. At the same time, ways to act out their intentions also became more concrete for some participants. For example, at Time 2, Andre was better able to identify specific instances in which he engaged in purposeful work than at Time 1. In this case, growth in purposeful work meant that Andre expanded the reach of his work to affect a wider range of people through identifying more tangible strategies.

Over time, those with stable purposeful work intentions diversified the ways they contributed within their workplaces through pursuing expanding roles, even within the same job. Perhaps the defining feature for these cases that distinguish them from some job crafting (Wrzesniewski et al., 2013) descriptions, however, is that they were anchored by the individual's clear desire to contribute. For example, Andre listed more ways at Time 2 than at Time 1 in which he could make a difference, including serving food to the elderly while on the job or serving as a role model to his co-workers. Along the same lines, Leah, showed how her aspirations to be of benefit to other people directly influenced her behavior at work over time. She was in charge of contacting customers and mentioned that her company's marketing policy caused her to reconsider her actions within this role. She made sure to only send e-mails when absolutely necessary or when it was requested by the customer. Although Leah adopted this practice to comply with regulations, she also did so out of respect for consumers' privacy. In respecting consumers' right to privacy regarding their contact information, she felt as if she was making a difference at her place of work. Furthermore, Leah engaged in purposeful work with her colleagues. In addition to volunteering with many community service organizations outside of work, she ran a boot camp for her co-workers during their lunch break. She said that being of service to others was the driving force behind this action as she trained people three times a week:

> I can donate that extra three hours . . . to something else that benefits somebody else, not just me. . . . I do boot camp, which benefits other people. . . . I wouldn't do boot camp if it didn't benefit the team. I would just go work out on my own.

Thus, Leah's purposeful work intentions came to be expressed through various roles at work, as employee and co-worker, some which she took on her own initiative. Her actions also demonstrate how behaviors that are driven by intentions to benefit something other than oneself can impact others on both small and large scales even within the confines of the workplace. In this case, they can benefit people with whom Leah had an interpersonal relationship (co-workers) and people she may have never met in person (customers).

Overall, the examples of stable purposeful work illustrate how purposeful work intentions can actually grow. Growth meant that participants exhibited two orientations to their work over time. First, participants broadened the reach of their purposeful intentions to reference and target larger, or other, groups of people in their immediate workplace or broader field. Second, participants identified—and actually listed—more ways to contribute at or through work, and the examples they listed became more concrete. Finally, some participants described growth through expanding or reconsidering their roles at work and how they performed their tasks; this suggests that participants became more effective and impactful in these tasks.

Coherent Yet Dynamic Career Goals

Participants who maintained purposeful work intentions exhibited a fair degree of coherence in how they spoke about career-related aspirations over time. This was shown by some expressing specific career goals at Time 1 and then putting them directly into action at Time 2, whereas for other participants, the goal-to-action relationship between Time 1 and Time 2 was less pronounced, yet still clearly present. In all five cases, however, a dynamic approach formed an underlying trend between the two time points.

Several examples illustrate how participants adopted a dynamic approach to their work while still maintaining a good degree of constancy in their career interests. Andre mentioned several career-related goals at Time 1 and Time 2, including becoming a manager, teaching, getting involved in philanthropy, achieving independence, and providing for his family. However, by Time 2 Andre had changed his major focus of study and no longer showed interest in becoming a realtor. Olivia professed interest in going to medical school, becoming independent, and going to or graduating from college at Time 1 and Time 2. By Time 2, however, she mentioned additional goals, including the desire to work in a hospital, enroll in medical school, and provide for herself and her family. The third participant, Leah, wanted to work at a company at Time 1 and by Time 2 had been hired by that same company. At both time points, Leah expressed an interest in marketing, wanting to work at a job that impacted others such as the Boys and Girls Club, graduating from college, and getting a job to buy a house. By Time 2, Leah had also phased out several career-related goals such as retiring young, being able to travel, keeping a steady job, and securing a job in a close-knit community, although her core interests remained stable. At Time 2 Leah was working constantly and had interviewed with companies out of state, but no longer wanted to move around as much. In the fourth case, that of Grace, a career goal in science persisted between Time 1 and Time 2, which was expressed through her interests in graduate school, research in biotechnology, and a well-defined sense of a professional identity. With Grace, some career goals changed slightly over time but maintained a similar focus. For example, Grace expressed an interest in medicine and physics (Time 1) that may have led to an interest in biotechnology (Time 2). She discussed wanting to bring education to more people (Time 1), which may have then informed her desire to perform health-related volunteer work (Time 2). Nonetheless, by Time 2 several of Grace's career-related goals mentioned at Time 1 had disappeared (i.e., developmental biology or immunology, to make money traveling with her mother, fashion design, getting a PhD). Finally, for Aiyana, goals to teach and be credentialed to do so persisted over time, but by Time 2, the desire to be financially independent surfaced in her interviews as very important.

These examples indicate that at least some change in career goals was common among participants. Even as participants mentioned the same goals across time, they usually added to their Time 1 list, detracted from it, or clarified it, showing a fair degree of flexibility in response to time and contextual factors, albeit maintaining core interests.

Positive and Negative Influences on Career Goals Impacting Purposeful Work

Psychological Support

Participants mentioned several sources of psychological support that served as positive influences on their career goals. Psychological support sources were personal mental and emotional states and competencies affecting participants' orientation to purposeful work. These sources fell into four categories: perspective, work ethic, enjoyment, and skill match. First, participants noted the importance of perspective in terms of having a positive mindset. For example, Olivia kept perspective in regards to her coursework at Time 1. She stated, "If I'm really motivated I'll get it done. The struggle might be hard, but I'll get it done." Her positive mindset was maintained in Time 2 as evidenced by reframing failure as something not to be concerned about. Second, participants emphasized work ethic by talking about their approach to work as being motivated, hard-working, or goal-oriented. At Time 1, Leah said that others would describe her as hard-working and went on to say that the most important thing for her are her goals. She reiterated this at Time 2 by saying that she is passionate about what she does and gives it her all. Third, participants enjoyed some aspect of their chosen career or field of study. Andre spoke at Time 1 about his chosen career as a realtor with enthusiasm by stating that he really enjoyed houses. He was also positive about pursuing a degree at Time 2, stating that he likes to learn. Fourth, participants indicated that they had skills in an area that would serve them well in the workplace. At Time 1 Grace said she had competencies in communication and interpersonal skills. She reiterated a good fit with her skills in the workplace at Time 2 by stating "I think I am good at customer service. . . . I am also good at computers. . . . I am good at science." In these ways, participants demonstrated instances of psychological support with respect to their career goals in terms of purposeful work.

Social Support

Participants outlined a considerable number of sources of social support, which are influences that participants referenced as being derived from their environment. Four categories emerged: experiential influences, support from a network, job environment, and financial incentives. First, participants mentioned the positive influence of experiences that led them to pursue a given career. For example, Aiyana spoke at Time 1 about how her involvement in a summer camp for children with disabilities resulted in her changing her field of study from biology to teaching. She reiterated the impact of that experience at Time 2, by saying that the summer camp caused her to re-evaluate her career path: "I need to stop being a bio major and switch over to this because this is what I want." Second, participants commented at length about the supportive influence experienced from their network. Networks included people such as family members, significant others, teachers, and on-the-job mentors. At Time 1, Andre mentioned that speaking with management at his job helped him learn. He repeated the importance of support at work at Time 2, mentioning how helpful it was for him to learn while on the job. Third, participants spoke about the job environment as a positive influence on their career goals. Leah spoke at Time 1 about the positive experience of beginning her employment as an intern at a start-up company. Her positive experience continued at Time 2 because the internship resulted in a more permanent career opportunity. Fourth, participants cited financial incentives as supporting their career goals. Financial incentives included pursuing higher education and financing college through work. Grace talked about the positive aspect of the financial compensation that her job provided at Time 1, which allowed her to continue studying and which put her in a better position for future opportunities. At Time 2, Grace reiterated the importance of the financial compensation but added that while money was important, so was "my personal professional satisfaction just by working." Thus, participants experienced various forms of social support, all of which contributed to their navigation of the school-to-work transition.

Behavioral Support

Participants mentioned several ways in which their own behaviors supported their career goals. Behavioral supports were described as practices or strategies. Although these supports were mentioned much less often than psychological and social ones, they were evident and fell into three categories: practice of financial acumen, practice of self-care, and practice of spirituality. First, participants described how tending to their monetary well-being benefited them and their career. Practices included acquiring scholarships or saving money. Leah spoke about staying responsible with her finances at Time 1 by mentioning how important it was that she be able to buy a house and retire at a decent age. She continued her commitment to financial responsibility at Time 2 by saving money and getting scholarships and grants for school. Second, the steps that participants took to practice self-care helped them succeed on the job. Examples of self-care strategies were practicing time management and taking measures to reduce stress. Olivia utilized a stress management strategy at Time 1 by considering alternative options in case she did not get accepted to the medical school of her choice. She also engaged in stress management at Time 2 by planning time to relax after completing her work. Third, participants mentioned practicing spirituality as a source of strength through cultivating beliefs that afforded hope during difficult times. For example, at Time 1 Grace described a perfect world as one that included being spiritual and doing things for the community. At Time 2, she also mentioned her belief in God as something that helped her overcome unexpected obstacles along her career path. Thus, although behavioral supports were overall less salient than social or psychological supports, they nonetheless appeared to exert a significant amount of influence on purposeful work among participants.

Financial and Time Obstacles

Participants mentioned positive supports of career goals more frequently than negative influences. Finances and time were the primary factors cited as negative influences on career goals, and sometimes participants mentioned them together. Money was described as an obstacle because the economy was uncertain and there was a lack of funding to support career enterprises. At Time 1, Andre mentioned funding as an obstacle to his creating a charitable organization. He referred to money as an obstacle again at Time 2, saying that it was a complicating factor in helping others. Additional financial concerns included the cost of tuition or rent. For example, at Time 1, Grace mentioned that her father had stopped paying for her education and this presented a challenge. At Time 2, Grace again cited financial limitations as an obstacle to her career path. Time was cited as an obstacle in regards to educational achievement, especially while pursuing a challenging course of study. Aiyana experienced this at Time 1 and mentioned time as an obstacle for success in school. She reiterated her position at Time 2 by describing student teaching as very demanding in terms of time in addition to being an unpaid position. Participants also cited lack of time management skills as an obstacle to career growth. At Time 1, Andre mentioned that the time to get things organized was an obstacle in his career. He also referred to this obstacle at Time 2 by citing time, or the lack thereof, as a barrier to helping people.

Discussion

This study explored supportive factors for purposeful work over time among six emerging adults, with emphasis on five participants who exhibited stable purposeful work and who accomplished this during a time of economic challenge (the Great Recession). Our analysis identified psychological, social, and behavioral supports of purposeful work, some negative influences, and described purpose growth dynamics over a two- to three year period. The findings substantiate other research related to purpose (but not always about purpose per se) and also indicate strategies for helping youth achieve successful school-to-work transitions.

At the heart of the findings is that a family of factors across domains (psychological, social/environmental, and behavioral) supported emerging adults' achievement of purposeful work over time. This ecological, multifactor perspective is corroborated in research on positive youth development. Moreover, many of the more specific factors we identified show up in previous research on constructs related to purposeful work or about healthy transitions to adulthood. This study therefore contributes additional insights on purposeful work. For instance, multiple social supports of purposeful work were mentioned by the participants: social experiences, support from a network, workplace environment, and financial incentives. In other research, social support demonstrates a substantial amount of influence on the experience of emerging adults as they transition into the workplace (Arnett, 2004), including expectations of initial employment opportunities and overall well-being (Kenny, Blustein, Chaves, Grossman, & Gallagher, 2003). Indeed, social supports facilitate the transition during emerging adulthood, while the absence of such supports may lead to decreased happiness, self-worth, and adjustment (Galambos et al., 2006; Mortimer et al., 2002; Polach, 2004). Furthermore, we found that maintaining and acting on spiritual beliefs, categorized as a behavioral influence in our study, served to support purposeful work, which aligns with studies showing that spiritual activities result in positive life purpose outcomes (Smith & Snell, 2009, p. 297)

Evidently, other research is consistent with many of the single factors that our emerging adults said support purposeful work and also shares a multifactor perspective on supports of thriving. The most interesting observation in this study was participants' ability to change and adapt to their circumstances in ways that augment their sense of purpose in work. Work adaptability is "readiness to cope with changing work and working conditions" (Super & Knasel, 1981, p. 195); the five emerging adults exhibited this capability through simultaneously adopting a coherent and dynamic approach to their career goals. They managed to maintain their core interests but also exercised flexibility in modifying these interests over time. In a general sense, this finding mirrors ideas on career adaptability mentioned in the literature on career calling (a concept closely akin to purposeful work; see Hall & Chandler, 2005), on maintaining purpose in one's work through job crafting (Wrzesniewski et al., 2013), and on how one's purpose in work grows as a result of focusing on something larger than oneself (Grant, 2008).

Our findings also mirror research on how young adults maintained purpose during the Great Recession in Greece (Bronk et al., 2018). Like the young people in the Greek study, our emerging adults were keenly aware of the social and economic obstacles to their success. Yet, they neither emphasized those obstacles (i.e., negative influences were infrequently mentioned) nor allowed these barriers to deter them. The purposeful Greek youth avoided demoralization by looking past present challenges and focusing on a positive future; they stayed hopeful by focusing on how they could support others (e.g. family, friends, community, country). They chose jobs that helped them grow and in which they found joy (Bronk et al., 2018). Our emerging adults reported similar attitudes, adopting a positive mindset (a sense of perspective, or reframing of failures), a motivated work ethic, an enthusiasm in their work, and a feeling that their work matched their skill set. Beyond these attitudes, however, the current study reveals additional insights by deeply explicating the ways in which growth in beyond-the-self work intentions happens, as well as the mechanisms by which this occurs. These included expanding the targets of one's contribution, identifying more concrete ways to contribute through work, and expanding one's role at work.

The results suggest consideration of how those who work with emerging adults might help them achieve purpose in their careers as they transition to the work world. For instance, those in professions such as teaching, career counseling, and higher education administration may find these results informative. The findings most obviously point to coaching young people in the psychological approaches, behavioral practices, and strategies related to purposeful work that emerged from this study, as well as exposing them to the types of social support that were mentioned. Certainly, to maximize purposeful work for young people everywhere, it is essential to remove or reduce obstacles such as finances and time, to include everyone in strong social networks, to cultivate good workplace environments, and to provide fair and viable financial incentives. From a broader perspective, however, the ability to adapt appears to be a most important feature in sustaining purpose, especially in times of any transition. To help young people develop this capability may require fostering a keener understanding of what being purposeful actually means, particularly as pertains to career goals. One common view is that purpose is about sticking to one's guns; having single, clear, and specific goal targets; and persisting toward these self-defined targets come what may (Malin, 2018). Realistically, however, purpose suggests a broader and more flexible approach since one's purpose may be constantly explored and expressed in multiple ways (i.e., one may have multiple purposes; Malin, 2018). Metaphorically, purpose is better conceived as "a beacon guiding one over open waters"—often not in a straight line—than as a smooth and clear path (Malin, 2018, p. 33). Perhaps, if educators foster this broader view of purpose, it could help youth build hope for the future and avoid demoralization when their immediate goals are not met, especially in times of uncertainty.

Study Limitations and Future Directions

This study was a secondary analysis of interview data that were about purpose in general, thus limiting a single focus on participants' discussion of purpose in the domain of work that may have yielded more extensive findings. The size of the sample and the qualitative nature of the data limit generalizability of the findings. Following initial case selection using precoded career labels, we read interviews closely to identify appropriate data for our study; however, a reading of each interview within the full sample might have captured important and additional experiences pertinent to our research focus. The five cases were all examples of stable purposeful work: Without a comparison group, we could not identify whether any of the factors were unique to those with purposeful work intentions. Future investigations should explore this topic among larger samples that are more differentiated in the stability of their purpose in work.

Furthermore, while our sample was relatively diverse, we did not consider how gender or cultural factors associated with ethnicity, socioeconomic status, or faith may have impacted findings. Future research could consider the impact of these variables on how purposeful work is expressed and defined by youth themselves, rather than use an a priori definition. For instance, Sofia, who identified as Mexican-American and Catholic, was the one participant who did not evince stable purposeful work by our definition and was thus not considered in the bulk of our analyses. A closer look at her interviews indicated endorsement of culturally specific character traits pertaining to traditional gender roles (e.g., *marianismo*; Piña-Watson, Castillo, Jung, Ojeda, & Castillo-Reyes, 2014) and the primary importance of family (*familismo*; Castillo & Cano, 2007) that are apparent in Latino culture. Sofia was the first in her family to go to college and at Time 2 speaks about plans for additional schooling, which include graduate degree programs. An examination of her case through the lens of culture could reveal other contributors to her career aspirations that were missed in the current analysis. Information such as this could shed more light on motivational factors that contribute to the development of purposeful work intentions.

Conclusion

There seems to be a growing trend for emerging or young adults to look for and even expect to find work that feels purposeful to them. It is promising therefore that the current study reveals factors that may contribute to a sense of purpose in work for this population and thereby help them to build hopeful futures and experience well-being, even in challenging times.

Acknowledgments

This research was supported in part from grants from the John Templeton Foundation to William Damon at Stanford University. The authors are grateful to the young people who participated and the school administrators who made it possible. We thank the researchers at the Stanford Center on Adolescence who collected and/or the coded data for primary analyses, including the following individuals and any others we have missed here: Matthew Andrews, Kendall Cotton Bronk, Matthew Joseph, Amina Jones, Heather Malin, Seana Moran, Brandy Quinn, Tim Reilly, and David Yeager.

References

Andrews, M., Bundick, M., Jones, A., Bronk, K. C., Mariano, J. M., & Damon, W. (2006). *Revised youth purpose interview.* Stanford, CA: Stanford Center on Adolescence.

Arnett, J. J. (2004). *Emerging adulthood: The winding road from the late teens through the twenties.* New York, NY: Oxford University Press.

Bronk, K. C. (2011). The role of purpose in life in healthy identity formation: A grounded model. *New Directions for Youth Development, 132,* 31–44.

Bronk, K. C. (2014). *Purpose in life: A component of optimal youth development.* New York, NY: Springer.

Bronk, K. C., Leontopoulou, S., & McConchie, J. (2018). Youth purpose during the great recession: A mixed-methods study. *The Journal of Positive Psychology, 14,* 405–416.

Bundick, M. J. (2011). The benefits of reflecting on and discussing purpose in life in emerging adulthood. *New Directions in Youth Development, 132,* 89–104.

Burrow, A. L., & Hill, P. L. (2011). Purpose as a form of identity capital for positive youth adjustment. *Developmental Psychology, 47,* 1196–1206.

Campbell, J. L., Quincy, C., Osserman, J., & Pedersen, O. K. (2013). Coding in-depth semistructured interviews: Problems of unitization and intercoder reliability and agreement. *Sociological Methods and Research, 42,* 294–320.

Castillo, L. G., & Cano, M. A. (2007). Mexican American psychology: Theory and clinical application. In C. Negy, (Ed.), *Cross-cultural psychotherapy: Toward a critical understanding of diverse client populations* (2nd ed., pp. 85–102). Reno, NV: Bent Tree Press.

Chao, G. T., & Gardner, P. D. (2017). Healthy transitions to work. In L. M. Padilla-Walker & L. J. Nelson (Eds.), *Flourishing in emerging adulthood: Positive development during the third decade of life* (pp. 104–128). New York, NY: Oxford University Press.

Costello, J., E., Erkanali, A., & Angold, A. (2006). Is there an epidemic of child and adolescent depression? *Journal of Child Psychology and Psychiatry, 47,* 1263–71.

Crocetti, E., Tagliabue, S., Sugimura, K., Nelson, L. J., Takahashi, A., Niwa, T., . . . Jinno, M. (2015). Perceptions of emerging adulthood: A study with Italian and Japanese university students and young workers. *Emerging Adulthood, 3,* 229–243.

Damon, W. (2008). *The path to purpose: How young people find their calling in life.* New York, NY: The Free Press.

Damon, W., Menon, J., & Bronk, K. C. (2003). The development of purpose during adolescence. *Applied Developmental Science, 7*(3), 119–128.

Deci, E. L., & Ryan, R. M. (2008). Self-determination theory: A macrotheory of human motivation, development, and health. *Canadian psychology/Psychologie canadienne, 49,* 182.

Erikson, E. H. (1968). *Identity, youth, and crisis.* New York, NY: Norton.

Galambos, N. L., Barker, E. T., & Krahn, H. J. (2006). Depression, self-esteem, and anger in emerging adulthood: Seven-year trajectories. *Developmental Psychology, 42,* 350–365.

Galinsky, L. (2011). *Work on purpose.* New York, NY: Echoing Green.

Grant, A. M. (2008). Does intrinsic motivation fuel the prosocial fire? Motivational synergy in predicting persistence, performance, and productivity. *Journal of Applied Psychology, 93*(1), 48–58.

Grant, A. M., & Hofmann, D. A. (2011). It's not all about me: Motivating hospital hand hygiene by focusing on patients. *Psychological Science, 22,* 1494–1499.

Hall, D. T., & Chandler, D. E. (2005). Psychological success: When the career is a calling. *Journal of Organizational Behavior, 26,* 155–176.

Hill, P. L., Burrow, A. L., Brandenberger, J. W., Lapsley, D. K., & Quaranto, J. C. (2010). Collegiate purpose orientations and well-being in early and middle adulthood. *Journal of Applied Developmental Psychology, 31,* 173–179.

Hill, P. L., Sumner, R., & Burrow, A. L. (2014). Understanding the pathways to purpose: Examining personality and well-being correlates across adulthood. *The Journal of Positive Psychology, 9*, 227–234.

Hruschka, D. J., Schwartz, D., St. John, D. C., Picone-Descaro, J. E., Jenkins, R. A., & Carey, J. W. (2004). Reliability in coding open-ended data: Lessons learned from HIV behavioral research. *Field Methods, 16*, 307–331.

Kashdan, T. B., & McKnight, P. E. (2009). Origins of purpose in life: Refining our understanding of a life well lived. *Psychological Topics, 18*, 303–316.

Kenny, M. E., Blustein, D. L., Chaves, A., Grossman, J. M., & Gallagher, L. A. (2003). The role of perceived barriers and relational support in the educational and vocational lives of urban high school students. *Journal of Counseling Psychology, 50*, 142–155.

Malin, H. (2015). Arts participation as a context for youth purpose. *Studies in Art Education, 56*, 268–280.

Malin, H., Reilly, T. S., Quinn, B., & Moran, S. (2014). Adolescent purpose development: Exploring pathways, discovering roles, shifting priorities, and creating pathways. *Journal of Research on Adolescence, 24*(1), 186–199.

Malin, H., Reilly, T. S., Yeager, D., Moran, S., Andrews, M., Bundick, M., & Damon, W. (2008). *Interview coding process for forms of purpose determination.* Stanford, CA: Stanford Center on Adolescence.

Mariano, J. M., Going, J., Schrock, K., & Sweeting, K. (2011). Youth purpose and perception of social supports among African-American girls. *Journal of Youth Studies, 14*, 921–937.

Mariano, J. M., & Vaillant, G. E. (2012).Youth purpose among the "greatest generation." *The Journal of Positive Psychology, 7*, 281–293.

Mortimer, J. T., Zimmer-Gembeck, M. J., Holmes, M., & Shanahan, M. J. (2002). The process of occupational decision making: Patterns during the transition to adulthood. *Journal of Vocational Behavior, 61*, 439–465.

Nurmi, J-E. (1991). How do adolescents see their future? A review of the development of future orientation and planning. *Developmental Review, 11*, 1–59.

Park, H., Twenge, J. M., & Greenfield, P. M. (2014). The Great Recession: Implications for adolescent values and behavior. *Social Psychological and Personality Science, 5*(3), 310–318.

Piña-Watson, B., Castillo, L. G., Jung, E., Ojeda, L., & Castillo-Reyes, R. (2014). The Marianismo Beliefs Scale: Validation with Mexican American adolescent girls and boys. *Journal of Latina/o Psychology, 2*, 113.

Polach, J. L. (2004). Understanding the experience of college graduates during their first year of employment. *Human Resource Development Quarterly, 15*(1), 5–23.

Ryan, L. (2016, December 20). It's not supposed to be fun—That's why they call it work. *Forbes.* Retrieved from https://www.forbes.com/sites/lizryan/2016/12/20/its-not-supposed-to-be-fun-thats-why-they-call-it-work/#48ceb4b310d0

Schwandt, H. (2019). Recession graduates: The long-lasting effects of an unlucky draw. *Stanford Institute for Economic Policy Research.* Retrieved from https://siepr.stanford.edu/sites/default/files/publications/PolicyBrief-Apr2019.pdf

Schwandt, H., & von Wachter, T. (2018). Unlucky cohorts: Estimating the long-term effects of entering the labor market in a recession in large cross-sectional data sets. *Journal of Labor Economics, 37*(1), 161–198.

Schwartz, S. J., Côté, J. E., & Arnett, J. J. (2005). Identity and agency in emerging adulthood: Two developmental routes in the individualization process. *Youth & Society, 37*, 201–229.

Smith, C., & Snell, P. (2009). *Souls in transition: The religious and spiritual lives of emerging adults.* New York, NY: Oxford University Press.

Super, D. E., & Knasel, E. G. (1981). Career development in adulthood: Some theoretical problems and a possible solution. *British Journal of Guidance and Counselling, 9*, 194–201.

Tanner, J. L., Arnett, J. J., & Leis, J. A. (2009). Emerging adulthood: Learning and development during the first stage of adulthood. In M. C. Smith & N. DeFrates-Densch (Eds.), *Handbook of research on adult learning and development* (pp. 34–67). Routledge/Taylor & Francis Group.

Vansteenkiste, M., Duriez, B., Simons, J., & Soenens, B. (2006). Materialistic values and well-being among business students: Further evidence of their detrimental effect. *Journal of Applied Social Psychology, 36*, 2892–2908.

Wrzesniewski, A., LoBuglio, N., Dutton, J. E., & Berg, J. M. (2013). Job crafting and cultivating positive meaning and identity in work. *Advances in Positive Organizational Psychology, 1*, 281–302.

Yeager, D. S., Bundick. M. J., & Johnson, R. (2012). The role of future work goal motives in adolescent identity development: A longitudinal mixed-methods investigation. *Contemporary Educational Psychology, 37*, 206–217

4

Ready, Set, Go!

School-to-Work Transition in the New Career

Jos Akkermans, Rowena Blokker, Corine Buers, Beatrice Van der Heijden, and Ans De Vos

Introduction

The transition that young adults experience during their emerging adulthood when they finish their education and enter the labor market has been a prominent topic of discussion for decades. This period is extremely turbulent for those young individuals, as they go through many major changes—such as facing the responsibilities of a job for the first time and exploring one's vocational identity in new ways—in a relatively brief period of time (Arnett, 2000, 2007; McKee-Ryan, Song, Wanberg, & Kinicki, 2005). Moreover, a large body of scientific literature has shown that individual pathways at the school-to-work transition (STWT) are of crucial importance for young adults' chances of attaining long-term career success (e.g., Pinquart, Juang, & Silbereisen, 2003; Schoon & Silbereisen, 2009). In addition, the STWT also has important implications for employing organizations and society in general, in terms of costs related to sickness absence and unused potential (Morrison, 2002). Following from this, it is clear that the STWT is an essential period during emerging adulthood that young people need to manage as successfully as possible to provide a basis for securing sustainable labor participation.

Research on the STWT from a careers perspective has a rich tradition starting approximately halfway through the 20th century. For example, Super (1957) and Holland (1959) touched upon this topic in their discussions of several career development models. Traditionally, the STWT was positioned as a predictable, structured career path in which individuals would either finish education or drop out and then enter stable employment and preferably remain with that employer for life (i.e., lifetime employment). Accordingly, obtaining long-term employment and learning job-related skills were conceived to be core indicators of a smooth STWT.

Jos Akkermans, Rowena Blokker, Corine Buers, Beatrice Van der Heijden, and Ans De Vos, *Ready, Set, Go!* In: *Young Adult Development at the School-to-Work Transition.* E. Anne Marshall and Jennifer E. Symonds, Oxford University Press (2021).
 DOI: 10.1093/oso/9780190941512.003.0004.

Yet, during the past few decades, many major changes in the labor markets have caused the STWT to become more complex and challenging (Brzinsky-Fay & Solga, 2016; Cebulla & Whetton, 2018), making it harder and more complex for young adults to successfully transition to the labor market than before (Lechner, Tomasik & Silbereisen, 2016). In general, careers have become longer and more complex as the result of several key labor market developments (Vuori, Toppinen-Tanner, & Mutanen, 2012).

First, labor markets have changed, from being primarily oriented on manufacturing, toward a service-oriented sharing economy. This has led to a fundamental shift in necessary knowledge and skills and, as a result, has increased the difficulty level of many jobs (Schoon, 2007). This development also puts additional pressure on young individuals from different educational levels and with different types of jobs (e.g., blue collar vs. white collar).

Second, the contemporary labor market is characterized by discontinuities in work (e.g., being laid off after reorganization or the "last in, first out" principle) and by serious challenges all working staff have to deal with, such as unemployment and underemployment (Haase, Heckhausen, & Köller, 2008; McKee-Ryan & Harvey, 2011). In fact, these issues have been most problematic for young adults entering the labor market for the first time (Akkermans, Nykänen, & Vuori, 2015b) also because they are often employed in temporary positions (Aronson, Callahan, & Davis, 2015; De Lange, Gesthuizen, & Wolbers, 2012).

Third, students are increasingly overloaded with information during their studies (e.g., because of massive online opportunities for information) and at the same time face a trend toward mass higher education (Tomlinson, 2008) and an increasingly complex labor market (MacLeod, Riehl, Saavedra, & Urquiola, 2017). Therefore, the importance of paying careful attention to connecting education with work is increasing. Unfortunately, scholars have argued that the coordination between the two has actually been declining (Heinz, 2009). As a result, these two worlds are still not especially well-connected academically nor in the perception of young adults, and this creates serious problems for graduates during the STWT.

Fourth, traditional definitions of a successful STWT have typically focused on success criteria such as obtaining stable and long-term employment. However, this is no longer the case in many countries as work has become more flexible and short-term and there is a growing number of self-employed workers (Kalleberg, 2009). Indeed, it is taking young adults ever longer to find their first job (Koivisto, Vuori, & Vinokur, 2010), let alone find stable employment (Ling & O'Brien, 2013).

Following from the previous discussion, it is not surprising that young adults have recently been described as the losers in a globalizing world (Blossfeld, Klijzing, Mills, & Kurz, 2005) and "the lost generation" (Wolbers, 2016, p. 51). For these reasons, we argue that to gain a thorough understanding of the STWT in today's dynamic world of work, it needs to be analyzed from a careers perspective. The primary aim of this chapter, therefore, is to examine the STWT through the lens of the contemporary career. In doing so, we will shed light on some of the major developments that are influential in explaining whether and how young adults might thrive during emerging adulthood and, particularly, in their early careers.

There are integral connections between the concepts of the STWT and the contemporary career, for in both people need fundamentally different knowledge, skills, and abilities to flourish in their education and work than before. Contrary to the traditional perspective, young adults can no longer expect predictable career patterns, nor can they passively wait until opportunities come "knocking at the door" (Ng & Feldman, 2007; Vogt, 2018). Indeed, today's young adults are expected to take ownership of their own career and proactively craft their own careers to be successful (Akkermans, Brenninkmeijer, Schaufeli, & Blonk, 2015a; Akkermans & Tims, 2017). Thus, the concept of agency has become dominant in discussions of an adaptive STWT. At the same time, it would be too simple to state that young adults are the only responsible party in their own career success. Career agency always occurs in context (De Vos, Van der Heijden, & Akkermans, 2020; Schoon, 2007; Schoon & Lyons-Amos, 2016) and even with growing individualization and the need for proactivity, the educational and vocational contexts in which the STWT takes place have a major influence on this process (Schoon & Lyons-Amos, 2017; Anders & Dorsett, 2017). In sum, this requires linking micro, meso, and macro frames of references to be able to examine the process accurately and understand which factors contribute to an adaptive STWT.

This chapter focuses on the STWT in the contemporary career. First, given that the STWT occurs within an organizational and societal context, both individual (i.e., micro-level) and structural (i.e., meso-level and macro-level) factors will be discussed that are at the foundation of a sustainable and adaptive STWT. Second, because research has clearly established the role of education and skill level (also see Akkermans et al., 2015b), we will argue that an adaptive STWT may be different for young individuals from different educational backgrounds. Next, we will introduce two topics that have a crucial role in contemporary early career success: career competencies and employability.

Finally, we will present and discuss several issues that we argue need further scientific exploration and testing.

Before we proceed, it is important to reflect on what we define as a successful way to transition to the labor market. To do so, we clarify our use of the term *adaptive STWT*. Scholars have used many different words in researching the STWT, most notably *successful STWT*. However, this term has a normative element, which would suggest that there is "only one right way" to transition into working life. For this reason, we choose the term *adaptive*, which suggests a process in which young adults manage to adapt to their new circumstances well (cf. person–career fit; Cha, Kim, & Kim, 2009; De Vos et al., 2020) and which has already been used by many prominent STWT scholars (e.g., Blustein, Philips, Jobin-Davis, Finkelberg, & Roarke, 1997; Tomasik, Hardy, Haase, & Heckhausen, 2009). It is also consistent with the core tenet of the protean career literature, which states that that self-awareness and adaptability are the key ingredients of contemporary careers (Hall, 2002). Although an adaptive transition can take many forms (Blustein et al., 1997), it generally concerns both objective/structural elements (e.g., finding a job and preventing underemployment) and subjective/individual elements (e.g., job and career satisfaction). Following from this, we define an adaptive STWT as the process during which young adults are able to transition into the labor market, perform well, achieve person–career fit, and develop in their work and early career, with the aim of securing employment and laying the foundation for a sustainable career.

Adaptive STWT and Sustainable Careers: The Role of Agency and Structure

The importance of an adaptive STWT as described here, calls for further understanding of those factors facilitating this state. In this section, we explore the role of individual agency as well as structural factors, thereby taking a broad career perspective. From a careers perspective, the notion of an adaptive STWT is closely linked with the recent notion of sustainable careers, that is, the sequence of an individual's career experiences, reflected through a variety of patterns of continuity over time, crossing several social spaces, and characterized by individual agency, herewith providing meaning to the individual (De Vos et al., 2020; Van der Heijden & De Vos, 2015). One could say that the transition from school to work represents an important initial sequence within an individual's career sustainability.

STWT From the Perspective of Sustainable Careers

Based on the work of Van der Heijden and De Vos (2015), De Vos et al. (2020) describe three dimensions that have important implications for the sustainability (i.e., long-term happiness, health, and productivity) of the careers of all workers: the person, the context, and time. We argue that these changes also pose particular challenges when it comes to realizing an adaptive STWT for young people.

First, the *person* is connected to changes in individual agency and meaning. Notwithstanding the many influential (structural) factors on all levels (i.e., personal circumstances, job, organization, profession, and society) that shape careers, a career is owned by an individual, and he or she is the one that has to idiosyncratically deal with, and respond to, stability and/or change in the world of work (Briscoe & Hall, 2006). In contemporary careers, individual agency is the key to continuous career success. Indeed, the individual—with young adults entering the labor market being no exception—is considered as the primary owner of their career, and this ownership comes together with an increased responsibility in a world wherein everything is extremely complex, with a mass of choices. Related to this, the *meaning* within careers has also changed over time. That is, careers are typically no longer a mere succession of related jobs, arranged in a hierarchy, through which persons move in an ordered sequence (Baruch, 2006). In that perspective, there is a rather narrow view on what a successful career entails (i.e., realizing upward progress through the hierarchy of an organization). In contrast, nowadays, subjective career success has come to the forefront. This refers to all kinds of aspects of career experiences that are valued by an individual, such as making an impact, having meaningful relations, and being satisfied with one's career (Mayhofer et al., 2016; Shockley et al., 2016; Spurk, Hirschi, & Dries, 2019). This implies that the meaning of career success will be determined by matching one's experience to one's internal career anchors (Schein, 1985). In terms of the STWT, such changes in career meaningfulness have important implications for how careers are examined and evolve. More specifically, not only do young workers need to learn how to do their jobs and self-manage this process, they also need to develop strong reflective skills and think about what their careers mean to them.

Second, regarding the *time* dimension: Careers have not only become longer but also less predictable due to a rapidly changing socioeconomic environment (Vickerstaff, 2003). For young people, this means that it is harder to predict where their early career steps might bring them. To illustrate, a recent report by the World Economic Forum (2016) states that even for technical studies, almost 50% of the knowledge and know-how acquired during the first year of a four-year study is outdated at the time of graduation. Furthermore, certain events can occur during the STWT that were unforeseen, such as unexpectedly losing one's first job due to a large reorganization or finding one's first job much earlier than expected (cf. career shocks; Akkermans, Seibert, & Mol, 2018) and that can have a long-term impact in one's career sustainability. From a broader view, this means that STWT is not a one-off event but rather a dynamic process that evolves over time.

Third, there are changes in the *context* within which careers evolve. Careers reflect the relationships between people and employing organizations or institutions and how these relationships fluctuate over time (Arthur, Hall, & Lawrence, 1989). Careers are at the intersection between both and, as such, are influenced by factors that stem from individuals' life spheres (e.g., family or one's broader life context) and by factors situated in the organization (e.g., recruitment policies and developmental opportunities). Both, in turn, are situated within a broader societal context that is also affecting individuals' career experiences (Greenhaus & Kossek, 2014). This element of context has also undergone substantial changes over the past decades. Obviously, these changes have made careers more complex. As an individual's career is no longer limited to a single or only a few employment settings over time, the "career playing field" is seemingly endless. Especially young individuals may perceive more career opportunities than ever before, but this also brings uncertainty, higher risks, and a variety of potential transition pathways (Brzinsky-Fay & Solga, 2016). Consequently, this stresses the need for individuals to actively take charge of their career, as we emphasized earlier, while trying to navigate the various contexts in which they operate.

Individual Agency and Adaptive STWT

Individuals change psychologically as they go through important transitions in life and this is especially the case for young graduates (Koen, Klehe, & Van Vianen, 2012; Mackenzie Davey & Arnold, 2000). Graduates are confronted with the challenges of defining career goals, searching for a job, and discovering what is expected from them, which often leads to feelings of uncertainty (Mackenzie Davey & Arnold, 2000; Sturges, Guest, & Mackenzie Davey, 2000). Added to these challenges, and as previously argued, they also need to proactively self-manage their early career: figuring out in which types of jobs, organizations, or sectors they would like to work. Identifying their competencies and relevant experiences, writing their CV, scanning job advertisements, attending job fairs, and preparing themselves for job interviews are just a few of the many actions young adults need to undertake to find a satisfying job. These behaviors are examples of what has been called "proactive career behaviors," that is, individuals' active attempts to build their careers rather than a passive response to the situation as a given (Seibert, Kraimer, & Crant, 2001). They include both a reflective (e.g., career planning and self-awareness about career ambitions and talents) and a behavioral (e.g., networking, sending out one's CV, and asking for advice) component (De Vos & Soens, 2008).

Within the career literature, there appears to be a consensus among contemporary academics that proactive career behaviors often help people to attain desired career outcomes and to experience general feelings of career success throughout the life course (e.g., Sturges, Conway, Guest, & Liefooghe, 2005; Sturges, Guest, Conway, & Mackenzie Davey, 2002). Although a major body of research in this field focuses on employees who are already at work and, recently, also on older workers, individual agency is no doubt also a critical success factor for young graduates entering the labor market (e.g., Akkermans & Tims, 2017; De Vos & Segers, 2013; Sturges et al., 2002; 2005). Indeed, agency might be even more important for young people given the many decisions they must make in the exploration stage of their career, the uncertain and ambiguous context they face, and the lack of a structural framework offered by an organizational context or chosen occupational path. In other words, from the perspective of situational strength theory (Barrick & Mount, 1993), the STWT represents a "weak" situation characterized by many ambiguous demands, absence of a fixed script, and lack of strong cues signaling what behavior is needed for successful adaptation. Consequently, individuals have considerable discretion in how to behave, making it more likely that individual factors come to the forefront in explaining an adaptive STWT.

From the perspective of sustainable careers, proactive career behaviors are important as they might have a long-term impact on vocational outcomes and future career success (Koen et al., 2012). Given that career sequences are becoming increasingly unpredictable throughout the life course and careers, more "boundaryless" (considering time and context dimensions of sustainable careers), it is important for young adults to develop career competencies that allow them to navigate their own career in view of their personal career success criteria (considering agency and meaning dimensions of sustainable careers). Otherwise, they might find themselves passively responding to those job opportunities to which they have the most easy access, despite these mismatching with their real interests or talents, and possibly resulting in underemployment (Koen et al., 2012).

Existing scholarly work supports the idea that proactivity facilitates an adaptive STWT. To illustrate, Brown, Cober, Kane, Levy, and Shalhoop (2006) found that proactive personality affects successful job searching and that this relationship is mediated by job search self-efficacy and job search behaviors. In another study, it was shown that young graduates who enacted networking behaviors before graduation reported higher levels of both objective and subjective career success in the early years of their career (De Vos, De Clippeleer, & Dewilde, 2009). Thus, in parallel with what has been found in studies addressing employed individuals, young people who are aware of their personal motives, their talents, and the labor market context and who engage in self-management behaviors like career exploration, networking, and planning (e.g., Zikic & Hall, 2009) are more likely to find a job that is in line with their expectations. In other words, individual agency affects both the likelihood of finding a job (i.e., *quantitative dimension*), and the likelihood of that job matching their expectations and providing stable employment prospects (i.e., *qualitative dimension*; e.g., Taylor, 2005).

Moreover, individual factors such as career self-efficacy (i.e., employees' beliefs about the capacity to realize a successful career), optimism, and ambition (De Vos et al., 2009) will impact the likelihood that young adults engage in proactive career behaviors. Nurmi, Salmela-Aro, and Koivisto (2002) summarize this in terms of three requirements: (a) a high level of interest in personal goals, (b) perceptions of efficacy to attain those goals, and (c) positive emotions that motivate behavior toward attainment of those goals. This is consistent with the dimensions of proactive motivation discerned by Parker, Bindl and Strauss (2010): "can do" (self-efficacy and context beliefs), "reason to" (autonomous career goals), and "energized to" (positive affect; p.830). Hirschi, Lee, Porfeli, and Vondracek (2013) found that these three types of motivation significantly predict career behaviors, and we argue that they might, therefore, be important indicators of an adaptive STWT.

Together, these findings point out that individual characteristics and proactive behaviors are important for an adaptive STWT. Therefore, to facilitate young adults in their STWT in the contemporary career landscape, it is important to make them aware of the important role they are playing in their own career development. Interventions such as career guidance can help them become more aware of their career expectations and learn more about what types of proactive career behaviors are needed to find relevant job opportunities and increase their chances for an adaptive STWT.

Structural Factors and Adaptive STWT

Despite the current emphasis on agency in contemporary careers literature, individuals' careers do not develop in a vacuum but are affected by the multiple contexts in which they evolve: the organizational context and the broader labor market, the policy measures taken by governments, initiatives from labor market intermediaries, and also the private context of individuals' personal lives (Arthur et al., 1989; De Vos et al., 2020; Greenhaus & Kossek, 2014). Applied to the STWT, contextual elements will determine the opportunities but also the obstacles that individuals may have to overcome in making an adaptive transition from school to work (Okay-Sommerville & Scholarios, 2014; Akkermans et al., 2015b).

More specifically, careers are part of a wide eco-system, which operates across internal and external labor markets and in which many different interrelated actors and factors may impact the career opportunities and outcomes of individuals (Baruch, 2015). To fully understand (early) careers, one must realize the influences of these multiple career contexts and the changes occurring within them, the career actors who take part in the play, and the dynamic nature of the system. The sustainability of individuals' careers relies not on their stability but on their ability to adjust, develop, and fit an ever-changing work environment (Baruch, 2015). These factors are situated in different levels of context.

Think, for instance, about labor market policies determined by policymakers or recruitment policies of companies (cf. Baruch & Rousseau, 2019). With little prior work experience or professional networks, young people often have difficulties finding suitable employment when they enter the labor market because employers can set high expectations in terms of previous work experience. Especially during economically hard times, when there are fewer vacancies and young graduates have to compete with more senior profiles, an adaptive STWT might not be self-evident (Aronson, Callahan & Davis, 2015; De Lange, Gesthuizen & Wolbers, 2014). This might not only be demotivating for young adults; it might also be risky for the sustainability of their careers in the long run. And, even worse, recurrently receiving negative answers from employers about their candidacy for job vacancies might lower their self-efficacy and their motivation for sustained effort in searching for a job that is in line with their career interests and talents. The setbacks and barriers experienced during the transition from school to work thus threaten the successful start of one's career (cf. Blokker, Akkermans, Tims, Jansen, & Khapova, 2019), and they might also have a longer-lasting impact on the sustainability of a career when this leads to quantitative or qualitative underemployment, prolonged unemployment, and negative consequences for career motivation (Koen et al., 2012).

Contextual factors affecting the sustainability of careers are not only situated at the societal and organizational level. Also, young people's personal context might facilitate or hinder an adaptive STWT. For instance, Blustein et al. (2002) found that social class plays a pivotal role in how young workers' experience the transition into working life: young people working in low-skilled jobs reported lower interest in work as a source of personal satisfaction, less crystallization of their self-concept, less access to external resources, and lower levels of career adaptability compared to peers from a higher social class. This implies that young peoples' personal context (i.e., social class) provides boundary conditions that facilitate (i.e., higher social class) or hinder (i.e., lower social class) the STWT.

Accordingly, we can conclude that career sustainability might already be at risk during emerging adulthood for certain groups of young adults, herewith making an adaptive STWT especially crucial. Indeed, it calls attention to ensuring an inclusive approach for schools or career counselors guiding young adults in their early career choices in order to avoid the so-called Matthew effect (De Vos, Dujardin, Gielens, & Meyers, 2017; Forrier, De Cuyper, & Akkermans, 2018): Those individuals who are already more intrinsically motivated when it comes to their career development, who are more ambitious, or who have a higher work centrality are more likely to also engage in proactive career behaviors, which might, in turn, increase their chances for an adaptive STWT. Contrarily, those individuals scoring lower on intrinsic career motivation, ambition, or work centrality are less likely to take a proactive stance toward their career, thereby lowering their chances for an adaptive STWT. In this context, interventions meant to enhance young people's career resources, such as their career competencies (e.g., Akkermans et al., 2015a; Koen et al., 2012), are of utmost importance. For example Akkermans et al. (2015a) demonstrated how a relatively short career development intervention (i.e., five sessions lasting four hours each) can be effectively implemented within an educational or organizational context to help young employees develop their career competencies, self-efficacy, resilience against setbacks, career self-management behaviors, employability, and work engagement.

In sum, in an increasingly unpredictable and complex world of work, individuals are viewed as the primary responsible agent for their own career and career success and for aligning these with their subjective values. Yet, at the same time, we cannot ignore the social context in which careers take place, as this has a major influence on attaining an adaptive STWT.

In the previous section, we reflected on the four dimensions of sustainable careers applied to the early career of young adults. However, to fully examine and understand the potential of creating sustainable early careers, it is important to consider several further issues. First, we will discuss the role of educational level, as extant literature has shown its important role during the STWT. Second, we will argue that especially career competencies and employability may be crucial indicators of an adaptive STWT during early careers.

STWT Differences Between and Within Educational Groups

Research has indicated that young adults experience and cope with the STWT very differently. Some young adults start their careers smoothly and integrate well into the labor market, whereas others face more difficulties after leaving education (Blossfeld, 2008; Buyens, De Vos, Heylen, Mortelmans, & Soens, 2006). Although many factors impact the STWT of young adults, educational credentials are one of the key determinants of an adaptive STWT (e.g., Yates, 2005; Müller, 2005; Di Stasio, 2014).

Differences Between Educational Levels

Studies investigating differences *between* educational levels show that an individual's level of education positively impacts the STWT in terms of employment status, job quality, and career prospects. Highly educated (i.e., higher vocational and university level) labor market entrants are less likely to be unemployed and more rapidly attain their first employment (Eurostat, 2016; Kogan & Müller, 2003; Noelke, Gebel, & Kogan, 2012) compared to their less-educated counterparts. Higher-educated labor market entrants are also more likely to attain objective and subjective forms of career success than lesser-educated young adults. For example, they are more often employed in jobs matching their educational qualifications (Groot & Van Den Brink, 2000; Wolbers, 2003), earn significantly more (Ng, Eby, Sorensen, & Feldman, 2005; Van der Velden & Wolbers, 2007), are more likely to be promoted (Ng et al., 2005), and experience higher levels of work-related well-being and health than lesser-educated labor market entrants (Akkermans, Brenninkmeijer, Van den Bossche, Blonk, & Schaufeli, 2013b; Creed, Patton, & Hood, 2010).

Furthermore, the higher the attained level of education is, the more favorable the career prospects continue to be, both at the time of labor market entry as well as in young adults' early careers. Research has indicated that the upward trend in temporary employment at the expense of permanent employment is weaker for higher-educated youth than for lower-educated youth (De Lange et al., 2012). Also, of those young adults who start their careers in temporary or nonoptimal employment, higher-educated labor market entrants are more capable of improving their position with each employer change and are faster in recovering from initial job mismatches (Schmelzer, 2011).

In contrast, lesser educated labor market entrants are hit particularly hard by the detrimental effects of flexible employment and unemployment in the early career. Research has shown that these labor market entrants more often return to unemployment after accepting a job (Ferrall, 1997; Schmelzer, 2011) and have a higher risk of becoming long-term unemployed after a spell of unemployment early in their careers (Eurostat, 2013, 2016; Ling & O'Brien, 2013; Yates, 2005). Yet, although initial negative consequences of precarious employment at labor market entry can have persistent negative effects, these effects do not differ between lower- and higher-educated school-leavers and often diminish during the early career (De Lange, Gesthuizen, & Wolbers, 2012; Skans, 2011).

To conclude so far, young adults with fewer educational credentials seem to encounter more challenges and difficulties in coping with the STWT compared to their higher-educated counterparts. However, considering these groups as homogeneous is not a fully accurate representation of reality, as research has also demonstrated differences *within* these educational groups.

Differences Within Educational Levels

Studies investigating differences within educational levels have shown that although lower-educated young adults appear to encounter more difficulties during the STWT, their lower educational credentials do not necessarily lead to a less adaptive STWT in the end. In particular, previous research has demonstrated that, within categories of educational groups, certain skills are more important than others for young adults who are starting their career. For example, in the German vocational education and training system, employers often prefer noncognitive skills (e.g., work attitude, motivation) over cognitive skills (e.g., grades) when selecting apprenticeship candidates among students with an intermediate-level school attainment (Protsch & Solga, 2015; Solga & Kohlrausch, 2013). In line with these findings, several scholars have proposed that training noncognitive skills—frequently referred to as "soft skills"—may provide opportunities to improve the situation of young individuals in the labor market. Indeed, career-related interventions aimed at developing noncognitive skills, such as career competencies and career adaptability, have raised young adults' chances to have a more adaptive STWT in terms of employability, career development, and well-being (Akkermans et al., 2015a; Koen et al., 2012; Koivisto, Vuori, & Nykyri, 2007).

Unfortunately, research on differences within educational levels in the STWT is still relatively scarce and this makes it difficult to draw strong conclusions for educational systems across the globe. In addition, employers react to educational credentials differently due to variation in institutional contexts across countries (Di Stasio & Van de Werfhorst, 2016) and to vocational characteristics such as field of education and industry (De Lange et al., 2012). A recent study by Middeldorp, Edzes, and Van Dijk (2018), for example, demonstrates that young people are more likely to have an adaptive STWT if they graduate with a vocational degree compared to a general degree. Specifically, young people with general education tend to obtain lower starting wages and more often end up in trajectories dominated by nonstandard employment, unemployment, and inactivity. However, this effect is not persistent, as young people with a general degree catch up within two to five years and are paid similar or better wages than those with a vocational degree. This suggests that, depending on the perspective one takes (i.e., between or within educational levels), other factors and mechanisms may play an important role. Therefore, it is crucial to further examine both differences between and within educational levels in the STWT.

In sum, we conclude that young adults with different educational backgrounds face various opportunities and challenges during the STWT. Although we know quite well that educational credentials are among the key determinants of an adaptive STWT, much less is known about the underlying factors causing these differences in the early career development of young adults with different educational backgrounds. We will elaborate on this later in this chapter when we present avenues for future research.

STWT in the New Career: Career Competencies and Employability

In the previous sections, we analyzed the STWT from the perspective of the contemporary career, discussing how both individual and structural factors might contribute to creating sustainable careers and how this may differ between and within educational groups. Now, we look forward and discuss two constructs that we argue are crucial for young adults in attaining an adaptive STWT: career competencies and employability.

Career Competencies

Ever since the new career started to gain traction among scholars and practitioners, around the early 1990s, career competencies have been an important topic of study. Influential new career perspectives, such as the boundaryless career (e.g., DeFillippi & Arthur, 1994) and the protean career (e.g., Hall & Mirvis, 1995) examined which competencies would be especially important in managing contemporary careers. Recently, Akkermans, Brenninkmeijer, Huibers, and Blonk (2013a) reviewed the available literature on career competencies and presented an integrated framework, which was specifically designed in the context of young adults and the STWT. They defined career competencies as "knowledge, skills, and abilities central to career development, which can be influenced and developed by the individual" (p. 249). Specifically, they synthesized four perspectives on career competencies: (a) the three ways of knowing (e.g., Eby, Butts, & Lockwood, 2003), (b) career metacompetencies (e.g., Briscoe & Hall, 2006), (c) career self-management (e.g., De Vos et al., 2009), and (d) the human capital perspective (e.g., Kuijpers, Schyns, & Scheerens, 2006). Based on these perspectives, they argued that young adults would especially need three types of career competencies: *reflective career competencies*, *communicative career competencies*, and *behavioral career competencies*.

Each of these three dimensions consists of two specific career competencies. The first reflective career competency is *reflection on motivation*: reflection on values, passions, and motivations about one's career. The second one is *reflection on qualities*, which refers to reflection on strengths, shortcomings, and skills in relation to one's career. Next, the first communicative career competency is *networking*, which focuses on the awareness of the presence and professional value of one's network. It also relates to the ability to expand this network for career-related purposes. *Self-profiling* is the second communicative competency, and it entails presenting and communicating personal knowledge, abilities, and skills to the internal and external labor market. Finally, the first behavioral career competency is *work exploration*, which is actively exploring and searching for work-related and career-related opportunities on the internal and external labor market. The second one is *career control*, which focuses on actively influencing learning and work processes related to one's career by setting goals and planning how to reach them.

Research has convincingly shown that developing career competencies in today's career has many benefits for employees. For example, career competencies can enhance career satisfaction (Eby et al., 2003), career success (Kuijpers et al., 2006), and vocational adjustment (King, 2004). Moreover, recent studies have elucidated that career competencies are important for young adults during their early career. For example, Akkermans, Paradniké, Van der Heijden, and De Vos (2018) showed that career competencies could enhance students' study engagement, well-being, and academic performance. Furthermore, Akkermans, Schaufeli, Brenninkmeijer, and Blonk (2013c) demonstrated that career competencies can interact with job resources to enhance work engagement. Specifically, career competencies and job resources interacted to enhance young workers' engagement at work. Similarly, young workers can benefit from developing career competencies because these can enhance their problem-solving skills, self-efficacy, and employability (Akkermans et al., 2015a) and are positively related to employee well-being in terms of job satisfaction and health (Plomp, Tims, Akkermans, Khapova, Jansen, & Bakker, 2016) and work engagement (Tims & Akkermans, 2017). Finally, Akkermans and Tims (2017) showed that career competencies can help young workers to proactively craft their jobs and enhance career success in terms of employability and work–home interaction. For instance, young workers who are better at reflecting on their skills and motivation, are more likely to proactively enhance their job resources, and are ultimately experience higher levels of career success.

Taken together, it is clear that career competencies are an important means for young adults to successfully navigate their early careers. Both during and after their studies (cf. Akkermans et al., 2015a), career competencies are a crucial building block for organizing and shaping their work and career. Given the current turbulent labor market, young adults need to be actively supported and encouraged in developing these competencies, thereby allowing them to adaptively transition into the labor market and successfully build their employability.

Employability

Whereas career competencies form an important *input* for young workers' careers (i.e., developing these competencies may benefit them in all kinds of ways), a crucial *outcome* of these would be employability. Traditionally, careers were linear and predictable. However, given the major changes that we described at the beginning of this chapter, traditional outcomes such as "lifetime employment" are in many cases no longer the norm. Rather, for young adults it is important to become and remain employable; that is, they are expected to develop the necessary competencies required to be able to obtain and retain employment, both on the internal and external labor market (Dacre Pool & Sewell, 2007; Vanhercke, De Cuyper, Peeters, & De Witte, 2014; Van der Heijde & Van der Heijden, 2006).

Although employability research originates from around the 1950s, there has recently been a resurgence of this topic within the context of the new career. Several perspectives on employability exist, of which the three most well-known are the dispositional perspective (e.g., Fugate, Kinicki, & Ashforth, 2004), the competence-based perspective (e.g., Van der Heijde & Van der Heijden, 2006), and the perceived employability perspective (e.g., Vanhercke et al., 2014). The dispositional and competence-based perspectives both describe certain abilities and competencies that identify to what degree a person is employable (e.g., adaptability, expertise), whereas the perceived employability perspective mainly emphasizes worker's own perceptions of their—internal and external—employability.

Despite these differences, the three perspectives share the notion that today's employees need to ensure they can obtain and retain employment when necessary and desired. For example, the competence-based perspective would argue that individuals need to develop occupational expertise and the ability to adapt to changes, whereas the perceived employability perspective would dictate that a person can differ in their perceptions of opportunities for employment both with their current employer and on the external labor market. Recently, Forrier, Verbruggen, and De Cuyper (2015) presented a dynamic model in which these different notions of employability are integrated. Specifically, they hypothesized that *movement capital* (i.e., integrating the dispositional and competence-based perspectives) forms an input for perceived employability. That is, when employees develop certain skills and abilities—such as adaptability, resilience, and expertise—they might subsequently perceive themselves to be more employable. These perceptions of employability would subsequently enhance individual career outcomes and mobility.

This renewed emphasis on employability is an important development for attaining adaptive STWTs. Given our earlier reasoning that career competencies are crucial for young adults to adaptively transition to the labor market in today's dynamic career landscape, it makes sense that employability would be an indicator of early career success (cf. Akkermans & Tims, 2017). Contrary to the traditional career notion, where students would graduate and then be employed for life within a single organization, they now need to ensure that they can be flexible when necessary and desired. In other words, already during emerging adulthood, it is essential for young adults to constantly be aware of their employability and to strive to enhance it.

Indeed, research has convincingly shown that employability is an important phenomenon for thriving in today's career. For example, becoming and remaining employable can lead individuals to be more healthy (Berntson & Marklund, 2007), perform better (De Cuyper & De Witte, 2011), experience less job insecurity (De Cuyper, Mäkikangas, Kinnunen, Mauno, & De Witte, 2012), better cope with organizational changes (Fugate & Kinicki, 2008), and achieve higher levels of career success (De Vos, De Hauw, & Van der Heijden, 2011) and workplace learning (Van der Heijden, Gorgievski, & De Lange, 2016). Given the relevance of these issues for young adults entering the labor market—they have to learn, deal with changes, cope with uncertainty, and maintain their health, performance, and career success—we underline the importance of employability enhancement for young adults going through the STWT.

However, it should be noted that there are also risks associated with this emphasis on employability. Related to our earlier discussions of career sustainability and differences between and within educational groups, there might be unequal opportunities among young people for becoming employable. In this regard, the earlier mentioned Matthew effect might come into play: It is conceivable that those young people who already have many resources (e.g., good grades, family support, competencies) are the ones who can be agentic and achieve career success, whereas the ones without such resources might lack the necessary tools to be agentic, thereby risking the loss of even more resources and potentially ending up in a nonadaptive STWT (cf. Forrier, De Cuyper, & Akkermans, 2018).

Taken together, when analyzing the STWT using a contemporary career perspective, we should take into particular account the development of career competencies and employability. The former seems especially applicable for young adults to enable them to navigate their early career, and the latter will provide them with a strong position on the labor market and a foundation for sustainable employment with high levels of person–career fit.

Looking Forward: What's Next?

In this chapter, we have analyzed the STWT from the perspective of the contemporary career. Among other things, we reflected on sustainable careers as a valuable framework for STWT, we zoomed in on educational differences, and we argued that career competencies and employability are crucial phenomena in today's STWT. In this final section, we will look forward and discuss several potentially fruitful avenues for future research.

The first suggestion we would like to make is for research on STWT in the contemporary career to integrate individual-level, organizational-level, and societal factors that impact this crucial transition. Most research thus far has taken a monodisciplinary view on the STWT, thereby adopting an either/or approach. We urge scholars to aim for more integration between these domains, as the STWT is an incredibly complex process during which many factors can play an important role. For example, when examining the predictive role of individual factors such as motivation, skills, and abilities in an adaptive STWT, it would also be crucial to look at factors such as actual job availability and institutional support. Similarly, when examining the STWT from a more sociological perspective, researchers would need to include micro-level factors such as individual perceptions of employability. Integrating disciplines is especially important because the labor market has rapidly changed, and these changes might significantly impact the STWT, for example, because of new ways of organizing work, new demands on individuals, and general trends in society. In all, we argue that a true understanding of the STWT in today's complex career landscape can only be obtained when studying it from an *interdisciplinary* perspective. A good first step to achieve this would be to systematically integrate the available literature on the STWT from different disciplines. Once this has been done, the overview that is created can serve as a foundation for future interdisciplinary research on the STWT.

Second, as a concrete example of crossing disciplines, current research on adaptive STWTs could focus more on integrating knowledge from the careers literature and human resource management literature with available knowledge from health and clinical psychology literature. Recently, the media have been presenting shocking statistics on students and young workers dropping out due to stress and burnout (see, e.g., "Companies Are Facing," 2018; "Burnout Is Everywhere," 2013; " How Burnout Became a Sinister," 2018) as a consequence of the major demands they are facing during their early career. From a career and human resource management perspective, there is a lot of available knowledge about the challenges young adults face during and after the STWT. However, a thorough understanding of the consequences of these challenges for their mental and health and well-being is still lacking. Therefore, it would be a valuable addition to existing knowledge on the STWT if future research could include theories and models—such as back-to-work integration programs—from health psychology to obtain a firmer grasp on the crucial factors that determine which young workers thrive and which of them do not survive. Subsequently, this improved understanding would be input for interventions and career counseling aimed at supporting emerging adults.

Our third suggestion would be to initiate more research on adaptive STWT processes in different contexts. As an example, it would be valuable to study vulnerable and disadvantaged groups. Most research thus far has looked at STWT as a general process that is equally applicable to all young adults. However, given recent developments, it would be likely that attaining an adaptive STWT would be fundamentally different for certain groups. For example, young adults with disabilities face truly different challenges compared to those who are relatively healthy (see, e.g., Dean et al., 2019). As an illustration, the increasingly dynamic and flexible world of work as we have described it in this chapter might be especially difficult to successfully enter for young adults with autism spectrum disorder, who face additional barriers, and who have unique needs when starting their careers (see e.g., Griffiths, Giannantonio, Hurley-Hanson, & Cardinal, 2016). Similarly, immigrants entering new labor markets will also face significantly different challenges when attempting to find their first jobs (Protsch & Solga, 2017). In both examples, there will be additional personal challenges and contextual factors that impact the STWT process. Another related trend is the increase of entrepreneurship and self-employed workers. In many countries, their numbers are dramatically increasing. It is likely that persons who become self-employed after graduation face a different STWT process compared to those who enter working organizations and obtain employment there (see, e.g., Rummel et al., 2019). For instance, they might need to be even more proactive, and their networking and profiling skills could be especially important. Taken together, we would suggest that future research examines adaptive STWTs not just from a general perspective but also from specific perspectives on certain groups.

Finally, we would suggest that future research on the STWT examines unexpected events that impact early career development. The vast majority of recent career and STWT literature has focused on individual agency and on the importance of being proactive, that is, how young adults can control their own career success. While we certainly support this notion, we also stress the importance of researching so-called *career shocks*, which are disruptive and extraordinary events that are, at least to some degree, caused by factors outside the focal individual's control and that trigger a deliberate thought process concerning one's career (Akkermans et al., 2018). Such shocks can be negative (e.g., getting rejected at a major job opening after graduation) or positive (e.g., receiving an unexpected job offer). For example, Blokker et al. (2019) recently showed that the interaction between individual agency (i.e., development of career competencies) and contextual factors (i.e., career shocks) plays an important role in young professionals' immediate (i.e., career satisfaction) and long-term career success (i.e., employability). Specifically, negative career shocks undermined young professionals' efforts to build their employability, whereas positive shocks strengthened this relationship. Yet, we still have a very limited understanding of the impact of career shocks on the STWT and sustainable career development of young adults, and we therefore urge scholars to perform more research in this area.

In conclusion, in this chapter we have examined the STWT from a sustainable careers perspective and argued that an adaptive STWT is crucial as a building block for long-term sustainability of careers. We showed that the STWT has become more challenging for young adults and we underlined how individual agency and structural factors can interact to lay an early foundation for sustainable career development. In particular, career competencies and employability were highlighted as crucial concepts for today's STWT. Finally, we discussed potentially interesting research areas for future research to further our understanding of the contemporary STWT.

References

Akkermans, J., Brenninkmeijer, V., Huibers, M., & Blonk, R. W. B. (2013a). Competencies for the contemporary career: Development and preliminary validation of the career competencies questionnaire. *Journal of Career Development*, *40*(3), 245–267. doi:10.1177/0894845312467501

Akkermans, J., Brenninkmeijer, V., Schaufeli, W. B., & Blonk, R. W. B. (2015a). It's all about CareerSKILLS: Effectiveness of a career development intervention for young employees. *Human Resource Management*, *54*(4), 533–551. doi:10.1002/hrm.21633

Akkermans, J., Brenninkmeijer, V., Van den Bossche, S. N. J., Blonk, R. W. B., & Schaufeli, W. B. (2013b). Young and going strong? A longitudinal study on occupational health among young employees of different educational levels. *Career Development International*, *18*(4), 416–435. doi:10.1108/CDI-02-2013-0024

Akkermans, J., Nykänen, M., & Vuori, J. (2015b). Practice makes perfect? Antecedents and consequences of an adaptive school-to-work transition. In J. Vuori, R. W. B. Blonk, & R. Price (Eds.), *Sustainable working lives: Managing work transitions and health throughout the life course.* (pp. 65–86). London, England: Springer.

Akkermans, J., Paradniké, K., Van der Heijden, B. I. J. M., & De Vos, A. (2018). The best of both worlds: The role of career adaptability and career competencies in students' well-being and performance. *Frontiers in Psychology*, *9*, 1678. doi:10.3389/fpsyg.2018.01678

Akkermans, J., Schaufeli, W. B., Brenninkmeijer, V., & Blonk, R. W. B. (2013c). The role of career competencies in the job demands-resources model. *Journal of Vocational Behavior*, *83*(3), 356–366. doi:10.1016/j.jvb.2013.06.011

Akkermans, J., Seibert, S. E., & Mol, S. T. (2018). Tales of the unexpected: Integrating career shocks in the contemporary careers literature. *SA Journal of Industrial Psychology*, *44*, e1503. doi:10.4102/sajip.v44i0.1503

Anders, J., & Dorsett, R. (2017). What young English people do once they reach school-leaving age: A cross-cohort comparison for the last 30 years. *Longitudinal and Life Course Studies, 8*(1), 75–103.

Arnett, J. J. (2000). Emerging adulthood: A theory of development from the late teens through the twenties. *American Psychologist, 55*(5), 469–480. doi:10.1037//0003-066X.55.5.469

Arnett, J. J. (2007). Emerging adulthood: What is it, and what is it good for? *Child Development Perspectives, 1*(2), 68–73.

Arthur, M. B., Hall, D. T., & Lawrence, B. S. (1989). *Handbook of career theory*. Cambridge, England: Cambridge University Press.

Aronson, P., Callahan, T., & Davis, T. (2015). The transition from college to work during the great recession: employment, financial, and identity challenges. *Journal of Youth Studies, 18*(9), 1097–1118. doi:10.1080/13676261.2015.1020931

Barrick, M. R., & Mount, M. K. (1993). Autonomy as a moderator of the relationships between the Big Five personality dimensions and job performance. *Journal of Applied Psychology, 78*(1), 111–118. doi:10.1037/0021-9010.78.1.111

Baruch, Y. (2006). Career development in organizations and beyond: Balancing traditional and contemporary viewpoints. *Human Resource Management Review, 16*(2), 125–138. doi:10.1016/j.hrmr.2006.03.002

Baruch, Y. (2015). Organizational and labor market as career eco-system. In A. De Vos & B. I. J. M. Van Der Heijden (Eds.), *Handbook of research on sustainable careers* (pp. 164–180). Cheltenham, England: Edward Elgar.

Baruch, Y., & Rousseau, D. M. (2019). Integrating psychological contracts and ecosystems in career studies and management. *Academy of Management Annals, 13*(1), 84–111. doi:10.5465/annals.2016.0103

Berntson, E., & Marklund, S. (2007). The relationship between perceived employability and subsequent health. *Work & Stress, 21*(3), 279–292. doi:10.1080/02678370701659215

Blokker, R., Akkermans, J., Tims, M., Jansen, P., & Khapova, S. (2019). Building a sustainable start: The role of career competencies, career success, and career shocks in young professionals' employability. *Journal of Vocational Behavior, 112*, 172–184. doi:10.1016/j.jvb.2019.02.013

Blossfeld, H. P. (Ed.). (2008). *Young workers, globalization and the labor market: Comparing early working life in eleven countries*. Edward Elgar Publishing.

Blossfeld, H. P., Klijzing, E., Mills, M., & Kurz, K. (2005). *Globalization, uncertainty, and youth in society. The losers in a globalizing world*. New York, NY: Routledge.

Blustein, D. L., Chaves, A. P., Diemer, M. A., Gallagher, L. A., Marshall, K. G., Sirin, S., & Bhati, K. S. (2002). Voices of the forgotten half: The role of social class in the school-to-work transition. *Journal of Counseling Psychology, 49*(3), 311–323. doi:10.1037/0022-0167.49.3.311

Blustein, D. L., Phillips, S. D., Jobin-Davis, K., Finkelberg, S. L., & Roarke, A. E. (1997). A theory-building investigation of the school-to-work transition. *The Counseling Psychologist, 25*(3), 364–402. doi:10.1177/0011000097253002

Briscoe, J. P., & Hall, D. T. (2006). The interplay of boundaryless and protean careers: Combinations and implications. *Journal of Vocational Behavior, 69*(1), 4–18. doi:10.1016/j.jvb.2005.09.002

Brown, D. J., Cober, R. T., Kane, K., Levy, P. E., & Shalhoop, J. (2006). Proactive personality and the successful job search: A field investigation with college graduates. *Journal of Applied Psychology, 91*(3), 717–726. doi:10.1037/0021-9010.91.3.717

Brzinsky-Fay, C., & Solga, H. (2016). Compressed, postponed, or disadvantaged? School-to-work-transition patterns and early occupational attainment in West Germany. *Research in Social Stratification and Mobility, 46*, 21–36. doi: 10.1016/j.rssm.2016.01.004

Burnout is everywhere—Here's what countries are doing to fix it. (2013). *Huffington Post.* Retrieved from https://www.huffingtonpost.com/2013/07/30/

worker-burnout-worldwide-governments_n_3678460.html?ncid=engmodushpmg00000004

Buyens, D., De Vos, A., Heylen, L., Mortelmans, D., & Soens, N. (2006). Vast, voltijds en levenslang: Het onwrikbare eenbaanskarakter van de loopbaan. *Tijdschrift voor HRM, 2*, 6–27.

Cebulla, A., & Whetton, S. (2018). All roads leading to Rome? The medium term outcomes of Australian youth's transition pathways from education. *Journal of Youth Studies, 21*(3), 304–323. doi:10.1080/13676261.2017.1373754

Cha, J., Kim, Y., & Kim, T.-Y. (2009). Person-career fit and employee outcomes among research and development professionals. *Human Relations, 62*(12), 1857–1886. doi:10.1177/0018726709338638

Companies are facing an employee burnout crisis. (2018). *CNBC*. Retrieved from https://www.cnbc.com/2018/08/14/5-ways-workers-can-avoid-employee-burnout.html

Creed, P. A., Patton, W., & Hood, M. (2010). Career development and personal functioning differences between work-bound and non-work bound students. *Journal of Vocational Behavior, 76*(1), 37–41. doi:10.1016/j.jvb.2009.06.004

Dacre Pool, L., & Sewell, P. (2007). The key to employability: developing a practical model of graduate employability. *Education + Training, 49*(4), 277–289. doi:0.1108/00400910710754435

Dean, D., Pepper, J., Schmidt, R., & Stern, S. (2019). The effects of youth transition programs on labor market outcomes of youth with disabilities. *Economics of Education Review, 68*, 68–88.

De Cuyper, N., & De Witte, H. (2011). The management paradox: Self-rated employability and organizational commitment and performance. *Personnel Review, 40*(2), 152–172. doi:10.1108/00483481111106057

De Cuyper, N., Mäkikangas, A., Kinnunen, U., Mauno, S., & Witte, H. D. (2012). Cross-lagged associations between perceived external employability, job insecurity, and exhaustion: Testing gain and loss spirals according to the Conservation of Resources Theory. *Journal of Organizational Behavior, 33*(6), 770–788. doi:10.1002/job.1800

DeFillippi, R. J., & Arthur, M. B. (1994). The boundaryless career: A competency-based perspective. *Journal of Organizational Behavior, 15*(4), 307–324. doi:10.1002/job.4030150403

De Lange, M., Gesthuizen, M., & Wolbers, M. H. (2012). Trends in labour market flexibilization among Dutch school-leavers: The impact of economic globalization on educational differences. *International Sociology, 27*(4), 529–550. doi:10.1177/0268580911423052

De Lange, M., Gesthuizen, M., & Wolbers, M. H. (2014). Youth labour market integration across Europe: The impact of cyclical, structural, and institutional characteristics. *European Societies, 16*(2), 194–212. doi:10.1080/14616696.2013.821621

De Vos, A., De Clippeleer, I., & Dewilde, T. (2009). Proactive career behaviours and career success during the early career. *Journal of Occupational and Organizational Psychology, 82*(4), 761–777. doi:10.1348/096317909X471013

De Vos, A., De Hauw, S., & Van der Heijden, B. I. J. M. (2011). Competency development and career success: The mediating role of employability. *Journal of Vocational Behavior, 79*(2), 438–447. doi:10.1016/j.jvb.2011.05.010

De Vos, A., Dujardin, J. M., Gielens, T., & Meyers, C. (2017). *Developing sustainable careers across the lifespan*. Cham, Switzerland: Springer International Publishing.

De Vos, A., & Segers, J. (2013). Self-directed career attitude and retirement intentions. *Career Development International, 18*(2), 155–172. doi:10.1108/CDI-04-2012-0041

De Vos, A., & Soens, N. (2008). Protean attitude and career success: The mediating role of self-management. *Journal of Vocational Behavior, 73*(3), 449–456. doi:10.1016/j.jvb.2008.08.007

De Vos, A., Van der Heijden, B. I. J. M., & Akkermans, J. (2020). Sustainable careers: Towards a conceptual model. *Journal of Vocational Behavior, 117*, 103196. doi:10.1016/j.jvb.2018.06.011

Di Stasio, V. (2014). Education as a signal of trainability: Results from a vignette study with Italian employers. *European Sociological Review*, *30*(6), 796–809. doi:10.1093/esr/jcu074

Di Stasio, V., & Van de Werfhorst, H. G. (2016). Why does education matter to employers in different institutional contexts? A vignette study in England and the Netherlands. *Social Forces*, *95*(1), 77–106. doi:10.1093/sf/sow027

Eby, L. T., Butts, M., & Lockwood, A. (2003). Predictors of success in the era of the boundaryless career. *Journal of Organizational Behavior*, *24*(6), 689–708. doi:10.1002/job.214

Eurostat. (2013). Labour market. *Statistics Explained.* Retrieved from https://ec.europa.eu/eurostat/statistics-explained/index.php?title=Labour_market

Eurostat. (2016). The EU in the world: Labour market. *Statistics Explained.* Retrieved from https://ec.europa.eu/eurostat/statistics-explained/index.php/The_EU_in_the_world_-_labour_market

Ferrall, C. (1997). Unemployment insurance eligibility and the school-to-work transition in Canada and the United States. *Journal of Business & Economic Statistics*, *15*(2), 115–129. doi:10.1080/07350015.1997.10524695

Forrier, A., De Cuyper, N., & Akkermans, J. (2018). The winner takes it all, the loser has to fall: Provoking the agency perspective in employability research. *Human Resource Management Journal*, *28*(4), 511–524. doi: 10.1111/1748-8583.12206

Forrier, A., Verbruggen, M., & De Cuyper, N. (2015). Integrating different notions of employability in a dynamic chain: The relationship between job transitions, movement capital and perceived employability. *Journal of Vocational Behavior*, *89*, 56–64. doi:10.1016/j.jvb.2015.04.007

Fugate, M., & Kinicki, A. J. (2008). A dispositional approach to employability: Development of a measure and test of implications for employee reactions to organizational change. *Journal of Occupational and Organizational Psychology*, *81*(3), 503–527. doi:10.1348/096317907X241579

Fugate, M., Kinicki, A. J., & Ashforth, B. E. (2004). Employability: A psycho-social construct, its dimensions, and applications. *Journal of Vocational Behavior*, *65*(1), 14–38. doi:10.1016/j.jvb.2003.10.005

Greenhaus, J. H., & Kossek, E. E. (2014). The contemporary career: A work–home perspective. *Annual Review of Organizational Psychology and Organizational Behavior*, *1*(1), 361–388. doi:10.1146/annurev-orgpsych-031413-091324

Griffiths, A. J., Giannantonio, C. M., Hurley-Hanson, A. E., & Cardinal, D. N. (2016). Autism in the workplace: Assessing the transition needs of young adults with autism spectrum disorder. *Journal of Business and Management*, *22*(1), 5–22.

Groot, W., & Maassen van den Brink, H. (2000). Overeducation in the labor market: a meta-analysis. *Economics of Education Review*, *19*(2), 149–158. doi:10.1016/S0272-7757(99)00057-6

Haase, C. M., Heckhausen, J., & Köller, O. (2008). Goal engagement during the school–work transition: Beneficial for all, particularly for girls. *Journal of Research on Adolescence*, *18*(4), 671–698. doi:10.1111/j.1532-7795.2008.00576.x

Hall, D. T. (2002). *Careers in and out of Organizations.* Thousand Oaks, CA: SAGE.

Hall, D. T., & Mirvis, P. H. (1995). The new career contract: Developing the whole person at midlife and beyond. *Journal of Vocational Behavior*, *47*(3), 269–289. doi:10.1006/jvbe.1995.0004

Heinz, W. R. (2009). Structure and agency in transition research. *Journal of Education and Work*, *22*(5), 391–404. doi:10.1080/13639080903454027

Hirschi, A., Lee, B., Porfeli, E. J., & Vondracek, F. W. (2013). Proactive motivation and engagement in career behaviors: Investigating direct, mediated, and moderated effects. *Journal of Vocational Behavior*, *83*(1), 31–40. doi:10.1016/j.jvb.2013.02.003

Holland, J. L. (1959). A theory of vocational choice. *Journal of Counseling Psychology*, *6*(1), 35–45. doi:10.1037/h0040767

How burnout became a sinister and insidious epidemic. (2018, February 21). *The Guardian*. Retrieved from https://www.theguardian.com/society/2018/feb/21/how-burnout-became-a-sinister-and-insidious-epidemic

Kalleberg, A. L. (2009). Precarious work, insecure workers: Employment relations in transition. *American Sociological Review*, *74*(1), 1–22. doi:10.1177/000312240907400101

King, Z. (2004). Career self-management: Its nature, causes and consequences. *Journal of Vocational Behavior*, *65*(1), 112–133. doi:10.1016/S0001-8791(03)00052-6

Koen, J., Klehe, U.-C., & Van Vianen, A. E. M. (2012). Training career adaptability to facilitate a successful school-to-work transition. *Journal of Vocational Behavior*, *81*(3), 395–408. doi:10.1016/j.jvb.2012.10.003

Kogan, I., & Müller, W. (2003). *School-to-work transitions in Europe: Analyses of the EU LFS 2000 ad hoc module*. Mannheim, Germany: Mannheimer Zentrum für Europäische Sozialforschung.

Koivisto, P., Vuori, J., & Nykyri, E. (2007). Effects of the School-to-Work Group Method among young people. *Journal of Vocational Behavior*, *70*(2), 277–296. doi:10.1016/j.jvb.2006.12.001

Koivisto, P., Vuori, J., & Vinokur, A. D. (2010). Transition to work: Effects of preparedness and goal construction on employment and depressive symptoms. *Journal of Research on Adolescence*, *20*(4), 869–892. doi:10.1111/j.1532-7795.2010.00667.x

Kuijpers, M. A. C. T., Schyns, B., & Scheerens, J. (2006). Career competencies for career success. *The Career Development Quarterly*, *55*(2), 168–178. doi:10.1002/j.2161-0045.2006.tb00011.x

Lechner, C. M., Tomasik, M. J., & Silbereisen, R. K. (2016). Preparing for uncertain careers: How youth deal with growing occupational uncertainties before the education-to-work transition. *Journal of Vocational Behavior*, *95*, 90–101. doi:10.1016/j.jvb.2016.08.002

Ling, T. J., & O'Brien, K. M. (2013). Connecting the forgotten half: The school-to-work transition of noncollege-bound youth. *Journal of Career Development*, *40*(4), 347–367. doi:10.1177/0894845312455506

MacKenzie Davey, K., & Arnold, J. (2000). A multi-method study of accounts of personal change by graduates starting work: Self-ratings, categories and women's discourses. *Journal of Occupational and Organizational Psychology*, *73*(4), 461–486. doi:10.1348/096317900167164

MacLeod, W. B., Riehl, E., Saavedra, J. E., & Urquiola, M. (2017). The big sort: College reputation and labor market outcomes. *American Economic Journal: Applied Economics*, *9*(3), 223–61. doi:10.1257/app.20160126

Mayrhofer, W., Briscoe, J. P., Hall, D. T., Dickmann, M., Dries, N., Dysvik, A., . . . Unite, J. (2016). Career success across the globe: Insights from the 5C project. *Organizational Dynamics*, *45*(3), 197–205. doi:10.1016/j.orgdyn.2016.07.005

McKee-Ryan, F., & Harvey, J. (2011). "I have a job, but . . .": A review of underemployment. *Journal of Management*, *37*(4), 962–996. doi:10.1177/0149206311398134

McKee-Ryan, F., Song, Z., Wanberg, C. R., & Kinicki, A. J. (2005). Psychological and physical well-being during unemployment: A meta-analytic study. *Journal of Applied Psychology*, *90*(1), 53–76. doi:10.1037/0021-9010.90.1.53

Middeldorp, M. M., Edzes, A. J., & van Dijk, J. (2018). Smoothness of the school-to-work transition: General versus vocational upper-secondary education. *European Sociological Review*, *35*(1), 81–97. doi:10.1093/esr/jcy043

Morrison, E. W. (2002). The school-to-work transition. In D. C. Feldman (Ed.), *Work careers: A developmental perspective* (pp. 126–158). San Francisco, CA: Jossey-Bass.

Müller, W. (2005). Education and youth integration into European labour markets. *International Journal of Comparative Sociology*, *46*(5–6), 461–485. doi:10.1177/0020715205060048

Ng, T. W. H., Eby, L. T., Sorensen, K. L., & Feldman, D. C. (2005). Predictors of objective and subjective career success: A meta-analysis. *Personnel Psychology*, *58*(2), 367–408. doi:10.1111/j.1744-6570.2005.00515.x

Ng, T. W. H., & Feldman, D. C. (2007). The school-to-work transition: A role identity perspective. *Journal of Vocational Behavior*, *71*(1), 114–134. doi:10.1016/j.jvb.2007.04.004

Noelke, C., Gebel, M., & Kogan, I. (2012). Uniform inequalities: Institutional differentiation and the transition from higher education to work in post-socialist Central and Eastern Europe. *European Sociological Review*, *28*(6), 704–716. doi:10.1093/esr/jcs008

Nordström Skans, O. (2011). Scarring effects of the first labor market experiences (IZA DP no. 5565). *IZA*. Retrieved from http://ftp.iza.org/dp5565.pdf

Nurmi, J.-E., Salmela-Aro, K., & Koivisto, P. (2002). Goal importance and related achievement beliefs and emotions during the transition from vocational school to work: Antecedents and consequences. *Journal of Vocational Behavior*, *60*(2), 241–261. doi:10.1006/jvbe.2001.1866

Okay-Somerville, B., & Scholarios, D. (2014). Coping with career boundaries and boundary-crossing in the graduate labour market. *Career Development International*, *19*(6), 668–682. doi: 10.1108/CDI-12-2013-0144

Parker, S. K., Bindl, U. K., & Strauss, K. (2010). Making things happen: A model of proactive motivation. *Journal of Management*, *36*(4), 827–856. doi:10.1177/0149206310363732

Pinquart, M., Juang, L. P., & Silbereisen, R. K. (2003). Self-efficacy and successful school-to-work transition: A longitudinal study. *Journal of Vocational Behavior*, *63*(3), 329–346. doi:10.1016/S0001-8791(02)00031-3

Plomp, J., Tims, M., Akkermans, J., Khapova, S. N., Jansen, P. G. W., & Bakker, A. B. (2016). Career competencies and job crafting: How proactive employees influence their well-being. *Career Development International*, *21*(6), 587–602. doi:10.1108/CDI-08-2016-0145

Protsch, P., & Solga, H. (2015). How employers use signals of cognitive and noncognitive skills at labour market entry: Insights from field experiments. *European Sociological Review*, *31*(5), 521–532. doi:10.1093/esr/jcv056

Protsch, P., & Solga, H. (2017). Going across Europe for an apprenticeship? A factorial survey experiment on employers' hiring preferences in Germany. *Journal of European Social Policy*, *27*(4), 387–399. doi: 10.1177/0958928717719200

Rummel, S., Akkermans, J., Blokker, R., & Van Gelderen, M. (2019, December 5). Shocks and entrepreneurship: A study of career shocks among newly graduated entrepreneurs. *Career Development International*. doi:10.1108/CDI-11-2018-0296 https://www.emerald.com/insight/content/doi/10.1108/CDI-11-2018-0296/full/html

Schein, E. H. (1985). *Career anchors*. San Diego: University Associates.

Schmelzer, P. (2011). Unemployment in early career in the UK: A trap or a stepping stone? *Acta Sociologica*, *54*(3), 251–265. doi:10.1177/0001699311412626

Schoon, I. (2007). Adaptations to changing times: Agency in context. *International Journal of Psychology*, *42*(2), 94–101. doi:10.1080/00207590600991252

Schoon, I., & Lyons-Amos, M. (2016). Diverse pathways in becoming an adult: The role of structure, agency and context. *Research in Social Stratification and Mobility*, *46*, 11–20. doi:10.1016/j.rssm.2016.02.008

Schoon, I., & Lyons-Amos, M. (2017). A socio-ecological model of agency: The role of structure and agency in shaping education and employment transitions in England. *Longitudinal and Life Course Studies*, *8*(1), 35–56.

Schoon, I., & Silbereisen, R. K. (2009). Conceptualising school-to-work transitions in context. In I. Schoon & R. K. Silbereisen (Eds.), *Transitions from school to work: Globalization, individualization and patterns of diversity* (pp. 3–29). Cambridge, England: Cambridge University Press.

Seibert, S. E., Kraimer, M. L., & Crant, J. M. (2001). What do proactive people do? A longitudinal model linking proactive personality and career success. *Personnel Psychology*, *54*(4), 845–874. doi:10.1111/j.1744-6570.2001.tb00234.x

Shockley, K. M., Ureksoy, H., Rodopman, O. B., Poteat, L. F., & Dullaghan, T. R. (2016). Development of a new scale to measure subjective career success: A mixed-methods study. *Journal of Organizational Behavior, 37*(1), 128–153. doi:10.1002/job.2046

Solga, H., & Kohlrausch, B. (2013). How low-achieving German youth beat the odds and gain access to vocational training: Insights from within-group variation. *European Sociological Review, 29*(5), 1068–1082. doi:10.1093/esr/jcs083

Spurk, D., Hirschi, A., & Dries, N. (2019). Antecedents and outcomes of objective versus subjective career success: Competing perspectives and future directions. *Journal of Management, 45*(1), 35–69. doi: 10.1177/0149206318786563

Sturges, J., Conway, N., Guest, D., & Liefooghe, A. (2005). Managing the career deal: the psychological contract as a framework for understanding career management, organizational commitment and work behavior. *Journal of Organizational Behavior, 26*(7), 821–838. doi:10.1002/job.341

Sturges, J., Guest, D., Conway, N., & MacKenzie Davey, K. (2002). A longitudinal study of the relationship between career management and organizational commitment among graduates in the first ten years at work. *Journal of Organizational Behavior, 23*(6), 731–748. doi:10.1002/job.164

Sturges, J., Guest, D., & MacKenzie Davey, K. (2000). Who's in charge? Graduates' attitudes to and experiences of career management and their relationship with organizational commitment. *European Journal of Work and Organizational Psychology, 9*(3), 351–370. doi:10.1080/135943200417966

Super, D. E. (1957). *The psychology of careers*. New York, NY: Harper & Row.

Taylor, A. (2005). "Re-culturing" students and selling futures: school-to-work policy in Ontario. *Journal of Education and Work, 18*(3), 321–340. doi:10.1080/13639080500200567

Tims, M., & Akkermans, J. (2017). Core self-evaluations and work engagement: Testing a perception, action, and development path. *PLOS ONE, 12*(8), e0182745. doi:10.1371/journal.pone.0182745

Tomasik, M. J., Hardy, S., Haase, C. M., & Heckhausen, J. (2009). Adaptive adjustment of vocational aspirations among German youths during the transition from school to work. *Journal of Vocational Behavior, 74*(1), 38–46. doi:10.1016/j.jvb.2008.10.003

Tomlinson, M. (2008). "The degree is not enough": students' perceptions of the role of higher education credentials for graduate work and employability. *British Journal of Sociology of Education, 29*(1), 49–61. doi:10.1080/01425690701737457

Van der Heijde, C. M., & Van Der Heijden, B. I. J. M. (2006). A competence-based and multidimensional operationalization and measurement of employability. *Human Resource Management, 45*(3), 449–476. doi:10.1002/hrm.20119

Van der Heijden, B. I. J. M., & De Vos, A. (2015). Sustainable careers: Introductory chapter. In A. De Vos & B. I. J. M. Van Der Heijden (Eds.), *Handbook of research on sustainable careers* (pp. 1–19). Cheltenham, England: Edward Elgar.

Van der Heijden, B. I. J. M., Gorgievski, M. J., & De Lange, A. H. (2016). Learning at the workplace and sustainable employability: A multi-source model moderated by age. *European Journal of Work and Organizational Psychology, 25*(1), 13–30. doi:10.1080/1359432X.2015.1007130

Van der Velden, R. K. W., & Wolbers, M. H. J. (2007). How much does education matter and why? The effects of education on socio-economic outcomes among school-leavers in the Netherlands. *European Sociological Review, 23*(1), 65–80. doi:10.1093/esr/jcl020

Vanhercke, D., De Cuyper, N., Peeters, E., & De Witte, H. (2014). Defining perceived employability: A psychological approach. *Personnel Review, 43*(4), 592–605. doi:10.1108/PR-07-2012-0110

Vickerstaff, S. A. (2003). Apprenticeship in the "Golden Age": Were youth transitions really smooth and unproblematic back then? *Work, Employment and Society, 17*(2), 269–287.

Vogt, K. C. (2018). From Job-seekers to self-searchers: Changing contexts and understandings of school-to-work transitions. *Young, 26*(4S), 18S–33S. doi:10.1177/1103308817741006

Vuori, J., Toppinen-Tanner, S., & Mutanen, P. (2012). Effects of resource-building group intervention on career management and mental health in work organizations: Randomized controlled field trial. *Journal of Applied Psychology, 97*(2), 273–286. doi:10.1037/a0025584

Wolbers, M. H. J. (2003). Job mismatches and their labour-market effects among school-leavers in Europe. *European Sociological Review, 19*(3), 249–266. doi:10.1093/esr/19.3.249

Wolbers, M. H. J. (2016). A generation lost?: Prolonged effects of labour market entry in times of high unemployment in the Netherlands. *Research in Social Stratification and Mobility, 46*, 51–59. doi:10.1016/j.rssm.2016.01.001

World Economic Forum. (2016, January). The future of jobs. employment, skills and workforce strategy for the Fourth Industrial Revolution. Retrieved from http://www3.weforum.org/docs/WEF_Future_of_Jobs.pdf

Yates, J. A. (2005). The transition from school to work: Education and work experiences. *Monthly Labor Review, 128*, 21.

Zikic, J., & Hall, D. T. (2009). Toward a more complex view of career exploration. *The Career Development Quarterly, 58*(2), 181–191. doi:10.1002/j.2161-0045.2009.tb00055.x

SECTION 2
SOCIAL RESOURCES

5

Romantic Relationships and the Transition to Work

Intersections, Practice Recommendations, and an Illustrative Case

José F. Domene and Sarah M. Johnson

Introduction

Emerging adulthood is a developmental period characterized by exploration and new experiences. For many people, it is a time of widespread changes, as possibilities in love, work, and world views are explored, leading to great diversity of subsequent life-course trajectories (Arnett, 2000, 2015). In this chapter, we address the intersection of two major changes that typically occur during emerging adulthood: the establishment of more serious, longer-term romantic relationships and the transition from education into the workforce. The chapter begins with a description of the nature of romantic relationships in emerging adulthood, focusing on what research has revealed about the types of romantic attachments that tend to develop at this time. We then explore the ways in which these romantic relationships are connected to the transition to work and provide practice recommendations that emerge from the research about these connections. We close the chapter with a case illustration to ground our discussion about how romantic relationships intersect with the transition to work in a real-life example, drawn from the first author's program of research, and some concluding thoughts.

It should be noted that our discussion of the nature of romantic relationships during this developmental period is a brief overview designed to introduce the primary focus of the chapter—that is, the roles and functions of romantic relationships within the transition to work. A more thorough explorations about the nature, functions, and associations of emerging adult romantic relationships in general can be found in the edited volumes on this topic by Crouter and Booth (2006) and Fincham and Cui (2011), as well as Chapter 11

José F. Domene and Sarah M. Johnson, *Romantic Relationships and the Transition to Work* In: *Young Adult Development at the School-to-Work Transition.* E. Anne Marshall and Jennifer E. Symonds, Oxford University Press (2021). © Oxford University Press. DOI: 10.1093/oso/9780190941512.003.0005.

of Young et al.'s (2010) book on the transition to adulthood and Shulman and Connolly's (2016) chapter on the subject in the *Oxford Handbook of Emerging Adulthood.*

Romantic Relationship Patterns in Emerging Adulthood

It is during emerging adulthood that the turbulent and short-lived romantic relationships experienced by individuals earlier in life begin to shift in nature, taking on an increased seriousness and level of importance. Achieving intimacy in the form of committed romantic relationships is considered to be one of the key developmental markers of the entry into adulthood (Conger, Cui, Bryant, & Elder, 2000). In industrialized societies, entering into these kinds of committed romantic relationships has historically taken place in what was considered the early years of adulthood. Arnett (2000) reported that, as recently as 1970, the median age of marriage in the United States was about 21 for women and 23 for men. However, substantial shifts in socialization patterns and cultural expectations have taken place in recent decades, including changes in patterns of marriage and having children. In these societies, an increasing number of individuals are choosing to delay these relationship commitments in favor of unmarried cohabitation and taking more time to explore pursuits such as extending education and focusing on career roles, with age at first childbirth following a similar pattern (Stanley, Rhoades, & Fincham, 2011; Shulman, & Connolly, 2016). For example, recent reports have indicated the average age at first marriage is now 27.3 for women and 29.3 for men in the United States (U.S. Census Bureau, 2015), 30.9 for women and 33.6 for men in Germany (Eurostat, 2017), and 29.3 for women and 30.9 for men in Japan (Statistics Bureau, Japan, 2014).

Despite these changes in historical markers of relationship commitment such as marriage and first childbirth, research evidence demonstrates that emerging adulthood remains a pivotal period for the development of romantic relationships. Compared to earlier life stages, romantic relationships in this developmental period are more likely to be steady, exclusive, and characterized by a higher level of intimacy and increased sense of commitment (Arnett, 2015; Collins, 2003). As Arnett and Collins explain, in contrast to dating practices earlier in life, which often take place in groups, in tandem with shared recreational activities, dating in emerging adulthood is more likely to happen one-on-one, as a couple. Consequently, the focus tends to move away from recreation toward exploring the potential for emotional and physical intimacy. Additionally, young adults' romantic relationships often last longer than adolescents' relationships and are more likely to include sexual intercourse and cohabitation (Young et al., 2010).

Research evidence also indicates that the diverse developmental and life-course trajectories found in adolescence have repercussions on the subsequent progression of people's romantic relationships, resulting in the development of different romantic relationship patterns through emerging adulthood (Boisvert & Poulin, 2016). A study by Rauer, Pettit, Lansford, Bates, and Dodge (2013) examined developmental transitions in romantic relationships from age 18 through age 25 in a sample of 511 young people from the United States. Cluster analyses revealed five different patterns of romantic relationships, which included variation in timing, duration, and frequency of participation. The *steady involvement* and *long-term committed* patterns featured steady involvement and the tendency to remain with the same partner, with *steady involvement* characterized by significant romantic relationship involvement with two partners over the study period, while *long-term committed* was limited to a single relationship. The pattern of *sporadic involvement* was characterized by alternating periods of involvement and non-involvement, while the *frequent involvement* pattern also involved repeated partner changes, but featured almost continuous involvement in some relationship. Finally, the *later involvement* pattern was characterized by later initial entry into romantic relationships, typically not reporting a relationship until two to three years later than other groups, and had the fewest partners and least romantic involvement overall. These different trajectories were predicted by variations in their experience and competency in their family and peer relationships, suggesting a connection between the nature of nonromantic relationships and subsequent development of different romantic relationship patterns.

A 13-year longitudinal study by Boisvert and Poulin (2016) sought to identify and describe the distinct relationship patterns that develop from adolescence to adulthood in a sample of 281 French-Canadian youth. Participants were assessed for dimensions of family and peer relationships at age 12 and subsequently asked to identify all their romantic partners and the duration of each relationship every year from age 16 to 24. Latent class analysis of this data revealed five distinct patterns of romantic relationship. They identified the same *long-term involvement*, *sporadic involvement*, *frequent involvement*, and *later involvement* patterns as Rauer and colleagues (2013). They also identified an *intense involvement* pattern; this involved having a large number of romantic partners (11.58 partners on average, compared to 1.3–7.08 for other groups throughout the study period) and being in relationship for a long period of time. These patterns were found to differ according to gender, with more young men having romantic relationships that fell into the sporadic and later involvement patterns while participants in the other three patterns were mostly young women. Additionally, substantial associations were found between patterns of romantic relationship involvement in emerging adulthood and family and peer relationships in early adolescence. Together, the findings of Rauer and colleagues (2013) and Boisvert and Poulin (2016) combine to reveal important variations in the patterns of romantic relationships that can occur during emerging adulthood and suggest that there are links between these patterns and individuals' close relationships earlier in life.

It is evident that there are many variations in the ways that emerging adults engage in romantic relationships. Shulman and Connolly (2013, 2016) have theorized that this variation, which contrasts to the more stable and committed relationships typically found in mature adult romantic relationships, may be explained by the presence of a separate, transitional stage of romantic relationship development. They describe this stage as being characterized by efforts to coordinate romantic relationships with other life plans, such as transition into the workforce. Shulman and Connolly further postulate that during this distinct stage of romantic relationship development, emerging adults strive to integrate their career paths and life plans with those of their romantic partner. Consequently, resolution of this stage would provide a foundation for ensuing long-term commitment to a life partner and potentially other areas of life such as work and careers. As we describe in the subsequent section, there is a growing body of evidence to support these theoretical propositions, at least in terms of the ways that emerging adults' romantic relationships tend to intersect with their career development.

The Intersection of Romantic Relationships and Career Development

Although some research has revealed work and family are perceived to be distinct domains of life for 16- to 19-year-olds (Cinamon & Hason, 2009), a shift in thinking appears to occur later in emerging adulthood. A growing body of evidence indicates that romantic relationships and career issues intersect through the transition to work. For example, within a larger study of developmental transitions and parent–child relationships in Germany, Masche (2008) found that being in the workforce significantly predicted subsequent cohabitation and marriage, but neither cohabitation nor marriage predicted being in the workforce. In contrast, Branje, Laninga-Wijnen, Yu, and Meeus (2014) found employment status to be predictive of relationship status and relational commitment (a dimension of relational identity) and relationships status to be predictive of employment status and work exploration (a dimension of work identity) in a sample from the Netherlands. Further, in a U.S. study of 18- to 24-year-olds in dating relationships, 72% of participants reported it was important to be in a financially secure relationship and believed their romantic partners had a "bright financial future" (Manning, Giordano, Longmore, & Hocevar, 2011, p. 324). In contrast, only 14% stated that they were unconcerned about their partners' financial future. Together, these studies reveal multiple and substantial connections between emerging adults' romantic relationships and their work life.

These connections are also evident in the way that difficulties within the romantic relationship can lead to difficulties in the domain of work, and vice versa. In a sample of Israeli emerging adults, Shulman, Laursen, and Dickson (2014) found that, although there were important gender differences in the nature of the spillover between work and romantic relationships, negative experiences in one domain were associated with negative subsequent experiences in the other domain. Ranta, Dietrich, and Salmela-Aro (2014) found that work-related goals and concerns were associated with romantic relationship status: It was typical for people who had financial concerns to be cohabiting and atypical for people who had financial goals to be in a more casual dating relationship. Finally, in an exploratory study of transition to work conducted with a sample of Canadian university students in committed romantic relationships, Domene and colleagues (2012) found that these couples created and worked toward achieving goals for the future by attending to both career and relationship issues together, rather than treating goals in these two domains as separate from each other.

Romantic partners have also been found to be an important source of support and influence on the transition to work. In a sample of Canadians who self-defined as being in a committed romantic relationship of at least one year, Brosseau, Domene, and Dutka (2010) found that higher levels of partner involvement in career decision-making were associated with lower levels of career decision-making difficulties. Similarly, romantic partners were identified as an important source of influence and support for young men's and young women's career development during the transition to adulthood in a large-scale, qualitative study conducted by Mortimer, Zimmer-Gembeck, Holmes, and Shanahan (2002) in the United States. These studies suggest that romantic partners can provide support for at least some aspects of the transition to work. Additionally, findings from the qualitative component of Manning et al.'s (2011) study of emerging adults in dating relationships reveal the nature of this influence. These participants explained that romantic partners provided encouragement and advice, served as models for positive behavior, and were a source of motivation to pursue educational and occupational goals. This study also revealed that romantic partners can have a negative influence during the transition to work, by taking time and energy away from the pursuit of educational and occupational goals. The findings, however, need to be tempered by the fact that romantic partners emerged as only one among many identified influences in Mortimer et al. (2002) and Manning et al. (2011), and there was a relatively small effect size in the study by Brosseau and colleagues (2010). Nonetheless, the evidence suggests that an individual's romantic partner can provide an important source of influence and support in the transition to work, even if he or she is only one among many sources of influence.

Concerns About Balancing Relationship and Career Goals

Despite the support that romantic partners can provide during the transition to work, many emerging adults are concerned about how to achieve both their career goals and their relationship goals and about how these domains may interfere with each other. For example, in a study of the future goals and concerns of Finnish students, Ranta and colleagues (2014) found that their three most prominent concerns were education, work, and romantic relationships. Research conducted in Canada, the United Kingdom, and the United States suggest that emerging adults are also concerned about potential conflicts between their future work and relationship responsibilities, such as moving in and living together, making and pursuing plans that meet both partners' goals for the future, and having children (Basuil & Casper, 2012; Caroll et al., 2007; Domene et al., 2012; Friedman & Weissbrod, 2005; Marks & Huston, 2002).

At the same time, there is considerable variation in the relative importance that emerging adults place on their work and romantic relationships and how they balance concerns about these roles (Deutsch, Kokot, & Binder, 2007; Kerpelman & Schvaneveldt, 1999). Existing evidence suggests that there are individual differences that systematically influence the importance that is placed on these roles. Not surprisingly, the salience of these concerns appears to be associated with young people's perceived time horizon for entry into different roles. Research from the United States suggests that those who are closer to transitioning into the workforce or transitioning into the next phase of their romantic relationship (e.g., marriage, having a child) are more likely to be concerned about how these worlds intersect (Barnett, Gareis, James, &

Steele, 2003; Caroll et al., 2007). Concern about managing the intersections of career and relationship goals has also been linked to efficacy beliefs. Specifically, in a sample of university students from the United States, Basuil and Casper (2012) found that participants who perceived themselves as more capable of managing these different life roles reported having more knowledge about and commitment to balancing work and family than those with lower levels of self-efficacy in this domain.

There is also research exploring how emerging adults engage with their concerns about balancing career and relationship goals. In a U.S. study with women in the final year of their undergraduate degree, Deutsch and colleagues (2007) explored different potential ways of balancing these goals. Their participants more frequently anticipated achieving balance in egalitarian ways (i.e., both partners would cut back on work responsibilities or rearrange schedules to accommodate household responsibilities) than other solutions (e.g., one partner having a reduced work role while the other has a reduced household role or outsourcing household responsibilities). Furthermore, there significant associations were found between individual characteristics (e.g., ideas about gender roles, parenting, and motherhood) and participants' preferences for how to achieve this balance. Thus, these findings indicate that the current generation of emerging adult women is concerned with the issue of how to balance their various life goals and have somewhat of a preference for seeking egalitarian approaches to achieving this balance, although their preferred solutions vary depending on their beliefs and values.

Domene and colleagues' (2012) qualitative exploration of how heterosexual couples navigate the transition to work provides further evidence to support the idea that emerging adults actively seek to balance their career and relationship goals. In this sample of Canadian university students, many also prioritized egalitarian ways of resolving their concerns about balancing career and relationship goals. Strategies included providing instrumental and emotional support to each other as they were attempting to make the transition, delaying the pursuit of relationship goals (e.g., marriage, having children) so that both members of the couple could focus on career goals and finding creative solutions to problems (e.g., where to reside after graduation) that would allow them to reach their career and relationship goals. This study also identified the strategy of "turn-taking" as a way to resolve their multiple competing responsibilities. Some couples decided to prioritize one partner's career goals at a time, with the understanding that the partner whose career was put on hold would have the opportunity to pursue those goals at a later date. It would require longer-term follow-up to determine whether turn-taking truly resulted in an egalitarian solution; that is, when the time came for the second person's "turn" to have their career prioritized, did this actually happen? In the study, there was no consistent pattern in whose turn would be first for couples using a turn-taking approach to balancing relationship and career goals. However, a gendered pattern did emerge in the minority of participants who resolved potential conflicts by prioritizing only on one partner's career. In these cases, it was the man's career that took precedence.

These two findings (i.e., some couples seek to balance relationships and careers while other couples prioritize the man's career) are important to consider in light of two studies connecting these issues to life satisfaction. Examining identity configurations in love and work in a sample from Germany, Luyckx, Seiffge-Krenke, Schwartz, Crocetti, and Klimstra (2014) identified numerous differences between individuals with different identity configurations. In contrast to Deutsch et al. (2007) and Domene et al. (2012), only a minority of the participants in this study had made strong commitments in both careers and romantic relationships. However, those who had done so also reported the lowest levels of internalizing and externalizing symptoms and conflicts between family and work, as well as the highest levels of life satisfaction. Additionally, Facio and Resett (2014) found that both job satisfaction and romantic relationship satisfaction predicted life satisfaction at ages 23 and 27 in a sample of Argentinian emerging adults. In their study, higher levels of satisfaction in each of these domains independently contributed to participants' overall sense of satisfaction. Although more research clearly needs to be conducted on this subject, the results of these two studies indicate that there may be psychological benefits to resolving concerns about the balance between relationship and career goals in a way that allows young people to maintain a commitment to their goals in both these domains.

To summarize, the period surrounding the transition to work is a time when many emerging adults are focused on attaining career and relationships goals and concerned about how to balance potential conflicts between these goals. They do not appear to experience one dominant pattern of prioritizing career and relationship goals for themselves or for their partners. Rather, the prioritization process is influenced by multiple and intersecting factors such as the anticipated time horizon for making the transition, self-efficacy beliefs, the type of work that individuals and their partners are seeking, and aspects of their relationship. Many emerging adults seek egalitarian solutions to managing future work and household responsibilities, although specific solutions vary from couple to couple. There is also some suggestion that there are benefits associated with addressing these concerns in a way that allows emerging adults to develop strong identities in both career and relationship domains. In light of this evidence, it is worthwhile to consider how educators, advisors, and career practitioners can best assist their clients to make an optimal transition into the workforce.

Practice Recommendations for Facilitating the Transition to Work in the Context of Romantic Relationships

The existing research examining romantic relationships in the transition to work is relatively small. Nonetheless, it provides evidence that emerging adults involve their romantic partners in their transition to work in numerous ways and are concerned with managing their various goals for the future. This body of literature yields several implications for career development practitioners, counselors, psychologists, social workers, and other professionals working with individuals who are making the transition into the workforce within the context of a romantic relationship. The following recommendations should be conceptualized as complementing rather than replacing existing recommendations for career counseling practice with this population, including those described in other chapters within this volume and the strategies suggested by Domene, Landine, and Stewart (2015) in their chapter addressing emerging adults within the *APA Handbook of Career Interventions.*

First, these relationships should not be ignored or treated as unimportant. Although this statement may appear to be self-evident, it needs to be stated explicitly because, historically, career counseling interventions for young people have included little if any focus on romantic relationships. Due to the many different ways that a romantic partner may influence career development and the various ways in which an emerging adult may prioritize relationship goals relative to career goals, it is important to assess the role and meaning of a client's current and potential future romantic relationship in relation to their career planning. This is certainly the case for clients who are in a committed romantic relationship, but it may also be true for clients who are single, in light of the evidence that many emerging adults are concerned about balancing career and relationship goals (Barnett et al., 2003; Basuil & Casper, 2012; Caroll et al., 2007; Deutsch et al., 2007; Kerpelman & Schvaneveldt, 1999).

Second, for clients who are in conflict with their romantic partners about issues related to the transition to work, it is possible that this conflict is reflective of larger conflicts or problems within the romantic relationship. If this is the case, then the client may benefit from relationship counseling to address any communication problems that the couple may be experiencing, as well as conflicts in their expectations for each other in the future. The experience of participants in Domene and colleagues' (2012) study suggests that clear and supportive communication is important for couples' pursuit of future goals. Couples counseling may also involve assisting emerging adults to evaluate whether it is worthwhile to remain in a relationship that is dominated by conflict and barriers to the pursuit of their life goals.

Finally, it may be beneficial to move beyond traditional (e.g., person–environment correspondence) theories of career development and approaches to career counseling when working with clients who are transitioning to work in the context of a committed romantic relationship. These theories and approaches tend to assume that clients make career decisions as autonomous individuals and, consequently, are ill-equipped to address the intersection of relationship and career (Collin, 2006). Instead, it may be more beneficial to adopt meaning-oriented approaches to career counseling that are designed address the relational contexts of clients lives, such as Savickas's (2011) career construction counseling, career counseling from a contextual action theory framework (Domene, Valach, & Young, 2014; Young et al., 2010), or one of the narrative career counseling approaches that have been described in the literature (e.g., Cochran, 1997; Gibbons & Shurts, 2010; McMahon & Watson, 2012). In addition, practitioners should consider the possibility of involving romantic partners in counseling sessions, even when that process is focused on the client's future career (Amundson, 2009; Gibbons & Shurts, 2010). Adopting one of these approaches will open up room for clients to describe the relational components of their career development and for practitioners to bring the romantic relationship to the foreground of the career counseling process.

Case Illustration: Marie and Bryn's Transition From Postsecondary Education Into the Workforce

This case illustrates several key issues and conclusions found in the literature on romantic relationships and the transition to work. It is drawn from an exploratory study of university student couples' career development, conducted in New Brunswick, Canada. The study uses Young and colleagues' *action project method* (Young, Valach, & Domene, 2005), a qualitative method of inquiry that has been described as falling within a constructivist research paradigm and informed by the theoretical tenets of *contextual action theory* (Young et al., 2005, 2010). Information was collected from this couple using a multistage interview that included interviewing the couple together, video-recorded observation of the couple having a discussion about their future, and video-assisted reflection about the discussion separately with each member of the couple. A discursive, consensus-based approach to thematic analysis was used to identify salient themes and processes across the multiple forms of data and to generate narrative descriptions of the couple's individual and joint experience, which were presented back to them for validation. Names and other demographic characteristics have been altered to preserve the confidentiality of the research participants.

Marie and Bryn are a couple who have been dating for approximately eight months and are planning to move in together in four months. Marie is a 23-year-old woman from eastern New Brunswick who moved to Fredericton over three years ago to pursue a bachelor of science degree in engineering at a local university. She currently lives in a dorm on campus. Her cultural background is Acadian, and her first language is French, although she is also fluent in English. She is a full-time student who works a few hours per week as a research assistant. Her history of romantic relationships appears to fall within the steady involvement pattern identified by Rauer and colleagues (2013). Bryn is a 21-year-old man from a rural community near Fredericton. He has been living in Fredericton for several years in a basement apartment with a roommate. Bryn's adoptive parents are English-Canadian; he is unaware of the cultural background of his birth parents. He is a unilingual Anglophone. Bryn has just completed an information systems specialist diploma at a local community college and is preparing to write certification exams. He also recently began working at a fast-food restaurant "to pay the bills" until he completes his certification and obtains employment in the information technology field, which he hopes will occur within the next year. Bryn's romantic relationship history fits the late involvement pattern. Marie and Bryn intend to live in Fredericton at least until Marie completes her degree and would prefer to remain in New Brunswick afterwards. However, they recognize they may have to relocate for employment purposes.

Over the course of their research involvement, it became evident that Marie is closely involved in Bryn's transition to work, providing support and motivation for Bryn to complete his certification and to find employment. For example, in the following sequence from their conversation together, Marie attempted to focus the conversation on Bryn's transition to work:

BRYN: I just don't feel like doing it [studying for certification exams] right now.

MARIE: No, I know. And I know, like, during your work term, you were just getting used to, like, working and stuff. (laughs)

BRYN: Yes.

MARIE: If it were me, I would have, like, started studying and stuff during my work term.

BRYN: Yeah, but I really hate studying. (sighs)

MARIE: I know. And I'm also a bit of a workaholic, you know. . . . Um (laughs)

BRYN: (sighs)

MARIE: So were there lots of things [job postings], like . . . in Saint John and Moncton?

BRYN: Ah, there were a few, yeah. I mean, it wasn't super popular. I thought I had this conversation with you too.

MARIE: Well, I knew you'd looked at stuff out of town, but like-

BRYN: Yeah. Well, it's not like they were, like, oozing off the walls or anything. But there were quite a few more . . . so . . . yeah.

MARIE: I'm just, I don't know. I thought, like, you, you went and looked but you didn't, like . . . look a whole lot.

BRYN: No, I didn't look a whole lot. I only looked once or twice.

In the individual interview, Marie clarified that she attempts to motivate and encourage Bryn to move toward his transition-to-work goals on an ongoing basis:

> When he had his work term in the summer at the hospital, I would be like, "shouldn't you start looking for jobs, shouldn't you start, like, working on getting your certs so you can get the job," and he wasn't ready for that yet. So just knowing, that's like, but you knew you were on a deadline. (laughs) Because when I have a deadline, I always try to get finished. . . . I knew he's looked at some positions. But I hadn't thought he looked a whole lot, so I was, like, when it came up in the interview, I was, like, "but you didn't look very much." (laughs)

In addition to direct support and motivation, Bryn's relationship with Marie was also linked to his transition to work in another way. Specifically, in his individual interview, Bryn reported that part of his motivation to accept employment in a fast-food restaurant so quickly was to relieve pressure that Marie was experiencing, "Her mom was like, 'Does he have a job yet, does he have a job yet, does he have a job yet.' So her mom was worrying the whole time, which was stressing [Marie], 'cause she gets stressed pretty easy." Although the specific ways in which Bryn's relationship with Marie have influenced his process of transitioning to work is complex, it is evident that elements in this romantic relationship has intersected with Bryn's career development.

This case also illustrates the research finding that many emerging adults are concerned about balancing relationship and career goals during the transition to work. For example, much of the conversation between Bryn and Marie was focused on their plans to move in together in a few months and considering options for where to live. A key determinant of this decision was finding a location that would allow for convenient transit to Marie's school and Bryn's employment. Additionally, the couple were considering the question of having children and how to balance children with career and employment issues. For example, Bryn described how having a child before they were financially stable and Marie was still in school was impractical:

BRYN: Obviously we're not planning to have children right now. And while we both, like, really want children. Like, if we were to have one right now, we probably wouldn't go to the abortion clinic or anything, we could have the child. But we, at this time [pause]

INTERVIEWER: It's not in the plan?

BRYN: Yes. We understand right now that we are not financially stable enough to support a child and our families would slaughter us. So it—we do talk about children quite a bit.

At the same time, they also discuss how children may influence career options in the future, and although they do not come to a resolution about this issue, their concern for balancing these responsibilities is evident in their interaction:

MARIE: Like . . . what's gonna happen, like, I kinda wonder, like . . . once we have kids and stuff, like, how's that gonna . . . change things?

BRYN: How do you mean?

MARIE: Well like, you can't just get up and move if you find a good job then.

BRYN: Why not? Lots of families do.

MARIE: I don't know. I'd feel bad, like, just making people move.

BRYN: Well I mean, if they're under a certain age it wouldn't really matter.

MARIE: Well, yeah, no. I get that.

BRYN: But, I mean, you know, you gotta go where the money is.

MARIE: Yeah. Well, just—my cousins had to move a lot, and—

BRYN: (interrupts) Oh yeah, so did I.

MARIE: And got screwed up.

BRYN: I'm not screwed up, am I?

MARIE: (laughs) Sometimes. (laughs)

BRYN: (laughs).

MARIE: Yeah.

BRYN: No, I don't know. You just gotta go where you gotta go.

Finally, it should be noted that these interactions are taking place in a couple who, despite their relatively young age, are both strongly committed to their romantic relationship and to their career goals. This suggests that Marie and Bryn would both fall into Luyckx et al.'s (2014) subset of emerging adults who have the lowest levels of internalizing and externalizing symptoms and the highest levels of life satisfaction. Although there was no formal assessment of these constructs in this couple, they presented to the interviewers as having relatively high satisfaction despite the external stressors that they were experiencing (e.g., financial pressures, parental pressures). Indeed, their functioning in both the relationship and career domains was such that they do not appear to be in need of counseling for their transition to work at the present time. However, the situation may change if Bryn fails to complete his certification or otherwise experiences an extended delay in obtaining a position in the information technology field.

Future Directions and Conclusion

Although there is a growing body of research examining the connections between romantic relationships and emerging adults' transition to work, it is also important to recognize three gaps in the existing knowledge-base, which should be prioritized as direction for future research on this subject. First, an overwhelming majority of the studies that have explored romantic relationships and the transition to work have been conducted in North America and western Europe. As Facio and Resett (2014) point out, additional research in this area needs to be conducted in other parts of the world, due to potential cultural differences in the nature of romantic relationships, as well as wide variations across countries in terms of the process of transitioning into the workforce. Until additional research is conducted, scholars' and practitioners' understanding of the phenomenon is incomplete.

Second, much of the existing research has been conducted with university students. Far less is known about the role of romantic relationships when individuals are transitioning into the workforce from high school. This gap in knowledge is especially problematic, given the previously described differences in the length, purposes, and activities of romantic relationships that typically occur during high school versus those that typically occur during the transition out of postsecondary education (Arnett, 2015; Collins, 2003; Young et al., 2010). Consequently, clear directions for future research are to explore the intersection of romantic relationships and entry into the workforce from high school and to identify similarities and differences in the role of romantic relationships when the transition to work occurs following the completion of high school versus postsecondary education.

Finally, building on existing research that has identified distinct patterns of romantic relationship involvement during emerging adulthood (Boisvert & Poulin, 2016; Rauer et al., 2013), it appears important to determine whether and how these patterns may be connected with different processes and outcomes related to the transition to work. For example, which patterns of romantic relationship involvement are associated with more rapid entry into the workforce? Do individuals who engage in shorter-term romantic relationship patterns (e.g., sporadic involvement, frequent involvement) also tend to have employment that is shorter term? Or could the opposite be true; that is, perhaps higher commitment to a job or career path is associated with lower commitment to romantic relationships? Additional research evidence is required to move the discussion of possible connections between young people's patterns of relationship involvement and their transition to work beyond speculation.

Although there are clear directions for future research that should be prioritized by scholars working in this area, the existing evidence base is sufficient to conclude that emerging adults' romantic relationships must be considered to more fully understand the transition to work. This chapter reveals a growing body of literature examining ways in which romantic relationship factors intersect with the transition to work experience. Findings from numerous countries converge to reveal that emerging adults' current romantic relationships, as well as thinking about future romantic relationship goals and responsibilities, are connected to numerous aspects of the transition. Indeed, sufficient evidence has emerged to warrant the recommendations presented in this chapter for practitioners who are assisting emerging adults to make an optimal transition to work: (a) Relationship status and relationship goals should be attended to and assessed in career practice; (b) for some emerging adult clients, it may be beneficial to recommend couples counseling prior to or alongside career counseling; and (c) contextual and meaning-oriented approaches may be more effective that person–environment correspondence models of career counseling for addressing issues related to the intersection of relationship and career. Finally, the case of Marie and Bryn has revealed some of the ways that the body of research evidence can manifest in the lives of one particular emerging adult couple.

References

Amundson, N. E. (2009). *Active engagement* (3rd ed.). Richmond, BC: Ergon Communication.

Arnett, J. J. (2000). Emerging adulthood: A theory of development from the late teens through the twenties. *American Psychologist, 55,* 469–480. doi:10.1037/0003-066X.55.5.469

Arnett, J. J. (2015). *Emerging adulthood: The winding road from the late teens through the twenties* (2nd ed.). New York, NY: Oxford University Press. doi:10.1093/oxfordhb/9780199795574.013.9

Barnett, R. C., Gareis, K. C., James, J. B., & Steele, J. (2003). Planning ahead: College seniors' concerns about career-marriage conflict. *Journal of Vocational Behavior, 62,* 305–319. doi:/10.1016/S0001-8791(02)00028-3

Basuil, D. A., & Casper, W. J. (2012). Work–family planning attitudes among emerging adults. *Journal of Vocational Behavior, 80,* 629–637. doi:10.1016/j.jvb.2012.01.017

Boisvert, S., & Poulin, F. J. (2016). Romantic relationship patterns from adolescence to emerging adulthood: Associations with family and peer experiences in early adolescence. *Youth Adolescence, 45,* 945–958. doi:10.1007/s10964-016-0435-0

Branje, S., Laninga-Wijnen, L., Yu, R., & Meeus, W. (2014). Associations among school and friendship identity in adolescence and romantic relationships and work in emerging adulthood. *Emerging Adulthood, 2,* 6–16. doi:10.1177/2167696813515851

Brosseau, D. C., Domene, J. F., & Dutka, T. (2010). The importance of partner involvement in determining career decision-making difficulties. *Canadian Journal of Career Development, 9,* 35–41.

Caroll, J. S., Willougby, B., Badger, S., Nelson, L. J., McNamara Barry, C., & Madsen, S. D. (2007). So close, yet so far away: The impact of varying marital horizons on emerging adulthood. *Journal of Adolescent Research, 22,* 219–247. doi:10.1177/0743558407299697

Cinamon, R. G., & Hason, I. (2009). Facing the future: Barriers and resources in work and family plans of at-risk Israeli youth. *Youth & Society, 40,* 502–525. doi:10.1177/0044118X08328008

Cochran, L. (1997). *Career counseling: A narrative approach*. Thousand Oaks, CA: SAGE.

Collin, A. (2006). Conceptualising the family-friendly career: The contribution of career theories and a systems approach. *British Journal of Guidance & Counselling, 34,* 295–307. doi:10.1080/03069880600769225

Collins, W. A. (2003). More than myth: The developmental significance of romantic relationships during adolescence. *Journal of Research on Adolescence, 13,* 1–24. doi:10.1111/1532-7795.1301001

Conger, R. D., Cui, M., Bryant, C. M., & Elder, G. H. (2000). Competence in early adult romantic relationships: A developmental perspective on family influences. *Journal of Personality and Social Psychology, 79,* 224–237. doi:10.1037/0022-3514.79.2.224

Crouter, A. C., & Booth, A. (2006). *Romance and sex in adolescence and emerging adulthood: Risks and opportunities*. Mahwah, NJ: Erlbaum.

Deutsch, F. M., Kokot, A. P., & Binder, K. S. (2007). College women's plans for different types of egalitarian marriages. *Journal of Marriage and Family, 69,* 916–929. doi:10.1111/j.1741-3737.2007.00421.x

Domene, J. F., Landine, J., & Stewart, J. (2015). Emerging adult career transitions. In P. J. Hartung, M. L. Savickas, & W. B. Walsh (Eds.), *APA handbook of career intervention* (Vol. 2, pp. 479–494). Washington, DC: American Psychological Association.

Domene, J. F., Nee, J. J., Cavanaugh, A. K., McLelland, S., Stewart, B. L., Stephenson, M., . . . Young, R. A. (2012). Young adult couples transitioning to work: The intersection of career and relationship. *Journal of Vocational Behavior, 18,* 17–25. doi:10.1016/j.jvb.2012.03.005

Domene, J. F., Valach, L., & Young, R. A. (2014). Action in counseling: A contextual action theory perspective. In R. A. Young, J. F. Domene, & L. Valach (Eds.), *Counseling and action: Toward life-enhancing work, relationships and identity* (pp. 151–166). New York, NY: Springer.

Eurostat. (2017). Marriage indicators. Retrieved from https://ec.europa.eu/eurostat/web/products-datasets/-/demo_nind

Facio, A., & Resett, S. (2014). Work, romantic relationships, and life satisfaction in Argentinean emerging adults. *Emerging Adulthood, 2*, 27–35. doi:10.1177/2167696813515854

Fincham, F. D., & Cui, M. (2011). *Romantic relationships in emerging adulthood.* New York, NY: Cambridge University Press.

Friedman, S. R., & Weissbrod, C. S. (2005). Work and family commitment and decision-making status among emerging adults. *Sex Roles, 53*, 317–325. doi:10.1007/s11199-005-6755-2

Gibbons, M. M., & Shurts, W. M. (2010). Combining career and couples counseling for college students: A narrative approach. *Journal of College Counseling, 13*, 169–181. doi:10.1002/j.2161-1882.2010.tb00057.x

Kerpelman, J. L., & Schvaneveldt, P. L. (1999). Young adults' anticipated identity importance of career, marital, and parental roles: Comparisons of men and women with different role balance orientations. *Sex Roles, 41*, 189–217. doi:10.1023/A:1018802228288

Luyckx, K., Seiffge-Krenke, I., Schwartz, S. J., Crocetti, E., & Klimstra, T. A. (2014). Identity configurations across love and work in emerging adults in romantic relationships. *Journal of Applied Developmental Psychology, 35*, 192–203. doi:10.1016/j.appdev.2014.03.007

Manning, W. D., Giordano, P. C., Longmore, M. A., & Hocevar, A. (2011). Romantic relationships and academic/career trajectories in emerging adulthood. In F. D. Fincham & M. Cui (Eds.), *Romantic relationships in emerging adulthood* (pp. 317–333). New York, NY: Cambridge University Press.

Marks, G., & Huston, D. M. (2002). The determinants of young women's intentions about education, career development and family life. *Journal of Education and Work, 15*, 321–336. doi:10.1080/1363908022000012085

Masche, J. G. (2008). Reciprocal influences between developmental transitions and parent–child relationships in young adulthood. *International Journal of Behavioral Development, 32*, 401–411. doi:10.1177/0165025408093658

McMahon, M., & Watson, M. (2012). Story crafting: Strategies for facilitating narrative career counselling. *International Journal for Educational and Vocational Guidance, 12*, 211–224. doi:10.1007/s10775-012-9228-5

Mortimer, J. T., Zimmer-Gembeck, M. J., Holmes, M., & Shanahan, M. J. (2002). The process of occupational decision making: Patterns during the transition to adulthood. *Journal of Vocational Behavior, 61*, 439–465. doi:10.1006/jvbe.2002.1885

Ranta, M., Dietrich, J., & Salmela-Aro, K. (2014). Career and romantic relationship goals and concerns during emerging adulthood. *Emerging Adulthood, 2*, 17–26. doi:10.1177/2167696813515852

Rauer, A. J., Pettit, G. S., Lansford, J. E., Bates, J. E., & Dodge, K. A. (2013). Romantic relationship patterns in young adulthood and their developmental antecedents. *Developmental Psychology, 49*, 2159–2171. doi:10.1037/a0031845.

Savickas, M. L. (2011). *Career counseling.* Washington, DC: American Psychological Association.

Shulman, S., & Connolly, J. (2013). The challenge of romantic relationships in emerging adulthood: Reconceptualization of the field. *Emerging Adulthood, 1*, 27–39. doi:10.1177/2167696812467330

Shulman, S., & Connolly, J. (2016). The challenge of romantic relationships in emerging adulthood. In J. J. Arnett (Ed.), *The Oxford handbook of emerging adulthood* (pp. 230–244). New York, NY: Oxford University Press.

Shulman, S., Laursen, B., & Dickson, D. J. (2014). Gender differences in the spillover between romantic experiences, work experiences, and individual adjustment across emerging adulthood. *Emerging Adulthood, 2*, 36–47. doi:10.1177/2167696813515853

Stanley, S. M., Rhoades, G. K., & Fincham, F. D. (2011). Understanding romantic relationships among emerging adults: The significant roles of cohabitation and ambiguity. In F. D. Fincham & M. Cui (Eds.), *Romantic relationships in emerging adulthood* (pp. 234–251). New York, NY: Cambridge University Press.

Statistics Bureau, Japan. (2014). Mean age of first marriage. *Statistical handbook of Japan 2014.* Retrieved from http://www.stat.go.jp/english/data/handbook/pdf/2014all.pdf

U.S. Census Bureau. (2015). Median age at first marriage. *2011–2015 American Community Survey 5-year estimates.* Retrieved from https://www.census.gov/programs-surveys/acs/technical-documentation/table-and-geography-changes/2015/5-year.html

Young, R. A., Valach, L., & Domene, J. F. (2005). The action-project method in counseling psychology. *Journal of Counseling Psychology, 52,* 215–223. doi:10.1037/0022-0167.52.2.215

Young, R. A., Valach, L., Marshall, S. K., Domene, J. F., Graham, M. D., & Zaidman-Zait, A. (2010). *Transition to adulthood: Action, projects and counseling.* New York, NY: Springer.

6

Narrative Approach to Career Identity Development

Parental Influence in the Italian Context

Luigia Simona Sica, Laura Aleni Sestito, and Tiziana Di Palma

Introduction

Since Erikson's (1980) conceptualization, identity development is placed at the intersection of characteristics of individuals and those from transactions between individuals and their environment (Adams & Marshall, 1996; Bosma & Kunnen, 2001; Kroger, 2000; 2004). A contextual trend within the developmental systems theory (Ford & Lerner, 1992; Thelen & Smith, 1994) has highlighted development as a co-constructed process occurring between the active individual and his/her active context, in particular within the family context that represents the first microsystem in which individual development occurs (Bronfenbrenner, 1979) and also within ongoing long-term relationships (Kuczynski, 2003; Lollis, 2003). Further, the family cannot be considered a "neutral environment because it deeply affects the individual process, starting during adolescence, that leads to the development of one' s identity" (Scabini & Manzi, 2011, p. 573). Therefore, parents are seen as *co-authors* (Koepke & Denissen, 2012) and as *identity agents* who actively interact with their offspring, thereby participating in identity formation (Schachter & Ventura, 2008). Some longitudinal studies have especially emphasized the interplay of family relationships and identity in college students (Beyers & Goossens, 2008; Kroger & Haslett, 1988; Luyckx, Soenens, Vansteenkiste, Goossens, & Berzonsky, 2007).

Even in the case of vocational identity, a number of studies emphasize that parents exert important influences on their children's career development (Bryant et al., 2006; Keller & Whiston, 2008; Paa & Whirter, 2000). For example, Keller and Whiston (2008) focus on the impact of parental behavior and attitude on children's career development; Xiao, Newman, and Chu

Luigia Simona Sica, Laura Aleni Sestito, and Tiziana Di Palma, *Narrative Approach to Career Identity Development* In: *Young Adult Development at the School-to-Work Transition*. E. Anne Marshall and Jennifer E. Symonds, Oxford University Press (2021).
 DOI: 10.1093/oso/9780190941512.003.0006.

(2016) have studied the interactions with parents and career planning and future thinking.

The present chapter focuses on the vocational identity formation process as a key factor for transition to adulthood and on vocational identity co-authoring between parents and young people within the narrative approach to career identity development (Meijer & Lengelle, 2012). Starting from the historical background of vocational identity in Italy and in light of the theoretical background of narrative vocational identity, the chapter underlines the parental influence on Italian youth's career development. Specifically, assuming that identity formation, and especially career construction, is a co-constructed process (Kuczynski, 2003; Lollis, 2003) in which parents can be interpreted as identity agents (Schachter & Ventura, 2008), the chapter presents and discusses the main results of a new piece of research in the Italian context and proposes a model of vocational identity co-authoring between parents and young people. In particular, this latter section explores the narrative interview with Italian students attending the last year of high school and the final year of university studies, carried out to understand how young people make sense of parental influence in their career development by incorporating it as a part of the larger life story (Young, Friesen, & Borycki, 1994). In addition to the parental influence on career construction processes, the chapter also considers the features of the social, cultural, and economic context of contemporary Italian society. With regard to these features, there are two main elements that are helpful to better understand young Italian people's career identity development: the social and economic changes, especially relating to the job market, and the crucial role of family in supporting and helping their children's identity development.

Insofar as the first is concerned, it is worth referring to the swift changes that have occurred in the world of work of postindustrial societies over the last few decades; these have produced a variety of contractual typologies as well as greater flexibility for entering the job market. This has led to a reduction in being able to predict outcomes for career development and, at the same time, to an increase in being at risk of remaining excluded or marginalized from the job market. The main problems in the Italian context include high rates of youth unemployment (ranging approximately from 35% to 58.3% in 2013; Eurostat 2016), which appear to be higher than the European average; widespread job precariousness (e.g., Cortini, Tanucci, & Morin 2011); and a deep-rooted crisis of confidence in the social institutions (e.g., Pharr & Putnam, 2000). Because the Italian job market is characterized by a particular difficulty for young people, larger numbers of youth are classified as NEET or "Not in Education, Employment, or Training" (Bynner & Parsons 2002). In fact, even after concluding their prolonged programs of study, young Italians have been found to experience additional periods of instability, insecurity, and economic uncertainty (Berton, Richiardi, & Sacchi 2009; Iezzi & Mastrobuoni 2010; ISTAT, 2014). Thus, for a large part of them, career commitment is likely to be unattainable (Aleni Sestito, Sica, & Nasti, 2013).

The difficult socioeconomic conditions outlined are associated with more general changes affecting all countries of contemporary postindustrial society, for example, destandardization of youth's transition to adulthood, modernization, globalization (Larson, 2011) that produce meaningful changes in developmental pathways.

In this regard, demographer Livi Bacci (2008) identified in the Italian context a "delay syndrome," which is characterized by five symptoms: (a) prolongation of education; (b) deferral of entry into the job market and high rates of unemployment; (c) tendency to remain in the parental home until the late 20s or 30s; (d) postponing entry into a committed partnership; and (e) delayed transition to parenthood. Many recent studies also confirm this delay in identity development and emphasize that this identity postponement could increase identity instability and hinder identity consolidation (Crocetti, Rabaglietti, & Sica, 2012; Sica, Aleni Sestito, & Ragozini, 2014). When compared with their northern European peers, young Italians demonstrate that the share of young Italians (as well as Greek) aged 20 to 29 living with their parents is higher (between 70% and 84.2%) than the share of young Germans (between 50% and 70%) and young French (between 30% and 50%).

Furthermore, the image of the future as a controllable and governable time is shrinking, and, as a result, "the present looks like the only temporal dimension available for defining choices, an authentic existential horizon that, in a certain sense, includes and replaces future and past" (Leccardi, 2006, p. 41). This situation for young Italian people is also characterized by the limits of the welfare system in which, compared to other European countries, social policies (such as public expenditure for families and children) toward younger generations are limited.

Therefore, in Italy as well as in other countries of southern Europe, the family plays a central role in the welfare system, acting as the main provider of care and welfare for children and dependent individuals (Banfield, 1958; Ferrera, 1996, 1997; León & Migliavacca, 2013; Moreno & Marí-Klose, 2013; Moreno Mínguez, 2010; Saraceno, 2003). In addition, the family represents the main social safety net that supports young people in facing challenges related to transition to work in a context characterized by high levels of job insecurity and unemployment and a general distrust in political institutions (Albertini & Kohli, 2013). In this respect, some scholars have pointed out that in Mediterranean countries the transition to adulthood occurs within the family context (Scabini, Marta, & Lanz, 2006); a very high percentage of young people tend to live with their parents for much longer than their peers in central and northern Europe and the United States (Aassve, Billari, Mazzuco, & Ongaro, 2002). In Italy, for instance, the mean age at which young people leave home is 29.5 years for females and 31 years for males (European Union, 2012). To underscore that in Italy the transition to adulthood is no longer an individual transition but a joint transition involving both parents and their children, Scabini and Donati (1988) proposed a conceptualization: "the long family life of the young adult." In other words, parents tend to support their children mainly through prolonged co-residence, and children are expected to leave the parental home only after they complete their educational career, find a stable job, and marry.

It has been shown that continued co-residence with parents during the 20s and 30s might slow down the process of transition from school to university/work and toward becoming a self-sufficient and independent adult (Aleni Sestito, Sica, 2014; Ingoglia, & Allen, 2010; Scabini, Marta, & Lanz, 2006). The extended period of cohabitation of young people with the family of origin can also produce a slowdown in the autonomy acquisition process (Arnett, 2000; Roisman, Masten, Coatsworth, & Tellegen, 2004).

Historical Background of Vocational Identity in Italy

From late adolescence and gradually throughout the transition to adulthood, the vocational identity formation process is a central element for individual development (Porfeli, Lee, Vondracek, & Weigold, 2011). Since Erikson and Marcia's early contributions, it has been shown that the acquisition of a relatively stable identity constitutes the main developmental task (Havighurst, 1953, 1972; Holland, Daiger, & Power, 1980; McCormick, Kuo, & Masten, 2011) of young people in the years of transition from adolescence to adulthood. Thus, the vocational identity process is intertwined with the development, in a more global view, of personal identity, and in a contextual view, it is affected in a concrete way by the historical, economic, and cultural environment in which the individual grows.

Specifically, vocational identity is conceived as a domain-specific aspect of overall identity, providing young people with a framework to regulate the pursuit of their academic and career objectives (Hirschi, 2011). People who show greater career planning and decidedness also show more advanced identity (Meeus, 1993; Skorikov & Vondracek, 1998). Numerous studies also confirm the positive association between vocational and overall identity (Nauta & Kahn, 2007; Savickas, 1985; Skorikov & Vondraceck, 1998), finding that engaging in occupational exploration and making occupational commitments promote identity development from childhood through to adulthood (Flum & Blustein, 2006; Kroger, 2007). Work experience was found to be the primary influence on overall identity development for college students, young workers, and unemployed (Danielsen, Loren, & Kroger, 2000). Vocational identity is, therefore, believed to be a defining feature in adolescent and young adult life, a leading aspect of global identity development, and fostered by work experience (Skorikov & Vondraceck, 2011). Indeed, adolescents tend to leave behind a vague sense of self as a "worker," inspired by childhood images of stereotypical or idealized work activities, and move toward an adult vocational identity that is more concrete, realistic, and alive in the real world of work, according to a developmental model of vocational identity that is boosted by developing a sense of industry and positive view of the working world (Porfeli, Lee, & Weigold, 2011).

Despite the general regularity of vocational identity development exhibited on the population across the late adolescent and emerging adulthood period, appreciable variability is observed also in the pathways and timing of vocational identity progress from person to person and across different cultural and socioeconomic contexts (Skorikov & Patton, 2007; Skorikov & Vondracek, 2011). Thus, the impact of globalization and global economic changes on the nature of work and career and how that may relate to changes in vocational identity processes and structure (Ashkenas, Ulrich, Jick, & Kerr, 1995) serves as a backdrop for the present study.

With regard to the specific context of the present chapter, many cross-cultural studies have focused on the peculiar trajectories of the transition to adulthood of young Italian people as compared to those in other countries. In particular, some studies on university students have found that delayed transition to adult life has a particular impact not only on global (Aleni Sestito, Sica, & Ragozini, 2012; Crocetti, Luyckx, Scrignaro, & Sica, 2011; Crocetti, Scrignaro, Sica, & Magrin, 2012) but also on vocational identity (Aleni Sestito, Sica, & Nasti, 2013). In a recent study on young Italians' vocational identity (Sica, Aleni Sestito, & Ragozini, 2014), results reveal that they are coping with a very difficult labor market by either (a) committing to careers with moderate to little exploration and appreciable flexibility and doubt or (b) avoiding career commitment and remaining in career exploration and flexibility patterns. These vocational patterns may be contributing to students choosing an academic pathway well before and possibly in isolation from or even in the absence of any personal career plans (Checchi & Ballarino, 2006).

Furthermore, these results confirm that identity develops and operates differently in different life domains (Goossens, 2001). With respect to vocational identity, even though it is conceived as a major component of one's overall sense of identity (Kroger, 2007; Skorikov & Vondrecek, 2007, 2011), this identity domain appears particularly sensitive to the labor context. In Italy, the work context clearly seems to be contributing to the definition of vocational identity. Indeed, this distressed economic situation in Italy, and specifically for young people who are in the throes of career decision-making, influences the distribution and nature of vocational identity statuses.

Parental Influence on Italian Youth

In addition to the specific Italian context described as being crucial to vocational identity development, there is also the impact of the family on young peoples' identity formation. It has been shown that continued co-residence with parents during the transition to adulthood may slow down the process by which an individual moves toward becoming a self-sufficient and independent adult, largely because parents do not facilitate their autonomy (Arnett, 2000; Roisman, Masten, Coastworth, & Tellegan, 2004). Within the transformations occurring in the family system (Carrà, Lanz, & Tagliabue, 2014), research has been emphasized the role played by Italian parents and their propensity to be relatively supportive in the search for an adaptive balance between autonomy and closeness to their sons and daughters, and in their autonomous choices. In a recent Italian study (Aleni Sestito & Sica, 2014), the results show that different profiles of parental influence on overall identity formation can be identified; the life stories of second-year university students revealed two basic profiles interpreted as "suitable and adaptive co-residency" and "conflict co-residency." In the first profile, comprising the majority of students, the association between responsiveness and autonomy support in the absence of conflict and control (for parenting), and identity commitment (for identity) pointed out that parental warmth and support were positively associated with commitment. Life stories showed that perceived parenting has a positive influence on identity development as well as on well-being. In the second profile, namely "conflict co-residency," dimensions of conflict and psychological control with moderate responsiveness and autonomy support were associated with commitment and in depth-exploration. Life stories, characterized by a vertical relationship with parents, showed a different family context, not only less pleasant than the one previously described but also less supportive of autonomy and outside experimentation. Moreover, parental contribution in the identity co-authoring of children seems to support a lack of development. As such, the research indicated that parents contribute to the maintenance of a relational dynamic of conflict type and do not promote adolescent detachment, independence, or the evolution toward a more in-depth exploration of identity or developmental change.

Indeed, the family and intergenerational bonds seem particularly strong, so the transition to adulthood is accomplished not only when young people perceive that they have become capable of assuming personal responsibilities, but especially when they feel capable of establishing equal relationships with parents (Aleni Sestito & Sica, 2014). These features seem to configure a Mediterranean model, in which "the prolonged co-residence with parents; the absence of financial support from the state and increased psychological uncertainty are hypothesized to be substituted by family support, especially parental support"(Tagliabue, Lanz, & Beyers, 2014, p. 3). This would also explain why most young Italians, similar to young Spanish people, leave the parental home primarily because of marriage (Lanz & Tagliabue, 2007), whereas for young northern and central Europeans, these two experiences are more frequently dissociated. In the specifically Italian context, the concept of "familism" has been proposed to explain the demographic and social policy distinctiveness of southern Europe, where the family, as previously described, plays a central role in the welfare system, acting as the main provider of care and welfare for young people (e.g., Leon & Migliavacca, 2013).

In the light of research tradition where personal agency and features of social context are combined (Adams & Marshall, 1996; Côté & Levine, 2002), Schachter and Ventura have recently introduced the concept of *parental identity agency* to underline that parents are active and purposeful co-participants in their children's identity formation. Indeed, they conceptualize parents as liaising internally between the macro-social context of development and the micro-social context of parent–child interactions. Focusing on parents as identity agents may therefore enable other agents, apart from young people, to be examined. Such an approach is based on Kuczynski's (2003) description of agents as "actors with the ability to make sense of the environment, initiate change, and make choices" (p. 9). This also involves the conceptualization of parents and children as a two-way interrelated identity system (Kerpelman & Lamke, 1997), enabling connections between parents and children and long-term related changes in parenting dimensions and identity dimensions to be drawn (Koepke & Denissen, 2012, p. 81). Such parental agency can be seen as co-authorship, and it appears more evident in the contemporary, postindustrial context in which the trajectories of a progressive acquisition of autonomy by young people and the construction of personal life plans are configured as more complex and uncertain and entail family involvement and an active role of parents both as material support and as actors of identity formation.

Identity could be seen as a co-authorship process for children and parents and especially vocational identity could be interpreted, supported, and fostered by focusing on a co-jointed autobiographical project. In other words, vocational identity could be seen as a narration in which personal desires, attitudes, and plans and parental support and influence are the actors. Young (1994) gave evidence on this point, identifying four different (progressive and regressive) narrative types of parental influence as retrospectively constructed by young people: progressive narrative with a dramatic turning point; progressive narrative with a positive evaluation frame; progressive narrative with negative evaluated stages; and anticipated regressive narratives. In this research, the four narrative types provide a useful way to understand the role of parental influence on the career and life direction of young people.

The Narrative Identity Approach as a Framework for Career Identity Development

Considering the main focus of the present chapter—namely, Italian parents' role in the career identity development of young people, above all on the co-construction processes of career projects—career identity development is explored in depth within the narrative identity approach. Although the narrative thinking and the ability to produce stories about oneself appears in early childhood, McAdams (2011) points out that only from late adolescence are young people able to understand and represent their identity through the construction of stories that give their lives coherence, unity, and direction. In particular, it has been underlined that the new social and cognitive skills gained during adolescence increase the capacity of meaning-making and self-connection, thanks to which young people can start thinking about their own self related to their own past and future selves (McAdams, 1988). In this sense, such a capacity is considered a prerogative of young people (McAdams, 1993, 2001). Even Habermas and Bluck (2000) believe that it is only from adolescence onward that young people gain the self-reflection needed to be able to integrate the different and sometimes contradictory experiences and required within the framework of meaning-making processes that substantiate the narrative identity. In this perspective, other authors have associated the increase of meaning-making capacities (McLean & Breen, 2009; McLean, Breen, & Fournier, 2010), beyond that of production capacities of interpretive narratives (Pasupathi & Wainryb, 2010) at a young age, to the increase in ability to understand and manage the contradictions of their own personal history.

The narrative identity approach places specific emphasis on individuals' subjective assessment of their personal experiences and the stories that they tell about them (McAdams, 1993). The autobiographical narratives enable individuals to structure their experiences in a format that facilitates subjective reflection and thus the process of making sense of life or of life's specific events, which is critical to identity development (Bruner, 1993; Kunnen & Bosma, 2000).

With particular reference to young people living in contemporary society, McAdams (2011) believes that the latter can more appropriately deal with the challenges inherent in their development tasks by building "integrative narratives" that may enable them to explain "how they came to be, where their lives are going, and how they hope to fit into the adult world that awaits them" (p. 100).

Therefore, the narrative approach is useful to evaluate the characteristics of vocational identity. In this perspective, it is believed that identity can be not only and not so much explored and investigated but also built through the reflection that everyone applies to herself or himself, in the *hic et nunc* of the act of narration, in the course of his or her interactions and in the context of his or her usual social, discursive, and communicative behaviors (i.e., the *situated story*; McLean & Pasupathi, 2010). In so doing, the narratives are conceived as subjective productions in ever-changing, *lifelong processes* that provide the key to a dynamic understanding of the whole person and shed light on the subjective interpretations much better than questionnaires and other self-report instruments and measures (Alisat & Pratt, 2012).

The narrative approaches can investigate the way in which each person manages the inevitable changes that may be perceived as a threat to the sense of personal continuity (Pasupathi, Brubaker, & Mansour, 2007). Autobiographical processes can contribute to vocational and career identity formation especially during the turning points, when people have to explore, define, and reconsider their vocational projects.

Co-Authoring Vocational Identity: A Research

According to the previously described theoretical framework and on the basis of the evidence available that parental influence and support in Italy persist even at the beginning of university (Aleni Sestito & Sica, 2014), we explore how career identity development is co-constructed by parents and children to identify descriptive typologies that could be useful to interpret the vocational identity process of Italian youth (henceforth in this study, we will refer to these as *vocational identity co-authorship typologies*). In this regard, research has indicated that family relationships influence youngsters' career aspirations (Wahl & Blackhurst, 2000), that parents continue to play a major role in the psychosocial development of adolescents especially where their career development is concerned (Kracke, 1997; Palladino-Schultheiss & Blustein, 1994; Young, 1994), and that young adults are more likely to freely explore career options when their parents grant them autonomy, gradual independence, and support and waive the obligation of intergenerational professional choices (Crockett & Bingham, 2000; Tziner, Loberman, Dekel, & Sharoni, 2012). Many research studies in this field were interviewed-based in the attempt to explore the parental behaviors that young people perceive to be influential in their career development (Phillips, Blustein, Jobin-Davis, & White, 2002; Schultheiss, Kress, Manzi, & Glasscock, 2001). For these reasons the aim of this present study is to focus on perceived parental influence in the career development of young people in the Italian context, through the narrative of students attending the last year of high school and final year of university. Indeed, we used a narrative approach to career identity development (Meijer & Lengelle, 2012) that seems the most helpful to understand how young people make sense of parental influence in their career development by incorporating it as a part of their larger life story (Chope, 2005; Young, Friesen, & Borycki, 1994).

Method

The participants consisted of 20 Italian university students aged 17 to 26 (M = 20.65 years, SD = 2.28): 10 students (5 males and 5 females) attending the last year of high school and 10 (5 males and 5 females) attending the final year of university courses. All the participants lived on a permanent basis with their parents at the time of this research, and none was an only child. They also came from intact families (i.e., both parents still together). The participants were all students attending high schools and university courses in a large Italian city (Naples). The school students were recruited by trainee psychology university students involved in the ideation phase of the project whereas the final-year university student-participants responded to notices posted on the website of University of Naples "Federico II." The notice called for students to take part in a study on transition to adulthood in Italy, but no mention was made of vocational identity. Participation in the study was voluntary and anonymity was guaranteed, and the respondents did not receive payment for their participation. Of the total number of respondents, 90% took part in the research. All participants were assigned pseudonyms and are referred to by this pseudonym when quoting them.

We adopted the open interview, based on the Sankey and Young approach (see Sankey & Young, 1996) and adapted for the Italian context (Pizzorno, Benozzo, Fina, Sabato, & Scopesi, 2014). Stated briefly, the participants were invited to talk about their own lives and were encouraged to develop each individual life story, focusing especially on where they were in their career development, what was important to them, what their goals were, and the influence they perceived their parents (both mother and father) had on their career choices. The questions addressed to the participants were (a) Where are you in your life and how have you arrived there? Start from whatever point you like; (b) Were there any turning points in your story? On these occasions what choices did you make, what difficulties did you encounter, and how did you take things forward? (c) Now, do you remember any specific episodes in which your parents played a role in your career path? Could you describe this episode? (d) What are your projects for the future? and (e) What role can your parents play in these projects?

Two psychology researchers familiar with the topics of the study conducted the interviews in an informal and relaxed setting. The female psychologist conducted half of the interviews and a male research assistant conducted the other half. Both interviewers interviewed an equal number of male and female respondents. The interviewers' actions were limited to nondirective requests to clarify or expand on unclear remarks, to elicit explanations when these were not given, or, more frequently, to request stories exemplifying statements made by the interviewee (e.g., "Can you recall an episode that illustrates what you have just told me?"). The interviews were digitally recorded with the informed consent of participants and lasted on average 25 to 40 minutes. Verbatim transcripts of the interviews served as the raw data for textual analysis in this study.

Data Analysis

We analyzed the interviews using content analysis through the guided multiple reading approach (Schachter, 2004; Tappan, 1990). Initially, each interview was read several times, bearing in mind the different concepts regarding young people's perception of the parental role on their vocational identity and career construction. Passages in the text with content bearing on each concept were highlighted for future observation. At this point the content of the interviews was codified. The coding system was developed by the authors, consistent with the interview questions and in the light of literature described before to capture young Italians' perception of parental influence on their career identity and explore the three dimensions involved, namely, the vocational identity formation processes, personal career project, and parental influence perception (henceforth *identity co-authorship markers*). Table 6.1 shows the template of the coding system.

Table 6.1 Coding System Template (The Identity co-Authorship Markers)

Category	Thematic Category	Description
Vocational identity	Commitment	Refers to enduring choices that individuals have made with regard to various developmental domains and to the self-confidence they derive from these choices (Crocetti, Rubini, & Meeus, 2008)
	In-depth exploration	Represents the extent to which individuals think actively about the commitments they have enacted (Crocetti et al., 2008)
	Reconsideration of commitment	Refers to the comparison of present commitments with possible alternative commitments because the current ones are no longer satisfactory (Crocetti et al., 2008)
Perceived parental influence	Responsiveness	Refers to the degree to which adolescents experience a positive and supportive relationship with their parents (Barber & Harmon, 2002; Maccoby & Martin, 1983)
	Control	Behavioral: involves child behavior regulation by communicating clear expectations and monitoring Psychological: refers to parental behaviors that intrude upon children's thoughts and feelings and has been characterized as typical of parents who excessively use manipulative parenting techniques such as guilt-induction and love withdrawal (Barber, 1996)
	Autonomy support	Refers to parents who encourage their children to behave on the basis of self-endorsed interests (Ryan, Deci, Grolnick, & La Guardia, 2006)
	Conflict	Refers to temporary perturbations instrumental to the transformation of parent–adolescent relationships (Buchanan, Eccles, & Becker, 1992; McLean &Thorne, 2003; Paikoff & Brooks-Gunn, 1991; Silbereisen & Kracke, 1993; Steinberg, 1990)
Career project	School project	A descriptive category that refers to the presence and the typology of a career project based on formation and school/university studies
	Work project	A descriptive category that refers to the presence and the typology of a personal project based on work/job/career issues

The third step was to aggregate the different interviews across the sample in an attempt to create typologies of *co-authorship* (Aleni Sestito et al., 2013; Aleni Sestito & Sica, 2014), using the prevalence of identity co-authorship markers.

Results

The Identity Co-Authorship Marker: Descriptive Findings

In terms of parental influence perception, we found that both high school (75%) and university students (84%) perceive their parents as responsive, active, and co-participatory in their own life story and in their career path.

> I've grown up in a family that has always supported me, and I especially have a super relationship with my mother, . . . my father's a bit detached but I know he means well even though he doesn't always show it. (F, 21, university student)

However this supportive role of parents mainly (80%) concerns the material and economic provision, aimed at facilitating completion of university studies and at overcoming difficulties, uncertainties, and failures, mainly because of the value traditionally placed on education and on its function as a social ladder (Skorikov & Vondracek, 2011).

> Ideally, my plan would be for instance to start up a preschool center one day. . . . I wish . . . but it's not easy because you have to invest, and we know that investing these days is not that simple, but if this opportunity arose, my parents would certainly help me out, yes definitely. (F, 26, university student)

Nevertheless, parents are mostly perceived as incompetent and inadequate in providing more effective support with regard to school/career, unable to give guidelines because of their noninvolvement with the academic world.

> No, in actual fact they have no practical knowledge of university life . . . They're people with menial jobs and so they can't have any idea of the context. . . . When I speak to them, they say "You can do this . . . you can do that" based on whatever I tell them. (F, 26, university student)
>
> So, my parents, I have to be honest, at that difficult time for me . . . would always judge me compared to others who were on the ball. I reckon they had no idea of

how to help me at all . . . All they would say is "you're wasting your time." (F, 25, university student)

Sometimes (the remaining18%) young people attribute to their parents a personal project for social mobility that they, the parents, want to achieve through their children. They feel involved in the aspirations that their parents have not attained for themselves and, moreover, feel that they have to accept and fulfill a project that is not of their own making.

> Ever since I was a child, wanting to be a doctor was an idea that I felt would be appreciated in my family. My folks, not having seen anyone in the family with a degree, would feel extremely proud of me. So, in a way they've had an influence . . . but they did not pressurize me. . . . Right up to the last year at school I've always wanted to be a doctor because, coming from a family, let's say not well off, I saw this career as the only way to get on in life. (M, 24, university student)

Alongside these, only in a few narrative accounts (2%) are parents perceived as authoritarian. The parents, especially the father, are perceived as controlling and providing little support for autonomy. In these accounts the mother often plays a complementary role to the father's even though she is perceived as an intermediary between the different needs and demands of the father and son or daughter.

> Eh, my mother . . . my mother is the only one who tries to understand me, I often I vent to her, we have a good relationship, compared to my father . . . but unfortunately, she gets convinced and therefore supports my father's choices. . . . Sometimes she also tries to mediate, but . . . . (F, 17, school student)

In analyzing more specifically the parental influence perceptions of young people regarding their career choices, the majority of respondents, mainly the high school students, deny such parental influence explicitly. However, they do highlight their influence in the construction process of narrative episodes, in particular when they describe experiences of turning points, where they give meaning to the crucial moments of transition through the dynamic interaction of suggestions received from various sources of influence.

> I grew up in a family that actually has always supported me. . . I remember that the day of the exam, after that rejection, I felt defeated, I did not have the courage to go home and tell that to my parents. . . . I started to wonder if I was really capable and suitable for that faculty. . . . After this experience I went through a period in which

> I was completely blocked. . . . My father on the other hand hardly understand these things, for him if you do not pass an exam it means that you have not committed enough, he doesn't realize the difficulties that maybe we were. So I was afraid even of his judgment but in the end I realized that if I had to commit myself I had to do it for myself, and now, a bit at a time. (F, 21, university student)

The Career Identity Co-Authorship Typologies

The analysis of interviews in the third stage was conducted so as to create specific profiles. In doing so, we aggregated the youngsters on the basis of the prevalence of the different co-authorship markers. Despite this approach as regarding the issue of external validity of qualitative studies, Bryman (1988) states that "the issue should be couched in terms of the generalizability of cases to theoretical propositions rather than to populations" (p. 90). Furthermore, our research attempts to identify different descriptive typologies of co-authorship and not to assess their relative frequencies in the general Italian emerging adult population. We shall describe briefly the profiles identified. These were as follows:

1. *Balanced co-authorship* comprising the respective career projects of parents and their sons or daughters (co-authorship within a peer transaction)
2. *Soft co-authorship* with prevalence of the young person's career projects
3. *Unbalanced co-authorship with conflict*, tending toward greater parental role (parental assignment of their own career project within a conflicting relationship)
4. *Unbalanced co-authorship without conflict* tending toward greater parental role without conflict

The first profile (balanced co-authorship) seems to be characterized not only by the sharing of a career project that the son or daughter has already undertaken or planned but especially by the sharing of motivations based on the career project itself. This sharing takes the form of progressive integration between perceptions, evaluations, and aspirations of the son or daughter for himself or herself and of the parent for the son or daughter. Joint sharing in the study and career project is substantially the result of a balance that springs from mutual progressive transitions based on reciprocity. The recollected events of turning points highlight parental active and proactive participation in the vocational identity formation process, but at the same time, they also support the autonomy of their son or daughter. In this profile the motivations based on vocational choices are intrinsic to parents and their children and focus mostly on self-realization goals and the concept of work as a career (Skorikov & Vondracek, 2011).

> As for choosing the right university course for me, I always did well at school, and perhaps that's why my father left me free to decide. Even when I decided to get a part-time job, he said I could do what I wanted, though without neglecting the rest, my studies above all because university requires a lot of sacrifices, especially financial, to be able to aspire to better things. To tell the truth, I don't have a very demanding father. (F, 22, university)

The second profile, soft co-authorship, identifies the parent–son/daughter relationship in which vocational identity developmental processes and career construction processes evolve largely independent from each other. The son's or daughter's planning seems to be, in this sense, little influenced by parental intervention, aspirations, motivations, and advice. This does not mean that parents are not perceived as affectively supportive, active, or involved in their development but, rather, less involved where career construction is concerned. It seems that sons and daughters feel their parents are ill-equipped and lack any resources or clear ideas for their future and are therefore not able to give guidance and provide a reference point to plan their future. What characterizes this profile is the absence of a comparison on educational/career themes, on work, and on the possible implications of the complex Italian context.

> My parents have always kept out of my decisions, I mean I choose for myself, I do everything myself. . . . They always felt that the university is there to make you into a more responsible person. . . . So, when it comes to advice and other stuff . . . no, nothing . . . on the contrary, I'd go up to my mother and say "Hey, Mum, do you think it'd be better for me to do this exam or that one?" and she'd answer "You decide." . . . But my folks have always been important because, otherwise, I'd never have graduated . . . even in the future they'll be there to encourage me, or at least I hope so. (F, 22, university student)

The third profile, unbalanced co-authorship with conflict, is characterized by the divergence of points of views, motivations, and evaluations about career construction between parents and their son or daughter. As a result, the parental perspective does not coincide with that of the son or daughter but remains an unresolved conflict relationship. This profile was most frequent

(63%) among the high school students. The narrative accounts that characterize this profile underline an accentuated difficulty of young people to elaborate their own vocational identity, to identify their own project, and to make autonomous decisions that show personal motivations, wishes, and aspirations. Indeed, the vagueness of the son or daughter's personal project seems to be linked to parental imposition on their perspectives and aspirations, more than to a lack of personal aspirations. Parents are perceived as officious even if affectively or emotionally supportive. In this profile, the career projects are different and discordant, including the motivations based on those that are intrinsic for sons or daughters and extrinsic for parents. Likewise, the conceptualization of work is different, since it is viewed as a career and a calling for young people on the one hand and as a job and social ladder from the parents' point of view (Skorikov & Vondracek, 2011). In some narrative accounts, the youngsters reported that parents tried to impose on them their own career path, displaying it as an opportunity to be taken, but overestimating its positive aspects.

> Here I am halfway through the story of my life and . . . I feel it's been uphill for me so far. . . . I think my parents have only got in the way, they haven't done much in this journey of mine other than decide . . . prevail over my, I don't know the word for super-I, over my sense of duty, . . . so I am only the product of all the obligations they've imposed on me. . . . They know they have a great hold on me, they know how much their judgment weighs on me, how much I ponder about my way of thinking on the basis of theirs . . . even where university is concerned, an important choice in life to have to make, and I did so partly because I was forced to do what they considered was right for me, and not what I felt I wanted to do. What I mean is that if I were to re-enroll for a degree course today, I would not choose economics. (F, 22, university student)

The fourth profile presents a unbalanced co-authorship without conflict, tending toward a stronger parental role, although without conflict in the parent–son/daughter relationship. Here, the latter perceive their parents as directly and explicitly active and involved in their own vocational identity exploration and career construction while perceiving themselves less active and inadequate with respect to vocational identity achievement. Our respondents seem, in fact, particularly confused, uncertain, and very much inclined to accept the proposals of their parents.

> My parents leave me free to do what I want, but they take for granted that once I finish high school I will go to university. What I mean is that in our family going

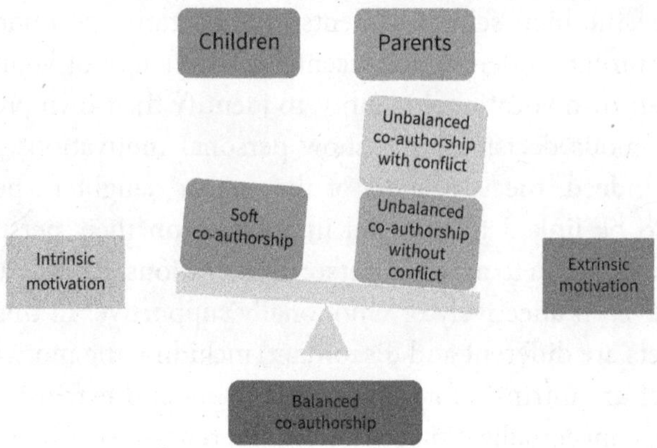

Figure 6.1 Career identity co-authorship: the unbalance between parental and child influence.

> to university after school is a must. It has never crossed their minds that I might start to work straightaway, but then nor have I ever thought of doing so. . . . In other words it's not been an obligation. . . . The problem is that I haven't really made a choice . . . so . . . my mother tells me, for example, not to do . . . for example, she says to do law. My mother sees me as a lawyer, but in the end it's not that they're forcing me, . . . they're advising me. (F, 17, high school student)

Summarizing, the profiles configure the presence of different modalities of co-authorship in which the parental influence could have a different leverage on their children's career identity formation. In some cases the parental influence is more significant in the definition of a career project, enough to unbalance the project toward the extrinsic motivation (desires and expectations by parents). In a few cases, where respondents have a major role in their career project definition, the intrinsic motivation has a significant role in unbalancing the co-authorship, and even attenuating it (Figure 6.1).

Conclusion

In this chapter we describe a specific cultural situation, namely the Italian context. However, the Italian socioeconomic, cultural, and relational features could be quite common to other Mediterranean countries where the instability of modern times has provoked changes in individual life trajectories. Specifically, vocational identity has changed for that section of young people who have a less stable reference of development, individualized life paths, and flexible contextual resources. In this chapter we identify two main effects related to career identity development in the Italian context: the delayed or interrupted vocational identity definition for youth (and particularly the exploration of future plans) and the active role of parents in the vocational identity definition of their children. In our opinion, addressing both these elements is crucial for planning intervention programs for supporting youth in the vocational/career project.

Italian students, as part of contemporary youth, must make difficult and demanding career choices at the end of high school, largely due to the weak and noninclusive labor market, characterized by continuous transformations. Indeed, students at the end of high school choose to find a job or go to university, where they must decide what field of study to undertake, without having had any practical experience or guidance in making choices during their school years. Guidance and counseling provided by schools are mostly informative and are not addressed mainly to a restricted group of students. They are expected, without due educational support, to make decisions about their educational and future career. First, they are required to decide whether or not to continue their studies and in what field. This happens despite results from recent research that demonstrate that a lot of high school students and students in their first year of university studies experience difficulties related to their career project construction (Sica at al., 2014; Sica & Aleni Sestito, 2016) and to their own vocational identity definition (Aleni Sestito et al., 2015), and they are mostly in moratorium and/or diffusion identity statuses (Sica et al., 2014) because they have not yet elaborated an identity definition (i.e., delay syndrome; Livi Bacci, 2008).

In addition, young Italians are subjected to a peculiar parental influence owing to prolonged cohabitation with parents (Aleni Sestito & Sica, 2014). Both these characteristics (delayed career identity and prolonged intimate relationships with parents) allowed us to hypothesize that career identity formation could be a co-authored process between Italian youth and their parents. Exploring this idea through a narrative empirical study involving 20 young people, we have identified four co-authorship typologies that reveal the effective presence of a career identity co-authorship, the prevalence of unbalanced co-authorship, and the prevalent parental role on the career identity project of their children.

In terms of narrative career identity development theory, our results confirm that the autobiographical process of integration of personal experiences and relationships with significant others is a key-element for the individual career project construction. Indeed, the narrative descriptions provided by students revealed to us the presence of a process of identification of future plans and project co-constructed by them and parents. They also revealed that this process became conscious for youth during the interview when they were encouraged to construct and reconstruct their story. According to this evidence, the need for supportive activities (in terms of narrative construction of vocational identity and career planning through activation and enhancement of self-reflection capacities) during the years of school and university is evident.

Limitations and Future Directions

The qualitative and somewhat exploratory nature of this study requires that the findings presented be carefully evaluated further. Longitudinal research is needed to support a more specific set of conclusions around career identity development in Italian youth. Further research works could study more in depth the different co-authorship typologies, the adaptive dimension of which will need to be carefully assessed, including consideration of the differences between mother and father. A cross-cultural study is also needed to highlight differences and commonalities in the Mediterranean context and between these and other cultures and societies characterized by a relatively more collectivist culture.

References

Aassve, A., Billari, F. C., Mazzuco, S., & Ongaro, F. (2002). Leaving home: A comparative analysis of ECHP data. *Journal of European Social Policy, 12*, 259–275.

Adams, G. R., & Marshall, S. K. (1996). A developmental social psychology identity. *Journal of Adolescence, 19*, 429–442.

Albertini, M., & Kohli, M. (2013). The generational contract in the family: an analysis of transfer regimes in Europe. *European Sociological Review, 29*, 828–840. doi:10.1093/esr/jcs061.

Aleni Sestito, L., & Sica, L. S. (2014). Identity formation of Italian emerging adults living with parents: A narrative study, *Journal of Adolescence, 37*, 1435–1447.

Aleni Sestito, L, Sica, L. S., & Nasti, M. (2013). La generazione dei giovani senza lavoro: Transizioni all'età adulta in condizioni di precarietà, disoccupazione e sottoccupazione. *Ricerche di psicologia, 3*, 411–444.

Aleni Sestito, L., Sica, L. S., & Ragozini, G. (2012). I primi anni dell'università: processi di definizione dell'identità tra confusione e consolidamento. *Giornale Italiano Di Psicologia Dello Sviluppo, 99*, 23–35

Aleni Sestito, L., Sica, L. S., Ragozini, G., Porfeli, E., Weisblat, G., & Di Palma, T. (2015). Vocational and overall identity: A person-centered approach in Italian university students, *Journal of Vocational Behavior, 91*, 157–169.

Alisat, S., & Pratt, M. W. (2012). Characteristics of young adults' personal religious narratives and their relation with the identity status model: A longitudinal, mixed methods study. *Identity, 12*, 29–52.

Arnett, J. J. (2000). Emerging adulthood: A theory of development from the late teens through the twenties. *American Psychologist, 55*, 469–480.

Ashkenas, R., Ulrich, D., Jick, T., & Kerr, S. (1995). *The boundaryless organization*. San Francisco, CA: Jossey-Bass.

Banfield, E. C. (1958). *The moral basis of a backward society*. New York, NY: Free Press.

Barber, B. K. (1996). Parental psychological control: revisiting a neglected construct. *Child Development, 67*, 3296–3319. doi:10.2307/1131780

Barber, B. K., & Harmon, E. L. (2002). Violating the self: parental psychological control of children and adolescents. In B. K. Barber (Ed.), *Intrusive parenting: How psychological control affects children and adolescents* (pp. 15–52). Washington, DC: American Psychological Association. doi:10.1037/10422-002

Berton, F., Richiardi, M., & Sacchi, S. (2009). *Flex-insecurity. Perché in Italia la flessibilità diventa precarietà*. Bologna, IL: Il Mulino.

Beyers, W., & Goossens, L. (2008). Dynamics of perceived parenting and identity formation in late adolescence. *Journal of Adolescence, 31*(2), 165–184. doi:10.1016/j.adolescence.2007.04.003

Bosma, H. A., & Kunnen, E. S. (2001). Determinants and mechanisms in ego identity development: A review and synthesis. *Developmental Review, 21*(1), 39–66. https://doi.org/10.1006/drev.2000.0514

Bronfenbrenner, U. (1979). *The ecology of human development: Experiments by nature and design*. Cambridge, MA: Harvard University Press

Bruner, J. S. (1993). The autobiographical process. In R. Folfenflik (Eds.), *The culture of autobiography: construction of self-representation* (pp. 38–56). Stanford, CA: Stanford University Press.

Bryant, B. K., Zvonkovic, A. M., & Reynolds, P. (2006). Parenting in relation to child and adolescent vocational development. *Journal of Vocational Behavior, 69*(1), 149–175.

Bryman, A. (1988). *Quality and quantity in social psychology*. New York, NY: Routledge.

Buchanan, C. M., Eccles, J. S., & Becker, J. B. (1992). Are adolescents the victims of raging hormones on moods and behavior at adolescence? *Psychological Bulletin, 111*, 62–107. doi:10.1037/0033-2909.111.1.62

Bynner, J., & Parsons, S. (2002) Social exclusion and the transition from school to work: The case of young people not in education, employment or training, *Journal of Vocational Behavior, 60*, 289–309.

Carrà, E., Lanz, M., & Tagliabue, S. (2014). Transition to adulthood in Italy: An intergenerational perspective. *Journal of Comparative Family Studies, 45*(2), 235–248.

Checchi, D., & Ballarino, G. (2006). *Scelte individuali e vincoli strutturali: Sistema scolastico e disuguaglianza sociale* [Individual choices and structural constraints: Educational system and social inequality]. Bologna, IL: il Mulino.

Cherlin, A., Scabini, E., & Rossi, G. (1997). Still in the nest: delayed home leaving in Europe and the United States. *Journal of Family Issues, 18*, 572–575. doi:10.1177/019251397018006001

Chope, R. C. (2005). Qualitatively assessing family influence in career decision making. *Journal of Career Assessment, 13* (4), 395–414.

Cortini, G., Tanucci, & Morin, E. (Eds.). (2011). Boundaryless careers and occupational well-being: An interdisciplinary approach. Houndmills, England: Palgrave MacMillan

Côté, J. E., & Levine, C. G. (2002). *Identity formation, agency, and culture: A social psychological synthesis*. Mahwah, NJ: Erlbaum.

Crocetti, E., Luyckx, K., Scrignaro, M., & Sica, L. S. (2011). Identity formation in Italian emerging adults: A cluster-analytic approach and associations with psychosocial functioning. *European Journal of Developmental Psychology*, *8*(5), 558–572.

Crocetti, E., Rabaglietti, E., & Sica, L. S. (2012). Personal identity in Italy. *New Directions for Child and Adolescent Development*, *138*, 87–102. doi:10.1002/cad.20023

Crocetti, E., Rubini, M., & Meeus, W. (2008). Capturing the dynamics of identity formation in various ethnic groups: Development and validation of a three-dimensional model. *Journal of Adolescence*, *31*, 207–222. doi:10.1016/j.adolescence.2007.09.002

Crocetti, E., Scrignaro, M., Sica, L. S., & Magrin, M. E. (2012). Correlates of identity configurations: Three studies with adolescent and emerging adult cohorts. *Journal of Youth and Adolescence*, *41*, 732–748. doi:10.1007/s10964-011-9702-2

Crockett, L. J., & Bingham, C. R. (2000). Anticipating adulthood: Expected timing of work and family transitions among rural youth. *Journal of Research on Adolescence*, *10*, 109–119.

Danielsen, L. M., Loren, A. E., & Kroger, J. (2000). The impact of social context on the identity formation process of Norwegian late adolescents. *Youth & Society*, *31*, 332–362.

Erikson, E. H. (1980). *Identity and the life cycle: A reissue*. New York, NY: Norton.

European Union. (2012). EU youth report. Retrieved from http://ec.europa.eu/youth/library/reports/eu-youth-report-2012

Eurostat. (2016). Youth: overview. Retrieved from http://ec.europa.eu/eurostat/web/youth

Ferrera, M. (1996). The "Southern model" of welfare in social Europe. *Journal of European Social Policy*, *6*(1), 17–37.

Ferrera, M. (1997). The uncertain future of the Italian welfare state. *West European Politics*, *20*(1), 231–249.

Flum, H., & Blustein, D. L. (2006). Reinvigorating the study of vocational exploration: A framework for research. *Journal of Vocational Behavior*, *56*, 380–404.

Ford, D. H., & Lerner, R. M. (1992). *Developmental systems theory: An integrative approach*. Thousand Oaks, CA: SAGE.

Goossens, L. (2001). Global versus domain-specific statuses in identity research: A comparison of two self-report measures. *Journal of Adolescence*, *24*(6), 681–699.

Habermas, T., & Bluck, S. (2000). Getting a life: the emergence of the life story in adolescence. *Psychological Bulletin*, *126*(5), 748.

Holland, J. L., Daiger, D. C., & Power, P. G. (1980). *My vocational situation: Description of an experimental diagnostic form for the selection of vocational assistance*. Palo Alto, CA: Consulting Psychologists Press.

Hirschi, A. (2011). Career choice readiness in adolescence: Developmental trajectories and individual differences. *Journal of Vocational Behavior*, *79*, 340–348.

Havighurst, R. J. (1953). *Human development and education*. White Plains, NY: Longmans.

Havighurst, R. J. (1972). *Development tasks and education*. New York, NY: McKay.

ISTAT. (2014). Il mercato del lavoro negli anni della crisi: dinamiche e divari. *Rapporto annuale istat*, *3*, 83–138.

Iezzi, M., & Mastrobuoni, T. (2010). *Gioventù sprecata*. Bari, Italy: Editori Laterza.

Ingoglia, S., & Allen, J. P. (Eds.). (2010). *Autonomia e connessione nella relazione genitori-adolescenti: Una procedura d'osservazione delle interazioni familiari*. Milano, Italy: Unicopli.

Keller, B. K., & Whiston, S. C. (2008). The role of parental influences on young adolescents' career development. *Journal of Career Assessment*, *16*(2), 198–217.

Kerpelman, J. L., Pittman, J. F., & Lamke, L. K. (1997). Toward a microprocess perspective on adolescent identity development: An identity control theory approach. *Journal of Adolescent Research*, *12*, 325–346.

Koepke, S., & Denissen, J. J. A. (2012). Dynamics of identity development and separation-individuation in parent–child relationships during adolescence and emerging adulthood: A conceptual integration. *Developmental Review*, *32*, 68–88.

Kracke, B. (1997). Parental behaviours and adolescents' career exploration. *Career Development Quarterly, 45*, 341–350.

Kroger, J. (2000). *Identity development: Adolescence through adulthood.* Thousand Oaks, CA: Sage.

Kroger, J. (2004). *Identity in adolescence. The balance between self and other.* London, England: Routledge.

Kroger, J. (2007). *Identity development: Adolescence through adulthood* (2nd ed.). Thousnad Oaks, CA: Sage.

Kroger, J., & Haslett, S. J. (1988). Separation–individuation and ego identity status in late adolescence: a two-year longitudinal study. *Journal of Youth and Adolescence, 17*, 59–79.

Kuczynski, L. (2003). Beyond bidirectionality: bilateral conceptual frameworks for understanding dynamics in parent–child relations. In L. Kuczynski (Ed.), *Handbook of dynamics in parent–child relations* (pp. 3–24). Thousand Oaks, CA: Sage.

Kunnen, E., & Bosma, H. (2000). Development of meaning making: A dynamic systems approach. *New Ideas in Psychology, 18*(1), 57–82. doi:10.1016/S0732-118X(99)00037-9

Lanz, M., & Tagliabue, S. (2007). Do I really need someone in order to become an adult? Romantic relationships during emerging adulthood in Italy. *Journal of Adolescent Research, 22*(5), 531–549.

Larson, R. W. (2011). Positive development in a disorderly world. *Journal of Research on Adolescence, 21*(2), 317–334.

Leccardi, C. (2006). Facing uncertainty. Temprality and biographies in the new century. In C. Leccardi & E. Ruspini (Eds.), *A new youth? Young people, generations and family life.* Hampshire, England: Ashgate.

Leon, M., & Migliavacca, M. (2013). Italy and Spain: Still the case of familistic welfare models? *Population Review, 52*(1), 25–42.

Livi Bacci, M. (2008). *Avanti giovani, alla riscossa!*. Bologna, Italy: il Mulino.

Lollis, S. (2003). Conceptualizing the influence of the past and future in present parent–child relationships. In L. Kuczynski (Ed.), *Handbook of dynamics in parent–child relations* (pp. 67–87). Thousand Oaks, CA: Sage.

Luyckx, K., Soenens, B., Vansteenkiste, M., Goossens, L., & Berzonsky, M. D. (2007). Parental psychological control and dimensions of identity formation in emerging adulthood. *Journal of Family Psychology, 21*(3), 546–550. doi:10.1037/0893-3200.21.3.546

Maccoby, E., & Martin, J. (1983). Socialization in the context of the family: parent-child interaction. In E M. Hetherington (Vol. Ed.) & P. H. Mussen, (Series Ed.), *Handbook of child psychology: Vol. 4, Socialization, personality, and social development* (4th ed., pp. 414–430). New York, NY: Wiley.

McAdams, D. P. (1988). Biography, narrative, and lives. *Journal of Personality, 56*, 1–18. doi:10.1111/j.1467-6494.1988.tb00460.x

McAdams, D. P. (1993). *The stories we live by*. New York, NY: Harper Collins.

McAdams, D. P. (2001). The psychology of life stories. *Review of General Psychology, 5*, 100–122. doi:10.1037/1089-2680.5.2.100

McAdams, D. P. (2011). Narrative identity. In *Handbook of identity theory and research* (pp. 99–115). New York, NY: Springer.

McCormick, C. M., Kuo, S. I.-C., & Masten, A. S. (2011). Developmental tasks across the lifespan. In K. L. Fingerman, C. A. Berg, J. Smith, & T. C. Antonucci (Eds.), *Handbook of lifespan development* (pp. 117–140). New York, NY: Springer.

McLean, K. C., & Breen, A. V. (2009). Processes and content of narrative identity development in adolescence: gender and well-being. *Developmental Psychology, 45*(3), 702–710.

McLean, K. C., Breen, A. V., & Fournier, M. A. (2010). Constructing the self in early, middle, and late adolescent boys: Narrative identity, individuation, and well-being. *Journal of Research on Adolescence, 20*(1), 166–187.

McLean, K. C., & Pasupathi, M. D. (2010). *Narrative development in adolescence.* New York, NY: Springer.

McLean, K. C., & Thorne, A. (2003). Late adolescents' self-defining memories about relationships. *Developmental Psychology, 39*(4), 635–645. doi:10.1037/0012-1649.39.4.635

Meeus, W. (1993). Occupational identity development, school performance, and social support in adolescence: Findings of a Dutch study. *Adolescence, 28*(112), 809–818.

Mínguez, A. M. (2010). Family and gender roles in Spain from a comparative perspective. *European Societies, 12*(1), 85–111.

Moreno, L., & Marí-Klose, P. (2013). Youth, family change and welfare arrangements: Is the South still so different? *European Societies, 15*(4), 493–513.

Nauta, N. M., & Kahn, J. H. (2007). Identity status, consistency and differentiation of interest and career decision self-efficacy. *Journal of Career Assessment, 15*(1), 55–65.

Paikoff, R. L., & Brooks-Gunn, J. (1991). Do parent–child relationships change during puberty? *Psychological Bulletin, 110*, 47–66.

Palladino-Schultheiss, D., & Blustein, D. (1994). Contributions of family relationship factors to the identity formation process. *Journal of Counseling and Development, 73*, 159–166.

Pasupathi, M., & Wainryb, C. (2010). On telling the whole story: facts and interpretations in autobiographical memory narratives from childhood through mid-adolescence. *Developmental Psychology, 46*(3), 735–745.

Pharr, S. J., & Putnam, R. D. (Eds.). (2000). *Disaffected democracies: What is troubling the what's troubling the trilateral countries?* Princeton, NJ: Princeton University Press.

Phillips, S. D., Blustein, D. L., Jobin-Davis, K., & White, S. F. (2002). Preparation for the school-to-work transition: The views of high school students. *Journal of Vocational Behavior, 61*(2), 202–216.

Pizzorno, M. C., Benozzo, A., Fina, A., Sabato, S., & Scopesi, M. (2014). Parent–child career construction: A narrative study from a gender perspective. *Journal of Vocational Behavior, 84*(3), 420–430.

Porfeli, E. J., Lee, B., Vondracek, F., & Weigold, I. K. (2011). A multidimensional measure of vocational identity status. *Journal of Adolescence, 34*, 853–871

Roisman, G. I., Masten, A. S., Coastworth, J. D., & Tellegan, A. (2004). Salient and emerging developmental tasks in the transition to adulthood. *Child Development, 75*(1), 123–133. doi:10.1111/j.1467-8624.2004.00658.x

Ryan, R. M., Deci, E. L., Grolnick, W. S., & La Guardia, J. G. (2006). The significance of autonomy and autonomy support in psychological development and psychopathology In D. Cicchetti & D. J. Cohen (Eds), *Developmental psychopathology: Theory and method* (Vol. 1, 2nd ed.). Hoboken, NJ: Wiley.

Sankey, A. M., & Young, R. A. (1996). Ego identity status and narrative structure in retrospective accounts of parental career influence. *Journal of Adolescence, 19*, 141–153.

Saraceno, C. (2003). *Family changes and social policies in Italy*. Bologna, Italy: il Mulino.

Savickas, M. L. (1985). Identity in vocational development. *Journal of Vocational Behavior, 27*(3), 329–337.

Scabini, P., & Donati, E. (1988). *La famiglia lunga del giovane adulto: verso nuovi compiti evolutivi* (Studi interdisciplinari sulla famiglia 7). Milano, Italy: Vita e Pensiero.

Scabini, E., & Manzi, C. (2011). Family processes and identity. In S. J. Schwartz, K. Luyckx, & V. L. Vignoles (Eds.), *Handbook of identity theory and research* (pp. 565–584). New York, NY: Springer Science.

Scabini, E., Marta, E., & Lanz, M. (2006). *The transition to adulthood and family relationship: An intergenerational Perspective.* London, England: Psychology Press.

Schachter, E. P. (2004). Identity configurations: a new perspective on identity formation in contemporary society. *Journal of Personality, 72*(1), 167–200. doi:10.1111/j.0022-3506.2004.00260.x

Schachter, E. P., & Ventura, J. J. (2008). Identity agents: parents as active and reflective participants in their children's identity formation. *Journal of Research on Adolescence, 18*, 449–476. doi:10.1111/j.1532-7795.2008.00567.x

Schultheiss, D. E. P., Kress, H. M., Manzi, A. J., & Glasscock, M. J. (2001). Relational influences in career development: A qualitative inquiry. *Counselling Psychologist, 29*, 214–239.

Sica, L. S., & Aleni Sestito, L. (2016). The "futuring" dilemma in narrative identity. *Psychology Research, 6*(6), 361–370. doi:10.17265/2159-5542/2016.06.004

Sica, L. S., Aleni Sestito, L., & Ragozini G. (2014). Coping for identity in the first years of university: Identity diffusion, adjustment, and identity distress. *Journal of Adult Development, 21*, 159–172. doi:10.1007/s10804-014-9188-8

Sica, L.S., Crocetti, E., Aleni Sestito, L., Ragozini, G., & Serafini, T. (2016). Future-oriented or present-focused? The role of social support and identity styles on "futuring" in Italian late adolescents and emerging adults. *Journal of Youth Studies, 19*(2), 183–203, doi:10.1080/13676261.2015.1059925

Silbereisen, R. K., & Kracke, B. (1993) Variation in maturational timing and adjustment in adolescence. In S. Jackson & H. Rodriguez-Tomé (Eds.), *Adolescence and its social worlds* (pp. 67–94). Hillsdale, NJ: Erlbaum.

Skorikov, V. B., & Patton, W. (2007). *Career development in childhood and adolescence*. Rotterdam, The Netherlands: Sense.

Skorikov, V. B., & Vondracek, F. W. (1998). Vocational identity development: Its relationship to other identity domains and to overall identity development. *Journal of Career Assessment, 6*, 13–35.

Skorikov, V. B., & Vondrecek, F. W. (2007). Vocational Identity. In V. B. Skorikow & W. Patton (Eds.), *Career development in childhood and adolescence* (pp. 143–168). Rotterdam, The Netherlands: Sense.

Skorikov, V. B., & Vondracek, F. W. (2011). Occupational identity. In S. J. Schwartz, K. Luyckx, & V. L. Vignoles (Eds.), *Handbook of identity theory and research* (pp. 693–714). New York, NY: Springer.

Steinberg, L. (1990). Autonomy, conflict, and harmony in the family relationship. In S. Feldman, & G. Elliot (Eds.), *At the threshold: The developing adolescent* (pp. 255–276). Cambridge, MA: Harvard University Press.

Tagliabue, S., Lanz, M., & Beyers, W. (2014). The transition to adulthood around the Mediterranean: contributions of the special issue. *Journal of Adolescence*, 37(8), 1405–1408.

Tappan, M. (1990). Hermeneutics and moral development: interpreting narrative representations of moral experience. *Developmental Review, 10*, 239–265. doi:10.1016/0273-2297(90)90012-S

Thelen, E., & Smith, L. B. (1994). *A dynamic systems approach to the development of cognition and action*. Cambridge, England: MIT Press.

Tziner, A., Loberman, G., Dekel, Z., & Sharoni, G. (2012). The influence of the parent offspring relationship on young people's career preferences. *Revista de Psicologia del Trabajo y de las Organizaciones, 28*(2), 99–105.

Wahl, K. H., & Blackhurst, A. (2000). Factors affecting the occupational and educational aspirations of children and adolescents. *Professional School Counselling, 3*, 367–374.

Xiao, J.J., Newman, B. M., & Chu, B. (2018). Career preparation of high school students: A multi-country study. *Youth & Society, 50*(6), 818–840. doi:10.1177/0044118X16638690

Young, R. (1994). Helping adolescents with career development: The active role of parents. *The Career Development Quarterly, 42*, 195–203.

Young, R. A., Friesen, J. D., & Borycki, B. (1994). Narrative structure and parental influence in career development. *Journal of Adolescence, 17*, 173–191.

7

Youth Work Transitions in the South of Europe

Pathways, Priorities, and Expectations

Filomena Parada

Introduction

This chapter focuses on the work transitions of southern European youth. Southern European or Mediterranean countries (Greece, Italy, Portugal, and Spain) were severely hit by the 2008 economic crisis, or Great Recession as it is also known. The crisis strongly impacted labor market participation and aggravated both income inequalities and the risk of poverty, exposing enduring systemic weaknesses and providing the worst image of the performance of the Mediterranean model of welfare capitalism (Gutiérrez, 2014). While all age, gender, education, and wage groups were affected in these countries, the crisis at the heart of the Great Recession had a particularly significant impact on youth. Young people facing labor market integration, that is, between ages 25 and 29, were among the groups most intensely affected by the generalized decline in employment levels, as well as by precarious employment and poverty (European Commission, 2012, 2015). Not only do youth unemployment rates in the South remain among the highest in Europe, but these countries also perform poorly in at least two of the three dimensions of job quality, that is, earnings quality or the extent to which workers' job earnings contribute to their well-being, labor market security, and quality of the working environment (OECD, 2016). Young people are also one of the groups most affected by poor job quality and are more at risk of poverty despite having a job (OECD, 2016; International Labour Organization [ILO], 2016).

To address the distinctive features of southern European youth transitions to work, we conducted an in-depth review of the literature examining the topic. We start by outlining the cultural and institutional features of the Mediterranean context that influence the timing and patterns of youth transitions in these countries. Next, we address the general patterns and the

Filomena Parada, *Youth Work Transitions in the South of Europe* In: *Young Adult Development at the School-to-Work Transition.* E. Anne Marshall and Jennifer E. Symonds, Oxford University Press (2021). © Oxford University Press.
DOI: 10.1093/oso/9780190941512.003.0007.

timings of work transitions for emerging adults in these countries. Finally, we discuss how prolonged and less predictable transitions to work affect other relevant dimensions of young people's transitions to adulthood. We conclude that the complexity of the situation underlying youth's transitions to work and to adulthood sheds light on the socially situated nature of agency, that is, the impact changing (adverse) social contexts have on how young people approach and live their lives.

Southern European Youth Transitions: The Influence of Culture and Context

The diverse patterns and timing of youth transitions to work or to adulthood across Europe are well established in the literature, and the influence of context and culture on these transitions has often been highlighted by ongoing debates on the topic (Arnett, Kloep, Hendry, & Tanner, 2011; Bynner, 2005; Côté & Bynner, 2008; Hendry & Kloep, 2010; Kloep & Hendry, 2014; Young et al., 2011). Youth transition behavior and socially structured opportunities establish a complex and frequently constraining interplay. Such interplay is crucial for how young people negotiate, perceive, and experience transitions, as well as address the tasks and their respective components associated with these transitions (Shanahan, 2000). Consequently, emerging adults' responses to opportunities and constraints cannot be understood as independent from the *transition regime*, that is, the "complex system of socioeconomic structures, institutional arrangements and cultural patterns" (Walther, 2006, p. 124) in which the transition occurs. Transition regimes are embedded in a specific constellation of relationships between the individual, the family, and the state, determining not only how social resources are distributed but also what individuals and society can legitimately aspire to or demand from one another (Biggart et al., 2007).

The timing, duration, and order of the multiple micro and macro transitions occurring during the transition to adult life or to the labor market vary considerably depending on individuals' characteristics, as well as on a person's country of origin and culture (Scabini, Marta, & Lanz, 2006). Southern European countries share some social, economic, political, historic, and cultural characteristics distinguishing them as a specific cluster or subregion known as the subprotective transition regime (Biggart et al., 2007; Buchman & Kriesi, 2011; Walther, 2006). To understand the distinctive features of the Mediterranean or subprotective model of transition, it is important to address three key areas of institutional settings that influence pathways to work and adulthood: the welfare regime, the education system and its linkages to the labor market, and labor market regulation (Buchman & Kriesi, 2011).

The Mediterranean Welfare Family System

What distinguishes Mediterranean countries *welfare regime* is its underdevelopment, linked to overall low levels of welfare provision by the state and a strong reliance on family for providing basic economic security and care for its members (Buchman & Kriesi, 2011). The regime essentially operates as a *welfare family* system where it is up to the family to provide for youth and compensate for minimal or nonexistent state provisions (Biggart et al., 2007). This precarious equilibrium underlies to a system of mutual protection where familial support is morally justified by a culture characterized by strong family ties and conservative values and reinforced by a deeply rooted, ancient religious heritage that emphasizes reciprocity and solidarity among members of a family (Cuzzocrea, 2011; Saraiva & Matos, 2016). Youth reliance on family resources, both symbolic and material, results in longer and often complete financial dependency on the family, as well as prolonged cohabitation with parents. It makes the transition to adulthood "very much a family project" (Biggart et al., 2007, p. 15).

In the South of Europe, prolonged cohabitation with parents is the cultural norm, and the transition to work and adulthood tends to occur while living with one's family of origin (Scabini et al., 2006). As youth progress to adulthood, such living arrangements create new demands on intergenerational relationships, and emerging adults and their parents are asked to engage in a negotiation that requires both parties to reconcile different lifestyles, create alternative roles and rules, and devise autonomy spaces for the young person (Pappámikail, 2004). At the same time, staying in the parental household until the late 20s or 30s appears a "voluntary and pragmatic coping behavior" perceived as advantageous by both parents and young adult children (Saraiva & Matos, 2016, p. 120). Labor market instability and adverse employment conditions make Mediterranean youth who live independently from their parents vulnerable to poverty (Abrantes, 2010). In fact, there is evidence that family's economic support is not temporally bound and that it may be extended beyond the period of intergenerational cohabitation (Cuzzocrea, 2011). By postponing the transition to independent housing, young people find themselves exempt from financial responsibilities that could compromise living standards. It also allows them to save money and invest in aspirations and life plans regarding leisure, education, work, or family formation that are often shared with parents and might not otherwise be possible (Biggart et al., 2007; Saraiva & Matos, 2016).

Traditionally, young people left school early and with very low qualifications (Müller, 2005). However, in the last two to three decades, this pattern changed, and there has been a clear growth in the number of individuals pursuing upper secondary and tertiary education as a means of overcoming labor market entry difficulties and accessing more stable, well-paid, and skilled jobs (Abrantes, 2010). Nowadays, young people in the South of Europe finish initial education at a relatively late mean age (Buchman & Kriesi, 2011). It is only through relying on family that young people guarantee the economic support and safety required for the longer education pathways that increase the odds of an effective labor market integration and financial independence (Biggart et al., 2007). Obtaining a stable position in the labor market is the main reason for moving out of the parental home, and once such position is secured, other transitions rapidly follow (Buchman & Kriesi, 2011).

This sequencing of events points to rather traditional role expectations, where the successful achievement of a transition in a specific area appears as a precondition for progress in other life domains (Saraiva & Matos, 2016). Delays in finishing one's studies lead to a postponement in access to employment and to financial independence, which contributes to deferments in settling down into independent housing or a committed romantic relationship, as well as to the subsequent decision of becoming a parent (Crocetti &Tagliabue, 2016). With the mean age for leaving school rising, normative subsequent steps also take place later in life. Crocetti and Tagliabue (2016) refer to the work of the Italian demographer Livi Bacci (2008) who labeled this postponement of typical adult roles and responsibilities as a *delay syndrome*. Combined with the previously discussed institutional, cultural, and economic features, these circumstances shed light on Mediterranean youth extended trajectory to adult roles, where major normative transitions are protracted and occur later in life (Crocetti & Tagliabue, 2016).

Transition Timings and Pathways to Work of Youth in the South of Europe

The educational system and its relations to the labor market and how the latter is regulated are the other two key areas influencing youth transitions to work and adulthood. Similarly to the welfare regime, countries in the South exhibit distinctive patterns in these two areas that distinguish them from the remaining Europe (e.g., Brzinsky-Fay, 2011; Gangl, 2001; Müller, 2005; Walther,

2006; Wolbers, 2007). As entrants to a segmented labor market, that is a labor market organized into subgroups with little to no crossover capability, young people from the Mediterranean often remain outsiders to a system with lower employment rates, precarious employment conditions, and higher unemployment rates than those of the overall population (European Commission, 2014). Therefore, these emerging adults find themselves in an extremely vulnerable position especially when trying to access or maintain a (stable) position in the labor market (e.g., Brzinsky-Fay, 2011; Gangl, 2001; Müller, 2005; Walther, 2006; Wolbers, 2007, 2014). The weakening of policies and programs supporting labor market integration brought about by the Great Recession only accentuated young people's vulnerability (Serracant, 2015). As de Lange and colleagues (2014) observed, southern European youth school-to-work transitions can be problematic. They combine "historical disadvantages of *time* and *place*" (Nico, 2011, p. 4; emphasis in original). While entering the labor market, young people from the Mediterranean not only start from the relatively disadvantageous position typical of those that are newcomers to the system but also face a time of economic recession, austerity, and increased unemployment, underemployment, and precarious employment.

Labor markets in the Mediterranean are characterized by (a) the influence of a conservative family model, where males are the main household breadwinners; (b) a reduced and secondary participation of youth of both genders and often also of adult females in employment; and (c) a dualism between insiders and outsiders to the labor market that is usually linked to strict employment protection legislation and low levels of overall unemployment (Gutiérrez, 2014). Consequently, a "smooth labour market integration is crucial for young people" (Wolbers, 2014, p. 167). As Wolbers (2014) noted, initial positions in the labor market determine to a large extent individuals' working careers, influencing the risks of unemployment and inactivity both during the transition to employment and in the long run. Qualifications play a decisive role in this process (Brzinsky-Fay, 2011; Gangl, 2001; Müller, 2005; Wolbers, 2007, 2014). Traditionally, southern European countries "lack ready-to-use and reliably signalled vocational qualifications" (Müller, 2005, p. 474) that send employers strong, unequivocal signals about job seekers' skills. Combined with high levels of employment protection legislation, this circumstance helps induce a rather static labor market that favors Mediterranean youth high levels of unemployment and low levels of labor market participation (Gangl, 2001; Wolbers, 2007). School-leavers with higher qualification levels are among the most affected by these circumstances.

Two distinct patterns of labor market entry for youth in the South of Europe result from this complex mix of structural features. In Italy, Greece, and

Portugal, the onset of young people's employment careers is characterized by (a) low levels of mobility once initial employment has been secured, regardless of how soon after leaving school such employment is obtained; (b) low qualification effects on labor market exclusion, especially on unemployment whose inherent levels are almost reached while youth transition to the labor market; and (c) high qualification effects on status attainment, in as much as higher qualifications typically help individuals avoid low-skilled positions (Gangl, 2001). Spain, on the other hand, has the peculiarity of exhibiting a rather flexible, deregulated youth labor market that combines low experience effects on unemployment and on variations in occupational attainment with a reduced bias toward low-skilled jobs in external recruitment (Gangl, 2001). However, like for Italy, Greece, and Portugal, the risk of unemployment at the outset of employment careers is very high in Spain. High unemployment rates are an indication of the "genuine problems in locating job offers" (Gangl, 2001, p. 491) experienced by youth in these four countries.

Indicators of Mediterranean Youth Labor Market Integration

Despite reforms implemented between the mid-1990s and the mid-2000s, the economic and financial crisis of 2008 had a significant impact not only on southern European countries' employment rates, which place them "well below the average level of the eurozone" (Gutiérrez, 2014, p. 375), but also on the composition of the labor force. According to Gutiérrez (2014), in 2012, in Greece, Italy, and Spain, approximately one in three emerging adults aged 20 to 24 who had just finished compulsory education had a job. In Portugal, this number rose to one in two. Although high unemployment levels of unqualified youth pre-existed the Great Recession, the recession aggravated the problem and not even recent improvements in these countries' labor market performance reversed the situation. In 2015, Portugal had 14% of early education and training leavers; in Italy, the number rose to 15%; and in Spain, it reached 20% (Eurostat, 2016b). Only in Greece (7.9%) was this percentage lower than the EU-28 rate of 11% of early education and training leavers, that is, the percentage of the population aged 18 to 24 with at most lower secondary education and who are not in further education or training during the four weeks that preceded the inquiry. Most of these youth are not employed, and among these, the majority would like to work. Greece and Italy also recorded the highest EU-28 rates of young people aged 20 to 34 that in 2015 were not in education, employment, or training (NEET): 32.4% and 31.6%, respectively (Eurostat, 2016d). The percentage of Spanish young people in these circumstances (24.2%) is also higher than the 18.6% average identified for the EU-28.

According to Eurostat (2015), Greece is among the countries with the highest increase in NEET rates during the years of the Great Recession: 9% between 2008 and 2013. The typical profile of NEETs in Italy and Greece is one of inactive individuals with little to no work experience who, in many cases, completed tertiary education and are discouraged from searching employment (Eurofound, 2012). Another specificity concerns the high share of Greek and Italian young women with the NEET status, which is much higher than the EU average. Contrarily to what happens in Italy and Greece, NEETs in Portugal and Spain are mostly unemployed and have work experience. However, like their Italian and Greek counterparts, a share higher than the European average are discouraged workers and have obtained tertiary education degrees. Regardless, like for the remaining Europe, people under the age of 35 who left education less than three years ago and have higher levels of education show a higher likelihood of being employed than those in the same age group who left education at least three years ago (European Commission, 2014). Young people in the 20 to 34 age group that left education or training in the last three years are the ones recording the lowest employment rates, irrespective of their level of education (Eurostat, 2016a). According to Eurostat (2016a), this is a likely reflection of the difficulties experienced by recent graduates in accessing their first job. School-leavers in Italy, Greece, and especially Spain find it substantially harder than their counterparts from other parts of Europe to access a first significant job, that is, a nonmarginal job of at least about 20 hours a week lasting at least six months (Wolbers, 2007).

Except for Portugal (six months), the average period for finding a first significant job after leaving formal education in the South is among the highest in Europe (Eurostat, 2015). Also in Portugal, and contrarily to what happens in most of Europe, there are almost no differences in the length of the period young people of all education levels take to transition from education to employment. In 2009, the EU-27 average for this transition is 6.5 months. In Spain, it ascends to 8 months, and in Italy and Greece, to 10 and 13 months, respectively (Eurostat, 2015). Between 2008 and mid-2014, Spain (−3.4 million), Italy (−1.2 million), and Greece (−1 million) were the countries in Europe where the highest amount of jobs was destroyed (European Commission, 2014). Spain was also the country where access to the labor market by young people aged 15 to 24 decreased the most (Eurostat, 2015). Between 2008 and

2013, the country lost 19% of the existing jobs for this group of the population. According to Eurostat (2015), in Greece, the same happened with the 25 to 29 age group, which lost 24% of the existing jobs. During this period, the loss in the overall employment rate of youth in the EU-28 is 5% (Eurostat, 2015). Hence, in 2013, almost one in two young people in Greece and Spain were exclusively in education, and less than 5% in Italy and Greece combined education and employment (Eurostat, 2015). According to Eurostat (2015), in 2012, Spain and Greece have a higher percentage than the EU-28 average of youth aged 20 to 24 enrolled in education (44.6%, 41.6%, and 41.1%, respectively). However, for the 25 to 29 age group, only in Greece the rate of young people enrolled in education is higher than that of the EU-28. In Portugal and Italy, for both age groups, these numbers are always lower than the EU-28 average.

In 2015, all southern European countries but Greece had a lower percentage than the EU-28 average of young people aged 20 to 24 completing at least upper secondary education (Eurostat, 2016c). The percentage of young women completing at least upper secondary education is always higher than the percentage of young men in similar circumstances. Simultaneously, in 2013, in Greece (49%) and Italy (53%), approximately one in two young people aged 25 to 29 were in employment (Eurostat, 2015). Together with Spain (58%), these two countries have the lowest employment rates for this age group, which is 71% in the EU-28. Since 2013, the youth unemployment rates in the EU-28 and per country started to exhibit a declining trend that was projected to extend to 2018; that was accompanied by a slight increase in employment rates and in the proportion of young people in education and training (European Commission, 2016a; ILO, 2016). Nonetheless, in 2014, in the four Mediterranean countries, the percentage of young people out of employment not only doubled the one of 2008 but also exceeded 30% (ILO, 2015). According to ILO (2015), in 2014, the youth unemployment rate was 53.2% in Spain, 52.4% in Greece, 42.7% in Italy, and 34.8% in Portugal. Long-term youth unemployment rates (i.e., the share of young people who are unemployed for a period of at least 12 months relative to the total number of persons active in the labor market)—although exhibiting a declining trend between 2013 and 2015—remained very high in the South of Europe (European Commission, 2016a). In 2013, youth long-term unemployment rates in Greece (30%), Spain (22%) and Italy (21%) more than doubled the EU-28 average. In Portugal this number was 14%, which was still rather high in comparison to the EU-28 rate of 8%.

Characteristics of the Jobs Offered to Youth in the South of Europe

Even before the financial and economic crisis of 2008, jobs made available to young people going through the school-to-work transition were precarious and of low quality, with reforms directed toward an increased flexibility of the labor market being insufficient to tackle the difficulties experienced by youth during this transition (Brzinsky-Fay, 2011, Kretsos, 2014; Wolbers, 2007, 2014). Nonetheless, the 2008 crisis "acted as a catalyst" that further deteriorated emerging adults' work and living conditions (Kretsos, 2014, p. 38). Although postcrisis trends of employment destruction started to be reversed after the first quarter of 2013, most of the jobs created meanwhile are precarious (European Commission, 2014). In 2015, temporary employment corresponded to about 14% of the employment in the European Union, and in countries like Spain, it exceeded 20% of the total employment (European Commission, 2016a). According to the European Commission (2014), these circumstances raise "concerns about the robustness of the recovery" (p. 15) and are an indication of the degree to which the recession affected European labor markets, in particular the quality of jobs offered to young people. Employed young people are not only overrepresented in temporary employment, but they also exhibit rather high levels of underemployment or involuntary part-time work (European Commission, 2014, 2016a; ILO, 2015). Italy, Portugal, and Spain are among the countries in Europe with the highest rates of youth employment precariousness (ILO, 2015). In Italy, the share of young people with temporary employment contracts in 2015 was higher than 50%, and in Spain and Portugal, this rate exceeded 60% (European Commission, 2016a; ILO, 2015). Furthermore, in 2015, nearly half or more of the young people in Portugal (67.9%), Greece (60.5%), and Italy (46.1%) were in temporary employment involuntarily (ILO, 2016). In Spain, at least 80% of youth in temporary employment wanted a permanent position.

Temporary employees in these four countries, especially in Spain, are among the most vulnerable in Europe (European Commission, 2016b). These individuals exhibit very high transition rates into unemployment and relatively low or very low rates of transition to permanent jobs. For example, in 2013, the share of temporary workers becoming inactive or unemployed the following year was approximately 25% in Portugal and Greece and at least 30% in Spain (European Commission, 2014). From 2008 to 2015, underemployment (i.e., part-time working by those who would like and are available to work more hours) increased significantly especially for the 15 to 24 age group (European Commission, 2016a). In 2015, of total part-time employment, the share of youth in involuntary part-time employment was above 70% in Italy and around 60% in Greece and Spain (ILO, 2016). Particularly for young Spaniards, underemployment often emerges as the only alternative to unemployment (European Commission, 2016a). As the European Commission (2014, 2016a, 2016b) noted, a scenario such as this may indicate that instead of operating as a stepping stone toward permanent employment, temporary and part-time contracts are trapping youth in dead-end jobs with rather detrimental effects on their employment prospects, specifically on their ability to access stable and better paid positions that offer adequate social security coverage and opportunities for lifelong learning. Likewise, hardships experienced by youth during school-to-work transitions appear to be pushing them to positions for which they are overqualified (European Commission, 2014, 2016a). According to Cedefop (2015), in 2014, this was the situation of about 25% of the labor market entrants with higher levels of qualification.

The segmentation and the rigidity typical of southern European labor markets only accentuates the difficulties emerging adults experience in finding a job that meets their actual skills level (European Commission, 2014). Even strategies such as mobilizing family and other informal supportive networks, frequently used by Mediterranean youth to address risks associated with problems in accessing the labor market, appear to have lost some of its efficacy (Kretsos, 2014). Formal recruitment also is perceived with some cynicism (Cuzzocrea, 2011). As Cuzzocrea (2011) observed, adverts directed toward recent graduates often require applicants to meet recruitment criteria, such as considerable work experience, that in Italy (as well as in other southern European countries) are not realistic. Therefore, accepting positions below one's qualifications or skills level, as well as undeclared work or "work with 'envelope' wages" (European Commission, 2014, p. 48) appear as alternative paths to employment that are becoming increasingly more common among (Mediterranean) youth (European Commission, 2014; ILO, 2015). Not surprisingly, young adults (i.e., young people aged 20 to 29) are the group of the population registering the highest increase in the at-risk-of-poverty rate in Europe (European Commission, 2016a). Between 2007 and 2014, such risk rose from 15.4% to 20%. Greece, Portugal, and Spain are among the countries in Europe where the situation of young people deteriorated the most. Income reductions induced by the 2008 crisis and subsequent years of austerity in conjunction with wage penalties associated with precarious employment, as well as low transition rates from temporary to permanent employment, increased significantly Mediterranean youth's likelihood of living in poverty despite having a job (European Commission, 2014, 2016a; ILO, 2016).

Work Transitions in the South of Europe: Impact on Youth's Experiences and Pathways to Adulthood

Young adulthood is characterized by overlapping transitions with significant choices in domains as diverse as education, employment, intimate relationships, and living arrangements being considered and implemented simultaneously (Domene, Landine & Stewart, 2015). Through the timing and sequencing of transitions, as well as individual experiences during these transitions, young people formulate their world views and establish unique pathways to adulthood. Although these pathways are increasingly flexible, complex, and heterogeneous, the role of labor market integration as a key transition enabling youth to engage in other adult roles and responsibilities remains unchanged (Parada, 2007). Especially for emerging adults in the South of Europe, financial independence operates as the driver for development in other relevant areas. However, the growing uncertainty that accompanies work transitions, particularly in these four countries where large numbers of individuals face unemployment and precarious employment, makes it increasingly hard for youth to "achieve even modest goals of affluence and job security" (Shulman et al., 2014, p. 1505). Such circumstances impact the ways in which young people from the Mediterranean approach and live their lives, including how they navigate ongoing, multiple, and interconnected transitions to adulthood.

Uncertainty About the Future, Deferment of Commitments and Disorientation

In the years following the Great Recession, youth circumstances in the South of Europe deteriorated drastically (Sica, Crocetti, Ragozini, Sestito & Serafini, 2016). Findings from several studies from Portugal and Italy suggest that increased hardships imposed on youth by the economic crisis and ensuing austerity, affected how emerging adults envisioned the future and addressed specific developmental tasks such individuation and identity construction. For example, a study exploring the effects of the crisis on the imagined futures of Portuguese tertiary education students showed respondents were pessimistic about their prospects in multiple life domains (Cairns, Growiec, & Alves, 2014). Study participants not only indicated a decreased sense of well-being but also made negative appraisals of their life chances in areas as diverse as those concerning employment opportunities, expected academic success, obtaining financial independence, and starting a family. As the authors highlighted, these findings were a "rude awakening" to the "apparent scale of the loss of hope" (Cairns et al., 2014, p. 1508) experienced by these young people. Awareness of adverse contextual conditions also appears to have influenced youth individuation processes. Additional findings from Portugal revealed that the perception of financial hardships translated into a decreased sense of well-being (lower self-esteem and higher depression levels), which was associated with difficulties in autonomy and differentiation toward the romantic partner during late adolescence and young adulthood (Brandão, Matos, & Saraiva, 2013).

In Italy, studies conducted by Aleni Sestito and colleagues (e.g., Aleni Sestito & Sica, 2010, 2014; Aleni Sestito, Sica, & Nasti, 2013; Aleni Sestito, Sica, & Ragozini, 2011; Sica et al., 2016) highlighted the strong impact of challenges with work transitions and financial independence on identity formation. Specifically, these studies suggest a delay in identity consolidation co-occurs with delays in adopting adult roles and responsibilities, particularly those pertaining to labor market integration. Such postponement also negatively impacts on young people's well-being (Aleni Sestito, Sica, & Ragazoni, 2011, Aleni Sestito, Sica, & Nasti, 2013). Both parents and youth report the lack of financial independence and a "weak social welfare system," to be main obstacles emerging adults must overcome to achieve autonomy (Aleni Sestito & Sica, 2014, p. 1443). Italian youth are aware that the outcome of their plans, especially in the career domain, does not exclusively depend on their personal ability and commitment (Aleni Sestito & Sica, 2010, 2014; Sica et al., 2016). Young people, especially those nearing the end of their higher education studies, grow apprehensive about their uncertain future, and appear to be "mainly in moratorium, disoriented and frightened" (Aleni Sestito & Sica, 2014, p. 1443).

Similarly, in Portugal, findings from the Families and Transitions in Europe research project show that, even before the economic crisis, parents and youth felt fear, anxiety, and worry about the future, especially about finding and keeping (stable) employment (Biggart et al., 2007). Particularly for parents, planning was sometimes seen as "absolutely counterproductive" (Biggart et al., 2007, p. 83) given the high risk of youth failing to achieve their goals. Furthermore, lack of resources and an external locus of control result in maladaptive strategies, which hinder young Italians ability to define and implement plans and achieve labor market integration (Aleni Sestito, Sica, & Nasti, 2013; Aleni Sestito, Sica, & Ragozini, 2011). Unemployed or precariously employed youth appear more oriented to external factors, such as securing a stable job or income. They also are more oriented to not taking responsibility for the consequences of their actions. These emerging adults not only blamed other people or the circumstances for their dissatisfaction and failure to achieve their goals (e.g., degrees that do not offer employment opportunities, no meritocracy) but also exhibit a general discomfort and distress with regards to the future. The previously described phenomenon corresponds to Italian youth *postponed identity*, that is, an identity configuration characterized by moratorium and/or diffusion identity statuses (Aleni Sestito & Sica, 2010, 2014; Aleni Sestito et al., 2011), delayed entry into adult roles, lack of future orientation, and external occupational locus of control (Aleni Sestito, Sica, & Ragazoni, 2011, Aleni Sestito, Sica, & Nasti, 2013).

As Crocetti and colleagues (e.g., Crocetti, Rabaglietti, & Sica, 2012; Crocetti, Schwartz, Fermani, Klimstra, & Meeus 2012; Crocetti, Scrignaro, Sica, & Magrin, 2012) noted, the postponed identity configuration involves a propensity to procrastinate commitments, avoid making decisions regarding the future, and delay identity consolidation. Italian youth, like their peers from the Mediterranean, find it extremely difficult to envision their future and the *extended present* emerges as "the only temporal dimension available for defining choices" (Leccardi, 2006, p. 41). These young people seize whatever opportunities present themselves and heavily rely on family support for survival (Cuzzocrea, 2011). Families are often the main or only source of income for youth. At the same time, families play a crucial role in how these young people address developmental tasks like individuation or identity formation (Saraiva & Matos, 2016). Young Italians about to end their university studies show a growing need for parental support and are "still far from achieving a relationship with parents characterized by autonomy and connectedness" (Sestito & Sica, 2014, p. 1443). Not only are emerging adults' ties to the family strong but also the emotional bond with the family of origin is crucial for identity formation and has a strong impact on youth satisfaction with life (Crocetti & Meeus, 2014).

Likewise, studies from Portugal consistently show that young adults who experience higher levels of parental support usually are more satisfied with their relationship with parents (Saraiva & Matos, 2016). As Saraiva and Matos (2016) highlight, the ways in which parents support and encourage autonomy appears crucial to how Portuguese young people construct meaningful pathways to adulthood. Parents' financial support and support to autonomy are a necessary foundation from which young adults develop their sense of agency and operationalize active approaches for managing uncertainty (Oliveira, Mendonça, Coimbra, & Fontaine, 2014). However, support to autonomy appears more effective than financial support in fostering youth agency and the use of action-based strategies to cope with uncertainty, which are strongly tied to psychological well-being. Particularly target-focused uncertainty management strategies are perceived by parents as most effective in helping their young adult children ensure successful implementation of life plans and priorities within the context of economic crisis. Peer support also plays an important role in how Italian emerging adults define the future and envisage their self-development (Sica et al., 2016). As Sica and colleagues (2016) note, support from friends has a major impact on young people's *futuring*, that is on their ability to consider, imagine, and plan for the future. By either deepening or undermining a person's identity processing style, friends' support brings young people closer to or further away from achieving an adaptive future orientation.

Delaying Transitions, Avoiding Poverty, and the Feeling of Being Excluded

The deferral of adult roles and responsibilities by a significant proportion of young people is one of the most relevant and widely acknowledged changes in contemporary youth transitions to adulthood (Côté & Bynner, 2008). Especially in the South of Europe, the precariousness of the labor market, which is also difficult for newcomers to access; the overall weak assistance the state provides to youth, including a lack of affordable housing; and the strong, familial cultural heritage results in significantly delayed transitions and independence from the family of origin (Moreno, 2012). Not only is prolonged cohabitation with parents a behavior consistent with Mediterranean emerging adults' lifestyle, but starting family of one's own is often postponed to the mid- to late 20s or 30s. In 2013, in Italy, the mean age for leaving the parental home was 30 years or above, and in Greece, Portugal, and Spain, it was higher than 28 years (Eurostat, 2015). During the same period, the average mean age for moving out of the parental home in Europe was 26 years (25 years for young women and 27 years for young men). Also according to Eurostat, Greece, Italy, Portugal, and Spain have relatively low fertility rates and the lowest percentage of babies born from mothers aged less than 30 years. In Italy and Spain, this was lower than 40%.

As an Italian study reveals, female unemployment and employment precariousness is a strong dissuasive factor to childbearing for couples with medium or low-income levels and for young women (Modena & Sabatini, 2010). As Modena and Sabatini (2010) observe if young women are unemployed or hold a precarious position in the labor market, they and/or the couple are less likely to have the time and material resources to have children. Female workers with temporary or atypical employment usually are not entitled to sick or parental leaves, and pregnancy often leads to contract termination. Under such circumstances, parenthood is not sustainable, and these women appear to face a dilemma between motherhood and labor market participation (Modena & Sabatini, 2010). Simultaneously, having a relationship and having a child do not appear to be prominent reasons for Portuguese higher education students to consider living independently (Cairns, 2011). Only 25.3% cited having a child and 36.4% cited a relationship as very important reasons to move forward with such a transition. In contrast, the same participants rated concerns about financial stability (74.4%) and having a job security (61.3%) as overwhelmingly important to the decision to move out of the parental home. Overall, 95% and 83.5% of the participants, respectively, considered those as important factors to emancipate.

Pursuing studies at the tertiary level, being unemployed, or employed in temporary and unskilled jobs are factors that increase southern European emerging adults' likelihood of remaining in the parental household (Moreno, 2012). For these youth, leaving home late is a defensive strategy that keeps them out of poverty. As studies consistently show, leaving early home in these countries increases the probability of being poor (Ayllón, 2009). For example, estimates from Spain suggest if all youth aged 26 to 35 years became independent, social exclusion rates would reach 45% (Moreno, 2012). This number would rise to 57% if young people had to pay for housing costs such as rent or mortgage. Therefore, staying longer in the family home, far from being a lifestyle choice, often results from a lack of opportunities and reflects what can be considered "imposed family dependence" (Moreno, López & Segado, 2012, p. 118). By living longer with parents, Mediterranean youth not only shield themselves against economic and employment downturns or poverty but also accumulate financial and symbolic resources, ensuring a smooth residential emancipation and a lifestyle similar to that they enjoy in the parental household (Ayllón, 2009).

Nonetheless, young people appear to live comfortably in their parents' home (Cairns, 2011). Even while living with their parents, Mediterranean youth appear to receive a high level and broad range of support, along with substantial autonomy. Parents usually do not demand financial contribution or participation in household chores from their emerging adult children (Crocetti & Tagliabue, 2016). These young people have fewer responsibilities and benefit from considerable freedom such as the absence of time restrictions, inviting friends or a romantic partner to visit, access to the family car, and unlimited Internet access (Cairns, 2011; Crocetti & Tagliabue, 2016). As Moreno (2012) highlights, especially during the last three decades, families provide autonomy and support to younger generations in exchange for prolonged family dependence. While getting help from parents during young adulthood is perceived as "something normative and unquestionable," young people also anticipate being able to give back to their parents the support received in the future (Coimbra & Mendonça, 2013, p. 166). According to Coimbra and Mendonça (2013), the support received and the anticipation of support to be returned are associated with higher rates of life satisfaction.

Leaving the nest late does not appear to affect the quality of parent–child relationships or individuation processes during young adulthood (Mendonça & Fontaine, 2013). As Mendonça and Fontaine suggest, prolonged cohabitation does not disrupt parent–child relationships during emerging adulthood. Living arrangements (co-residence, semi-autonomy, and independent living) not only are not associated with conflictual independence or parent–child relationship quality, but also are independent from the association between individuation and the quality of parent–child relationships. Financial independence is what ends up facilitating a complete individuation from the parents and triggering family development. Thus, even though postponing key transitions such as living independently or forming a family appear fundamental to Mediterranean youth survival and well-being, it is important to reflect on how a prolonged sense of preparation and uncertainty affects development, specifically a sense of biographical coherence (Saraiva & Matos, 2016). There is a growing disconnect not only between life goals and plans in different domains, but also within specific areas of commitment such as education, family, and work (Oliveira & Fontaine, 2012).

A sense of disconnection makes it harder for young people to achieve a sense of identity and role coherence, as well as to develop temporal continuity allowing them to attach biographical meaning to their goals and plans within and across life domains (Oliveira & Fontaine, 2012). In line with what is observed elsewhere, for young people in these four countries perceiving oneself as an adult does not necessarily depend on criteria attached to traditional adulthood markers, such as finding a job, marrying, moving out of the parental household, or having children (Crocetti & Tagliabue, 2016; Mendonça, Andrade & Fontaine, 2009; Petrogiannis, 2011; Zacarés, Serra, & Torres, 2015). As these studies suggest, psychological, internal, or emotional dimensions of personal autonomy and self-sufficiency (e.g., accepting responsibility for the consequences of own actions, decisions based on personal beliefs and values independent from parents or other influences) are what determine most participants' self-perception of adulthood. However, as findings also indicate, perceiving oneself as an adult is a complex phenomenon that results from a multitude of interconnected criteria in multiple domains of development (Crocetti & Tagliabue, 2016). For example, Italian (Crocetti and

Tagliabue, 2016) and Greek (Petrogiannis, 2011) youth rated settling into a long-term career as 1 of the 10 most important criteria they used to define themselves as adults.

As Petrogiannis (2011) notes, long-term career usually implies full autonomy and financial independence. At the same time, the recent rise in unemployment and underemployment in these countries led youth to view a long-term career as a "mirage" (Crocetti & Tagliabue, 2016, p. 46). According to the 2016 Eurobarometer, youth in the South of Europe overwhelmingly felt marginalized and excluded from the economic and social life of their countries as a consequence of the 2008 crisis (European Parliament, 2016). The proportion of young people feeling excluded because of the crisis rose to 93% in Greece, 86% in Portugal, 79% in Spain, and 78% in Italy. In addition, 41% of young people aged 16 to 30 years interviewed in Greece felt forced to become mobile and go study or work abroad. This number rose to 41% in Portugal. Following the economic crisis many emerging adults from the South of Europe moved to another country in search of work or education. These countries were among those most affected by the "brain drain" phenomenon (Patrutiu-Baltes, 2014), and, at least in Portugal, the phenomenon of emigration has been accompanied by an increased sense of loss and anxiety about the future (Saraiva & Matos, 2016). In these four countries, emigration appears to have emerged as a possible pathway for youth transitions to work or to adulthood; it entails a "potential loss of talent and human capital" that will certainly have a negative impact on these nations productive structures and economic development and on the sense of family typical of their cultural or institutional environment (Moreno et al., 2012, p. 46).

Conclusion

The transition from school to work has recently emerged as an "important, modern rite de passage" (Wolbers, 2014, p. 167). In Europe, especially in countries most hardly hit by the financial and economic crisis of 2008, work transitions are not only "far from smooth" (Wolbers, 2014, p. 167) but often also transform emerging adults into the "biggest losers, because they suffer first and most" with the uncertainty and turbulence characterizing this period of their lives (Wolbers, 2014, p. 168). As the literature consistently demonstrates, the timing and sequencing of events in domains such as education and work have long-term effects and strategically important consequences for individuals' life course and related outcomes (Billari & Liefbroer, 2010). Specifically, they affect other relevant dimensions of youth transitions to adulthood, such as living independently or becoming a parent, as well as young people's priorities and experiences concerning work and their imagined future possibilities in this domain. The lack of consistency as well as the scarcity or absence of institutional resources supporting southern European youth transitions to work and adulthood brings to light not only the low social visibility of these young people but also the socially situated nature of agency. How Mediterranean emerging adults approach and live their lives is reflective of how they construct meaning across time, that is, of their "past and imagined future possibilities, which guide and shape actions in the present together with subjective perceptions of the structures they have to negotiate" (Evans, 2007, p. 92) within a social context as fluid and adverse as the one these young people currently live in. As we expect our review of the literature illustrated, the risks associated to such a context led southern European youth to find new or alternative ways of negotiating institutional rules, norms, and conventions that often challenge the traditional organization of the Mediterranean society and place their lives in a sort of a limbo, with material and symbolic consequences in terms of both how these young people experience the present and the types of opportunities the future will open to them.

References

Abrantes, P. (2010). Towards a new relation with education and work? Youth transitions in Europe and in Latin America (CIES e-Working Paper no. 86/2010). *Centro de Investigação e Estudos de Sociologia*. Retrieved from http://cies.iscte-iul.pt/destaques/documents/CIES-WP86Abrantes_000.pdf

Aleni Sestito, L., & Sica (2010). La formazione dell'identitá nella tranzione dalla scuola superiore all'università: Dimensione processuali e stili [Identity formation during the transition from high school to university: Processual dimensions and styles]. *Rassegna di Psicologia*, *3*, 59–82.

Aleni Sestito, L., & Sica, L. S. (2014). Identity formation of Italian emerging adults living with parents: A narrative study. *Journal of Adolescence*, *37*, 1435–1447. doi:10.1016/j.adolescence.2014.02.013

Aleni Sestito, L., Sica, L. S. & Nasti, M. (2013). The generation of youth without work: Transitions to adulthood in conditions of precariousness, unemployment and underemployment. *Ricerche di Psicologia*, *3*, 411–444.

Aleni Sestito, L., Sica, L. S., & Ragozini, G. (2011). First years of university: Identity formation processes between confusion and consolidation. *Giornale di Psicologia dello Sviluppo*, *99*, 22–35.

Arnett, J. J., Kloep, M., Hendry, L. B., & Tanner, J. L. (2011). Debating emerging adulthood: Stage or process? Oxford, England: Oxford University Press.

Ayllón, S. (2009, November). Modelling state dependence and feedback effects between poverty, employment and parental home emancipation among European youth (SOEPapers on

Multidisciplinary Panel Data Research). *Deutsches Institut für Wirtschaftsforschung Berlin*. Retrieved from https://www.diw.de/documents/publikationen/73/diw_01.c.343251.de/diw_sp0235.pdf

Biggart, A., Engelsted, N., Post, A., Rodriguez, G.C., Jilov, N., Fontanesi, M., Richter, I. & Stein, G. (2007). *Families and transitions in Europe (FATE)—Final report*. Luxembourg: Publications Office of the European Union.

Billari, F. C., & Liefbroer, A. C. (2010). Towards a new patter of transition to adulthood? *Advances in Life Course Research, 15*, 59–75. doi:10.1016/j.alcr.2010.10.003.

Brandão, T., Saraiva, L. M., & Matos, P. M. (2013, June). *A perceção da situação financeira e o processo de separação-individuação em adultos emergentes: O papel mediador da autoestima e depressão* [Perceived financial situation and separation-individuation in emerging adults: The mediating role of self-esteem and depression]. Paper presented at the VIII Simpósio Nacional de Investigação em Psicologia. Aveiro, Portugal.

Brzinsky-Fay, C. (2011). What difference does it make? The outcome effects of the European Employment Strategy on the transition from education to work. *German Policy Studies, 7*, 45–72.

Buchman, M. C., & Kriesi, I. (2011). Transition to adulthood in Europe. *Annual Review of Sociology, 37*, 481–503. doi:10.1146/annurev-soc-081309-150212

Bynner, J. (2005). Rethinking the youth phase of the life course: The case for emerging adulthood?. *Journal of Youth Studies, 8*, 367–384. doi:10.1080/13676260500431628

Cairns, D. (2011). Youth, precarity and the future: Housing transitions in Portugal during the economic crisis (CIES e-Working Paper no. 111/2011). *Centro de Investigação e Estudos de Sociologia*. Retrieved from http://cies.iscte-iul.pt/destaques/documents/CIES-WP111_Cairns_000.pdf

Cairns, D., Growiec, K., & Alves, N. A. (2014). Another "missing middle"? The marginalised majority of tertiary-educated youth in Portugal during the economic crisis, *Journal of Youth Studies, 17*, 1046–1060. doi:10.1080/13676261.2013.878789

Cedefop. (2015). *Matching skills and jobs in Europe: Insights from Cedefop's European skills and jobs survey*. Thessaloniki, Germany: Cedefop, European Centre for the Development of Vocational Training.

Coimbra, S., & Mendonça, M. G. (2013). Intergenerational solidarity and satisfaction with life: Mediation effects with emerging adults. *Paidéia, 23*, 161–169. doi:10.1590/1982-43272355201303

Côté, J., & Bynner, J. M. (2008). Changes in the transition to adulthood in the UK and Canada: The role of structure and agency in emerging adulthood. *Journal of Youth Studies, 11*, 251–268. doi:10.1080/13676260801946464

Crocetti, E., & Meeus, W. (2014). "Family comes first!" Relationships with family and friends in Italian emerging adults. *Journal of Adolescence, 37*, 1463–1473. doi:10.1016/j.adolescence.2014.02.012

Crocetti, E., Rabaglietti, E., & Sica, L. S. (2012). Personal identity in Italy. *New Directions for Child and Adolescent Development, 138*, 87–102. doi:10.1002/cad.20023

Crocetti, E., Schwartz, S., Fermani, A., Klimstra, T., & Meeus, W. (2012). A cross-national study of identity statuses in Dutch and Italian adolescents: Status distributions and correlates. *European Psychologist, 17*, 171–181. doi:10.1027/1016-9040/a000076

Crocetti, E., Scrignaro, M., Sica, L. S., & Magrin, M. E. (2012). Correlates of identity configurations: Three studies with adolescent and emerging adult cohorts. *Journal of Youth and Adolescence, 41*, 732–748. doi:10.1007/s10964-011-9702-2

Crocetti, E., & Tagliabue, S. (2016). Are being responsible, having a job, and caring for the family important to adulthood? Examining the importance of different criteria for adulthood in Italian emerging adults. In R. Žukauskiene (Ed.), *Emerging adulthood in a European context* (pp. 33–53). London, England: Routledge.

Cuzzocrea, V. (2011). Squeezing or blurring: Young adulthood in the career strategies of professionals based in Italy and England. *Journal of Youth Studies, 14*, 657–674. doi:10.1080/13676261.2011.571664

de Lange, M., Gesthuizen, M., & Wolbers, M. H. J. (2014). Youth labour market integration across Europe: The impact of cyclical, structural, and institutional characteristics. *European Societies, 16*, 194–212. doi:10.1080/14616696.2013.821621

Domene, J. F., Landine, J., & Stewart, J. (2015). Emerging adult career transitions. In P. J. Hartung, M. L. Savickas, & W. B. Walsh (Eds.), *APA handbook of career intervention: Vol. 2, Applications* (pp. 479–494). Washington, DC: American Psychological Association. doi:10.1037/14439-035

Eurofound. (2012). *NEETs—Young people not in employment, education or training: Characteristics, costs and policy responses in Europe*. Luxembourg: Publications Office of the European Union. doi:10.2806/41578

European Commission. (2012). *Employment and social developments in Europe 2012*. Luxembourg: Publications Office of the European Union. doi:10.2767/86080.

European Commission. (2014). *Employment and social developments in Europe 2014*. Luxembourg: Publications Office of the European Union. doi:10.2767/33738.

European Commission. (2015). *Employment and social developments in Europe 2015*. Luxembourg: Publications Office of the European Union. doi:10.2767/42590.

European Commission. (2016a). *Employment and social developments in Europe: Annual review 2016*. Luxembourg: Publications Office of the European Union. doi:10.2767/062945.

European Commission. (2016b). Labour market transitions: Analytical web note 1/2016. Retrieved from http://ec.europa.eu/social/BlobServlet?docId=15716&langId=en

European Parliament. (2016). *European youth in 2016: Special Eurobarometer of the European Parliament*. Brussels, Belgium: Directorate-General for Communication, European Parliament. doi:10.2861/837451.

Eurostat. (2015). *Being young in Europe today: Eurostat statistical books*. Luxembourg: Publications Office of the European Union. doi:10.2785/59267

Eurostat. (2016a). Educational attainment statistics. *Statistics Explained*. Retrieved from http://ec.europa.eu/eurostat/statistics-explained/index.php/Educational_attainment_statistics

Eurostat. (2016b). Employment rates of recent graduates. *Statistics Explained*. Retrieved from http://ec.europa.eu/eurostat/statistics-explained/index.php/Employment_rates_of_recent_graduates

Eurostat. (2016c). *Key figures on Europe: 2016 edition*. Luxembourg: Publications Office of the European Union. doi:10.2785/326769.

Eurostat. (2016d). Statistics on young people neither in employment nor in education or training. *Statistics Explained*. Retrieved from http://ec.europa.eu/eurostat/statistics-explained/index.php/Statistics_on_young_people_neither_in_employment_nor_in_education_or_training

Evans, K. (2007). Concepts of bounded agency in education, work and the personal lives of young adults. *International Journal of Psychology, 42*, 85–93.

Gangl, M. (2001). European patterns of labour market entry: A dichotomy of occupationalized vs. non-occupationalized systems. *European Societies, 3*, 471–494. doi:10.1080/14616690120112226

Gutiérrez, R. (2014). Welfare performance in Southern Europe: Employment crisis and poverty risk. *Journal of South European Society and Politics, 19*, 371–392. doi:10.1080/13608746.2014.948592

Hendry, L. B. & Kloep, M. (2010). How universal is emerging adulthood? An empirical example. *Journal of Youth Studies, 13*, 169–179. doi:10.1080/13676260903295067

International Labour Organization. (2015). *Global employment trends for youth 2015: Scaling up investments for decent jobs for youth*. Geneva, Switzerland: Author.

International Labour Organisation. (2016). *World employment and social outlook 2016: Trends for youth*. Geneva, Switzerland: Author.

Kloep, M., & Hendry, L. (2014). Some ideas on the emerging future of developmental research. *Journal of Adolescence, 37*, 1541–1545. doi:10.1016/j.adolescence.2014.09.002

Kretsos, L. (2014). Youth policy in austerity Europe: The case of Greece. *International Journal of Adolescence and Youth, 19*, 35–47. doi:10.1080/02673843.2013.862730

Leccardi, C. (2006). Redefining the future: Youthful biographical constructions in the 21st century. *New Directions for Child and Adolescent Development, 113*, 37–48. doi:10.1002/cd.167

Livi Bacci, M. (2008). *Avanti giovani, alla riscossa* [Go ahead young people, to the rescue]. Bologna, Italy: il Mulino.

Mendonça, M., Andrade, C., & Fontaine, A. M. (2009). Transição para a idade adulta e adultez emergente: Adaptação do Questionário de Marcadores da Adultez junto de jovens portugueses [Transition to adulthood and emerging adulthood: Adaptation of the Questionnaire of Markers of Adulthood among Portuguese youth]. *Psychologica, 51*, 147–168. doi:10.14195/1647-8606_51_10

Mendonça, M., & Fontaine, A. M. (2013). Late nest leaving in Portugal: Its effects on individuation and parent-child relationships. *Emerging Adulthood, 1*, 233–244. doi:10.1177/2167696813481773

Modena, F., & Sabatini, F. (2010). *I would if I could: Precarious employment and childbearing intentions in Italy* (Discussion paper no. 13/2010). Trento, Italy: University of Trento, Department of Economics.

Moreno, A. (2012). The transition to adulthood in Spain in a comparative perspective: The incidence of structural factors. *Young, 20*, 19–48. doi:10.1177/110330881102000102

Moreno, A., López, A. & Segado, S. (2012). *The transition to adulthood in Spain: Economic crisis and late emancipation* (Social Studies Collections 34). Barcelona, Spain: Fundación La Caixa.

Müller, W. (2005). Education and youth integration into European labour markets. *International Journal of Comparative Sociology, 46*, 461–485. doi:10.1177/0020715205060048

Nico, M. (2011). Young adults of the Great Recession: Individual and historical times, present and future biographies (CIES e-Working Paper no. 101/2010). *Centro de Investigação e Estudos de Sociologia*. Retrieved from http://cies.iscte-iul.pt/destaques/documents/CIES-WP_105Nico_000.pdf

OECD. (2016). *How good is your job? Measuring and assessing job quality*. Paris, France: OECD.

Oliveira, J. E., Mendonça. M., Coimbra, S., & Fontaine, A. M. (2014). Family support in the transition to adulthood in Portugal: Its effects on identity capital development, uncertainty management and psychological well-being. *Journal of Adolescence, 37*, 1449–1462. doi:10.1016/j.adolescence.2014.07.004

Oliveira, J. E., & Fontaine, A. M. (2012). Uncertainty management in the transition to adulthood. In E. Scabini & G. Rossi (Eds.), *Family transitions and families in transition* (pp. 111–124). Milano, Italy: Vita e Pensiero.

Pappámikail, L. (2004). Relações intergeracionais, apoio familiar e transições juvenis para a vida adulta em Portugal [Intergenerational relationships, family support and youth transitions to adult life in Portugal]. *Sociologia, Problemas e Práticas, 46*, 91–116.

Parada, F. (2007). *Significados e transições para o trabalho em jovens adultos* [Young adults' meanings and transitions to work] (Unpublished PhD thesis), University of Porto, Portugal.

Patrutiu-Baltes, L. (2014, September). The brain-drain phenomenon within the European Union. *One Europe*. Retrieved from http://one-europe.net/brain-drain-eu.

Petrogiannis, K. (2011). Conceptions of the transition to adulthood in a sample of Greek higher education students. *International Journal of Psychology & Psychological Therapy, 11*, 121–137.

Saraiva, L., & Matos, P. M. (2016). Becoming an adult in Portugal: Negotiating pathways between opportunities and constraints. In R. Žukauskiene, (Ed), *Emerging adulthood in a European context* (pp. 117–137). London, England: Routledge.

Scabini, E., Marta, E., & Lanz, M. (2006). The transition to adulthood and family relations: An intergenerational perspective. Sussex, England: Psychology Press.

Serracant, P. (2015). The impact of the economic crisis on youth trajectories: A case study from Southern Europe. *Young, 23*, 39–58. doi:10.1177/1103308814557398

Shanahan, M. J. (2000). Pathways to adulthood in changing societies: Variability and mechanisms in life course perspective. *Annual Review of Sociology, 26*, 667–692. doi:10.1146/annurev.soc.26.1.667

Shulman, S., Vasalampi, K., Barr, T., Livne, Y., Nurmi, J., & Pratt, M. (2014). Typologies and precursors of career adaptability patterns among emerging adults: A seven-year longitudinal study. *Journal of Adolescence, 37*, 1505–1515. doi:10.1016/j.adolescence.2014.06.003

Sica, L. S., Crocetti, E., Ragozini, G., Sestito, L. A., & Serafini, T. (2016). Future-oriented or present-focused? The role of social support and identity styles on "futuring" in Italian late adolescents and emerging adults. *Journal of Youth Studies, 19*, 183–203. doi:10.1080/13676261.2015.1059925

Walther, A. (2006). Regimes of youth transitions: Choice, flexibility and security in young people's experiences across different European contexts. *Young, 14*, 119–139. doi:10.1177/1103308806062737

Wolbers, M. H. J. (2007). Patters of labour market entry: A comparative perspective on school-to-work transitions in 11 European countries. *Acta Sociologica, 50*, 189–210. doi:10.1177/0001699307080924

Wolbers, M. H. J. (2014). Introduction: Research on school-to-work transitions in Europe. *European Societies, 16*, 167–174. doi: 10.1080/14616696.2013.827230

Young, R. A., Marshall, S. K., Valach, L., Domene, J. F., Graham, M. D., & Zaidman-Zait, A. (2011). *Transition to adulthood: Actions, projects, and counseling*. New York, NY: Springer.

Zacarés, J. J., Serra, E., & Torres, F. (2015). Becoming an adult: A proposed typology of adult status based on a study of Spanish youths. *Scandinavian Journal of Psychology, 56*, 273–282. doi:10.1111/sjop.12205

8

Policies to Enhance Transition to Work

A Case Study in Canada

Lorraine Godden and Christopher DeLuca

Introduction

This chapter highlights the role of policy in the continued struggles faced by Canadian youth in their transition from school to work (STW). In July 2016 the unemployment rate for youth (aged 15–24) in Canada stood at 13.3% compared to the general unemployment rate of 6.9% (Statistics Canada, 2016). Moreover, for emerging adults under the age of 30 who are employed, many are working in increasingly precarious conditions (e.g., temporary, contract, part-time, or low paid) or nonpermanent jobs (Foster, 2012). Within the member states of the OECD, Canada has the highest proportion of degree holders earning poverty-rate incomes (OECD, 2014). In fact, the OECD highlights that 18% of university graduates in Canada are employed in jobs where they earn at or below the poverty line (Bell, Benes, & Redekopp, 2016).

The associated economic costs of such unemployment and precarious employment are well known. In Ontario, Canada's most densely populated province, the mismatch between skills learned and labor market needs is estimated by the Conference Board of Canada (2013) to cost the Ontario economy $24.3 billion in foregone gross domestic product as well as $4.4 billion in federal tax revenues and $3.7 billion in provincial tax revenues annually. This cost, the Conference Board of Canada stated, was a result of too many Ontarians not obtaining adequate levels of education or the right skills to find employment in today's economy. Consequently, the Canadian Chamber of Commerce (2014), a national body that represents businesses across Canada, has argued that improving transitions from education to employment for emerging adults is a matter of national importance (Bell, et al., 2016).

In this chapter we focus particularly upon current secondary school–based policy developments in Ontario that aim to enhance the transition from STW for emerging adults. We have selected Ontario as a focal province for this chapter due to its being the most densely populated province in Canada and

Lorraine Godden and Christopher DeLuca, *Policies to Enhance Transition to Work* In: *Young Adult Development at the School-to-Work Transition.* E. Anne Marshall and Jennifer E. Symonds, Oxford University Press (2021). © Oxford University Press.
DOI: 10.1093/oso/9780190941512.003.0008.

having a significant number of youth unemployed—14.3% in February 2016 compared to the unemployment rate of 5.7% for the adult population aged 25 to 54 (Ontario Ministry of Advanced Education and Skills Development, 2017). In addition, the unemployment rate of Ontario youth aged 15 to 24 remains above the 13.3% average seen across Canada (Statistics Canada, 2016).

Ontario has been addressing this issue, most notably through the introduction of two policy documents aimed at supporting all students in the public education system with transitions through school and into initial postsecondary destinations, including work. The first policy, Creating Pathways to Success: An Education and Career/Life Planning Program for Ontario Schools, promotes "opportunities and support for all students to plan their individual pathways through school and for each to make a successful transition to his or her initial postsecondary destination" (Ontario Ministry of Education, 2013a, p. 3). The second policy, currently awaiting full implementation due to a change of government in 2018, Community Connected Experiential Learning: A Policy Framework for Ontario Schools, Kindergarten to Grade 12, introduces "policy, procedures, and mechanisms for deepening and broadening the role of experiential learning for students from Kindergarten to Grade 12" (Ontario Ministry of Education, 2016, p. 4). Both policies emphasize the value of experiential and/or work-based learning to effectively prepare emerging adults for successful transition into the workplace. In this chapter, we review these policies in an effort to identify common messages and underlying assumptions that shape the policy discourse on youth transition in Ontario. In particular, we consider how these policies respond to the needs of youth at-risk of noncompletion of compulsory schooling. Accordingly, this analysis serves to articulate the current discourse aimed at addressing youth disengagement from school and work, and the efforts to promote greater workforce attachment.

Youth Caught in Transition

Globally, the current generation of youth have been called *a generation at-risk* as a result of declining workforce opportunities and more challenging entrance requirements to postsecondary institutions (International Labour Office, 2013). Some of these emerging adults are classified as Not in Education, Employment, or Training (NEET; Hutchinson & Kettlewell, 2015). Youth that are described as NEET are not a homogenized group and are not necessarily long-term unemployed. For example, under normal circumstances they may present as socially advantaged but are currently NEET while undertaking a gap year or preparing for university entrance (Spielhofer et al., 2009). However, within the heterogenous NEET group is a subgroup of youth who might be considered at risk. These are youth who remain disengaged or who are likely to disengage due to a number of social, personal, or cultural factors (DeLuca, Godden, Hutchinson, & Versnel, 2015). These emerging adults have often had negative school experiences and difficulty identifying a pathway to a meaningful postsecondary destination. They can lack educational mastery, which makes their educational careers problematic, including obtaining end-of-school or vocational education qualifications; hence, they are less competitive for the few jobs available to them (Ziguras, 2006). Research has continuously demonstrated that at-risk youth can hold negative peer relationships and experience adverse family contexts often influenced by social prejudices (Scarpetta, Sonnet, and Manfredi, 2010). These emerging adults, in Canada and elsewhere, are caught between previous negative school experiences and an unreachable workforce.

Research worldwide has identified that transitions policies and processes are required to effectively engage at-risk youth in work, preventing them from becoming NEET (e.g., Cardoso & Moreira, 2009; Mawn et al., 2017; Perreira et al., 2007). Transition begins in secondary school with continued supports until meaningful engagement. Based on our previous empirical research and systematic review of studies focused on youth in transition to work, we noted that effective transition systems that create resilient contexts for at-risk youth are demarked by four characteristics (DeLuca et al., 2015):

1. Transition systems should attend to individual facets shaping disengagement. These factors include one's capacity for agency and self-advocacy within contexts of school, family and peers, (e.g., Cardoso & Moreira 2009).
2. Transition systems should employ tracking of student progress and enable differentiated pathways into school and work (e.g., Smyth et al. 2001).
3. Transition systems have "built-in" partnerships between school and work (e.g., cooperative education placements).
4. Transition systems are purposefully built to provide students with meaningful skills/knowledge intended for meaningful work (e.g., Perreira et al. 2007).

Overall, these characteristics describe effective transition models that help curtail youth unemployment. Policies aimed at engaging emerging adults into work or other postsecondary destinations should likely integrate these tenets as fundamental considerations for localized transition structures. Features that facilitate successful transitions for emerging adults have been identified in a number of international studies (e.g., Bell, Benes, & Redekopp, 2016; European Training Foundation, 2008; OECD, 2000) with the role of educational and training systems and the interfaces linking education and work (e.g., career guidance) prominent as successful features of effective STW transition.

Canadian Policies to Support STW Transitions

Given the provincial governance of education in Canada, there is not currently any specific pan-Canadian STW policy per se (Bell, Benes, & Redekopp, 2016), although the Council of Ministers of Education (CMEC) produced the first pan-Canadian student transitions reference framework in July 2017 (CMEC, 2017). Table 8.1 shows the diversity of policies, initiatives, and programs at the Canadian provincial and territorial level—it can be seen that most areas have some form of ongoing career education; however, there are multiple and varied more specific programs for senior secondary students (usually aged 16–18). STW policies in other countries that also have provincial, state, or regional jurisdiction for education could be similarly diverse.

Across the country, the federal government's overarching response to youth employment is outlined in the Youth Employment Strategy (Government of Canada, 2016), which is principally a work experience program providing opportunities within federal departments that are broadly aimed at the general youth population. Indigenous youth aged 18 to 34 are further supported by the First Nations and Inuit Skills Link Program, managed by the Federal Government of Canada (Government of Canada, 2019). In addition, a number of provinces and territories are supported through co-funded Youth Employment Funds targeted at long-term unemployed 18- to 29-year-old youth that help youth gain work experience and develop basic transferable skills through workplace training, mentorship, and coaching (Bell, Benes, & Redekopp, 2016). Given the developing policy context for STW in Canada and globally, there remains a need to monitor common messages and underlying assumptions that shape the policy discourse on youth transitions, to provide timely contributions to understanding how schools can support young people's successful transition to postsecondary destinations and the labor market.

Table 8.1 Policies to Support School-to-Work Transitions

Province or Territory	Initiative or Program
Alberta	Mandatory high school Career and Life Management (CALM) course (senior high) Career Technology Foundations (grades 5–9) Career and Technology Studies (grades 9–12)
British Columbia	Career development (K–12) Apprenticeships Youth employment services Get Youth Working program (work experience) S.U.C.C.E.S.S. program (youth employment)
Manitoba	Career Education (high school) Blueprint for life/work (K–12) MB4Youth (20 employment programs)
New Brunswick	Career development (grades 3–12). Career Cruising development portfolios Labour Market Information (LMI) initiatives Transition policies for youth with disabilities under consultation
Newfoundland and Labrador	Career strategy PD for appropriate educators Professional learning for teachers Reviewing graduation requirements Elementary level career development Youth apprenticeship program *All of the previously listed items are currently under development.
Northwest Territories	Blueprint for life/work (K–12) Adopted Alberta's Career and Technology Studies (grades 9–12)
Nova Scotia	Action Plan for Education (2015–2020) includes strengthening career education Community-based learning Cooperative Learning Entrepreneurship Establishing Business-Education Council Career development program (grades 4–12) is under development (includes uniquely experiential programming targeted at at-risk youth)
Nunavut	Inuit Youth Summer Work Experience Program
Ontario	Creating Pathways to Success (K–12) Community Connected Experiential Learning Program (K–12) (draft) Specialist High Skills Majors Ontario Youth Apprenticeship program Expanded Cooperative Education program Dual Credit programs Ontario Youth Jobs Strategy Youth Job Connection Experience Ontario

Table 8.1 *Continued*

Province or Territory	Initiative or Program
Prince Edward Island	Career Education Strategy (K–12) including compulsory Career Education course at grade 10
Quebec	Stratégie d'action jeunesse 2009–2014 Ministère du Travail, de l'Emploi et de la Solidarité sociale (includes job integration companies, volunteering, internships and job shadowing)
Saskatchewan	Broad K–12 career education goals for essential skills and career management competencies Saskatchewan Youth Apprenticeship (SYA) program
Yukon	Department of Education Strategic Plan (2011–2016) includes goal of creating inclusive, adaptable, and productive workforce Essential skills and trades training programs Apprenticeships Supporting transitions programs Yukon Youth Connections Program Youth employment services (Skookum Jim Friendship Centre)

Analyzing Policies

This chapter reports on the examination of two purposefully selected policy documents relating to STW transitions in the province of Ontario, Canada: (a) Creating Pathways to Success: An Education and Career/Life Planning Program for Ontario Schools (CPS; Ontario Ministry of Education, 2013a) and (b) Community Connected Experiential Learning: A Policy Framework for Ontario Schools, Kindergarten to Grade 12 (CCEL; Ontario Ministry of Education, 2016). Our analytic approach to these policies was informed by Prior (2003) and Miller and Alvarado's (2005) content analytic approach to document analysis. Prior discussed how policy documents could be taken as a field of research in their own right, and that "processes of production and consumption of written materials" (p. 166) provide two robust areas for crucial research. Miller and Alvarado argued that greater attention to documents, as primary or supplementary sources of data, was needed in qualitative research, especially within evolving educational policy contexts (such as STW transition). In their study, they explored the nature of documents, the distinctive features of research with documents, as well as how documents might be analyzed, and produced a framework to consider the spectrum of available approaches to document analysis. Miller and Alvarado identified three distinct approaches to the analysis of documents: (a) content (content analytic);

(b) commentary (context analytic); and, (c) documents as actors (context analytic). In this chapter, we use Miller and Alvarado's content analytic approach.

We initiated data analysis for this study by examining the content of the two selected policy documents to identify key themes. In this approach, documents were seen to be "conduits of communication" (Prior, 2008) that contained meaningful messages. Our examination of the CPS and CCEL documents involved a deductive content analysis (Miller & Alvarado, 2005). Our analytic framework purposefully sought to examine how four characteristics related to successful transitions (DeLuca et al., 2015) were conceptualized in the two policy documents. These characteristics were introduced earlier and are described in more detail as follows:

1. *Agency and self-advocacy within contexts of school, family, and peers.* This characteristic refers to the capacity for these STW policies to enable student agency and advocacy within and across contexts so that needs can be effectively met. Two conditions are required here: first, explicit teaching about needs and how to advocate for needs and, second, receptive contexts in which needs are addressed and student agency respected. The extent to which these two conditions are explicated, identified, and supported within policies suggests the intention of the STW policy in fulfilling this key characteristic of successful transitions.
2. *Tracking of student progress to enable differentiated pathways into school and work.* This characteristic involves systematic monitoring and tracking of student progress through various pathways leading ideally to meaningful work. By following and following-up on student progress, more purposeful and productive matches between student and work experiences can be facilitated. Moreover, through monitoring student progress and identifying gaps in student learning, explicit instruction and resources can be supplied to students to enable more successful transitions earlier in the process, diverting at-risk instances. The extent to which policies explicitly describe tracking and monitoring processes signal their intentions to facilitate this important dimension of STW transition.
3. *Built-in partnerships between school and work (e.g., cooperative education work placements in the community).* This characteristic relates to the need for established partnerships between schools and workplaces with known and proven records of success. If school educators and workplace supervisors have productive relationships, then they are more likely to work together to support emerging adults as they experience work placements. Leveraging these transitional cooperative education

experiences provides students with a positive and productive experience that could equip them with required experience and skills to seek meaningful employment on their own after school. If policies make provisions that nurture school and workplace relationships through appropriate work placements, then students stand to benefit through smoother and more effective transitions.

4. *Purposefully built to provide students with meaningful skills/knowledge intended for meaningful work.* This final characteristic relates to the match between the student's work interests and their workplace experience. The greater the fit between what the emerging adult wants to learn and do and what they experience during the work placement, the more likely the experience will be meaningful and successful. Spending time purposefully matching work placements with emerging adult interests and skills will increase the value of the experience. Policies that provide explicit guidance on how to match placements with students' interests, dispositions, attitudes, backgrounds, and career goals will work to provide purposefully built work experiences for students, leading to more meaningful work placements.

Prior to presenting the results of this analysis, we provide additional contextual details in the following section. Specifically, we set the stage for interpreting the STW transition context within our focal province, Ontario.

Ontario Educational Policy Context

Education policy within Ontario is generated at the provincially managed Ministry of Education (MOE) level; school boards receive these policies and implement them at either board or school level, dependent upon the individual requirement of the particular policy. School boards are responsible for developing necessary procedures and allocating resources to support schools to implement policies and meet provincial mandate requirements. Teachers, although employed by individual school boards, are regulated as a profession by the Ontario College of Teachers (Kutsyuruba, Burgess, Walker, & Donlevy, 2013). Since 2018, the MOE under the Progressive Conservative Government has held the overarching priority of ensuring "from the early years through to postsecondary, children and students can get the skills and knowledge they need to reach their full potential" (Ontario Ministry of Education, 2019). In addition to this overarching priority, the MOE has introduced a number of policies and strategies to support transitions, career, and life planning, which have been introduced as revised, expanded, or new polices and curricula across to province to support this overarching aim.

A results-based plan briefing document (Ontario Ministry of Education, 2013b) outlined the following four priorities: *Success for Students, Strong People, Strong Economy, Better Health,* and *Safer Communities.* The priority of Strong People, Strong Economy encompassed a number of significant programs and initiatives including specialist high skills majors, expanded cooperative education, dual credits, student success teachers and teams, student voice, Grade 8 to Grade 9 transition teams, homework help, student success school support initiative, supervised alternative learning, and the 21st-century teaching and learning initiative. Although many of these activities were existing and established areas of policy and curriculum prior to 2013 in Ontario, the results-based plan briefing document detailed how they would be renewed or expanded over the fiscal year of 2013–2014 (Ontario Ministry of Education 2013b).

In addition to the focus on programs and initiatives through Strong People, Strong Economy, the Ontario Government launched Stepping Up, a strategic framework to help Ontario's youth to succeed (Government of Ontario, 2014). The framework was structured around seven themes:

- Health and wellness
- Strong, supportive friends and families
- Education, training, and apprenticeships
- Employment and entrepreneurship
- Diversity, social inclusion, and safety
- Civic engagement and emerging adult leadership
- Coordinated and youth friendly communities

To support the implementation of this framework, the Ontario Government created (in consultation with researchers, youth, community leaders, and service providers), *Stepping Stones: A Resource on Youth Development* (Ontario Ministry of Education, 2014), a resource intended to support those who work with youth aged 12 to 25. Included in this resource was an overview of emerging adult development, a series of developmental maps, and tips for implementation.

A brief examination of the documents identified in the previous two paragraphs reveals some common issues relevant to this chapter. In the programs linked to Strong People, Strong Economy priorities, significant attention was given to describing the economic and social benefit for Ontario students to graduate with their high school diploma. The provision of specialist high skills majors, cooperative education, and dual-credit programs were described as key strategies for students to focus their interests and learning toward employment and specific economic sectors, while simultaneously earning necessary credits for successful graduation. All of the documents provided descriptions of available support for student transitions and student engagement. For example, the assistance available to students via dedicated student success teams and the CPS career/life planning process. The documents, like both the CPS and CCEL, have an all-encompassing, holistic approach, with language consistent in its description of programming, learning goals, outcomes, and evaluations across different documents. The two documents examined were aimed at K–12 student populations and were targeted across school and district school board job roles.

CPS, one of the focal policies used in our analysis, was introduced by the Ontario Ministry of Education during 2013, with full implementation rolled out during September 2014. Described by the Ministry as "the new career development policy for Ontario schools" (Ontario Ministry of Education, 2013a, p. 3), the policy outlined an education and career/life planning program for all Kindergarten to Grade 12 (K–12) students. CPS is intended as a "whole-school program delivered through classroom instruction linked to the curriculum and through broader school programs and activities" (p. 3).

CCEL, the second focal policy used in our analysis, was introduced by the Ontario Ministry of Education as a draft for consultation during the winter of 2016, with full implementation planned for fall 2016. At the time of writing this chapter, the policy has yet to be implemented in full across Ontario schools due to a change of government in Ontario in 2018. The CCEL document outlines Ontario's "vision and plan of action for the province based on a commitment to the success and well-being of every student and child" (Ontario Ministry of Education, 2016, p. 4). In particular, the document outlines "policy, procedures, and mechanisms for deepening and broadening the role of experiential learning for students from Kindergarten to Grade 12" (p. 4).

Analysis of Ontario STW Policies

Our goal in analyzing the CPS and CCEL documents was to establish how the four characteristics related to successful transitions drawn from our previous work (DeLuca et al., 2015) were conceptualized in education and career/life planning programs for Ontario K–12 public schools. These conceptualizations could represent common messages and underlying assumptions that shape the policy discourse on youth STW transition in Ontario. This analysis conveys the current discourse aimed at addressing youth disengagement from school, work, and postsecondary education and the efforts to promote greater workforce attachment.

Agency and Self-Advocacy Within Contexts of School, Family and Peers

Agency

CPS defines the importance of positive "beliefs about student success" (Ontario Ministry of Education, 2013b, p. 9) early in the document, highlighting that all students can be successful, that success came in many forms and there were many pathways to success. Social equity, when mentioned in CPS, is linked with ensuring all emerging adults were supported with transitions, and with equal opportunities to successfully transition from Grade 8 to Grade 9 and from Grade 12 to their postsecondary destination. Successful transitions are very much expressed as an outcome of successful learning within the education and career/life planning program. To facilitate this, schools are required to provide orientation programs to support transitions and "multiple and varied opportunities and resources to inform the planning process" (p. 23). Section 4 of CPS details transition planning efforts that must be made by all schools and district school boards. A small section refers specifically to students with special educational needs, and to transitions, which include all those a student might face, for example, entry to school, transitions between grades, transitions between various settings and classrooms, moving from school to school or school to outside agency, and transitioning from elementary to secondary and from secondary to postsecondary destinations. The responsibility for coordinating and developing this transition support falls ultimately to the school principal.

Within CCEL, experiential learning is seen as being able to assist students to see connections between course content and its application in other contexts, which is argued to more broadly support transitions. The CCEL document cites the Canadian Council on Learning (2009) view that experiential learning has "psycho-social benefits for students, including increased self-esteem and engagement in the workplace or school, improved motivation, and improved social and leadership skills" (p. 6). In the CCEL, experiential learning requires students to become immersed in an experience, reflect upon their experience, make meaning from it, and identify what they have learned.

Self-Advocacy

In CPS, there is an often-repeated emphasis on students being expected to develop knowledge of themselves and their decision-making processes to determine education and life planning goals. In CCEL, technology is described as having a significant role in enabling enrichment and expansion of learning opportunities through experiential learning for all students. The CCEL document asserts that "innovative technologies allow for more equitable access to experiential learning opportunities by removing barriers to participation that may have stood in the way for some students, including those living in remote areas and those with special educational needs" (Ontario Ministry of Education, 2016, p. 18). Our analysis findings related to the themes of *agency* and student *self-advocacy* found in CPS and CCEL are presented in Table 8.2.

Tracking of Student Progress to Enable Differentiated Pathways

Student Progress

In Ontario, students are expected to successfully navigate a summative assessment process necessary for successful acquisition of the Ontario Secondary School Diploma (Ontario Ministry of Education, 2013a, p. 22). To prompt students to gather evidence of their learning in CPS, students are expected to respond to the "Framework: Areas of Learning and Enquiry Questions" (p. 12) of *Who am I? What are my opportunities? Who do I want to become?* and *What is my plan for achieving my goals?* Students subsequently work through a diagnostic assessment process to "document and reflect on their experiences and learning, discuss what they are learning, and weight their options for next steps, their competence in education, and career/life planning grows" (p. 16). A major goal of CPS is to enable students "to become confident, independent, and effective education and career/life planners throughout their lives" (p. 13).

The CPS determines that a "process must be in place for all students to capture evidence of learning in a portfolio called 'All About Me' for Kindergarten to Grade 6, and in the Individual Pathways Plan (IPP) for Grades 7 to 12" (Ontario Ministry of Education, 2013a, p. 20). A procedure must also be in place for students to "summarize and transfer their key learning" between these portfolios as they moved from Grade 6 to Grade 7. Educators are advised on how to support students to utilize their IPP, a web-based portfolio to track and record all of their learning. Educators are expected to utilize a variety of methods of learning to provide students with numerous and varied opportunities to successfully engage in, undertake, reflect upon, and document their

Table 8.2 Agency and Self-Advocacy Within Contexts of School, Family, and Peers

	Agency	Self-Advocacy	Context
Creating Pathways to Success	• Supporting students in identifying their personal interests, strengths, needs, and aspirations (p. 3) • Students are responsible for building and updating their portfolios and Individual Pathways Plans (IPP) (p. 4) • Students are to identify the qualities that describe who they are (p. 4) • All students can be successful, success comes in many forms, there are many pathways to success • Ensuring all students are supported with transitions (p. 16) • Successful transitions are seen as desirable outcome for students (p. 21) • Schools are responsible for providing orientation to support transitions (p. 22) • Principal's role in supporting transition planning is identified (p. 23)	• Students able to use knowledge of themselves to inform choices of programs and learning opportunities (p. 12) • Students use decision-making processes to determine their education and life planning goals (p. 17) • Students identify the demands, rewards, and features of other opportunities that have explored (p. 17) • A goal of the CPS program is to teach students to understand themselves better and plan for the future (p. 8)	• Students • Parents • Teachers • Principals/administrators • Broader community
Community Connected Experiential Learning	• All students can become immersed in an experience, make meaning from it, and identify what they have learned (p. 8) • Students are more engaged in their learning and are more motivated to learn (p. 9) • Educators can adjust complexity, focus, and depth of process to suit developmental needs of students (p. 9) • Student is an active participant (p. 9) • Students develop habits of looking for learning that can be drawn from life experiences (p. 9) • Reflection is a strategy that develops metacognition (p. 9)	• Acquiring knowledge and skills to make informed education and life choices (p. 8) • Students develop the ability to monitor their own progress towards achieving a learning goal (p. 9) • Students consider how their learning stimulates further inquiry (p. 9) • Three questions—What? So what? Now what? (p. 9)	• Students • Teachers • Principals/administrators • Community mentor • Industry education councils • Post-secondary institutions • Non-for-profit organizations • Training organizations • Community living associations • Local businesses

learning in the education and career life planning program. There is also a requirement for schools to establish an education and career life planning program advisory committee, responsible for coordinating the "development, implementation, and evaluation" (p. 37) of a school's program. The committee must include representatives of all members of the school community including administrators, teachers, students, parents, and members of the broader community. In secondary schools, the committee extends to include guidance staff who, it is suggested, "may play a key role in coordinating the development and implementation process" (Ontario Ministry of Education, 2013a, p. 35).

Differentiated Pathways

Instructional strategies consisted of classroom instruction, program-related activities, teaching and learning activities, Universal Design for Learning, and diverse and engaging learning opportunities. Within these strategies, educators are provided with clear examples of how they might transpire into practice within schools and classrooms, and expected learning outcomes are explicit and aligned to the learning experiences and opportunities. For example, as noted in CPS (Ontario Ministry of Education, 2013a),

> the experiences students have as they actively develop answers to the four key inquiry questions allow them to gather information about themselves and their opportunities; consider feedback from their teachers, parents, and peers; make decisions and set goals; and develop plans for achieving their goals. (p. 16)

Within the CPS, emphasis is placed on strategies to encourage students to achieve deeper levels of understanding through the program content. For example, by providing students with opportunities to "review evidence of their learning" (Ontario Ministry of Education, 2013a, p. 18) and "see the connections between what they are learning in school and its relevance and application beyond the classroom" (p. 28).

The CCEL document defines the goals of community-connected experiential learning as

- deepening their [students] understanding of the knowledge and skills within the curriculum and of their life experience beyond the curriculum;
- acquiring the knowledge and skills needed to make informed education and career/life choices;
- developing their capacities for deeper learning, including learning for transfer, and helping them to acquire important 21st-century

competencies (such as critical thinking and problem-solving, communication, and collaboration) so that they have the talent and skills they need to succeed and lead in the global community; and

- contributing to a local, national, or global community and developing competencies related to the identity as individuals and as members of their community, society, and the world.

Within the CCEL program, provisions are "being introduced to make it possible for students to earn experiential learning credits though a formal evaluation and accreditation process known as the Experiential Learning Assessment and Recognition (ELAR)" (Ontario Ministry of Education, 2016, p. 35). The CCEL document describes how it will be possible for students enrolled in Ontario secondary schools to "earn credit for the skills and knowledge articulated in their ELAR learning plan and demonstrated through their ELAR culminating activity" (p. 35). A summary of pointers to tracking student progress and differentiated pathways were summarized from analysis of CPS and CCEL and are outlined in Appendix 8.A.

Evaluation of the Tracking Student Progress Process

The CPS document expects provision for students learning within their education and career/life planning to be evaluated within the overall program evaluation. Students are also expected to gather evidence of their learning within their portfolios and IPPs. Students are expected to build a range of evidence from actively developing answers to four key questions that help them to both gather information about themselves and to develop plans for achieving their goals. Schools and district school boards are expected to develop and implement evaluation strategies that aligns with indicators for pathways planning (e.g., School Effectiveness Framework) and put processes into place to gather varied types of data to measure program effectiveness. Included is the requirement to gather student feedback, and inclusion of student voice featured prominently throughout CPS.

An overarching goal of CPS program evaluation is to assess "how well the program is succeeding in helping students develop the knowledge and skills they need for effective education and career/life planning" (Ontario Ministry of Education, 2013a, p. 39). Throughout Section 6 (pp. 35-41) of the CPS, the role and responsibility of a number of policy actors in contributing to evaluation of the CPS is determined. Policy actors included teachers, guidance counselors, principals, district school boards, parents, students, and community partners. Limited information is provided toward how such a wide-ranging contribution from so many parties could be effectively and meaningfully coordinated and collated, and we suspect schools will rely heavily on existing structures for such evaluation.

Inadequate information is provided in the CCEL document regarding program evaluation; however, given this is a draft consultation document, we would expect that the final policy document would include more deeply consider appropriate program and policy evaluation that takes account of the policy's ability to support individual student progress.

Partnerships Between School and Work

Partnerships With Employers

CPS clearly places value on emerging adults participating in vocational and work-related programs, highlighting a variety of intentional vocational education and training (VET) programming available in Ontario public schools. Particular mention was made of experiential learning, cooperative education, dual credit, specialist high skills majors, and the Ontario Youth Apprenticeship. All of these programs were highlighted as being able to provide students with "learning opportunities that allow them to apply their knowledge and skills to real-life work-related situations" (Ontario Ministry of Education, 2013a, p. 28). All the VET programs and options for students were included in section 5 of the document and were described as "the where of learning" (p. 26). The CPS also highlights the compulsory Grade 10 Careers Studies course that is available for all students that is available through the guidance and career education curriculum. This curriculum also includes a number of optional career education courses that students can take during Grades 11 and 12.

The VET options and programs are described as providing students with "a wide range of opportunities in and outside of the classroom to practice education and career/life planning" (Ontario Ministry of Education, 2013a, p. 27). Such opportunities are also deliberately linked to all of the other subject area curriculum policy documents. For Grades 1 to 8, all curriculum policy documents in the current review cycle of the MOE contain a chapter called "Some Considerations for Program Planning" with a subsection called Building Career Awareness, which is "focused on students' exploration of their strengths and skills and on career exploration opportunities" (p. 28). For grades 9 to 12 documents, there is a section that is focused on career education. Any curriculum documents released during 2013 onwards align fully with the CPS.

Work-Related Learning

A range of education and career/life exploration activities and experiential learning are delivered in connection with the Ontario secondary school curriculum, and they may also be provided on a school-wide basis as part of a career education program. For example, CPS outlines guidance and career education courses, experiential learning, cooperative education programs, and Specialist High Skills Majors programs as being education and career/life planning programming available for schools (Ministry of Education, 2013b, pp. 26–36). Within this structure, the curriculum included the opportunity for students to take cooperative education programs that provided students with the opportunity to earn credits toward their secondary school diploma while completing a work placement that is directly related to the learning expectations of a secondary school course. Students received mentorship from a workplace supervisor and cooperative education teacher while they were completing their cooperative education credit. The CPS highlighted the *Cooperative Education and Other Forms of Experiential Learning: Policies and Procedures for Ontario Secondary Schools, 2000* (Ministry of Education, 2000) as a further resource.

In addition to cooperative education, the CPS emphasized that many secondary schools and district school boards provide programs that "focus on students' preparation for postsecondary endeavors and to address particular interests" (Ontario Ministry of Education, 2013a, p.31). Such programs included dual credit, Ontario Youth Apprenticeship Program, Specialist High School Majors, and STW transition programs. Throughout the brief descriptions of these options, terminology and language were targeted toward providing students with flexible and varied opportunities to achieve success in their learning and facilitating students to subsequently transfer that learning success to life after their compulsory schooling.

The CCEL policy utilizes three components to ensure that the Experiential Learning Assessment and Recognition (ELAR) process "duly addresses student learning, student demonstration and application of learning, and requirements governing recognition of learning" (Ontario Ministry of Education, 2016, p. 36). Students must submit a detailed proposal of their planned experiential learning to a designated teacher, who subsequently reviews the proposal. Should the proposal be agreed, the student, student's parent (if the student is under 18), and the teacher meet to formulate a detailed ELAR learning plan. The emerging adult then undertakes the experiential learning experience, and this is followed by a recognition process during which the student demonstrates that they have successfully completed the experiential learning experience, evidenced their ongoing reflection on formal and informal learning, and applied their learning. A summary of pointers to tracking partnerships with employers and work-related learning were summarized from analysis of CPS and CCEL are outlined in Appendix 8.B.

Opportunities for Learning and Purposeful Skills Building

Knowledge of Skills

The requirements for providing opportunities for learning for students in a deliberately planned manner is embedded throughout the CPS. Given the far-reaching scope K–12 of the CPS policy, this is not unexpected. The CPS seems to be structured in such a way as to allow a wide variety of educator policy actors room for individual interpretation and subsequent implementation of the CPS appropriate to their educational institution needs. For example, the policy includes sections on education and career/life planning through "school-wide activities" (Ontario Ministry of Education, 2013a, p. 32), and "activities in the community" (p. 33). Schoolwide activities are varied and include experiential learning opportunities linked with community outside of school. Community activities include undertaking civic responsibilities, volunteering, and part-time employment. All schools are required to establish an "Education and Career/Life Planning Program Advisory Committee" (p. 36) that must, among other duties, develop a "communication plan that fosters support among all stakeholders for the implementation of the program in the school, at home, and in the community" (p. 36).

A great deal of emphasis is placed upon emerging adults learning within the education and career/life planning program, with a detailed framework that "provides a starting point and a process for ongoing program development and student learning" (Ontario Ministry of Education, 2013a, p. 13). Educators are encouraged to apply the framework to structure and develop appropriate learning activities for all students. Although not extensively detailed within CPS, there is a requirement to provide opportunities for students to develop skills and knowledge of the labor market, gain exposure to and/or explore the labor market, and form habits of mind to help them prepare for future career/life planning including entering the labor market. Where skills are mentioned, they include job search, employment retention, and essential skills and knowledge includes gathering information about different occupations and technical skills related to specific work sectors. In addition, students are expected to have opportunities to develop their knowledge about future work and occupations.

Purposeful Skills Building

Assessing students' knowledge, skills, and expertise as they relate to the labor market, or of matters connected to the labor market are seen as important in the CPS. For example, students are required to develop knowledge of "a variety of fields of work, occupations, and careers, and develop an awareness of local and global trends (e.g., demographic, technological, economic, social) on the opportunities connected to them" (Ontario Ministry of Education, 2013a, p. 15).

The CCEL is strongly connected to CPS, and educators are expected to

> create alignment and coherence among the experiential policy framework; the policy governing the education and career/life planning program in Ontario schools, articulated in Creating Pathways to Success, policies outlined in the Kindergarten program document and the Ontario curriculum documents, and other ministry policies and initiatives. (Ontario Ministry of Education, 2016, p. 15)

There is an emphasis within CCEL for students to develop deeper levels of skills building that are linked with "21st century competencies" (Ontario Ministry of Education, 2016, p. 8), and the specific "knowledge and skills related to education and career/life planning" (p. 34). A summary of pointers to opportunities for learning and purposeful skills building were summarized from analysis of CPS and CCEL and are outlined in Table 8.3.

Discussion

Within CPS, much of the focus toward agency and self-advocacy seems to be linked with the need for emerging adults to be prepared for transitions. For example, students are to be encouraged to take increasing responsibility for compiling IPP's that contain evidence of their qualities, skills, and aptitudes. This in turn is linked with students developing a "fuller understanding of the education and career/life planning process" (Ontario Ministry of Education, 2013a, p. 19). Ultimately, knowing the "value the process will have for them in their post-secondary planning" (p. 19) is described as being essential for a successful transition. Within CCEL, undertaking an experiential learning experience is seen as facilitating students to see connections between course content, its application to other contexts, and its ability to support ongoing transitions. This certainly speaks to and aligns with the agency and self-advocacy characteristic in the person-in-context model of DeLuca et al. (2015). Both policies rely heavily upon students' possessing agency and self-advocacy to undertake

Table 8.3 Opportunities for Learning and Purposeful Skills building

	Knowledge of skills	Building and applying skills	Context
Creating Pathways to Success (CPS)	• Career— the development of the knowledge and skills needed to set short-term and long-term goals in planning for the future (p. 4). • The inquiry process and the related knowledge and skills must be taught explicitly before students learn to apply it habituall (p. 13). • Through the education and career/life planning program, students from Kindergarten to Grade 12 acquire knowledge and skills in four areas of learning—Knowing Yourself, Exploring Opportunities, Making Decisions and Setting Goals, and Achieving Goals and Making Transitions (p. 14).	• Education and career/life planning refers to a process that assists in the development and application of the knowledge and skills (p. 6). • From Kindergarten to Grade 12, as students develop their knowledge and skills in education and career/life planning, they document and reflect on their experiences and learning and weigh their options for next steps (p. 21). • Explore employment opportunities and develop job search skills and employment retention skills (p. 23).	• Students • Teachers
Community Connected Experiential Learning CCEL)	• Providing our learners with opportunities to develop the knowledge and skills that will lead them to become personally successful, economically productive, and actively engaged citizens remains at the core of Ontario's education system (p. 4). • They may also support students in developing knowledge and skills that will better prepare them for the jobs of tomorrow (p. 29). • Students to track and reflect on their learning, including but not limited to the OSP Essential Skills, 21st-century competencies, the learning skills and work habits, and knowledge and skills related to the education and career/life planning program (p. 37). • Ontario Skills Passport (OSP). A web-based resource that provides clear descriptions of the "Essential Skills" and "work habits" that are important for work, learning, and life. The Essential Skills are used in virtually all occupations and are transferable from school to work, job to job, and sector to sector (p. 43).	• Deepening their understanding of the knowledge and skills within the curriculum and of their life experiences beyond the curriculum (p. 7). • Developing their capacities for deeper learning, including learning for transfer, and helping them to acquire important 21st-century competencies (such as critical thinking and problem solving, communication, and collaboration) so that they have the talent and skills they need to succeed and lead in the global economy (p. 8). • Students and their parents should be encouraged to reflect on the importance of activities in the community to students' development of knowledge and skills related to education and career/life planning (p. 34).	• Students • Teachers

the IPP process and create appropriately evidenced IPP portfolios. It should be noted that the CCEL policy introduces an opportunity for students to complete ELAR and gain credit for their Ontario Secondary School Diploma. Through this process, students need to demonstrate agency in collating evidence and completing the summative tasks.

We know that an emerging adult's motivation and personal agency are important factors in their ability to meet learning and transition goals, and these are significantly impacted by their ability to overcome barriers and challenges within the transitions process (e.g., Bandura et al., 2001; Rojewski & Yang, 1997; Schoon & Parsons, 2002). We also know that explicit teaching and targeted support focused on learning how to advocate for particular needs are effective (e.g., Hatch, Shelton, & Monk, 2009; Howard & Solberg, 2006). However, lower achieving emerging adults and minority youth were reported by Demereth, Lynch, and Davidson (2008) as not being comfortable and effective in advocating for themselves when compared to their higher achieving and majority peers. Subsequently, lower achieving emerging adults with special education needs and at-risk youth may well be significantly disadvantaged within the outlined IPP and ELAR processes contained in CPS and CCEL. More research is needed to address the needs of these populations.

The CPS relies heavily on students building their IPPs as demonstration of evidence for their learning and achievement, and this is linked to growth in "education and career/life planning competence" (Ontario Ministry of Education, 2013a,p. 16). Emphasis is placed upon the IPP being a "vehicle through which students can provide feedback about the kinds of school experiences and learning activities that have been most helpful to them" (p. 16). Clearly, thought has been given to the benefits of providing students with opportunities to engage in a reflective, self-monitoring process that will nurture their ability to self-advocate. However, little detail is provided in CPS regarding the provision of purposeful and productive matches in their career/life planning and work experiences, combined with rigorous and systematic monitoring processes focused at supporting at-risk learners' individual transition needs that are necessary to adequately support lower achieving students, students with special education needs, and at-risk youth. Thus, the appropriateness of matching career/life planning with work experiences, and effectiveness of support provided for at-risk learners is open to interpretation by all educational staff who have responsibility for STW transitions.

Within the CCEL, the ELAR is divided into three components that (a) develop an ELAR learning plan and ELAR agreement, (b) outline participation in the experience including the setting of learning goals and evaluation procedures, and (c) recognize how the student will evidence their learning based upon an experiential learning cycle, consisting of *participate*, *reflect*, and *apply* (Ontario Ministry of Education, 2016, p. 7). This recognition process involves many components and seems to depend upon students agentic and self-advocating capabilities. Although the overarching scope of ELAR is wide, facilitating differentiated pathways is implicit in the process and is not defined as a clearly linked objective.

Both the CPS and CCEL policies assign significant attention to the value of developing partnerships to support students in career and postsecondary planning. In the CPS, these are described as the broader school community, and in the CCEL, there is a greater focus on the relationships schools can form with workplaces. Where community involvement is described in the CPS (Ontario Ministry of Education, 2013a, p. 33), the focus is on encouraging students and parents to reflect upon the value of undertaking community involved opportunities. However, the CCEL does recognize the need for establishing and sustaining strong partnerships and expounds the necessity for district school boards to work with partnerships to ensure mutual goals and benefits of experiential learning are established and that partners and their contributions are supported and valued. We see this as important, as where educators and workplace supervisors have productive relationships, it is more likely they will work together to support students as they experience work placements.

The delineation of the need to *carefully* and *purposefully* match the hopes students hold for education, career/life planning, experiential learning, and work-related outcomes with their actual work-related learning experienced through CPS and/or CCEL (e.g., cooperative education placement) are not explicit in either policy. Both policies promote an intention for students to develop increased awareness of how they can connect their learning, skills, and aptitudes with clear postsecondary planning. However, as research conducted by Hutchinson et al. (2011) has demonstrated, schools play a critical role in helping at-risk youth understand and navigate the varied layers of labor market conditions driven by societal, political, and economic forces. We therefore suggest that although the matching process is important for all students undertaking CPS and CCEL programs, it is crucial for at-risk youth who need purposefully crafted work placements to maximize their chances of experiencing a meaningful work-related experience.

Conclusion

Evident from our review of the STW policy context in Canada and our analysis of documents from Ontario, there exist many initiatives and programs to support youth in transition across the nation. The continued development of new policies further suggests that STW is an active policy area for government, at both national and provincial levels. Through our analysis of two focal documents from Ontario, the CPS and CCEL, we denote alignments between policy statements, mandates, and programs using four characteristics of supportive STW transition models that have been identified in previous research (DeLuca et al., 2015). Specifically, these two policies articulate various strategies that attend to (a) agency and self-advocacy within contexts of school, family and peers; (b) tracking of student progress and enable differentiated pathways into school and work; (c) "built-in" partnerships between school and work (e.g., cooperative education placements); and (d) purposeful development to provide students with meaningful skills/knowledge intended for meaningful work.

Based on our earlier work and the research of others (Cardoso & Moreira 2009; Perreira et al. 2007; Smyth et al. 2001; Ziguras 2006), we know that these characteristics facilitate resilient contexts for emerging adults in transition and support mobility toward positive labor market attachment in Canada and in other countries. Policies help shape contexts of resilience (Schoon & Bynner 2003; Ungar, 2005). Discourses, mandates, and programs articulated through policies provide the backbone for enabling productive transitions for our youth. The two K–12 "across the grade and subject area" policies examined in this chapter reflect a growing policy trend in Canada and other nations, for example, England (MacDonald, Britton, Ellis, Stewart, & Neary, 2019), Finland (Felt et al., 2019), and Korea (Lee, Jeong, Lee, Kim, & Kim, 2019) where implementing youth transition policy and programming moves beyond that of the traditional guidance counsellor to include a broader range of educators and community partners working in many different roles and contexts. This brings about challenges in enabling effective contexts for emerging adults transition due to the multiple stakeholders involved in interpreting the requirements of the policy.

Accordingly, in Ontario, school administration needs to be confident that CPS and CCEL policies are being interpreted and implemented to best meet the needs of *all* students within the school. As Ball, Maguire, Braun, and Hoskins (2011) remind us, we need to understand how individuals and their organizational roles are combining to make such policies happen. Consequently, we suggest a number of considerations are important. First, the availability of an engaged educator coordinator who is able to facilitate appropriately matched work placement and experiential learning opportunities that are aligned to individual student needs and interests is crucial. Second, careful consideration needs to be made of the evidence-gathering processes undertaken by students as they create their IPP or undertake the ELAR process. In particular, the ELAR process is highly metacognitive and academic in its approach. Consequently, it is not theoretically well placed to meet the needs of lower-achieving youth. We urge further consideration of revised assessment protocols that are vocationally competence-based.

Third, research has shown (e.g., Hutchinson et al., 2011) that matching vocational education programming (e.g., cooperative education and career education) with individual student needs is crucial to effectively support *all* students, including those students who are at-risk or have disabilities. The shift toward K–12 transition policies is creating increasingly complex policy arenas. Within such arenas, assessable and additional student support services (e.g., careers advisors, social workers, and guidance counselors) could enhance the work of educators and community partners in responding to the many facets that contribute to making successful STW transition so difficult for some youth.

In Canadian mainstream education, there has been increased policy focus on the role of career education as a mechanism to support student transitions. Two important frameworks have been endorsed by ministers of public and postsecondary education: *Future in Focus—Atlantic Career Development Framework for Public Education: 2015-2020* (Council of Atlantic Ministers of Education and Training, CAMET, 2015) and *Reference Framework for Successful Student Transitions* (CMEC, 2017). These frameworks, if implemented, could both transform access to career development and provide a sustainable framework that supports smooth transitions to postsecondary destinations (including work) for all students. Given Canada's decentralized system, there is no mechanism at present for holding individual provinces and territories accountable for such outcomes. Subsequently, implementation and evaluation across the diverse regions and student cohorts across Canada remain the potential weak links. We conclude that aligned and coherent interpretation of both CPS and CCEL and other K–12 transition policies is essential to (a) initiate effective working practices with multiple stakeholders and (b) explicitly signpost programming that matches student needs. We deem both as vital in facilitating appropriate support for effective student postsecondary transitions through the implementation of career/life planning, experiential learning, and other STW transition policies.

References

Ball, S. J., Maguire, M., Braun, A., & Hoskins, K. (2011). Policy actors: Doing policy work in schools. *Discourse, 32*(4), 625–639.

Bandura, A., Barbaranelli, C., Vittorio Caprara, G., & Pastorelli, C. (2001). Self-efficacy beliefs as shapers of children's aspirations and career trajectories. *Child Development, 72*, 187–206.

Bell, D., Benes, K., & Redekopp, D. (2016). *Improving the school-to-work transitions of youth in Canada: A scoping review*. Ottawa, ON: The Canadian Career Development Foundation.

Canadian Chamber of Commerce. (2014). A battle we can't afford to lose: getting young Canadians from education to employment. Retrieved from http://www.chamber.ca/media/blog/141014-a-battle-we-cant-afford-to-lose-getting-young-canadians-from-education-to-employment/

Canadian Council on Learning. (2009). *The impact of experiential learning programs on student success*. Ottawa, ON: Ontario Ministry of Education.

Cardoso, P., & Moreira, J. M. (2009). Self-efficacy beliefs and the relation between career planning and perception of barriers. *International Journal for Educational and Vocational Guidance, 9*, 177–188.

Conference Board of Canada. (2013, June). The need to make skills work: The cost of Ontario's skills gap. Retrieved from https://www.conferenceboard.ca/infographics/skills-gap-info.aspx

Council of Atlantic Ministers of Education and Training. (2015). Future in focus: Atlantic career development framework for public education: 2015–2020. Retrieved from https://www.princeedwardisland.ca/sites/default/files/publications/eelc_future_in_focus_camet.pdf

Council of Ministers of Education of Canada. (2017). CMEC reference framework for successful student transitions. Retrieved from https://www.cmec.ca/Publications/Lists/Publications/Attachments/372/CMEC-Reference-Framework-for-Successful-Student-Transitions-EN.pdf

DeLuca, C., Godden, L., Hutchinson, N. L., & Versnel, J. (2015). Preparing at-risk youth for a changing world: Revisiting a person-in-context model for transition to employment. *Educational Research, 57*(2), 182–200.

European Training Foundation (ETF). (2008). *Transition for education to work in EU neighbouring countries*. Luxemburg: Author.

Foster, K. (2012, October). Youth employment and un(der) employment in Canada: More than a temporary problem? *Canadian Centre for Policy Alternatives*. Retrieved from https://www.policyalternatives.ca/sites/default/files/uploads/publications/National%20Office/2012/10/Youth%20Unemployment.pdf

Government of Canada. (2016). Youth employment strategy. Retrieved from http://www.esdc.gc.ca/en/funding/youth_employment_strategy.page

Government of Canada. (2019). First nations and Inuit skills link program. Retrieved from: https://www.canada.ca/en/employment-social-development/services/funding/youth-employment-strategy/skills-link.html

Demereth, P., Lynch, J., & Davidson, M. (2008). Dimensions of psychological capital in a U.S. suburb and high School: Identities for neoliberal times. *Anthropology & Education Quarterly, 39*, 270–292.

Felt, T., Heinivirta, K., Heinonen, V., Kettunen, J., Toni, A., & Vuorinen, R. (2019). *Leading career development services into an uncertain future: Ensuring access, integration and innovation*. Finland country paper presented at the International Centre for Career Development and Public Policy International Symposium, Norway. Retrieved from https://www.kompetansenorge.no/globalassets/iccdpp/finland-country-paper-is2019.pdf

Hatch, T., Shelton, T., & Monk, G. (2009). Making the invisible visible: School counselors empowering students with disabilities through self-advocacy training. *Journal of School Counseling, 7*, 1–14.

Howard, K. A. S., & Solberg, V. S. (2006). School-based social justice: The achieving success identity pathways program. *Professional School Counseling, 94*(4), 278–287.

Hutchinson, J., & Kettlewell, K. (2015). Education to employment: Complicated transitions in a changing world (Editorial). *Educational Research, 57*(2), 113–120.

Hutchinson, N. L., Versnel J., Poth, C., Berg, D., deLugt, J., Dalton, C. J., Chin, P., & Munby, H. (2011). "They want to come to school": Work-based education programs to prevent the social exclusion of vulnerable youth. *Work, 40*(2011), 195–209.

International Labour Office. (2013). *Global employment trends for youth 2013.* Retrieved from http://www.ilo.org/wcmsp5/groups/public/---dgreports/---dcomm/documents/publication/wcms_212423.pdf

Kutsyuruba, B., Burgess, D., Walker, K., & Donlevy, J. K. (2013). *A guide to Ontario school law.* Kingston, ON: Turning Point Global.

Lee, J-Y., Jeong, J., Lee, D., Kim, H. J., & Kim, N. (2019). *Leading career development services into an uncertain future: Ensuring access, integration and innovation. Korea country paper presented at the International Centre for Career Development and Public Policy International Symposium*, Norway. Retrieved from https://www.kompetansenorge.no/globalassets/iccdpp/iccdpp2019-country-paper-korea.pdf

MacDonald, C., Britton, A., Ellis, J., Stewart, S., & Neary, S. (2019). *Leading career development services into an uncertain future: Ensuring access, integration and innovation. England country paper presented at the International Centre for Career Development and Public Policy International Symposium*, Norway. Retrieved from https://www.kompetansenorge.no/globalassets/iccdpp/england-country-paper-iccdpp2019.pdf

Mawn, L., Oliver, E. J., Akhter, N., Bambra, C. L., Torgerson, C., Bridle, C., & Stain, H. J. (2017). Are we failing young people not in employment, education or training (NEETs)? A systematic review and meta-analysis of re-engagement interventions. *Systematic Reviews, 6*, 16–26.

Miller, F. A., & Alvarado, K. (2005). Incorporating documents into qualitative nursing research. *Journal of Nursing Scholarship, 37*(4), 348–353.

OECD. (2000). *From initial education to working life: Making transitions work.* Paris, France: Author.

OECD. (2014). *Education at a glance 2014: OECD indicators.* Retrieved from http://www.oecd-ilibrary.org/education/education-at-a-glance-2014_eag-2014-en

Ontario Ministry of Advanced Education and Skills Development. (2017). Ontario Labour Market Statistics, February 2016. Retrieved from https://www150.statcan.gc.ca/n1/daily-quotidien/160311/dq160311a-eng.htm

Ontario Ministry of Education. (2000). Cooperative education and other forms of experiential learning: policies and procedures for Ontario secondary schools. Retrieved from http://www.edu.gov.on.ca/eng/document/curricul/secondary/coop/cooped.pdf

Ontario Ministry of Education. (2010). Growing success: assessment, evaluation, and reporting in Ontario schools, first edition covering grades 1 to 12. Retrieved from http://www.edu.gov.on.ca/eng/policyfunding/growSuccess.pdf

Ontario Ministry of Education. (2013a). Creating Pathways to Success: An education and career/life planning program for Ontario schools. Retrieved from: http://www.edu.gov.on.ca/eng/document/policy/cps/creatingpathwayssuccess.pdf

Ontario Ministry of Education. (2013b). Results-based plan briefing book 2013–2014. (ISSN#1718-6463). Retrieved from http://www.children.gov.on.ca/htdocs/English/documents/about/Results_2013-2014.pdf

Ontario Ministry of Education. (2014). Stepping up: A strategic framework to help Ontario's youth succeed. Retrieved from http://www.children.gov.on.ca/htdocs/English/professionals/steppingup/contents.aspx

Ontario Ministry of Education. (2016). Community-connected experiential learning: A policy framework for Ontario schools, kindergarten to grade 12. (Draft for consultation). Retrieved from http://edu.gov.on.ca/eng/general/elemsec/job/passport/CommunityConnected_ExperientialLearningEng.pdf

Ontario Ministry of Education. (2019). Education in Ontario. Retrieved from https://www.ontario.ca/page/education-ontario#section-6

Perreira, K. M., Mullen Harris, K., & Lee, D. (2007). Immigrant youth in the labor market. *Work and Occupations, 34*, 5–34.

Prior, L. (2003). *Using documents in social research*. London, England: SAGE.

Prior, L. (2008). Document Analysis. In L. M. Given (Ed.) *The SAGE encyclopedia of qualitative research methods*. (pp. 230–232) Thousand Oaks, CA: SAGE.

Rojewski, J. W., & Yang, B. (1997). Longitudinal analysis of select influences on adolescents' occupational aspirations. *Journal of Vocational Behavior, 51*, 375–410.

Scarpetta, S., Sonnett, A., & Manfredi, T. (2010). *Rising youth unemployment during the crisis: How to prevent negative long-term consequences on a generation?* Paris, France: OECD.

Schoon, I., & Bynner, J. (2003). Risk and resilience in the life course: Implications for interventions and social policies. *Journal of Youth Studies, 6*, 21–31.

Schoon, I., & Parsons, S. (2002). Competence in the face of adversity: The influence of early family environment and long-term consequences. *Children & Society, 16*, 260–272.

Smyth, E. M., Gangl, D., Raffe, D., Hannan, D., & McCoy, S. (2001). A comparative analysis of transitions from education to work in Europe (CATEWE). Retrieved from https://www.researchgate.net/publication/234760045_A_Comparative_Analysis_of_Transitions_from_Education_to_Work_in_Europe_CATEWE_Final_Report_and_Annex_to_the_Final_Report

Spielhofer, T., Benton, T., Evans, K., Featherstone, G., Golden, S., Nelson, J., & Smith, P. (2009). Increasing Participation understanding young people who do not participate in education or training at 16 and 17. *National Foundation for Educational Research*. Retrieved from https://www.nfer.ac.uk/publications/PEJ01/PEJ01.pdf

Statistics Canada. (2016, February). Labour force survey, February 2016. Retrieved from http://www.statcan.gc.ca/daily-quotidien/160311/dq160311a-eng.htm

Statistics Canada. (2016, June). Labour force survey, June 2016. Retrieved from http://www.statcan.gc.ca/daily-quotidien/160805/dq160805a-eng.htm?HPA=1&indid=3587-2&indgeo=0.

Ungar, M. (2005). Pathways to resilience among children in child welfare, corrections, mental health, and educational settings: Navigation and negotiation. *Child and Youth Care Forum, 34*(6), 423–442.

Ziguras, S. (2006). Labour market transitions and risks of exclusion. *Australian Bulletin of Labour, 32*(3), 203–226.

Appendix 8.A Tracking of Student Progress to Enable Differentiated Pathways

	Student Progress	Differentiated Pathways	Context
Creating Pathways to Success	• As students document and reflect on their experiences and learning, discuss what they are learning, and weigh their options for next steps, their competence in education and career/life planning grows (p. 16). • The "All About Me" portfolio in Kindergarten to Grade 6 and the Individual Pathways Plan (IPP) in Grades 7 to 12 provide a structure for, and serve as a record of, this learning process (p. 16). • Students capture evidence related to the four areas of learning for their portfolio or IPP in all their subjects or courses at school and in various endeavours and activities at home and in the community (p. 16). • The portfolio and the IPP could inform parent interviews and student-led conferences at which students share and reflect on their learning (p. 16).	• The twice-yearly review can be conducted in a variety of ways, including an individual interview or presentation or a student-led teacher/parent conference or, if the student wishes, a small-group presentation or seminar that may also involve peers (p. 17). • Through this collaborative process, parents and teachers gain insight into the options students are considering, the challenges they face, the learning opportunities they have identified, and the plans they have started to develop (p. 17). • All students to have information about the types of courses offered, and how best to design their personal secondary school program based on their interests, strength, needs, and aspirations. • Specialized programs and board-wide programs, extracurricular activities, and additional support programs (p. 22).	• Students • Parents • Teachers • Guidance counselors • Principals/ administrators
	• Both these tools can also help students manage key transitions (p. 17). • Students must be given the opportunity to review and share evidence of their developing knowledge and skills at least twice a year with their teacher and, where possible, their parents (p. 17).	• Strategies for completing the community involvement requirement (p. 22). • The full range of postsecondary opportunities (apprenticeship training, college, community living, university, and the workplace) (p. 22).	

	Student Progress	Differentiated Pathways	Context
Community Connected Experiential Learning	• To improve student outcomes, assessment and evaluation procedures and practices must align with the principles outlined in Growing Success: Assessment, Evaluation, and Reporting in Ontario Schools (Ontario Ministry of Education, 2010) (p. 19) • Student success in all community-connected experiential learning opportunities requires the establishment of clear learning goals and success criteria that are tied to the expectations of the learning opportunity (p. 19) • When determining a grade, educators should consider evidence of student learning gleaned through conversation, observation, and the completion of products or performances (p. 20) • Gathering evidence of student learning from multiple and varied sources ensures that evaluation will be both valid and reliable and will most accurately reflect the learning that has occurred through the experiential learning opportunity (p. 20)	• Expanding "learning opportunities outside the school to include community-based, civic, humanitarian, scientific, and artistic activities, as well as cross-cultural and international experiences (p. 4). • Creating and sustaining authentic community connections is essential in order to provide students with rich opportunities, appropriate to their age and stage of development, that will deepen their understanding of the curriculum, inspire them to explore learning beyond the curriculum, and enable them to apply their learning in varied, engaging environments (p. 11). • Innovative technologies allow for more equitable access to experiential learning opportunities by removing barriers to participation that may have stood in the way of some students, including those living in remote areas and those with special education needs (p. 18).	• Students • Parents • Community partners • Teachers

Appendix 8.B Partnerships Between School and Work

	Partnerships With Employers	Work-Related Learning	Context
Creating Pathways to Success	• The IPP must include evidence of the student's investigations that addresses the four areas of learning . . .[and] may include . . . presentations about postsecondary education and training by . . . *workplace representatives* (p. 23). • The principal is responsible for ensuring the coordination and development of any transition plan required for students with special education needs. *In the case of the transition from secondary school to work* . . . this could include making provisions to help the student connect with . . . community agencies, and/or the workplace, as appropriate (p. 24).	• The IPP, starting in Grade 10, requires students to record: Their initial post-secondary destination (e.g., with respect to education, training, *the workplace*, or community living) (p. 23). • Most students have their initial *employment experiences* while they are in elementary or secondary school. These early experiences provide rich opportunities for students to develop self-awareness with respect to their skills, strengths, and interests and the kind of work they like to do, as well as an awareness of the *world of work* (p. 34).	• Students • Employers • Workplace representatives • Teachers • Principals/ administrators

SECTION 3

SCHOOL EXPERIENCES

9

School Experiences and Postschool Pathways in the Republic of Ireland

Emer Smyth and Selina McCoy

Introduction

There is a large body of international research that examines the way in which gender and social class background influence the postschool destinations of young adults (also called emerging adults) and the extent to which these differences operate indirectly through academic achievement or directly through differences in aspirations and expectations. However, comparatively little attention has been paid to the way in which schools can shape young people's postschool pathways. This chapter draws on a mixed-methods longitudinal study (McCoy et al., 2014) of a cohort of young people in the Republic of Ireland (hereafter "Ireland") who were followed from their entry to secondary education to their outcomes three to four years after completing upper secondary education. The chapter explores the extent to which the social composition of the school shapes young people's postschool outcomes and whether other factors such as school climate can play a role, particularly in channeling young people toward (or away from) higher education (HE).

School Influences on Postschool Pathways

In spite of some commentators emphasizing the increasing fragmentation and individualization of transition pathways (see, e.g., Beck, 1992), there is consistent evidence that social background characteristics and gender continue to influence the routes taken by young people upon leaving school. Studies point to the continued advantage of middle-class young people in securing entry to HE and to the most prestigious institutions and fields of study within that sector (Sullivan et al., 2011; Boliver, 2011). Changes in the nature of gender inequality have been more marked than shifts in social differentiation, with

Emer Smyth and Selina McCoy, *School Experiences and Postschool Pathways in the Republic of Ireland* In: *Young Adult Development at the School-to-Work Transition.* E. Anne Marshall and Jennifer E. Symonds, Oxford University Press (2021).
 DOI: 10.1093/oso/9780190941512.003.0009.

female tertiary education participation rates now outstripping those of males in most Western countries (DiPrete & Buchmann, 2013). However, gender differences in early labor market outcomes remain evident, with higher unemployment rates among young women in many countries and the persistence of occupational segregation by gender (Blossfeld et al., 2015.).

The schooling system plays a crucial role in shaping these postschool trajectories. In systems with a differentiation between academic and vocational tracks, as in Germany, early selection is found to be influenced by social class background and by teacher recommendation (Breen & Jonsson, 2005). In contrast, in systems where subject choice and/or examination grades matter for access to education, training, and employment, as in Ireland, Scotland, and England, schools can influence young people's opportunities through the subjects they provide and the quality of learning experience offered (Iannelli, 2013). However, relatively few studies have sought to unpack the direct and indirect influences of the individual school attended on postschool pathways. The exceptions to this lacuna largely center on the adaptation of Bourdieu's notion of habitus to describe the way in which certain options (such as HE) become "unthinkable" for young people in more disadvantaged schools (see Reay et al., 2001, 2005). McDonough's (1997) study carefully delineated the way in which two U.S. high schools shaped the expectations of students regarding college entry. These schools each had a distinct "institutional habitus" where college assumed a taken-for-granted status for the student population, and these expectations were facilitated through the provision of more advanced level subjects along with educational advice and guidance. In this way, assumptions about the social composition of the school were firmly embedded in school practices, which enhanced the chances of students achieving the goal of HE entry. Taking a cross-national perspective, research by Iannelli (2004) pointed to the way in young people's postschool destinations in Scotland, Ireland, and the Netherlands were influenced by the individual school they attended. Further research on Ireland showed variation between individual schools in the proportion of students applying to HE, differences that reflected academic expectations at the school level and the amount of time devoted to career guidance (Smyth & Hannan, 2007).

The concept of institutional habitus has not been without critique. Atkinson (2011) highlights the way in which the concept glosses over potential internal differentiation within the school. In addition, Donnelly (2015) argues for the need to incorporate insights from school effectiveness research and suggests that the relationship between the characteristics of the student population and the school culture is not as simple as assumed by those using the habitus perspective.

This chapter builds upon this research by using survey and interview material to show the extent to which the social mix of the school results in a distinctive habitus, which shapes postschool pathways, particularly entry to HE. In doing so, it also takes account of the fact that different students in the same school may have very different learning experiences. Furthermore, the longitudinal nature of the study allows for the exploration of the extent to which these broader school experiences, particularly the nature of teacher–student relationships, influence subsequent trajectories.

The Irish Educational and Postschool Landscape

Secondary education in Ireland consists of a three-year lower secondary program (junior cycle—generally ages 12–13 to 16), followed by an optional Transition Year program and two years of upper secondary education (senior cycle—ages 16–17 to 18). Both lower and upper secondary education culminate in a set of nationally standardized examinations, with Leaving Certificate (upper secondary) grades determining access to HE and to good quality employment. Secondary education can be characterized from a comparative perspective as general or academic in nature (Hannan et al., 1996), with only a small proportion (around 6% of the cohort) taking a separate prevocational upper secondary track, the Leaving Certificate Applied program, which does not facilitate direct access to HE. There is a considerable degree of active school choice in the Irish context, with around half of the cohort not attending their nearest or most accessible school (Hannan et al., 1996). As a result, schools vary significantly in the social background and prior achievement levels of their student body. Due to the persistence of a significant single-sex sector in Irish education, schools also differ in their gender composition. The extent to which variation in school social mix leads to a distinctive institutional habitus in particular schools is explored in the remainder of the chapter.

Over time, higher (tertiary) education has become the dominant postschool pathway in Ireland (Department of Education and Skills, 2013). Within Irish HE, there are two main types of institutions: universities and institutes of technology.[1] There are now eight institutions with university status while the university structure also encompasses recognized colleges, including colleges of education and art colleges. From the late 1960s, Regional Technical Colleges were set up to offer subdegree courses in technical areas; these colleges were

[1] Since the Leaving School in Ireland study was conducted, a new model, the technological university, has been introduced. At the time of writing, one such university has been designated.

intended to cater to regional labor markets and promote economic development at the local level (Clancy, 2008). Over the period 1992 to 2006, these colleges were redesignated as Institutes of Technology, of which there are now 13, and their function has evolved considerably in that they now offer degree and postgraduate degree courses across a range of disciplines. In addition to universities and institutes of technology, there are several private colleges that provide degree-level courses.

Other options open to school-leavers include further education and direct labor market entry. Further education is comprised of Post-Leaving Certificate (PLC) courses and apprenticeship (McGuinness et al., 2014). PLC courses vary from one to three years and are provided in further education colleges and secondary schools. PLC qualifications can lead directly to employment or be used to access (some) HE courses. The national apprenticeship system has a legislative basis and is organized around competency-based standards with a modular structure leading to a recognized qualification. The apprenticeship combines periods of on-the-job and off-the-job learning and the apprentice is employed by an approved employer.[2] Apprenticeships had been largely confined to traditionally male craft occupations, mainly in the construction sector, but have recently been the subject of reform to expand the domains they cover; the number of new entrants to apprenticeships decreased significantly over the course of the recession. The cohort of young people studied in this chapter left school in 2007 or 2008, a time of increasing labor market uncertainty. As in most other countries, young people in Ireland were particularly negatively affected by the recession (McGinnity et al., 2014). Youth unemployment increased from 9.1% in 2007 to 24% in 2009, peaking at 30.4% in 2012.

Data and Methodology

This chapter draws on data from a longitudinal study of secondary students in 12 case-study schools in Ireland. The 12 schools were selected on the basis of three dimensions identified in a survey of all secondary principals: the school's approach to ability grouping (whether mixed ability or streamed[3] base classes), the timing of subject choice (whether pre- or postentry to secondary schooling, and whether a taster program was provided), and the

[2] Prior to 2016, apprentices received a training allowance while engaged in off-the-job learning; since 2016, apprentices are paid by their employer for the duration of the apprenticeship.

[3] Streamed systems allocate students to higher, middle, or lower streamed classes on the basis of their assessed ability. Students typically take most or all of their subjects within the same class grouping.

degree of emphasis on student integration structures for first-year students. The schools were also chosen to give a good geographical spread. A particular focus in the selection of schools was capturing variation in the social class profile of student intake, given the role of school choice in the Irish context. Two of the schools were middle-class in profile, one of these being a fee-paying school; five of the schools had a mix of students from different social class backgrounds while five of the schools served a predominantly working-class population. During their school career, this cohort of students, who entered secondary education in 2002, completed a questionnaire annually (twice in first year), and groups of students were interviewed to explore their experiences in greater depth. This cohort of young people was surveyed again three to four years after leaving school[4] using a multimode approach (web, post, telephone, or face-to-face contact with an interviewer). The total target sample was 1,251 school-leavers, representing 714 who sat the Leaving Certificate in 2007, with the remaining 537 doing so in 2008. The final sample size achieved was 753, representing a response rate of just over 60%.

To gain a better understanding of the trajectories of young people after school, life-course interviews were conducted with a subset of 27 school-leavers (15 females and 12 males) between the ages of 21 and 23, drawn from those who responded to the survey of school-leavers. The selection of interviewees was based on detailed information from the survey on the young people's educational and work histories; this information was used to construct the main pathways they had pursued on leaving school rather than focusing on outcomes at one point in time only. Five main pathway groups were distinguished: those who entered the labor market directly, those who entered an apprenticeship program, those who pursued a PLC course, those who entered HE following completion of a PLC course, and direct entrants into HE. This chapter draws on both survey and interview data to explore the influence of school factors on young people's postschool trajectories.

School Experiences and Postschool Pathways

The dominant postschool pathway among the young people was HE entry, with 61% of young people in the survey sample taking this route. Over a fifth

[4] The cohort completed secondary education over two school years because many had taken the optional Transition Year program at the end of lower secondary education.

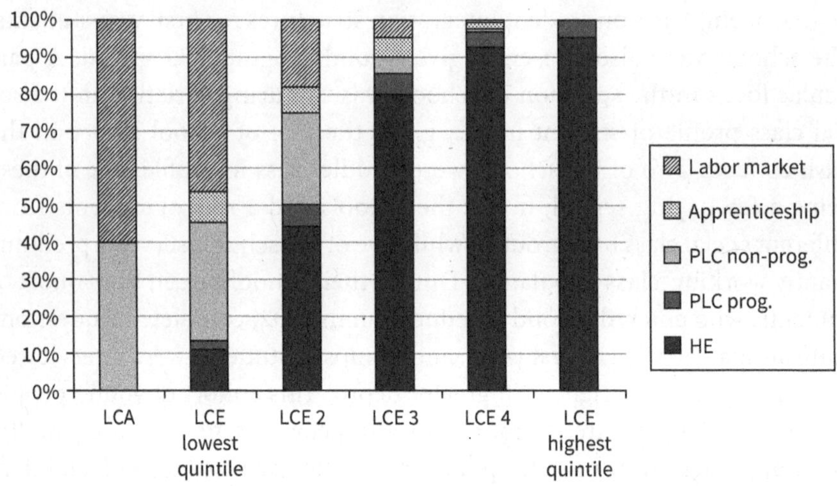

Figure 9.1 Main postschool pathway by Leaving Certificate performance.

(22%) of the group took part in further education (a PLC course or apprenticeship training) while one in six (17%) entered the labor market. None of this group of Leaving Certificate leavers were inactive (outside the labor market) for reasons other than participation in education/training. Young women and men in the sample were equally likely to go on to HE, but other pathways were highly gendered. Young men were significantly more likely to enter the labor market than young women (21% men vs. 14% women). Within further education, males were overrepresented among apprenticeships (8% men vs. 0.5% women) and underrepresented on PLC courses (10% men vs. 26% women).

The high stakes nature of the Leaving Certificate exam in Ireland means that there is a very direct relationship between the grades achieved and the pathways pursued. Figure 9.1 shows the postschool pathways associated with Leaving Certificate Applied (LCA) and different Leaving Certificate Established (LCE) performance levels. Almost all of those in the top quintile (fifth) of Leaving Certificate performance went directly on to HE, with the remainder later entering HE via a PLC course (PLC progression). In contrast, those with low levels of performance (the lowest quintile) and those who took the noncollege bound LCA program were much more likely to enter the labor market directly or, if they continued in education, to take PLC courses. Given that the school attended affects Leaving Certificate grades (Hannan et al., 1996; Smyth, 1999), then school experiences would be expected to play, at the very least, an indirect role in shaping postschool pathways. But do

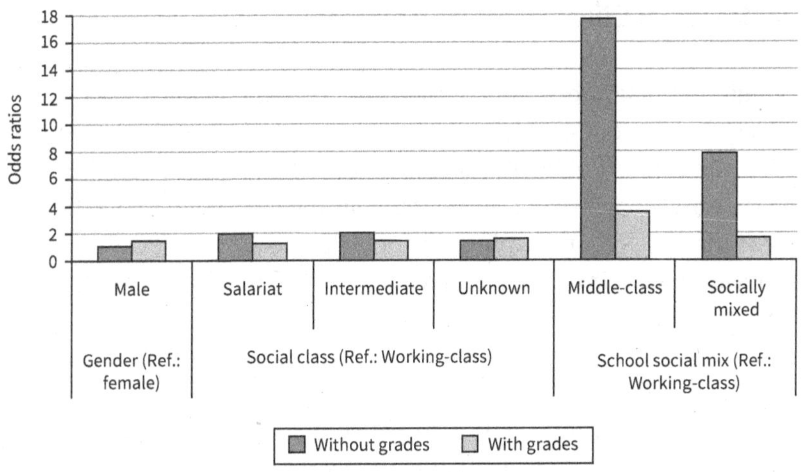

Figure 9.2 Odds ratios of HE entry compared to LM entry by individual and school social class. HE = higher education. LCA = Leaving Certificate Applied. LCE = Leaving Certificate Established. LM = labor market. non-prog. = non-progression. PLC = Post-Leaving Certificate. prog. = progression.

they play a direct role? And what influences does the social class mix of the school have?

Figure 9.2 presents the results of a multilevel model showing the chances of going on to HE compared to the labor market, controlling for gender, migrant status,[5] and having a special educational need, as reported by the young person themselves. The first set of columns shows the influence without taking account of Leaving Certificate (upper secondary) grades while the second set of columns adjusts for exam performance. Young people from the salariat and intermediate classes were around twice as likely as working-class youth to go to HE, with some of this class difference mediated through exam grades. Differences by school social mix were much stronger than those found by individual social class background. Those who attended middle-class schools were 17 times more likely than those from working-class schools to go on to HE while those from socially mixed schools were eight times more likely to do so. Most of the effects of school social mix were mediated through exam grades, although the differences remained substantial (at 3.6 and 1.6 times, respectively) even when these were taken into account.

[5] Because of the relatively small number of immigrant students in the sample, they cannot be disaggregated by length of time in Ireland or by nationality of origin.

Expectational Climate of the School

The longitudinal nature of the study allows us to explore the processes underlying the emergence of distinct orientations to particular pathways in different schools. The concept of institutional habitus is based on the idea that certain routes assume a taken-for-granted status in more middle-class schools (see previous discussion). In keeping with this perspective, our analyses showed that educational aspirations among young people in the study emerged early; aspirations expressed in third year (the final year of lower secondary education) were found to be highly predictive of the actual pathway pursued upon leaving school (Figure 9.3). Over four fifths of those who had aspired to a degree-level qualification went on to HE compared with just over a third of those who expected to go no further than secondary education. Young people who had held lower educational aspirations were much more likely to enter the labor market directly upon leaving school or to enter further education (PLC or apprenticeship). Among labor market entrants, those with lower educational aspirations were found to have higher levels of unemployment three to four years after leaving school than those who had higher aspirations; 53% of those with no educational aspirations to go beyond secondary schooling were unemployed compared with 38% of those who aspired to a degree.

Interviews with the young people highlighted the roles of both family habitus and school habitus in shaping their educational decision-making. In most middle-class families, it was taken for granted that they would go on

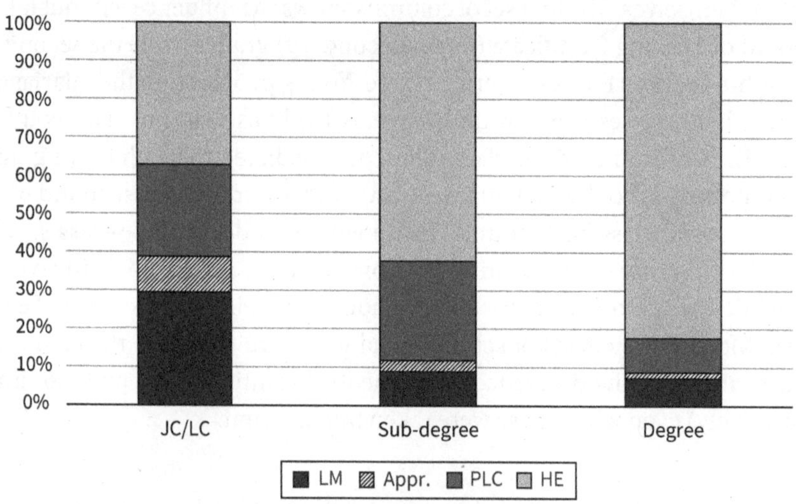

Figure 9.3 Main postschool pathway by educational aspirations in lower secondary education. JC/LC = Junior/Leaving Certificate.

to postschool education. For these young people, going on to further education or HE was seen as a natural progression from school, meaning that decision-making focused on what college[6] or which course to attend rather than *whether* to attend college (see Smyth & Banks, 2012, for similar findings when this group were in their Leaving Certificate year; also see McCoy et al., 2010, for parallel findings on a different group of school-leavers). Denise,[7] who had attended a middle-class school, described how her parents "one hundred percent" thought she should go on to HE. For her, this decision was "expected . . . just kind of like routine. . . . I mean my older brothers did it." Even though Fiona attended a working-class school, her middle-class parents reinforced her own aspirations to go on to HE:

> All I knew is that definitely college was an option. There was no way that I'm not going to college, like I did want to go to college no matter what it was. I never saw it as like okay, this is the end of the road, once I've done my Leaving Cert[ificate] I can now start working, it was always college.

In the in-depth interviews, several young people from working-class backgrounds highlighted the lack of detailed parental knowledge on the college entry process since their parents had not themselves gone on to HE. In these cases, parents "didn't really know a lot about . . . the college process" (Deirdre) while Carol felt that "there should be more information for parents." Dermot, who attended a working-class school, saw his parents as supportive in general but as lacking knowledge as to what was involved:

> I never even discussed college with me parents or anything like that, never, because they're real old fashioned. . . . They left school when they were fourteen, fifteen. . . . So . . . they're happy I'm in college but they don't really understand what college is all about or they know it's obviously good ... but I don't think they know what it takes.

Thus, young people had access to differential resources and information depending on the educational background of their parents. In some instances, the local neighborhood was seen as contributing to the lack of aspirations:

> I think the problem there was that there was a lack of dreams . . . the social dynamic is based around, we'll say to be frank, alcohol, and they're at the local bars there,

[6] Respondents tended to use the term *college* to refer to both HE and PLC institutions.
[7] Pseudonyms are used for the young people interviewed.

> that's where a lot of the socializing would have gone on and that's where a lot of the parents would remain. . . . I think the other lads were unfortunate in the sense that they weren't really told that, you know, you can have these kind of dreams and, you know, push forwards like, and there's nothing stopping you other than yourself. So I think it's not so much that they didn't realize their own dreams, I just think that they may not have had as many of them. (Conall, working-class school)

While these accounts show the role of family habitus in shaping the decision to go on to HE, the concentration of groups of middle-class or working-class young people in particular schools resulted in an institutional habitus, which often reinforced the expectations being fostered at home. Thus, in one of the middle-class schools in the study, high expectations were supported by guidance strategies that involved college visits, assisting with college applications, and contacting college representatives. The guidance counselor in this middle-class school used their social capital to organize tours of the campus and opportunities for students to meet with college staff and students outside of the regular open day schedule:

> They [students] were given a general kind of admissions talk on all the programs and they were then brought off in groups on average of about ten, on tours of the campus, by present students of that institution, and they found that fantastic and they were able to ask the questions. And then they were brought back and certain faculty heads then spoke to them about their own individual faculties and the course on offer. And they were treated to lunch then and brought back.

This approach provided unique information on college life, thus normalizing college entry (Smyth & Banks, 2012).

In working-class schools, students were more dependent on formal guidance provided in school. Throughout their school career, young people in our study relied on their parents as the main source of advice around educational decisions (Smyth, 2016). As they approached the end of lower secondary education, formal guidance through the school guidance counselor assumed an increasingly important role. The extent of reliance on different sources of advice varied by school social mix, with young people attending working-class schools much more likely to see the advice from the guidance counselor as most helpful than those in middle-class schools (see Figure 9.4). In contrast, those in middle-class schools were more likely to see their mothers as the most helpful source of advice.

The greater reliance on school-based guidance in working-class schools served in some instances to reinforce low expectations. In one working-class

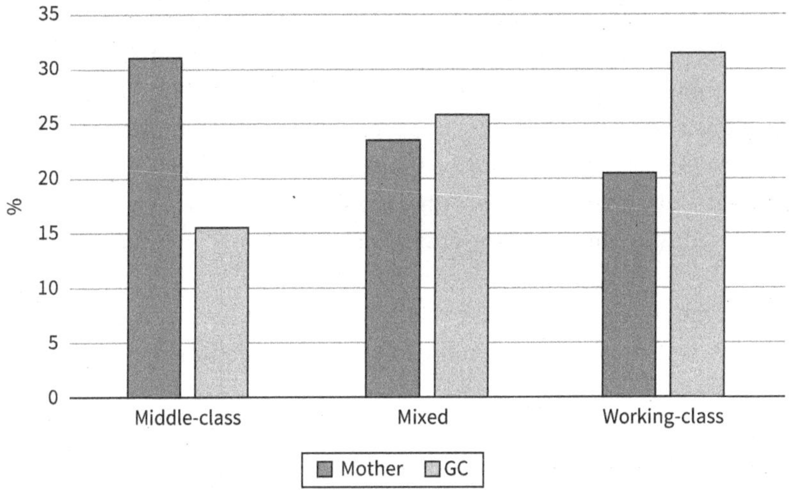

Figure 9.4 Most helpful source of advice on postschool pathways by school social mix. GC = guidance counsellor.

school, students at upper secondary level felt that their guidance counselor was encouraging them to go on to further education rather than HE. Students described feeling "put down" by the choices suggested to them and felt they were being encouraged to be "realistic" in their goals rather than applying for HE (Smyth & Banks, 2012):

> The career guidance counsellor always puts us down as well . . . she says "I don't think . . . you have to be realistic [name of student]," I go "what do you mean realistic, that's what I want, I'll work for them points if that's what I want to do." "Ah but you have to be realistic, why don't you go for this [a PLC course]?" I don't want to go for that like. (Working-class school)

Low expectations were also evident in how staff at the school blurred the boundaries between further education and HE in discussing postschool options by using the term *college*. The guidance counselor used the term *college* for any education where students go "a little bit further": "Going to college is important for them, college is, so they can take pride in going a little bit further and getting a good qualification." However, this does not recognize the real difference in life chances resulting from a degree as opposed to a further education qualification.

In the same school, Fiona described how the low expectations of teachers were expressed in day-to-day interaction as well as through formal guidance:

> I think it's also like the school that we went to . . . like you'd have expectations but it's not like high expectations, you know, it wouldn't be the thing of like "okay, try to all be doctors or try to all be lawyers" and things like that, it was kind of like "okay, just get past your Leaving Cert or just get past your Junior Cert," kind of attitude, you know. So I don't think a lot of the students that were in my class even thought of college as like an option. . . . But [there was] no drive [from the teachers] to say like you can do it. (Fiona, working-class school)

The theme of teacher–student relationships, and their role in shaping expectations, is further explored in the following subsection.

The Social Climate of the School

Relationships between teachers and students are a key component of the social landscape of a school (Roorda et al., 2011; Martin & Dowson, 2009).[8] Throughout their secondary school career, young people in the study cohort were asked a number of questions about the nature of their interaction with teachers. These questions formed two scales: positive interaction, which assessed the frequency with which students received praise or positive feedback from teachers, and negative interaction, which measured the frequency with which students were reprimanded or told off by teachers either in relation to schoolwork or for misbehavior. No social class differences were found in levels of positive interaction with teachers. However, young people from working-class and nonemployed backgrounds experienced much higher levels of negative feedback from their teachers than from their middle-class peers. Furthermore, schools with a concentration of working-class students had quite different school climates than other schools, having greater levels of both positive and negative interaction, suggesting greater surveillance, positive and negative, in working-class schools.

The quality of teacher–student relationships was found to have both direct and indirect effects on postschool pathways. Praise and positive feedback from teachers were associated with enhanced academic self-image while frequent reprimands were associated with reduced academic self-image; academic self-image, in turn, influenced educational aspirations. Taking account

[8] Relations with peers are also a key component of the school climate, but the focus in this chapter is on relations with teachers and their variation by school social class mix. The broader study upon which this chapter draws examines the role of peers in decision-making (McCoy et al., 2014), complementing earlier research on the same cohort which highlighted the role of bullying and class disruption by peers in early school-leaving (Byrne, Smyth, 2010).

of a range of other background and school factors, young people who had experienced negative interaction with their teachers in second year received lower grades on the Junior Certificate exam taken at the end of third year (Smyth et al., 2008). This influence persisted even when taking into account the extent of negative teacher–student interaction in third year, suggesting that second year is a crucial period in setting the tone for student–teacher relations. Interestingly, the level of positive interaction with teachers did not explain variation in exam performance, indicating that the prevalence of negative interaction is a stronger driver of (under)performance than positive interaction. Thus, negative teacher–student relations had an indirect effect on postschool pathways through their influence on academic self-confidence and grades. However, a direct effect was also evident. Even taking into account young people's social class background and prior achievement levels, labor market entrants were found to have had significantly higher levels of negative interaction with teachers during lower and upper secondary education than HE, PLC, and apprenticeship entrants. Thus, negative relationships with teachers emerged as discouraging young people from pursuing postschool education and training of any kind and this effect was even stronger in relation to HE entry.

The Academic Climate of the School

As well as providing guidance geared toward college entry, McDonough (1997) highlights the way in which more middle-class schools provide the kinds of advanced learning opportunities that facilitate the transition to postschool education. In Irish secondary education, students take subjects at higher or ordinary level (with a further foundation level in English, math, and Irish). The influence of the school's approach to ability grouping as well as the interaction of teacher and student expectations resulted in marked differences in the number of higher-level subjects studied according to the social composition of the school. In the lower secondary exam, students in working-class schools[9] took an average of 3.2 higher level subjects compared to 6.3 in socially mixed schools and 7.5 in middle-class schools. Differences by school social class mix remain evident even taking account of reading and math test scores on entry to secondary education (see Smyth et al., 2008).

[9] These figures relate to the cohort in this chapter who went on to complete upper secondary education. Between-school differences are even greater when those who left school early are included in the averages.

To what extent then did early educational success play a role in channeling young people toward or away from HE? Figure 9.5 shows the predicted likelihood of going on to HE by lower secondary (Junior Certificate) grade point average. Junior Certificate grade point average takes account of both the grade achieved and the level taken in the subject. All else being equal, those who took a large number of higher-level subjects are almost all predicted to go on to HE, irrespective of the composition of the school they attended. However, looking at those with a fairly low to medium number of higher level subjects, school social class mix makes a very significant difference, with much higher rates of HE transition among those who had attended middle-class schools, reflecting the taken-for-granted nature of college entry for this group. Thus, for example, among those taking three higher level subjects, 41% of students from middle-class schools are predicted to go on to HE compared with 22% of those from socially mixed schools and just 9% from working-class schools.

The number of higher level subjects studied at lower secondary level was found to have a direct effect on access to higher level subjects at upper secondary level and therefore on the points awarded to students for the purposes of HE entry. Young people attending middle-class schools took an average of 4.5 higher level subjects for the Leaving Certificate compared with 3.9 for those from socially mixed schools and 1.4 for those from working-class schools. This pattern therefore influenced whether they could access HE, what kind of institution they attended (university or institute of technology), and the type of course (field of study) entered.

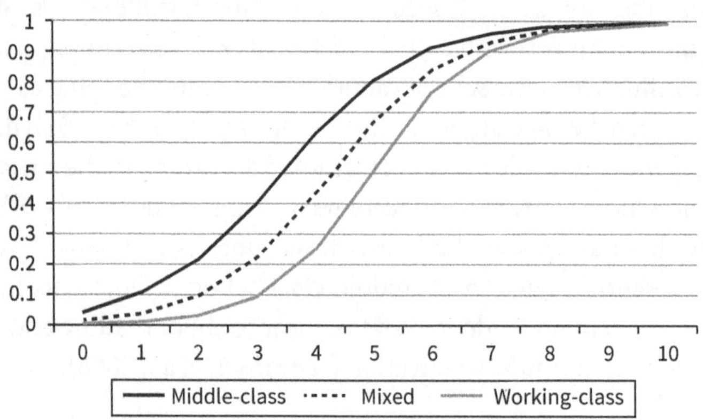

Figure 9.5 Predicted probability of higher education entry by lower secondary (Junior Certificate) grade point average and school social mix. Controls for individual social class, gender, migrant status, and having a special educational need.

Conclusions

In keeping with previous international research, the study findings show that the main pathways taken by young adults in Ireland reflected their gender, social class background, and academic performance. However, the analyses go further than previous work by indicating the way in which the nature of postschool transitions is firmly embedded in earlier school experiences. In particular, the chapter contributes to the ongoing debate on the effects of school composition to show that school social mix has a very significant impact on postschool outcomes, with those who attended middle-class schools having particularly high levels of participation in HE. In contrast, young people who had attended working-class schools are much more likely than those in middle-class or socially mixed schools to enter the labor market directly upon leaving school, even taking account of their Leaving Certificate grades.

Educational decision-making reflects family habitus, with parental expectations and encouragement found to be associated with the likelihood of going on to HE. Over and above the influence of family background, school social class mix is found to have a strong influence on postschool transitions. This influence operates through three aspects of school culture: the expectational climate, the social climate, and the academic climate. Educational aspirations are formed as early as lower secondary education, remaining relatively stable thereafter, and are highly predictive of the actual routes taken two to three years later. These aspirations are not only influenced by parental expectations but also by the way in which the institutional habitus is expressed through formal and informal guidance within the school. The quality of teacher–student relationships plays an important role, with negative relations with teachers serving to discourage young people from remaining on in any form of education/training. Schools differ too in the extent to which they facilitate and encourage students taking subjects at a higher level; the number of higher level subjects studied is an important reflection as well as a driver of educational success and serves to channel young people in more middle-class schools into college-bound pathways. The findings therefore illustrate the value of the concept of institutional habitus in capturing the way in which assumptions based on the social composition of the school are embedded in school practices and culture. At the same time, some differences are evident among students in the same school in terms of their gender, level of engagement, and aspirations for the future, reflecting the need to take account of the potential heterogeneity of school cultures (see Atkinson, 2011). Even among schools with similar profiles, school practice and climate can vary (Donnelly,

2015), with, for example, significant variation among socially mixed schools in the number of higher level subjects taken by students (Smyth et al., 2008).

The findings presented in this chapter highlight the importance of locating an analysis of youth transitions within the context of an understanding of school effects and effectiveness. They show the complex way in which individual social class background and school social mix can interact to shape very different pathways for young people leaving school. In a context such as Ireland, with relatively high employment and earning returns to tertiary qualifications, this pattern has very significant consequences for the reproduction of social inequality across generations.

References

Atkinson, W. (2011). From sociological fictions to social fictions: Some Bourdieusian reflections on the concepts of "institutional habitus" and "family habitus." *British Journal of Sociology of Education, 32*(3), 331–347.

Beck, U. (1992). *Risk society: Towards a new modernity.* London, England: SAGE.

Blossfeld, H. P., Skopek, J., Triventi, M., & Buchholz, S. (Eds.). (2015). *Gender, education and employment: An international comparison of school-to-work transitions.* Cheltenham, England: Edward Elgar.

Boliver, V. (2011). Expansion, differentiation, and the persistence of social class inequalities in British higher education. *Higher Education, 61*(3), 229–242.

Breen, R., & Jonsson, J. O. (2005). Inequality of opportunity in comparative perspective: Recent research on educational attainment and social mobility. *Annual Review of Sociology, 31,* 223–243.

Byrne, D., & Smyth, E. (2010). *No way back? The dynamics of early school leaving.* Dublin, Ireland: Liffey Press/ESRI.

Clancy, P. (2008). The non-university sector in Irish higher education. In J. S. Taylor, B. S. Ferreira, M. L. Machado, & R. Santiago (Eds.), *Non-university higher education in Europe* (pp. 123–145). Amsterdam, The Netherlands: Springer.

Department of Education and Skills. (2013). *Supporting a better transition from second level to higher education.* Dublin, Ireland: Author.

DiPrete, T. A., & Buchmann, C. (2013). *The rise of women: The growing gender gap in education and what it means for American schools.* New York, NY: Russell Sage Foundation.

Donnelly, M. (2015). A new approach to researching school effects on higher education participation. *British Journal of Sociology of Education, 36*(7), 1073–1090.

Hannan, D., Raffe, D., & Smyth, E. (1996). *Cross-national research on school to work transitions: An analytical framework.* Paris, France: OECD.

Hannan, D. F., Smyth, E., McCullagh, J., O'Leary, R., & McMahon, D. (1996). *Coeducation and gender equality.* Dublin, Ireland: Oak Tree Press/ESRI.

Iannelli, C. (2004). School variation in youth transitions in Ireland, Scotland and the Netherlands. *Comparative Education, 40*(3), 401–425.

Iannelli, C. (2013). The role of the school curriculum in social mobility. *British Journal of Sociology of Education, 34*(5–6), 907–928.

Martin, A. J., & Dowson, M. (2009). Interpersonal relationships, motivation, engagement, and achievement: Yields for theory, current issues, and educational practice. *Review of Educational Research, 79*(1), 327–365.

McCoy, S., Byrne, D., O'Connell, P., Kelly, E., & Doherty, C. (2010). *Hidden disadvantage? A study of the low participation in higher education by the non-manual group*, Dublin, Ireland: Higher Education Authority.

McCoy, S., Smyth, E., Watson, D., & Darmody, M. (2014). *Leaving school in Ireland: A longitudinal study of post-school transitions*. Dublin, Ireland: ESRI.

McDonough, P. M. (1997). *Choosing colleges: How social class and schools structure opportunity*. New York, NY: SUNY Press.

McGinnity, F., Russell, H., Watson, D., Kingston, G., & Kelly, E. (2014). *Winners and losers? The equality impact of the great recession in Ireland*. Dublin, Ireland: Equality Authority/ESRI.

McGuinness, S., Bergin, A., Kelly, E., McCoy, S., Smyth, E., Whelan, A., & Banks, J. (2014). *Further education and training in Ireland: Past, present and future*. Dublin, Ireland: ESRI/ SOLAS.

Reay, D., David, M., & Ball, S. J. (2005). *Degrees of choice: Social class, race, gender and higher education*. Stoke-on-Trent, England: Trentham Books.

Reay, D., Davies, J., David, M., & Ball, S. (2001). Choices of degree or degrees of choice? Class, "race" and the higher education choice process. *Sociology, 35*(4), 855–874.

Roorda, D. L., Koomen, H. M., Spilt, J. L., & Oort, F. J. (2011). The influence of affective teacher–student relationships on students' school engagement and achievement: A meta-analytic approach. *Review of Educational Research, 81*(4), 493–529.

Smyth, E. (1999). *Do schools differ?* Dublin, Ireland: Oak Tree Press/ESRI.

Smyth, E. (2016). *Students' experiences and perspectives on secondary education: Institutions, transitions and policy*. Basingstoke, England: Palgrave Macmillan.

Smyth, E., & Banks, J. (2012). "There was never really any question of anything else": young people's agency, institutional habitus and the transition to higher education. *British Journal of Sociology of Education, 33*(2), 263–281.

Smyth, E., Dunne, A., Darmody, M., & McCoy, S. (2008). *Gearing up for the exam? The experiences of Junior Certificate students*. Dublin, Ireland: Liffey Press/ESRI.

Smyth, E., & Hannan, C. (2007). School process and the transition to higher education. *Oxford Review of Education, 33*(2), 175–194.

Sullivan, A., Heath, A., & Rothon, C. (2011). Equalisation or inflation? Social class and gender differentials in England and Wales. *Oxford Review of Education, 37*(2), 215–240.

10

Smooth, Staggered, or Stopped?

Educational Transitions in the South African Youth Panel Survey

Kathryn S. Isdale, Vijay Reddy, Lolita D. Winnaar, and Tia Linda Zuze

Introduction

South African learners perform poorly based on both local and international standards (Department of Basic Education, 2012; Ross, Saito, Dolata, Hungi, & Makuwa, 2007). At a country level, a high proportion of young people exit the school system prematurely, but the considerable grade repetition within the education system itself further exacerbates both low average levels of schooling and high educational inequalities (Branson & Lam, 2010; Branson & Zuze, 2012). Understanding educational transitions is vital to address the country's basic skills shortages and improve the life chances of all South African learners.

Efforts to examine in detail young people's educational pathways in South Africa have, however, been hampered by a lack of high-quality, longitudinal data. In response, the first wave of the South African Youth Panel Study (SAYPS) was administered in 2011. SAYPS is a longitudinal panel study based on Grade 9 learners who participated in the Trends in International Mathematics and Science Study (TIMSS) in 2011, designed specifically to examine learners' educational pathways. The study provides the first national longitudinal data collected annually on young people in South Africa, making it possible to study the detail of individual transitions over a consecutive four-year period.

This chapter uses SAYPS to investigate educational transitions and patterns of early school-leaving. We analyze the characteristics of young people with different transition pathways between Grades 9 and 12 and explore key predictors of the various routes taken. Our key objective is to move beyond a simple, cross-sectional definition of school transition and describe in detail the dynamics of learner pathways through the postcompulsory phase of

Kathryn S. Isdale, Vijay Reddy, Lolita D. Winnaar, and Tia Linda Zuze, *Smooth, Staggered, or Stopped?* In: *Young Adult Development at the School-to-Work Transition.* E. Anne Marshall and Jennifer E. Symonds, Oxford University Press (2021).
 DOI: 10.1093/oso/9780190941512.003.0010.

secondary school.[1] We also analyze how those on a "smooth," (i.e., a grade repetition-free) progression differ from young people with more protracted routes through the system to better inform pedagogical practices and policies designed to improve staying-on rates and ease entry into the labor market.

We begin by outlining the current educational context in South Africa and review existing evidence on the various individual-, family-, and school-level factors associated with educational transitions. We describe the data used in the analysis, as well as outline the analytic strategy and some of the issues surrounding missing data and bias in our sample. We then report the results of each stage of the analyses and, subsequently, offer concluding comments and an overview of policy implications.

Background

The South African Context

The 2015 TIMSS reports that South African Grade 9 learners perform poorly in comparison with their international counterparts: Roughly two thirds of students achieve below the minimum benchmark levels set out by TIMSS, denoting the minimal level of competence, and just 1% reaching the advanced level (Reddy et al., 2016). While there have been improvements over the last 20 years, the pace of progress continues to be slow, and overall achievement remains vastly unequal with the wealthiest 20% of schools achieving results far and above the rest of the student population (see also Fiske & Ladd, 2004; Fleisch, 2008; Van der Berg, 2009).

Grade repetition in sub-Saharan Africa is particularly severe with rates often as high as 20% per grade (Lee, Zuze, & Ross, 2005) and becomes increasingly staggered as learners move through the education system. Branson, Hofmeyr, and Lam (2014), for example, used data from the National Income Dynamics Study (NIDS) to examine schooling transitions between 2008 and 2010 for learners across Grades 1 to 12 and observe patterns of grade repetition, rates of year-on-year progress, and school dropout. Their results showed that prior to Grade 9, successful progression rates sit between 65% and 80%.

[1] Two government departments oversee South African education. The Department of Basic Education is responsible for Grades R (preprimary school), Grades 1 to 7 (primary school), and Grades 8 to 12 (secondary school). Grades R through 9 are collectively referred to as the General Education and Training phase. Grades 10 to 12 are known as the Further Education and Training phase. At the end of secondary school, South African learners write a National School Certificate examination (commonly referred to as matric).

However, from Grade 9 onwards, there was a large increase in both the proportion repeating grades and those who were not enrolled in any form of education at all (see also Bhorat et al., 2015; Lam et al., 2011). Examination of who repeats reflects inequalities elsewhere in the education system, with learners in the most advantaged schools more likely to progress smoothly (Branson & Lam, 2010). Such patterns persist despite evidence to suggest that grade repetition is largely ineffective in addressing underachievement and is more often simply a prelude to school dropout (Jimerson et al., 2002).

Internationally, early exit from education is linked to less favorable labor market outcomes, and South Africa is no exception (Bhorat et al., 2015; also see Crawford, Duckworth, Vignoles, & Wyness, 2012, for evidence from the United Kingdom). Learners with a Grade 12 certificate—those who "matriculate"—are between 30% and 60% more likely to be employed than individuals who do not, and some level of tertiary qualification nearly doubles the likelihood of finding employment when compared to a matric-only certificate (Cloete, 2009; Ranchhod, 2013). School dropout has also been linked to teenage pregnancy and substance abuse in some communities (Strassburg, Meny-Gibert, & Russell, 2010). These risks are compounded by the high and growing level of unemployment in South Africa—in 2012, unemployment among young people (including discouraged job seekers[2]) was estimated to be around 66% (Southern African Labour and Development Research Unit, 2013)—and periods of youth unemployment increase the risk of further spells of unemployment (Bell & Blanchflower, 2010).

Individual and Family Influences

One of the most consistent findings in the developmental literature is that early cognitive performance predicts later achievement and educational outcomes (Kowleski-Jones & Duncan, 1999; McCall, Applebaum, & Hogarty, 1973). This is equally true in the South African context with Lam, Ardington, and Leibbrandt (2011) reporting that baseline cognitive skills are key determinants of progress through secondary school. In international contexts, poor prior achievement is the biggest predictor of both low

[2] According to Statistics South Africa (2016), a *discouraged worker* is defined as someone who is not working but is available to work and wants to work but did not actively do anything to find a job in the previous four weeks. To be categorized as a discouraged job seeker, the main reason for not looking for work needs to be one of the following: there were no available jobs in the area where the job seeker lives, there were no jobs to match the job seeker's skills set, and/or the job seeker lost hope of finding employment.

educational participation and problematic transitions into the labor market (Crawford et al., 2012; McVicar & Rice, 2001).

Evidence on individual-level factors associated with educational progress also shows that male learners are more likely than female to repeat a grade (Zuze & Reddy, 2014), as well as to drop out of school altogether (Branson et al., 2014). In addition, the younger the learner is, the less likely they are to dropout of secondary school: an older learner observed in the post-Grade 9 period being already more likely to have repeated earlier grades (Bhorat et al., 2015).

Research also shows a positive relationship between academic beliefs and attitudes and achievement over time (Watts et al., 2015) and highlights, for example, that positive school attitudes and ability self-concept are important components in developing ability (George, 2006; Juan, Reddy, & Hannan, 2014; Watts et al., 2015). In contrast, the experience of being bullied has been shown to have an adverse effect on educational attainment and human capital accumulation beyond school (Brown & Taylor, 2008).

Demographic factors, such as race[3] and socioeconomic status, including income and parental education, are repeatedly shown to correlate with the decision to drop out of school (Bhorat et al., 2015; Branson et al., 2014; Lam et al., 2011). Fleisch, Shindler, and Perry (2012), for example, used data from a large South African Community Survey of 7- to 15-year-olds not attending school to paint a picture of the racial pattern evident in dropout statistics: Coloured youth had the highest rate of nonattendance followed by Black Africans, with Whites and Indian/Asian youth recording nonattendance rates of just 1%.[4] Lam, Ardington, and Leibbrandt (2011) reported similarly large racial differences in school progression and found that the impact of earlier achievement in literacy and numeracy was stronger for White, Indian/Asian and Coloured students than for African students (see also Reddy et al., 2012). The authors concluded that grade progression in historically African schools is often poorly linked to actual ability and learning and argued that a greater understanding of educational transitions, and which students advance to higher grades, is a critical, understudied dimension of school quality.

[3] Racial categorization was a feature of the apartheid government and has not been used to differentiate groups since 1994. However, to track the achievement toward equity in the country, we disaggregate some statistics by racial categories.

[4] Statistics South Africa asks people to describe themselves in terms of five racial population groups. The 2011 census figures for these categories were Black African (76.4%), White (9.1%), Coloured (8.9%), Asian (2.5%), and Other/Unspecified (0.5%).

School Background Factors

The South African schooling system is made up of approximately 7% independent schools and 93% public schools (Reddy et al. 2016). Within the public sector particularly there is considerable variation in the physical conditions of schools and the contexts in which they are located. This variation is captured by a school poverty index (quintile rankings 1 [low] to 5 [high]), with schools in quintiles 1, 2, and 3 receiving subsidies from the government's pro-poor strategies that make it possible to exempt learners from paying fees. The public sector is thus differentiated into fee-paying (quintile 4 and 5) and no-fee paying schools, with 55% of SAYPS learners attending public no-fee schools; 36%, public fee-paying schools; and 9%, independent schools.

Students in the richest quintile (quintile 5) substantially outperform those in the other four quintiles (van der Berg, 2008). Branson et al. (2014) also showed evidence of a strong correlation between learner progression and school type and further demonstrated that those who are lagging behind for their age are partially protected from dropping out if they attend a higher quality school. For example, 30% of the poorest Grade 11 learners had repeated at least one grade, compared with just 8% of the richest.

Data and Procedures

Data

Data for this chapter come from the SAYPS, a longitudinal panel study that started in 2011. SAYPS targeted learners from Grade 9 (aged approximately 15 years old) who took part in the TIMSS in 2011 (see Mullis et al., 2012, for further details) ensuring that the baseline sample was drawn from a nationally representative sample of schools and their learners. Following the baseline data collection and matching with TIMSS, three further annual waves of information were collected in 2012 (aged 16), 2013 (aged 17), and, most recently, in 2014 (aged 18),[5] providing four waves of individual data tracking learners from Grade 9, approximately aged 15, onwards.[6] The

[5] A fifth wave of data was collected in 2015 but was not available for analyses at the time of writing.

[6] Learners begin primary school in Grade 1, typically the year they turn 7 years old. Those who move smoothly through the grade system without repetition would therefore turn 15 years old in Grade 9, 16 years old in Grade 10, 17 years old in Grade 11, and finally 18 years old in Grade 12. In practice, however, there is a considerable spread of ages in each grade owing to the high levels of grade repetition present throughout the system.

Table 10.1 Sample Size by Wave and Year

Wave	1	2	3	4
Year	2011	2012	2013	2014
Sample *N*	11,895	5,946	5,872	3,613
% of Wave 1 sample		50.0	49.4	30.4

data provides a wealth of information on individual characteristics and family background and, through matching with TIMSS, achievement scores in mathematics and science, school-level detail, and student and family characteristics.

The SAYPS baseline survey interviewed 11,895 young people. As shown in Table 10.1, 30% of learners opted out of further follow-ups after this baseline, and study dropout in the first follow-up brought the overall sample down to just below half of the original sample. In the most recent sweep of data collection, the sample size has fallen to 30% of the original group of learners.

Measures

The main aim of this chapter is to explore the educational activities and transitions of young people in South Africa over time, thus our key outcome of interest was the young person's main activity across each of the four waves. Table 10.2 provides a snapshot of what the sample of learners are doing at any one point in time.

In addition to this central measure of interest, our analysis employed a set of additional background factors known to correlate with and influence educational pathways, including the following:

Table 10.2 Percentage in Each of the Four Main Activity Statuses, by Wave

	Wave 1	Wave 2	Wave 3	Wave 4
	2011	2012	2013	2014
Still at school	100	98.0	96.2	92.3
Moved to TVET college		0.7	1.4	1.1
Working		0.2	0.5	1.0
Not studying and not working		1.2	1.9	5.7

Note: TVET = technical, vocational, education, and training and community colleges.

- Individual characteristics (age and gender)
- Social background and household resources (highest household education, social position, race, language spoken, number of books in the home)
- Student attitudes, educational expectations, and experience of bullying
- School-context characteristics (school quintile, economic background of learners)
- Achievement in mathematics and science

Detailed descriptions on how all variables were constructed are provided in Appendix 10.A and summary statistics are provided in Appendixes 10.B and 10.C.

Analytic Strategy

Our analysis first considered the main activity statuses of young people using transition matrices to explore year-on-year changes in what individuals were doing and, for those remaining in school, how they were progressing through the grade system. Based on these patterns, we then differentiated four main pathways, describing the characteristics of young people following these different tracks through school and exploring how individual-, family-, and school-level factors predicted different educational transitions.

Missing Data

As noted in Table 10.1, the SAYPS sample size in the fourth wave was only 30% of its initial population. This level of sample attrition is problematic and makes generalization to the wider population difficult. Analysis of the missingness across the four waves of SAYPS[7] suggested that learners missing after the baseline sweep were more likely to:

- be male;
- come from more disadvantaged backgrounds (lower levels of household education, lower self-ranked social status position, and fewer books in the home);

[7] Attrition analysis is not reported here for reasons of brevity but is available from the researchers on request.

- have lower educational expectations;
- attend poorer schools; and
- score significantly lower in TIMSS mathematics and science assessments.

However, because complex weighting procedures were not available and a priori oversampling methodologies were not employed, the analyses presented in this chapter focus on the rich, longitudinal sample of 3,613 learners present at all four waves, while acknowledging the upward bias inherent in this reduced sample. For example, Branson and Lam (2009) reported figures from NIDS, the 2007 Community Survey, and the Labour Force Survey, which showed between 93% and 97% of 15-year-olds as enrolled in school, in comparison with the SAYPS core sample, which has 100% enrollment at Grade 9. Similarly, Branson and colleagues (2014) reported, using NIDS only, that after Grade 8, dropout rates increased year on year, with 15.3% of those exiting the school system by Grade 12 without completing matric, compared to just 7.7% in our core analytic sample.

Variable level attrition for the 3,613 sample was very low, and so imputation strategies[8] within this population were performed ahead of the multivariate analysis.

Results

Learner Pathways: Main Activity Transitions

Table 10.3 shows what young people are doing at Wave 4 in 2014 given their main activity state at Wave 3 in 2013. Looking first at activity persistence, the figures on the diagonal (highlighted) show the proportion of learners who carried on doing what they were in the previous year and show considerable evidence of continuity, particularly for those in school, with 94.8% of those in school at Wave 3 (98% of the complete 3,613, case sample) remaining there a year later. The other main movement for the in-school group is to become not in education, employment, or training (NEET): 3.8% have left school and not entered the workforce. Interestingly, just over half, 52.0%, of those who were in a technical vocational education and training and community (TVET) college in Wave 3 have moved back into school by Wave 4, indicating some fluidity between educational settings. More than 4 in 10 young people (42.1%),

[8] Missing values were set to the variable's average value for continuous variables, mode for categorical variables, and zero for categorical ones and indicated by a 0/1 dummy variable in all regression analyses.

Table 10.3 Main Activity Transitions Between Wave 3 (2013) and Wave 4 (2014)

		Still at school	TVET college	Working	NEET	Total
Wave 3: 2013	% in W2			Wave 4: 2014		
Still at school	98.0	94.8	0.8	0.6	3.8	100
TVET college	0.7	52.0	18.0	8.0	22.0	100
Working	0.2	0	0	42.1	57.9	100
NEET	1.2	18.6	2.9	7.1	71.4	100
Total		92.3	1.1	1.0	5.7	100

Note: *N* = 3,613. TVET = technical, vocational, education, and training and community colleges. NEET = not in education, employment, or training.

who were working in Wave 3, continue to be employed in Wave 4, but over half (57.9%) become unemployed and remain out of education.

Table 10.3 also shows evidence of considerable entrenchment amongst the NEET group, with over two thirds (71.4%) of those not studying or working at Wave 3 remaining economically inactive a year later. On a more positive note, however, one in five returned to some kind of education, 18.6% to school and 2.9% to college.

Learner Pathways: Grade Transitions

Table 10.3 shows that the majority of the SAYPS sample remained in school across the four waves of SAYPS. South Africa's education system has a policy of grade repetition if learners fail to pass the year: If progression through school were "smooth," there would be neat year-on-year transitions, with all young people moving to the next grade or exiting the school system altogether. However, in line with the previously reviewed literature reviewed, the cross-sectional view in Table 10.4 shows evidence of clear repetition at each wave.

Column 3 of Table 10.4, for example, shows the degree of grade progression by Wave 3: 3.4% of learners remained in Grade 9 two years on, just under a third (30.0%) progressed just one year, and almost two thirds (62.8%) made the expected of two year's progress. To put these figures from our reduced, more advantaged sample in context with a more nationally representative picture of South African learners, Branson et al. (2014) reported that less than half (just 43.3%) of the NIDS sample who were in Grade 9 in 2008 progressed smoothly to Grade 11 by 2010, with 28.0% repeating one year and 3.9%

Table 10.4 School Grades, by Wave

Wave	Wave 1	Wave 2	Wave 3	Wave 4
Year	2011	2012	2013	2014
Grade 9	100	14.4	3.4	0.9
Grade 10		83.6	30.0	10.0
Grade 11			62.8	34.0
Grade 12				47.4
n/a		2.0	3.8	7.8

making no progress at all. Note, however, their corresponding dropout rate is 24.8%, considerably higher than the 3.8% in the SAYPS data, suggesting that the majority of our "missing" sample is most likely to be from the population of early school-leavers.

Table 10.5 reports grade progression between Waves 3 and 4 and shows both the smooth progress of some learners (77.4% of those in Grade 11 at Wave 3 continued on into Grade 12), as well as evidence of discontinuity (i.e., off-diagonal movement; 22.6% of those in Grade 11 at Wave 3 remained there at Wave 4). There is also movement for those young people previously "stuck": More than two thirds of learners progressed from Grade 9 to Grade 10 (67.4%) and Grade 10 to Grade 11 (71.2%), respectively.

The final row of Table 10.5 shows grade progression for those in school across all four waves. Only half (51.6%) progressed smoothly from Grades 9 to 12 over the four-year period observed with 1% remaining stuck in Grade 9 at all four waves. Again, for context, Bhorat et al. (2015) reported that in the NIDS data only 31.4% of young people in Grade 9 in 2008 progressed at the desired, year-on-year rate, completing their high school education and

Table 10.5 Grade Transitions Between Wave 3 and Wave4

		Grade 9	Grade 10	Grade 11	Grade 12	Total
Wave 3: 2013	% in W3			Wave 4: 2014		
Grade 9	3.6	32.6	67.4	0	0	100
Grade 10	31.2	0	28.8	71.2	0	100
Grade 11	65.2	0	0	22.6	77.4	100
Total		0.9	10.7	36.8	51.6	100

Note: N = 3,294.

exiting the pipeline by 2012, with 30.3% repeating grades, 2% moving to tertiary education, and 36.3% dropping out of education altogether.

Examination of the main activity state and grade transitions revealed complex patterns of continuity and discontinuity in terms of young people's educational and early employment pathways: Approximately half of the sample of young people in SAYPS does not follow a neat, school-based track through the education system. Next, we focus on capturing the different pathways young people take to understand some of the key differences between those following a smooth pathway and those who do not.

A More Detailed Look at Individual Transitions Across Four Waves of SAYPS

Taking into account the full analytic sample of SAYPS used here ($N = 3{,}613$; i.e., including those who leave the education system), the proportion of learners with a smooth year-on-year transition through school fell to just below half (46.9%). Detailed examination of transitions at an individual level yielded four main pathway types (see Appendix 10.C for further detail on these groupings):

- *Smooth*: Neat, year-on-year grade progression through school
- *Staggered*:
  - Learners in school for all waves, who made some grade progress but have at least one episode of grade repetition or a move to a TVET college and
  - Individuals who returned to school in Wave 4 but are out of education (either working or NEET) for at least one wave
- *Stuck*: Learners in school for all waves, but stuck in Grade 9 or 10 for three or more periods
- *Stopped*: Individuals who leave school before the Wave 4 and do not return

After the smooth group, those with staggered transitions were the next most common group with 4 in 10 (39.4%) young people following this more protracted pathway through school. Stuck learners represented a small (6.9%), but problematic group of young people who appear trapped in the system, while the stopped group (6.8%) represent those who exit education prematurely.

Table 10.6 presents summary statistics for several key variables by these four transition groups. In line with the extant literature, male learners are

Table 10.6 Descriptive Statistics for Reduced Transition Pattern Groups

	Freq.	Percentage	Girl		Baseline Age (in 2011)		Highest Household Education		Number of Books in the Home (Scale)		TIMSS Achievement Score: Mathematics		TIMSS Achievement Score: Science	
			Mean	Std. Dev.	Mean	Std. Dev.	Mean	Std. Dev.	Mean	Std. Dev.	Mean	Std. Dev.	Mean	Std. Dev.
All			.58	0.49	15.7	1.1	4.8	1.7	2.0	1.0	366.8	77.28	351.2	101.18
Smooth	1,697	47.0	.63	0.48	15.4	0.8	5.1	1.8	2.2	1.1	408.6	81.39	406.5	102.28
Staggered	1,422	39.4	.54	0.50	15.8	1.1	4.6	1.6	1.9	1.0	343.4	55.37	321.3	75.55
Stuck	250	6.9	.54	0.50	16.0	1.2	4.5	1.6	1.8	.9	318.4	51.34	286.0	71.52
Stopped	244	6.8	.43	0.50	17.0	1.3	4.3	1.4	1.9	1.0	309.2	55.62	271.0	78.41
Total	3,613	100												

more likely to drop out than females: 63% of the smooth group are girls, while just 43% of those in the stopped group are. Those in the smooth group are also the youngest at the Wave 1 baseline, indicating that up to that point they had similarly been following a smooth grade progression through school, while those who are stuck or stopped are older, suggesting grade repetition prior to our baseline observation in Grade 9.

Across the four groups, young people following a smooth educational pathway come from the most advantaged households, namely, those with higher levels of parental education and social standing, as well as more resources as measured by number of books in the home. Those who stop and exit the education system prematurely appear to come from the most disadvantaged backgrounds. Those in the smooth group also have higher than average achievement scores as measured by the TIMSS assessments in mathematics and science.

Predicting Young People's Educational Transitions: What Differentiates the Smooth Group?

Table 10.7 reports the results from logistic regression models predicting learner pathways. We identify factors associated with having a smooth transition, that is, which characteristics learners who have a smooth pathway are more or less likely to have in comparison to those who have any other type of transition (staggered, stuck, or stopped). Given the particular importance of achievement in influencing educational pathways, we show the regression models with and without controls for TIMSS performance. In so doing, we were able to examine some of the relationships that might be masked once achievement is included in the model. Next, we adopted the same analytic approach to tease out the characteristics of those in the remaining groups, namely, predicting the likelihood of having a staggered transition in contrast to one which is stuck or stopped, excluding those in the smooth category entirely, again with and without controls for achievement.

As in the earlier descriptive analysis, even when controlling for key features of social background, individual characteristics and school factors, girls are 1.3 times more likely than boys to have a smooth transition through school. Column 2 of Table 10.7 shows that this is also the case conditional on achievement. As expected, those who are younger were also more likely to have a smooth pathway through school; age is negatively and significantly associated with the likelihood of being in the smooth group, indicating that members of this category are younger than those who are in other types of transition

Table 10.7 Odds Ratios: Predicting the Likelihood of Having a Smooth or Staggered Transition

	Smooth (Vs. All Others)				Staggered (Vs. "Stuck" and "Stopped")			
	Excl. ACH		Inc. ACH		Excl. ACH		Inc. ACH	
	OR	S.E.	OR	S.E.	OR	S.E.	OR	S.E.
Individual characteristics								
Girl	1.31	0.13**	1.59	0.17***	1.03	0.15	1.08	0.16
Age	0.64	0.03***	0.73	0.04***	0.64	0.04***	0.67	0.04 ***
Social background								
Highest household education (ref: none/low)								
Completed Grade 9 only	0.90	0.20	0.90	0.22	1.12	0.36	1.16	0.37
Completed Grade 12	0.93	0.18	0.96	0.21	0.92	0.25	0.91	0.24
Postmatric certificate/diploma	0.92	0.20	0.90	0.21	1.01	0.33	1.00	0.33
Degree and higher	0.82	0.18	0.82	0.19	1.09	0.36	1.16	0.38
Perceived position on social ladder	.91	0.04	0.91	0.05	0.98	0.06	0.98	0.06
Race (ref: Black African)								
Coloured	0.99	0.21	0.93	0.20	0.60	0.18	0.56	0.17
White, Indian/Asian, other	2.50	0.52***	1.53	0.34	0.35	0.14**	.36	0.15*
Frequency language of TIMSS test spoken in home (ref: always/almost always)								
Sometimes	0.74	0.09**	1.11	0.14	1.16	0.23	1.27	0.26
Never	0.43	0.10***	0.73	0.18	0.87	0.26	1.03	0.33
Household resources								
Number of books in the home								
Student academic perceptions	1.03	0.05	1.02	0.06	0.91	0.07	0.92	0.07
Attitudes and beliefs about mathematics	1.12	0.06*	1.04	0.06	1.18	0.10	1.17	0.11

Continued

Table 10.7 Continued

	Smooth (Vs. All Others)				Staggered (Vs. "Stuck" and "Stopped")			
	Excl. ACH		Inc. ACH		Excl. ACH		Inc. ACH	
	OR	S.E.	OR	S.E.	OR	S.E.	OR	S.E.
Attitudes and beliefs about science	1.01	0.05	0.92	0.05	1.03	0.10	0.95	0.09
Not bullied at school scale (high = never/rarely bullied)	1.21	0.06***	1.08	0.06	1.16	0.09	1.11	0.09
Educational expectations (ref: finish Grade 9 only)								
Finish Grade 12	1.47	0.51	1.33	0.43	0.57	0.18	0.51	0.17*
Finish post-matric certificate	1.21	0.45	0.85	0.31	0.57	0.22	0.49	0.19
Finish diploma	1.90	0.69	1.28	0.43	0.84	0.33	0.68	0.28
Finish degree	2.61	0.93**	1.48	0.50	0.80	0.30	0.62	0.24
Finish honors degree or higher	3.39	1.11***	1.58	0.48	1.16	0.38	0.83	0.29
School factors								
School quintile (ref: quintile 1 = low)								
Quintile 2	1.31	0.21	1.33	.022	1.02	0.22	1.03	0.22
Quintile 3	1.02	0.17	0.80	0.14	1.13	0.24	1.00	0.22
Quintile 4	1.10	0.18	0.77	0.13	1.28	0.29	1.10	0.25
Quintile 5	1.91	0.37***	0.90	0.19	2.51	.87**	2.01	0.69*
Independent school	2.32	0.47***	0.87	0.20	1.57	0.60	1.22	0.48
Economic background of school's pupils (ref: 0%–10% disadvantaged)								
11%–25%	0.84	0.22	0.55	0.18	0.76	0.35	0.62	0.29
26%–50%	0.48	0.12**	0.34	0.10***	1.28	0.57	1.12	0.51
More than 50%	0.53	0.12**	0.45	0.12**	1.20	0.42	1.08	0.38
Achievement								
TIMMS Mathematics score			1.79	0.26***			1.03	0.21
TIMMS Science score			1.99	0.29***			1.52	0.31*
R^2		0.18		0.25		0.11		0.12

group. White and Indian/Asian learners are 2.5 times more likely than Black Africans to be in the smooth group, while those who sometimes or never speak the language of the TIMSS test at home are significantly less likely to have smooth transition through school. Interestingly, in contrast to the literature reviewed, there is no significant association between social background—as measured by highest household education and the young person's own perception of the family's social position—and educational transitions even in the model that does not include learner achievement. We discuss this result further in our concluding section.

Table 10.7 also shows that those with more positive attitudes and beliefs about mathematics, those who are not bullied,[9] and those with higher educational expectations were also more likely to have a smooth transition through school. Finally, in line with Branson et al. (2014), our results showed that young people attending the best resourced fee-paying public schools (quintile 5) and those in the independent school sector were also more likely to have repetition-free pathways, while those in schools with higher proportions of economically disadvantaged learners were less likely to do so.

However, as predicted, once prior achievement is controlled for (see Table 10.7, column 2), most of the significant relationships fall away, suggesting that many of these associations are mediated by (i.e., their relationship operates through) individual achievement: Learners with greater educational expectations for themselves—those in quintile 5 fee-paying public schools as well as those in the independent sector, for example—are also more likely to have higher levels of TIMSS achievement, and the association between being in the smooth transition group and prior achievement is stronger. Only gender, age, and the economic background of the schools' learners remain significant alongside TIMSS achievement scores in predicting the likelihood of having a smooth transition through school.

By contrast, those in the staggered group (vs. being in either the stuck or stopped groups) were less likely to be White or Indian/Asian than Black African, even controlling for prior achievement (Table 10.7, column 6) and had lower educational expectations. Similar to the smooth grouping, young people with a staggered pathway were also more likely to be from fee-paying rather than no-fee public schools, although interestingly not from independent schools. Note, however, that 70% of independent school students (9% of the overall sample) had smooth pathways, making the numbers here quite

[9] A positive coefficient on the "Not bullied at school" scale here reflects that those who are never or rarely bullied are more likely to be in the smooth group than any other, since the measure is scaled such that a high score means less or no bullying.

small. On the whole, however, there are fewer characteristics that appeared to differentiate those in the staggered group from those in the stuck and stopped groups than there were for distinguishing those in the smooth category from the other three transition pathways, at least with respect to the set of individual, family, and school factors considered here.

And Finally: A Good News Story?

This final analytic section looks beyond the somewhat predictable pattern of advantage and "achievement begets achievement," to examine whether our data show evidence of young people succeeding despite the odds. For example, the regression analyses showed that those in the most advantaged schools were more likely to have a smooth transition through school, but the data nevertheless revealed a surprising number of young people from the lowest-ranking schools make comparable educational progress.

Table 10.8 shows that while almost 57% of the smooth group came from fee-paying or independent schools, a corresponding 43% of this group came from non-fee paying, low-quintile schools. Moreover, almost 3 in 10 (29.1%) of those in the stopped group came from fee-paying or independent schools. For comparison in the more nationally representative NIDS data, Branson et al. (2014) reported that dropout rates between the richest and poorest schools were far more similar than the proportions achieving smooth progression routes: 20% of Grade 10 learners from the poorest-quintile schools progressed successfully, compared to 50% of the richest Grade 10 learners, versus around 40% of Grade 11 learners dropping out in the poorest schools with 30% of the richest Grade 11 learners. In addition, while the results presented in Table 10.7 showed that achievement scores are one of the most important predictors

Table 10.8 Transition Group, by Quintile of School Attended in Grade 9

	School Quintile						
	Non-Fee-Paying			Fee-Paying			
Transition Group	Q1	Q2	Q3	Q4	Q5	Independent	Total
Smooth	11.1	15.9	16.2	18.0	25.0	13.9	100
Staggered	16.0	21.8	24.8	20.8	10.6	5.9	100
Stuck	22.4	28.0	23.6	16.4	5.6	4.0	100
Stopped	19.3	23.8	27.9	20.5	6.6	2.1	100
Total	14.4	19.6	20.9	19.2	16.8	9.2	100

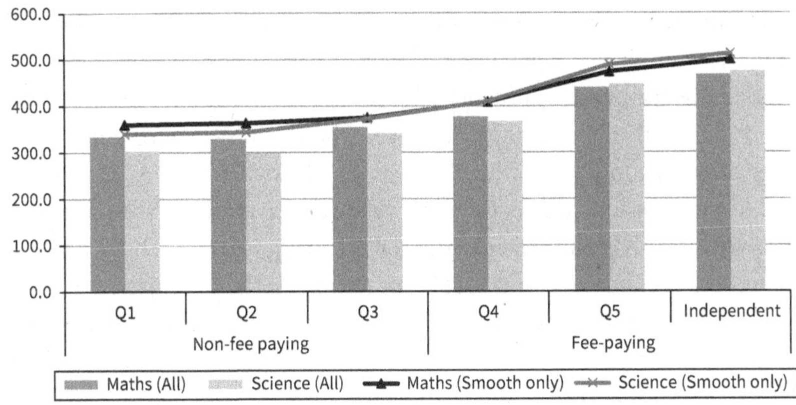

Figure 10.1 TIMSS average and smooth transition group only achievement, by school quintile.

of educational pathways, Figure 10.1 highlights that not only are young people with low average scores in the TIMSS assessments following smooth progression pathways, but they are doing so from the least well-off schools and with performance levels well below the TIMSS lowest benchmark cut-offs.

Conclusions and Implications

SAYPS provides the first national longitudinal data collected annually on young people in South Africa, making it possible to study the detail of individual transitions over a four-year period. This chapter examines the educational and early labor market transitions of the SAYPS cohort and provides the first in-depth look at what young people are doing, how they move through the education system, and how background and school-level characteristics influence those pathways in South Africa.

The Predictable Story Versus a New One

The SAYPS data confirm much of what is already known in the literature with respect to school progress and successful educational transitions: learners who followed a smooth transition tended to have higher scores in the TIMSS mathematics and science assessments measured at baseline and attended more socially advantaged schools. In addition, boys and those with previous episodes of grade repetition were more likely to experience interrupted pathways through school. Our results also supported previous findings concerning the high levels of grade repetition and increasingly staggered school progression in the postcompulsory phase.

Just under half of the sample achieved the desired rate of smooth year-on-year progression from Grade 9 to Grade 12, with a further 39.4% having staggered progression routes, 6.9% being stuck for at least three consecutive periods within the grade system, and 6.8% exiting leaving school altogether. These figures are, however, upwardly biased given the prevalence of missing data in the cohort particularly with respect to those who exit the system prematurely—the so-called stopped group—with national estimates from NIDS indicating that those with a smooth transition comprised roughly only a third of learners while those who dropout altogether made up around 30% to 40% of the cohort (Branson et al., 2014).

But, interestingly, in addition to the predictable, confirmatory story, our results also tell a new one for South Africa, highlighting that it is possible to beat the odds and succeed academically despite apparent disadvantage (see Duckworth & Schoon, 2012, for comparable evidence for the United Kingdom). There are, for example, a surprising number of young people from the poorest schools and with low scores on the TIMSS assessment who nevertheless had smooth pathways through school. We also found evidence of a significant role for individual's own academic attitudes and beliefs, as well as educational expectations, in predicting educational transitions that has not previously been demonstrated in South African data sets: Young people who expected more for themselves were more likely to have a smooth, repetition-free pathway through school.

While the role of advantage is clearly evident in our findings, it does not appear to be one driven by family background alone as one might expect. Rather the advantage stems from being in the better off public or independent schools, where the proportion of disadvantaged learners is lower and overall achievement is higher. However, in a cohort where less than 20% of learners come from households where at least one parent has a degree and 42.9% of the sample has no more than a high school education, it may not be that surprising that we do not see a stronger relationship between socioeconomic status and educational transitions. One possible explanation here might be that the parents of this sample had a lower level of education than they were actually capable of achieving—a reflection of the sociohistorical context particular to South Africa—and so want more for their children, which manifests itself in high educational expectations and, in turn, stronger academic motivation among children. The importance of learners' own attitudes and expectations may then act as a mediator of the effect of parents' own education observed in so much of the international extant literature (see Feinstein, Duckworth, & Sabates, 2008, for a review).

An alternative explanation is simply that the measure of parents' education and the indicator of social standing in the SAYPS data are not very reliable: Socioeconomic status is drawn from learner reports, and there is evidence to suggest that young people are not always accurate in estimating these indicators of social background (Buchmann, 2002; Lien, Friestad, & Klepp, 2001; West, Sweeting, & Speed, 2001). Jerrim and Micklewright (2014), for example, used data from two large international surveys of pupil achievement, PISA and PIRLS, and showed that while children's reports of their father's occupation were fairly reliable, their reports of number of books in the home and parental education were more prone to measurement error. Measures of socioeconomic status, such as family income, used by others (e.g. Lam et al., 2011) might show a stronger relationship between family background and educational transitions but were not available in SAYPS.

Policy Implications

The results here provide an additional lens to policies focused on expanding postschool educational opportunities by showing what progress through school looks like for different types of learners. While our predictable story supports commitments to increasing educational opportunities and ensuring that learners thrive at school, lending support to the National Development Plan's focus on early interventions to address opportunity gaps, it also demonstrates the systemic challenges faced by boys at school that require further attention.

Our findings highlight patterns of fluidity across the achievement spectrum and transition pathways that require further investigation. In particular, shifts in and out of the schooling system might be more frequent than previously thought, and so it is important that the country's schooling and postschooling system is well-integrated to allow for these movements. Equally important is clarifying what options are available for learners, in terms of TVET colleges, the terrain of which is currently very complicated. Finally, evidence of persistent grade repetition suggests a need to understand how the current progression policy is applied practically across different schools.

Limitations of the Study

As noted throughout the chapter, the SAYPS data has a high level of missing data and the resulting analytic sample overrepresents those who do better in school and are from more advantaged households, attending better off schools. Nevertheless, our findings are in line with much of the extant literature and show interesting variation within this likely narrower, more advantaged group of learners that can inform policies across all South African learners.

Moreover, our methodological approach uses the best available data to address the issues of diverse educational transitions and has considerable advantages over those adopted by others in attempting to describe learner transitions through school. To date, there are no other nationally representative, annually collected, longitudinal South African studies of learners that can offer such a detailed insight into the educational transitions of young people. Reddy et al. (2012) and Taylor et al. (2015), for example, used a quasi-panel rather than a longitudinal one, with heavy, and most likely similar, levels of biased attrition (details unreported), while Lam et al. (2011) used a small area-specific study in the Western Cape, which is similarly likely to overrepresent advantaged groups and have limited broad generalization.

Thus, while there are limitations in the extent to which we can draw broad brush conclusions based on the core SAYPS sample used here and the relative size of these different transition groups on a national scale, our results nevertheless add to a growing body of research on South African youth transitions using the best available data possible, contextualizing estimates with national data where available. In the fullness of time, these findings will be supplemented by the parallel SAYPS II study and other emerging longitudinal resources.

References

Bell, D. N. F. & Blanchflower, D. G. (2010). UK unemployment in the Great Recession. *National Institute Economic Review, 214*, 3–25.

Bhorat, H., Lilenstein, K., Magadla, S., & Steenkamp, F. (2015). *Youth transitions from schooling to the labour market in South Africa: Characteristics, determinants and solutions* (Unpublished concept note). Development Policy Research Unit, University of Cape Town, Cape Town, South Africa.

Branson, N., Hofmeyr, C., & Lam, D. (2014). Progress through school and the determinants of school dropout in South Africa. *Development Southern Africa, 31*(1), 106–126.

Branson, N., & Lam, D. (2009). *Education: Analysis of the NIDS Wave 1 dataset* (Discussion paper no. 3). Cape Town, South Africa: Southern Africa Labour and Development Research Unit, University of Cape Town.

Branson, N., & Lam, D. (2010). Education Inequality in South Africa: Evidence from the National Income Dynamics Study. *Studies in Economics and Econometrics, 34*(3), 85–109.

Branson, N., & Zuze, T. L. (2012). Education, the great equaliser: Improving access to quality education. In K. Hall, I. Woolards, L. Lake, & C. Smith (Eds.), *2012 South African child gauge* (pp. 69–74). Cape Town, South Africa: Children's Institute.

Brown, S., & Taylor, K. (2008). Bullying, education and earnings: Evidence from the National Child Development Survey. *Economics of Education Review, 27*(4), 387–401.

Buchmann, C. (2002). Measuring family background in international studies of education: conceptual issues and methodological challenges. In A. Porter & A. Gamoran (Eds.), *Methodological advances in cross-national surveys of educational achievement* (pp. 150–197). Washington, DC: National Academy Press.

Cloete, N. (2009). *Responding to the educational needs of post-school youth: Determining the scope of the problem and developing a capacity-building model.* Cape Town, South Africa: Centre for Higher Education and Transformation.

Crawford, C., Duckworth, K., Vignoles, A., & Wyness, G. (2012). *Young people's education and labour market choices aged 16 to 19.* London, England: Centre for Analysis of Youth Transitions, Department for Education.

Department of Basic Education. (2012). *Report on the annual national assessments of 2011.* Pretoria, South Africa: Author.

Duckworth, K., & Schoon, I (2012). Beating the odds: Exploring the impact of social risk on young people's school-to-work transitions during recession in the UK. *National Institute Economic Review, 222*, 38–51

Feinstein, L., Duckworth, K., & Sabates, R. (2008). *Education and the family: Passing success across the generations.* Oxford, England: Routledge.

Fiske, E. B., & Ladd, H. F. (2004). *Elusive equity: Education reform in post-apartheid South Africa.* Washington, DC: Brookings Institution Press.

Fleisch, B. (2008). *Primary education in crisis: Why South African schoolchildren underachieve in reading and mathematics.* Cape Town, South Africa: Juta.

Fleisch, B., Shindler, J., & Perry, H. (2012). Who is out of school? Evidence from the Community Survey 2007, South Africa. *International Journal of Educational Development, 32*, 529–536.

George, R. (2006). A cross-domain analysis of change in students' attitudes towards science and attitudes about the utility of science. *International Journal of Science Education, 28*(6), 571–589.

Jerrim, J., & Micklewright, J. (2014). Socio-economic gradients in children's cognitive skills: Are cross-country comparisons robust to who reports family background? *European Sociological Review, 30*, 766–781.

Jimerson, S. R., Anderson, G. E., & Whipple, A. D. (2002). Winning the battle and losing the war: Examining the relation between grade retention and dropping out of high school. *Psychology in the Schools, 39*(4), 441–457.

Juan, A., Reddy, V., & Hannan S. (2014). Attitudes to science: Part of the puzzle to improve educational achievement? *African Growth Agenda, 11*(3-4), 13–16.

Kowleski-Jones, L., & Duncan, G. J. (1999). The structure of achievement and behavior across middle childhood. *Child Development, 70*(4), 930–943.

Lam, D., Ardington, C., & Leibbrandt, M. (2011). Schooling as a lottery: Racial differences in school advancement in urban South Africa. *Journal of Development Economics, 95*(2), 121–136.

Lee, V. E., Zuze, T. L., & Ross, K. N. (2005). School effectiveness in 14 sub-Saharan African countries: Links with 6th graders' reading achievement. *Studies in Educational Evaluation, 31*, 207–246.

Lien, N., Friestad, C., & Klepp, K. (2001). Adolescents' proxy reports of parents' socioeconomic status: how valid are they? *Journal of Epidemiology and Community Health, 55*, 731–737.

McCall, R. B., Appelbaum, M. I., & Hogarty, P. S. (1973). Developmental changes in mental performance. *Monographs of the Society for Research in Child Development, 38*(3), 1–84.

McVicar, D., & Rice, P. (2001). Participation in full-time further education in England and Wales: an analysis of post-war trends. *Oxford Economic Papers, 53*, 47–56.

Mullis, I. V. S., Martin, M. O., Foy, P., & Arora, A. (2012). *TIMSS 2011 International results in mathematics.* Chestnut Hill, MA: TIMSS & PIRLS International Study Center, Boston College.

Ranchhod, V. (2013). *Earnings volatility in South Africa.* (NIDS discussion paper 2013/3; Working paper series no. 121). Cape Town, South Africa: Southern Africa Labour and Development Research Unit, University of Cape Town.

Reddy, V., van der Berg, S., Janse van Rensburg, D., & Taylor, S. (2012). Educational outcomes: Pathways and performance in South African high schools. *South African Journal of Science, 108*(3–4), a620.

Reddy, V., Visser, M., Winnaar, L., Arends, F., Juan, A., Prinsloo, C. H., & Isdale, K. (2016). *TIMSS 2015: Highlights of mathematics and science achievement of Grade 9 South African learners.* Pretoria, South Africa: Human Sciences Research Council.

Ross, K. N., Saito, M., Dolata, S., Hungi, N., & Makuwa, D. (2007). *Data Archive for the SACMEQ II Project.* Paris, France: UNESCO-IIEP.

Southern African Labour and Development Research Unit. (2013). *Youth unemployment and social protection.* Cape Town, South Africa: SALDRU, University of Cape Town.

Statistics South Africa. (2016). *Quarterly labour force survey: Quarter 1: 2016.* Pretoria, South Africa: Author.

Strassburg, S., Meny-Gibert, S., & Russell, B. (2010). *Left unfinished: Temporary absence and drop-out from South African schools.* Johannesburg, South Africa: Social Surveys Africa.

Taylor, S., van der Berg, S., Reddy, V., & Janse van Rensburg, D. (2015). The evolution of educational inequalities through secondary school: Evidence from a South African panel study. *Development Southern Africa, 32*(4), 425–442.

Van der Berg, S. (2008). How effective are poor schools? Poverty and educational outcomes in South Africa. *Studies in Educational Evaluation, 34*(3), 145–154.

Van der Berg, S. (2009). *The persistence of inequalities in education.* Oxford, England: Oxford University Press.

Watts, T. W., Duncan, G. J., Chen, M., Classens, A., Davis-Kean, P. E., Duckworth, K., . . . Susperreguy, M. I. (2015). The role of mediators in the development of longitudinal mathematics achievement associations. *Child Development, 86*(6), 1892–1907.

West, P., Sweeting, H., & Speed, E. (2001). We really do know what you do: a comparison of reports from 11 year olds and their parents in respect of parental economic activity and occupation. *Sociology, 35*, 539–59.

Zuze, T. L., & Reddy, V. (2014). School resources and the gender reading literacy gap in South African schools. *International Journal of Educational Development, 36*, 100–107.

Appendix 10.A Variable Descriptions

Girl: The young person's gender was coded 0 = boy; 1 = girl.

Age: Age was measured in years at the 2011 baseline interview.

Highest household education: Measured in the TIMSS questionnaire, young people were asked "What is the highest level of education completed by your mother and father (or step-mother/father or female/male guardian)." The variable was coded separately for each parent as *none/low*, *completed Grade 9 only*, *completed Grade 12*, *completed a postmatric certificate/diploma*, or *completed a first degree or higher*. A highest household indicator was created as the higher of the two values where both parents are present and for the one in single parent households.

Perceived position on the social ladder: In the SAYPS baseline questionnaire, young people were asked to "imagine that society is a ladder, with the richest person at the top and the poorest at the bottom. Where would your family be on the ladder?" The variable ranges from 1 to 10, with a larger score indicating a higher social ranking.

Race: Race was assessed using five categories: Black African (84.8%), Coloured (6.5%), Indian or Asian (1.4%), White (6.8%), and Other (0.4%). Since the Indian/Asian, White, and Other groups are so small, these groups were recoded into one, creating a threefold variable.

Frequency language of the TIMSS test spoken at home: Young people were asked how often they spoke the language the TIMSS assessment *was* given in (English or Afrikaans) at home. The variable was coded as *always/almost always*, *sometimes*, or *never*.

Number of books in the home: Individuals were asked about the approximate number of books in their home, excluding magazines, newspapers, and school books. The variable was coded on a 5-point scale from *none or very few* (0–10 books) to *enough to fill three or more bookcases* (more than 200).

Attitudes and beliefs about mathematics and science: On completing the TIMSS assessments, learners were asked about their attitudes towards and beliefs about mathematics and science separately, covering their liking, valuation of, confidence in, and engagement with the two subjects. These four subject specific scales were then factor analyzed to create one measure of positive attitudes towards and beliefs about each subject.

Not bullied at school scale: As part of an assessment of school climate, young people are asked six questions about how often, on a 4-point scale ranging from *at least once a week* to *neve*, they experienced bullying behaviors. Bullying behaviors included how often they were made fun of, left out of games of activities, stolen from, and hit or hurt. A score ranging from low (*frequent experience of bullying*) to high (*rare experience of bullying*) was created by TIMSS (see Mullis et al., 2012, for further details) and was used here.

Educational expectations: Asked in the TIMSS questionnaire, young people were asked "How far in your education do you expect to go?" The variable was coded with the same values as for mother's and father's highest level of education achieved, ranging from *finishing Grade 9* to *finishing a first honors degree or higher*.

School type: Public school type was measured through quintile membership (no-fee schools: quintiles 1 to 3) and fee-paying schools (quintiles 4 and 5).

Independent school: Coded as 1 if the young person attended an independent school, and zero otherwise.

Economic background of school's learners: Measured by the TIMSS school-level questionnaire, this variable categorized the proportion of a school's learners who come from disadvantaged backgrounds: 0% to 10%, 11% to 25%, 26% to 50%, and more than 50%.

TIMSS achievement: First conducted in 1994–1995 across 45 countries, the TIMSS is a cross-national assessment of the mathematics and science knowledge of fourth- and eighth-grade learners. The TIMSS assessments are designed to align broadly with the mathematics and science curricula in participating countries and, in 2011, was administered to 11,969 Grade 9 learners in 285 schools across South Africa.

For mathematics, TIMSS 2011 assessed the content areas of numbers, algebra, geometry, and data and chance. For science, TIMSS 2011 assessed biology, chemistry, physics, and earth sciences.

TIMSS achievement test scores were measured out of a possible 1,000 scale points, with a center point set at 500 and a standard deviation of 100, and were divided into four international benchmarks:

- Low: 400–475
- Intermediate: 475–500
- High: 550–625
- Advanced: over 625

Learners scoring less than 400 points are deemed below the level of the test and not able to demonstrate the level of knowledge required for their grade.

Appendix 10.B Descriptive Statistics

	Mean	Std. Dev.	Min	Max
Individual characteristics				
Girl	0.58	(0.49)	0	1
Age	15.7	(1.06)	10	19.8
Social background				
Highest household education (ref: none/low):				
Completed Grade 9 only	0.10	(0.29)	0	1
Completed Grade 12	0.25	(0.43)	0	1
Postmatric certificate/diploma	0.15	(0.36)	0	1
Degree and higher	0.19	(0.39)	0	1
Perceived position on social ladder	5.5	(2.06)	1	10
Race (ref: Black African):				
Coloured	0.07	(0.25)	0	1
White, Indian/Asian, Other	0.09	(0.28)	0	1
Frequency lang. of TIMSS test spoken in home (ref: always/almost always):				
Sometimes	0.64	(0.48)	0	1
Never	0.05	(0.22)	0	1
Household resources				
Number of books in the home	2.00	(1.03)	1	5
Student academic perceptions				
Attitudes and beliefs about mathematics	0.15	(0.98)	–4.2	2.6

	Mean	Std. Dev.	Min	Max
Attitudes and beliefs about science	0.14	(0.98)	−4.5	2.3
Not bullied at school scale (high = never/rarely bullied)	8.7	(1.57)	2.9	13.0
Educational expectations (ref: finish Grade 9 only)				
Finish Grade 12	0.12	(0.33)	0	1
Finish postmatric certificate	0.06	(0.23)	0	1
Finish diploma	0.07	(0.25)	0	1
Finish degree	0.08	(0.27)	0	1
Finish honors degree or higher	0.52	(0.50)	0	1
School factors				
School quintile (ref: quintile 1 = low)				
Quintile 2	0.20	(0.40)	0	1
Quintile 3	0.21	(0.41)	0	1
Quintile 4	0.19	(0.39)	0	1
Quintile 5	0.17	(0.37)	0	1
Independent school	0.09	(0.29)	0	1
Economic background of school's pupils (ref: 0%–10% disadvantaged)				
11%–25%	0.11	(0.32)	0	1
26%–50%	0.08	(0.28)	0	1
More than 50%	0.71	(0.45)	0	1
Achievement				
TIMMS Mathematics score	366.8	(77.28)	193.6	746.0
TIMMS Science score	351.2	(101.18)	98.8	756.2

Appendix 10.C Detailed Transitions Across Four Waves of SAYPS

Transition Detail					Frequency	Percentage
	W1	W2	W3	W4		
Smooth						
	9	10	11	12	1,697	47.0
Staggered						
	9	TVET	TVET	TVET	5	0.1
	9	9	10	10	133	3.7

Transition Detail					Frequency	Percentage
	9	9	10	11	212	5.9
	9	10	10	11	496	13.7
	9	10	11	11	496	13.7
	SCH & TVET combos				61	1.7
Subtotal					1,403	38.8
Returners						
	9	N	N	SCH	6	0.2
	9	N	SCH	SCH	5	0.1
	9	SCH	N	SCH	7	0.2
	9	W	10	11	1	0.0
Subtotal					19	0.5
Stuck						
	9	9	9	9	31	0.9
	9	9	9	10	64	1.8
	9	10	10	10	155	4.3
Subtotal					250	6.9
Stopped						
	9	X	X	X	45	1.3
	9	9	X	X	18	0.5
	9	10	X	X	29	0.8
	9	9	9	X	25	0.7
	9	9	10	X	16	0.4
	9	10	10	X	52	1.4
	9	10	11	X	59	1.6
Subtotal					244	6.8
Total					3,613	100

Notes: N = not studying or in work. SCH = in school. TVET = technical, vocational, education, and training and community colleges. W = working. X = not in school or FET college.

11

High School Dropouts' Movements In and Out of Work and Education During the Transition to Adulthood

Laurence Lavoie, Éliane Thouin, Véronique Dupéré, and Eric Dion

Introduction

The transition from adolescence to adulthood is a major junction in the life course, especially when it comes to education and work. In advanced economies, through compulsory schooling, the vast majority of children and adolescents share some common educational experiences. This common core typically ends with high school in North America or with upper or lower secondary education in Europe, after which educational and professional pathways multiply and branch out in starkly different directions. However, even before that point, a small but significant proportion of youth diverge on a separate track, because they quit high school or upper secondary education prior to graduation. In Western countries, around 10% of young adults aged under 25 years old have no upper secondary qualifications and are no longer in training (Eurostat, 2016; Gilmore, 2010; U.S. Department of Education, 2016). These emerging adults, often referred to as high school dropouts in North America and early school-leavers in Europe (in this chapter, the two terms are used interchangeably), are vulnerable to an array of negative outcomes during the school-to-work transitions, notably in terms of employment prospects and earnings, both because dropout reflects pre-existing long-term difficulties and because it creates new problems and restrictions in its own right (Campbell, 2015a, 2015b; Rumberger, 2011). Despite the significant challenges that early leavers experience as a group during the school-to-work transition, some are likely to fare better than others because, for instance, they successfully return to school or find satisfying employment regardless of unfavorable odds. Understanding how resilience emerges among

Laurence Lavoie, Éliane Thouin, Véronique Dupéré, and Eric Dion, *High School Dropouts' Movements In and Out of Work and Education During the Transition to Adulthood* In: *Young Adult Development at the School-to-Work Transition*. E. Anne Marshall and Jennifer E. Symonds, Oxford University Press (2021). © Oxford University Press. DOI: 10.1093/oso/9780190941512.003.0011.

this highly vulnerable group is important to guide policy and practice aiming at better supporting those most in need during the transition to adulthood (see DeLuca, Clampet-Lundquist, & Edin, 2016).

The goal of this chapter is to describe, via a selected review of the literature, the heterogeneous school-to-work pathways experienced by high school dropouts during emerging adulthood, as well as the processes underlying risk and resiliency. Even though the early factors leading to dropout can be identified and addressed via preventive early interventions, this chapter is limited in scope to post-dropout pathways. We start with an overview of the various terms used in the literature on the transition to adulthood to refer to youth without high school credentials. We then describe the major educational and employment pathways that dropouts experience during emerging adulthood and their main associated consequences, followed by a brief presentation of the individual and contextual antecedents of these pathways. We then present examples of programs and policies that have been found to help early school-leavers in the transition to adulthood, and conclude with a discussion of gaps in the existing literature and recommendations for future studies.

Terminology

In the literature on school-to-work transition, relatively few studies focus specifically on dropouts or early school-leavers. In fact, dropouts are often engulfed in wider categories that also include youth with high school credentials but who interrupt their postsecondary educational or professional activities for various reasons. The terms used to designate these categories and their specific outlines tend to vary in European and in North American studies, as described next.

In Europe, dropouts are routinely found within the NEET category, representing young adults who are "Not in Employment, Education, or Training" (Mascherini, Salvatore, Meierkord, & Jungblut, 2012). As underscored by Furlong (2006) and Yates and Payne (2006), among others, the NEET category is extremely heterogeneous. It notably includes young people not in school with and without secondary credentials who unsuccessfully look for work, who interrupt their activities because of disabilities or to take care of their children, as well as those who take a break to travel or to invest in artistic projects or in volunteer activities. It thus amalgamates vulnerable youth in need (e.g., those who desire to work but remain unemployed) with others who probably do not need any particular assistance (e.g., those involved in voluntary work abroad). Importantly, the NEET category excludes some vulnerable youth who experience difficult transitions and who could benefit from external support, such as dropouts who work, but in low-paid, unstable, and unsatisfying jobs (sometimes referred to as youths in "jobs without training," another heterogeneous category; see Lawy, Quinn, & Diment, 2009; Roberts, 2011). The exclusion of these youth limit the usefulness of NEET studies for understanding the full range of challenges experienced by high school dropouts during the school-to-work transition.

Although the school-to-work transitions of early school-leavers are often examined within a NEET framework in Europe, the parallel literature from the United States often approaches the question using categories such as the "forgotten half" or the "disconnected." The term *forgotten half* was coined in the late 1980s to underscore the neglect of noncollege-bound youth in the literature on school-to-work transitions (Rosenbaum, 2001; W. T. Grant Foundation Commission on Work, 1988). "Forgotten half" youth include all young people who, upon exiting high school with or without a diploma, do not attend college but rather directly make the transition to work or, in some case, to unemployment. Today, according to recent estimates, the proportion of youth in this category in OECD countries is closer to a third (OECD, 2018). The "forgotten half" category is broader in some ways than the NEET one because it includes youth who are not in college whether they are working or not. However, by definition, it does not distinguish between noncollege-bound youth and dropouts and their peers who graduated from high school. The specific school-to-work experiences of dropouts are thus often hard to pin down in studies adopting a "forgotten half" lens.

The term *disconnected* is also used in the United States to designate young adults who are not in education or employment, regardless of whether or not they possess high school credentials (Bray, Depro, McMahon, Siegle, & Mobley, 2016; Burd-Sharps & Lewis, 2012; Hair, Moore, Ling, McPhee-Baker, & Brown, 2009; Levin-Epstein & Greenberg, 2003). This term is thus analogous to NEETs and, as such, is sometimes used in European studies, notably from the United Kingdom (e.g., MacDonald, 2008). However, like other analogous terms, its definition varies across studies, and some authors specifically use it to refer to young adults who dropped out of high school and who encounter significant challenges during the transition to adulthood (Bloom, 2010; Bloom, Thompson, & Ivry, 2010). However, most authors use the term more broadly, and as a result dropouts' experiences are often hard to distinguish from that of other "disconnected" peers with a high school diploma.

In short, even if many studies examine challenging school-to-work transitions among vulnerable youth, relatively few focus on these transitions among high school dropouts or early school-leavers in the emerging adulthood period. Given this paucity, in the next sections we review not only studies that consider dropouts separately, but also studies that consider them as a part of broader at-risk groups, such as studies focusing on NEETs, "forgotten-half," or "disconnected" youth. However, it is important to bear in mind that the extent to which the findings of these studies specifically apply to dropouts remains an open question.

Heterogeneous Pathways: Description and Associated Consequences

There are many reasons why young people leave high school prior to graduation, and this heterogeneity of pathways continue following their departure (Schoon, 2015). Contrary to what is often assumed, not all dropouts become NEET or disconnected after they leave school. Some decide to go back to school not long after their initial departure, and others go directly into the labor market. There are a multitude of possible trajectories, but they can be grouped into four broad categories, described next, along with the main outcomes associated with these pathways during the school-to-work transition.

Youth Who Go Back to School

In North America and Europe, studies show that many if not most students who drop out of high school before graduation eventually re-engage in educational activities (Barrat, Berliner, & Fong, 2012; Hango & De Broucker, 2007; Looker & Thiessen, 2008; Rumberger & Rotermund, 2008; Schoon & Duckworth, 2010). Some return to their former high school, and others reenroll in second-chance programs and schools. The second-chance options take a variety of forms, two of which are particularly common.

First, many dropouts re-enroll in adult education centers that offer the possibility to take examinations and receive credentials that are considered equivalent to a high school diploma. For instance, in the United States, many dropouts go back into the educational world via General Educational Development (GED) programs. These programs offer high school dropouts the possibility to take a test that measures their skills in four different subjects (science, mathematics, social studies, and reading). Those who succeed get a certification stating that they have skills equivalent to those necessary to obtain an American high school diploma. Second, others re-enroll in technical or vocational programs that do not necessarily require full high school credentials. This second option is favored by large proportions of dropouts in countries where this option is available, such as Canada, Australia, and a number of European countries (Janosz, Bisset, Pagani, & Levin, 2011; Quintini & Manfredi, 2009; Rumberger & Lamb, 2003).

Associated Outcomes

Dropouts who obtain accreditations and diplomas via second-chance systems in general fare better in terms of employment than dropouts who remain without secondary education credentials or equivalents (e.g., Hango & De Broucker, 2007). In particular, vocational programs seem to increase successful school-to-work transitions among dropouts (e.g., Quintini & Manfredi, 2009). However, the apparent added value of alternative second-chance credentials should not be assumed but rather thoroughly evaluated, as in some cases (most notably that of the GED program available in the Unied States; see Heckman, Humphries, & Kautz, 2014), it may mostly reflect preexisting differences between dropouts who re-enroll and those who do not, rather than true gains due to a second-chance program. Also, a number of studies suggest that those who return to education to obtain some form of postsecondary training, through trade schools, for example, but who leave before completing their program may not fare better and perhaps do even worse in some respects than high school graduates and even dropouts (DeLuca et al., 2016; Hango & De Broucker, 2007; Rosenbaum, Ahearn, Becker, & Rosenbaum, 2015). For instance, DeLuca et al. (2016) described a crippling cycle of debt in which some low-educated young adults become entangled following enrollment in costly private programs from which they never graduate. Because failed attempts are costly both for dropouts individually and for society, dropouts who wish to return to school should receive counseling to help them choose the right program given their personal goal and situation, as well as support until their program is complete to help them anticipate and navigate setbacks (Bloom, 2010; Bloom et al., 2010).

Youth Who Go Directly Into the Labor Market

The desire or need to work is cited by a significant proportion of dropouts to explain their early departure from school (e.g., about a third according to Bridgeland, DiIulio, & Morison, 2006; Dalton, Glennie, & Ingels, 2009). In accordance with these aspirations, many dropouts enter the labor market and become productive workers. For instance, a study focusing on Australian and American dropouts found that two years after quitting, about half of the dropouts in both countries were working full time, and about 10% were working part time (Rumberger & Lamb, 2003). Similarly, in Canada, about 70% of dropouts in their early 20s were found to be employed (Hango & De Broucker, 2007). However, these rates of employment were observed among youth who attended high school in the 1990s or before and may not adequately represent current circumstances. In fact, employment rates are likely to be highly volatile among low-skilled youth, a segment of the workforce that is particularly vulnerable in times of economic downturns. For instance, in the context of the 2008 economic crisis, the employment rate among young dropouts in the United States dropped to 46%, a rate 50% lower than that of high school graduates, a pattern that persisted in following years (Sum, Khatiwada, & McLaughlin, 2009; Sum, Khatiwada, Trubskyy, & Palma, 2014). Apparently, this decline is not only the result of short-term crises, but also of long-term trends toward deteriorating employment prospects for low-skilled youth in advanced economies (Berlingieri et al., 2014; Brunello & De Paola, 2014; Kalleberg, 2011; Sum, Khatiwada, McLaughlin, & Palma, 2011).

Associated Outcomes

For dropouts, jobs are not only increasingly harder to find and to keep, as reflected by comparatively higher unemployment rates; for them, available jobs tend to be unstable, low paid, and without benefits (see Kalleberg, 2011; OECD, 2008, 2015). Moreover, the consequences of unemployment among young people often stretch into their future in a negative feedback loop, because marginal employment means less work experience and thus less chance to obtain a job in the future (Sum et al., 2014). Similarly, youth who cannot find a job are more likely to engage in crime, and those who subsequently get a criminal record further reduce their chances of reintegration into work (Levitan, 2005; McNally & Telhaj, 2007; Sum et al., 2009).

The experiences of low-skilled youth in the labor market may have consequences that are not limited to the work sphere. Marginal employment is often the source of a plethora of secondary stressors such as economic hardship, spousal conflict, and inadequate housing, stressors that in turn negatively impact mental and physical health and thus potentially the ability to work (Conger, Conger, & Martin, 2010; Pearlin & Bierman, 2013). Such negative feedback loops sparked by inadequate employment opportunities for low-skilled workers are thought to contribute to underlying troubling health trends, such as the recent increase in mortality rates observed among low-educated middle-aged White Americans (Case & Deaton, 2015). In sum, even if they find work, low-educated youth may still experience disproportionate hardships.

Youth Who Are NEET or Disconnected

Some dropouts do not re-enroll in school and do not participate in the labor market, either by choice or because of constrained opportunities and resources. The employment rate statistics presented previously suggest that among dropouts who do not re-enroll in school and remain nongraduates as emerging adults, one third to one half are not in employment either (Berlingieri, 2014; Hango & De Broucker, 2007; Sum et al., 2014). In other words, a substantial proportion of high school dropouts belong to the disconnected or NEET category.

Associated Outcomes

Among early school-leavers, those who do not reintegrate into school and who do not work are the most vulnerable, and most in need of support (Bloom, 2010; Bloom et al., 2010). For instance, these youth are particularly at risk of becoming homeless and living in conditions of extreme poverty (Sum et al., 2009; Zweig, 2003). For them, long-term disconnection from training and employment appears most harmful (Ralston, Feng, Everington, & Dibben, 2016).

Unfortunately, addressing the considerable needs of these dropouts is difficult for at least four reasons. First, as already mentioned, the longer one is out of school and out of work, the harder it is to reintegrate either educational or professional activities both because of scarring effects, and because long periods of inactivity can weaken motivation and erode the skills needed to reconnect (e.g., Ralston et al., 2016; Sum et al., 2014). Second, these youth are often particularly hard to locate and to reach, a significant problem for service delivery (Bloom, 2010). Third, youth with no ties to educational or labor market institutions do not have access to the services provided via these institutions directly or indirectly (e.g., career counseling for enrolled students, services available via employer-sponsored insurance programs). Fourth, in the absence of links with formal institutions, informal ones, first and foremost the family, become the only source of material, social, and emotional support (Booth, Brown, Landale, Manning, & McHale, 2012). Unfortunately, low-educated youth often have low-educated parents and relatives with comparatively few resources available to support grown-up children (Schoeni & Ross, 2005; Settersten Jr & Ray, 2010; Vargas Lascano, Galambos, Krahn, &

Lachman, 2015). Taken together, these challenges make it difficult to address the needs of disconnected youth.

Mixed Pathways

After dropping out of high school, most youth do not fall into neat trajectories characterized by continuous engagement or reengagement in school, work, or neither (e.g., Roberts, 2011; Schoon, 2015). Rather, dropouts' postsecondary experiences are often characterized by fits and starts and by overlapping and intersecting periods of work, education, and disconnection (Zaff, Ginsberg, Boyd, & Kakli, 2014). Mixed pathways appear to be the norm rather than the exception, and frequent changes are apparently common both in the United States and Europe (Brzinsky-Fay, 2007; Quintini & Manfredi, 2009; Schoon & Lyons-Amos, 2016).

Associated Outcomes

Mixed pathways can be positive or not, depending on context. Stable pathways can be positive; for instance staying in education longer following a re-entry is generally considered a good outcome especially when it leads to a diploma, but it can also be negative, for instance, when it means long-term unemployment. Some results focusing primarily on high school graduates show that youth with gaps and interruptions in their educational pathways during the transition to adulthood tend not to fare as well as those who are consistently enrolled until they complete their postsecondary education (Hango & De Broucker, 2007; Rosenbaum et al., 2015). Similarly, employment instability in early adulthood has been linked with suboptimal employment outcomes later in terms of wages and job satisfaction (Fuller, 2008; Krahn, Howard, & Galambos, 2015). Presumably, such gaps and instabilities are also harmful to dropouts, but more research is needed to fully grasp the consequences and underlying factors associated with mixed pathways among this specific group.

Antecedents of Contrasted Pathways Among Dropouts

The four pathways previously described (in education, in employment, not in education or employment, and mixed) are associated with different consequences; they are also foreshadowed by different antecedents. These antecedents are better known for some pathways than for others. Namely, much more is known about the factors that distinguish dropouts who return to school or who are either in school or employed than for those who are considered disconnected. We thus focus on this particular contrast between connected and disconnected youth, even though this dual approach does not do justice to the full heterogeneity of pathways (Schoon, 2015). An overview of individual antecedents associated with these two pathways is presented first, followed by a brief discussion of more distal family- and school-related antecedents.

Individual Factors

Many studies show that dropouts who go back to school had, on average, a more favorable individual profile during high school or before than those who do not. For instance, their academic aspirations and grades were initially higher; they also had repeated fewer grades and had a more resilient temperament (Berktold, Geis, & Kaufman, 1998; Entwisle, Alexander, & Olson, 2004; Sacker & Schoon, 2007). Furthermore, those who dropped out later and who had thus accumulated more course credits prior to dropout were more likely to return to school than those who dropped out earlier and with fewer credits (Suh & Suh, 2004). Re-enrollment was also found to be higher among females as compared to male dropouts, although becoming a parent before or shortly after dropout generally reduces the chances of re-enrollment and graduation, especially among females (Berliner, Barrat, Fong, & Shirk, 2008; Boylan & Renzulli, 2014; Looker & Thiessen, 2008; Raymond, 2008). Finally, dropouts with a history of disability or of involvement in the juvenile justice system were also found to be less likely to re-enroll, as compared to those without such histories (Altschuler & Brash, 2004; Blum, White, & Gallay, 2005; Wertheimer, 2002; Wyckoff, Cooney, Djakovic, & McClanahan, 2008).

Family Background

In addition to individual characteristics, family background is also associated with post-dropout pathways. As compared with dropouts who do not re-enroll, dropouts who return to school tend to come from families with a higher socioeconomic status, who belong to advantaged racial or ethnic groups, and in which parents value education more (Berliner et al., 2008; Hurst, Kelly, & Princiotta, 2004; Looker & Thiessen, 2008; Schoon & Lyons-Amos, 2016). Similar patterns are found in studies comparing dropouts who work to those who are unemployed. In the United States for instance, employment rates are higher among White dropouts than among their Black or Hispanic counterparts (Levitan, 2005). Also, among immigrant dropouts, those whose family immigrated later in their life course are more at risk of disconnection, because immigration during adolescence as opposed to childhood is associated with less language and cultural fluency in the host country (e.g., Carhill, Suárez-Orozco, & Páez, 2008; Fine & Jaffe-Walter, 2007).

School-Related Factors

A number of school-related factors may also influence dropouts' pathways during the transition to adulthood. Re-enrollment may be affected by policies and practices implemented in schools prior or after to dropout. Prior to dropout, school-related factors that are associated with higher risks for dropout, such as harsh disciplinary policies and poor school climate (Lamont et al., 2013), could also have a lingering impact after dropout has occurred. For instance, those who cite conflicts with teachers or peers as a reason why they left school were found to be less likely to enroll afterwards (Boylan & Renzulli, 2014). After dropout, the availability of a variety of second-chance programs, including not only GED-like programs that offer high school equivalencies but also apprenticeships and vocational training options may also facilitate reengagement in education and employment (Sum et al., 2014). This connects dropout to the issue of vocational specificity, which is covered in detail by Muja, Gesthuizen, and Wolbers (this volume).

Wider Social and Economic Factors

The fortunes of low-educated emerging adults do not depend only on themselves, their families, and their local schools: They also depend on broader social and economic forces. As already discussed, economic cycles and long-term trends influence the levels of employment among low-educated young adults. In general, the situation has deteriorated in recent years, as fewer jobs are available to them, and the remaining ones are often of poor quality (e.g., Kalleberg, 2011; Sum et al., 2014). In the face of these trends, disconnected young dropouts need strong supports and attractive and affordable options to successfully reconnect to the labor market, for instance, through subsidized programs that offer paid work opportunities (Bloom, 2010; Settersten & Ray, 2010; Sum et al., 2014). The willingness of policymakers to fund such programs may depend on how emerging adults are generally perceived. For instance, common misconceptions may diminish support for such initiatives, such as those suggesting that instability at this life stage is normal and harmless (Côté, 2014). Research on the transition to adulthood among highly vulnerable youth such as dropouts may help dispel such misconceptions. The next section provides some examples of policies and programs that could facilitate school-to-work transitions among low-educated, vulnerable youth.

Programs and Policies

A comprehensive review of programs and policies aiming at facilitating the school-to-work transition among high school dropouts is beyond the scope of this chapter; rather, the next paragraphs aim at providing a general overview of a range of approaches. To do so, we draw on recent reviews of programs and policies designed to re-engage disconnected youth in North America (Bloom, 2010; Sum et al., 2014) and Europe (Berlingieri, 2014; Kluve, 2010; Symonds & O'Sullivan, 2017). We focus on programs for high school dropouts offering concrete training or job opportunities. Following Bloom et al. (2010), we categorize these programs in three broad types and provide case examples of programs that have been rigorously evaluated.

A first type of program focuses on work and aims at providing paid work experiences for high school dropouts. One example is the Youth Incentive Entitlement Pilot Projects (Farkas et al., 1984). In this program, high school dropouts between 16 and 19 years old were offered full-time employment during the summer and part-time employment during the school year at minimum-wage jobs on the condition that they return to school. The program led to significant improvement in employment and earnings during and after the program but had no impact on school enrollment and graduation.

Other examples come from Ireland and the United Kingdom (Symonds & O'Sullivan, 2017), where national programs take work-first approaches to get emerging adults quickly into employment, using work experience, career counseling, financial incentives, and sanctions. These programs are targeting all young people but could be particularly helpful for dropouts who show more difficulty in their integration into employment. For example, the JobBridge program in Ireland allows young people between the ages of 18 and 25 who have been actively seeking employment for at least three months to obtain internships. A financial compensation of €50 per week for a total of 30 to 40 hours a week is given over a nine-month period. However, the results of a recent assessment of the program are mixed (Doorley, 2015) finding that while most participants were satisfied with their experience, there was only a minority who succeeded in obtaining a position after their internship. The United Kingdom's National Youth Contract program, similar to the JobBridge program in Ireland, also helps young people between the ages of 16 and 24 in their transition to the labor market by providing paid training courses aimed at developing pre-employment skills, work experience placement, and access to job interviews (see Symonds & O'Sullivan, 2017).

A second type of program focuses primarily on education and job training. For instance, in the National Guard Youth ChalleNGe program (Millenky, Bloom, Muller-Ravett, & Broadus, 2011), dropouts spend about five months in residence and receive education and character and skills training sessions, as well as career counseling and planning. After this initial phase, participants transition to a final 12-month, nonresidential phase involving structured mentoring and placement in productive educational or work activities. In terms of outcomes, this program was found to have positive impacts on education credentials, employment, and earnings three years after initial enrollment when the participants were in their early 20s. The Youth Build program, another program conceived in the United States that is also available in several countries such as South Africa and Canada, has similar objectives: to enable young people from very disadvantaged backgrounds between the ages of 16 to 24 to graduate or to enter the labor market. This program provides high school dropouts or other vulnerable young people with different kinds of training such as academic training, on-site construction training, and leadership training. Participants also have access to assistance regarding different problems they could encounter during the program (e.g., job placement, counseling, social services) and continue to have access to those services for a 12-month period following the end of the program. An evaluation of this program showed that youth who participated were more likely to obtain employment compared to a control group (Mitchell, Jenkins, Nguyen, Lerman, & DeBarry, 2003). Also, of all the participants who enrolled in the program without any high school qualifications, approximatively 29% obtained new credentials.

A third type of approach consists of mandatory welfare-based programs designed to support school enrollment and attendance via various incentives and social services. For instance, the Ohio Learning, Earning, and Parenting (LEAP) program provided financial incentive and services including case management, child care, and transportation to adolescent mothers on welfare (Bos & Fellerath, 1997). Positive outcomes in terms of GED receipt and earnings were observed.

Overall, these types of programs can confer gains in education and employment at least in the short-term, but few evaluations included long-term follow-ups; those that did found that the impacts tended to fade over time, even though in some cases significant impacts remained after a few years (Bloom, 2010; Millenky et al., 2011). Also, many of these programs aimed at helping students obtain alternative credentials like the GED were successful, but that does not ensure improved labor market outcomes because many employers do not see the GED as being equivalent to a high school diploma (Heckman et al., 2014). Existing programs are also limited because dropouts enrolling in those program choose to do so, which implies that they were motivated to change their paths (Bloom, 2010). It is thus uncertain whether the reviewed programs would work to the same extent with those who do not typically enroll. National programs that do not specifically target dropouts, such as JobBridge or Youth Contract, also have some shortcomings. As raised by Symonds and O'Sullivan in their recent program review (2017), the quality of the mentors helping the youth in learning new skills and the presence of a good support system are sometimes lacking in those programs. These authors also stressed that many programs were not evidence-based and that a lot of programs did not pay much attention to work preparation skills. Further research and development is thus apparently needed to generate options that durably improve both education and employment outcomes among dropouts with different profiles.

Limits of Extant Literature on the School-to-Work Transition Among High School Dropouts

Despite the relevance of the reviewed studies on the school-to-work transitions among high school dropouts, this literature remains limited in several ways. A first set of limits stems from the use of heterogeneous categories that do not distinguish dropouts from youth with a secondary school qualification. Many studies on the school-to-work transition include high school dropouts in their sample, but dropouts' experiences are often not singled out for separate analyses. Rather, as exemplified in the section about terminology, dropouts are often collapsed in categories also including youth who have a high school diploma but who do not work or pursue their education further after graduation. Accordingly, it is difficult to parse out the factors that are specifically associated with dropouts' educational and employment outcomes in early adulthood.

Second, even in studies considering dropouts separately, the unfolding of their school-to-work pathways is often unclear because of suboptimal or inconsistent time frames and measurement strategies used to determine educational and employment over time. For instance, dropouts are often identified rather crudely by singling out youth who are not in education and who do not have high school credentials at the time of data collection in early adulthood (e.g., see Ralston et al., 2016). With such an approach, those who dropped out and successfully returned to school before they were surveyed are indistinguishable from those who never dropped out. This means it is impossible to study the experiences of dropouts who successfully returned to school, along with the factors associated with their resilience. To avoid these problems and fully understand the full range of post-dropout pathways, it will be necessary to use longitudinal designs that regularly and consistently assess dropouts' educational and employment status starting when they first quit high school or before, along with analytic techniques that allow for a thorough treatment of such data (for a recent interesting example, see Schoon & Lyons-Amos, 2016). Such approaches would allow for a deeper understanding of the factors that support or hinder successful transitions in this group. Moreover, standard definitions of post–high school pathways would highly facilitate interpretation and comparisons across studies.

A third limit is related to the sparse research base on the processes underlying dropouts' difficulties and successes in the school-to-work transition. Beyond highlighting associations between dropout and poor outcomes in the labor market, it is necessary to understand how and why the gap between dropouts and more educated peers emerges, so as to develop policies and practices with the potential to bridge this gap. Even though important progress has been made in this regard (Sum et al., 2014), researchers still need to examine the extent to which the gap reflects deficient skills, biased hiring practices, wider labor market dynamics, lack of adequate training options or of knowledge about available options, mental and physical health problems associated with high school dropout, family and child care issues, financial hardship, etc. (Campbell, 2015a). The interplay between such factors can be complex, as highlighted by recent work on the transition to adulthood among highly disadvantaged youth (DeLuca et al., 2016).

Finally, as noted by Bloom (2010), there is a lack of research thoroughly evaluating programs and policies aimed at supporting high school dropouts as a specific group independent of broader groups such as NEET during the transition to adulthood. This kind of research is essential to identify what works best, for whom, and under what circumstances and, in turn, to truly help emerging adults who need it most at a strategic junction of the life course.

Conclusion

In advanced economies, young people who drop out of high school are likely to experience a number of difficulties during the school-to-work transition. However, even within this at-risk group, there is considerable heterogeneity, with some faring better than others as they transition to adulthood. Understanding this heterogeneity, and the processes behind it, is necessary to better understand and answer the needs of dropouts and early school leavers with different profiles.

Acknowledgment

Financial support for the preparation of this article was provided to Véronique Dupéré by Canada's Social Sciences and Humanities Research Council (SSHRC), Fonds de recherche du Québec—Santé (FRQS), and Société et culture (FRQSC) and IRSPUM.

References

Altschuler, D. M., & Brash, R. (2004). Adolescent and teenage offenders confronting the challenges and opportunities of reentry. *Youth Violence and Juvenile Justice*, *2*(1), 72–87. doi:10.1177/1541204003260048

Barrat, V. X., Berliner, B., & Fong, A. B. (2012). When dropping out is not a permanent high school outcome: Student characteristics, motivations, and reenrollment challenges. *Journal of Education for Students Placed at Risk*, *17*(4), 217–233. doi:10.1080/10824669.2012.717028

Berktold, J., Geis, S., & Kaufman, P. (1998). *Subsequent educational attainment of high school dropouts*. Washington, DC: National Center for Educational Statistics.

Berliner, B., Barrat, V. X., Fong, A. B., & Shirk, P. B. (2008). *Reenrollment of high school dropouts in a large, urban school district*. Washington, DC: U.S. Department of Education.

Berlingieri, F., Bonin, H., Sprietsma, M. (2014). *Youth unemployment in Europe: Appraisal and policy options*. Mannheim, Germany: Centre for European Economic Research.

Bloom, D. (2010). Programs and policies to assist high school dropouts in the transition to adulthood. *The Future of Children*, *20*, 89–108. doi:10.1353/foc.0.0039

Bloom, D., Thompson, S. L., & Ivry, R. (2010). *Building a learning agenda around disconnected youth*. New York, NY: MDRC.

Blum, R., White, P. H., & Gallay, L. (2005). Moving into adulthood for youth with disabilities and serious health concerns (Policy brief no. 26). Philadelphia, PA: University of Pennsylvania, MacArthur Research Network on Transitions to Adulthood and Public Policy.

Booth, A., Brown, S. L., Landale, N. S., Manning, W. D., & McHale, S. M. (2012). *Early adulthood in a family context*. New York, NY: Springer.

Bos, J. M., & Fellerath, V. (1997). *LEAP: Final report on Ohio's welfare initiative to improve school attendance among teenage parents*. New York, NY: Manpower Demonstration Research Corporation.

Boylan, R. L., & Renzulli, L. (2014). Routes and reasons out, paths back: The influence of push and pull reasons for leaving school on students' school reengagement. *Youth & Society*, *49*(1), 46–71. doi:10.1177/0044118x14522078

Bray, J. W., Depro, B., McMahon, D., Siegle, M., & Mobley, L. (2016). Disconnected geography: A spatial analysis of disconnected youth in the United States. *Journal of Labor Research*, *37*, 317–342. doi:10.1007/s12122-016-9228-1

Bridgeland, J. M., DiIulio, J. J., Jr., & Morison, K. B. (2006). *The silent epidemic: Perspectives of high school dropouts.* Washington, DC: Civic Enterprises in association with Peter D. Hart Research Associates for the Bill & Melinda Gates Foundation.

Brunello, G., & De Paola, M. (2014). The costs of early school leaving in Europe. *IZA Journal of Labor Policy*, *3*, 22. doi:10.1186/2193-9004-3-22

Brzinsky-Fay, C. (2007). Lost in transition? Labour market entry sequences of school leavers in Europe. *European Sociological Review*, *23*(4), 409–422. doi:10.1093/esr/jcm011

Burd-Sharps, S., & Lewis, K. (2012). One in seven: Ranking youth disconnection in the 25 largest metro areas. *Measure of America.* Retrieved from http://www.measureofamerica.org/wp-content/uploads/2012/09/MOA-One_in_Seven09-14.pdf

Campbell, C. (2015a). High school dropouts after they exit school: Challenges and directions for sociological research. *Sociology Compass*, *9*(7), 619–629. doi:10.1111/soc4.12279

Campbell, C. (2015b). The socioeconomic consequences of dropping out of high school: Evidence from an analysis of siblings. *Social Science Research*, *51*, 108–118. doi:10.1016/j.ssresearch.2014.12.011

Carhill, A., Suárez-Orozco, C., & Páez, M. (2008). Explaining English language proficiency among adolescent immigrant students. *American Educational Research Journal*, *45*(4), 1155–1179. doi:10.3102/0002831204500411 55

Case, A., & Deaton, A. (2015). Rising morbidity and mortality in midlife among white non-Hispanic Americans in the 21st century. *Proceedings of the National Academy of Sciences*, *112*, 15078–15083. doi:10.1073/pnas.1518393112

Conger, R. D., Conger, K. J., & Martin, M. J. (2010). Socioeconomic status, family processes, and individual development. *Journal of Marriage and Family*, *72*, 685–704. doi:10.1111/j.1741-3737.2010.00725.x

Côté, J. E. (2014). The dangerous myth of emerging adulthood: An evidence-based critique of a flawed developmental theory. *Applied Developmental Science*, *18*(4), 177–188. doi:10.1080/10888691.2014.954451

Dalton, B., Glennie, E., & Ingels, S. J. (2009). Late high school dropouts: Characteristics, experiences, and changes across cohorts. *National Center for Education Statistics, Institute of Education Sciences, U.S. Department of Education.* Retrieved from http://nces.ed.gov/pubs2009/2009307.pdf

DeLuca, S., Clampet-Lundquist, S., & Edin, K. (2016). *Coming of age in the other America.* New York, NY: Russell Sage Foundation.

Doorley, J. (2015). *Jobbridge: Stepping stone or dead end?* Dublin, Ireland: National Youth Council of Ireland.

Entwisle, D. R., Alexander, K. L., & Olson, L. S. (2004). Temporary as compared to permanent high school dropout. *Social Forces*, *82*(3), 1181–1205. doi:10.1353/sof.2004.0036

Eurostat. (2016). Early leavers from education and training. *Statistics Explained.* Retrieved from https://ec.europa.eu/eurostat/statistics-explained/index.php?title=Early_leavers_from_education_and_training#Overview

Farkas, G., Olsen, R., Stromsdorfer, E., Sharpe, L., Skidmore, F., Smith, D. A., & Merrill, S. (1984). *Post-program impacts of the youth incentive entitlement pilot projects.* New York, NY: Manpower Demonstration Research Corporation.

Fine, M., & Jaffe-Walter, R. (2007). Swimming: On oxygen, resistance, and possibility for immigrant youth under siege. *Anthropology & Education Quarterly, 38*(1), 76–96. doi:10.1525/aeq.2007.38.1.76

Fuller, S. (2008). Job mobility and wage trajectories for men and women in the United States. *American Sociological Review, 73*(1), 158–183. doi:10.1177/000312240807300108

Furlong, A. (2006). Not a very NEET solution: representing problematic labour market transitions among early school-leavers. *Work, Employment and Society, 20*(3), 553–569. doi:10.1177/0950017006067001

Gilmore, J. (2010). Trends in dropout rates and the labour market outcomes of young dropouts. *Statistics Canada*. Retrieved from http://www.statcan.gc.ca/pub/81-004-x/2010004/article/11339-eng.htm#f

Hair, E. C., Moore, K. A., Ling, T. J., McPhee-Baker, C., & Brown, B. V. (2009). Youth who are "disconnected" and those who then reconnect: Assessing the influence of family, programs, peers and communities. *Child Trends, 37*, 1–8.

Hango, D. W., & De Broucker, P. (2007). *Education-to-labour market pathways of Canadian youth: Findings from the youth in transition survey* (Vol. 5). Ottawa, ON: Culture, Tourism and the Center for Education Statistics, Statistics Canada.

Heckman, J. J., Humphries, J. E., & Kautz, T. (2014). *The myth of achievement tests: The GED and the role of character in American life*. Chicago, IL: University of Chicago Press.

Hurst, D., Kelly, D., & Princiotta, D. (2004). *Educational attainment of high school dropouts 8 years later* (NCES 005-026). Washington, DC: US Department of Education, National Center for Education Statistics.

Janosz, M., Bisset, S. L., Pagani, L. S., & Levin, B. (2011). Educational systems and school dropout in Canada. In S. Lamb, E. Markussen, R. Teese, N. Sandberg, & J. Polesel (Eds.), *School dropout and completion: International comparative studies in theory and policy* (pp. 295–320). Dordrecht, The Netherlands: Springer.

Kalleberg, A. L. (2011). *Good jobs, bad jobs: The rise of polarized and precarious employment systems in the United States 1970s to 2000s*. New York, NY: Russell Sage Foundation.

Kluve, J. (2010). The effectiveness of European active labor market programs. *Labour Economics, 17*(6), 904–918. doi:10.1016/j.labeco.2010.02.004

Krahn, H. J., Howard, A. L., & Galambos, N. L. (2015). Exploring or floundering? The meaning of employment and educational fluctuations in emerging adulthood. *Youth & Society, 47*(2), 245–266. doi:10.1177/0044118x12459061

Lamont, J. H., Devore, C. D., Allison, M., Ancona, R., Barnett, S. E., Gunther, R., . . . Wheeler, L. S. (2013). Out-of-school suspension and expulsion. *Pediatrics, 131*(3), e1000–e1007. doi:10.1542/peds.2012-3932

Lawy, R., Quinn, J., & Diment, K. (2009). Listening to "the thick bunch": (Mis) understanding and (mis) representation of young people in jobs without training in the south west of England. *British Journal of Sociology of Education, 30*(6), 741–755. doi:10.1080/01425690903235284

Levin-Epstein, J., & Greenberg, M. H. (2003). *Leave no youth behind: Opportunities for congress to reach disconnected youth*. Washington, DC: Center for Law and Social Policy.

Levitan, M. (2005). Out of school, out of work . . . Out of luck? New York City's disconnected youth. *Community Service Society of New York*. Retrieved from http://betterfutures.fcny.org/betterfutures/out_of_school_out_of_luck.pdf

Looker, E. D., & Thiessen, V. (2008). *The second chance system: Results from the three cycles of the youth in transition Survey*. Gatineau, QC: Human Resources and Social Development Canada.

MacDonald, R. (2008). Disconnected youth? Social exclusion, the "underclass" & economic marginality. *Social Work & Society, 6*(2), 236–248.

Mascherini, M., Salvatore, L., Meierkord, A., & Jungblut, J.-M. (2012). *NEETs: Young people not in employment, education or training: Characteristics, costs and policy responses in Europe*. Luxembourg: Publications Office of the European Union.

McNally, S., & Telhaj, S. (2007). *The cost of exclusion: Counting the cost of youth disadvantage in the UK*. London, England: The Prince's Trust.

Millenky, M., Bloom, D., Muller-Ravett, S., & Broadus, J. (2011). *Staying on course: Three-year results of the National Guard Youth ChalleNGe evaluation*. New York, NY: MDRC.

Mitchell, M., Jenkins, D., Nguyen, D., Lerman, A., & DeBarry, M. (2003). *Evaluation of the Youthbuild Program. U.S. Department of Housing and Urban Development, Office of Policy Development and Research*. Retrieved from https://www.huduser.gov/Publications/PDF/YouthBuild.pdf

OECD. (2008). *Cutting school drop-out rates key to improve job prospects for disadvantaged youth*. Paris, France: Author.

OECD. (2015). *Education at a Glance 2015: OECD* Indicators. Paris, France: Author.

OECD. (2018). Education at a Glance 2018: OECD Indicators. Paris, France: Author.

Pearlin, L. I., & Bierman, A. (2013). Current issues and future directions in research into the stress process. In C. S. Aneshenzel, J. C. Phelan, & A. Bierman (Eds.), *Handbook of the sociology of mental health* (2nd ed., pp. 325–340). Dordrecht, The Netherlands: Springer.

Quintini, G., & Manfredi, T. (2009). *Going separate ways? School-to-work transitions in the United States and Europe*. Paris, France: OECD.

Ralston, K., Feng, Z., Everington, D., & Dibben, C. (2016). Do young people not in education, employment or training experience long-term occupational scarring? A longitudinal analysis over 20 years of follow-up. *Contemporary Social Science, 11*(2–3), 203–221. doi:10.1080/21582041.2016.1194452

Raymond, M. (2008). *High school dropouts returning to school*. Ottawa, ON: Statistics Canada, Culture, Tourism and the Centre for Education Statistics.

Roberts, S. (2011). Beyond "NEET" and "tidy" pathways: considering the "missing middle" of youth transition studies. *Journal of Youth Studies, 14*(1), 21–39. doi:10.1080/13676261.2010.489604

Rosenbaum, J. E. (2001). *Beyond college for all: Career paths for the forgotten half*. New York, NY: Russell Sage Foundation.

Rosenbaum, J. E., Ahearn, C., Becker, K., & Rosenbaum, J. (2015). *The new forgotten half and research directions to support them*. New York, NY: William T. Grant Foundation.

Rumberger, R. W. (2011). *Dropping out: Why students drop out of high school and what can be done about it*. Cambridge, MA: Harvard University Press.

Rumberger, R. W., & Lamb, S. P. (2003). The early employment and further education experiences of high school dropouts: A comparative study of the United States and Australia. *Economics of Education Review, 22*(4), 353–366. doi:10.1016/S0272-7757(02)00038-9

Rumberger, R. W., & Rotermund, S. (2008). *What happened to dropouts from the high school class of 2004?* Santa Barbara, CA: University of California.

Sacker, A., & Schoon, I. (2007). Educational resilience in later life: Resources and assets in adolescence and return to education after leaving school at age 16. *Social Science Research, 36*(3), 873–896. doi:10.1016/j.ssresearch.2006.06.002

Schoeni, R. F., & Ross, K. E. (2005). Material assistance from families during the transition to adulthood. In R. A. Settersten, F. F. Furstenberg, & R. G. Rumbaut (Eds.), *On the frontier of adulthood: Theory, research, and public policy* (pp. 396–416). Chicago, IL: University of Chicago Press.

Schoon, I. (2015). Diverse pathways: Rethinking the transition to adulthood. In P. R Amato, A. Booth, S. M McHale, & J. Van Hook (Eds.), *Families in an era of increasing inequality* (pp. 115–136). Cham, Switzerland: Springer International.

Schoon, I., & Duckworth, K. (2010). Leaving school early— and making it! *European Psychologist, 15*(4), 283–292. doi:10.1027/1016-9040/a000063

Schoon, I., & Lyons-Amos, M. (2016). Diverse pathways in becoming an adult: The role of structure, agency and context. *Research in Social Stratification and Mobility, 46*, 11–20. doi:10.1016/j.rssm.2016.02.008

Settersten, R. A., Jr., & Ray, B. (2010). What's going on with young people today? The long and twisting path to adulthood. *The Future of Children, 20*(1), 19–41. doi:10.1353/foc.0.0044

Suh, S., & Suh, J. (2004). Focusing on second chance education: High school completion among dropouts. *Journal of Educational Research & Policy Studies, 4*(1), 59–73.

Sum, A., Khatiwada, I., & McLaughlin, J., & Palma, S. (2009). *The consequences of dropping out of high school: Joblessness and jailing for high school dropouts and the high cost for taxpayers.* Boston, MA: Center for Labor Market Studies, Northeastern University.

Sum, A., Khatiwada, I., McLaughlin, J., & Palma, S. (2011). No country for young men: Deteriorating labor market prospects for low-skilled men in the United States. *The Annals of the American Academy of Political and Social Science, 635*(1), 24–55. doi:10.1177/0002716210393694

Sum, A., Khatiwada, I., Trubskyy, M., Ross, M., McHugh, W., & Palma, S. (2014). *The plummeting labor market fortunes of teens and young adults.* Washington, DC: Brookings Institution.

Symonds, J. E., & O'Sullivan, C. (2017). Educating young adults to be work-ready in Ireland and the United Kingdom: A review of programmes and outcomes. *Review of Education, 5*(3), 229–263. doi:10.1002/rev3.3099

U.S. Department of Education. (2016). *The condition of education 2016* (NCES 2016-144). Washington, DC: National Center for Education Statistics.

Vargas Lascano, D. I., Galambos, N. L., Krahn, H. J., & Lachman, M. E. (2015). Growth in perceived control across 25 years from the late teens to midlife: The role of personal and parents' education. *Developmental Psychology, 51*(1), 124–135. doi:10.1037/a0038433

W. T. Grant Foundation Commission on Work, Family, and Citizenship. (1988). *The forgotten half: Pathways to success for America's youth and young families.* New York, NY: W. T. Grant Foundation.

Wertheimer, R. F. (2002). Youth who" age out" of foster care: Troubled lives, troubling prospects. *Child Trends Research Brief*, 59, 1–8. Retrieved from http://www.childtrends.org/Files/Child_Trends-2002_12_01_RB_FosterCare.pd

Wyckoff, L., Cooney, S. M., Djakovic, D. K., & McClanahan, W. S. (2008). *Disconnected young people in New York City: Crisis and opportunity.* New York, NY: Public/Private Ventures.

Yates, S., & Payne, M. (2006). Not so NEET? A critique of the use of "NEET" in setting targets for interventions with young people. *Journal of Youth Studies, 9*(3), 329–344. doi:10.1080/13676260600805671

Zaff, J. F., Ginsberg, K. K., Boyd, M. J., & Kakli, Z. (2014). Reconnecting disconnected youth: Examining the development of productive engagement. *Journal of Research on Adolescence, 24*(3), 526–540. doi:10.1111/jora.12109

Zweig, J. M. (2003). *Vulnerable youth: Identifying their need for alternative educational settings.* Washington, DC: Urban Institute.

12

Vocational Education and Youth Labor Market Integration

The Role of Vocational Specificity at the Level of School-Leavers, Study Programs, and Education Systems

Ardita Muja, Maurice Gesthuizen, and Maarten H. J. Wolbers

Introduction

The transition from school to work is an important rite of passage in young people's lives, in which educational qualifications have a profound impact on young people's integration into the labor market. It refers to the period between the end of young people's enrollment in school-based education and their first job position in the labor market. Youth's initial labor market entry after leaving school is one of the crucial changes young people experience in emerging adulthood (Arnett, 2000; Bynner, 2005). The transition from school to work is regarded as a decisive stage in the process of becoming an adult and is closely related with other transitions in youth, such as leaving the parental home and starting a family (Wolbers, 2007a). The impact of this transition goes beyond the initial labor market position, given the substantial empirical evidence that the first steps taken in the labor market determine subsequent employment chances, labor market outcomes and life chances (Barone & Schizzerotto, 2011; De Lange, Gesthuizen & Wolbers, 2014a; De Lange; Wolbers, Gesthuizen & Ultee, 2014). This is especially true for young people from upper vocational education compared to their counterparts from higher education, as they experience the final stage of occupational identity formation within the period of emerging adulthood (Bynner, 2005). Hence, a smooth transition from school to work is not only crucial during young people's early labor market career during emerging adulthood, as it prevents unemployment or inactivity when leaving school, but also in terms of long-term effects on their future careers and overall future life prospects.

Ardita Muja, Maurice Gesthuizen, and Maarten H. J. Wolbers, *Vocational Education and Youth Labor Market Integration* In: *Young Adult Development at the School-to-Work Transition.* E. Anne Marshall and Jennifer E. Symonds, Oxford University Press (2021).
 DOI: 10.1093/oso/9780190941512.003.0012.

With regard to the significant impact of education on labor market integration and outcomes, one of the key functions of education is to prepare young people for the labor market (Van de Werfhorst, 2014). However, in many Western societies, including the Netherlands, social scientists and policymakers are concerned about the difficulties young people face when entering the labor market. Previous comparative research has found that the share of unemployment and temporary employment is high among youth in Europe (Scherer, 2005; De Lange, Gesthuizen, & Wolbers, 2014b). These concerns are even greater for school-leavers with lower educational qualifications, as they have higher risks of unemployment or, if employed, have higher risks of attaining less stable, less autonomous, lower-skilled, and lower-paid jobs (De Grip & Wolbers, 2005).

The vocational specificity of the education system is regarded as a central component for allocating young people to the labor market (Van de Werfhorst, 2014), helping school-leavers to avoid risks of unemployment, and becoming skilled rather than unskilled workers (Arum & Shavit, 1995). Most upper secondary education systems distinguish a vocationally and academically oriented track. The vocational orientation in upper secondary education is the extent to which vocational-specific skills are emphasized as opposed to more academic skills. Different existing theoretical frameworks yield contrasting notions about the impact of vocational skills on labor market returns. Two dominant theories in the current literature are human capital theory (Becker, 1964) and job competition theory (Thurow, 1975; Spence, 1973). According to human capital theory, investment in vocational education equips students with relevant job-specific skills that make them immediately productive in the labor market as opposed to investment in academic education. Human capital theory holds the assumption that employers act rationally and prefer employees with higher levels of labor productivity. On the other hand, job competition theory predicts that vocational school-leavers are stigmatized by employers as being less motivated or having less (cognitive) abilities than academic school-leavers (Iannelli & Raffe, 2007). This presumed negative signal of vocational qualifications might place vocationally educated school-leavers lower in the job queue, resulting in risks of unemployment and a troublesome transition from school to work.

In this chapter, we discuss the role of vocational specificity in upper secondary education in promoting (or not) youth labor market integration. The first reason why this is an important issue to consider is that social inequality manifests itself within a society through young people's labor market opportunities, which are, at least partly, shaped by the way institutional arrangements of an education system are organized (Shavit & Müller, 1998). Second, even though the impact of vocational specificity runs through at least three levels—that is, individual vocational-specific skills, the vocational specificity of study programs, and the vocational orientation of national education systems—research on the impact of vocational education on youth labor market integration usually focuses at a subset of these levels. To establish more clarity in the overall impact of vocational education, we argue that an overview of the theoretical insights and empirical evidence regarding this field of research is necessary, paying special attention to the levels through which the impact of vocational education might operate. This should lead then to the development of a structured set of indicators that measure the vocational specificity of education on all three levels, integrating relevant social-scientific knowledge from different disciplines in one, coherent indicator system.

To examine the role of vocational education during the transition from school to work, it is important to adequately define the various aspects of both vocational specificity and youth labor market integration. In the existing literature, the latter often refers to various labor market outcomes of young people: risks of unemployment, instability of employment (i.e., fixed-term or temporary employment; Gebel & Giesecke, 2016; De Lange et al., 2014b), the duration of job search (Wolbers, 2007b), and the quality of the (first) job (e.g., occupational status and wage level; Wolbers, 2007b; Muller, 2005). Young people with better employment prospects are more integrated into the labor market.

As we have indicated, the vocational specificity of education manifests itself at three levels: individuals (or school-leavers), study programs, and education systems. These three levels are closely related to one other. A country's structure of the education system affects the design of the study programs within that country, and this consequently has an influence on the type of knowledge, skills, and competencies that are obtained by the individuals participating in that particular study program within that particular education system. In addition, as education plays a large role in the socialization of students, it is at least plausible that school-leavers' values, preferences, and goals are influenced by the education system and study program attended. In the search for a job, school-leavers' choices of action on the one hand depend on educational requirements (e.g., vocational or academic qualifications), individual preferences, and resources. On the other hand, the institutional context restricts and predefines school-leavers' resources and opportunities, influencing their search for a job and their labor market integration.

On the level of individual school-leavers, vocational specificity reflects the distinction in their acquisition of either generic or specific competences (Meng, 2006). Generic competences refer to general or academic knowledge and skills that can be applied in a wide variety of contexts, whereas specific competences refer to vocational or job-specific knowledge and skills that can be applied in a limited number of occupation-specific contexts (Van der Velden, 2011). In general, it is assumed that school-leavers from vocationally oriented study programs are equipped with job-specific knowledge and skills, making them immediately productive on the job compared to their counterparts from more generally or academically oriented education (Bishop, 1995; Shavit & Muller, 2000). This immediate labor productivity is what makes vocationally trained school-leavers valuable and more in demand by employers, which may in turn also enhance their employment opportunities (Hanushek, Woessmann, & Zhang, 2011).

On the level of study programs within a country, vocational specificity usually refers to the relative degree to which study programs equip their students with job-specific knowledge and skills required to practice a particular occupation or profession. As such, and independent of the individual skills of school-leavers, programs emit signals to employers regarding the potentiality of the students that completed them. Previous research has argued that school-leavers from more vocationally oriented study programs are more in demand by employers, because they require less on-the-job training than school-leavers from generally or academically oriented study programs (Glebbeek, 1988; Van der Velden, & Wolbers, 2007).

On the level of national education systems, vocational specificity reflects the institutional linkage between education and the labor market (Allmendinger, 1989; Shavit & Muller, 2000). The strength of the institutional linkage depends on the degree to which the labor market system in a country is involved in the design and the administration of the education system (Shavit & Muller, 2000). There are various ways in which this institutional linkage can be organized, which basically refers to the extent to which theoretical learning is combined with practical work experience. In general, vocationally oriented education systems are considered to be strongly linked to the labor market, whereas generally oriented education systems are considered to be weakly associated to the labor market (Wolbers, 2003, 2007b).

Figure 12.1 illustrates the manifestation of the vocational specificity of education on all three levels in relation to youth labor market integration.

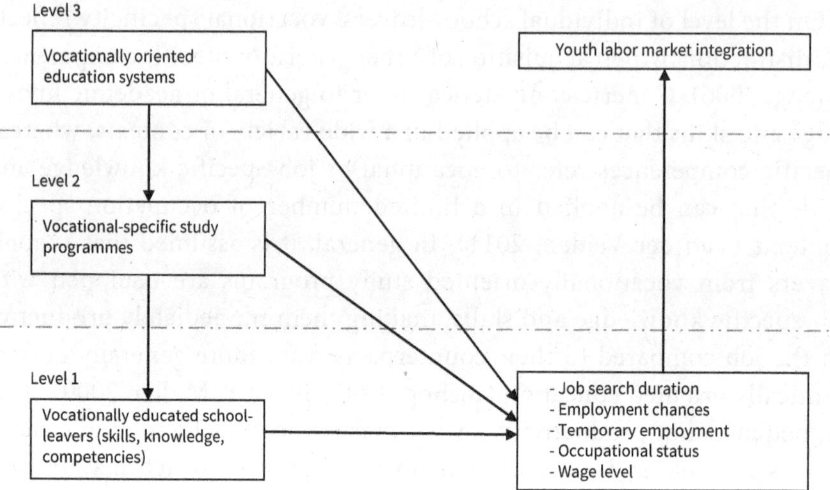

Figure 12.1 Schematic overview of the role of vocational specificity on youth labor market integration.

The Role of Vocational Specificity at the Level of School-Leavers

Various individual mechanisms are at play in how education impacts youth labor market integration. This section give an overview of some of these mechanisms to offer an insight into why education provides different labor market returns between school-leavers.

Level of Education

According to human capital theory (Becker, 1964), the acquisition of knowledge and skills through schooling is a form of capital. Individual expenditures on human resources, such as education, can be seen as the product of deliberate self-investment (Schultz, 1961). By investing in education, people acquire more skills, knowledge, and competencies that directly affect their labor productivity, valued and rewarded by employers, which improves their prospects in the labor market, including an increase in employment opportunities (Schultz, 1961; Bishop, 1995; Borghans & Heijke, 2005). Over the years, studies have continually found that more educated people have better employment opportunities, higher occupational status, higher salaries, and better employment contracts than less educated people (e.g., Andersen & Van de Werfhorst, 2010). Thus, increasing educational input typically leads to higher labor market outputs through the acquisition of skills, knowledge and competencies (Hanushek & Woessmann, 2005).

However, level of education is just one piece of the big puzzle in how education promotes youth labor market integration. Large differences in labor market integration are found even between school-leavers with the same level of education (Iannelli & Raffe 2007, Levels et al., 2014; Pfeffer, 2015; Shavit & Muller, 2000). These findings indicate that horizontal differentiation in education matters as well and is related to the type of education attained, specifically vocational versus general education, and the way its organization prepares school-leavers for the labor market (Pfeffer, 2008).

Vocational Versus General Skills

The distinction between vocationally and generally oriented education received much attention in the literature, and this form of horizontal differentiation has led to an ongoing debate as to whether vocational or general skills are more effective in facilitating youths' employment opportunities and their school-to-work transition. General or academic education provides students with generic or academic skills, which can be defined as cognitive, analytical, communicative, and problem-solving skills that can be applied in a wide range of contexts (Heijke, Meng, & Ris, 2003; Meng, 2006). Thus, generic skills are occupation-independent and are transferable to other occupational fields. General or comprehensive education often prepares students for higher levels of education. In contrast, vocational education refers to the extent to which students are provided with work-specific skills, which can be defined as job-specific knowledge directly applicable in the labor market. These skills can only be applied in a limited number of occupation-specific contexts (Van der Velden, 2011).

Within the framework of human capital theory—with its focus on skills of productive value in the labor market—an important question is, What type of skills should be learned at school that bring forth productive workers in the workplace? A central assumption is that school-leavers from vocational education programs are equipped with job-specific skills that make them immediately productive on the job as opposed to their counterparts from general education (Bishop, 1995; Shavit & Muller, 2000). Because of their immediate job productivity, vocationally trained school-leavers are more valuable and in demand from employers, which enhances their chances of entering the labor market successfully (Hanushek, Woessmann, & Zang, 2011).

Contrariwise, job competition theory (Thurow, 1975) gives little weight to teaching vocational skills in schools. This theory assumes that labor productivity is determined by occupational characteristics rather than individual ones. It also assumes that vocational skills are mainly acquired through on-the-job training and not in education. Education does not really provide students with productive skills but instead provides general cognitive skills that are seen as important signals of school-leavers' learning abilities, motivation, and perseverance in obtaining new job-relevant skills (Van der Velden & Wolbers, 2007). In this perspective, education serves as a "screening device" or "signal" to future employers (Spence, 1973). Job seekers with more education signal higher levels of productivity (Bol & Van de Werfhorst, 2011). Employers use educational degrees or credentials to screen job applicants and put them in an imaginary labor queue (Thurow, 1975).

Related to this theory is the notion that educational degrees can be expressed as credentials that act as a mechanism for education as a means of social closure by the elites, where people are not selected for their productivity per se, but for the external standards of what they possess (Collins, 1979). In this perspective, diplomas, degrees, and certificates are replaced by a more loaded concept of credentials, set up to create legitimate social barriers that sustain social differences and structure the access to occupations (Bol & Van de Werfhorst, 2011). Credentials give access to higher-status occupations, and the higher the educational credentials, the more access to higher-status occupations school-leavers have. Following both signaling and credentialing mechanisms, degrees are not only rewarded because they signal the potential productivity of a job applicant but also because access to occupations is regulated on account of credentials (Bills & Wacker, 2003). Investing in academic (read: general) education rather than vocational education therefore enhances students' employment prospects.

Furthermore, the labor queue model yields negative predictions for the effect of vocational education on the labor market integration of school-leavers. Vocational education is often attended by academically weaker students and can inhibit further educational attainment (Shavit & Muller, 2000). As vocational students have fewer opportunities to enter higher education than academic students and tend to have earlier exits from school (Ryan, 2000), vocationally trained applicants may be stigmatized as being less motivated or having less (cognitive) abilities than academically trained applicants (Iannelli & Raffe, 2007; Spence, 1973). This stigmatization might place vocational school-leavers lower in the labor queue, resulting in (higher) risks of unemployment and a troublesome transition from school to work.

However, empirical studies have found that vocational education actually reduces unemployment risks compared to general education, which refutes the idea that vocational degrees serve as negative signals to employers (Bol & Van de Werfhorst, 2011; Breen, 2005; De Lange et al., 2014b; Muller, 2005). In terms of signaling, it may be the case that vocational credentials send employers stronger and clearer signals of school-leavers' productivity and abilities than general qualifications. Whether vocational credentials indeed act as positive or negative signals and whether these signals are strong and clear for employers most likely depends on the organization of study programs and institutional characteristics of education systems (Meng, 2006; Muller, 2005; Scherer, 2005). We will elaborate on this in more detail in the following sections.

To date, empirical research on school-to-work transitions deals with a crucial limitation in examining the impact of vocational (versus general) skills, that is, a lack of high-quality and cross-national comparable direct measures of the actual obtained vocational skills of school-leavers. In the majority of studies, an indirect approach is therefore applied, in which an educational qualification in upper secondary vocational education is seen as a suitable measure of the extent to which vocational skills are acquired (e.g., De Lange et al, 2014b; Heisig & Solga, 2015; Iannelli & Raffe, 2007; Levels et al., 2014; Wolbers, 2007b; Scherer, 2005). One reason for this is that vocational skills are acquired in and therefore mainly associated with upper secondary vocational education in many countries. Nevertheless, this type of qualification is a relatively crude measure of the actual vocational skills taught in these programs (Bol & Van de Werfhorst, 2013). Even within a vocational track, the degree of vocational specificity might vary between programs. Progress in this field of research can be made by developing a more direct measure of vocational skills.

Apprenticeship Training

Vocational education can be organized in various ways, whether this is entirely school-based or offered through a combination of school-based teaching and learning at the workplace, such as apprenticeships at firms. In this latter dual system, employers have an influence on the curriculum, which increases the likelihood that the acquired skills are in demand by employers (Ryan, 2001). In addition, apprenticeships are more standardized than firm-specific on-the-job training, and, therefore, the acquired skills are better transferable across employers, firms, or industries (De Grip & Wolbers, 2005). Apprenticeships offer advantages in the allocation process for both employers and school-leavers. For employers, school-leavers with apprenticeship experience are very attractive, since they have already acquired the skills required for the jobs, which saves firms additional training costs. Moreover, employers have the opportunity to screen potential workers during their apprenticeship, which also decreases selection and allocation costs. As for students, apprenticeships provide not only work experience within a firm but also allow students to become acquainted with the firm and its employees. From a network perspective, apprentices benefit from the social capital acquired at the workplace, which gives them easier or even immediate access to employers or their networks that recruit employees (Rosenbaum, Kariya, Settersten, & Maier, 1990). Furthermore, successful completion of an apprenticeship may increase the likelihood of staying employed within the same firm. Accordingly, research has found that apprenticeships are indeed effective in facilitating youth labor market integration (Lerman, 2009; Muller, 2005), in that school-leavers who obtained a vocational degree by combining learning and working in the dual system have lower unemployment risks than their counterparts from school-based vocational education.

Field of Study

Horizontal differentiation is a key mechanism in most education systems. This refers to the extent to which students are adequately sorted in study programs of different fields of study that matches their personal talents and interests. Choosing a field of study has a major impact on further direction and future prospects in the labor market. In this subsection, we discuss the varying skills acquisition between fields of study (Reimer, Noelke, & Kucel, 2008) that can impact youth labor market integration, whereas in the next section we focus on the relationship between study programs of different fields of study and the labor market integration of school-leavers.

Human capital theory brings forth a straightforward explanation of why different fields of study carry different labor market outcomes. Proponents of this theory assume that different fields of study represent different types of specialized human capital (Daymont & Andrisani, 1984; Paglin & Rufolo, 1990). Students invest in a specific field of study to accumulate skills and knowledge that increase labor productivity rewarded by employers. It seems plausible that different fields of study vary in their content provision for vocational knowledge and skills and that certain fields offer opportunities for students to develop more productive skills and thus better prepare students for the labor market than other fields of study (Van de Werfhorst & Kraaykamp, 2001).

Regarding specific fields of study, scholars have developed a comprehensive framework within the human capital approach, relating fields of study to four different types of skills: cultural, economic, communicative, and technical skills versus general skills (Kalmijn & Van der Lippe, 1997; Van de Werfhorst, 2002). For example, technical fields may require more vocational knowledge and skills for students to be sufficiently prepared for the labor market as opposed to cultural fields (Dronkers, 1993). Moreover, the labor market returns to different fields may also depend on the scarcity of the type of specific human capital they are associated with (Paglin & Rufolo, 1990). For example, if fields of study are associated with a scarce form of specific human capital that is in high demand in the labor market, such as computer programming skills, then this may have higher rewards for individuals in the labor market. As most empirical research on fields of study has not measured the actual acquisition of a certain group of skills, it would be interesting for future research to take this into account as well.

From a signaling perspective, some fields of study may be more challenging for students than others and require higher levels of prior ability compared to other fields. Therefore, even within the same broad educational level, fields of study act as a sorting mechanism where students are channeled through their ability, because only a select group can succeed in challenging fields that carry higher labor market rewards. Conversely, students with less prior ability may choose less challenging and less rewarding fields (Reimer et al., 2008). This may result in more challenging fields of study carrying a higher signaling value to employers than less challenging fields that depend less strongly on prior ability. Thus, ability differences are converted into different signal values in the labor market. For this reason, it would be of value to control for prior ability to examine whether specific fields of study impact labor market integration.

The Role of Vocational Specificity at the Level of Study Programs

In the previous section, we discussed the impact of vocational versus general education on individuals, through shaping and channeling individual knowledge, skills, and competencies and, consequentially, impacting young people's transition from school to work. In this section, we expand on that discussion by examining the impact of study program characteristics on school-leavers' employment opportunities. A study program can be described as a specific field of study at a particular level of education (Van der Velden & Wolbers, 2007).

Study programs do not only have an indirect influence on young people's labor market integration in interaction with individual knowledge, skills, and competencies as described, but they also have a direct impact, as the employment opportunities of school-leavers are found to vary widely between study programs, even within the same educational level (Wolbers & Van der Velden, 2007; Bishop, 1995; Xu, 2013). This implies that youth labor market integration not only depends on the type and amount of knowledge and skills acquired, but also on where individuals have acquired these assets. In this section, we focus on study programs in upper secondary education, given that much vocational education takes place here, and many students participate in vocational programs at this level before they enter the labor market (Bol & Van de Werfhorst, 2013).

Training Costs Model

Both human capital and job competition theory share the assumption that employers act rationally and prefer employees with higher levels of prospective labor productivity in relation to the effort it takes to train them. Glebbeek (1988) used this shared assumption to combine the theories into a model of training costs. This model assumes that students are selected based on their expected training costs, which employers cannot individually evaluate but are able to deduce from the average expected training costs of students across a particular study program (Van der Velden & Wolbers, 2007). The premise is that school-leavers with lower expected training costs will have an advantage in the process of employee selection. Following this model, the expected training costs of school-leavers are determined by three components of study programs: vocational specificity, program selectivity, and educational level.

Regarding vocational specificity, study programs differ in the degree to which they specifically prepare students for certain occupations in the labor market. The vocational specificity of study programs indicates the extent to which vocational skills are emphasized in a study program rather than more general knowledge and cognitive abilities. The more a study program provides job-specific skills required for a particular job (or the narrower the occupational profile of a study program is), the less additional on-the-job-training school-leavers need. From this line of reasoning, school-leavers from general study programs are less attractive for employers, because they require more additional on-the-job-training compared to those who finished vocationally oriented study programs. There is corroborating evidence for different labor market outcomes between vocational and academic programs, in which vocationally trained school-leavers have better employment opportunities than their generally trained counterparts (Arum & Shavit, 1995; Bishop, 1995).

Study program selectivity refers to having selective entrance criteria based on students' prestudy program ability and competencies (Klein, 2010). However, even very selective educational programs do not house homogenous groups of students, as there are differences in school-leavers' personal and professional qualities within study programs that can be hidden behind educational credentials (Glebbeek, Wim, & Schakelaar, 1989). Study programs differ in the risk they offer that school-leavers will pass the exam without having a minimum level of skills. Highly selective study programs offer low risks, and vice versa. For employers, this poses a problem because the overperformance of one school-leaver does not simply compensate the underperformance of another (Van der Velden & Wolbers, 2007). If we assume that employers are able to recognize such differences in performance, then this may have an impact on their recruitment behavior and, hence, on the labor market position of school-leavers.

Study programs can enhance their selectivity by closure strategies, which can take the form of student-intake restrictions through entrance requirements or tuition fees. Supply restrictions of school-leavers from certain programs are a result of social closure aimed to exclude some of the applicants. In response to restrictions of supply in these programs, labor market rewards tend to increase (Reimer et al., 2008). High labor market returns incite competition between applicants, and therefore, applicants who are more cognitively and/or financially equipped may have the greatest chance to earn a place. This may lead to an increase in average ability levels in more selective programs. As a consequence, highly selective programs offer less uncertainty and signal higher values about school-leavers' quality with regard to their abilities and competencies compared to weakly selective programs.

The training costs model assumes that employers are able to distinguish the different levels and types of selectivity between study programs, which may influence their recruitment behavior and, subsequently, school-leavers' employment opportunities in the labor market. Employers usually look for highly productive or trainable employees and are therefore keener to select school-leavers that graduate from more selective study programs, as they signal higher mean abilities, lower risks of a minimum possession of skills, and less expected training costs compared to school-leavers from less selective study programs. Thus, according to the training costs model, more selective study programs better facilitate school-leavers' employment opportunities than less selective study programs.

The third part of the model draws on the effort employers have to make to overcome existing skill deficiencies of potential employees. This component is closely related to the general learning abilities of school-leavers and can, therefore, be adequately measured through the educational level of study programs. Through the eyes of the employer, more educated school-leavers have greater learning capabilities, which lowers the required training costs to overcome school-leavers' skill deficiencies. This may mean that, despite the fact that a particular student possesses vocational-specific skills, general learning abilities are still of importance to bridge skill deficiencies.

To summarize, then, study programs that (a) have higher educational levels, (b) are more selective, and (c) are more vocational specific send clearer signals indicating lower additional training costs for employers. Previous empirical research has found that level of education has the most profound effect on (permanent) employment opportunities, job search duration, and income (Klein, 2010; Van der Velden & Wolbers, 2007). The selectivity of education has a subordinate signal for employers, but it is also found to have an impact on employment opportunities. Finally, the specificity of study programs has been found to reduce the job search duration (Klein, 2010) and to positively affect employment opportunities (Van der Velden & Wolbers, 2007), giving some evidence for the ecological validity of the training costs model.

Linkage Between Study Program and Labor Market

Various sociological studies posit that having educational qualifications with a close linkage to the labor market facilitates the school-to-work transition (Allmendinger, 1989; Shavit & Muller, 2000). It is argued there that study programs with a strong linkage to the labor market are characterized by having frequent contact and communication with employers, trade unions, and/or labor organizations, and importantly, by having these agents and agencies jointly involved in the design, updating, and evaluation of programmers' curricula (Iannelli & Raffe, 2007). This close communication and/or collaboration with the labor market sends very clear signals to employers about the potential productivity of school-leavers, suggesting that close linkages between study programs and the labor market may promote smoother school-to-work transitions.

In most Western countries, general study programs prepare students for higher education and tend to be weakly related to the labor market, resulting in employers having little insight into the precise knowledge and skills acquired by school-leavers on these programs (De Grip & Wolbers, 2005). In comparison, vocational study programs usually focus more on preparing students for immediate labor market entry and therefore tend to be more embedded in institutional relationships with the labor market (Breen, 2005). Vocational programs are argued to contribute more to students' human capital, because the skills acquired are more congruent with and more strongly reflect employers' demands, when employers are more involved in the design of the programs (Iannelli & Raffe, 2007). As a result, vocational programs send clear signals to employers about the productivity of school-leavers, and employers have direct knowledge of and are more readily to trust vocational credentials representing the actual skills required for the job. In addition, vocational study programs create stronger networks of students and employers, due to internship requirements in the curriculum, which facilitate school-leavers' access to potential future employers and recruitment networks. In addition, employers can gain additional information about interns and can use this knowledge for determining their hiring decisions.

The strength of the linkage can differ between study programs within the same education system, which has been referred to as the extent to which study programs are either generally or vocationally oriented. In general, vocational study programs maintain a closer linkage with the labor market as opposed to general programs. More recent research has moved away from dichotomizing study programs in either vocational or general programs (DiPrete, Bol, Ciocca, & Van de Werfhorst, 2017). In this research, the vocational specificity of study programs is measured by the linkage strength between study programs and occupational positions, in which both level of education and field of study are taken into account. This new approach measures the vocational specificity of study programs in a more sophisticated way than was done in Van der Velden and Wolbers (2007).

Field of Study

In the previous section we argued that both human capital and job competition theory bring forth a straightforward explanation of why different fields of study carry different labor market outcomes. Despite the fact that the assumed mechanisms focus on the individual (or school-leaver) level, such as the possession of specific skills and competencies, the majority of studies do not actually examine field-related skills. Instead, most research operationalizes these skills by means of the field of study attained (at a particular educational level), in which these theoretical mechanisms serve as an underlying explanation of differential fields of study effects on labor market outcomes.

Regarding specific fields of study, some scholars make a distinction between "hard" fields like mathematics, computer science, physics, and engineering versus "soft" fields like humanities and social studies. Other scholars differentiate between three fields, while some differentiate nine or even more fields (Reimer & Steinmetz, 2007; Smyth, 2005). This variety of classifications makes it somewhat difficult to compare results and discover consistent patterns of labor market returns across studies. However, there is somewhat consistent evidence that the fields of science, technology, engineering, and mathematics (STEM) result in higher labor market returns compared to humanitarian fields (Reimer et al., 2008).

Numerous studies have shown that, in general, employment chances (Reimer et al., 2008; Reimer & Steinmetz, 2007; Smyth, 2005) and occupational status attainment (Smyth, 2005; Van de Werfhorst, 2004) vary between different fields of study, in which soft fields have a disadvantage compared to hard fields (Reimer et al., 2008). Moreover, it was found that fields of study have an impact at labor market entry (Van de Werfhorst, 2002; Van de Werfhorst & Kraaykamp, 2001). Once again, soft fields have a disadvantage (Klein, 2010). One drawback of the current literature is that most research has focused on higher education and less so on upper secondary education. Considering the theoretical reasons why hard versus soft fields of study have differential labor market returns, it seems plausible that these differences may also apply for upper secondary study programs. As discussed, another drawback is that there is a lack of clarity around how field of study impacts school-leavers' labor market outcomes in relation to study program effects, individual skills effects, and the combination of both.

The Role of Vocational Specificity at the Level of Education Systems

Countries show considerable variation in youth labor market integration. One explanation for these cross-country differences is that macro-economic conditions play an important role in the labor market entry process of young people. Economic downturns increase risks of unemployment and temporary employment (Wolbers, 2014). Still, even when taking macro-economic conditions into account, school-leavers in some countries have to deal with a more problematic labor market integration than school-leavers in other countries, as we discuss later. These findings suggest that other factors than macro-economic circumstances are important in explaining cross-national differences in youth labor market integration.

Comparative research on school-to-work transitions has increasingly acknowledged the importance of institutional arrangements that shape the opportunities for school-leavers in entering the labor market. Many studies have stressed that cross-national differences in school-to-work transitions are shaped by the way that national education systems are organized (Shavit & Müller, 1998; Van der Velden & Wolbers, 2003; Breen, 2005; Wolbers, 2007b; Bol & Van de Werfhorst, 2011; De Lange et al., 2014b; Levels et al., 2014). There is substantial evidence that education systems with strong vocational characteristics have a closer relationship with labor market outcomes than education systems with less vocational characteristics (Andersen & Van de Werfhorst, 2010; Scherer, 2005). These findings imply that the relationship between vocational education and labor market integration is institutionally imbedded and that its pattern and strength differ between institutional systems of countries (Kerckhoff, 1995).

In this section, we consider institutional characteristics of education systems affecting school-leavers' labor market integration. The literature on school-to-work transitions often refers to three dimensions as the basis of education system's capacity to structure school-leavers' entry in the labor market, that is, stratification, standardization, and vocational specificity (Kerckhoff, 1995, 2001; Shavit & Muller, 2000). Here, we only focus on the last dimension. We discuss the institutional linkage between the education and employment system of a country and how this linkage impacts upon youth labor market integration.

Vocational Orientation

Education systems can provide students with either more general skills or more vocational skills, and the amount to which they do so varies between countries. It is well-established that vocationally oriented education systems help school-leavers in the transition process from education to the labor market (Andersen & Van de Werfhorst, 2010; Bol & Van de Werfhorst, 2011; Van der Velden & Wolbers, 2003; Wolbers, 2007b) and that in these countries youth unemployment is lower compared to countries with limited vocational components in their education system (Bol & Van de Werfhorst, 2013; Breen, 2005; Wolbers, 2007b; De Lange et al., 2014b).

From a theoretical point of view, these findings are generally explained by the acquired (occupational) skills and clear signaling of vocational qualifications that enhance access to the labor market (Van de Werfhorst,

2014). In a more extensive explanation, this means that students gain relevant job-specific skills in vocationally oriented education systems, and it is for this very reason that these education systems have a clear transparency of the skills acquired compared to more generally or academically oriented education systems. As a result, educational degrees obtained in vocationally oriented education systems send very clear and specific signals and information about school-leavers' abilities and potential productivity. It seems plausible that in countries where education is more vocationally oriented, educational degrees hold more information and are therefore more important for occupational attainment (Bol & Van de Werfhorst, 2011).

External Differentiation

The link between social inequality and education is that national education systems contribute to the processes that differentiate people into social strata. Within this perspective, education systems serve as a "sorting machine," given that they sort students into stratified levels of educational attainment, which are hierarchically ranked (higher vs. lower) by certified credentials. It refers to the extent to which educational opportunities are differentiated between and within educational levels and refers to the extent in which students are allocated to different tracks in upper secondary education based on achievement or demonstrated ability (Allmendinger, 1989).

Proponents of external differentiation in the form of tracking argue that sorting students into different tracks based on their ability increases classroom homogeneity, allowing more precisely targeted instruction that is more closely aligned with students' needs and is therefore beneficial for students' educational achievements (Figlio & Page, 2002). Moreover, as a result of more fine-grained distinctions made between students from various schools, tracks, or programs (Van der Velden, 2011), employers are not only better informed about school-leavers' abilities, but these abilities are also better recognizable through clearer qualification signals (Levels et al., 2014; Muller, 2005). This eases employers' selection and allocation process of potential employees to jobs. Numerous studies have found that countries with differentiated education systems (especially those with strong vocational components) facilitate youth's school-to-work transitions and lower unemployment risks compared to less differentiated education systems (Andersen & Van de Werfhorst, 2010; Breen, 2005; Kerckhoff, 2001; Shavit & Muller, 2000; Scherer, 2005; Van de Werfhorst & Mijs, 2010). These findings indicate that highly differentiated education systems may send stronger and clearer signals to employers about school-leavers' productivity, ability, and trainability compared to less differentiated systems, which enhances youth labor market integration.

Although tracking has been a common practice for decades in various Western countries, in recent years it has received a lot of criticism, as tracking affects social inequality in educational opportunities and subsequently occupational outcomes (Kocer & Van de Werfhorst, 2012; Shavit & Muller, 1998). Opponents to tracking argue that differentiation in education systems originated to stimulate the reproduction of social classes to maintain social class differences. Tracks are hierarchically ranked—not only in objective terms by means of cognitive level, but also in subjective terms by means of status and prestige—and it is clear which tracks are ranked higher or lower. Various studies on this institutional characteristic of differentiation found detrimental consequences for equality of educational opportunity. Countries with stratified education systems have larger dispersions of educational achievement than countries with less stratified systems (Hanushek & Woessmann, 2005; Heisig & Solga, 2015; Pfeffer, 2015; Van de Werfhorst & Mijs, 2010). This is especially the case when tracking takes place earlier in upper secondary education. From this perspective, highly differentiated systems legitimize and sustain inequality in educational attainment of individuals, which can also negatively influence their future labor market outcomes (Ainsworth & Roscigno, 2005). Thus, external differentiation of students into different tracks seems not solely based on ability but also on ascribed characteristics such as social class and has an impact on young people's opportunities in education and subsequent labor market entry (Andersen & Van de Werfhorst, 2010; Bol & Van de Werfhorst, 2011; Shavit & Muller, 2000).

Skills Transparency

In line with the empirical research that has found a positive impact of the two previously discussed institutional characteristics on youth labor market integration, the prevailing interpretation of these findings in more recent research is that vocational orientation and external differentiation promote "skills transparency" of both general and vocational skills (Heisig & Solga, 2015). Otherwise stated, the link between educational credentials and school-leavers' actual skills are strengthened by these two institutional characteristics (Andersen & Van de Werfhorst, 2010). The skills transparency refers to the extent to which educational credentials are predictive of actual skills, determining the signal's strength sent to employers about a school-leaver's actual skills. It is assumed that educational credentials send stronger signals about a school-leaver's actual skills—indicating a stronger skills transparency—when (a) the skills gap between different educational groups is larger and (b) the skills distribution within educational groups is more homogeneous. The first refers to differences between educational groups in the average level of skills. The larger this skills gap is between educational groups distinguished by their educational credentials, the more indicative signals these educational credentials send to employers about school-leavers' actual skills. The second refers to the homogeneity of skills within an educational group, in which the signal is stronger when educational groups are more homogeneous (Aigner & Cain, 1977).

Institutional Linkage

The institutional linkage is an important aspect and part of education systems that are vocationally oriented (Allmendinger, 1989). The strength of the institutional linkage depends on the degree to which the labor market is involved in the design and the administration of the education system (Shavit & Muller, 2000). Institutional linkages can be organized in various ways and refer to the extent to which theoretical learning is combined with practical work experience. This can be either entirely school-based teaching or a combination of school-based teaching and learning at the workplace (i.e., dual system). The stronger the institutional linkage, the higher the likelihood that skills taught in the curriculum are actually in demand by employers and the clearer the signals sent to employers about school-leavers' abilities and productive powers (Iannelli & Raffe, 2007). Empirical evidence shows that (vocationally oriented) education systems with strong institutional linkages (often in the form of the existence of a dual system) lead to a smoother school-to-work transition and lower chances of unemployment (Breen, 2005; Iannelli & Raffe, 2007; Levels et al., 2014; Raffe, 2008; Van der Velden & Wolbers, 2003).

Internal Versus Occupational Labor Markets

So far, it has been argued that cross-national variation in youth labor market integration reflects differences in institutional features of the national education and training system. But there are also scholars who have explained transition patterns through differences in labor market structures. Arguments in this respect are advanced from the perspective of a contrast between qualificational and organizational spaces (Maurice, Sellier, & Silvestre, 1986;

Shavit & Müller, 1998), and systems of internal labor markets (ILM) versus systems of occupational labor markets (OLM; Marsden, 1999; Gangl, 2001). The basis of such claims is an informational argument. Employers have to make hiring decisions under uncertainty conditions and imperfect information, because the match between job applicants' capabilities and the skills required on the work floor is something that cannot easily determined due to a screening problem (Arrow, 1973). This screening problem can be solved by using different sources of information about job seekers: on-the-job screening, probation periods, previous employment records, and educational qualifications. As employers generally opt for the least costly alternative providing an effective assessment of job applicants, the relative role of education in the job allocation process is larger, the more it offers reliable information about the actual capabilities and skills of individuals.

In the ILM–OLM dichotomy, countries are differentiated based on the extent to which education sends clear and reliable signals about individuals' skills. If education provides clear signals, this will form the basis for achieving adequate job–person matches at labor market entry. From an employer's point of view, then, there is no need to develop and institutionalize firm internal career structures, as recruitment from the external, occupational labor market into (highly) skilled positions is a more viable option. So, in countries with an education system providing vocational-specific skills, an OLM system exists, whereas in the absence of a sufficiently specific education system the ILM system is the baseline market arrangement.

Raffe (2008) argues that clustering countries in terms of institutional characteristics is one of the weakest and most arbitrary features of research in transition systems. He describes three challenges that this typology approach faces. First, typologies are only useful when a study covers few countries, but larger numbers of countries easily lead to national differences that cannot be explained by any available typology. In addition, a characteristic of an education system within a country can be internally heterogeneous. For instance, linkages between education and the labor market may vary across occupational sectors or between study programs within a country. A final challenge is the lack of robustness in empirical typologies. Studies differ in the way they have grouped countries into different clusters, depending often on the data and analytical techniques used.

Conclusion

Youth's integration into the labor market is one of the crucial changes young people experience in emerging adulthood (Arnett, 2000). As young people from upper secondary vocational education experience their final stage of occupational identity formation within the period of emerging adulthood (Bynner, 2005), their initial labor market entry (during this period) influences their future careers and life prospects (Barone & Schizzerotto, 2011; Wolbers, 2007a; Scherer, 2005). The presented overview of theoretical insights and empirical evidence regarding the role of vocational education in youth labor market integration and, more specific, the explicit attention paid to the three levels (i.e., school-leavers, study programs, and education systems) through which the vocational specificity of education operates, has resulted in an attempt to develop a coherent system of indicators that measure vocational specificity at the three levels. A summary of the key indicators is given in Table 12.1.

The next step therefore is to find adequate operationalizations of these indicators. A few examples are already given in the table. For instance, the attendance of apprenticeship training by upper secondary education students, aimed at acquiring job-specific skills, can be operationalized by various variables, such as the number of firms, the period of apprenticeship training, and the number of days per week an apprentice is gaining practical work experience. The task is now to define valid and reliable variables for all the relevant indicators. At the micro level, this may imply the development of new

Table 12.1 Key Indicators of Vocational Specificity on All Three Levels

School-Leavers	Study Programs	Education Systems
• General versus specific skills - Literacy skills - Numeracy skills - Analytical skills - Job-specific skills - Soft skills • General versus vocational education - Whether or not a person has followed upper secondary vocational education • Field of study • Attendance in apprenticeship - Number of firms - Duration of apprenticeship period - Number of days per week	• Vocational specificity of study program (linkage approach) - Linkage between study program and occupational domain • Narrow versus broad vocational education programs • Field of study	• Vocational specificity of education system - Percentage of students enrolled in upper secondary vocational education in the total of all upper secondary educational programs per country • Institutional linkage - Percentage of students enrolled in upper secondary vocational education that takes place in a dual system per country • Internal versus occupational labor markets

measurement instruments (and new data collection) to determine individuals' generic and job-specific skills levels; at the meso and macro level, the success of this task is dependent upon the availability of descriptions of the content and quality of offered study programs at educational institutions for vocational education and (time series of) existing databases from statistical offices (Eurostat, OECD).

When this step is taken, a multilevel analytical strategy will be necessary to simultaneously estimate the impact of these variables at the school-leaver, study program, and education system level to adequately test the total impact of the vocational specificity of education on the integration of young people into the labor market.

References

Aigner, D. J., & Cain, G. G. (1977). Statistical theories of discrimination in labor markets. *Industrial and Labor Relations Review, 30*, 175–187.

Ainsworth, J. W., & Roscigno, V. J. (2005). Stratification, school–work linkages and vocational education. *Social Forces, 84*, 257–284.

Allmendinger, J. (1989). Educational systems and labour market outcomes. *European Sociological Review, 5*, 231–250.

Andersen, R., & Van de Werfhorst, H. G. (2010). Education and occupational status in 14 countries: The role of educational institutions and labour market coordination. *The British Journal of Sociology, 61*, 336–355.

Arnett, J. J. (2000). Emerging adulthood: A theory of development from the late teens through the twenties. *American Psychologist, 55*, 469.

Arrow, K. (1973). Higher education as a filter. *Journal of Public Economics, 2*, 193–216.

Arum, R., & Shavit, Y. (1995). Secondary vocational education and the transition from school to work. *Sociology of Education, 68*, 187–204.

Barone, C., & Schizzerotto, A. (2011). Introduction: Career mobility, education and intergenerational reproduction in five European countries. *European Societies, 13*, 331–345.

Becker, G. (1964). *Human capital. A theoretical and empirical analysis, with special reference to education*. New York, NY: National Bureau of Economic Research.

Bills, D. B., & Wacker, M. E. (2003). Acquiring credentials when signals don't matter: Employers' support of employees who pursue postsecondary vocational degrees. *Sociology of Education, 76*, 170–187.

Bishop, J. H. (1995). Vocational education and at-risk youth in the United States. *Vocational Training European Journal, 6*, 34–42.

Bol, T., & Van de Werfhorst, H. G. (2011). Signals and closure by degrees: The education effect across 15 European countries. *Research in Social Stratification and Mobility, 29*, 119–132.

Bol, T., & Van de Werfhorst, H. G. (2013). Educational systems and the trade-off between labor market allocation and equality of educational opportunity. *Comparative Education Review, 57*, 258–308.

Borghans, L., & Heijke, H. (2005). The production and use of human capital: Introduction. *Education Economics, 13*, 133–142.

Breen, R. (2005). Explaining cross-national variation in youth unemployment. Market and institutional factors. *European Sociological Review, 21*, 125–134.

Bynner, J. (2005). Rethinking the youth phase of the life-course: The case for emerging adulthood? *Journal of Youth Studies, 8*, 367–384.

Collins, R. (1979). *The credential society. A historical sociology of education and stratification.* New York, NY: Academic Press.

Daymont, T. N., & Andrisani, P. J. (1984). Job preferences, college major, and the gender gap in earnings. *Journal of Human Resources, 19*, 408–28.

De Grip, A., & Wolbers, M. H. J. (2005). Cross-national differences in job quality among low-skilled young workers in Europe. *International Journal of Manpower, 27*, 420–433.

De Lange, M., Gesthuizen, M., & Wolbers, M. H. J. (2014a). Consequences of flexible employment at labour market entry for early career development in the Netherlands. *Economic and Industrial Democracy, 35*, 413–434.

De Lange, M., Gesthuizen, M., & Wolbers, M. H. J. (2014b). Youth labour market integration across Europe: The impact of cyclical, structural and institutional characteristics. *European Societies, 16*, 194–212.

De Lange, M., Wolbers, M. H. J., Gesthuizen, M., & Ultee, W. C. (2014). The impact of macro- and micro-economic uncertainty on family formation in the Netherlands. *European Journal of Population, 30*, 161–185.

DiPrete, T. A., Bol, T., Ciocca, C., & Van de Werfhorst, H. G. (2017). School-to-work linkages in the United States, Germany and France. *American Journal of Sociology, 122*(6), 1869–1938.

Dronkers, J. (1993). The precarious balance between general and vocational education in the Netherlands. *European Journal of Education, 28*, 197–207.

Figlio, D., & Page, M. (2002). School choice and the distributional effects of ability tracking: Does separation increase inequality? *Journal of Urban Economics, 51*, 497–514.

Gangl, M. (2001). European patterns of labour market entry. A dichotomy of occupationalized versus non-occupationalized systems. *European Societies, 3*, 471–494.

Gebel, M., & Giesecke, J. (2016). Does deregulation help? The impact of employment protection reforms on youths' unemployment and temporary employment risks in Europe. *European Sociological Review, 32*, 486–500.

Glebbeek, A. (1988). De arbeidsmarktpositie van opleidingen. Ontwikkeling en illustratie van een theoretisch model. *Tijdschrift voor Arbeidsvraagstukken, 4*, 75–89.

Glebbeek, A., Wim, N., & Schakelaar, R. (1989). The labor-market position of Dutch sociologists: An investigation guided by a theoretical model. *Netherlands Journal of Social Sciences, 25*, 57–74.

Hanushek, E. A., & Woessmann, L. (2005). Does educational tracking affect performance and inequality? Differences-in-differences evidence across countries. *Economic Journal, 116*, 63–76.

Hanushek, E. A., Woessmann, L., & Zhang, L. (2011). *General education, vocational education, and labor-market outcomes over the life-cycle* (Working paper no. 17504). National Bureau of Economic Research, New York, NY.

Heijke, H., Meng, C., & Ris, C. (2003). Fitting to the job: the role of generic and vocational competencies in adjustment and performance. *Labour Economics, 10*, 215–229.

Heisig, J. P., & Solga, H. (2015). Secondary education systems and the general skills of less- and intermediate-educated adults. A comparison of 18 countries. *Sociology of Education, 8*, 202–225.

Iannelli, C., & Raffe, D. (2007). Vocational upper-secondary education and the transition from school. *European Sociological Review 23*, 49–63.

Kalmijn, M., & Van der Lippe, T. (1997). Type of schooling and sex differences in earnings in the Netherlands. *European Sociological Review, 13*, 1–15.

Kerckhoff, A. (1995). Institutional arrangements and stratification processes in industrial societies. *Annual Review of Sociology, 15*, 323–47.

Kerckhoff, A. (2001). Education and social stratification processes in comparative perspective. *Sociology of Education*, 3–18.

Klein, M. (2010). *Mechanisms for the effect of field of study on the transition from higher education to work* (Working paper no. 2010/130). Mannheimer Zentrum für Europäische Sozialforschung, Mannheim, Germany.

Kocer, R. G., & Van de Werfhorst, H. G. (2012). Education systems and the formation of societal consensus on justice. *Quality and Quantity*, *46*, 451–470.

Lerman, R. I. (2009). *Training tomorrow's workforce: Community college and apprenticeship as collaborative routes to rewarding careers.* Washington, DC: Center for American Progress.

Levels, M., Van der Velden, R. K. W., & Di Stasio, V. (2014). From school to fitting work: How education-to-job matching of European school leavers is related to educational system characteristics. *Acta Sociologica*, *57*, 341–361.

Marsden, D. (1999). *A theory of employment systems: Micro-foundations of societal diversity.* Oxford, England: Oxford University Press.

Maurice, M., Sellier, F., & Silvestre, J.-J. (1986). *The social foundations of industrial power: A comparison of France and Germany.* Cambridge, MA: MIT Press.

Meng, C. (2006). *Discipline-specific or academic? Acquisition, role and value of higher education competencies* (PhD thesis). Research Centre for Education and the Labour Market, Maastricht.

Müller, W. (2005). Education and youth integration into European labour markets. *International Journal of Comparative Sociology*, *46*, 461–485.

Paglin, M., & Rufolo, A. (1990). Heterogeneous human capital, occupational choice, and male-female earnings differences. *Journal of Labor Economics*, *8*, 123–44.

Pfeffer, F. T. (2008). Persistent inequality in educational attainment and its institutional context. *European Sociological Review*, *24*, 543–565.

Pfeffer, F. T. (2015). Equality and quality in education: A comparative study of 19 countries. *Social Science Research*, *51*, 350–368.

Raffe, D. (2008). The concept of transition system. *Journal of Education and Work*, *21*, 277–296.

Reimer, D., Noelke, C., & Kucel, A. (2008). Labor market effects of field of study in comparative perspective. An analysis of 22 European countries. *International Journal of Comparative Sociology*, *49*, 233–256.

Reimer, D., & Steinmetz, S. (2007). *Gender differentiation in higher education: Educational specialization and labour market risks in Spain and Germany* (Working paper no. 2007/99). Mannheimer Zentrum für Europäische Sozialforschung, Mannheim, Germany.

Rosenbaum, J. E., Kariya, T., Settersten, R., & Maier, T. (1990). Market and network theories of the transition from high school to work: Their application to industrialized societies. *Annual Review of Sociology 16*, 263–299.

Ryan, P. (2000). The attributes and institutional requirements of apprenticeship: Evidence from smaller EU countries. *International Journal of Training and Development*, *4*, 42–65.

Ryan, P. (2001). The school-to-work transition: A cross-national perspective. *Journal of Economic Literature*, *39*, 34–92.

Scherer, S. (2005). Patterns of labour market entry: Long wait or career instability? An empirical comparison of Italy, Great Britain and West Germany. *European Sociological Review, 21*, 427–440.

Schultz, T. W. (1961). Investment in human capital. *American Economic Review*, *51*, 1–17.

Shavit, Y., & Müller, W. (Eds.). (1998). *From school to work. A comparative study of educational qualifications and occupational destinations.* Oxford, England: Oxford University Press.

Shavit, Y., & Muller, W. (2000). Vocational secondary education: Where diversion and where safety net? *European Societies*, *2*, 29–50.

Smyth, E. (2005). Gender differentiation and early labour market integration across Europe. *European Societies*, *7*, 451–79.

Spence, M. (1973). Job market signalling. *Quarterly Journal of Economics, 87*, 355–374.

Thurow, L. C. (1975). *Generating inequality.* New York, NY: Basic Books.

Van der Velden, R. K. W. (2011). De effecten van betrouwbaarheid van onderwijsdiploma's op arbeidsproductiviteit. In J. Dronkers (Ed.), *Goede bedoelingen in het onderwijs. Kansen en missers* (pp. 27–49). Amsterdam, The Netherlands: Amsterdam University Press.

Van der Velden, R. K. W., & Wolbers, M. H. J. (2003). The integration of young people into the labour market: The role of training systems and labour market regulation. In W. Müller & M. Gangl (Eds.), *Transitions from education to work in Europe. The integration of youth into EU Labour Markets* (pp. 186–211). Oxford, England: Oxford University Press.

Van der Velden, R. K. W., & Wolbers, M. H. J. (2007). How much does education matter and why? The effects of education on socio-economic outcomes among school-leavers in the Netherlands. *European Sociological Review, 23*, 65–80.

Van de Werfhorst, H. G. (2002). A detailed examination of the role of education in intergenerational social-class mobility. *Social Science Information, 41*, 407–438.

Van de Werfhorst, H. G. (2004). Systems of educational specialization and labor market outcomes in Norway, Australia, and the Netherlands. *International Journal of Comparative Sociology 45*, 315–35.

Van de Werfhorst, H. G. (2014). Changing societies and four tasks of schooling: Challenges for strongly differentiated educational systems. *International Review of Education, 60*, 123–144.

Van de Werfhorst, H. G., & Kraaykamp, G. (2001). Four field-related educational resources and their impact on labor, consumption, and socio-political orientation. *Sociology of Education, 74*, 296–317.

Van de Werfhorst, H. G., & Mijs, J. J. B. (2010). Achievement inequality and the institutional structure of educational systems: A comparative perspective. *Annual Review of Sociology, 36*, 407–28.

Wolbers, M. H. J. (2003). Job mismatches and their labour market effects among school-leavers in Europe. *European Sociological Review, 19*, 249–66.

Wolbers, M. H. J. (2007a). Employment insecurity at labour market entry and its impact on parental home leaving and family formation. A comparative study among recent graduates in eight European countries. *International Journal of Comparative Sociology, 48*, 481–507.

Wolbers, M. H. J. (2007b). Patterns of labour market entry: A comparative perspective on school-to-work transitions in eleven European countries. *Acta Sociologica, 50*(3), 189–210.

Wolbers, M. H. J. (2014). Introduction. Research on school-to-work transitions in Europe. *European Societies, 16*, 167–174.

Xu, Y. J. (2013). Career outcomes of STEM and non-STEM college graduates: Persistence in majored-field and influential factors in career choices. *Research in Higher Education, 54*, 349–382.

SECTION 4

DIVERSE PATHWAYS—VULNERABLE GROUPS

13

The Transition to Adulthood for Individuals With Intellectual Disability

A Joint Project

Deirdre Curle, Asmae El Bouhali, Ma Zhu, Sheila Marshall, John Murray, Filomena Parada, Tim Stainton, Jessie Wall, Siwei Wu, and Richard A. Young

Introduction

This chapter focuses on the school-to-work transition of emerging adults with intellectual disability (ID). Intellectual disability is defined by the fifth edition of the *Diagnostic and Statistical Manual of Mental Disorders* (DSM-V; American Psychiatric Association, 2013) as impairment of general mental abilities, beginning in the developmental period, that impact functioning in conceptual learning, social skills, and self-management in the activities of daily living. Since ID is identified in childhood, school systems become aware of the individual's learning needs early on and typically provide adaptations or modifications to curriculum and classroom environments, along with transition planning in high school to help prepare students for postsecondary life (Carter, Austin, & Trainor, 2012; Butcher & Wilton, 2008).

Upon leaving the school system, emerging adults with ID are three to four times less likely to be employed than their nondisabled peers, and they are more likely to work in segregated settings (Verdonschot, de Witte, Reichrath, Buntinx, & Curfs, 2009). Parents and guardians often remain the primary decision makers in the lives of individuals with ID and are usually involved in the transition process from school to postsecondary life (Leonard et al., 2016). Therefore the school-to-work transition for emerging adults with ID is more often not a solo process, but one of joint engagement between young

Deirdre Curle, Asmae El Bouhali, Ma Zhu, Sheila Marshall, John Murray, Filomena Parada, Tim Stainton, Jessie Wall, Siwei Wu, and Richard A. Young, *The Transition to Adulthood for Individuals With Intellectual Disability* In: *Young Adult Development at the School-to-Work Transition.* E. Anne Marshall and Jennifer E. Symonds, Oxford University Press (2021). © Oxford University Press. DOI: 10.1093/oso/9780190941512.003.0013.

adults, their parents, educators, and/or agencies that are involved in providing supported employment opportunities.

In this chapter we examine the transition to work for emerging adults with ID through the lens of intentional, goal-directed processes engaged in by the young adult and their parents or other family members who function in parent-like roles. This examination will use contextual action theory (CAT) as the conceptual framework, along with case studies to illustrate how parents and young people with ID jointly construct, articulate, and act on goals and strategies pertinent to the transition to adulthood and the search for employment.

Workforce Experiences of Youth with ID and Their Parents

There are many reasons why employment is a vital goal for individuals with ID and their families as well as policymakers. First, individuals with ID often have similar aspirations to their typically developing peers, desiring to participate in employment (Holwerda, van der Klink, Boer, Groothoff, & Brouwer, 2013; Wagner, Newman, Cameto, Garza, & Levine, 2005) and experience the fulfillment and economic autonomy that a paid job provides (Cooney, 2002). Employment promotes economic self-sufficiency and financial security and provides opportunities for independent living and meaningful community participation (Dixon & Reddacliff, 2001; Rabren, Dunn & Chambers, 2002; Test, Aspel & Everson, 2006; Steere, Rose, & Cavaiuolo, 2007; Lindstrom, Doren, Miesch, 2011). Employment also offers opportunities for social interactions with others, which in turn can contribute to the development of support networks (Donelly et al., 2010; Lysaght, Cobigo, & Hamilton, 2012; Lysaght, Ouellette-Kuntz, & Lin, 2012). Additionally, employment can contribute to well-being and sense of worth as a productive member of society (Eggleton, Robertson, Ryan, & Koban, 1999; Grant, 2008; Hensel, Kroese, & Rose, 2007; Joshi, Bouck, & Maeda, 2012; Steere et al., 2007; Test et al., 2006). Thus, reasons to include individuals with ID in the workplace are well grounded.

However, work experiences of individuals with ID are generally less positive than their typically developing peers. Researchers consistently find that employment rates of young adults with ID are considerably lower than their peers without disabilities (Grant, 2008; Hall, 2009; Hall, Butterworth, Winsor, Gilmore, & Metzel, 2007; Unger, Campbell, & McMahon, 2005; Rose, Saunders, Hensel, & Kroese, 2005; World Health Organization, 2011; Yamaki

& Fujiura, 2002). As they struggle to find and maintain employment (Garcia-Iriarte, Balcazar, &Taylor-Ritzler, 2007; Lindsay, 2011; Verdonschot et al., 2009; Wagner & Blackorby, 1996), young people with ID are more likely to be engaged in jobs requiring lower skill levels (Luftig & Muthert, 2005); furthermore, they often work fewer hours and earn a lower income than their typically developing peers (Jahoda, Kemp, Riddell, & Banks, 2008; Kirsh et al., 2009; Lysaght, Ouellette-Kuntz, et al., 2012). Moreover, they tend to have fewer interactions in the workplace and less positive relationships with co-workers (Vander Hart, 1998; Butterworth, Hagner, Helm, & Whelley, 2000; Hall, 2009) and may even be bullied by other staff (Andrews & Rose, 2010).

These poor employment outcomes are related to the unique barriers that emerging adults with ID face both internally and externally during the transition from school to work. Adults with ID have varying functional limitations in mobility, self-care, communication, and learning (Parish & Cloud, 2006), which can lead to difficulties in understanding instructions, learning new skills, and performing skills consistently (Bucholz, Brady, Duffy, Scott, & Kontosh, 2008; McConkey & Mezza, 2001). Some young adults with ID are aware of being stigmatized and thus distance themselves from employment services as well as from other people (Jahoda & Markova, 2004); this is associated with lower motivation to be employed (McConkey & Mezza, 2001). Externally, emerging adults with ID are viewed by their employers as needing more training and supervision, which may result in greater cost to companies compared to employees without disabilities (Olson, Cioffi, Yovanoff, & Mank, 2001). Furthermore, employers with and without experience in hiring individuals with ID express concern about safety issues, quality control problems, reduced productivity, and potential behavior problems (Morgan & Alexander, 2005).

Given the challenges facing emerging adults with ID during transition to work, parents play a critical role in facilitating and accessing employment. In addition to providing practical assistance, moral support, motivation, and modeling a strong work ethic, parents also often act as advocates for their young adult children even before the young adults obtain employment. Parents frequently describe "fighting" or "battling" for their children as they navigate and negotiate systems in their quest to help them find employment (Gillan & Coughlan, 2010). They often act as liaisons, networking in their respective communities while job hunting for and with their children (Dixon & Reddacliff, 2001; Freedman & Fesko, 1996). When young adults do find employment, parents may provide continuing support by reaching out to employers or employment agencies when difficulties crop up at work (Dixon & Reddacliff, 2001; Foley, Dyke, Girdler, Bourke, & Leonard, 2012).

However, while parents seek employment for their young adult children, they often struggle to find information about community supports available through private or government-funded agencies. As their children age out of school and pediatric care systems, parents report a lack of knowledge regarding work and living options for adults with ID (Chambers, Hughes, & Carter, 2004). Contending with an unfamiliar adult agency support system with uncertain outcomes can lead to feelings of powerlessness (Cooney, 2002).

Although many parents hope for their young adult child to be employed (Carter et al., 2012; Wehman et al., 2015), they may experience conflict between their aspirations for their young adult to work independently and their doubt that it will actually happen (Kraemer & Blacher, 2001). This tension can be exacerbated by feelings of wanting to protect young adults with ID from failure and exploitation at work (Freedman & Fesko, 1996; Thorin, Yofanoff, & Irvin, 1996).

Parents clearly play an important role in supporting the school-to-work transition of emerging adults with ID (Foley et al., 2012). But parents' actions should be viewed in the context of their relationship with their children. That is, they are not making decisions or acting without input from their young adult children. Rather, as we have found in previous studies, the school-to-work transition can be viewed as joint actions involving both the young adult and parents or guardians (Young et al., 2008). This approach posits that the school-to-work transition is jointly constructed during conversations and other activities between parents and young adults.

Contextual Action Theory

Much of the literature on the transition from school to work suggests, at least implicitly, that emerging adults have or should have goals and that they engage in actions toward those goals. This is a common-sense understanding. Most people understand their own and other's behavior as goal-directed. They often explain what they themselves and others do by identifying the goals of behavior. This type of explanation is also useful for understanding, researching, and intervening in the school-to-work transition.

Often the school-to-work literature relies on identifying the causes of behavior rather than the goals of behavior. Social policy and intervention programs are typically based on these causal explanations. Notwithstanding the value and success of these programs, it is important to understand the young person as an actor in his or her context. Moreover, a conceptual framework based on goal-directed action is helpful in examining this important transition because of the need for research, interventions, and policy to reflect the understanding and motivation of young people and significant others.

Research confirms that solely focusing on individuals' goals is insufficient. An adequate conceptual framework should include short-, medium-, and long-term goal-oriented processes. It needs to be able to address how individuals join others in constructing and implementing their actions. Young and colleagues (2002, 2011, 2015) propose Contextual Action Theory (CAT) as a conceptual framework to understand and describe human action in order to design interventions to support individuals.

In CAT, the term *action* refers to units of goal-directed, intentional behavior. When a series of actions is constructed over a medium length of time by the actor, most often with others, one can speak of a *project*. Project is a particularly meaningful and useful construct when considering school-to-work transition actions. For example, participating in an apprenticeship, graduating from high school, or getting a part-time job can all readily be identified as projects in the school-to-work transition, when they are constructed as such by the actors involved. When projects coalesce over a longer term, CAT uses the term *career*. Occupational careers provide one straightforward example of this construct. A long-term career as a draftsperson would likely have been constructed out of many actions and projects over a lifetime.

Another important aspect of CAT is its focus on the jointness of actions, projects, and careers. Most human action involves others. Consider the simple task of putting a book onto a sales counter for the clerk to ring in the sale. The expectations and coordination of goals and functions between these two people make this joint action possible. When one considers the decision to buy the book in the first place, other joint actions become apparent. Often, such decisions are made in concert with other people who are not present as part of a project. In the previous example, perhaps the individual was purchasing a book about Italy with the intention of taking a trip there with his or her partner.

The literature on goals is abundant. While this literature is critical to the view we are espousing, an action's goal in itself provides too limited a view of the complexity and dynamism of action. CAT frames goal-directed action within three levels. The first level refers explicitly to the goals of action. In this view, the individual's goals and the meaning of their actions are closely connected. An individual's goal of getting a job to earn a salary is connected to, if not identical to, the meaning of getting a job for that person. The second level of action identifies the tasks related to the goal or functions to accomplish the goal. For example, a task related to finding a job would be searching employment advertisements. Finally, the third level encompasses specific behaviors and resources needed to accomplish the task. These behaviors can typically be observed and counted and represent the actor's resources, skills, and unconscious processes. An example of a behavior related to the goal of finding a job would be spending time online looking at job postings, with the resource of having Internet access.

The following two case studies were selected from two studies on this topic (Marshall et al., 2018; Young et al., 2018) to illustrate the joint actions and projects parents or guardians and emerging adults with ID engage in while navigating the young person's transition to work. Although the studies from which these cases are drawn focus on the transition to adulthood—and not specifically on the school-to-work transition—transitions to postsecondary education and to employment were one of the main topics addressed by participants in their conversations. Often the actions and projects two parents and/or guardians engaged in between themselves, as well as the actions and projects between young adults and their parents, aimed to support the young person to enter postsecondary education or consistent, long-term employment.

Case example A illustrates how parents and their young adult child with ID work together over time to reach common goals in the youth's transition to postsecondary education or work. In this case, a father and daughter discuss the daughter's career possibilities, specifically going to college, with finding employment as a backup plan. They do this by using their relationship to explore different ways to help the daughter anticipate and prepare for the upcoming transition. Although the father takes the lead in the conversation, he ensures that his daughter has space to express herself, in particular her hopes and worries about the post–high school transition. This case example sheds light on the importance of the young adult's agency and provides insight into how to conceptualize interventions aimed at helping parents or guardians and young adults with ID to construct, articulate, and enact joint goals and strategies pertinent to the transition from school to work.

Case example B offers another illustration of some of the challenges parents face in trying to find employment for their young adult child. Specifically, it provides insight into the limitations of ID and the lack of opportunities available to these young adults may increase the complexity and extend the transition period. It also highlights the stress, frustration, and fatigue many parents feel as a result of trying to "navigate the system." At the age of 19, when youth with ID typically reach the end of secondary education, they also experience a concurrent transition from child to adult care and support systems. Significant changes in resources, services, and supports require parents to learn a new system to connect the young person to services and supports.

Parents often also struggle to meet their own needs, not only to manage their emotions, expectations, and hopes regarding their child's future, but also as they age and manage their own transitions to retirement and older age. By illustrating how parents and youth jointly navigate complex challenges and changes, the case example shows, at the level of goals and functional steps, how everyday actions and projects unfold. Such an understanding is valuable for planning interventions aimed at providing support, while recognizing individuals as goal-directed actors in their own development.

Case Example A

This dyad comprises a father and his 18-year-old daughter, Cynthia, who lives at home with her parents and one brother. Cynthia is in a postsecondary program at a special educational institute and plans to apply to a college. The parents are in the process of determining what is required for Cynthia's college application, while also considering alternative plans, such as employment. The father, who works as a social worker, describes Cynthia as needing little help with her daily activities but indicates that she has challenges in math and comprehension and experiences difficulties in managing emotions, particularly anxiety. In terms of the transition to adulthood, the father states he is trying to discover what his daughter wants and how he might support her. Cynthia shares that becoming an adult will be a big change for her. The uncertainty makes her nervous about the transition.

This dyad's project is to explore different ways to help Cynthia anticipate and prepare for the upcoming transition to work. In the following conversation, the father brings up the upcoming transition, Cynthia's hopes, fears, and expectations around her plans, what her peers are doing, and alternative or backup plans for her future.

During their conversation, Cynthia's father describes his work with another adolescent in transition, involving alternate post–high school plans. He then connects it to Cynthia's situation as a segue to exploring possible backup plans:

FATHER: So, if you weren't to get into the college program, what would you want to do?

CYNTHIA: I don't know.

FATHER: Is that one of the things that's kind of freaky?

CYNTHIA: Yes.

FATHER: Hmm. I kind of wondered about that.

CYNTHIA: Yeah.

FATHER: Right? So I think it would probably be good idea to have a just-in-case, right?

CYNTHIA: Hmm [name] and I should look in to that.

FATHER: Yeah, could be. I know that's kind of why I was looking at that coffee shop and just thinking, "Wow, I mean, if you did a couple of shifts a week. . . ."

CYNTHIA: Like, some people—

FATHER: Sorry?

CYNTHIA: Some people don't even go to college. They just do work and stuff.

FATHER: Yeah.

Later in the conversation, they continue this topic, and together they come up with other options for Cynthia:

FATHER: Yeah, that maybe also just, try walking little dogs. And you and I doing a little bit of it, right?

CYNTHIA: Like, remember? We did that at the SPCA.

FATHER: Yep. No, but I mean walking people's dogs for money.

CYNTHIA: Yep. That's what [name] does.

FATHER: Mhm.

CYNTHIA: She does that.

FATHER: And also, I mean there's stuff you can do too where you um, you know, where you're looking at taking care of people's houses. People go on vacation and they—

CYNTHIA: I kind of want to start babysitting too for little kids, because I like working with them at school, and—

FATHER: Oh you do?

CYNTHIA: I work with them at school.

FATHER: Well, well, well.

CYNTHIA: I volunteer for [teacher]'s um . . .

FATHER: Yeah.

CYNTHIA: Grade one class.

FATHER: I never thought that was something you'd want to do.

CYNTHIA: Yeah.

The previous segments illustrate some of the joint actions between Cynthia and her father in their conversation. Steps the father takes include asking questions, acknowledging or agreeing with Cynthia, and clarifying and elaborating her answers. He also normalizes her concerns and proposes alternative perspectives and options. He asks her follow-up questions to help her process what she experiences or actively problem-solve. The father is guided by a desire to make sure Cynthia's voice is heard in the discussion and that she has support from her parents during the transition. The father explains to the researcher that he introduced this topic to "unmask the unknowns so they are not so scary." He knew that once he "put it out there," Cynthia would "respond and respond over the next several months." He adds that he raised the topic of possible employment opportunities to keep it fresh in his own mind as he has not yet discussed backup plans for Cynthia with his wife. He also mentions that his approaching retirement would allow him to help Cynthia expand the dog walking business.

Steps Cynthia takes include answering her father's questions, clarifying her answers, agreeing with her father's suggestions, and sharing her own thoughts and feelings. Her actions are guided by a desire to respond to her father and engage in the discussion about what it would be like after she leaves high school. She is mostly comfortable and confident in her communication with her father. Although her father takes the lead in the conversation, she steers the conversation to topics she is interested in and away from topics she does not want to talk about.

Case Example B

A mother, Anwen, and father, Charles, of a 22-year-old son who has cerebral palsy comprise the second dyad case example. Anwen supports their son, Patrick, in his daily activities, and Charles is employed part-time. They also have two daughters, one of whom lives at home with them and Patrick. They describe Patrick as needing moderate support in his daily activities, although he wants to be as independent as possible. He has learned to get around independently by public transit and has a number of strengths, including operating his smartphone and computer, as well as academic skills such as spelling and arithmetic. Patrick loves sports and would like to find work in a sports-related field. He has been out of high school for three years. After an extra year of high school, he spent a year in a work experience program and then enrolled in a 12-month employment training program at a community college. Although he is employed at a local event center, his shifts are sporadic, with his most recent shift occurring nine months previous to the time of the interview. Anwen and Charles are working with an employment specialist agency to assist their son in finding consistent and stable work.

The parents' project focuses on problem-solving around Patrick's employment situation. They see this project as a means of fulfilling three important goals for Patrick: (a) having gainful employment so he will have the means to make purchases or engage in recreational activities without accruing debt, (b) living independently, and, (c) participating in the community and developing a social network for the future.

Project-related activities consist primarily of everyday conversations between Charles and Anwen regarding career fairs, job prospects, how to help their son find gainful employment, and communicating with the employment specialist/job coach. Other activities include volunteering as a family at a local sporting event to help Patrick network and become known in the community. In the action domain, Anwen and Charles frequently converse about how best to help Patrick obtain employment. Charles advocates for a more active approach both with the system and as parents, whereas Anwen prefers to wait and see what transpires with the employment agencies. Initially, Anwen takes the lead in the project as it aligns with her responsibilities as the primary caregiver for their son. However, over time, Charles moves from a supportive role to taking a more active role, including looking for jobs for Patrick and communicating with the job coach.

Steps Anwen's takes include maintaining contact with the employment specialist, attending meetings about the transition to adulthood for people with ID to gain information, networking and talking with others about possible pathways to employment and job opportunities, keeping Charles up to date and "translating knowledge," and volunteering at different events with Patrick to help him network and become known in their community. Her steps are guided by a sense of hope that they are doing the right things and eventually an opportunity will arise. She wants to be patient and wait for the employers or employment specialist, rather than be the "squeaky wheel." Reflecting on their project after 10 months, she states:

> I was really hoping by the time we came back to you now, that . . . we'd be on cloud nine and, you know, at least we'd have something positive to talk about. . . . I know things keep changing and there's a reason it takes a long time, because we don't rush into the first thing. . . . But it's still hard.

Charles' actions include encouraging Anwen to contact the employment specialist when they did not hear back, offering his opinion but deferring to Anwen, given her role as the primary caregiver ("not stepping on her toes"), making Patrick aware of their expectations, and helping Patrick update his resume, look for jobs, and attend job fairs. His actions are guided by a desire to support Anwen in her role and approach, despite a wish to be more assertive in communicating with the professionals. Over time, he becomes more involved in the process, both with the agencies and with Patrick, in hopes that Patrick will find employment before finishing his employment training program. He expresses that his own part-time job is often a barrier to the project, as it often takes priority and keeps him busy for periods of time.

There are significant barriers to these parents' project, mainly related to the employment agency and the employment training program. Limited communication, frequent organizational changes, and lack of opportunities were identified as barriers to the project. First, Anwen and Charles both express doubts about the agency and employment training program. Second, the parents report a lack of personal connections and networks. Both Anwen and Charles immigrated to Canada from another country 25 years previous to their participation in this study. Anwen expressed that a number of young people with ID obtain employment through personal connections and networks. She feared they were not connected well enough in the community to help their son in this way. Third, Patrick's lack of interest in managing his hygiene and taking initiative in the job search was a hindrance to finding employment. Anwen felt frustrated with Patrick's lack of interest in work, and, at times, she felt unappreciated for her efforts. Charles expresses that spending time with Patrick is demanding and, at times, irritating. Lastly, the employment-finding process is slow. They had been engaging in the project for three years. Anwen says, "It's a little discouraging to have got here with all the work that we and other individuals have put in and we still aren't at the finish line yet." They both indicate that they feel a "time crunch," especially as they look ahead to their future and their plans for retirement. They see this project as a stepping stone toward finding Patrick a supported living situation away from their home, as they anticipate that at some point they will no longer be able to care for him.

Discussion

In this chapter we sought to use CAT and the action-project method as a way to elucidate the transition from school to work for emerging adults with ID and their families. Parents of typically developing youth often engage in joint projects with them well before they reach adulthood, exploring possibilities for possible future work or careers, and many young adults seek career-related advice and assistance from their parents (Domene, Arim, & Young, 2007; Young et al., 2001, 2006). Parents of emerging adults with ID often play a larger role in constructing goals and planning their children's transition to work. In the first case example, we saw how a father led the conversation on preparing for the postsecondary education transition by presenting different educational and employment options to his daughter. In the second case, the parents' joint project of finding their son employment was hindered by their son's lack of interest in developing job-related skills, as well as a lack of communication from the agencies providing their son's training and employment. In both cases, there is a sense of the leading role parents may take in helping their young adult child with ID enter the work force. At the same time, it is clear that the young adults participate in the joint project through their choices and actions, which steer the project. These young adults' actions indicate whether the young adult shares the parents' goals of pursuing employment, or whether they have a different project in mind altogether.

Implications for Professionals

Counseling theories provide a framework for counselors to conceptualize their cases and to act jointly with their clients relative to the case (Young, Domene, & Valach, 2015). Counsellors supporting youth with ID can enhance their practice by integrating CAT with career exploration and individualized transition planning. By examining levels of action, such as internal processes, social meaning, communication and manifest behaviors, not only within the young person but also with their families can illuminate ways in which they can assist with the transition (Young et al., 2011). Previous research indicates that when youth with ID are transition-planning in high school, parents often take a passive role, leaving the planning to school-based professionals (DeFur, Todd-Allen, & Getzel, 2001; Garriott, Wandry, & Snyder, 2000). Thus, CAT may be a helpful framework for drawing parents into the transition process.

There are five key tasks in counselling from CAT that the client and counselor engage in together (Domene, Valach, & Young, 2015). The first is developing and maintaining an effective working alliance. Previous literature emphasizes the importance of positive relationships between families and professionals in transition planning (Defur et al., 2001; Nuehring & Sitlington, 2003; Stoner, Angell, House, & Bock, 2007). In the previous case examples, the only participants are parent–child (Case A) and mother–father (Case B), who already have an established working alliance. For a CAT intervention, the counselor needs to join this alliance to allow for this level of discussion to continue in the counseling setting.

The second task in CAT counseling is for the counselor and client to identify the actions, projects, and careers that are salient in the clients' lives. Parents' and young people's goals may be different—previous research shows that young people with ID are more concerned about being bullied or losing someone they depend upon than getting a job or having surplus money (Forte, Johada, & Dagnan, 2011). By examining the actions among young people and their parents, families can become more aware of differences in goals as well as their own roles in the transition process, and how their actions can facilitate or hinder the transition.

The third counseling task in CAT is to identify and address actions, projects, or careers that are problematic. Numerous barriers exist to employment for young people with ID, as previously stated in this chapter. Identifying the barriers and problems may help families and young people re-examine their goals and actions. Furthermore, CAT can be used to help resolve differences among couples, parents, professionals and/or the young person to work toward agreement on goals and functional steps that will facilitate finding and keeping employment.

The fourth task is to address emotion and emotional memory among clients. There are, understandably, emotional responses to any major life transition, and it can be expected that the transition from school to work may involve some concerns and worries among both young people and parents. Case A mentions the anxiety Cynthia felt about transitioning to adulthood, and the parents in Case B spoke of their frustration when they were unable to find their son employment. Additionally, counselors need to become familiar with the young person's specific diagnosis, as some diagnoses include emotional or behavioral symptoms. For example, the diagnosis of the young woman in Case A is associated with anxiety and depression. Addressing emotions can help parents or young people recognize and regulate their anxiety or frustration to minimize the impact of these feelings on the transition project.

Finally, the fifth task of CAT counseling is to translate counseling gains into daily life. This includes considering clients' contexts and experiences prior to counseling, as well as guiding clients to link insights to future goals, projects, and careers (Young et al., 2011). Valach and Young (2013) suggest giving clients the opportunity to construct narratives of their lives that help them see their action organization and action systems in a way that is understandable and relevant.

One suggested intervention for addressing the application and fulfillment of these tasks is a counseling intervention based on the action-project method (A-PM; Valach, Young, & Lynam, 2002; Young et al., 2001). This qualitative research method has been used in counseling psychology to investigate goal-directed, intentional behavior by accessing information from three perspectives: manifest behavior, internal processes, and social meaning (Young, Valach, & Domene, 2005). Counselors meet the five previously identified key tasks through (a) eliciting a narrative, (b) videotaped self-confrontation, (c) identifying project(s), (d) sharing the narrative, and (e) facilitating actions and projects over time. With such an intervention, the first phase, eliciting the narrative, is used to build the therapeutic alliance, as well as identify and explore actions in the context of important others.

It is possible for other counseling interventions to be combined with this approach, as long as the five key tasks are prioritized. Additionally, these interventions need to be matched to the young person's cognitive and linguistic developmental level. In the case of a young person who is more severely impacted by ID, counseling may need to focus more on supporting parents or parents in partnership with the professionals who support the young person's employment. The use of A-PM is not limited to young adults and their parents; it can be used in educational or supported work settings to elucidate the joint goals and projects of the teacher and student or support worker and client relevant to the transition from school to work.

Summary

In the previous section we discussed the essential components of counseling from a CAT perspective. We then briefly presented how these tasks could be addressed in a counselling intervention based on the A-PM research method. Using examples from the earlier case examples, we showed that the A-PM counseling intervention provides a unique way to address transition to career-related steps for young adults with ID and their families. Such a unique focus on goals, projects, and careers provides a way for young adults, parents, and agencies or supporting individuals to contextually structure both short- and long-term goals around transition to work.

References

American Psychiatric Association. (2013). *Diagnostic and statistical manual of mental disorders* (5th ed.). Arlington, VA: American Psychiatric Publishing.

Andrews, A., & Rose, J. L. (2010). A preliminary investigation of factors affecting employment motivation in people with intellectual disabilities. *Journal of Policy and Practice in Intellectual Disabilities, 7*(4), 239–244.

Bucholz, J. L., Brady, M. P., Duffy, M. L., Scott, J., & Kontosh, L. G. (2008). Using literacy-based behavioral interventions and social stories to improve work behavior in employees with developmental disabilities. *Education and Training in Developmental Disabilities, 43*(4), 486–501.

Butcher, S., & Wilton, R. (2008). Stuck in transition? Exploring the spaces of employment training for youth with intellectual disability. *Geoforum, 39*, 1079–1092.

Butterworth, J., Hagner, D., Helm, D. T., & Whelley, T. A. (2000). Workplace culture, social interactions, and supports for transition-age young adults. *Mental Retardation, 38*(4), 342–353.

Carter, E. W., Austin, D., & Trainor, A. A. (2012). Predictors of postschool employment outcomes for young adults with severe disabilities. *Journal of Disability Policy Studies, 23*(1), 50–63.

Chambers, C. R., Hughes, C., & Carter, E. W. (2004). Parent and sibling perspectives on the transition to adulthood. *Education and Training in Developmental Disabilities, 39*(2), 79–94.

Cooney, B. F. (2002). Exploring perspectives on transition of youth with disabilities: Voices of young adults, parents, and professionals. *Mental Retardation, 40*(6), 425–435.

Defur, S. H., Todd-Allen, M., & Getzel, E. E. (2001). Parent participation in the transition planning process. *Career Development for Exceptional Individuals, 24*(1), 19–36.

Dixon, R. M., & Reddacliff, C. A. (2001). Family contribution to the vocational lives of vocationally competent young adults with intellectual disabilities. *International Journal of Disability, Development and Education, 48*(2), 193–206.

Domene, J. F., Arim. R. G., & Young, R. A. (2007). Gender and career development projects in early adolescence: Similarities and differences between mother-daughter and mother-don dyads. *Qualitative Research in Psychology, 4*(1–2), 107–126.

Domene, J. F., Valach, L., & Young, R. A. (2015). Action in counseling: A contextual action theory perspective. In R. A. Young, J. D. Domene, & L. Valach (Eds.), *Counseling and action: Toward life-enhancing work, relationships, and identity* (pp. 151–166). New York, NY: Springer.

Donelly, M., Hillman, A., Stancliffe, R. J., Knox, M., Whitaker, L., & Parmenter, T. R. (2010). The role of informal networks in providing effective work opportunities for people with an intellectual disability. *Work, 36*(2), 227–237.

Eggleton, I., Robertson, S., Ryan, J., & Kober, R. (1999). The impact of employment on the quality of life of people with an intellectual disability. *Journal of Vocational Rehabilitation, 13*(2), 95–107.

Foley, K., Dyke, P., Girdler, S., Bourke, J., & Leonard, H. (2012). Young adults with intellectual disability transitioning from school to post-school: A literature review framed within the ICF. *Disability and Rehabilitation, 34*(20), 1747–1764.

Forte, M., Jahoda, A., & Dagnan, D. (2011). An anxious time? Exploring the nature of worries experienced by young people with a mild to moderate intellectual disability as they make the transition to adulthood. *British Journal of Clinical Psychology, 50*(4), 398–411.

Freedman, R. I., & Fesko, S. L. (1996). The meaning of work in the lives of people with significant disabilities: Consumer and family perspectives. *Journal of Rehabilitation, 62*(3), 49–55.

Garcia-Iriarte, E., Balcazar, F., & Taylor-Ritzler, T. (2007). Analysis of case managers' support of youth with disabilities transitioning from school to work. *Journal of Vocational Rehabilitation, 26*(3), 129–140.

Garriott, P. P., Wandry, D., & Snyder, L. (2000). Teachers as parents, parents as children: What's wrong with this picture? *Preventing School Failure, 45*(1), 37–43.

Gillan, D., & Coughlan, B. (2010). Transition from special education into postschool services for young adults with intellectual disability: Irish parents' experience. *Journal of Policy and Practice in Intellectual Disabilities, 7*(3), 196–203.

Grant, J. (2008). Paid work–A valued social role that is empowering more people with an intellectual disability and providing employers with dedicated employees! *Journal of Intellectual and Developmental Disability, 33*(1), 95–97.

Hall, A. C., Butterworth, J., Winsor, J., Gilmore, D., & Metzel, D. (2007). Pushing the employment agenda: Case study research of high performing states in integrated employment. *Intellectual and Developmental Disabilities, 45*(3), 182–198.

Hall, S. A. (2009). The social inclusion of young adults with intellectual disabilities: A phenomenology of their experiences. *Journal of Ethnographic & Qualitative Research, 4*(1), 24–40.

Hensel, E., Kroese, B. S., & Rose, J. (2007). Psychological factors associated with obtaining employment. *Journal of Applied Research in Intellectual Disabilities, 20*(2), 175–181.

Holwerda, A., van der Klink, J. J., de Boer, M. R., Groothoff, J. W., & Brouwer, S. (2013). Predictors of work participation of young adults with mild intellectual disabilities. *Research in Developmental Disabilities*, *34*(6), 1982–1990.

Jahoda, A., Kemp, J., Riddell, S., & Banks, P. (2008). Feelings about work: A review of the socio-emotional impact of Supported Employment on people with intellectual disabilities. *Journal of Applied Research in Intellectual Disabilities*, *21*(1), 1–18.

Jahoda, A., & Markova, I. (2004). Coping with social stigma: People with intellectual disabilities moving from institutions and family home. *Journal of Intellectual Disability Research*, *48*(8), 719–729.

Joshi, G. S., Bouck, E. C., & Maeda, Y. (2012). Exploring employment preparation and postschool outcomes for students with mild intellectual disability. *Career Development and Transition for Exceptional Individuals*, *35*(2), 97–107.

Kirsh, B., Stergiou-Kita, M., Gewurtz, R., Dawson, D., Krupa, T., Lysaght, R., & Shaw, L. (2009). From margins to mainstream: What do we know about work integration for persons with brain injury, mental illness and intellectual disability? *Work*, *32*(4), 391–405.

Kraemer, B. R., & Blacher, J. (2001). Transition for young adults with severe mental retardation: School preparation, parent expectations, and family involvement. *Mental Retardation*, *39*(6), 423–435.

Leonard, H., Foley, K., Pikora, T., Bourke, J., Wong, K., McPherson, L., . . . Downs, J. (2016). Transition to adulthood for young people with intellectual disability: the experiences of their families. *European Child & Adolescent Psychiatry*, *25*(12), 1365–1381.

Lindsay, S. (2011). Employment status and work characteristics among adolescents with disabilities. *Disability and Rehabilitation*, *33*(10), 843–854.

Lindstrom, L., Doren, B., & Miesch, J. (2011). Waging a living: Career development and long-term employment outcomes for young adults with disabilities. *Exceptional Children*, *77*(4), 423–434.

Luftig, R. L., & Muthert, D. (2005). Patterns of employment and independent living of adult graduates with learning disabilities and mental retardation of an inclusionary high school vocational program. *Research in Developmental Disabilities*, *26*(4), 317–325.

Lysaght, R., Cobigo, V., & Hamilton, K. (2012). Inclusion as a focus of employment-related research in intellectual disability from 2000 to 2010: A scoping review. *Disability and Rehabilitation*, *34*(16), 1339–1350.

Lysaght, R., Ouellette-Kuntz, H., & Lin, C. J. (2012). Untapped potential: Perspectives on the employment of people with intellectual disability. *Work*, *41*(4), 409–422.

Marshall, S. K., Stainton, T., Wall, J. M., Zhu, M., Murray, J., Wu, S., . . . Young, R. A. (2018). Transition to adulthood as a joint parent-youth project for young persons with intellectual and developmental disabilities. *Intellectual and Developmental Disabilities*, *56*(4), 263–277.

McConkey, R., & Mezza, F. (2001). Employment aspirations of people with learning disabilities attending day centres. *Journal of Intellectual Disabilities*, *5*(4), 309–318.

Morgan, R. L., & Alexander, M. (2005). The employer's perception: Employment of individuals with developmental disabilities. *Journal of Vocational Rehabilitation*, *23*(1), 39–49.

Nuehring, M. L., & Sitlington, P. L. (2003). Transition as a vehicle: Moving from high school to an adult vocational service provider. *Journal of Disability Policy Studies*, *14*(1), 23–35.

Olson, D., Cioffi, A., Yovanoff, P., & Mank, D. (2001). Employers' perceptions of employees with mental retardation. *Journal of Vocational Rehabilitation*, *16*(2), 125–133.

Parish, S. L., & Cloud, J. M. (2006). Financial well-being of young children with disabilities and their families. *Social Work*, *51*(3), 223–232.

Rabren, K., Dunn, C., & Chambers, D. (2002). Predictors of post-high school employment among young adults with disabilities. *Career Development for Exceptional Individuals*, *25*(1), 25–40.

Rose, J., Saunders, K., Hensel, E., & Kroese, B. S. (2005). Factors affecting the likelihood that people with intellectual disabilities will gain employment. *Journal of Intellectual Disabilities, 9*(1), 9–23.

Steere, D. E., Rose, E. D., & Cavaiuolo, D. (2007). *Growing up: Transition to adult life for students with disabilities*. Boston, MA: Allyn & Bacon.

Stoner, J. B., Angell, M. E., House, J. J., & Bock, S. J. (2007). Transitions: A parental perspective from parents of young children with Autism spectrum disorder (ASD). *Journal of Developmental and Physical Disabilities, 19*(1), 23–39.

Test, D. W., Aspel, N. P., & Everson, J. M. (2006). *Transition methods for youth with disabilities.* Upper Saddle River, NJ: Pearson Education.

Thorin, E., Yovanoff, P., & Irvin, L. (1996). Dilemmas faced by families during their young adults' transitions to adulthood: A brief report. *Mental Retardation, 34*, 117–120.

Unger, D. D., Campbell, L. R., & McMahon, B. T. (2005). Workplace discrimination and mental retardation: The national EEOC ADA research project. *Journal of Vocational Rehabilitation, 23*(3), 145–154.

Valach, L., & Young, R. A. (2013). The case study of therapy with a Swiss woman: An action theory perspective. In S. Poyrazli & C. E. Thompson (Eds.), *International case studies in mental health* (pp. 13–32). Los Angeles, CA: SAGE.

Valach, L., Young, R. A., & Lynam, M. J. (2002). *Action theory: A primer for applied research in the social sciences*. Westport, CT: Praeger.

Vander Hart, N. S. (1998). Social interactions between supported employees and their non-disabled co-workers in integrated work settings: Perceptions of supported employment professionals. *Dissertation Abstracts International, 59*, 1795.

Verdonschot, M. M., De Witte, L. P., Reichrath, E., Buntinx, W. H. E., & Curfs, L. M. (2009). Community participation of people with an intellectual disability: A review of empirical findings. *Journal of Intellectual Disability Research, 53*(4), 303–318.

Wagner, M., Newman, L., Cameto, R., Garza, N., & Levine, P. (2005, April). After high school: A first look at the postschool experiences of youth with disabilities. A report from the National Longitudinal Transition Study-2 (NLTS2). *SRI International*. Retrieved from https://files.eric.ed.gov/fulltext/ED494935.pdf

Wagner, M. M., & Blackorby, J. (1996). Transition from high school to work or college: How special education students fare. *The Future of Children, 6*(1), 103–120.

Wehman, P., Sima, A. P., Ketchum, J., West, M. D., Chan, F., & Luecking, R. (2015). Predictors of successful transition from school to employment for youth with disabilities. *Journal of Occupational Rehabilitation, 25*(2), 323–334.

World Health Organization. (2011). World report on disability. Retrieved from http://www.who.int/disabilities/world_report/2011/report.pdf

Yamaki, K., & Fujiura, G. T. (2002). Employment and income status of adults with developmental disabilities living in the community. *Mental Retardation, 40*(2), 132–141.

Young, R. A., Domene, J. F., & Valach, L. (2015). *Counseling and action: Towards life-enhancing work, relationships, and identity.* New York, NY: Springer.

Young, R. A., Marshall, S., Domene, J. F., Arato-Bolivar, J., Hayoun, R., Marshall, E., Zaidman-Zait, A., & Valach, L. (2006). Relationships, communication, and career in the parent-adolescent projects of families with and without challenges. *Journal of Vocational Behavior, 68*, 1–23.

Young, R. A., Marshall, S. K., Domene, J. F., Graham, M., Logan, C., Zaidman-Zait, A., & Lee, C. M. (2008). Transition to adulthood as a parent-youth project: Governance transfer, career promotion, and relational processes. *Journal of Counseling Psychology, 55*(3), 297–307.

Young, R. A., Marshall, S. K., Stainton, T., Wall, J. M., Curle, D., Zhu, M., . . . Zaidman-Zait, A. (2018). The transition to adulthood of young adults with IDD: Parents' joint projects. *Journal of Applied Research in Intellectual Disabilities, 31*(Suppl 2), 224–233. doi:10.1111/jar.12395

Young, R. A., Marshall, S. K., & Valach, L., Domene, J. F., Graham, M. D., & Zaidman-Zait, A. (2011). *Active transition to adulthood: A new approach for counseling*. New York, NY: Springer-Science.

Young, R. A., Valach, L., Ball, J., Paseluikho, M. A., Wong, Y. S., DeVries, R. J., & Turkel, H. (2001). Career development in adolescence as a family project. *Journal of Counseling Psychology*, *48*(2), 190–202.

Young, R. A., Valach, L., & Collin, A. (2002). A contextual explanation of career. In D. Brown (Ed.), *Career choice and development* (4th ed., pp. 206–250). San Francisco, CA: Jossey-Bass.

Young, R. A., Valach, L., & Domene, J. F. (2005). The action-project method in counseling psychology. *Journal of Counseling Psychology*, *52*, 215–223.

14

Supporting the School-to-Work Transition for Young Adults Formerly in Care

Hope-Informed Interventions

Rachel King, Chelsea Arsenault, and Denise Larsen

Introduction

The school-to-work (STW) transition is rife with a myriad of challenges, making this developmental period difficult for many young adults, regardless of their individual context (Young et al., 2011). However, young adults formerly in care (YAFC) experience the STW transition as especially complex and fraught with a number of barriers to success (Courtney, Terao, & Bost, 2004; M. Davis, 2003). For YAFC the STW transition coincides with moving out of the childcare system and into independent living. This accelerated transition to adulthood has significant impacts on the STW transition for YAFC. They face independence and adult responsibilities at a young age, while still dealing with the effects of developmental disruptions during their time in care. The STW transition sets the trajectory for adult life, determines financial stability, and holds the potential for adopting personally meaningful life roles that contribute to a sense of value and purpose (Stohler et al., 2008; Osgood et al., 2005). The complicated process of navigating the transition into work life is even more crucial, with potentially higher stakes, for youth formerly in care.

Unfortunately, many YAFC experience depression and hopelessness, which exacerbate—and often stem from—the challenges they already face (Lee & Whiting, 2007). Hopelessness and perceived lack of control can make it increasingly difficult for youth to engage in their transition in resilient ways (Widom, 1994). Certainly, it is possible to navigate the difficult landscape of the transition out of the childcare system, but to do so requires significant

Rachel King, Chelsea Arsenault, and Denise Larsen, *Supporting the School-to-Work Transition for Young Adults Formerly in Care* In: *Young Adult Development at the School-to-Work Transition.* E. Anne Marshall and Jennifer E. Symonds, Oxford University Press (2021). © Oxford University Press. DOI: 10.1093/oso/9780190941512.003.0014.

engagement with the future, determination to work toward that future, and capacity to tolerate setbacks and uncertainty. Hope is an important internal resource in the STW transition for all youth and may be especially pertinent in combating despondency and increasing engagement. Indeed, hope theory offers a practical and effective framework for understanding and supporting human change and flourishing, particularly in the face of uncertainty and difficulty (Scioli, Ricci, Nyugen, & Scioli, 2011). Further, a large body of research indicates that higher levels of hope are linked to resilience as well as improved educational and employment outcomes in the transition from adolescence to adulthood (Schmid et al., 2011).

This chapter outlines and explores the distinct barriers faced by YAFC as they embark on the STW transition. Hope is used as a practical heuristic for understanding and addressing these barriers, grounded in theory and research. Using hope as a foundation for understanding intervention, evidence-based recommendations for supporting a successful STW transition for YAFC are presented.

Who Are Young Adults Formerly in Care?

YAFC is an umbrella term that applies to all young adults who have aged out of the government care system. These individuals embark on the STW transition having lived in out-of-home placements, including foster care, group homes, residential treatment facilities, and juvenile detention centers (Canadian Child Welfare Research Portal, 2011). Most frequently, these placements are precipitated by the removal of the child or youth from their home of origin, when the survival, security, and development of the child are deemed to be insufficiently protected by their guardian (Child, Youth and Family Enhancement Act, R.S.A., 2000). Many of the children and youth who enter the government care system come from high-risk community and family backgrounds (Courtney et al., 2004). These young people are significantly more likely than their noncare peers to have experienced maltreatment including sexual and physical abuse, emotional trauma, neglect, trouble with the law, exposure to violence, and illicit drug use (Altschuler, Strangler, Berkley, & Burton, 2009; Osgood et al., 2005; Representative for Children and Youth, 2014; Tyler, 2006).

While the exact number of youth in care is difficult to determine, Jones, Sinha, and Trocmé (2015) estimated that in 2013 there were approximately 62,400 youth living in out-of-home care across Canada. That is, for every 1,000 children in the Canadian population, 8.5 were residing in an out-of-home care setting. This estimation represents a notable increase in the rates of young people being placed in government care in Canada since the 1990s. Additionally, there is a significant overrepresentation of Indigenous children in the youth in care population in Canada (Trocmé, Knoke, & Blackstock, 2004; Wray & Sinha, 2015). Indigenous children are twice as likely to be taken into care than non-Indigenous peers (Trocmé et al., 2004).

Postguardianship supports, which offer continued care from the government after youth reach adulthood, are highly conditional on behavior as well as the youth's level of disability and are typically only provided until 22 years of age (Government of New Brunswick, n.d.; Alberta Human Services, 2016), although some provincial governments have now extended that support to age 24 (Alberta Human Services, 2016). In research, young adults receiving postguardianship support have described a frustrating dialectic, in which continued government support is contingent on their being neither too successful nor too problematic in their behavior (Office of the Child and Youth Advocate, 2013). Some youth choose to exit the childcare system and end their guardianship status upon reaching the end of the "age of protection," which is 16 in the majority of provinces and territories (Canadian Child Welfare Research Portal, 2011). Ultimately, youth must fully assume adult roles and responsibilities after leaving government care, between the ages of 16 and 24 in Canada (Office of the Child and Youth Advocate of Alberta, 2013).

Barriers to Successful School-to-Work Transition

Young adulthood is a time of immense change, growth, and new responsibility (Young et al., 2011). It is a time to lay the foundation for occupational capacities and adult identity (Young et al., 2011). However, the process of transitioning out of government care and into independence has been described as "risky, complex, stigmatized and fast-tracked" (Abel & Fitzgerald, 2008, p. 365). While for many young adults the STW transition is an extended period of exploration (Bradley & Devadsen, 2008), former youth in care are often pushed to make premature career decisions to survive (Osgood, Foster, & Courtney, 2010). Furthermore, YAFC face systemic barriers throughout their development and during the STW transition itself. The following section will discuss three main types of barriers faced by YAFC in relation to the STW transition: developmental disruption, lack of normative supports or opportunities, and premature transition, as well as how these barriers threaten hope. While no two stories of government care are exactly alike, these are some common barriers faced by YAFC.

Developmental Disruption

The difficulties faced by YAFC during the STW transition begin long before they actually leave government care and have roots in child and adolescent developmental disruption. Experiences leading up to the transition greatly impact the ability to smoothly transition (Daining & DePanfilis, 2007). Children who eventually enter the foster care system are significantly more likely than the general population to have experienced maltreatment in their family of origin (Tyler, 2006). Attachment research indicates that individuals who face abuse and neglect in their formative years do not adequately develop executive functioning skills, such as emotional regulation and planning for the future (Colvert et al., 2008). Erik Erikson (1968) posits that a basic developmental task of early childhood is the development of hope. If a child's experiences leads her or him to the belief that others cannot be trusted to meet their basic needs, Erikson suggests that child will fail to adequately develop the capacity for hope. Therefore, both foundational theory and recent research suggest that at the heart of developmental disruption, hope is already threatened.

Experiences within care can further compromise hope. Being removed from one's home and placed in care is itself a disruption, which may be interpreted by the child or youth as traumatic (Folman, 1998). Children placed in care show an immediate increase in acting-out behavior, which is sustained over time, as well as higher levels of anxiety and depression than peers of similar family backgrounds who are not in care (Lawrence, Carlson, & Egeland, 2006), suggesting that experiences in care may contribute to hopelessness. Further, youth face an average of 15 separate moves during their time in care (Newton et al., 2000), and a greater number of placements are associated with poorer educational and career outcomes (Cashmore & Paxon, 2006). Childhood and adolescent involvement in government care can fundamentally threaten both hope and readiness for adulthood (Munson, Lee, Miller, Cole, & Nedelcu, 2013).

Lack of Normative Supports and Opportunities

In addition to any developmental deficits accrued, YAFC must also cope with fewer supports than their similarly aged peers. When scholar D. Wayne Osgood (2005) describes former foster youth as "on their own without a net" (p. 1), the net he refers to is social and financial support. YAFC are much less likely to have material or emotional support from parents (Avery

& Freundlich, 2009). Furthermore, the influence of peers during the transition to adulthood is extensive, and many youth in the foster care system experience troubled peer connections. Influences of negative peer relationships on at-risk youth have been shown to significantly impact adult outcomes (Rankin, & Quane, 2002), as well as negatively impacting career exploration, even when controlling for academic performance (Creed, Tilbury, Buys, & Crawford, 2011). Indeed, YAFC report that lack of social and emotional support was their largest concern during the transition from care (Goodkind, Schelbe, & Shook, 2011). Without these supports, YAFC find themselves in the precarious position of needing to succeed on their own in the STW transition because they lack a social and financial safety net. However, the lack of a nurturing social support network can further threaten hope and make it more difficult for YAFC to be successful in this essential transition (Collins, Spencer, & Ward, 2010; Croce, 2013).

Premature Transition

After exiting the government care system, YAFC are propelled into independent living and commonly face a premature transition to adulthood. While growing numbers of young adults in Canada have a prolonged reliance on familial support, sometimes into their late 20s (Kins, Beyers, Soenens, & Vansteenkiste, 2009), youth transitioning out of the care of the government have fewer supports and are expected to function independently at a much younger age. YAFC describe the STW transition as a time of accelerated responsibility with high stakes (Munson, Lee, Miller, Cole, & Nedelcu, 2013). In a qualitative study, YAFC describe the STW transition as a time, not of exploration, but rather of preparation for assuming adult responsibilities:

> I'm not exploring; I'm preparing. . . . I'm preparing mentally. I'm trying to prepare financially. . . . I'm not having fun while I'm doing it, and that's what I think of when somebody says "explore." I think of fun 'cause you're experiencing stuff. It's like "Wow. It's amazing." No, I'm preparing myself for life. That's how I feel, it's not a time to explore. (Munson et al., 2013, p. 927)

It is telling that the word YAFC used most frequently to define success in adulthood is simply *surviving* (Goodkind, Schelbe, & Shook, 2011). Clearly, the premature transition can limit YAFC's beliefs about possibilities for their adult lives. A deficit of hope in this population is clear.

Hope in the Face of Challenging Circumstances for YAFC

Given the numerous barriers encountered by YAFC, it is not surprising that the STW transition often leaves youth vulnerable and at risk for hopelessness. We suggest utilizing a framework of hope to support resilient transitions from care. A large corpus of human science research reveals hope as a positive human capacity, fundamental to effective human change processes within education, employment, and social domains. While hope is certainly not a panacea to address the systemic issues leading to inequality of opportunities, it may provide a theoretical framework to understand successful STW transitions in this population. Further, a growing body of research indicates that hope is essential to resilience for young adults and serves as a buffer against stress and adversity, in turn, fostering more positive and resilient outcomes (Lagace-Seguin & d'Entremont, 2012; Rew, Taylor-Seehafer, Thomas, & Tockey, 2001).

In the simplest terms, hope has been described as the capacity that allows individuals to "imagine a future in which they would wish to participate" (Jevne, 1994, p. 8). As a construct, hope has specific properties which support positive action in the face of difficulty. First, research indicates that the need for hope arises particularly during periods of difficulty or stress (Bruininks & Malle, 2005; Lagace-Seguin & d'Entremont, 2012). The STW transition for YAFC is inherently difficult and stressful, and the barriers faced during this transition leave YAFC vulnerable to despair. In the context of this difficulty and uncertainty, hope can offer a stable orientation to a positive possible future, despite adverse probabilities (Bruinincks & Malle, 2005; Jevne, 1994; Petit, 2004). In this way, hope is distinct from optimism (Bruinincks & Malle, 2005). Rather than expecting positive outcomes as optimistic individuals do, hoping individuals are oriented to a positive outcome despite probabilities. This means that with hope, one can be aware of the barriers faced but can still orient toward a desired outcome, as though directed by a compass toward their hoped-for future. Perhaps most important, hope motivates action toward hoped-for outcomes (Averill, Catlin, & Chon, 1990; Bruinincks & Malle, 2005; Morse & Doberneck, 1995). While this action may not culminate in the ultimate hoped-for outcome, it allows the individual to position themselves in a better trajectory than if hope were not present. In short, hope supports resilient behavior in the face of adversity.

To properly frame a discussion about how hope can be supportive in the context of transition, it is important to consider theories of hope that are particularly relevant to young adults. Two such theories pertain to career development for YAFC. First, Carl Snyder's (2002) cognitive-behavioral model of hope as related to goal attainment provides a helpful heuristic for understanding hope in relation to specific goals, such as work-life development. Second, Anthony Scioli and colleagues' (2011) more complex model of hope as consisting of four channels grounded in biological imperatives provides a perspective on the developmental nature of hope.

Snyder's (2002) hope theory identifies hope as consisting of three main parts: goals, agency ("the will") to achieve goals, and pathways ("the way") of thinking, including the capacity to envision several routes to one's ultimate goal and the capacity to change strategies. There is a natural fit between Snyder's hope theory and the STW transition for YAFC. For hope to be alive in this process, youth must have a desired outcome, be invested in working toward that outcome, and determine how to get there, while adopting a flexible and adaptive approach. The simple structure of Snyder's model has been extremely helpful for establishing quantitative support for the importance of hope in young adult development and career planning (e.g. Adams et al., 2002; Gilman, Dooley, & Florell, 2006; Snyder et al., 2002; Yeager & Bundick, 2009). As such, we see clear evidence for the value of Snyder's theoretical approach to understanding how hope may be related to success in the STW transition.

With respect to additional hope theory, Scioli and colleagues' (2011) model adds dimension to the construct of hope by maintaining that while hope can certainly be related to goal attainment (what Scioli et al. calls *mastery*), it is also important in other life domains. To elaborate, Scioli et al. posit that hope consists of four primary channels: mastery, attachment, survival, and spirituality. *Mastery hope* includes goals, skill development or expression, and empowerment beliefs. *Attachment hope* arises from interpersonal experiences and encompasses basic trust and openness. *Survival hope* is related to an individual's capacity to feel safe, meet basic needs, and self-regulate. Finally, *spiritual hope* is not necessarily religious in nature but encapsulates an individual's broader understanding about the world and how he or she attributes meaning. The four channels explicated in Scioli et al.'s model are all informed by developmental experiences, including social supports, cultural endowments, and individual traits. These experiences either nurture or challenge biological imperatives of hope (e.g., to survive or to connect).

There are several important implications of Scioli's et al. (2011) model for the STW transition in YAFC. Scioli et al.'s theory of hope is informed by both a biological foundation and developmental experiences implying that hope may be unique for youth formerly in care, given their unique developmental experiences. In addition, survival hope is likely to be particularly pertinent to the study of YAFC. Survival as a component of hope highlights the importance of hope even in the context of darkness or difficulty (Scioli et al., 2011). In Scioli et al.'s hope model, hope can act as the force that allows an individual to cope. Finally, because circumstances can change significantly during the transition period, Scioli et al.'s flexible model is useful in that it allows for certain facets of hope to take precedence depending on the current circumstances and needs. Different aspects of hope may be salient at different times during the transition. Practically, it provides professionals several access points for hope when working with a YAFC. For example, when mastery hope is threatened (e.g., school is going poorly), other aspects of hope can be emphasized and drawn upon.

These understandings of hope provide an important foundation for conceptualizing how hope can be useful for YAFC in transition. The following section will explore typical outcomes for YAFC and present research supporting the importance of hope in successful STW transitions.

Outcomes

Compared with noncare peers, YAFC typically experience poorer outcomes in essentially all domains of adult life, including educational attainment, employment and financial stability, mental and physical well-being, early parenthood, criminal engagement, and interpersonal relationships (Osgood et al., 2005; Representative for Children and Youth, 2014). However, research indicates that hope supports more resilient outcomes. In the following discussion, typical outcomes experienced by YAFC are outlined and the role of hope in ameliorating adverse outcomes is discussed.

Educational Attainment

Youth in care and formerly in care attain lower levels of academic achievement than their noncare peers (Osgood et al., 2005; Pecora et al., 2006; Representative for Children and Youth, 2014). While attending high school, youth in care demonstrate poorer performance on standardized testing, fail more grades, and are overall less likely to graduate (Barker et al., 2014; Ministry of Children and Family Development, 2012; Osgood et al., 2005; Representative for Children and Youth, 2014). Vacca (2008) reported that less than half of youth who are emancipated from government care experience successful high school completion compared to 85% of their same-age peers. YAFC who do eventually graduate are more likely to receive high school equivalency credentials as opposed to a high school diploma (Brownell et al., 2015; O'Brien et al., 2010).

Perhaps unsurprisingly, given the rates of high school graduation, YAFC are also less likely than the general population to pursue and successfully complete postsecondary education (Courtney, Dworsky, Lee, & Raap, 2010; R. J. Davis, 2006; Pecora et al., 2006; Representative for Children and Youth, 2014). A study focusing on the educational experiences of youth in care revealed that only 20% of youth in government care who graduated from high school went on to pursue postsecondary education, compared with 60% of their noncare peers (McMillen, Auslander, Elze, White, & Thompson, 2003). There appears to be further attrition once enrolled in postsecondary. Courtney and colleagues (2011) found that only 8% of YAFC (aged 25–27) had successfully completed a minimum of a two-year postsecondary degree while the general population maintained a graduation rate of 46%.

Prior to the transition, the majority of YAFC express a desire to graduate high school and pursue postsecondary education (Courtney, Charles, Okpych, Napolitano, & Halsted, 2014; McMillen et al., 2003; Rutman & Hubberstey, 2016), suggesting a foundation of hope is available to be built upon. Bolstering this hope during the transition may have a significant impact. There is a strong association between higher levels of hope and successful educational outcomes, particularly in supporting the educational resilience for youth from low socioeconomic backgrounds (Schmid et al., 2011). Schmid and her colleagues found that adolescents' level of hope for the future was a significant and strong predictor of a positive educational trajectory. Similarly, Worrell and Hale (2001) found that in youth at risk, hope predicted high-school graduation, where risk factors, perceived school climate, and belief in the importance of education did not differ between dropouts and graduates. This suggests hope may be a necessary and important prerequisite to pursuing educational goals. Indeed, Nurmi (2004) suggests that "in order to be active agents in the selection of their future developmental trajectories, adolescents' personal goals need to be evidenced in their positive thinking about the future and belief in personal control" (p. 99). This is supported by qualitative research with former foster youth who succeeded in higher education and who cited hope and belief in a positive future as an important determinant of their success (Lovitt & Emerson, 2008).

Employment and Financial Stability

For the majority of YAFC, outcomes do not improve after the transition from school to work. YAFC experience high rates of unemployment and underemployment (Goerge et al., 2002; Osgood et al., 2005; Representative for Children and Youth, 2014). In a quantitative study of 601 youth, Bender and colleagues (2015) found that only 20% of interviewees reported having maintained full-time employment in the six months prior to the interview. This study also revealed that three quarters of participants resorted to alternative means of meeting basic needs, including panhandling, dealing drugs, and theft.

YAFC's employment situations tend to be unstable and produce significantly lower earnings than those of the general young adult population (Dworsky, 2005; Goerge et al., 2002; Representative for Children and Youth, 2014). The typical employment patterns and earnings of YAFC frequently leave them living in poverty and struggling to obtain basic necessities (Barth, 1990; Dworsky & Courtney, 2001; Goerge et al., 2002; Gypen, Vanderfaeillie, De Maeyer, Belenger, & Van Holen, 2017; Osgood et al., 2005). As a result, many YAFC find themselves relying on social assistance programs to meet their financial needs (Courtney, Piliavin, Grogan-Kaylor, & Nesmith, 2001; Rutman, Hubberstey, & Feduniw, 2007). Sadly, many YAFC eventually face homelessness (Courtney et al., 2001; Osgood et al., 2005; Representative for Children and Youth, 2014).

Hope again plays an important role in supporting employment. Kenny and colleagues (2010) adapted Snyder's hope theory to investigate the importance of "work hope." They examined the importance of work hope on achievement motivation in STW transitions of high-risk adolescents. Work hope strongly predicted achievement motivation and was negatively correlated with skepticism. Further, work hope was significantly more important than career planning for achievement motivation and efficacy. In other research, hope was shown to be a better predictor of job performance (both self- and employer-rated) and job satisfaction than either resilience or optimism (Youssef & Luthans, 2007). Additionally, recent research highlights that higher levels of hope in young adults predicts career flexibility (Buyukgoze, 2016), suggesting that hope develops a capacity to adapt to a situation while maintaining focus on the overall goal of securing a career. Some initial work has been done to incorporate hope into programming designed to support employment in high-risk youth (Park-Taylor & Vargas, 2012; Robitschek, 1996; Taylor et al., 2015). However, given the evidence for hope as an important component of success throughout the STW transition, more applied research is certainly needed.

The importance of hope across the STW transition is clear. As we discuss recommendations for supporting YAFC throughout their STW transition, we will highlight how these interventions are grounded in nurturing hope. As a society and as professionals, our obligation to support these young people should not end when they enter young adulthood. Rather, it may be possible to help YAFC to envision and maintain a robust hope for the future that will support them through the very real challenges they face in the transition to adulthood.

Recommendations

As helping professionals, it is vital to foster a sense of hope and positive engagement in the youth we serve. The existing literature provides a number of evidence-based recommendations for supporting YAFC. We suggest using a framework of hope theory, by fostering both hope agency and hope pathways (Snyder, 2002), with clear links to additional hope research. Hope is a particularly important aspect of resilience in the STW transition because, unlike other resilience factors, which are static and unchangeable, such as intelligence (Masten, 2001) or academic achievement (Byrant, Schulenberg, O'Malley, Bachman, & Johnston, 2003), hope is an internal and changeable resilience factor (Drapeau, Saint-Jacques, Lepine, Begin, & Bernard, 2007; Maholmes, 2014). The recommendations presented next are conceptualized as serving a dual purpose by (a) providing supports and combatting barriers to success in pragmatic ways and (b) supporting hope for the future.

Hope Agency

To foster hope, professionals must first support youth to identify what they would like to see in their futures and increase their sense of capability and personal agency.

Fostering Supportive Relationships

One of the most widely agreed-upon recommendations to promote transitional success among YFAC is to foster positive and long-term relationships (Office of the Child and Youth Advocate Alberta, 2013; Representative for Children and Youth, 2014; Rutman & Hubberstey, 2016). Given the importance of attachment to hope (Dufault & Martocchio, 1985; Scioli et al., 2011), fostering these relationships can in turn increase a youth's sense of hope for themselves. There is a wealth of research, both across Canada and abroad, which suggests that youth in out-of-home care who possess strong social supports and maintain stable connections with their family systems and communities experience significantly better outcomes as they transition into adult life (Courtney et al., 2001; Reid & Dudding, 2006; Representative for Children and Youth, 2014).

Encouraging Family Contact

Positive relationships with family members are especially valuable and are associated with a greater sense of well-being and improved transitional outcomes for YAFC (Davidson & Cappelli, 2011; Reid & Dudding, 2006; Representative for Children and Youth, 2014). Given the importance of these relationships, there should be a distinct focus on improving the connections between youth in care and their families where appropriate (Biehal & Wade, 1996; Representative for Children and Youth, 2014). Some specific suggestions for strengthening family bonds include encouraging regular contact and communication between youth and their family members, encouraging family members to become increasingly involved in youths' transition planning, and providing access to specialized family counseling and mediation services (Biehal & Wade, 1996; Davidson & Cappelli, 2011; Reid & Dudding, 2006; Representative for Children and Youth, 2014). It is important to note that for many youth in care promoting relationships with specific family members may not be a viable option due past experiences of abuse or the unwillingness of families to provide support (Biehal & Wade, 1996). Therefore, the recommendation to promote family connections should be evaluated in each individual situation. In situations where parental relationships are not deemed possible or appropriate, connections to siblings and extended family members may be valuable sources of interpersonal support (Biehal & Wade, 1996; Reid & Dudding, 2006). Similarly, engagement in mentoring programs and extracurricular activities have shown promise in promoting success throughout the STW transition for youth in care by helping to establish meaningful relationships and connections to community, both of which have been directly linked to educational outcomes (Reid & Dudding, 2006; Rutman & Hubberstey, 2016).

Supporting Identity Development

One of the key processes of adolescence is identity development (Representative for Children and Youth, 2014). This process allows youth to examine their personal histories and discover who they are, what they value, and who they hope to be in the future (Representative for Children and Youth, 2014), a process clearly tied to hope. When youth have a strong sense of personal, cultural, and social identity, they are better able to set clear goals for the future (Representative for Children and Youth, 2014), whereas disconnection from cultural resources or supports can erode a sense of personal identity and pride (Bruskas, 2008). In addition to isolation from supports, many youth experience negative stigma and stereotypes (Reid & Dudding, 2006; Representative for Children and Youth, 2014). Sadly, youth are sometimes assumed to be delinquent or mentally ill simply due to their status in care.

Positive identity formation can be threatened by stigma (Representative for Children & Youth, 2014). As youth are exposed to toxic messages, they incorporate them into their own self-concept, leaving them feeling ashamed, undervalued, and lacking confidence in a desirable personal future (Representative for Children and Youth, 2014). Professionals working with this population must actively challenge this negative stigma, a clear and common threat to youth hope; recognize youths' individual strengths; and help them develop a personal sense of hope for the future (Representative for Children and Youth, 2014).

Increasing Agency and Engagement

Fostering youth engagement promotes hope and a successful STW transition. Youth living in care consistently report a desire to become more active participants in decisions made about their lives (Reid & Dudding, 2006). Allowing youth in care and transitioning from care a sense of control in their lives can help to support hope agency (Snyder, 1995), providing a sense of mastery and accomplishment (Scioli et al., 2011). Over time, youth should become incrementally more involved in decisions related to their living situations, school placements, decisions for the future, career planning, and service needs (Reid & Dudding, 2006). Developing and assuming more complex decision-making skills is a developmental process known as scaffolding. Youth in care want to know their opinions have value, rather than having decisions imposed upon them (Reid & Dudding, 2006). YAFC describe a paradox in which they are not encouraged to practice self-determination while in care and then are expected to have a range of skills and significant self-determination directly following their transition (Greenan & Powers, 2007). By hearing and respecting youths' voices, we can support a healthy sense of autonomy and encourage increasing ownership over their lives (Reid & Dudding, 2006).

Hope Pathways

Even when youth identify where they would like to go, they may have a hard time envisioning the steps needed to get there, which can threaten hope.

Educational Supports

Promoting educational success is essential to supporting the STW transition because educational success offers a pathway to possible positive futures (Reid & Dudding, 2006; Representative for Children and Youth, 2014). Supports for educational success may include individualized education plans, access to an academic tutor or mentor specifically trained to work with marginalized youth, or assigning teachers who possess an understanding of the distinct abilities and challenges experienced by these youth (Day, Riebschleger, Dworsky, & Damashek, 2012; Rutman & Hubberstey, 2016). Further, research has shown that the educational outcomes of youth in care are improved when there is increased collaboration between the education and relevant child welfare systems (Rutman & Hubberstey, 2016). Collaboration between systems allows professionals in each context to be better informed on the progress and particular needs of the youth they are working with and to become increasingly effective in providing required interventions in a timely fashion (Rutman & Hubberstey, 2016; Vacca, 2008).

The attitudes of caregivers and professionals working with the youth in care population are essential in promoting educational success (Dill, Flynn, Hollingshead, & Fernandes, 2012; Rutman & Hubberstey, 2016). It is important to foster motivation by setting academic expectations and holding youth accountable (Dill et al., 2012; Rutman & Hubberstey, 2016). By collaborating with youth in setting educational goals, educators can help youth identify specific goals, encourage motivation, and identify pathways toward achieving those goals (Snyder, 1995). For youth who are reluctant to set goals or who express fear of failure, it may be beneficial to use the language of "hope," rather than "goals" to speak about desired outcomes. Because hope inherently acknowledges and allows for uncertainty, young people who are more tentative in goal setting may feel more free to explore possibilities in this framework, rather than being asked to articulate goals (Larsen & Stege, 2010). For example, asking questions such as "What do you hope to do for work?" can invite a broader, and potentially less vulnerable, conversation about future aspirations, beginning the process of collaboration.

Fostering Development of Life-Skills

Another important element of increasing hope pathways and supporting a positive STW transition for YAFC is to assist them in developing essential life skills (Reid & Dudding, 2006). The development of life skills are especially important given that less than half of youth exiting the government care system feel adequately prepared to live independently (Office of Children's Administration Research, 2003). YAFC often struggle to acquire skills related to cooking, money management, career planning, interpersonal communication, self-care, accessing community services, decision-making, healthy relationships, sexual health, and parenting (Davidson & Cappelli, 2011; Office of Children's Administration Research, 2003; Office of the Child and Youth Advocate Alberta, 2013; Reid & Dudding, 2006). Considering Scioli et al.'s (2011) hope framework, developing specific life skills reflect three main channels of hope (mastery, attachment, and survival) and assist YAFC with more pathways to success when faced with challenges. Imparting life skills in helpful ways can constitute the endowments and supports, which Scioli et al. suggest contribute to the establishment of hope during human development. Further, independent living programs that aim to teach basic life skills are especially beneficial when delivered through a hands-on approach that encourage youth to practice their skills by integrating them into their day-to-day lives (Reid & Dudding, 2006; Representative for Children and Youth, 2014). Research also supports the importance of implementing skill development programs early in adolescence so youth are given time to adequately practice and learn under the support of the child welfare system before left on their own (Reid & Dudding, 2006; Representative for Children and Youth, 2014), a process known as scaffolding.

Mental Health Support

Pathways to accessing mental health supports are also crucial to supporting hope in the transition. Youth exiting the government care system report ongoing mental health concerns but struggle to access services (Reid & Dudding, 2006; Office of the Child and Youth Advocate Alberta, 2013). While in care, youth require mental health services to help them heal from the experiences that initially led to their being put into care. Sadly, the YAFC's mental health challenges are too often exacerbated by a myriad of challenges associated with living in the government care system and the distinct barriers that they face as they transition into adult life (Reid & Dudding, 2006; Representative for Children and Youth, 2014). Consistent access to mental health supports throughout the transition into adulthood is important for instilling hope and addressing hopelessness and despair (Representative for Children and Youth, 2014).

Advocacy and Information About Services

The final recommendation to improve the STW transition for YAFC emphasizes that transitional planning and integration into adult life should be understood as a shared responsibility of all involved parties, not delegated solely to the youth (Davidson & Cappelli, 2011). It can be extremely difficult to navigate various government departments, as well as not for profit agencies and their services (Office of the Child and Youth Advocate Alberta, 2013). Caregivers, including social workers, teachers, youth workers, counselors, and family members must take an active role in advocating for these young people to ensure they are well informed of the opportunities available to them and what services they may be eligible for (Office of the Child and Youth Advocate Alberta, 2013). This may include providing information related to career and educational pathways, as well as specialized assistance programs or financial aid (Representative for Children and Youth, 2014). Previous hope research indicated that accessing information about alternatives increases personal hope in individuals coping with HIV, another marginalized group (Harris & Larsen, 2007). This type of advocacy and information-giving may open up possible future pathways that a youth was not aware of or could not access without the advocacy of a professional. Ensuring proper training for professionals working with this population is essential to meeting this recommendation and addressing the unique needs of YAFC (Office of the Child and Youth Advocate, 2013). Making youth aware of services available to them can help to increase pathways of hope (Snyder, 1995) when youth have the "will" but not necessarily the "way" to move toward their desired future.

Beyond these specific recommendations, fostering hope and providing youth more control and agency over their futures will allow them to embark on their transition from care with a sense that they will be able to make a difference in their own lives. Therefore, inspiring hope during the transition from care may begin a lifelong process of living toward hope.

Summary

This chapter provides an overview of the barriers and outcomes experienced by youth in care during the STW transition, as well as the potentially beneficial impacts of hope. Understanding intervention with YAFC as a process of instilling and maintaining hope can provide a framework for facilitating movement toward positive futures. The previously outlined recommendations emphasize the areas of interpersonal relationships, education, life-skill development, mental health, identity development, youth engagement, and advocacy as essential in fostering hope and promoting transitional success among this population. Through recognizing the difficulties inherent in this transition and by providing mechanisms for hope, we may in turn assist these youth in looking toward their desired futures not with despondency, but with hope.

References

Abel, G. M., & Fitzgerald, L. J. (2008). On a fast-track into adulthood: An exploration of transitions into adulthood for street-based sex workers in New Zealand. *Journal of Youth Studies, 11*(4), 361–376.

Adams, V. H., Snyder, C. R., Rand, K. L., King, E. A., Sigmon, D. R., & Pulvers, K. M. (2002). Hope in the workplace. In R. A. Giacalone & C. L. Jurkiewicz (Eds.), *Handbook of workplace spirituality and organizational performance* (pp. 367–377). Armonk, NY: ME Sharpe.

Alberta Human Services. (2016). Enhancement policy manual. Retrieved from http://humanservices.alberta.ca/documents/ Enhancement-Act-Policy-Manual.pdf

Altschuler, D., Strangler, G., Berkley, K., & Burton, L. (2009). *Supporting youth in transition to adulthood: Lessons learned from child welfare and juvenile justice.* Washington, DC: Center for Juvenile Justice Reform.

Averill, J. R., Catlin, G., & Chon, K. K. (1990). *Rules of hope.* New York, NY: Springer-Verlag.

Avery, R. J., & Freundlich, M. (2009). You're all grown up now: Termination of foster care support at age 18. *Journal of Adolescence, 32*(2), 247–257.

Barker, B., Kerr, T., Alfred, G. T., Fortin, M., Nguyen, P., Wood, E., & DeBeck, K. (2014). High prevalence of exposure to the child welfare system among street-involved youth in a Canadian setting: Implications for policy and practice. *BMC Public Health, 14*(1), 1–15.

Barth, R. P. (1990). On their own: The experiences of youth after foster care. *Child and Adolescent Social Work Journal, 7*, 419–440.

Bender, K., Yang, J., Ferguson, K., & Thompson, S. (2015). Experiences and needs of homeless youth with a history of foster care. *Children and Youth Services Review, 55*, 222–231.

Biehal, N., & Wade, J. (1996). Looking back, looking forward: Care leavers, families and change. *Children and Youth Services Review, 18*, 425–445.

Bradley, H., & Devadason, R. (2008). Fractured transitions: Young adults' pathways into contemporary labour markets. *Sociology, 42*(1), 119–136.

Brownell, M., Chartier, M., Au, W., MacWilliam, L., Schultz, J., Guenette, W., & Valdivia, J. (2015). *The educational outcomes of children in care in Manitoba.* Winnipeg, MB: Manitoba Centre for Health Policy.

Bruininks, P., & Malle, B. F. (2005). Distinguishing hope from optimism and related affective states. *Motivation and Emotion, 29*(4), 324–352.

Bryant, A. L., Schulenberg, J. E., O'Malley, P. M., Bachman, J. G., & Johnston, L. D. (2003). How Academic Achievement, Attitudes, and Behaviors Relate to the Course of Substance Use During Adolescence: A 6-Year, Multiwave National Longitudinal Study. Journal of Research on Adolescence, 13(3), 361–397. https://doi.org/10.1111/1532-7795.1303005

Bruskas, D. (2008). Children in foster care: A vulnerable population at risk. *Journal of Child and Adolescent Psychiatric Nursing, 21*(2), 70–77.

Buyukgoze-Kavas, A. (2016). Predicting career adaptability from positive psychological traits. *Career Development Quarterly, 64*(2), 114–125.

Canadian Child Welfare Research Portal. (2011). How do Canadian child welfare systems work for Indigenous children? *Frequently Asked Questions (FAQs).* Retrieved from http://cwrp.ca/faqs#Q13

Canadian Child Welfare Research Portal. (2011). Out-of-home care. Retrieved from http://cwrp.ca/out-of-home-care

Cashmore, J., & Paxman, M. (2006). Wards leaving care: Follow up five years on. *Children Australia, 31*(3), 18–25.

Child, Youth and Family Enhancement Act, R.S.A. 2000, c C-12.

Collins, M. E., Spencer, R., & Ward, R. (2010). Supporting youth in the transition from foster care: Formal and informal connections. *Child Welfare, 89*(1), 125.

Colvert, E., Rutter, M., Kreppner, J., Beckett, C., Castle, J., Groothues, C., . . . Sonuga-Barke, E. J. (2008). Do theory of mind and executive function deficits underlie the adverse outcomes associated with profound early deprivation?: Findings from the English and Romanian adoptees study. *Journal of Abnormal Child Psychology, 36*(7), 1057–1068.

Courtney, M. E., Charles, P., Okpych, N. J., Napolitano, L., & Halsted, K. (2014). *Findings from the California youth transitions to adulthood study (CalYOUTH): Executive summary.* Chicago, IL: Chapin Hall at the University of Chicago.

Courtney, M. E., Dworksy, A., Brown, A., Cary, C., Love, K., & Vorhies, V. (2011). *Midwest evaluation of the adult functioning of former foster youth: Outcomes at age 26.* Chicago, IL: Chapin Hall Center for Children at the University of Chicago.

Courtney, M. E., Dworsky, A., Lee, J. S., & Raap, M. (2010). *Midwest evaluation of the adult functioning of former foster youth: Outcomes at ages 23 and 24.* Chicago, IL: Chapin Hall Center for Children at the University of Chicago.

Courtney, M. E., Piliavin, I., Grogan-Kaylor, A., & Nesmith, A. (2001). Foster youth transitions to adulthood: A longitudinal view of youth leaving care. *Child Welfare: Journal of Policy, Practice, and Program, 80*, 685–717.

Courtney, M., Terao, S., & Bost, N. (2004). *Midwest evaluation of the adult functioning of former foster youth: Conditions of youth preparing to leave state care.* Chicago, IL: Chapin Hall.

Creed, P., Tilbury, C., Buys, N., & Crawford, M. (2011). The career aspirations and action behaviours of Australian adolescents in out-of-home-care. *Children and Youth Services Review, 33*(9), 1720–1729.

Croce, M. (2013). Youth aging out of foster care: A study of youth sense of hope (Doctoral dissertation). Retrieved from http://pqdtopen.proquest.com/doc/1466022850.html?FMT=ABS

Daining, C., & DePanfilis, D. (2007). Resilience of youth in transition from out-of-home care to adulthood. *Children and Youth Services Review, 29*(9), 1158–1178.

Davidson, S., & Cappelli, M. (2011). *We've got growing up to do: Transitioning youth from child and adolescent mental health services to adult mental health services.* Ottawa, ON: Ontario Centre of Excellence for Child and Youth Mental Health.

Davis, M. (2003). Addressing the needs of youth in transition to adulthood. *Administration and Policy in Mental Health, 30*, 495–509.

Davis, R. J. (2006). *College access, financial aid, and college success for undergraduates from foster care.* Washington, DC: National Association of Student Financial Aid Directors.

Day, A., Riebschleger, J., Dworsky, A., Damashek, A., & Fogarty, K. (2012). Maximizing educational opportunities for youth aging out of foster care by engaging youth voices in a partnership for social change. *Children and Youth Services Review, 34*, 1007–1014.

Dill, K., Flynn, B., Hollingshead, M., & Fernandes, A. (2012). Improving the educational achievement of young people in out-of-home care. *Children and Youth Services Review, 34*, 1081–1083.

Drapeau, S., Saint-Jacques, M. C., Lepine, R., Bégin, G., & Bernard, M. (2007). Processes that contribute to resilience among youth in foster care. *Journal of Adolescence, 30*(6), 977–999.

Dufault, K., & Martocchio, B. C. (1985). Hope: Its spheres and dimensions. Symposium on compassionate care and the dying experience. *Nursing Clinics of North America, 20*, 379–391.

Dworsky, A. (2005). The economic self-sufficiency of Wisconsin's former foster youth. *Children and Youth Services Review, 27*, 1085–1118.

Dworsky, A., & Courtney, M.E. (2001). *Self-sufficiency of former foster youth in Wisconsin: Analysis of unemployment insurance wage data and public assistance data.* Washington, DC: US Department of Health and Human Services, Office of Assistant Secrettary for Planning and Evaluation.

Erikson, E. H. (1968). Life cycle. *International encyclopedia of the social sciences, 9*, 286–292.

Folman, R. D. (1998). "I was tooken": How children experience removal from their parents preliminary to placement into foster care. *Adoption Quarterly, 2*(2), 7–35.

Gilman, R., Dooley, J., & Florell, D. (2006). Relative levels of hope and their relationship with academic and psychological indicators among adolescents. *Journal of Social and Clinical Psychology, 25*(2), 166–178.

Goerge, R. M., Bilaver, L., Lee, B. J., Needell, B., Brookhart, A., & Jackman, W. (2002). *Employment outcomes for youth aging out of foster care.* Chicago, IL: Chapin Hall Center for Children, University of Chicago.

Goodkind, S., Schelbe, L. A., & Shook, J. J. (2011). Why youth leave care: Understandings of adulthood and transition successes and challenges among youth aging out of child welfare. *Children and Youth Services Review, 33*(6), 1039–1048.

Government of New Brunswick. (n.d.). *Children's residential services: Child care residential centres.* Retrieved from https://www2.gnb.ca/content/gnb/en/services/services_renderer.200590.Children_s_Residential_Services_-_Child_Care_Residential_Centres.html

Greenen, S., & Powers, L. E. (2007). "Tomorrow is another problem": The experiences of youth in foster care during their transition to adulthood. *Children and Youth Services Review, 29*, 1085–1101.

Gypen, L., Vanderfaeillie, J., De Maeyer, S., Belenger, L., & Van Holen, F. (2017). Outcomes of children who grew up in foster care: Systematic review. *Children and Youth Services Review, 76*, 64–83.

Harris, G. E., & Larsen, D. (2007). HIV peer counseling and the development of hope: Perspectives from peer counselors and peer counseling recipients. *AIDS, Patient Care and STDs, 21*(11), 843–859.

Jevne, R. (1994). *Voice of hope: Heard across the heart of life.* San Diego, CA: Lura.

Jones, A., Sinha, V., & Trocmé, N. (2015). *Children and Youth in Out-of- Home Care in the Canadian Provinces* (CWRP Information Sheet #167E). Montreal, QC: Centre for Research on Children and Families, McGill University.

Kenny, M. E., Walsh-Blair, L. Y., Blustein, D. L., Bempechat, J., & Seltzer, J. (2010). Achievement motivation among urban adolescents: Work hope, autonomy support, and achievement-related beliefs. *Journal of Vocational Behavior, 77*(2), 205–212.

Kins, E., Beyers, W., Soenens, B., & Vansteenkiste, M. (2009). Patterns of home leaving and subjective well-being in emerging adulthood: The role of motivational processes and parental autonomy support. *Developmental Psychology, 45*(5), 1416.

Lagace-Seguin, D., & d'Entremont, M-R. (2012). A scientific exploration of positive psychology in adolescence: The role of hope as a buffer against the influences of psychosocial negatives. *International Journal of Adolescence and Youth, 16*(1), 69–95.

Larsen, D., & Stege, R. (2010). Hope-focused practices during early psychotherapy sessions: Part II. Explicit approaches. *Journal of Psychotherapy Integration, 20*(3), 293–311.

Lawrence, C. R., Carlson, E. A., & Egeland, B. (2006). The impact of foster care on development. *Development and Psychopathology, 18*(01), 57–76.

Lee, R. E., & Whiting, J. B. (2007). Foster children's expression of ambiguous loss. *American Journal of Family Therapy, 35*, 417–428.

Lovitt, T., & Emerson, J. (2008). Foster youth who have succeeded in higher education: Common themes. *National Center on Secondary Education and Transition Information Brief, 7(1)*, 1–6.

Maholmes, V. (2014). *Fostering resilience and well-being in children and families in poverty: Why hope still matters.* New York, NY: Oxford University Press.

Masten, A. S. (2001). Ordinary magic: Resilience processes in development. *American Psychologist, 56*(3), 227–238.

McMillen, C., Auslander, W., Elze, D., White, T., & Thompson, R. (2003). Educational experiences and aspirations of older youth in foster care. *Child Welfare, 82*, 475–495.

Ministry of Children and Family Development. (2012). *Educational experiences of children under a continuing custody order.* Victoria, BC: Author.

Morse, J. M., & Doberneck, B. (1995). Delineating the concept of hope. *Image: The Journal of Nursing Scholarship, 27*(4), 277–285.

Munson, M. R., Lee, B. R., Miller, D., Cole, A., & Nedelcu, C. (2013). Emerging adulthood among former system youth: The ideal versus the real. *Children and Youth Services Review, 35*(6), 923–929.

Newton, R. R., Litrownik, A. J., & Landsverk, J. A. (2000). Children and youth in foster care: Disentangling the relationship between problem behaviors and number of placements. *Child Abuse & Neglect, 24*(10), 1363–1374.

Nurmi, J-E. (2004). Socialization and self-development: Channeling, selection, adjustment, and reflection. In R. M. Lerner & L. Steinberg (Eds.), *Handbook of adolescent psychology* (Vol. 2, pp. 85–124). Hoboken, NJ: Wiley.

O'Brien, K., Pecora, P., Echohawk, L., Evans-Campbell, T., Palmanteer-Holder, N., & White, C. R. (2010). Educational and employment achievements of American Indian/Alaska Native alumni of foster care. *Families in Society, 91*, 149–157.

Office of the Child and Youth Advocate (Alberta). (2013). *Where do we go from here? Youth aging out of care special report.* Edmonton, AB: Author.

Osgood, D. W., Foster, E. M., & Courtney, M. E. (2010). Vulnerable populations and the transition to adulthood. *The Future of Children, 20*(1), 209–229.

Osgood, D. W., Foster, E. M., Flanagan, C., & Ruth, G. R. (2005). *On your own without a net: The transition to adulthood for vulnerable populations.* Chicago, IL: University of Chicago Press.

Park-Taylor, J., & Vargas, A. (2012). Using the constructs multifinality, work hope, and possible selves with urban minority youth. *Career Development Quarterly, 60*, 243–253.

Pecora, P. J., Williams, J., Kessler, R. C., Hiripi, E., O'Brien, K., Emerson, J., . . . Torres, D. (2006). Assessing the educational achievements of adults who were formerly placed in family foster care. *Child & Family Social Work, 11*, 220–231.

Petit, P. (2004). Hope and it's place in mind. *Annals of the American Academy of Political and Social Science, 5*(92), 152–165.

Rankin, B. H., & Quane, J. M. (2002). Social contexts and urban adolescent outcomes: The interrelated effects of neighborhoods, families, and peers on African-American youth. *Social Problems, 49*(1), 79–100. doi:10.1525/sp.2002.49.1.79

Reid, C., & Dudding, P. (2006). *Building a future together: Issues and outcomes for transition-aged youth.* Ottawa, ON: Centre of Excellence for Child Welfare.

Representative for Children and Youth. (2014). *On their own: Examining the needs of B.C. youth as they leave government care.* Victoria, BC: Author.

Rew, L., Taylor-Seehafer, M., Thomas, N. Y., & Yockey, R. D. (2001). Correlates of resilience in homeless adolescents. *Journal of Nursing Scholarship, 33*(1), 33–40.

Robitschek, C. (1996). At-risk youth and hope: Incorporating a ropes course into a summer jobs program. *Career Development Quarterly, 45*, 163–169.

Rutman, D. & Hubberstey, C. (2016). *Fostering success: Improving educational outcomes for youth in/from care.* Victoria, BC: University of Victoria.

Rutman, D., Hubberstey, C., & Feduniw, A. (2007). *When youth age out of care: Where to from there?* Victoria, BC: University of Victoria.

Schmid, K. L., Phelps, E., Kiely, M. K., Napolitano, C. M., Boyd, M. J., & Lerner, R. M. (2011). The role of adolescents' hopeful futures in predicting positive and negative developmental trajectories: Findings from the 4-H study of positive youth development. *Journal of Positive Psychology, 6*(1), 45–56.

Scioli, A., Ricci, M., Nyugen, T., & Scioli, E. R. (2011). Hope: Its nature and measurement. *Psychology of Religion and Spirituality, 3*, 78–97.

Snyder, C. R. (2002). Hope theory: Rainbows in the mind. *Psychological Inquiry, 13*(4), 249–275.

Snyder, C. R., Shorey, H. S., Cheavens, J., Pulvers, K. M., Adams, V. H., III, & Wiklund, C. (2002). Hope and academic success in college. *Journal of Educational Psychology, 94*(4), 820–826.

Stohler, R., Storo, J., Vincent, D., Wade, J., Schröer, W., Zeller, M., Ward, H., Mendes, P., Pinkerton, J., Knorth, E. & Köngeter, S. (2008). *Young people's transitions from care to adulthood: international research and practice*. London: Jessica Kingsley Publishers.

Taylor, C. E., Hutchinson, N. L., Ingersoll, M., Dalton, C., Dods, J., Godden, L., . . . de Lugt, J. (2015). At-risk youth find work hope in work-based education. *Exceptionality Education International, 25*, 158–174.

Trocmé, N., Knoke, D., & Blackstock, C. (2004). Pathways to the overrepresentation of Aboriginal children in Canada's child welfare system. *Social Service Review, 78*, 577–600.

Tyler, K. A. (2006). A qualitative study of early family histories and transitions of homeless youth. *Journal of Interpersonal Violence, 21*(10), 1385–1393.

Vacca, J. S. (2008). Foster children need more help after they reach the age of eighteen. *Children and Youth Services Review, 30*, 485–492.

Widom, C. S. (1994). *Childhood victimization and adolescent problem behaviors.* Mahwah, NJ: Erlbaum.

Worrell, F. C., & Hale, R. L. (2001). The relationship of hope in the future and perceived school climate to school completion. *School Psychology Quarterly, 16*, 370–388.

Wray, M., & Sinha, V. (2015). *Foster care disparity for Aboriginal children in 2011* (CWRP information sheet #165E). Montreal, QC: Centre for Research on Children and Families.

Yeager, D. S., & Bundick, M. J. (2009). The role of purposeful work goals in promoting meaning in life and in schoolwork during adolescence. *Journal of Adolescent Research, 24*, 423–452.

Young, R. A., Marshall, S. K., Valach, L., Domene, J. F., Graham, M. D., & Zaidman-Zait, A. (2011). *Transition to adulthood: Action, projects, and counselling.* New York, NY: Springer.

Youssef, C. M., & Luthans, F. (2007). Positive organizational behavior in the workplace the impact of hope, optimism, and resilience. *Journal of Management, 33*, 774–800.

15

A Strategy for Building Transition-Focused Education Capacity to Support Disabled Students in Australian Schools

Todd Milford, Breanna Lawrence, Wendi Beamish, Michael Davies, and Denis W. Meadows

Introduction

Post–high school transitions are often exciting times for young people. Yet, decisions about employment, postsecondary education (PSE), and independent living can be daunting, particularly for students with disabilities. Increasingly, high school students expect to attend postsecondary institutes or university (Gothberg et al., 2015; Schneider, 2015). However, there is a gap in student readiness as many young people leaving high school feel underprepared (Conley, 2010). The importance of transition planning and successful transitions becomes even more pronounced for young people with disabilities as well as for their families. As suggested in the introductory chapter, successful transitions are often considered linear moves from school to the labor market or PSE into the labor market while unsuccessful transitions involve neither education nor employment. While the definition of successful transitions for young people with disabilities may be similar to peers without disabilities, additional outcomes may form a primary focus such as finding meaningful volunteer work, learning how to live independently away from parents, and community involvement. This chapter describes current research on supporting young people with disabilities to transition successfully from high school to adult life. An example of implementing evidence-based practice to support successful transitions in an Australian context is described.

Todd Milford, Breanna Lawrence, Wendi Beamish, Michael Davies, and Denis W. Meadows, *A Strategy for Building Transition-Focused Education Capacity to Support Disabled Students in Australian Schools* In: *Young Adult Development at the School-to-Work Transition.* E. Anne Marshall and Jennifer E. Symonds, Oxford University Press (2021). © Oxford University Press. DOI: 10.1093/oso/9780190941512.003.0015.

Background

Both educators and parents understand post–high school transitions are important for young people. However, there is also wide scale agreement of the complex environment associated with transition planning for young people with disabilities and their families (Gothberg et al., 2015, Halpern 1985). Early models of this transition process (see Figure 15.1) attempted to capture this complexity in a single dimension of service provided as youth move from high school to employment (Will, 1984).

This initial model was viewed as overly narrow as there is some agreement that outcomes associated with successful transitions from school to adult include a career path, some aspect of PSE, involvement in community activities, leisure and recreation participation, and some aspects of self-determined action (Morgan & Riesen, 2016). Halpern revised the initial postschool transition model to capture the idea that living in one's community should be the overall target of transitions for young people with disabilities. He argued that the addition of nonvocational adult adjustment is justifiable not only for its contribution to employment but also as an end in and of itself. These revised outcomes included residential environment and social and interpersonal networks, in addition to the original primary outcome of employment, as shown in Figure 15.2.

No matter the dimensions identified across pathways, the process of successful transition needs an educational environment that is willing to work toward the understanding of how best to support young people with disabilities. Inclusive education is an approach to providing educational services to young people with disabilities where these students spend the majority of their time

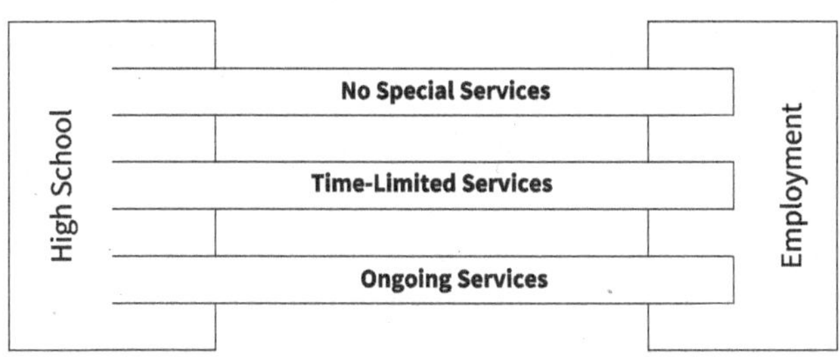

Figure 15.1 Early model of transition process.

Reprinted with permission from Halpern, A. S., 1985, Transition: A look at the foundations, *Exceptional Children, 51*(6), 479–486.

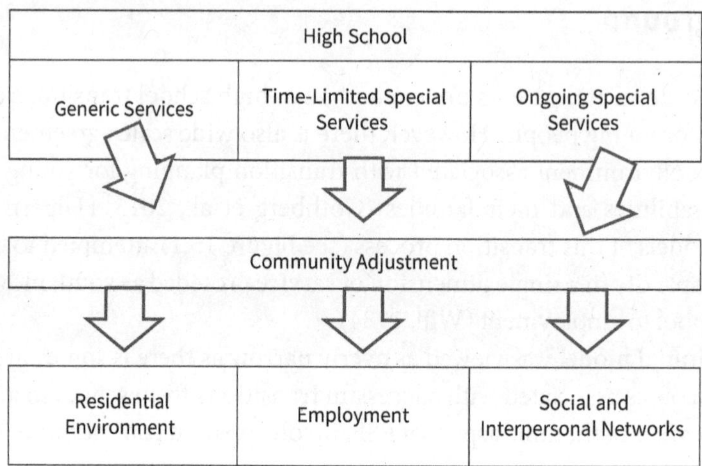

Figure 15.2 Revised model of transition process.
Reprinted with permission from A. S. Halpern, 1985, Transition: A look at the foundations, *Exceptional Children, 51*(6), 479–486.

with their peers in a general classroom setting and often at their neighborhood schools (Hutchinson, 2014). Examples of such service categories of students with disabilities include, but are not limited to, autism, blindness, intellectual disability, and learning disability. Inclusive education involves valuing and supporting the full participation of all people together within mainstream educational settings (Cologon, 2013). According to Cologon, the Australian Government expresses its commitment to inclusive education in an array of documents and policies, including the *National Disability Strategy*, the *Australian Curriculum*, the *Australian Professional Standards for Teachers*, the *National Quality Framework*, and the *Early Years Learning Framework for Australia*.

Despite the commitment from governments such as Australia to young people with disabilities, the transitions for youth from high school to adulthood are less favorable than those for students without disabilities. A large percentage of youth and young adults who had exited from special education programs were either unemployed or underemployed in the United States (Hasazi, Gordon, & Roe, 1985; Shandra & Hogan, 2008). More specifically, Butterworth et al. (2014) looked at individuals with intellectual and developmental disabilities (IDD) and same-aged peers without a disability who were two years out of high school. Approximately 23% of youth with IDD were employed compared to close to 60% of youth without disabilities. According to these authors, this relatively low employment rate was explained due to (a) lack of emphasis on integrated employment outcomes; (b) inadequate collaboration between schools and employment agencies; (c) limited vocational experiences in school; (d) inadequate transition support; and (e) limited development of self-determination and career-related skills during the transition years in schools.

Additional data out of the United States on employment, education, and independent living outcomes for young people with disabilities who have exited high school have been explored using the National Longitudinal Transition Study (NLTS) and the follow up NLTS-2. The follow-up study gathered data from a stratified random sample of 500 school districts and special schools in the United States. Wave 1 in 2001 began with 11,270 participants and concluded with Wave 5 in 2009 with about 4,810. This survey reported that 61% of those individuals with disabilities were employed (compared to 66% of youth overall) with 31% of young people with disabilities reporting that they had been employed at some point since leaving high school but were currently unemployed. Overall, these figures were higher than other results reported here; however, NLTS-2 focused on more general disabilities compared to the specific areas of IDD as reported previously (Morgan & Riesen, 2016).

Newman et al. (2011) also used the NLTS-2 findings to provide information on the PSE pursuits of young people with disabilities who had been out of school for up to eight years. Results were presented across the three outcomes of (a) current enrollment in PSE, (b) enrollment by program, and (c) enrollment by disability category. According to these authors, a smaller percentage of young people with disabilities had enrolled in PSE programs since graduation and were more often enrolled in two-year community college, and their disability category was associated with levels of enrollment.

The National Secondary Transition Technical Assistance Center (NSTTAC; 2010) out of the United States—as part of their mandate—offers information on how to improve transition services and postschool outcomes for young people with disabilities. To this end, they have identified a number of in school predicators associated with successful post–high school outcomes (i.e., PSE, employment, and independent living). Predictors associated with these outcomes involved inclusion practices in general education, paid employment/work experience, self-care and independent living activities and student support during the transition process. Predictors associated with PSE and employment included career awareness, interagency collaboration, occupational courses, self-advocacy/self-determination, social skills, transition program, and vocational evaluation. Although according to the NSTTAC's methodology, there were no identified strong predictors, the highest predictors were inclusion in general education, vocational education, employment/work experience, and parental expectations. Moreover, the

NSTTAC did not view these predictors as forming a checklist in evaluating effective school-based transition practices but more as a direction that schools and educators could explore more fully in their own settings. They felt that what mattered more than the existence of these predictors was the efficacy to which they were implemented (Morgan & Riesen, 2016).

Compared to the body of literature on the mostly poor postschool outcomes for young people with disabilities reported from the United States, there is relatively little known about the same student cohort and their postschool outcomes within Australia. Only two relatively large-scale studies have offered any data in regards to this issue. The first by Riches, Parameter, and Robertson (1996) who uncovered that approximately 50% of students who had left school in the state of New South Wales (NSW) were engaged in some form of employment; however, it was typically part time, causal, volunteer, sheltered, or unpaid. Additionally, these authors also found that those same young people tended to rely quite heavily upon parents and family for living arrangements as well as for access to social activities. The second study by Meadows et al. (2006) looked more specifically at the postschool transition of students identified with autism spectrum disorder (ASD), intellectual impairment (II), or the dual diagnosis of ASD/II who had left the school system within the previous five years in the state of Queensland. Similar to those results reported from the NSW study, only 25% of those studies had been involved in open employment, 13% has been involved in supported employment with the majority of the sample indicating participation in nonpaid day program type activities. Additionally, these young people also typically lived at home and experienced limited access to community engagement.

Current Study

There is a paucity of literature about students with disabilities and their postschool outcomes within Australia. The study outlined here seeks to address this lack of research by detailing efforts made by Meadows, Beamish, and Davies working in collaboration with a nongovernment educational authority, Brisbane Catholic Education (BCE), to apply recommended practices in postschool transitions for students with disabilities.

These practices of post–high school transitions for young people with disabilities, although linked to the previously mentioned model on postschool transitions forwarded by Halpern (1985), are grounded in the work of Kohler, her notions of transition-Focused Education (TFE), and the Taxonomy for Transition Programming (Kohler, 1996). Beamish, Meadows, and Davies

(2012) take the position that improving postschool outcomes for young people with disabilities requires schools to improve their capacity to adapt and develop these emerging best practices. The rest of this chapter details the application of the Taxonomy as a key tool used initially as a statewide audit of transition practice across the state and then for capacity-building across a number of secondary colleges (schools) within BCE in South East Queensland, Australia.

Australian Context

Australia has a total landmass of approximately 7.7 million square kilometers and is comprised of the mainland of Australia, Tasmania, and numerous smaller islands. It is divided into six states—New South Wales (NSW), Queensland (QLD), South Australia (SA), Tasmania (TAS), Victoria (VIC), and Western Australia (WA)—and two territories—the Australian Capital Territory (ACT) and the Northern Territory (NT). It is the sixth largest nation in the world by total area yet only ranks 53 in terms of total population (approximately 24 million). The majority of Australians have some British or Irish heritage; however, since the end of the First World War, the main population drivers have been in large part to immigration. Australia is now considered a multicultural nation. Figure 15.3 shows a map of the states and territories.

QLD is located in the northeast corner of Australia and is bordered by the NT on the west, SA in the south-west, and NSW to the south. It has a population of close to 5 million people who are concentrated along the coast (particularly in the south-east corner) and has an area close to 2 million square

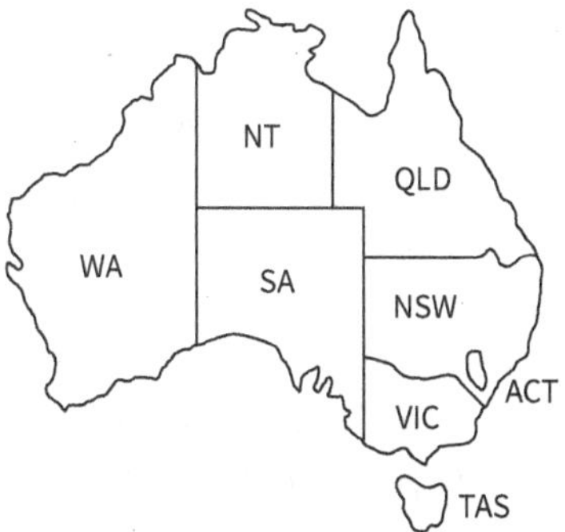

Figure 15.3 Map of states and territories in Australia.

kilometers. Brisbane, the state's capital, has a population of almost 2.5 million and is located in the south-east corner of the state close to the border of NSW.

The QLD education system is similar to other states and territories with each respective government providing both funding as well as regulating the public and private schools within its governing area. Typically, the school system follows the three-tier model which includes primary (Prep to year 6), secondary (year 7–12) and tertiary (years 12+). Education is compulsory between the ages of 5 and 15. The academic year typically runs from late January/ early February until early/mid-December for primary and secondary schools.

The school system is divided between government, Catholic, and independents schools, together with a small portion who are homeschooled. Government schools are free to attend for Australian citizens and permanent residents, while Catholic and independent schools typically charge a fee. Regardless of system, all schools are mandated to follow the Australian curriculum frameworks. In 2010, 65.5% of students in Australia attended government schools, 20% attended Catholic school sand 14.5% attended independent schools (Australian Bureau of Statistics, 2018). Students within the education system perform well and Australia typically places in the top 10 of international measures of academic achievement such as the Program for Student Assessment (PISA) and the Trends in Mathematics and Science Study (TIMSS; Ricci, 2015).

Initial Queensland Study

As part of a 2002 initiative from the Ministerial Task Force on Inclusive Education in QLD, a research team from Griffith University in Brisbane in 2005–2006 was engaged to study the relationship between transition practices and postschool outcomes for students with II, II/ASD, and ASD (Meadows et al., 2006). The results of this statewide study offered quantitative and qualitative data on postschool outcomes for this student population. The study was structured around the taxonomy of postschool transition planning as forwarded by Kohler (Kohler, 1996; Kohler & Field, 2003). The study comprised (a) a literature review of the factors associated with positive postschool outcomes for students with a disability (Meadows, Punch, Elias, Beamish & Davies, 2005); (b) a parent survey of students at school or who had left school system in the last five years (Davies & Beamish, 2009); (c) a teacher survey of their beliefs and use of key practices from the taxonomy (Beamish, et al.,

2012); and (d) statewide focus groups of stakeholders (parents, students, transition educators, and postschool service providers).

The literature review (Meadows et al., 2005) comprised a strong theoretical base around empirically supported postschool outcomes. Kohler's five key areas of TFE (student focused planning, student involvement, family-school-relations, interagency collaboration, and program structure) provided the structure. This structure was the framework for both survey design and question group focus in later parts of the study.

Results from the parent survey (Davies & Beamish, 2009) suggested the majority of parents indicated involvement in postschool transition process, limited work experience opportunities for youth, and insufficient postschool options in the community. Findings from the teacher survey (Beamish et al., 2012) indicated an agreement that the recommended transition practices were associated with program quality in secondary school, that transition practices should begin between the ages of 11 to 14, that areas such as professional development and documentation were inadequate, and that improvements were needed in the implementation of interagency collaboration.

The focus groups conducted with transition teachers and postschool service providers identified difficulties associated with gaining and adequately supervising work experience for students as a major barrier to improving postschool outcomes as were problems with establishing and maintaining relationships with postschool service providers. A lack of structured programs to develop student self-awareness and self-advocacy in students was also viewed as problematic. By comparison, establishing sound relationships with students' families at an early stage was seen as beneficial to student progress. In addition, school transition officers (a support staff position) were viewed as playing a major role in establishing sound transition practices on a regional basis and teachers identified the need for improved professional development.

The parent and student focus groups also identified a lack of work experience opportunities and the insufficient training of teachers in transition as barriers. Parents valued involvement in transition planning meetings with their son or daughter but were unsure about the degree to which their adolescents were taught how to self-advocate. Parents also wished their responsibilities during this period were more clearly defined, and they viewed the lack of coordination between government departments involved in postschool services and schools as an issue. Finally, parents commented, and students agreed, that a sense of loss was felt when the student left the supportive environment of the school (Davies & Beamish, 2009).

Background and Context for the Study

As an extension for the previous study and as the result of a request from the Queensland Catholic Education Commission, this same author team was tasked to respond to the 12 priority areas as highlighted in the previously noted document. Brisbane Catholic Education (BCE) subsequently identified the area of postschool transition for students with disabilities between stages of schooling or from schooling to further education, training, or employment as an area to target for improvement. BCE recommended that capacity-building should focus on the school-to-postschool transition process, and the research team from Griffith University in Brisbane was requested to design and implement a capacity-building approach at the college (i.e., secondary) level in concert with BCE.

As part of the Catholic school system, BCE provides education to over 70,000 students attending 137 schools from Prep (kindergarten) to year 12. (BCE, n.d.a). Its mission statement is as follows:

> Catholic education in this Archdiocese is promoted as a lifelong enterprise, inviting all those involved in educational ministry to be anchored in a Catholic vision that is personal and public, reflective and active, nurturing and transformative. The educational mission of Brisbane Catholic Education, as an evangelising agent of the Catholic Church, is to teach, challenge and transform the world through what it does and how it is done. Mission in this context is the result and lived out expression of an underpinning spirituality of communion. Mission is developed and expressed in ways that include individual, systemic and ecclesial dimensions.

Within their educational program, BCE promotes the ideals of inclusive education by ensuring that their schools are supportive and engaging places to attend. They provide for students who have a diverse range of personal characteristics and experiences attributable to physical, religious, cultural, personal health or well-being, intellectual, psychological, socioeconomic, or life experiences. Their public and online policy statement defines transitions as "when a student has to move from or into a new educational setting" (BCE, n.d.a). They also clearly identify how transitions involve the inclusion and support of parents and identify the support and personnel required to make the transition as smooth as possible.

From 2012 to 2013, the Australian Government made available and short-term grant of AUS$200 million to build the capacity for the state, Catholic and independent school systems in the areas of school transition pathways and postschool outcomes for students with disabilities. Within this process, the

Queensland Catholic Education Commission and more locally, BCE, sought to identify priorities around transition planning within their secondary schools (colleges; years/Grades 8–12). The senior education officer (SEO) within BCE targeted *effective transitions for students with disabilities between stages of schooling as well as from school into further education, training and/or employment.* Specifically, the SEO argued that capacity-building as identified by the Australian Government should focus on the process that facilitated transitions for these students (Maher, Raciti, Meadows, Beamish, & Davies, 2014).

This capacity-building partnership involved the SEO, an education officer from BCE, and the three academics from Griffith University. College-level participation included secondary college staff, parents, students, and relevant postschool providers. Of the 14 participating colleges, 4 were located in metropolitan Brisbane, 2 in urban areas close to Brisbane, 7 in urban regional centers, and 1 in a rural town 200 kilometers outside of Brisbane. The student enrollment across the colleges ranged from a low of 250 to close to 1,000, with a total of 307 students (out of a total of 8,295 students in years 8–12) identified with a disability (from 8 to 70 across all 14 colleges). The number of staff across the 14 colleges was 1,112.

Central to the capacity-building process was the benchmarking instrument with 46-item drawn from Kohler's (1996) Taxonomy and socially validated for the Queensland context in the previous 2005–2006 study (see Beamish et al., 2012). Items within the instrument were sorted according to five practice areas within the Taxonomy: (a) student-focused planning (9 items); (b) student involvement (10 items); (c) family–school relations (7 items); (d) interagency collaboration (7 items); and (e) program structure (13 items). Each college in the project selected one of these five practice areas for improvement as part of the capacity-building process.

Project Focus

Project focus and direction were framed by the following purpose, goals, and subgoals, as shown in Table 15.1.

The Capacity-Building Process With Outcomes

The capacity building process was driven by the university research team and education officer/transition who provided ongoing information, support, and

Table 15.1 Purpose, Goals, and Subgoals for Capacity-Building Process

Purpose	Building the capacity of schools to implement effective postschool pathways that support students with disabilities—specifically in terms of employment readiness, continued education, and social engagement.
Goal	Build the capacity of schools to work collaboratively with the development and implementation of quality school to postschool transition educational programs for students with disabilities.
Sub-goals	1. Schools to engage in a capacity-building process. 2. Stakeholders to improve their understanding of the Taxonomy for Transition Programming 3. Stakeholders to demonstrate an increase in agreement with the practices outlined in the Taxonomy for Transition Programming. 4. Stakeholders to demonstrate an increase in implementation of the practices outlined in the Taxonomy for Transition Programming. 5. Students to realise improved outcomes in relation to employment, continued education, and social engagement.

coaching so that each college would take control of their own process. The process involved five phases: Phase 1, informing and initial data gathering via surveys; Phase 2, data sharing, focus group meetings, open forums, and priority setting among stakeholders; Phase 3, goal setting and action planning for capacity-building by college staff and administrators; Phase 4, implementation, sharing, and coaching; and Phase 5, final data gathering via survey. Figure 15.4 details these phases.

Phase 1: Informing and Initial Data Gathering

Initially, staff and administrators from the 14 secondary colleges were invited to an information session where project aims and funding, Kohler's Taxonomy (1996), and the process model were outlined. Subsequently, colleges were asked to commit to and commence the project in either of two waves, a year apart. Six colleges committed to participate in Wave 1, and eight, in Wave 2.

Data-gathering for both waves commenced with an online survey for staff and administrators across the 14 colleges. Based on that used by Beamish et al. (2012), this survey comprised questions on 46 transition practices across the five areas of Kohler's Taxonomy (1996). Each practice was benchmarked for levels of agreement (belief) and use (implementation) in place at each college. Following this benchmarking, Wave 1 colleges gathered additional survey data from other stakeholders. Parents of both past and current students

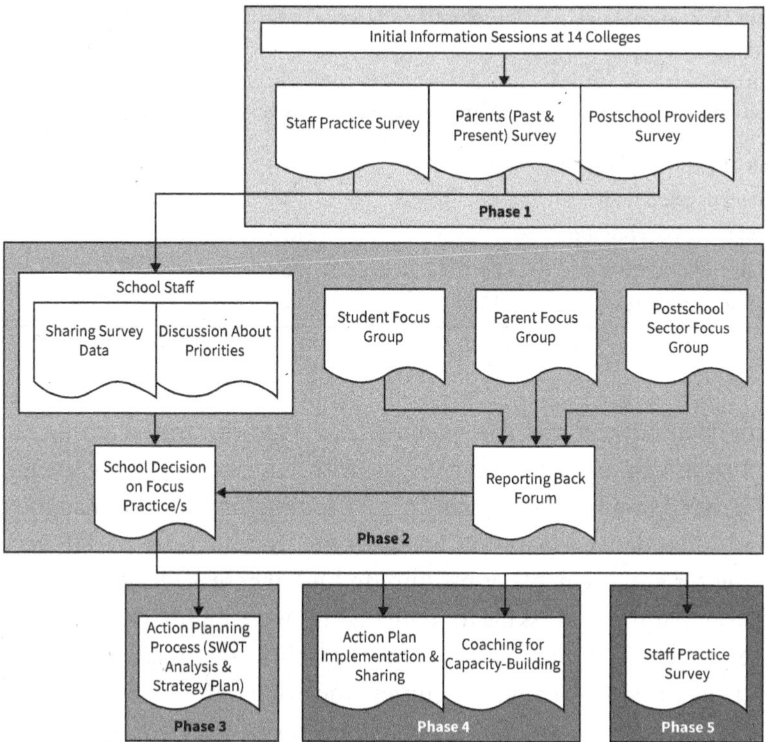

Figure 15.4 Five phases of the capacity-building process.

completed a parent survey (at home, by telephone, or in groups at school) that provided demographic data, information regarding student activities (e.g., work experience, employment, community access), and views about the transition process for their sons and daughters. Wave 2 colleges gathered this data in the following year.

Similarly, postschool service personnel in contact with each Wave 1 college complete an online survey based on practices contained in the interagency collaboration area of the staff online benchmarking survey. Information about their engagement levels with the college and role in the transition process was collected. This process was repeated by the Wave 2 colleges in the following year.

Data on the 46 transition practices from the online survey of staff and administrators ($N = 110$) are provided in Table 15.2 and presented graphically in Figure 15.5. High levels of agreement (belief) and use (implementation) were recorded in only one area, family–school relations. However, in the remaining four practice areas, levels of agreement met the 50% criterion level, but levels of use were below criterion.

Table 15.2 Mean Levels of Agreement and Use across the Five Practice Areas (as Percentages)

Practice Area	Number of Items	Level of Agreement	Level of Use
Student-focused planning	9	77	49
Student development	10	70	43
Interagency collaboration	7	64	30
Family–school relations	7	76	64
Program structures	13	62	28

Data from current and past parents (N = 194) confirmed strong family–school relationships across all colleges, with high ratings being assigned to the degree of family involvement in goal setting for sons and daughters. In relation to student preparation for adult life, the majority of parents rated "training for employment" at medium to high whereas ratings for "community participation" and "skills for daily living" were highly variable from college to college. In comparison to other stakeholder groups, feedback from postschool providers from the survey and focus group meeting was low (N = 25). However, participating personnel reported on two common issues. They identified the need for postschool providers to be more involved across a range of school-based activities related to transition planning and collectively

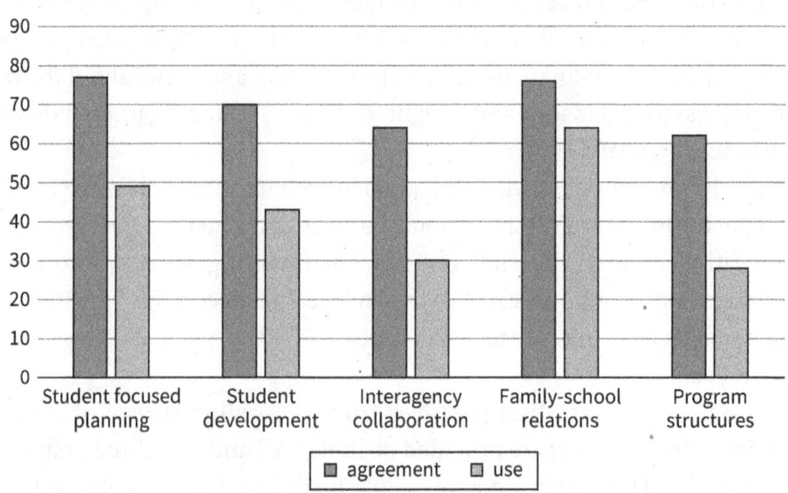

Figure 15.5 Phase 1 data from staff and administrators.

expressed a desire to be involved in joint professional development about transition. Taken together, these benchmark data provided an initial view of practice across the 14 colleges, and in doing so, the data provided a solid foundation for capacity-building at each college.

Phase 2: Data Sharing, Focus Group Meetings, Open Forum, and Priority Setting

Phase 2 was conducted at each college setting over a full day of four activities. First, the project team presented Phase 1 data to college administration and staff that included a comparison of college staff benchmark data with regional norms, parent survey summary, and responses from postschool providers wherever possible. Second, staff reviewed and discussed these data in conjunction with Kohler's taxonomy without intervention from the team. Meanwhile, parents, students, and postschool providers participated in separate focus group meetings and reflected on their overall satisfaction with the school and the school transition planning process. Third (following lunch), all stakeholders participated in an open forum that included a report back from each group and a response from college leadership. Finally, guided by the day's deliberation and stakeholder feedback, administration and staff met to discuss the issues raised and to make decisions about which of the Taxonomy's practice areas would be initially prioritized for capacity-building at their college.

Phase 3: Goal Setting and Action Plan Development

A full-day activity directly followed the Phase 2 day, focusing on goal setting in the specific practice area of the Taxonomy that was identified at the end of Phase 2 and the development of an action plan. A modified SWOT (strengths, weaknesses, opportunities, and threats) analysis developed by Kohler (2003) enabled TFE college staff and administrators to reflect on their current transition practice and identify strengths, needs, opportunities, and threats. These data helped to identify a measurable goal in the selected practice area. Subsequently, an action plan for capacity-building was developed and included the identification of activities required to meet the goal, the assigning of responsibilities, and specified timeframes. These activities were simultaneously projected on a screen as part of the developmental process, as were the determinations as an ongoing record of proceedings for the group make informed decisions. Across the two-year project, nine colleges developed action plans for practices related to the program structure area of the Taxonomy (Kohler, 1996), while eight colleges focused on the student development area. Additionally, two colleges used a job-coaching model to improve practices in the area of interagency collaboration.

Phase 4: Implementation, Sharing, and Coaching

School teams implemented their individual college action plans with support from the education officer/transition. Colleges focusing on similar goals met to workshop ideas and share strategies. For example, program structure was conducted between five colleges and a very productive full-day workshop provided new insights across the colleges. Additionally, the Wave 1 colleges presented their outputs to a full-day conference of representatives from the 14 colleges at the university. These presentations were recorded and distributed electronically to all colleges. Similarly, at the completion of the project, all 14 colleges presented poster sessions on their outputs at a conference held at the district office.

The education officer/transition, assisted by a university researcher, also adopted a coaching role to teams at individual colleges and when required, conducted workshops on relevant transition topics across colleges. For example, workshops on interagency collaboration and job coaching were conducted in response to specific needs. Additionally, colleges were encouraged, individually and collectively, to use regional facilities to progress work and share outcomes on their targeted goals for capacity building.

Phase 5: Final Data Gathering

Final data gathering, using the benchmarking survey, was completed, and the data from the online survey of staff and administrators ($N = 44$) are provided in Table 15.3 and presented graphically in Figure 15.6. These data revealed higher levels of agreement (belief) and use (implementation) across all areas in comparison with the initial data collected in Phase 1 (as seen in Table 15.2 and Figure 15.5). Improvement was substantial, with all areas meeting the 50% criterion, except for level of use in program structures.

Table 15.3 Mean Levels of Agreement and Use Across the Five Practice Areas (as Percentages)

Practice Area	Number of Items	Level of Agreement	Level of Use
Student-focused planning	9	84	71
Student development	10	86	69
Interagency collaboration	7	85	69
Family–school relations	7	94	85
Program structures	13	76	48

Outcomes and Recommendations

This project aimed to build capacity of colleges to implement effective postschool pathways for students with disabilities and additional educational needs. From an overarching perspective, all colleges embraced the importance of TFE as an integral component of secondary schooling for this student cohort and proactively engaged in project activities to build capacity in at least on area of Kohler's Taxonomy. This active engagement was driven by the education officer/transition who provided support and encouragement so that the colleges maintained their schedules in achieving their TFE goals. As

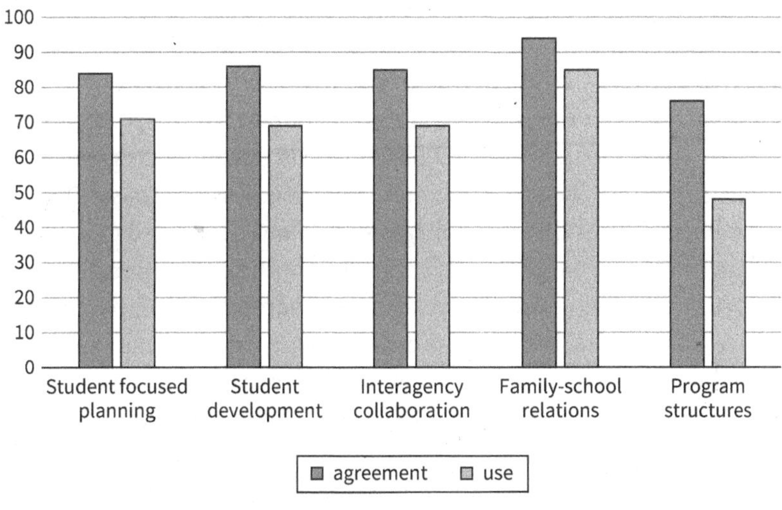

Figure 15.6 Phase 5 survey data from staff and administrators.

the project was data-driven, three key achievements provide evidence of the progress made by colleges over the two-year period. First, data from the online surveys show increased capacity in colleges from Phase 1 to Phase 4 across the region, as expressed by the improvement in levels of agreement and use of transition best practice. Second, these data are supported by the range of permanent products developed within and across colleges as a result of capacity-building activities and sharing at the symposia and regional meetings. Third, in both online surveys of staff and administration, family–school relations, was identified as the area of strength. This finding augurs well for the future of students as family involvement is a recognized predictor of postschool employment (Test et al., 2009).

Future Directions for Participating Colleges

To sustain and advance capacity building in and across colleges, a number of considerations were offered to regional administrators. The region was encouraged to consider developing a policy document on TFE in partnership with colleges to have a shared vision and to sustain capacity building over time. At regional and college levels, priority should be given to continuing professional development in TFE. The project has provided a basic knowledge and understanding of TFE and related practice implementation. However, staff engagement (as participants and presenters) in seminars and national conferences should be supported to sustain and advance TFE practice. Although levels of program structure improved across the region, this area had the lowest levels in both agreement and use of all practice areas. Since program structure is viewed as a foundation for successful TFE, colleges who have not targeted outcomes in this area should be encouraged to do so. Additionally, from Phase 1 (online survey) and Phase 2 (focus group meetings) postschool providers expressed the need to be more involved in school-based TFE activities. It followed that individual colleges should be encouraged to increase the involvement of external stakeholders in the transition planning process. In Phase 1 (online survey) and Phase 2 (focus group meetings), parents sought assistance from staff in fostering the development of daily living skills for their son/daughter. Individual colleges may wish to consider adding daily living skills to their TFE curriculum because these skills are predictors of postschool success (Test et al., 2009).

Based on these outcomes, the project was judged to be a success. From a practitioner perspective, the outputs in colleges and the outputs throughout the project stand as exemplars of practice for other secondary schools and colleges. From a research perspective, the capacity-building process undertaken across the project stands as a methodology that should be disseminated. To date, this process has been co-presented at national and international conferences and published in the transition literature (Beamish, Meadows, Davies, & Milford, 2016; Maher et al., 2014).

Conclusion

Post–high school transitions are crucial and complex developmental tasks. This chapter describes recent efforts between a team of researchers from Griffith University in Queensland, Australia, and a local BCE school region to address poor post–high school outcomes for students with disabilities. The data-gathering process presented here offers a template for other educational regions and researchers interested in improving transition practice so that young people with disabilities can transition successfully from high school to adult life.

References

Australian Bureau of Statistics. (2018). 4221.0: Schools, Australia: Summary of findings 2017. Retrieved from http://www.abs.gov.au/

Beamish, W., Meadows, D., & Davies, M. (2012). Benchmarking teacher practice in Queensland transition programs for youth with intellectual disability and autism. *The Journal of Special Education, 45*(4), 227–241.

Beamish, W., Meadows, D., Davies, M., & Milford, T. (2016). Benchmarking practice to improve post-school transition outcomes for students with special educational needs. *CAISE Review, 4*, 87–104. Available at http://dx.doi.org/10.12796/caise-review.2016V4.005

Brisbane Catholic Education. (n.d.a). Mission. Retrieved from https://www.bne.catholic.edu.au/vision/

Brisbane Catholic Education. (n.d.b). Supporting students: Inclusive education. Retrieved from https://www.bne.catholic.edu.au/students-parents/Pages/Supporting-Students.aspx

Butterworth, J., Winsor, J., Smith, F. A., Migliori, A., Domin, D., Timons, J. C., & Hall, A. C. (2014). *State data: The national report on employment services and outcomes.* Boston, MA: Institute for Community Inclusion.

Cologon, K. (2013). *Inclusion in education: Towards equity for students with disability.* Canberra, Australia: Children With Disability Australia.

Conley, D. T. (2010). *College and career ready: Helping all students success beyond high school.* San Francisco, CA: Jossey-Bass.

Davies, M., & Beamish, W. (2009). Transition from school for young adults with intellectual disability: Parental perspectives on "life as an adjustment." *Journal of Intellectual and Developmental Disabilities, 34*, 248–257

Gothberg, J. E., Peterson, L. Y., Peak, M., & Sedaghat, J. M. (2015). Successful transitions of students with disabilities to 21st century college and careers. *Teaching Exceptional Children, 47*(6), 344–351.

Halpern, A. S. (1985). Transition: A look at the foundations. *Exceptional Children, 51*(6), 479–486

Hasazi, S., Gordon, L., & Roe, C., Hull, M., Finck, K., & Salembier, G. (1985). A statewide follow-up on post high school employment and residential status of student labelled "mentally retarded." *Education and Training of the Mentally Retarded, 20*, 222–234.

Hutchinson, N. L. (2014). *Inclusion of exceptional learners in Canadian schools: A practical handbook for teachers.* Toronto, ON: Pearson Canada.

Kohler, P. D. (1996). Preparing youth with disabilities for future challenges: A taxonomy for transition programming. In P. D. Kohler (Ed.), *Taxonomy for transition programming: Linking research to practice* (pp. 1–62). Champaign, IL: Transition Research Institute, University of Illinois at Urbana–Champaign.

Kohler, P. D. (2003). *Reflecting on transition-focused education* (Unpublished manuscript), Western Michigan University, Kalamazoo, Michigan.

Kohler, P., & Field, S. (2003). TFE: Foundation for the future. *Journal of Special Education, 37*, 174–183

Maher, K., Raciti, N., Meadows, D., Beamish, W., & Davies, M. (2014). Improving postschool outcomes for students with a disability: A process for building school capacity in transition-focused education. *Special Education Perspectives, 23*(2), 3–12.

Meadows, D., Alcorn, I., Beamish, W., Davies, M., Elias, G., Grimbeek, P., & Punch, R. (2006). *Quality outcomes for students with a disability.* Queensland, Australia: Queensland Government, Department of Education, Training and the Arts.

Meadows, D., Punch, R., Elias, G., Beamish, W., & Davies, M. (2005). *Literature review: School to post-school transition* (Unpublished manuscript), Queensland Department of Education and the Arts and Griffith University, Brisbane, Australia.

Morgan, R. L., & Riesen, T. (2016). *Promoting successful transitions to adulthood for students with disabilities.* New York, NY: Guilford.

National Secondary Transition Technical Assistance Center. (2010). Improving postsecondary outcomes for all students with disabilities. Retrieved from http://transitionata.org/

Newman, L., Wagner, M., Huang, T., Shaver, D., Knokey, A. M., Yu, J., . . . Cameto, R. (2011). Secondary School programs and performance of students with disabilities: A special topic report of findings from the National Longitudinal Transition Study-2 (NLTS2; NCSER 2012-3000). *National Center for Special Education Research.* Retrieved from https://ies.ed.gov/ncser/pubs/20123000/pdf/20123000.pdf

Ricci, C. (2015, May 25). OECD education rankings show Australia slipping, Asian countries in the lead. *Sydney Morning Herald.* Retrieved from http://www.smh.com.au/national/education/oecd-education-rankings-show-australia-slipping-asian-countries-in-the-lead-20150525-gh94eu.html

Riches, V., Parameter, T., & Robertson, G. (1996). *Youth with disabilities in transition from school to community: Report of a follow-along of students with disabilities involved in the New South Wales transition initiative 1989–1994.* Sydney, Australia: Unit for Community Integration Studies, School of Education, Macquarie University, NSW Australia.

Schneider, B. (2015). The college ambition program: A realistic transition strategy for traditionally disadvantaged students. *Educational Researcher, 44*(7), 394–403.

Shandra, C. L., & Hogan, D. P. (2008). School-to-work program participation and the post-high school employment of young adults with disabilities. *Journal of Vocational Rehabilitation, 29*, 117–130.

Test, D. W., Mazzotti, V., Mustian, A. L., Fowler, Kortering, L., & Kohler, P. (2009). Evidence-based secondary transition predictors for improving postschool outcomes for students with disabilities. *Career Development for Exceptional Individuals*, *32*, 160–181.

Will, M. (1984). *OSERs programming for the transition of youth with disabilities: Bridges from school to working life.* Washington, DC: Office of Special Education and Rehabilitative Service.

SECTION 5

DIVERSE PATHWAYS—CULTURAL GROUPS AND GLOBALIZATION

16
A Cultural Perspective on School and Work Transitions for Indigenous Young Adults in Canada

E. Anne Marshall and Suzanne L. Stewart

Introduction

Work plays a central role in peoples' lives—it contributes to the overall social and economic welfare of a population and is also the way we establish meaning and identity in our lives (Blustein, 2006; Amundson, 2006). Work satisfaction or dissatisfaction has also been shown to be a significant predictor of overall mental health (Kirmayer, Brass, & Tait, 2000). Recently, there has been an increasing emphasis in career literature on the role of culture, broadly defined, as it relates to work, education, and other significant life decisions (Arnett, 2018; Arthur & Popadiuk, 2010). As Pedersen (1991) maintains, cultural factors play a significant role in all aspects of life and development, including work. Ethnic identity, family, and gender are cultural locations that affect life and work decisions. For young or emerging adults who are preparing to or just entering the workforce, these factors are particularly salient and can have far-reaching effects on their future work and life pathways.

Transitioning from school to work or higher education has been identified as a particularly high priority for one cultural group—Indigenous young adults in North America (Duran, 2006; Juntunen et al., 2001; Stewart & Marshall, 2011). Unemployment rates are consistently higher for Indigenous adolescents and young adults than for non-Indigenous. For example, among those aged 15 to 24 in Canada in 2018, unemployment rates for Indigenous youth averaged 17.2%, as compared to 10.8% for non-Indigenous youth (Statistics Canada, 2019). In the United States, the unemployment rate for Native Indians and Alaska Natives averaged 15% to 9% between 2010 and 2016, compared to 6% to 4% for nonnative populations (Bureau of Labor Statistics, 2018).

E. Anne Marshall and Suzanne L. Stewart, *A Cultural Perspective on School and Work Transitions for Indigenous Young Adults in Canada* In: *Young Adult Development at the School-to-Work Transition.* E. Anne Marshall and Jennifer E. Symonds, Oxford University Press (2021). © Oxford University Press. DOI: 10.1093/oso/9780190941512.003.0016.

Expressing concern with this workforce participation discrepancy, communities, individuals, and governments agree that increasing employment rates needs to be a high priority for Indigenous young adults and that school-to-work transitions are particularly important to achieve these employment goals (Kirkness & Barnhardt, 2001; Marshall, 2002; Stewart, 2008). While there are considerable survey data available that summarize young adult unemployment, there is limited in-depth qualitative research that explores the work and transition experiences of these young people from their perspective. In this chapter, we describe the issues, options, and pathways for Indigenous young adults and how these affect school and work transitions. We present results from three qualitative research studies with these young people and one study with employers. Our analysis and discussion conclude with several implications for more culturally oriented research, practice, and policy.

School and Work Transitions

Patterns of young adults' work-life transitions have changed over the last few decades, becoming more protracted and complex (Arnett, 2015; Lent, Hackett, & Brown, 1999; Worthington & Juntunen, 1997). Unlike generations before, the work–life transition has transformed from a relatively linear pathway to an often meandering, gradual, and individualized process. Work–life transitions are multifaceted processes that are significantly influenced by changing socioeconomic conditions. This, in turn, has resulted in less defined and predictable career pathways, greater competition and pressure for productivity, greater work/life complexity, more need for dual career planning, and increased pressure on families (Amundson, 2006; Marshall & Butler, 2015).

Identity formation is a crucial developmental task for adolescents and young adults (Arnett, 2018; Young, Marshall, & Vallach, 2007). In the 21st century, increased freedoms and more diverse social opportunities impact young people's development and growth. Jeffrey Arnett (2015, 2018) calls the years from 18 to 25 "emerging adulthood," characterized by multiple transitions and instability. It is a significant period of identity exploration in which young people explore work and personal selves and become more independent from their parents, but do not generally have the stable commitments of typical Western adult life such as a long-term job, marriage, and parenthood. During this period, work and educational choices are often based on underlying identity questions such as: "What kind of work am I good at? What kind of work would I find satisfying for the long term? What are my chances of getting a job in the field that seems to suit me best?" Through different work and life experiences, young people expand their repertoire of emerging, or "possible selves" (Markus & Nurius, 1986), by examining their abilities, interests, strengths, and weaknesses.

Writers such as Blustein, Schultheiss, and Flum, (2004) and Feller (2003) categorize the school-to-work transition as a developmental task that is strongly influenced by cultural, social, economic, and historical circumstances. Goodwin and O'Connor (2007) observe that the movement from "full-time education to employment has always been fraught with risk, uncertainty, insecurity, and individualization" (p. 570). Horowitz and Brominick (2007) draw attention to the increasing consensus that social change has transformed the transition to adulthood from a relatively straightforward and logical pathway to a more complex and perhaps fragmented process dependent on young peoples' abilities to manage diverse landmark events and transitions (Dwyer et al., 2003; Furlong & Cartmel, 1997).

In the 21st century, globalization, advances in technology and information, and significant demographic shifts have been significantly affecting work patterns and labor markets (Diemer & Blustein, 2007; Marshall & Butler, 2015). Formerly well-established local industries and companies are disappearing from the industrial landscape; jobs and trades once thought to be secure have vanished alongside these transformations (Goodwin & O'Connor, 2007). For example, in rural and coastal areas in Canada, restructuring in fishing and logging industries has resulted in widespread cutbacks and substantial job losses (Lawrence & Marshall, 2018; Marshall, 2002). Increasing demands for highly qualified and well-educated workers, flexible specialization in the workplace, and changes in social policies have far-reaching impacts on the work experiences of young people, especially at entry levels (Furlong & Cartmel, 1997). Rising qualification levels have been observed in most developed countries and the age when young people enter employment has been delayed due to increasing postsecondary participation. Given these transformations, Furlong and Cartmel (1997) assert that it is no longer appropriate to apply universal "grand theories" to the study of career and life development because work and individual life pathways are more diverse and less predictable. The current social and economic climate has created a challenging context for teachers, career counselors, and advisors supporting young people through work–life transitions (Blustein, 2006; Lawrence & Marshall, 2018).

Indigenous Young Adult Transitions

Indigenous or Aboriginal peoples are the fastest-growing segment of the population in Canada. Since 2006, the Aboriginal population (First Nations, Métis, and Inuit) has grown by 42.5%—more than four times the growth rate of the non-Aboriginal population over the same period (Statistics Canada, 2017). The increase for Indigenous youth and young adults is even more dramatic—from 2006 to 2016, the number of First Nations, Métis, and Inuit youth aged 15 to 34 increased by 39%, about six and a half times the 6% growth rate for their non-Indigenous youth counterparts (Statistics Canada, 2018). The Indigenous population is, on average, nearly a decade younger than the rest of the population in Canada. The numbers of Indigenous young people who are now and will be entering postsecondary institutions and the workforce will double and triple in the coming decades. Thus, knowledge of and support for their particular educational and work development needs are more important than ever before.

Sadly, employment has been a major challenge for Indigenous young people; figures from Statistics Canada (2019) demonstrate unemployment rates averaging over 17% (as compared to 10.8% for non-Indigenous youth aged 15–24). They face multiple employment barriers related to poverty, access, literacy weaknesses, discrimination, colonization, and the daunting legacy of residential school abuse (McCormick & Amundson, 1997; Stewart & Marshall, 2011). However, there has been little research relating to culturally appropriate methods of teaching and training with Indigenous youth in the context of work–life outcomes. Evidence exists to substantiate that Indigenous conceptualizations of both education and work–life differ from those of the majority Canadian society (Battiste, Bell, & Findlay, 2002; Kirkness & Barnhardt, 2001). The extent of these differences indicates that education, career exploration, and employment training should be reconsidered to incorporate Indigenous cultural conceptions of pedagogy and work. There is a need for more systemic exploration of Indigenous experiences of employment that are seen to be successful, because most existing research focuses on individual and community problems and barriers, not on educational and employment solutions (Mendelson 2006; Royal Commission on Indigenous Peoples, 2004). More focus on relevant and successful educational and work approaches, strategies, programs, and research is clearly needed (Stewart, 2009). Following six years of research and consultation, the Truth and Reconciliation Commission of Canada (2015) published 94 specific "calls to action" to address the current intergenerational negative impacts of the residential school system on the lives of individuals and communities and to restore relations between Indigenous peoples and nonnative Canadians. Several recommendations focus on providing information and training about Indigenous history, values, and customs in educational and workplace settings.

Postsecondary education, an important precursor to career success, is underaccessed by the Indigenous populations as a whole, and research suggests that this is, in part, because most institutions are based on non-Indigenous conceptions of education, community, work, and success (Kirkness & Barnhardt, 2001; Battiste et al., 2002). Instructors and institutions are not educated about Indigenous pedagogies and world views; instructors typically use Western-based teaching approaches that do not value Indigenous students' ways of knowing or learning (McCormick, Amundson, & Poehnell, 2002; Stewart, 2008). To address this gap, a range of programmatic interventions within higher education have been developed, falling along a spectrum from minimal Indigenous content in the curriculum to rethinking course delivery and institutional structures to better reflect Indigenous understandings of education (Guenette & Marshall, 2008; Marshall et al., 2009).

A study by Stewart (2009) looked at the success of urban postsecondary Indigenous students. Common themes in the students' narratives included self-awareness, integrating two worlds, trailblazing, and mentorship. Most had overcome issues related to historical struggles generally and isolation within the academy specifically. From their experiences, Stewart concluded that Indigenous students require strong role models and support systems within the institution if they are to complete their degree and carry on to successful employment outcomes.

Culture is inextricably bound to work–life issues. Ethnic identity, family, and gender play a significant role in all aspects of life and development affecting life and work decisions (Arnett, 2018; Shepard & Marshall, 2000; Young et al., 2007). Blustein (2006) calls for an expanded and more inclusive theoretical framework on work that takes cultural and human developmental contexts into account. The emphasis on individual choice and fulfillment of many career exploration and guidance frameworks is clearly at odds with the collective identity and community needs orientation held by many nonmajority populations. These differences would suggest that many Western-based education and work theories, programs, and resources are not appropriate for use with Indigenous young adults. There are many unanswered questions about the experiences of transition from school to work or to postsecondary education for Indigenous young adults that we have attempted to address in our research.

Our Research Studies With Indigenous Young Adults

Theoretical Models and Frameworks

Our research is guided by cultural and Indigenous formulations and social constructionist theoretical frameworks that emphasize the meaning of work and career transitions as embedded in social and cultural contexts (Amundson, 2006; Young et al., 2007). In particular, the work of David Blustein (2006) and others (Blustein et al., 2004; Blustein, McWhirter, & Perry, 2005; Kenny et al., 2007; Juntunen et al., 2001) includes less advantaged youth and young adults, including Indigenous groups. For these populations, the notion of work is often in sharp contrast to the majority of career development research participants. Cultural minority and Indigenous young people face multiple obstacles, both in the job search process and in the workplace itself.

Indigenous peoples are underrepresented in vocational psychology research and literature—little is understood about the issues that may be related to their successful career development and school-to-work transitions (Juntunen et al., 2001). In particular, the emphasis on individual choice and fulfillment may be at odds with the community-focused identity and goals evident in native and other community-oriented cultures (McCormick & Amundson, 1997). Additional factors to consider include community priorities, sense of place or ties to the land, family and kinship systems, spiritual values, and the role of cultural knowledge (Stewart & Marshall, 2016). These differences would suggest that many Western-based career theories, programs, and resources are not appropriate for use with Indigenous youth and young adults.

Much of the research with Indigenous populations focuses on deficits and problems; we strongly believe that it is important to shift our focus to a more positive orientation. What strengths do Indigenous young adults already possess that they can build on? How can they use their skills and strategies effectively in different contexts? How can we view diversity as an asset that adds value to world views and perspectives? The approaches of positive psychology and relational-cultural theory offer more positive orientations for culturally relevant exploration of transition-related issues with Indigenous young adults.

In his groundbreaking work, Seligman's (2005) positive psychology approach expanded the focus of psychology beyond the realm of treating disease, distress, and dysfunction to examining positive experiences and personal characteristics. Through emphasizing capabilities and strengths, a positive psychology approach is helpful for Indigenous young adults by acknowledging and honoring their social and cultural context.

Relational approaches have also been shown to be highly effective for culturally relevant work with students (Walker, 2004). Blustein et al. (2004) have applied relational approaches to career development and counseling. Popadiuk and Arthur (2004) found that international students' transition and adjustment issues were often linked to connections and disconnections in their relationships. These studies suggest that many career-type issues could be conceptualized as relational issues. Given that many Indigenous youth experience a high degree of family and community involvement in decision-making (Stewart, 2009), we need to carefully consider how we assist them with educational and career planning. Exploration must extend beyond the bounds of autonomous decision-making, to include an analysis of family and community expectations and personal duty, as well as the intersection of identity and cultural selves. Our research studies have included exploration of these key extended contexts.

Methodology

In this section we summarize three research studies investigating Indigenous late adolescent and young adult transitions to work and postsecondary education. The main focus of these studies (Marshall et al., 2013, 2016; Spowart & Marshall, 2015; Stewart & Marshall, 2011) was Indigenous young people's in-depth descriptions of the successes and challenges they have experienced in making transition from school to work or from secondary to postsecondary education. We also interviewed employers in one study (Marshall et al., 2015). Our overall research question has been, *What are the perceived factors contributing to successful postsecondary and school-to-work transitions for Indigenous young adults in Canada?* More specifically, we asked, What experiences, practices, and actions were seen to be helpful or hindering by the young adults themselves and by employers?

Consistent with Indigenous oral and storytelling traditions, we adopted a narrative methodology (Stewart, 2008) grounded in social constructionist and relational career development theory (Blustein et al., 2005; Savickas, 1999) and situated within a community partnership model. We have maintained ongoing relationships with several Indigenous community agency partners over more than 10 years of research—Native Canadian Centre of Toronto, Victoria Native Friendship Centre, Surrounded by Cedar Child and Family Services, First Peoples Cultural Council, and Saanich Adult Education Centre. Our partners have assisted with participant recruitment, provided space for meetings and interviews, convened community meetings for knowledge mobilization, and generously shared their time and local expertise with us. In turn, we have involved them in all phases of the research (partners decided when, how, and to what extent), provided research training for partner staff and community research assistants, helped with partner funding proposals, and contributed to programs and events as requested. These reciprocal and mutually supportive relationships are *essential elements* to the ongoing success of our research projects, guided by the four *R*s of respect, reciprocity, relevance, and responsibility described by Kirkness and Barnhardt (2001) in their seminal paper on First Nations and higher education. Mindful of the negative reputation of researchers whose actions have harmed Indigenous individuals and communities (Marshall & Batten, 2004; Smith, 2012), our commitment first and foremost is to ethically support and enhance the aspirations and experiences of our partners and research participants in culturally appropriate ways. In Canada, the Tri-Council Policy Statement on ethical research (Canadian Institutes, 2014) has an entire chapter on research principles and processes involving Indigenous peoples (First Nations, Metis, and Inuit); our university ethical research boards adhere to this policy.

We conducted our research in two urban sites in Canada: Marshall in Victoria, British Columbia (population 383,000), and Stewart in Toronto, Ontario (population 2.73 million). Across both sites we interviewed a total of 190 Indigenous late adolescent and young adult participants aged 17 to 29. They took part in individual ($N = 81$) and group ($N = 109$) narrative interviews of 45 to 90 minutes exploring cultural identity, work experiences, supports, and barriers. About a third also participated in "storymapping" (Stewart) and "possible selves mapping" (Marshall)—expressive narrative mapping techniques developed within our team in which participants explored work and identity goals, aspirations, fears, and actions across time (for details about these expressive interview techniques, see Shepard & Marshall, 2000; Spowart & Marshall, 2015; Stewart, 2008). In addition, 15 employers were interviewed individually about policies and practices related to employing Indigenous youth and young adults (Marshall et al., 2015; also see next section).

All group and individual interviews were audio-recorded, transcribed verbatim, and the transcripts analyzed for common and unique data themes following an inductive and iterative method adapted from Braun and Clarke (2006). This process involved the following eight steps: making notes during and immediately after interviews; listening to interview tapes without stopping and recording holistic impressions of key points; verbatim transcription of interview tapes; line-by-line coding of transcripts; reviewing and combining data codes into data themes within transcripts; listing, reviewing, and reassessing themes across transcripts; relistening to interview tapes to identify gaps and revise data themes; and grouping similar data themes into overarching metathemes. In the Toronto site, group interview participants contributed to initial data analysis by prioritizing concepts and themes immediately after the group interview. In the Victoria site, two Indigenous community knowledge keepers contributed to the thematic data analysis after initial coding was complete—these were respected community leaders who were knowledgeable about Indigenous culture, language, and customs but not yet considered elders. Including Indigenous young adults and community members in the analysis process was another way of integrating Kirkness and Barnhardt's (2001) four *R*s into the research process.

Discussion and Implications

Although the youth and young adult participants in the three research studies were from diverse Indigenous cultures, family backgrounds, and locations, we identified six common themes across the data relating to school-to-work transitions. These were importance of cultural identity, relational connectedness, need for respecting diversity, roles of family and community, roles of employers and co-workers (or instructors and fellow students), and overcoming the impact of discrimination. These common themes are discussed later, with connections to research in the literature. Other more individual themes identified in the data were typically related to particular cultural perspectives, community values, or local work conditions that are important contextual components for individuals or small groups of participants. A few illustrative examples will be presented to describe some of these particular perspectives.

Importance of Cultural Identity

As we expected, cultural identity was significant for all participants across our multiple research studies, although the impact and expression of cultural identity did, of course, differ. For these Indigenous young adults, a major task for many was finding a way to blend or integrate aspects of two or more cultures. sometimes in the face of resistance from their families and home communities (Duran, 2006; McCormick & Amundson, 1997; Stewart, 2009). This bicultural identity or "walking in two worlds" had both positive and negative aspects. Working in a culturally diverse urban setting after graduation, for example, provided many with an opportunity to successfully negotiate the coming together of both identities. However, this very integration of the new identity often created internal struggles about whether to stay or go back home, as well as relational struggles with family who may express concerns about an increasing emphasis on individualism, autonomy, and pursuing a career that is outside culturally valued trajectories.

Indigenous culture was a central and important theme within many facets of the youth's work life. For example, several of the participants chose to work within the Indigenous sector because they found a sense of place within a familiar cultural environment. Many participants indicated that they enjoyed and felt culturally and emotionally safe being in a place of work that shared their values and ways of being. Participants noted feelings of acceptance in terms of cultural identity within Indigenous organizations and a sense of united purpose in working to improve conditions for Indigenous peoples in various facts of society such as education, social services, politics, and health. In this sense, many participants felt a like-mindedness between their place of work and their own personal and cultural identity. Participants showed resourcefulness and used their cultural uniqueness to gain employment, through various traditional art forms and customs.

Relational Connectedness

Our participants consistently emphasized the importance of relationships when navigating transitions, as Blustein et al. (2004) and Walker (2004) have described in relational-cultural theory. Narratives of connection, and of disconnection, were seen to be instrumental in situations that were either successful and fulfilling or unsuccessful and distressing. Indigenous adolescents and young adults who established ongoing supportive relationships with older family members, mentors, or community champions often reported that these connections were significant factors in helping them to make cross-cultural adjustments, learn new institutional systems and procedures, overcome challenges, acquire new skills, find suitable work, and develop new relationships.

The importance of family and/or relational support systems was emphasized in the stories of work–life development. Participants described the tangible and emotional support that parents, elders, and extended family provided regarding secondary school completion, postsecondary studies, and work ethics. This included childhood experiences and family history (both positive and negative) related to confidence, determination, and self-efficacy with regard to finding and keeping work.

Community connection was defined by participants as relationship to an Indigenous community, whether it be a home urban or reserve community or a joined urban or rural/reserve community. Community connection described as either strong or tenuous was seen as a major factor in terms of employment success or failure, respectively. For example, participants revealed barriers associated with attaining work in Indigenous-run organizations; participants spoke of the importance of having the status of a "community insider" to gain employment in this sector. "Outsiders" faced barriers such as nepotism and hiring within circles of friends. Participants explained that if one is outside of such circles, there can often be challenges to accessing these types of work opportunities. Finally, some participants noted that many jobs in the Indigenous health and social service sector are taken by non-Indigenous people who often have competitively high levels of post-secondary education, yet do not possess the cultural knowledge or sensitivity required to be successful.

Respecting Diversity

Time and time again, participants spoke of respect and acceptance of themselves, their values, and their cultural ways as being critically important to the success of their transitions. Even small gestures were seen to be acknowledgment that could have a significant impact; lack of respect was consistently cited as very problematic with regard to self-esteem, identity development, adjustment to new settings, achievement, and work performance. Respect has been well established as a necessary component of cultural acceptance (Kirkness & Barnhardt, 2001). Yet the narratives of many of our participants who had experienced racism and discrimination indicate that acceptance continues to be a challenging issue within the dominant Canadian culture. Awareness and education were often mentioned as ways to increase respect for nondominant world views and cultural practices that are part of everyday school and work lives.

Roles of Family and Community

Family and community were often seen as what might be termed "mixed blessings." All participants described support they had received from their family members and communities when pursuing educational or work and career goals; however, many also described the conflicting values and expectations that resulted in additional stress and anxiety during the transition process and even throughout their academic experiences. These perceived pressures from loved ones and community members, who may have made substantial financial sacrifices to support the young person in a new environment, sometimes engendered feelings of disloyalty, shame, and isolation

Roles of Employers and Co-Workers (or Instructors and Fellow Students)

Whether these young people were making transitions to work settings or to further education, they related instances of support (or lack of it) from colleagues and employers, supervisors, or instructors. These people were part of daily interactions that tended to have a cumulative effect over time. With so much new learning necessary, an understanding boss or a fellow student could make a significant difference with regard to successful transitions (Amundson, 2006; Battiste et al., 2002). Frequently, our participants narrated stories of particular individuals who really had a major impact on their adjustment process, usually for better, although sometimes not. A friendly greeting, an invitation for coffee or an outing, an explanation of a new procedure, or acknowledgment of a cultural value, although perhaps a seemingly small gesture, could serve as a turning point for how participants viewed their transition progress.

Overcoming Discrimination

Current and historical themes of oppression were also salient across participant narratives. Almost all participants described having faced instances of discrimination and racism, particularly when working outside of Indigenous agencies and organizations. Several participants noted that they would hide their Indigenous ancestry to protect themselves from discriminatory treatment and to gain a sense of emotional and physical safety in their place of work. Many participants felt they were treated unfairly (e.g., working beyond their job description, working for unfair wages) due to their Indigenous identity. In terms of securing employment, some participants had experienced an abundance of work opportunities specifically geared to Indigenous young people, as well as training and assistance such as resume preparation and job search strategies. However, others observed that these opportunities may not be known to many and are thus inaccessible, particularly if one is not a postsecondary student and lacks information and other resources through school. Some participants also felt that community colonial experiences such as residential schools, forced land relocation, and the giving and taking of Indigenous status had a direct effect on their personal employment outcomes.

Not all participants shared stories of racism or discrimination, and it was sometimes difficult to assess the extent of discrimination that participants experienced due to differing degrees of comfort in sharing specific instances (Stewart, 2008). Although the topic is a sensitive one, it deserves more extensive and in-depth investigation as well as discussion of actions and interventions that have been found to be successful in addressing this problem.

Perspectives From Employers

A total of 15 non-Indigenous employers who worked with Indigenous youth and adults were interviewed individually in the Victoria site. Employer interviews took between 30 and 45 minutes and included questions such as "Can you tell us about your experiences with Indigenous workers?"; "What do you think helps and hinders Indigenous young people in the workplace?"; and "What suggestions do you have for employers and workers to increase success?" As with other participants, interviews were audio-recorded and transcribed verbatim. Interview data analysis followed the previously described eight-step process with the young adult participants.

Four main themes were identified among the employer participants: understanding Indigenous cultural values, being flexible, the importance of mentoring, and lack of policies and guidelines (Marshall et al., 2015). Each of these themes will be described briefly, with illustrative quotes from participants.

Understanding Indigenous Cultural Values

All employer participants endorsed the importance of knowing something about the values and customs of their Indigenous employees, such as their more collective or community orientation and the emphasis placed on respect for elders. One described, "For a lot of young Aboriginal folks in this area of the country, it's very hierarchical, the culture. . . . This means you don't talk to just anybody about some issues, you know, you have to ask a specific person." This employer explained that she needed to make sure that her Indigenous employees had a clear understanding of appropriate pathways for obtaining work-related information and procedures. Other participants described their efforts to get to know local Indigenous residents and attend a community event to learn more about cultural values and community priorities.

Being Flexible

Several employers described how they needed to be flexible about employees taking time off or leave without pay for important community events such as a naming ceremony or the death of a chief or elder. As one observed, "but there's some very intense cultural activity at certain times. . . . You have to be creative." This person suggested having discussions with employees about priorities and potential "make-up hours" if something came up suddenly. Other employers recognized the need for flexibility but indicated that the work demands and structure in their settings made that a challenge.

The Importance of Mentoring

Among Indigenous communities, mentoring and observational learning are critical learning processes. One employer shared a strategy that had been very successful in his workplace: "What does work is if somebody is given a buddy, like a person to share their experience with and to learn from." Others described examples of working "side by side" with Indigenous young people, explaining and demonstrating at the same time. Many said that their young Indigenous workers liked to have a more experienced worker who could guide and mentor them. One recalled what one of his workers had said to him: "If I had somebody, you know, that I could just talk to, like, not the boss or my supervisor, just somebody who was doing the job I was doing to sort of have a comfortable relationship with." Several employers noted that mentoring was helpful for all workers but that their Indigenous workers seemed to really benefit from these relationships: "It's similar to what happens in their communities."

Lack of Polices and Guidelines

Employers lamented that there was virtually no information available about recruiting, hiring, and retaining Indigenous employees. As one said "there's, like, nothing out there. . . . I called [the local employment service] and they said they had nothing." One employer said she had contacted an Indigenous agency director she knew to get information and advice: "It was really helpful to have someone to talk to when I had a question." Our team members were able to share some Indigenous employment resources with participants, such as the Guiding Circles program (McCormick et al., 2002), and there are government reports available online; however, employers said short, practical "tip sheets" and specific suggestions would be most helpful. "Cultural safety," for example, was something many had heard about but were not sure "what that might look like in the workplace." Workshops and training programs on cultural safety are increasingly available in large and publicly funded organizations (Ward, Branch, & Fridkin, 2016); however, access to or funding for these opportunities are a challenge for small businesses.

Overall, the findings from interviews with employers were mostly consistent with the common themes identified in the Indigenous young adult interviews. One notable difference was the apparent reluctance of these employers to discuss racism and discrimination—a significant theme in the young adult interviews. A few acknowledged its presence but declined to describe the extent or provide examples. This is clearly an area that needs more investigation. Most employers agreed that respect and acceptance were important—this speaks to the critical notion of cultural safety, the lack of which has been experienced as a barrier by Indigenous participants in the present and other studies (Kirmayer et al., 2000; Ward et al., 2016).

Limitations

There are boundaries and limitations associated with our research studies. As with all qualitative research, in-depth and detailed descriptions were generated that cannot be generalized to larger populations. However, the size of the sample and the extent of agreement on common themes indicate that the findings would be relevant to Indigenous young adults in medium to large size urban centers (although many participants had also lived in small towns and rural areas). Many of the participants were college or university students; their experiences would likely differ to at least some degree from those who are not or not yet in postsecondary settings. Further qualitative and qualitative investigations of the major data themes identified in the present studies with larger and more diverse population samples are recommended.

Implications

Several implications emerge from our studies. Most importantly, more inclusive and culturally sensitive transition theories and models are needed that take into account the diverse contextual forces in Indigenous young adult's lives, explain how cultural factors are influential in decision-making, and suggest appropriate support and intervention strategies. Most school-to-work or secondary-to-postsecondary transition theories and models are based on western dominant cultural assumptions about individuation, freedom of choice, affluence, and upward mobility notions of work or career success (Stewart 2009; Young et al., 2007). Indigenous young adults' values and priorities are more likely to align with community, collectivist, relational, and non-competitive perspectives that need to be considered when assisting them with education and work planning. Professionals and employers who are working with Indigenous young adults should be knowledgeable about and sensitized to the cultural perspectives and issues that affect them when entering workplaces and learning institutions.

Mentoring has been recognized as a facilitating factor for transitions (Battiste et al., 2002; Marshall et al., 2013); young adult participants in the present studies shared a number of examples of how mentoring relationships had helped them with decisions and actions related to school and work. Employer participants also found that mentoring relationships were helpful for their Indigenous employees. However, their diverse experiences would indicate that more than one mentor could be needed, because different perspectives are useful and people have different areas of strength and interest. For example, some people excel at social support and networking, whereas others are more comfortable providing information or explaining procedures. Optimally, Indigenous young people would have multiple mentors to assist them in work and life transitions. The findings also emphasize the need to address issues of racism, discrimination, and cultural safety throughout the system.

With regard to research methods, authentic community partnerships and the incorporation of traditional knowledge are key factors throughout the process, from design to dissemination. This project has demonstrated how to locate research within an Indigenous context and to collaborate with local knowledge keepers and community partners; this led to a more locally relevant interpretation of stories and more comprehensive data on the supports, challenges and barriers these youth faced. By beginning with this Indigenous lens and constantly grounding the work in notions of culture and community, the findings are more trustworthy and authentic for Aboriginal communities.

Conclusion

When speaking of cultural groups and identities, we must keep in mind that there is as much, if not more, diversity *within* a culture as there is *between* cultures (Pedersen, 1991). Rather than problematizing how Indigenous young or emerging adults are different, we can acknowledge that all peoples are different to varying degrees and look for points of relation and connection as well as consider key differences. If we are to assist Indigenous young people with their transitions from school to higher education and work, we need to help them to walk successfully in their multiple cultural worlds. All young people, regardless of their cultural affiliations, will benefit from an emphasis on respect, acceptance, and valuing diversity.

Cultural diversity brings the strengths of multiple knowledges and perspectives to education, to the workplace and to society as a whole. We have the opportunity to acknowledge and embrace the gifts that Indigenous young adults bring with them and to use these assets to build success for everyone. Significant and positive steps are in evidence that can be shared with and adapted by other countries, services, and individuals. The growing body of knowledge and research focusing on culturally oriented transition theory and promising practices will yield even more effective methods and resources to be used in the educational and work settings of the future.

References

Amundson, N. E. (2006). Challenges for career interventions in changing contexts. *International Journal for Educational and Vocational Guidance*, 6, 3–14.

Arnett, J. J. (2015). *Emerging adulthood. The winding road from the late teens through the twenties.* (2nd ed.). New York, NY: Oxford University Press.

Arnett, J. J. (2018). *Adolescence and emerging adulthood. A cultural formulation* (6th ed.). Upper Saddle River, NJ: Pearson Education.

Arthur, N., & Popadiuk, N. E. (2010). A cultural formulation approach to career counseling with international students. *Journal of Career Development*, *37*(1), 423–440.

Battiste, M., Bell, L., & Findlay, L. M. (2002). Decolonizing education in Canadian universities: An interdisciplinary, international, Indigenous research project. *Canadian Journal of Native Education*, *26*(2), 82–95.

Blustein, D. L. (2006). *The psychology of working. A new perspective for career development, counselling, and public policy.* Mahwah, NJ: Erlbaum.

Blustein, D. L., McWhirter, E. H., & Perry, J. C. (2005). An emancipatory communitarian approach to vocational development theory, research, and practice. *Counseling Psychologist*, *33*, 141–179.

Blustein, D. L., Schultheiss, D. E. P., & Flum, H. (2004). Toward a relational perspective of the psychology of careers and working: A social constructionist analysis. *Journal of Vocational Behavior*, *64*, 423–440.

Braun, V., & Clarke, V. (2006). Using thematic analysis in psychology. *Qualitative Research in Psychology*, *3*(2), 77–101. doi:10.1191/1478088706qp063oa

Bureau of Labor Statistics. (2018, November 8). Labor market trends for American Indians and Alaska Natives, 2000–17. *The Economics Daily.* Retrieved from https://www.bls.gov/opub/ted/2018/labor-market-trends-for-american-indians-and-alaska-natives-2000-17.htm

Canadian Institutes of Health Research, Natural Sciences and Engineering Research Council of Canada, and Social Sciences and Humanities Research Council of Canada. (2014, December). Tri-council policy statement: Ethical conduct for research involving humans. Retrieved from http://www.pre.ethics.gc.ca/eng/policy-politique/initiatives/tcps2-eptc2/Default/

Diemer, M. A., & Blustein, D. L. (2007). Vocational hope and vocational identity: Urban Adolescents' career development. *Journal of Career Assessment*, *15*, 98–118.

Duran, E. (2006). *Healing the soul wound: Counseling with American Indians and other native peoples*. New York, NY: Teachers College Press.

Dwyer, P., Smith, G., Tyler, D., & Wyn, J. (2003). *Life-patterns, career outcomes and adult choices.* Melbourne, Australia: Youth Research Centre.

Feller, R. W. (2003). Aligning school counseling, the changing workplace, and career development assumptions. *Professional School Counseling*, 6, 262–271.

Furlong, A., & Cartmel, F. (1997). *Young people and social change: Individualization and risk in late modernity.* Philadelphia, PA: Open University Press.

Goodwin, J., & O'Connor, H. (2007). Continuity and change in the experience of transition from school to work. *International Journal of Lifelong Education*, *26*, 555–572.

Guenette, F., & Marshall, E. A. (2008). Indigenizing counsellor education. Implementing post-secondary curriculum change. *Canadian Journal of Native Education*, *31*(1), 107–122.

Horowitz, A. D., & Brominick, R. D. (2007). Contestable adulthood: Variability and disparity in markers for negotiating the transition to adulthood. *Youth & Society, 39*, 209–231.

Juntunen, C. J., Barraclough, D. J., Broneck, C. L., Seibel, G. A. Winrow, S. A., & Morin, P. M. (2001). American Indian perspective on the career journey. *Journal of Counseling Psychology, 48*, 274–285.

Kenny, M. E., Gualdron, L., Scanlon, D., Sparks, E., Blustein, D. L., & Jernigan, M. (2007). Urban adolescents' constructions of supports and barriers to educational and career attainment. *Journal of Counseling Psychology, 54*, 336–343.

Kirkness, V. J., & Barnhardt, R. (2001). First Nations and higher education: The four R's—respect, relevance, reciprocity, responsibility. *Journal of American Indian Education, 30*(3), 1–15.

Kirmayer, L. J., Brass, G. M., & Tait, C. L. (2000). The mental health of Indigenous peoples: Transformation of identity and community. *Canadian Journal of Psychiatry, 45*(7), 607–616.

Lawrence, B. C., & Marshall, E. A. (2018). Work–life transitions for young, coastal adults: A qualitative follow-up study. *Canadian Journal of Career Development, 17*(1), 28–40.

Lent, R. W., Hackett, G., & Brown, S. D. (1999). A social cognitive view of school-to-work transition. *Career Development Quarterly, 47*, 297–311.

Markus, H., & Nurius, P. (1986). Possible selves. *American Psychologist, 41*(9), 954–969.

Marshall, A. (2002). Life-career counselling issues for youth in coastal and rural communities: The impact economic, social and environmental restructuring. *International Journal for the Advancement of Counselling, 24*, 69–87.

Marshall, A., & Batten, S. (2004). Researching across cultures: Issues of ethics and power. *Forum Qualitative Sozialforschung/Forum: Qualitative Social Research, 5*(3), Art. 39.

Marshall, E. A. (2016). Cultural identity and school-to-work transitions for post-secondary students. *International Journal of Arts and Sciences, 9*(2), 395–402.

Marshall, E. A., & Butler, K. (2015). School to work transitions. In J. J. Arnett (Ed.), *Oxford handbook of emerging adulthood* (pp. 316–333). New York, NY: Oxford University Press.

Marshall, E. A., Stewart, S. L. Coverdale, J., & Elliot, N. (2015, January). *Employer perspectives: Integrating Aboriginal cultural and work-life identities.* Paper presented at the 2015 Cannexus Conference, Ottawa, Ontario.

Marshall, E. A., Stewart, S. L., Popadiuk, N., & Lawrence, B. (2013). Walking in multiple worlds. Successful school-to-work transitions for Indigenous and cultural minority youth. In G. Tchibozo (Ed.), *Cultural and social diversity and the transition from education to work* (pp. 185–202). Rotterdam, The Netherlands: Springer.

Marshall, E. A., Williams, L., Emerson, L., Antoine, A., MacDougall, C., & Peterson, R. (2016). A'tola'nw. Indigenous-centred learning in a counselling graduate program. In S. Stewart, R. Moodley, & A. Hyatt (Eds.), *Indigenous cultures and mental health counselling. Four directions for integration with counselling psychology*. (pp. 182–198). New York, NY: Routledge.

McCormick, R. M., & Amundson, N. E. (1997). A career-life planning model for First Nations People. *Journal of Employment Counseling, 34*, 171–179.

McCormick, R. M., Amundson, N. E., & Poehnell, G. (2002). *Guiding circles. An Aboriginal guide to finding career paths.* Saskatoon, SK: Indigenous Human Resources Development Canada.

Mendelson, M. (2006). *Indigenous peoples and postsecondary education in Canada.* Ottawa, ON: Caledon Institute of Social Policy.

Pedersen, P. B. (1991). Multiculturalism as a generic approach to counselling. *Journal of Counseling and Development, 70*(1), 6–12.

Popadiuk, N. E., & Arthur, N. (2004). Counselling international students in Canadian schools. *International Journal for the Advancement of Counselling, 26*, 125–145.

Royal Commission on Indigenous Peoples. (2004). Highlights from the report of the Royal Commission on Indigenous Peoples: People to people, nation to nation. Retrieved from https://www.rcaanc-cirnac.gc.ca/eng/1100100014597/1572547985018

Savickas, M. L. (1999). The transition from school to work: A developmental perspective. *Career Development Quarterly, 47*, 326–336.

Seligman, M. E. P. (2005). Positive psychology, positive prevention, and positive therapy. In C. R. Snyder & S. J. Lopez (Eds.), *Handbook of positive psychology* (pp. 3–9). New York, NY: Oxford University Press.

Shepard, B., & Marshall, A. (2000). Career development and planning issues for rural adolescent girls. *Canadian Journal of Counselling, 34*(3), 155–171.

Smith, L. T. (2012). *Decolonizing methodologies: Research and indigenous peoples.* (2nd ed.). London, England: Zed Books.

Spowart, J. P., & Marshall, E. A. (2015). Relational and cultural impacts on the work life of young Indigenous men. *Canadian Journal of Counselling, 49*(3), 214–231.

Statistics Canada. (2017). Aboriginal peoples in Canada: Key results from the 2016 census. Retrieved from https://www150.statcan.gc.ca/n1/daily-quotidien/171025/dq171025a-eng.htm

Statistics Canada. (2018). First Nations people, Métis and Inuit in Canada: Diverse and growing populations. Retrieved from https://www150.statcan.gc.ca/n1/pub/89-659-x/89-659-x2018001-eng.htm

Statistics Canada. (2019). Labour force characteristics by province, region and Aboriginal group (ages 15–24) (Table 14-10-0364-01). Retrieved from https://www150.statcan.gc.ca/t1/tbl1/en/tv.action?pid=1410036401&pickMembers%5B0%5D=3.8&pickMembers%5B1%5D=4.1&pickMembers%5B2%5D=5.3

Stewart, S. (2008). Promoting Indigenous mental health: Cultural perspectives on healing from Native counsellors in Canada. *International Journal of Health Promotion and Education, 46*(2), 49–56.

Stewart, S. (2009). Exploring the successes of Indigenous graduate students. *Centre for Studies in Post Secondary Education Newsletter, 1*. Retrieved from http://css.oise.utoronto.ca/

Stewart, S. & Marshall, E. A. (2011, October). *Traditional cultural perspectives and interventions for supporting Indigenous youth in employment. Work–life and mental health and healing.* Paper presented at the annual Native Mental Health Association of Canada Conference. Victoria, BC.

Stewart, S. L., & Marshall, E. A. (2016). Counselling Indigenous peoples in Canada. In S. Stewart, R. Moodley, & A. Hyatt (Eds.), *Indigenous cultures and mental health counselling: Four directions for integration with counselling psychology.* (pp. 73–89). New York, NY: Routledge.

Truth and Reconciliation Commission of Canada. (2015). Calls to action. Retrieved from http://nctr.ca/reports.php

Walker, M. (2004). How relationships heal. In M. Walker & W. B. Rosen (Eds.), *How connections heal: Stories from relational-cultural therapy* (pp. 3–21). New York: Guilford Press.

Ward, C., Branch, C., & Fridkin, A. (2016). What is Indigenous cultural safety—and why should I care about it? *Visions, 11*(4), 29–32.

Worthington, R. L., & Juntunen, C. L. (1997). The vocational development of non-college-bound youth: Counseling psychology and the school-to-work transition movement. *Counseling Psychologist, 25*, 323–363.

Young, R. A., Marshall, S. K., & Valach, L. (2007). Making career theories more culturally sensitive: Implications for counselling. *Career Development Quarterly, 56*, 4–18.

17

Gateways to Occupational Success

Educational Mobility and Attainment for Australian Aboriginal and Torres Strait Islander Emerging Adults

Philip D. Parker, Gawaian Bodkin-Andrews, Michelle Trudgett, and Maggie Walter

Introduction

Choices made at transition points between levels of education, particularly relating to further education, are ongoing determinants of later life attainment (Dietrich, Parker, & Salmela-Aro, 2012; Lucas, 2001). Gaining a university degree is increasingly a requirement for a "good life." Jobs that once required a high school diploma now require a university degree, and increasingly youth are remaining in education to a postgraduate level to secure stable employment (Goldin & Katz, 2009; Piketty, 2014). Indeed, while the prospects of those with a university degree have not increased, the gap between those with and without a university degree has grown due to the considerable decline in the fortune of those with less than or only a high school level of education (Goldin & Katz, 2009; Heckman, 2006). It is thus problematic to note that considerable inequalities in educational attainment (IEA) exist, internationally, for at-risk groups in the transition to upper levels of education (e.g., immigrants, minorities, Indigenous populations, low socioeconomic groups; Lucas, 2001; OECD, 2011).

Although inequality is a concern across the life span, we are particularly interested in the period from late adolescence to age 25. Often called *emerging adulthood* this is a period of possibilities, exploration, and identity construction that is critical to young people's life chances (Arnett, 2007). The period can also be one of considerable angst for vulnerable groups, yet our previous research has suggested that Indigenous emerging adults have similar levels of well-being than non-Indigenous emerging adults (Parker, Bodkin-Andrews,

Philip D. Parker, Gawaian Bodkin-Andrews, Michelle Trudgett, and Maggie Walter, *Gateways to Occupational Success* In: *Young Adult Development at the School-to-Work Transition.* E. Anne Marshall and Jennifer E. Symonds, Oxford University Press (2021).
 DOI: 10.1093/oso/9780190941512.003.0017.

Parker, & Biddle, 2018).[1] Although this group has unique strengths that help facilitate development during emerging adulthood (Parker et al., 2018), these strengths are threatened by continued inequality and systematic oppression (Behrendt, 2016; Bodkin-Andrews, Bodkin, Andrews, & Evans, 2017; Paradies, 2016). Often this takes the form of unequal access to traditional avenues for advancement.

In absolute numbers there are more Indigenous youth in university than ever (Behrendt, Larkin, Greiw & Kelly, 2012; Department of Education, Employment, and Workplace Relations, 2008, p. 116). Yet this must be considered in context. The increase in Indigenous university enrollment has occurred during a period of remarkable higher educational expansion in Australia. Thus, it is the proportional uptake in different educational options and its relationship with changes in the structure of the current labor market that must be considered (Behrendt, Larkin, Greiw, & Kelly, 2012; Department of Education, Employment, and Workplace Relations, 2008). In particular increased demand for a university level education in the labor market has driven an increase in the proportion of all individuals seeking a university level education across much of the Western world (Piketty, 2014). This increase has led to a remarkable increase in participation rates in university for both Indigenous and non-Indigenous youth (Australia Bureau of Statistics, 2013; Bourke et al., 2000; Schwab, 2006; Zubrick et al., 2006). While this is positive, the end result has been an increase in the education qualification gap with the rate of university participation growing at a much greater rate in the non-Indigenous population, as seen in Figure 17.1). There is also evidence that the higher the level of university qualification is, the greater the disparity in Indigenous and non-Indigenous participation (Trudgett, 2013, 2014). This is not a pattern specific only to Australia, but this growing gap in educational outcomes along with a persistent gap in wages and employment is also present in Indigenous populations in Canada and New Zealand (Mitrou et al., 2014). Thus, exploring the predictors and mechanisms associated with higher education uptake among Indigenous people in Australia is important internationally.

[1] Within this article, we use the term *Indigenous Australian* to represent people of Aboriginal and Torres Strait Islander descent. We stress that readers should recognize not only that the label *Indigenous Australian* obscures the distinctiveness between Aboriginal and Torres Strait Islander peoples but also the immense diversity of language groups and cultural values across Aboriginal and Torres Strait Islander peoples (Purdie et al., 2010). We simply retain the label of Indigenous Australian to avoid confusion with previous research and policy.

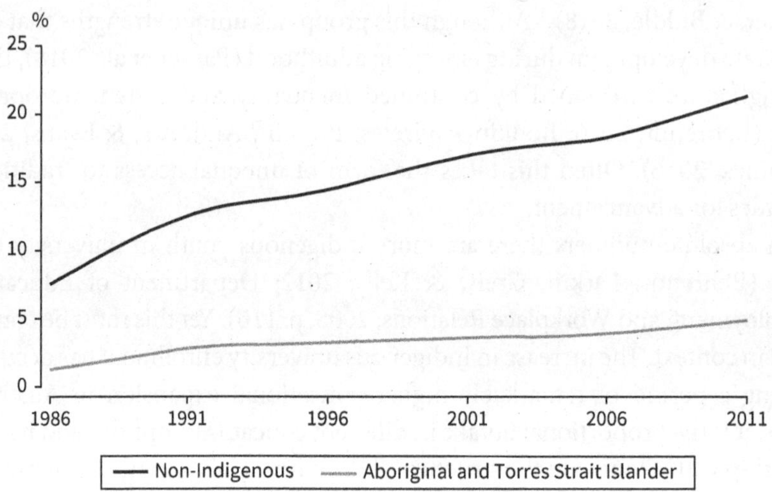

Figure 17.1 Proportion of youth (aged 15–24) who were higher education students by census year.

Image adapted from ABS (cat no. 4102.0; 2013). The image was adapted from an image licensed under creative commons.

For a long time the focus of IEA policy and research for Indigenous people has been on "closing the gap" in academic achievement. The presumption underpinning "closing the gap" is that the key to reducing racial inequality is the reduction or even elimination of the educational and employment disparities between Indigenous and non-Indigenous Australians. This discourse presumes that with similar educational and employment outcomes significant proportions of the Aboriginal and Torres Strait Islander population will be socially mobile, moving into different levels of socioeconomic prosperity in similar proportions to the non-Indigenous population. This presumption, however, is largely without supporting evidence. There is little literature on the social mobility patterns of Aboriginal and Torres Strait Islander people or, more critically, whether educational and employment outcomes translate into social mobility for Indigenous people in the same way that they do for non-Indigenous Australians. For example, empirical research suggests that achievement only accounts for around 50% of IEA for Indigenous youth (Parker, Bodkin-Andrews, Marsh, Jerrim, & Schoon, 2013). This suggests the need to focus more broadly on a full range of factors associated with university entry. Educational mobility and attainment results from multiple intertwined sources (e.g., locality, socioeconomic status, confidence, prior achievement) and thus should be investigated from a multidisciplinary perspective. It is for this reason we explore the issue from the perspective of multiple social science fields.

Education as a Gateway

Education has often been considered to be the key to increasing social mobility, stability of wages, and improving life chances. A consequence of this that is not often acknowledged is the effect education has on health. Education is the strongest predictors of all-cause mortality when compared to income, social class, and social status (Torssander & Erikson, 2009). On all these aspects Indigenous people trail behind their non-Indigenous peers. From an occupational perspective, Australian Bureau of Statistics (2014) modeling suggests that education is the driving force in the near 20-percentage point difference in labor force participation between Indigenous and non-Indigenous persons. Accounting for education reduced this gap by half. Accounting for differences in health and geography reduced the gap by only a further 1 percentage point. As will become salient later, however, controlling for these factors still left a sizable Indigenous disadvantage.

On this basis, it is worth considering education as a principally important area of policy and research for Indigenous youth. Our focus here is on two broad questions in relation to how inequality in educational outcomes might emerge:

1. Are educational mobility patterns qualitatively different for Indigenous and non-Indigenous youth or do they differ only in absolute rates?
2. Are the inequities in educational attainment endured by Indigenous Australians well-articulated by Western social science theories, or is such educational disadvantage influenced by forces outside of current Western epistemologies?

Education Mobility Patterns

To explore mobility patterns from parents' educational attainment to children's educational destination at age 19, we used all five cohorts of the Longitudinal Study of Australian youth (LSAY).[2] LSAY is a representative

[2] Attrition weights are used for all cohorts. Standard errors are corrected for school membership.

sample of Australian youth. The first two cohorts represent all children in year 9 (average age = 14) who were longitudinally followed for the next 10 years (average ages = 14–24). The final three cohorts are representative of all children aged 15 years in the year of testing who were also longitudinally followed for the next 10 years (ages 15–25). The cohorts represented individuals with modal birth years of 1981, 1984, 1987, 1990, and 1993 with initial data collected in 1995, 1998, 2003, 2006, and 2009. In total, the models explore data from 27,681 Australian youth of whom 2.25% ($N = 614$) were Indigenous.

From this data we first focus on two variables. First, we use the highest of mother's and father's educational attainment as a measure of education origin. Second, we use the child's educational attainment as a measure of education destination. Age 19 was chosen as the point for evaluating education destinations to ensure a reasonable sample size (attrition in subsequent waves leads to very small samples of Indigenous youth). Given the relatively young age at which education destination attainment was assessed, we used broad categories of education origin and destination: (a) had not completed high school by 19 (noHS), (b) had completed high school by 19 (HS), and (c) had enrolled in university at a bachelor level by age 19 (Uni). It may be argued that 19 is too young to evaluate educational attainment; however, most young people in Australia are no longer at school by age 18 (Parker, Jerrim, Anders, & Astell-Burt, 2016). Likewise, it may be argued that this is missing a distinctive feature of the Indigenous educational landscape—namely, late university entry (Asmar, Page, & Radloff, 2015; Wilks & Wilson, 2015). However, as we have argued elsewhere, timing of attainment during emerging adulthood and not just acquisition is important (Dietrich et al., 2012; Parker et al., 2016). Indeed, occupational and wage outcomes can be significantly lower in individuals who delay entry into the next level of education, even by a single year (Parker, Thoemmes, Duineveld, & Salmela-Aro, 2015). As such, we believe that age 19, an age where the initial outcomes of postschool transition attempts should be clear for the majority of the sample, is an appropriate assessment point.

We calculated outflow mobility tables over the five cohorts combined and separately. These tables provide the percentage of youth of parents with a particular level of education (e.g., parents are university graduates) who end up with different levels of educational attainment (e.g., university or just high school). We refer to these parental levels of education as educational origins. To simplify our exploration of absolute rates of mobility, we concentrate our discussion of outflow percentages (row percentages) for the combined cohorts of youth from the LSAY, presented in Table 17.1. The five outflow tables by cohort can be found in Appendix Tables 17.A1 to 17.A5. We first considered the degree of dissimilarity between the outflow percentages for the Indigenous and non-Indigenous participants. Dissimilarity is a summary statistic of the

Table 17.1 Outflow (Row Percentage) Mobility Tables

	Destination					
	Indigenous Row Percentages			Non-Indigenous Row Percentages		
Origin	noHS	HS	Uni	noHS	HS	Uni
noHS	26.3	56.5	17.2	16.5	50.3	33.1
HS	23.8	58.0	18.2	16.8	45.4	37.8
Uni	14.5	54.4	31.1	6.2	28.4	65.4

Notes: Origin = the highest level of education of the parents. Destination = the youth's current educational attainment position. noHS = did not finish high school. HS = completed high school but did not go on to tertiary education. Uni = enrolled in university at some point. Diagonals in grey represent youth having the same educational attainment as their parents by age 19. Off-diagonals in white thus represent youth who have different educational attainment than their parents at age 19. Thus the proportion of individuals in the off-diagonals represents the absolute rate of mobility.

overall difference between the outflow table for Indigenous youth and the outflow table for non-Indigenous youth. In Table 17.1, this was 0.233. That is 23.3% of Indigenous group members would have needed different educational outcomes for the outflow tables of both groups to look the same. Most of this difference between the groups related to Indigenous youths' greater likelihood of being in the HS and not the Uni category.

Another striking feature of the outflow tables was their implications for absolute mobility (comprising upward and downward movement). Indeed, the results suggest that absolute mobility is higher in Indigenous youth. There, 61.5% are mobile compared to 57.5% of non-Indigenous youth (the proportion of individuals in the off-diagonals of Table 17.1). Unfortunately, much of this mobility was downward. Indeed, from each origin (i.e., highest parental educational attainment), non-Indigenous individuals were more likely to be enrolled in university compared to their Indigenous peers. These absolute rates of mobility suggest a barrier to university entry for Indigenous youth and a propensity for larger downward mobility not shared by their non-Indigenous peers.

However, this may mistake differences in the marginal distribution of the data with qualitatively different mobility processes (i.e., relative mobility; Erikson & Goldthorpe, 1992). That is, Indigenous status may be associated only with lower educational attainment of both parents and children (an additive model) but not with significantly different mobility processes in the transmission of education attainment from parents to their children. To account for this, we ran a set of log-linear models on the same data focused on the relative rates of movement between origins and destinations.

Education Mobility Processes

We ran a series of mobility models on the data that are presented in Appendix Tables 17.A1 to 17.A5 using log-linear models (see Hout, 1983, for an overview). Our focus in these models was to separate out the marginal effects of Indigenous status (i.e., that Indigenous parents and children tend to be underrepresented in higher educational attainment categories) from relative effects (i.e., that the processes underlying educational mobility were qualitatively different for Indigenous and non-Indigenous individuals). We tested two sets of models: (a) a constant education fluidity model (cnEF; Erikson & Goldthorpe, 1992), which hypothesized that there was little trend in increased or decreased educational mobility from cohort to cohort, and (b) a universal difference model (uniDiff; Erikson & Goldthorpe, 1992), which hypothesized a trend from cohort to cohort in the changes in mobility. All models included an interaction by Indigenous status as a last step as a means of identifying whether mobility processes differed between groups.

The results from all these models fit the data well, as seen in Table 17.2. Indeed, the models are so well fitting it is difficult to choose between them. For example, while the uniDiff model misclassified less than 1% of cases, it was not much better than the simpler cnEF model.

Indeed, as can be seen from Figure 17.2, which plots the log-odds increase in immobility, there is little evidence of a trend except for some small movement toward greater immobility in the 2006 and 2009 cohorts (positive log-odds indicate that mobility at time t was greater than at time $t + 1$). As such, it is hard to recommend this model over the cnEF model.

Regardless of which model one chooses, under no circumstance were mobility processes moderated by Indigenous status (see Table 17.2). Put simply,

Table 17.2 Mobility Models

	χ^2 (df)	ID	Comparison: $\Delta\chi^2$ (df)
M0: null model	2,086 (32)**	13.63	—
M1: main effect	28 (28)	1.05	M0: 2,058 (4)**
M2: moderated by Indigenous status	23 (24)	1.02	M1: 6 (4)
M3: main effect	22 (25)	0.61	M0: 2,064 (7)**
M4: moderated by Indigenous status	17 (21)	0.57	M3: 6 (4)

Notes: All models are built upon a quasi-perfect mobility model (M0) where we expect there to be significantly greater number of cases on the diagonals (i.e., that children will have the same educational attainment than their parents). ID = Index of dissimilarity. $^{**}P < 0.001$.

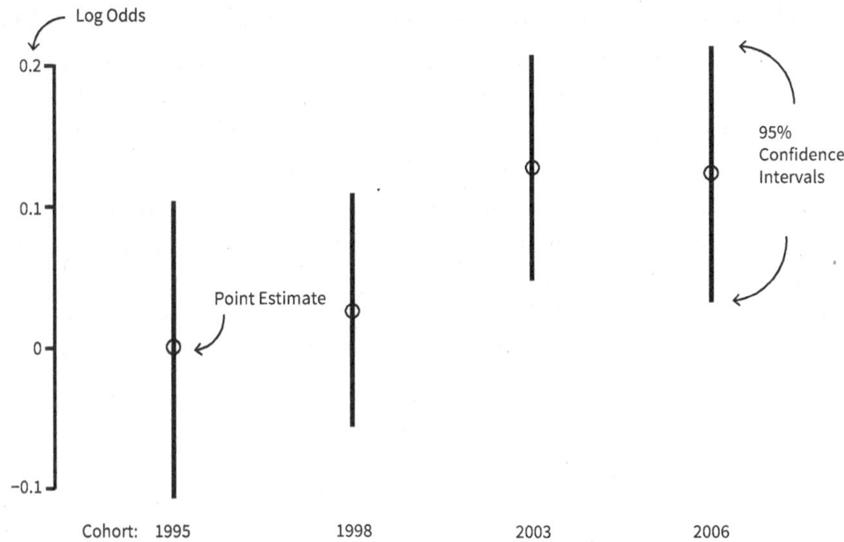

Figure 17.2 Model of log-odds increases in immobility. Using the 1995 cohort as reference category, each bar represents log-odds of the movement toward greater similarity between parents' educational origin and child's educational destination. Confidence intervals represent 95% confidence intervals based on quasi standard errors.

Indigenous participants did not have greater difficulty progressing upward from their parents' educational background nor less difficulty falling downward. Rather the results of these models suggested that Indigenous status played a unique additive effect on educational attainment. Indigenous status predicted that both parents and children would have lower educational attainment but we did not find that the transmission process between Indigenous and non-Indigenous emerging adults differed. It is this additive effect we turn to in the next section.

Models Explaining Educational Attainment in Indigenous People

The previously described results suggest that while there is a difference in the mobility of Indigenous and non-Indigenous youth (additive model), the mobility mechanisms appear to be relatively similar (nonsignificant multiplicative model). Thus, we next turned to exploring what might account for the additive effect of Indigenous status on educational attainment. We ran a series of models, each of which represented common approaches present in social science literature to explain IEA. In this way, we follow similar approaches to understanding socioeconomic inequality used by Dardanoni et al. (2006) and Jencks and Tach (2006). Dardanoni et al. distinguish between several types of predictors of IEA: (a) circumstances, (b) ability, and (c) noncognitive factors. Jencks and Tach likewise distinguish between (a) family background, (b) cognitive factors (like ability and IQ), and (c) noncognitive factors. In both cases, empirical results suggest associations remain between origin socioeconomic status and destination status after controlling for these factors. We aim to explore if similar residual effects exist for the Indigenous versus non-Indigenous educational attainment divide before turning to what factors such residual effects may represent.

We start with a base model (base) that includes only Indigenous status as a predictor of educational attainment. We then build on this model by adding in groups of variables suggested by Western models to explain the Indigenous disadvantage. The aim of this process is to see if the effect of Indigenous status on educational attainment is reduced to nonsignificance by the addition of these sets of variables. Model H1 adds variables related to individual circumstances (e.g., parents' education, parents' occupational status, neighborhood educational and occupational status, and geographic location). In our models these factors represent circumstances into which the child is born and/or develops (Dardanoni et al., 2006). From here we use Breen and Goldthorpe's (1997) rational action theory as a theoretical framework to justify including cognitive (Model H2) and noncognitive factors (Model H3). After both H2 and H3, we ask whether accounting for these additional processes explains the Indigenous effect (i.e., is the effect now nonsignificant).

The classic Breen and Goldthorpe (1997) model suggests that differences in educational attainment are generally the results of rational responses to differing situational affordances and constraints. In particular,

1. Children have a strong preference for maintaining a status in society at least equal with their parents and will tend to shy away from attempting to advance beyond their parents' social status if they think failure is a realistic possibility (i.e., relative risk aversion);
2. Children with lower levels of resources (both financial and otherwise) are less likely to move on to the next level of education; and
3. Children with lower ability and by extension noncognitive factors related to negative perceptions about ability are less likely to move on to the next level of education.

All three factors become inputs into rational cost–benefit calculations about whether attempts at upward mobility can be undertaken with manageable risk. In previous research, we illustrated the double disadvantage this implies for Indigenous youth. Reproduced here as Figure 17.3 (Parker et al., 2015), we can see that Indigenous youth both (a) require a higher threshold of underlying ability before considering university (the right shift in the probability curves between Indigenous and non-Indigenous youth) and (b) have lower academic ability from which such a threshold could be met (the left shift in academic achievement between Indigenous and non-Indigenous youth). Put simply, Indigenous youth require a higher level of academic excellence before considering enrollment in university despite, on average, having lower levels of academic performance to start with. The decision of whether or not to enroll in university is likely perceived as a riskier proposition for an Indigenous youth than for a non-Indigenous youth.

When evaluated in relation to social class, the Breen and Goldthorpe model is remarkably robust (Goldthorpe, 2007). It is also, as with all rational choice theories, extremely parsimonious. In particular, this model explicitly rejects cultural differences as mechanisms that explain differences in educational attainment. For example, there is no space in this model to suggest qualitatively different social costs and benefits between groups explain different choices at

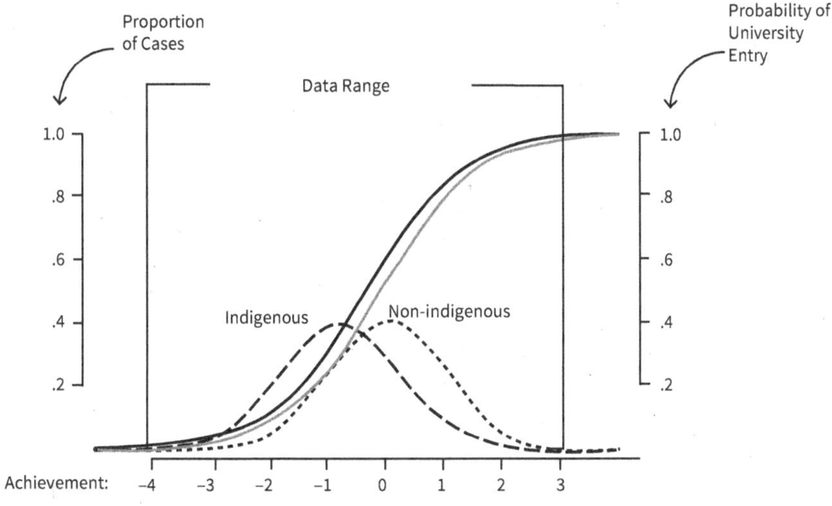

Figure 17.3 Double disadvantage of University Entry for Indigenous and non-Indigenous youth.
Adapted from Parker et al. (2015).

educational decision points. Thus, rational action theory explicitly rejects the concept that specific cultural processes are factored into decisions surrounding educational attainment and rather focuses only on situational affordances and constraints. For the current chapter, this model can be extended to make clear and precise hypotheses about the Indigenous/non-Indigenous gap in educational attainment based on the following minimal set of assumptions:

1. The effect of Indigenous status reflects a historical tendency for Indigenous people to grow up in circumstances associated with lower social status (e.g., lower socioeconomic status and locations with poorer access to educational institutions).
2. As a result, Indigenous children will have a greater tendency than their non-Indigenous peers to come from families with lower social status.
3. Thus, the Indigenous/non-Indigenous difference in educational attainment can be explained purely in rational action theory terms:
   a. Indigenous children have a greater tendency to have working class backgrounds with parents having high school or lower educational attainment, resulting in their relative risk aversion at educational transition points.
   b. Indigenous children will have achievement levels and resources consummate with other working class children.

This suggests several hypotheses.

1. H1: Conditioning on circumstances should essentially eliminate the effect of Indigenous status on educational attainment (model H1).
2. H2: As circumstances are rarely measured with perfect reliability, controlling for variables associated with rational action theory should further reduce the effect of Indigenous status. In particular, we include academic performance on standardized tests in math, reading, and science (model H2).
3. H3: Given noncognitive factors are formed rationally in response to resources and academic performance, conditioning on these aspects will have essentially no further explanatory role in educational attainment nor have any meaningful effect on the size of the Indigenous effect (model H3).

Table 17.3 presents the results of a multinomial model of educational attainment using the 2003, 2006, and 2009 cohorts of the LSAY database (the only three LSAY cohorts with consistent measures of all variables of

Table 17.3 Models of Educational Attainment

Model	HS over noHS Log odds [S.E.] (OR = Indig/ Non-Indig)	Uni Over HS Log Odds [S.E.] (OR = Indig/ Non-Indig)	Covariates
Base	−0.17 [0.14] (OR = 2.78/3.31)	−1.22 [0.12] (OR = 0.54/1.83)**	Cohort
H1	−0.04 [0.14] (OR = 3.22/3.36)	−0.99 [0.14] (OR = 0.68/1.82)**	+ Parent education, parent status, postcode status, location
H2	0.16 [0.15] (OR = 5.28/4.51)	−0.61 [0.14] (OR = 0.97/1.79)**	+Math, reading, science achievement
H3	0.27 [0.17] (OR = 8.72/6.67)	−0.54 [0.14] (OR = 1.57/2.69)**	+Parents and students aspirations, academic self-concept, utility task value

Notes: Indig = Indigenous. noHS = did not finish high school. HS = completed high school but did not go on to tertiary education. Non-Indig = non-Indigenous. OR = odds ratio. S.E. = standard error. Uni = enrolled in university at some point. ** $P < 0.001$.

interest).[3] Hypotheses H1 to H3 are then tested sequentially, building on a base multinomial model in which educational attainment was predicted by Indigenous status alone. The results suggest a few important points. First, Indigenous status was unrelated to whether or not an individual obtained or did not obtain a high school level of education. However, our findings had significant implications for university entry, with all the action being centered there.

As can be seen, conditioning on circumstances and rational action theory variables reduces the effect of Indigenous status by some margin. Nevertheless, even in model H3, which contains a large number of covariates, the probability of an Indigenous emerging adult entering university was 0.61 compared to 0.73 for a similar positioned non-Indigenous emerging adult. Simply put, while circumstances and rational action theory accounts for a proportion of the Indigenous effect on university entry, it leaves much left unexplained (non-Indigenous youth were still more likely to go to university in all models). Thus, the effect of Indigenous status on educational attainment cannot solely be explained by rational action theory or a wide array of common social science predictors. This suggests the need to consider cultural distinct processes and discriminatory practices to account for the residual effect. We consider what this residual effect of Indigenous status might be in the following section but briefly touch on an important finding that is somewhat tangential but has considerable practical implications.

[3] Attrition and population weights used as well as balanced repeated replication weights to account for the complex design of the LSAY database.

Influence of Noncognitive Variable

Model H3 indicates the incremental improvement in explaining educational attainment when considering noncognitive factors in addition to demographics and academic achievement. This model is particularly interesting and has practical implications given the noncognitive revolution (Heckman, 2006). It is now not uncommon for noncognitive factors to be promoted as critical targets in intervention for disadvantaged populations, particularly in relation to adolescents (Heckman, 2006). The evidence for their effectiveness for explaining mobility, however, remains surprisingly weak (Jenks & Tach, 2006). For Indigenous youth, research has focused on factors tied closely to the academic domain such as academic aspirations, self-concept, and task value (Craven & Marsh, 2004; A. J. Martin, 2006; McInerney, 1995; Mooney, Seaton, Kaur, Marsh, & Yeung, 2016). A number of empirical studies have indeed found lower levels of these factors in Indigenous populations (Ahrens, Bodkin-Andrews, Craven, & Yeung, 2014; Bodkin-Andrews, et al., 2013; De Bortoli & Cresswell, 2004; Magson, et al., 2014; A. J. Martin, Ginns, Papworth, & Nejad, 2013; Purdie & McCrindle, 2004). These studies, however, typically occur in the presence of rather weak controls.

Rational action theory suggests there is unlikely to be group specific factors which distort the development of self-beliefs and attitudes toward education, and thus the only difference in these factors we would expect is on the basis of differences in academic achievement alone. Thus, aspirations, self-concept, and task value represent rational assessment based on sober reflection of an individual's objective academic attainment. Indeed, this model accounted for the data quite well in two respects. First, it is important to note that that the decline in the effect size from model H2 to model H3 was extremely small (see Table 17.3). Second, rational action theory would indeed suggest this is the case as such factors are dependent on rational assessments of achievement and thus, once achievement is taken into account, should not differ. Table 17.4 shows this was indeed the case.

Indigenous youth do have lower levels of aspirations, self-concept, and utility task value. But once achievement is taken into account only one of these effects remains significant. The remaining effect is a just significant difference in youths' perception of parents' aspirations for their educational career. Taken together, we remain skeptical of claims that enhancing academic specific noncognitive skills will help close the gap in educational attainment for Indigenous youth given the current state of evidence.

Table 17.4 Indigenous Effect on Mediators of Educational Attainment

Outcome	M1 [S.E.]	M2 [S.E.]
Math	−0.52 [0.06]**	—
Reading	−0.48 [0.06]**	—
Science	−0.48 [0.06]**	—
Parents' aspirations[a]	−0.50 [0.12]**	−0.25 [0.11]*
Students' aspirations[a]	−0.48 [0.12]**	−0.20 [0.12]
Academic self-concept	−0.25 [0.04]**	−0.08 [0.04]
Academic utility value	−0.01 [0.04]	0.07 [0.04]

Notes: M1 conditioned on circumstance variables (birth cohort, parent education, parent status, postcode status, location). M2 conditioned on circumstance and math, read, and science achievement variables. S.E. = standard error. $*P < 0.05$; $**P < 0.001$.

[a]Log-odds.

Altering Rational Action Theory to Account for Indigenous Specific Mechanisms

Rational action theory is a parsimonious and well-supported model of educational attainment from a Westernized perspective. However, we show that there remains a significant and sizable Indigenous effect when predicting university controlling for rational action theory processes. We argue that the reason for this is that rational action theory does not and cannot incorporate the distinctive additional situational affordances and constraints present for the Indigenous youth (i.e., the portion of the additive effect of Indigenous status left unexplained by rational action theory predictors). Here we draw on Maggie Walter's (2015) exposition of the "distinctive patterns of Indigenous social capital" (p. 69). In particular, we claim that educational and further social mobility for Indigenous children contain a distinctive set of "hazards and costs" that are not shared by non-Indigenous people are thus missing from standard models of attainment and mobility (p. 70). Examples include the negative impact of multiple levels of racism on patterns of educational achievement, engagement, and aspirations for Indigenous students documented across nearly all levels of education (Bodkin-Andrews, Denson, & Bansel, 2013; Gair, Miles, Savage, & Zuchowski, 2015; Wainwright, Gridley, & Sampson, 2012). We discuss these issues in relation to racial capital both within and outside the education system.

Social Capital

Portes (1998) provides a broad review of social capital and all its competing definitions. He notes a critical aspect of multiple definitions of social capital is that it can both promote and constrain educational and occupational advancement in minority and marginalized groups. As Walter (2015) identifies, the double-edged sword of social capital "has resonance for Indigenous Australians" (p. 75). For Indigenous individuals in particular, bonding capital (i.e., close social bonds within one's community) may represent a potential cost of attending university, as such attendance may require leaving the community. We make a similar argument in relation to the unique negative effect of rural and remote location on university entrance in Australia (Parker et al., 2016). There we argue that a possible unique effect of rural status on university participation may be due to close connections to community, increasing the emotional cost of leaving home to attend university—an issue not shared by urban individuals who may not need to leave home at all and also tend to have weaker ties to the local community.

School achievement patterns in remote communities suggest that the interaction between remoteness and Indigeneity is also important to consider. That is, government reports have repeatedly shown that while there is a notable decline in the achievement rates of Indigenous students based on increasing levels of remoteness, this effect is not visible for non-Indigenous students, to the extent that non-Indigenous students in remote locations perform better than Indigenous students in metropolitan locations (Steering Committee for the Review of Government Service Provision, 2014). These results suggest that the path to educational inequity for Indigenous emerging adults is not only due to their greater likelihood of living in rural communities. As Walter (2015) argues, the distinctive patterns of Indigenous social capital aligned with race relations barriers to educational and occupational attainment suggest that the connection between education and social capital for Aboriginal and Torres Strait Islander people is not a replica of that experienced by the non-Indigenous population. Put simply, emerging adulthood is likely to be a fundamentally different experience for Indigenous than non-Indigenous people.

It is also possible to frame the issue of social capital in other ways. For example, it may be the case that Indigenous social networks are more economically homogeneous than non-Indigenous networks (individuals engaged in a limited number of distinct occupations), and as such, there is a redundancy in the available career models within a given community. Again, this is an argument we have made previously in relation to rural and remote communities that tend to have relatively little economic diversity (Parker, et al., 2016). Finally, the argument could be kept within standard human capital models of economics (Becker, 2009). Essentially, the standard human capital model hypothesizes that individuals pursue a level of education up to the level at which costs of continuing education outweigh the benefits. As Akerlof and Kranton (2010) note, one can easily include social costs in this equation, and it may be that Indigenous youth have greater social costs to comparable non-Indigenous youth (e.g., caring costs; see Walter, 2015). This may lead Indigenous youth to evaluate university entry using different standards than non-Indigenous youth. Summarizing these perspectives, we claim that Indigenous culture leads youth to evaluate costs and benefits differently than their non-Indigenous peers. However, we simply do not yet have the empirical evidence available to address these claims. As we argue in the final section of this chapter, there needs to be a revolutionary alliance between qualitative and quantitative research and Western and Indigenous research methods to address this issue.

Racial Capital

While there is a strong consensus among many Indigenous scholars that race, as a biological construct, does not meaningfully exist, the social construction of race, particularly under the subjugating historical and contemporary lens of dominant Western epistemological frameworks, ensures that race is a meaningful and impacting construct (K. L. Martin, 2008; Moreton-Robinson, 2009; Page, Trudgett & Bodkin-Andrews, 2016; Tuhiwai Smith, 2012; Walter & Anderson, 2013). Aligned to this is a plethora of scholarly research that has noted the systemic nature in which Indigenous Australians are repeatedly subjugated through the likes of being denied: acknowledgement of a voice in defining their own diverse histories (Behrendt, 2016); identifying with their culture (Bond, Brough, & Cox, 2014; Bennett, 2014; Fredericks, 2013); and high expectations for achieving at school (Dandy, Durkon, Barber, & Houghton, 2015; De Plevitz, 2007) and the workplace (Cunningham & Paradies, 2013; Hunter, 2000). This pattern of findings, also aligned with empirical research suggesting that interpersonal forms of racism are common lived experiences for Indigenous students and their families (Bodkin-Andrews & Carlson, 2016; Paradies, Harris, & Anderson, 2008), paints a picture of systemic and perpetual oppression that ensures that the disadvantaged and "othered" status of Indigenous Australians is still sustained today (Moreton-Robinson, 2009). From this, it is not surprising that Walter (2010) highlights the notion of racial capital:

> Societally produced and reproduced race is still a potent explanatory of why one group, distinguished by skin color, culture, or place of origin, differ in life chances to

> others. Race as a social relation of power is underpinned by a society's system, usually entrenched, of racial stratification. Population differentiation into hierarchically superposed racial groups . . . establishes the capital power of a particular race position. Thus race capital, like other capitals, is distributed unequally prefigured as a sphere of relational societal resource: both a predictor and determinant of our social positioning. (p. 47)

The importance of recognizing the impact of racial capital and how it may interact with social capital includes the way in which Aboriginal and Torres Strait Islander peoples, families, and communities are forced into positionings repeatedly associated with socioeconomic disadvantage. It also includes unique cultural and social strengths within and across Indigenous communities are repeatedly overlooked and ignored within wider academic and political discourses (Parker et al., 2018; Walter, 2015).

Taken together, we develop a model that aims to integrate rational action theory with theories related to social and racial capital specific to Indigenous Australians. The focus on social and racial capital and its requirement for strong, clear, and qualitatively distinct mechanisms would seem to go against rational action theory as it moves some explanatory focus away from individuals making choices on the basis on quantitatively different levels of resources and risk aversion and onto the normative influence of culture. However, as Goldthorpe (2007) argues cultural forces may be in operation for social divides other than social class. Cultural forces have not been included in rational action theory because social class does not have the sort of normative pressure such models would require. In groups in which such normative pressures do hold, however, one presumes cultural mechanisms would play a much stronger role. This is clearly the case when considering educational attainment from an Indigenous perspective (Walter, 2015). Further, it suggests the need to bring together theories, which focus on individual decision-making in the context of situational affordances and constraints with identity economic models focusing on the influence of cultural specific factors.

Intersectionality

In the attempt to provide evidence of causal processes, social scientists interested in disadvantage and inequality have been obsessed with average causal effects. We could also be accused of taking this perspective in our chapter. While our focus was on whether Indigenous status represented an additive or multiplicative cause on educational mobility and attainment, we did not explore the issue of intersectionality between Indigenous status and other forms of minority or marginalized status. This intersectionality was once the domain solely of qualitative researchers. This is despite the quantitative methods for engaging in this research being well developed (i.e., moderation analysis, moderated-mediation, and mixture models; Else-Quest & Hyde, 2016). This suggests the potential for fruitful collaboration between qualitative and quantitative approaches, as well as Indigenous and non-Indigenous approaches, to research could indeed occur.

As Walter (2015) notes, intersectional perspectives for Indigenous issues, particularly in relation to social class, gender, and geography, are critical. To rectify our initial lack of attention to intersection, we used the quantitative approach to intersectionality proposed by Else-Quest and Hyde (2016) in which the interaction between multiple forms of marginalized or minority status are considered. We did this in relation to the base and H3 models seen in Table 17.3. There was a significant moderator for parents' occupational status for the base model (log odds: −0.255 [standard error =0.108], $P < 0.05$) and marginally significant effect in the full H3 model (log odds: −0.262 [standard error = 0.146], $P = 0.074$). Similar to the issues related to the tenuous nature of the benefits of middle class status for Indigenous people proposed by Walters (2015), the results seem to suggest that high parental occupational prestige provides less advantage to Indigenous youth than non-Indigenous youth as seen in Figure 17.4.

Implications and Warnings

For this reason, among others, we must be careful when making recommendations based on our analysis. Largely our basis for this paper is that increased educational attainment for Indigenous youth will help many gain high positions of status and thus help build the fledgling Indigenous middle class (Walter, 2015). While education is indeed a primary predictor of access to professional occupations, it would be naive to suggest education as a panacea (Walter, 2015).

It must also be recognized that the imposed racial label of Indigenous Australia itself is problematic, as it ignores the diverse contexts, histories, values, and languages of the 500-plus Indigenous clans and language groups that exist throughout Australia. The implications of this mass generalization is not just limited to locality, social, and class based variations but also have strong relevance to the ongoing development of the Australian Professional Standards for Teachers (Australian Institute for Learning and School

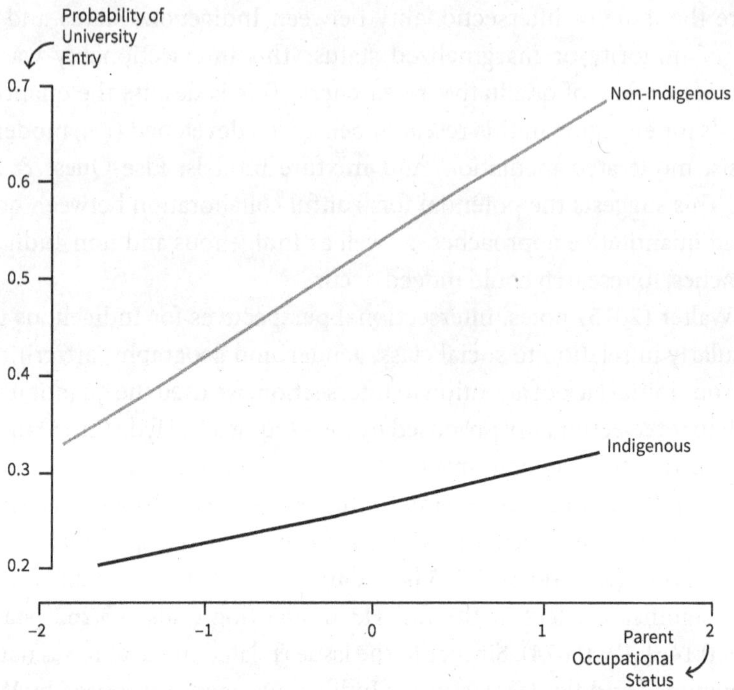

Figure 17.4 Intersectional findings: Probability of entering university given parental occupational status. Results based on interaction included in the base model and plotted from the 5th to the 95th percentile in *z*-scored occupational status.

Leadership, 2011). Initiated and sponsored by the Australian Government, these standards define quality teaching across all levels of education within Australia have a range specific standards relating to the professional knowledge of teachers. More specially, Section 1.4 of the standards relates to the teaching of Indigenous Australian students, and Section 2.4 relates to the teaching of understand and respect for Indigenous Australian peoples and communities. Imbedded within this recommendation is a knowledge of and engagement with diverse identities, histories, cultures, and languages of Indigenous Australian peoples and communities. To put it simply, future teaching and research practices must investigate more deeply than broad racial labels such as *Indigenous Australian*.

Our results also challenge the standard modernization theory of increasing merit selection, which postulates that academic achievement is increasingly the basis for entry into education and prestigious jobs. This model has disputed for some time (Brown, 2013; Erikson & Goldthorpe, 1992). Yet its effect on emerging adults' aspirations remains strong and is beginning to have damaging effects. There is increasing frustration among emerging adults given the broken promise of modernization theory and its implications for economic stability and success (Brown, 2013). This appears to be even more evident for Indigenous people where education and even occupational success do not appear to have the same pay-offs as they do for non-Indigenous Australians (Walters, 2015). Further, there are many compelling issues that Indigenous students need to contend with and overcome once enrolled in university to succeed (i.e., culture shock; Trudgett & Franklin, 2011). Thus, while we remain convinced that closing the educational attainment gap remains a critical policy goal we should not be naive in thinking that this alone will be sufficient to completely resolve Indigenous disadvantage.

Implications for Research

Clearly representative data sets like the Australian census, LSAY, and, more broadly, international databases like the program for international student assessment (PISA) and Trends in International Mathematics and Science Study (TIMSS) provide critical insight for monitoring the degree to which gaps in occupational and educational attainment exist for Indigenous people and exploring the degree to which standard Western models account for such gaps. However, as we previously note, standard models do not have the power to explain all of the "Indigenous effect." Unfortunately, Western-based research and policy has a long history of ignoring both the complexities and strengths that can be found within Indigenous Australian communities (Maddison, 2012). Indeed, Indigenous scholarly literature has revealed a wide range of successful social and educational initiatives and strategies that have closely engaged with the immense diversities within "Indigenous Australia." Examples include the teaching of varying Indigenous Australian approaches to science (Riley & Genner, 2011), literature (Phillips, 2015), art (Blacklock, 2015), mathematics (Matthews, 2012), sports (Evans, Wilson, Dalton, & Georgakis, 2015), business (Foley, 2003), law (Wood, 2011), and history (Maynard, 2007). The limited measures and labels that our chapter had access to are a classic example of the methodological ignorance of Indigenous standpoints, methods, and practices. Part of the reason for this is that these large databases simply do not contain measures of factors like bonding social capital, discrimination, and Indigenous epistemologies and ontologies that are likely quantitatively more important for Indigenous youth, nor can they include factors specific to Indigenous people. What we suggest is a revolutionary partnership between quantitative analysis of large-scale databases with qualitative research and a joining together of Western and Indigenous research methodologies and knowledges to redress this imbalance.

References

Akerlof, G. A., & Kranton, R. E. (2010). *Identity economics: How our identities shape our work, wages, and well-being*. Princeton, NJ: Princeton University Press.

Arnett, J. J. (2007). Emerging adulthood: What is it, and what is it good for? *Child Development Perspectives, 1*, 68–73. https://doi.org/10.1111/j.1750-8606.2007.00016.x

Asmar, C., Page, S., & Radloff, A. (2015). Exploring anomalies in Indigenous student engagement: Findings from a national Australian survey of undergraduates. *Higher Education Research & Development, 34*, 15–29.

Australia Bureau of Statistics. (2010). Hitting the books: Characteristics of higher education students (Cat no. 4102.0). Retrieved from http://www.abs.gov.au/AUSSTATS/abs@.nsf/Lookup/4102.0Main+Features20July+2013

Australia Bureau of Statistics. (2014). Exploring the gap in labour market outcomes for Aboriginal and Torres Strait Islander peoples (Cat no. 4102.0). Retrieved from http://www.abs.gov.au/ausstats/abs@.nsf/Lookup/4102.0main+features72014#EQUAL

Australian Institute for Training and School Leadership. (2011). National professional standards for teachers. Retrieved August 25, 2016, from: http://www.aitsl.edu.au/docs/default-source/apst-resources/australian_professional_standard_for_teachers_final.pdf

Becker, G. S. (2009). *Human capital: A theoretical and empirical analysis, with special reference to education*. Chicago, IL: University of Chicago Press.

Behrendt, L. (2016). *Finding Eliza: Power and colonial storytelling*. Saint Lucia, Australia: University of Queensland Press.

Behrendt, L., Larkin, S., Griew, R., & Kelly, P. (2012). *Review of higher education access and outcomes for Aboriginal and Torres Strait Islander people—Final report*. Canberra, Australia: Commonwealth of Australia.

Bennett, B. (2014). How do light-skinned Aboriginal Australians experience racism? Implications for social work. *AlterNative, 102*, 180–192.

Blacklock, F. (2015). Art: Connecting cultures. In K. Price (Ed), *Knowledge of life: Aboriginal and Torres Strait Islander Australia* (pp. 77–97). Victoria, Australia: Cambridge University Press.

Bodkin-Andrews, G., Bodkin, F., Andrews, G., & Evans, R. (2017). Aboriginal identity, worldviews, research, and the story of the Burra'gorang. In C. Kickett-Tucker, D. Bessarab,M. Wright, & J. Coffin (Eds.), *Mia Mia Aboriginal community development: Fostering cultural security* (pp. 19–36). Cambridge, England: Cambridge University Press.

Bodkin-Andrews, G., & Carlson, B. (2016). The legacy of racism and Indigenous Australian identity within education. *Race, Ethnicity and Education, 19*, 784–807.

Bodkin-Andrews, G., Craven, R. G., Parker, P., Kaur, G., & Yeung, A. S. (2013). Motivational cognitions and behaviours for metropolitan Aboriginal and non-Aboriginal Australian students: Assessing the relations between motivation and school engagement. In G. A. D. Liem & A. B. I. Bernardo (Eds.), *Advancing cross-cultural perspectives on educational psychology: A festschrift for Dennis M. McInerney* (pp. 295–316). Charlotte, NC: Information Age Press.

Bodkin-Andrews, G. H., Denson, N., & Bansel, P. (2013). Teacher racism, academic self-concept, and multiculturation: Investigating adaptive and maladaptive relations with academic disengagement and self-sabotage for Indigenous and non-Indigenous Australian students. *Australian Psychologist, 48*, 226–237.

Bond, C., Brough, M., & Cox, L. (2014). Blood in our hearts or blood on our hands? The viscosity, vitality and validity of Aboriginal "blood talk." *International Journal of Critical Indigenous Studies, 7*, 2–14.

Bourke, C., Rigby, K., & Burden, J. (2000). *Better practice in school attendance: Improving the school attendance of Indigenous students* (Tech. rep.). Melbourne:, Australia: Monash University.

Breen, R., & Goldthorpe, J. H. (1997). Explaining educational differentials: Towards a formal rational action theory. *Rationality and Society*, *9*, 275–305.

Brown, P. (2013). Education, opportunity and the prospects for social mobility. *British Journal of Sociology of Education*, *34*, 678–700.

Craven, R. G., & Marsh, H. W. (2004). The challenge for counsellors: Understanding and addressing Indigenous secondary students' aspirations, self-concepts and barriers to achieving their aspirations. *Australian Journal of Guidance and Counselling*, *14*, 16–33.

Cunningham, J., & Paradies, Y. C. (2013). Patterns and correlates of self-reported racial discrimination among Australian Aboriginal and Torres Strait Islander adults, 2008–09: Analysis of national survey data. *International Journal for Equity in Health*, *12*, 47.

Dandy, J., Durkin, K., Barber, B. L., & Houghton, S. (2015). Academic expectations of Australian students from Aboriginal, Asian and Anglo backgrounds: Perspectives of teachers, trainee-teachers and students. *International Journal of Disability, Development and Education*, *62*, 60–82.

Dardanoni, V., Fields, G. S., Roemer, J., & Puerta, M. L. S. (2006). How demanding should inequality be, and how much have we achieved. In S. L. Morgan, D. B. Grunsky, & G. S. Fields (Eds.), *Mobility and Inequality* (pp. 59–84). Stanford, CA: Stanford University Press.

De Bortoli, L., & Cresswell, J. (2004). *Australia's Indigenous students in PISA 2000: Results from an international study* (ACER research monograph no 59). Victoria, Australia: Australian Council for Educational Research.

De Plevitz, L. (2007). Systemic racism: The hidden barrier to educational success for Indigenous school students. *Australian Journal of Education*, *51*, 54–71.

Department of Education, Employment, and Workplace Relations. (2008). *National report to parliament on Indigenous education, science, and training: 2008* (Tech. rep.). Canberra, Australia: Commonwealth of Australia.

Dietrich, J., Parker, P., & Salmela-Aro, K. (2012). Phase-adequate engagement at the post-school transition. *Developmental Psychology*, *48*, 1575–1593.

Else-Quest, N. M., & Hyde, J. S. (2016). Intersectionality in quantitative psychological research: II. Methods and techniques. *Psychology of Women Quarterly*, *40*, 319–336.

Erikson, R., & Goldthorpe, J. H. (1992). *The constant flux: A study of class mobility in industrial societies*. New York, NY: Oxford University Press.

Evans, J. R., Wilson, R., Dalton, B., & Georgakis, S. (2015). Indigenous participation in Australian sport: The perils of the "panacea" proposition. *Cosmopolitan Civil Societies*, *7*, 53–79.

Fredericks, B. (2013). "We don't leave our identities at the city limits": Aboriginal and Torres Strait Islander people living in urban localities. *Australian Aboriginal Studies*, *1*, 4–16.

Foley, D. (2003). An examination of indigenous Australian entrepreneurs. *Journal of Developmental Entrepreneurship*, *8*, 133–151.

Gair, S., Miles, D., Savage, D., & Zuchowski, I. (2015). Racism unmasked: The experiences of Aboriginal and Torres Strait Islander students in social work field placements. *Australian Social Work*, *68*, 32–48.

Goldin, C. D., & Katz, L. F. (2009). *The race between education and technology*. Cambridge, MA: Harvard University Press.

Goldthorpe, J. H. (2007). *On sociology*. Stanford, CA: Stanford University Press.

Heckman, J. J. (2006). Skill formation and the economics of investing in disadvantaged children. *Science*, *312*(5782), 1900–1902.

Hout, M. (1983). *Mobility Tables*. SAGE Publications, Inc. https://doi.org/10.4135/9781412985086.

Hunter, B. (2000). *Social exclusion, social capital, and Indigenous Australians: Measuring the social costs of unemployment*. Canberra, Australia: Centre for Aboriginal Economic Policy Research, Australian National University.

Jencks, C., & Tach, L. (2006). Would equal opportunity mean more mobility?. *Mobility and inequality: Frontiers of research from sociology and economics.* In S. L. Morgan, D. B. Grunsky, & G. S. Fields (Eds.), *Mobility and Inequality* (pp. 23–58). Stanford, CA: Stanford University Press.

Lucas, S. R. (2001). Effectively maintained inequality: Education transitions, track mobility, and social background effects. *American Journal of Sociology, 106*, 1642–1690.

Maddison, S. (2012). Evidence and contestation in the Indigenous policy domain: Voice, ideology and institutional inequality. *Australian Journal of Public Administration, 71*, 269–277.

Magson, N. R., Craven, R. G., Nelson, G. F., Yeung, A. S., Bodkin-Andrews, G. H., & McInerney, D. M. (2014). Motivation matters: Profiling Indigenous and non-Indigenous students' motivational goals. *Australian Journal of Indigenous Education, 43*, 96–112.

Martin, A. J. (2006). A motivational psychology for the education of Indigenous Australian students. *Australian Journal of Indigenous Education, 35*, 30–43.

Martin, A. J., Ginns, P., Papworth, B., & Nejad, H. (2013). Aboriginal/Indigenous students in high school: Understanding their motivation, engagement, academic buoyancy, and achievement. In G. A. D. Liem & A. B. I. Bernardo (Eds.), *Advancing cross-cultural perspectives on educational psychology: A festschrift for Dennis M. McInerney* (pp. 273–294). Charlotte, NC: Information Age Press.

Martin, K. L. (2008). *Please knock before you enter: Aboriginal regulation of outsiders and the implications for researchers.* Brisbane, Australia: Post Pressed.

Matthews, C. (2012). Maths as storytelling: Maths is beautiful. In K. Price (Ed.), *Aboriginal and Torres Strait Islander education: An introduction for the teaching profession,* (pp. 94–112). Victoria, Australia: Cambridge University Press.

Maynard, J. (2007). Circles in the sand: An Indigenous framework of historical practice. *Australian Journal of Indigenous Education, 36*, 117–120.

McInerney, D. M. (1995). Goal theory and indigenous minority school motivation: Relevance and application. *Advances in motivation and achievement, 9*, 153–181.

Mitrou, F., Francis, M., Martin, C., David, L., David, P., Elena, M., . . . Zubrick, S. R. (2014). Gaps in Indigenous disadvantage not closing: A census cohort study of social determinants of health in Australia, Canada, and New Zealand from 1981–2006. *BMC Public Health, 14*, 201. doi:10.1186/1471-2458-14-201

Mooney, J., Seaton, M., Kaur, G., Marsh, H. W., & Yeung, A. S. (2016). Cultural perspectives on Indigenous and non-Indigenous Australian students' school motivation and engagement. *Contemporary Educational Psychology, 47*, 11–23.

Moreton-Robinson, A. (2009). Imagining the good indigenous citizen: Race war and the pathology of patriarchal white sovereignty. *Cultural Studies Review, 15*, 61–79.

OECD. (2011). *Education at a glance: 2011 OECD indicators.* Paris, France: Author.

Page, S., Trudgett, M., & Bodkin-Andrews, G. (2016). Exploring an Indigenous graduate attribute project through a critical race theory lens. In M. Davis & A. Goody (Eds.), *Research and development in higher education: The shape of higher education* (Vol. 39, pp. 258–267). Hammondville, Australia: HERDSA.

Paradies, Y. (2016). Colonisation, racism and Indigenous health. *Journal of Population Research, 33*(1), 83–96.

Paradies, Y., Harris, R., & Anderson, I. (2008). *The impact of racism on Indigenous health in Australia and Aotearoa: Towards a research agenda* (J. Yule & C. Edmonds, Eds.). Casuarina, Australia: Cooperative Research Centre for Aboriginal Health.

Parker, P. D., Bodkin-Andrews, G., Marsh, H. W., Jerrim, J., & Schoon, I. (2013). Will closing the achievement gap solve the problem? An analysis of primary and secondary effects for indigenous university entry. *Journal of Sociology, 51*, 1085–1102.

Parker, P. D., Bodkin-Andrews, G., Parker, R. B., & Biddle, N. (2018). Trends in Indigenous and Non-Indigenous multidomain well-being. Decomposing persistent, maturation, and period effects in emerging adulthood. *Emerging Adulthood*, 216769681878201. https://doi.org/10.1177/2167696818782018

Parker, P. D., Jerrim, J., Anders, J., & Astell-Burt, T. (2016). Does living closer to a university increase educational attainment? A longitudinal study of aspirations, university entry, and elite university enrolment of Australian youth. *Journal of Youth and Adolescence*, *45*, 1156–1175.

Parker, P. D., Thoemmes, F., Duineveld, J. J., & Salmela-Aro, K. (2015). I wish I had (not) taken a gap-year? The psychological and attainment outcomes of different post-school pathways. *Developmental Psychology*, *51*, 323–333.

Phillips, S. R. (2015). Literature: Writing ourselves. In K. Price (Ed), *Knowledge of life: Aboriginal and Torres Strait Islander Australia* (pp. 98–117). Victoria, Australia: Cambridge University Press.

Piketty, T. (2014). *Capital in the twenty-first century*. Cambridge, MA: Harvard University Press.

Portes, A. (1998). Social capital: Its origins and applications in modern sociology. *Annual Review of Sociology*, *24*, 1–24.

Purdie, N., Dudgeon, P., & Walker, R. (2010). *Working together: Aboriginal and Torres Strait Islander mental health and wellbeing principles and practice* (Tech. rep.). Canberra, Australia: Office of Aboriginal and Torres Strait Islander Health, Department of Ageing.

Purdie, N., & McCrindle, A. (2004). Measurement of self-concept among Indigenous and non-Indigenous Australian students. *Australian Journal of Psychology*, *56*, 50–62.

Riley, L., & Genner, M. (2011). Bemel-Gardoo: Embedding cultural content in the science and technology syllabus. In N. Purdie, G. Milgate, & H. R. Bell (Eds), *Two way teaching and learning: Toward cultural reflective and relevant education* (pp. 119–154). Victoria, Australia: ACER Press.

Schwab, R. G. (2006) *Kids, skidoos and caribou: The junior Canadian ranger program as a model for re-engaging indigenous Australian youth in remote areas* (CAEPR discussion paper no. 281/2006). Canberra, Australia: Centre for Aboriginal Economic Policy Research, Australian National University.

Steering Committee for the Review of Government Service Provision. (2014). *Overcoming Indigenous disadvantage: Key indicators*. Canberra, Australia: Productivity Commission.

Torssander, J., & Erikson, R. (2009). Stratification and mortality: A comparison of education, class, status, and income. *European Sociological Review*, *26*, 465–474.

Trudgett, M. (2013). Stop, collaborate and listen: A guide to seeding success for Indigenous higher degree research students. In R. G. Craven & J. Mooney (Eds.), *Seeding success in indigenous Australian higher education* (pp. 137–155). Bingley, England: Emerald.

Trudgett, M. (2014). Supervision provided to Indigenous Australian doctoral students: A Black and White issue. *Higher Education Research & Development*, *33*, 1035–1048.

Trudgett, M., & Franklin, C. (2011). Not in my backyard: The impact of culture shock on Indigenous Australians in higher education. In *Proceedings of the 1st International Australasian Conference on Enabling Access to Higher Education* (pp. 33–40). Adelaide, Australia: University of South Australia National Committee of Enabling Educators

Tuhiwai Smith, L. (2012). *Decolonizing methodologies: Research and indigenous peoples*. London, England: Zed Books.

Wainwright, J., Gridley, H., & Sampson, E. (2012). Facing a world of NO: How accessible is a career in psychology for Aboriginal and Torres Strait Islander Australians?. *Australian Community Psychologist*, *24*, 143–151.

Walter, M. (2010). The politics of the data: How the Australian statistical Indigene is constructed. *International Journal of Critical Indigenous Studies*, *3*, 45–56.

Walter, M. (2015). The vexed link between social capital and social mobility for Aboriginal and Torres Strait Islander people. *Australian Journal of Social Issues*, *50*, 69–88.

Walter, M., & Andersen, C. (2013). *Indigenous statistics: A quantitative research methodology.* Walnut Creek, CA: Left Coast Press.

Wilks, J., & Wilson, K. (2015). A profile of the Aboriginal and Torres Strait Islander higher education student population. *Australian Universities' Review, 57*, 17–30.

Wood, A. (2011). Law studies and indigenous students' wellbeing: Closing the (many) gap(s). *Legal Education Review, 21*(2), 6.

Zubrick, S., Silburn, S. R., De Maio, J. A., Shepherd, C., Griffin, J. A., & Dalby, R. B. (2006). *The Western Australian Aboriginal Child Health Survey: Improving the educational experiences of Aboriginal children and young people* (Tech. rep.). Perth, Australia: Curtin University of Technology and Telethon Institute for Child Health Research.

Appendix Individual Cohort Mobility Tables

Table 17.A1 Mobility Table: 1995

	Destination					
	Indigenous			Non-Indigenous		
Origin	noHS	HS	Uni	noHS	HS	Uni
noHS	0.310	0.434	0.256	0.169	0.386	0.444
HS	0.323	0.425	0.252	0.118	0.371	0.511
Uni	0.049	0.479	0.472	0.047	0.205	0.748

Notes: Origin = the highest level of education of the parents. Destination = the youth's current educational attainment position. noHS = did not finish high school. HS = completed high school but did not go on to tertiary education. Uni = enrolled in university at some point. Diagonals in grey represent youth having the same educational attainment as their parents by age 19. Off-diagonals in white thus represent youth who have different educational attainment than their parents at age 19. Thus the proportion of individuals in the off-diagonals represents the absolute rate of mobility.

Table 17.A2 Mobility Table: 1998

	Destination					
	Indigenous			Non-Indigenous		
Origin	noHS	HS	Uni	noHS	HS	Uni
noHS	0.226	0.522	0.253	0.089	0.580	0.332
HS	0.282	0.509	0.209	0.090	0.514	0.396
Uni	0.081	0.688	0.231	0.035	0.321	0.644

Notes: Origin = the highest level of education of the parents. Destination = the youth's current educational attainment position. noHS = did not finish high school. HS = completed high school but did not go on to tertiary education. Uni = enrolled in university at some point. Diagonals in grey represent youth having the same educational attainment as their parents by age 19. Off-diagonals in white thus represent youth who have different educational attainment than their parents at age 19. Thus the proportion of individuals in the off-diagonals represents the absolute rate of mobility.

Table 17.A3 Mobility Table: 2003 Cohorts

	Destination					
	Indigenous Row Percentages			Non-Indigenous Row Percentages		
Origin	noHS	HS	Uni	noHS	HS	Uni
noHS	33.2	58.9	7.9	24.6	50.6	24.8
HS	30.9	53.8	15.3	20.9	49.3	29.8
Uni	23.5	51.3	25.2	8.8	34.6	56.5

Notes: Origin = the highest level of education of the parents. Destination = the youth's current educational attainment position. noHS = did not finish high school. HS = completed high school but did not go on to tertiary education. Uni = enrolled in university at some point. Diagonals in grey represent youth having the same educational attainment as their parents by age 19. Off-diagonals in white thus represent youth who have different educational attainment than their parents at age 19. Thus the proportion of individuals in the off-diagonals represents the absolute rate of mobility.

Table 17.A4 Mobility Table: 2006 Cohorts

	Destination					
	Indigenous Row Percentages			Non-Indigenous Row Percentages		
Origin	noHS	HS	Uni	noHS	HS	Uni
noHS	26.1	62.3	1.17	23.9	45.2	31.0
HS	17.8	63.1	19.1	19.1	45.4	35.4
Uni	17.8	49.7	32.5	6.8	27.1	66.0

Notes: Origin = the highest level of education of the parents. Destination = the youth's current educational attainment position. noHS = did not finish high school. HS = completed high school but did not go on to tertiary education. Uni = enrolled in university at some point. Diagonals in grey represent youth having the same educational attainment as their parents by age 19. Off-diagonals in white thus represent youth who have different educational attainment than their parents at age 19. Thus the proportion of individuals in the off-diagonals represents the absolute rate of mobility.

Table 17.A5 Mobility Table: 2009 Cohorts

	Destination					
	Indigenous Row Percentages			Non-Indigenous Row Percentages		
Origin	noHS	HS	Uni	noHS	HS	Uni
noHS	8.1	85.2	6.7	17.1	42.6	40.3
HS	23.2	59.5	17.4	15.2	43.0	41.8
Uni	11.0	53.5	35.5	5.0	24.2	70.9

Notes: Origin = the highest level of education of the parents. Destination = the youth's current educational attainment position. noHS = did not finish high school. HS = completed high school but did not go on to tertiary education. Uni = enrolled in university at some point. Diagonals in grey represent youth having the same educational attainment as their parents by age 19. Off-diagonals in white thus represent youth who have different educational attainment than their parents at age 19. Thus the proportion of individuals in the off-diagonals represents the absolute rate of mobility.

18

University-to-Work Transition for Emerging Adult International Students in Canada

Natalee Popadiuk and Nancy Arthur

Introduction

One key element of globalization includes the movement or exchange of people and ideas from one part of the world to another, often for reasons related to education and employment (Arthur, 2014; Prilleltensky & Stead, 2012). International students are a growing population in higher education, with increasing numbers of younger international students pursuing secondary education in other countries prior to commencing higher education (Kuo & Rorsircar, 2006; Popadiuk, 2009, 2010). In addition to revenue generation, international student recruitment is a key aspect of campus internationalization to promote intercultural exchange between learners and to develop future international partnerships (Altbach & Knight, 2007; Brennan & Dellow, 2013). Countries such as the United States, Australia, the United Kingdom, and Germany have historically held the largest market share of international students, with other countries such as Canada, New Zealand, and countries within Europe attracting increasing numbers. Recently, there has been growth in the international student market within Asian countries and more students from other continents pursuing international education in Asia. These patterns of mobility reflect shifting trends in destination markets and the perceived economic, social, and employment advantages of studying in particular countries and regions of the world for future employability (Arthur & Nunes, 2014; Wintre, Kandasamy, Chavoshi, & Wright, 2015).

Research on the transition experiences of international students has predominantly focused on their initial entry into a new country and culture and related issues of cultural adjustment (Arthur, 2016). Depending on the

Natalee Popadiuk and Nancy Arthur, *University-to-Work Transition for Emerging Adult International Students in Canada* In: *Young Adult Development at the School-to-Work Transition.* E. Anne Marshall and Jennifer E. Symonds, Oxford University Press (2021).
 DOI: 10.1093/oso/9780190941512.003.0018.

degree of perceived differences between home and host countries, international students may experience major or minor changes in cultural norms, educational practices, language, or social interactions (Pedersen, 1991). Although such adjustments may be challenging, and at time be viewed as negative or overwhelming, experiencing cultural contrasts is a primary source of learning. Although many of the adjustments faced by international students are similar to local students who enter new educational systems in the transition to higher education, the experience of cross-cultural transition often adds additional layers of complexity to their identity development. It is through cross-cultural transitions that international students gain new perspectives about themselves, other people, and the world around them. In essence, international students embark on academic journeys, but the learning that occurs in a new country and cultural context can profoundly impact their identity development (Arthur, 2016).

The purpose of this chapter is to examine the university-to-work transition for emerging adult international students, with particular reference to our experience in the Canadian context. Although we categorically describe students who study in another country as international students, who often share common experiences, it is important to recognize the diversity of countries and cultures and subgroups within specific countries that are represented in the international student population. International students represent heterogeneous populations, and they have a myriad of influences on their cultural identities. The intersections of gender, race, social class, religion, and sexual orientation can shift during their experiences of living and learning across cultures and through the ways that other people in destination countries perceive them (Arthur, 2016; Arthur & Popadiuk, 2010).

Our examination of the university-to-work transition considers the broader context of international and cross-cultural transitions and related influences for the identity development of international students as emerging adults. We consider the strong connections between international education and work, as countries consider ways to recruit and retain international students, connected to national immigration strategies. The discussion of these contextual influences lays the groundwork for an examination of the identity development of international students as emerging adults. The connections between social relationships and social capital are explored from the perspective of supporting students to implement their academic and career goals and to foster positive personal identity and social integration. International students' experiences of university–work transition are integrally linked to more than their academic success; while navigating the immediate demands and customs of the local culture, they also must build social capital and social support for the university-to-work transition when they graduate.

Contextual Influences on the Identity Development of International Students

An examination of the identity development of international students goes beyond their initial transition to the destination country where they are studying. Transition experiences are ongoing, from the time of preparing to study in another country, through the phases of initially entering the new country, living and learning in the new country, and preparing for and implementing postgraduate plans (Arthur, 2007). Another key period of their cross-cultural journey occurs when international students approach the end of their university education and begin to implement plans for where they will live, continue studying, or work postgraduation.

There are multiple influences on international students' university-to-work transition, beginning with the decision to pursue international education. Motivations for pursuing international education are highly variable and depend on perceived conditions in both the host and home countries (Bohman, 2014; Mazzarol & Soutar, 2002). Common motivations for international education include the quality of education, lifestyle options, and pursuit of language and cross-cultural competencies. However, one of the main reasons that individuals and their families elect to study in other countries is the perceived advantage for future career options (Arthur, 2013). International education is often selected with the hope of a career advantage, including better prospects of future employment and immigration (She & Wotherspoon, 2013). Consequently, it is important to consider that the school-to-work transition of international students is not only a matter of planning for education in another country. There are complex and ever-changing influences on identity development while they are studying, and new issues may surface as they prepare for plans postgraduation.

Historically, international students were considered temporary sojourners, who were required as a condition of their student visa status to return home when they finished their studies. However, changing immigration policies in many countries afford opportunities for international students to gain work experience while studying, to gain work experience postgraduation, and to apply for permanent residency (Arthur & Nunes, 2014). These changes in immigration policy are connected to the view that international students are preferred immigrants and a desirable source of human capital; they bring experience and contacts from their home countries, they have completed degrees in the host country, and they have already been enculturated to local cultural norms (Arthur, 2013; Ziguras & Law, 2006).

For example, in 2015, Canada attracted a record number of 353,000 international students, who stated that they valued the quality of the educational system, the perceived safety, and quality of lifestyles in Canadian society (Canadian Bureau for International Education [CBIE], 2016). Approximately 51% of international students reported that they had plans to apply for permanent residency once they graduated (CBIE, 2016). Countries such as Australia, Canada, and New Zealand have also linked international students to immigration strategies for attracting skilled labor, while some countries such as the United States and the United Kingdom have restricted access. Immigration policies can change with little notice, reflecting shifting sentiments toward newcomers, including international students. Correspondingly, regulations and access to work permits can change rapidly, adversely impacting the university-to-work plans of international students. As a result, international students often hold precarious identities related to their plans for connecting education, employment, and immigration (Arthur & Nunes, 2014).

International Students as Emerging Adults

As noted in the introductory chapter to this book, the concept of emerging adulthood has gained popularity in studying the experiences of young people who are transitioning from school-to-work and/or between educational systems (Marshall & Symonds, this volume). As such, the concept "emerging adulthood" has been used extensively to describe young adults from affluent Western countries who spend extended periods of time obtaining postsecondary education before becoming self-sufficient adults (Arnett 2000, 2008). Arnett has characterized emerging adulthood with five features: (a) identity exploration ("Who am I in relation to school, work, and relationships?"), (b) self-focus ("What do I want to do and who do I want to be before taking on responsibilities?"), (c) instability ("Which university will I go to and where will I live? How will my family still support me in these changes?"), (d) feeling in-between ("In which ways am I responsible for myself, and how am I still dependent on my family?"), and (e) possibilities/optimism ("What will my future career and romantic relationships be like?")

Although these features may resonate for some, researchers have critiqued the overrepresentation of research participants as young White students at four-year colleges. Critics contend that the majority of students in the emerging adulthood literature hold a higher socioeconomic status (SES), who have the luxury and financial support from parents to attend postsecondary education and spend time contemplating their careers (e.g., Cote, 2014; Schoon, Chen, Kneale, & Jager, 2012). These criticisms are congruent with Blustein's (2006) assessment of dominant career theories as largely based on a relatively affluent, privileged, White North American demographic. Even Arnett (2000) acknowledges that there is little evidence to suggest that emerging adulthood is relevant across diverse cultural groups. Some researchers have offered that cultural beliefs and practices in countries like China (Nelson, Badger, & Wu, 2004; Nelson & Chen, 2007) and India (Seiter & Nelson, 2011) differ substantially, and therefore, the concept of emerging adulthood is not transferable to other cultures.

Therefore, the extent to which the concept of emerging adulthood transcends cultural contexts requires critical examination. For example, some have critiqued the emphasis on autonomy and independence as markers of adulthood within an individualistic world view, in contrast to a collectivist world view of valuing connection and interdependent family and community relations throughout the life course (Oyserman, Coon, & Kemmelmeier, 2002). There has also been criticism levied against perspectives of human development that fail to acknowledge variations due to gender and cultural constructions of norms and expectations for career and life roles (Schultheiss, 2007). The assumptions of linear progress and autonomy in the developmental milestones associated with adolescence and adulthood and related markers in people's career development is problematic when uniformly applied (Flores, 2009). As such, there is an assumption held by many people in industrialized societies that individuals will complete their education prior to working and establishing a family. In reality, many students are holding employment while pursuing education and managing extensive family and community responsibilities as caregivers to their own children or taking care of parents or other family members. The social caretaking roles are often overshadowed by the predominant view of paid employment as the more important role in conceptualizing people's transition to adulthood (Richardson, 2012).

Despite these critiques, a recent qualitative study on international student motivations by Wintre and her colleagues (2015) found support for the emerging adulthood concept with a group of 64 undergraduate students from 26 countries. Five out of eight themes developed from the data matched the five hallmark features of Arnett's emerging adulthood. First, Wintre et al.'s motivational theme of new experiences (e.g., to meet new people, self-understanding) matched Arnett's (2000) concept of identity exploration. Second, education (e.g., improving career opportunities) mapped onto Arnett's (2000) concept of self-focus. Third, the themes of location (e.g., choosing which city to live in) and friends/relatives in Canada (e.g., deciding to live with relatives) fit into the concept of instability. Financial reasons (e.g., locating affordable tuition and accommodation), the fourth theme, matched Arnett's feeling in-between feature. Finally, future prospects of career/immigration to the host country (e.g., improving English fluency, getting a good job) corresponded with the feature of possibilities/optimism. The results of this study demonstrated that many of the key features of emerging adulthood are relevant and applicable to some international students.

Three themes, however, were unique and fell outside of Arnett's five hallmark features. The issues included the additional financial strain due to higher international student tuition fees, restrictions on paid employment, the strength of social support to study abroad, the role of parental involvement, having family or friends already living in the host city, and peer support (Wintre et al., 2015). The findings regarding social support, family involvement, and peer support are congruent with our study that examined the importance of international students' key relationships at home and abroad in supporting international student adjustment and academic success (Popadiuk & Arthur, 2014). Thus, the concept of emerging adulthood might be a salient construct for many international students, although more research is needed to test the concept with this diverse student population.

International Student Identity Development

No single theory or definition is linked to international student identity development in the literature. Instead, researchers draw upon a variety of theories and concepts when examining identity issues with this population. For example, Li, Marbley, Bradly, and Lan (2016) utilized ethnic identity as described by Helms (1993) and Phinney (1996) when studying help-seeking attitudes of Chinese international students. Some researchers (e.g., Imamura & Zhang, 2014) have used the Common Ingroup Identity Model developed by Gaertner, Rust, Dovidio, Bachman, and Anastasio (1994). Others have used the rejection-identification model and found that when international students were rejected by the host culture, they identified with other international students of different linguistic, ethnic, and national backgrounds (Schmitt, Spears, & Branscombe, 2003). Given the sheer number of identity theories and culturally relevant concepts utilized in international student research, we will only explore a few pertinent ideas.

One of the dominant theories about identity and culture stems from the work of Markus and Kitayama (1991). These researchers postulated that people in Western countries (e.g., North America) are primarily oriented toward independence, while people in Eastern cultures (e.g., Japan) tend to be interdependent with others and the social context. Similarly, Triandis (1995) developed a theory based on individualism and collectivism, which he portrayed as cultural syndromes. Despite evidence to the contrary, researchers and practitioners have continued to perpetuate these early ideas that have reified the dualistic notion of Western individualism and independence and Eastern collectivism and interdependence (Oyserman et al., 2002). More recently, research headed by Vignoles et al. (2016), along with 70 multinational co-researchers, conducted studies to determine whether the traditional concepts of Markus and Kitayama's (1991) identity theory could be better understood and clarified. Their results showed that, contrary to popular belief, people and regions of the world cannot be categorized as either collectivist or individualist and instead individual differences need to be assessed along a continuum using a multifaceted approach (Vignoles et al., 2016).

Vignoles and her team (2016) suggest that a shift is required for cultural identity research. They recommend that researchers avoid using ethnicity and geography, or the East versus West dichotomy, when discussing people from other regions and cultural backgrounds. Their findings showed that "much cultural variation was within, rather than between, these regions" (Vignoles et al., 2016, p. 992). This finding is consistent with other research about within-group variability (e.g., Lee & Chen, 2015), and strengthens Crenshaw's (1991) assertion that "ignoring difference within groups contributes to tension among groups" (p. 1242). From their data, these researchers developed a seven-dimensional model of self-construal that assessed independence and interdependence across seven domains of personal and social functioning: (a) defining the self: difference to similarity; (b) experiencing the self: self-containment to connection to others; (c) making decisions: self-direction to receptiveness to influence; (d) looking after oneself: self-reliance to dependence on others; (e) moving between contexts: consistency to variability; (6) communicating with others: self-expression to harmony; (7) dealing with conflicting interests: self-interest to commitment to others (see Vignoles et al., 2016, for a full description of the model). Instead of applying a simplistic East–West or individualism–collectivism label to individuals and groups, this seven-dimensional model provides the framework for examining the range and nuances of behavior within and across cultures.

Another common and well-known theory relevant to better understanding international student identity development is social identity theory, which states that people tacitly develop their identity and sense of self by being a member in one or more social groups in which they are invested emotionally (Tajfel & Turner, 1979). These researchers stated that individuals count on being able to make positive comparisons to people in other groups (outgroups), as well as within their own group (ingroups). The theory explains that when the comparison is negative, and the person feels stigmatized or marginalized for one or more of their social group memberships (e.g., ethnicity, nationality), they might attempt to leave the group. Alternatively, they might decide to stay in the group but become more distinctive and disengaged from the group that has rejected them. Social identity theory (Tajfel & Turner, 1979) is relevant to international student identity, in that lived experiences during their transition largely depend on their ingroup–outgroup statuses in the host country.

In essence, each time an international student turns around and talks to someone new in a different context, they need to renegotiate their identities (Popadiuk & Marshall, 2011). Many international students have experiences that negatively and, unexpectedly, make them question who they are. Thus, whether their sense of self-worth increases or decreases partly depends on the implicit and unspoken power differentials they bump up against and must negotiate in the new context. Consider an international student who leaves home to study abroad and suddenly finds that they have gone from in-group to outgroup, from dominant to nondominant, from high-status to low-status, from fluent language speaker to English language learner. For example, research has shown that many Chinese and Korean international students face prejudice and discrimination when studying abroad (e.g., Lin & Flores, 2013), which would effectively lower their social status. For international students who might be seen negatively and treated poorly by some members of the host country, it is not difficult to imagine that these experiences would negatively impact a person's sense of identity and be a barrier for reaching outside their own social groups.

Finally, the idea that emerging adulthood can represent marked changes in lifestyle, mental health, relationships, and identity (see Schwartz, 2016, for background studies) goes beyond the ways that typical life trajectories in developmental literature have been portrayed. Instead, international students' emerging identity development can evolve into areas of new-found autonomy that is culturally relevant and goes beyond geographic and ethnic distinctions to engage in ways outside the protection of, or conversely, abuse from, parents, peers, and teachers. Specifically, Schwartz (2016) theorizes that there are two faces associated with this developmental stage:

> Someone who experienced a difficult childhood can develop a positive and successful life trajectory in his or her 20s, and someone whose early life was fairly

> comfortable can become involved in personally or socially destructive activities as an emerging adult. Such a redirection can be more than a gain or a loss—it represents a wholesale change in how one's life is experienced. (p. 307)

This idea is supported by other researchers who have emphasized the motivation for international education as a strategy to overcome obstacles found in students' home countries (e.g., Yan, 2017). One narrative includes an in-depth case study about a 27-year-old female international student who had grown up in an abusive family, but who reconstructed her relationship dynamics with others (Martinez, 2006). Similarly, while interviewing international students over the years, we have also heard some participants recount stories of being bullied, battered, or belittled by peers, romantic partners, and parents during their adolescence or early adulthood. Of the participants who shared difficult personal stories, they reported a drastic improvement in their well-being, sense of identity, and relational experiences upon arriving and living in Canada. These particular international students actively sought out a culturally acceptable escape by seeking education half-way around the world to re-invent themselves and "experience a wholesale change" (Schwartz, 2016) in their identities and lives. Thus, international students who leave difficult relational histories have the opportunity to start a new life, to reinvent oneself, to have a new beginning divergent from their past struggles.

These identity theories provide a snapshot into only a handful of perspectives that could be applicable to international student identity development. The absence of an evidence-based or standardized definition leaves room for many challenges, including a lack of a coherent theory and a common language for researchers and practitioners alike. On the other hand, the ability to select identity theories that are relevant for the context helps to ensure a fluidity and openness to new ways of seeing and knowing the experiences of international students. It also mitigates the rigidity that might be found when using stage, categorical, or outdated theories that tend to narrow the focus and limit the view of the full experience of people's lives. Reviewing these theories here demonstrates the importance of thinking broadly by continuing to expand our understanding with new ideas, research, and fluid ways of conceptualizing international student identities.

Building Social Capital and Social Support

Given the opportunity to welcome large numbers of educated young adults into Canadian society each year, it is important that university administrators, employers in workplaces, and government policymakers understand the factors that promote success during the university-to-work transition. Specifically, we need knowledge about the individual, relational, organizational, and societal contexts that contribute to effective international student job obtainment within the Canadian labor market. For this purpose, we will first discuss the concept of social capital and then highlight examples of four key sources of social support, through which international students can build social capital to facilitate the university-to-work transition (Arthur, 2017; Beech, 2014; Popadiuk & Arthur, 2014). These sources include family, peers, academic faculty and supervisors, and institutional support.

Social capital is a popular term with a long tradition that spans disciplinary boundaries (see Engbers, Thompson, & Slaper, 2017, for a history and description of the methodological challenges of this concept). Common definitions hinge on the value or benefit one derives from belonging to social groups, networks, or institutions, which can be gained from shared culture, purposes, or norms (Jensen & Jetten, 2015; Putnam, 2000). While there are a variety of definitions, there are two key components: (a) accessibility or network extension (family, friends, or institutions that one is connected to) and (b) mobilization, which is the ability to gain resources from these networks (e.g., a job, inside information; other connections; Engbers et al., 2017; Perna & Titus, 2005). Thus, students from educated middle class professional families will have far greater social capital than students of color from poor or working class background for better paying, high-status positions. For example, a young adult with professional parents working in business may approach their parents or friends of their parents for a corporate summer job while attending university. This is in contrast to research that finds that poor, minority, or first-generation students may not have role models who can support them in pursuing education and are, therefore, less likely to attend university or to complete their studies (e.g., Simmons, 2011).

Two additional concepts that are associated with social capital are bonding (strong ties) and bridging (weak ties; Putnam, 2000). Those who have more in common, such as cultural background or linguistic commonality, typically experience greater bonding or closeness with others in their network. This, in turn, creates strong social ties and high social capital. For example, an international student who already has family living and working in the host destination will have immediate access to more local knowledge and supports than new international students without family. Alternatively, bridging social capital or weak ties are the more tenuous connections that are created outside of one's network. For example, professors may be considered bridging social capital; that is, they are not close to new international students, but given the academic relationship, the student has access to and can request help from the professor. Bridging ties can develop into bonding or strong ties with time and greater emotional connection.

Family Sources of Social Capital

Tierney (2000) and Bordieu (1986) have suggested that the social capital found in one's family background can either facilitate or hinder academic persistence at university. Family members are a key source of social capital by providing (a) instrumental support predeparture regarding the decision to study in another country, (b) financial and emotional support while they are studying in the host country, and (c) ideas and influence toward implementing plans postgraduation. One of the issues for international students is that social capital from their family's connections or from their educational success at home may or may not be relevant or accessible in the new cultural context. An example of international student social capital highlighted in Wintre and colleagues' (2015) study discussed earlier was the finding that many international students lived in a city and country in which they already had relatives. We have also noticed this in a number of our studies (e.g., Popadiuk & Arthur, 2014) in which we found that a portion of international students used their own or their families' social capital to locate a personal resource in the host country (person/family/home) where they could live while attending school or who they could reach out to for assistance and a sense of social belonging.

One of the biases in the international student literature is the tendency to focus on their experiences as autonomous and independent from family members who accompany them (Chittooran & Sankar-Gomes, 2007). Spouses, or accompanying partners, can be a tremendous source of social capital as they are often the ones who are primarily responsible for navigating the household responsibilities, school and childcare, and building neighborhood resources (Cui, Arthur, & Domene, 2017). In essence, this source of social capital frees international students to focus on their academic work while the accompanying partner figures out how to navigate local resources and builds community connections. Similar to the literature that focuses exclusively on international student adjustment, the limited literature on families tends to focus on their corresponding issues of adjustment (Chittooran & Sankar-Gomes, 2007), thereby ignoring the social capital that family members often contribute toward supporting international student success (Cui et al., 2017).

Peers and Friendships as Sources of Social Capital

Besides bonding relationships or strong ties, social capital theory also suggests that individuals can reach across groups to create bridging relationships or weak ties with others in the social network who have less in common with them. In terms of international students, they might use bridging social capital to reach beyond their own co-national group to connect with domestically born students (weak ties). However, research has consistently shown that it tends to be very difficult for many international students to develop friendships with domestic students (e.g., Sakurai, McCall-Wolf, & Kashima, 2010). Thus, many international students make friends with co-nationals from the same region in the world, nationality, and language, where they feel accepted and understand the cultural context of friendship.

Yet others find it easier to become friends with other new international students from diverse ethnicities and languages, based on their shared international student status, struggles with learning English, and difficulties connecting with local domestic students (Schmidt, Spears, & Branscombe, 2003). Although bonding social capital with other students can facilitate their sense of belonging by creating a safety net, this type of bonding can also hinder academic identity development by creating groups with their own set of norms and social control (Jensen & Jetten, 2015; Putnam, 2000). One negative outcome of strong ties with other students can be the limited bridging interactions with educators (Tinto, 1993), who have been identified as making the most impact on students' academic and professional identities (Jensen & Jetten, 2015).

Despite the emphasis on challenges faced by international students in seeking friendship and social connection (Johnson & Sandhu, 2007), many are able to develop close and meaningful relationships in the host country. Social bonds can last beyond the international education experience and global friendships can be maintained for years, with the advantages of the Internet and other forms of social media. For some international students, serious issues of perceived relationship loss can surface as they face the realities of graduation, returning home, or moving to another destination to pursue additional educational or employment opportunities. With the culmination of several years, many international students realize the close connections and bonds that they have developed in a country that is their current home (Arthur, 2016). These deep friendships, which some international students refer to as their new family, are one key reason for deciding to permanently immigrate to the host country (Popadiuk & Arthur, 2014). Relationships that were initially only bridging social capital became bonding social capital.

Academic Faculty and Supervisors

A large part of identity development for international students occurs through academic roles and their perception of mastery or failure at managing the demands of their academic program in a new educational environment. It is critical that academic faculty are prepared to support international students' academic success through teaching, supervision, and mentoring (Arthur, 2017; Glass, Kociolek, Wongtrirat, Lynch, & Cong, 2015).

For many international students, faculty members are more than instructors; they are a key source of social capital for international students to navigate the academic system and prepare for the university-to-work transition (Arthur, 2017; Popadiuk & Arthur, 2014). Additionally, the supervisory relationship has been implicated in the perceived quality of the academic experience and whether or not international students have a strong sense of belonging in the local environment (Curtin, Stewart & Ostrove, 2013; Glass et al., 2015; Gopal, 2016). Presumably, the supervisory relationship can offer a secure base (Bowlby, 1988) from which international students can feel more confident in testing out new directions as a learner, thereby promoting positive identity development. In many ways, international students rely on their academic supervisors for information sharing, advice, and guidance related to their academic program, but that relationship often extends to managing many other aspects of their transition experiences.

Academic supervisors have a unique role in mentoring students and preparing them for their future career development, particularly for graduate students (Gopal, 2016). Academic supervisors not only can guide international students about local expectations for academic standards, but they also help them appreciate the connections between academic content and the knowledge and skills sought by employers. When academic faculty members share knowledge about employment opportunities and help international students to build a network of employment contacts, they are opening a door for future career success (Popadiuk & Arthur, 2014). To quote an international student who participated in one of our research studies, "We have a network, but it is at home." International students require support to build social capital for employment. Research has suggested that prior experience in their home country may not be viewed as important as local experience. Similar to the job-seeking experiences of other new immigrants, some employers favor local credentials and experience, which can be used to screen out international applicants (Nunes & Arthur, 2013).

For students planning to stay in the destination country, academic faculty and supervisors can open doors for employment while international students are studying, help them link to university employment programs, such as co-op terms, and help them to understand expectations in the local employment context. Alternatively, international students may need help to represent their international credentials to employers and make the most of their unique experience. Academic supervisors are a valuable source of information; they can help students to make contacts and provide references for employment. The supervisory and mentoring role is particularly important in supporting international students to learn about options that support the transition to employment following graduation (Arthur, 2017). For students who are returning to their home destination or pursuing educational or employment opportunities in other countries, references from faculty and particularly the academic supervisor are a critical form of "academic currency" for attesting to the transferability of credentials and their suitability for employment (Campbell, 2010). It is through the academic record, local work experience, and the references provided to students that both local and international experience can be represented as assets in job-seeking during the university-to-work transition.

In summary, academic faculty, and particularly academic supervisors, are key relationships for international students to build social capital. Faculty and supervisors are a critical resource for guiding students during the initial adjustment to the academic environment, for helping them to build new relationships with other students, and for helping them gain employment experience while studying and postgraduation. Faculty and academic supervisors are often the pivotal relationship for helping international students expand their local network and for seeking additional resources. Additionally, when students experience major adjustment issues, including mental health issues, faculty members can offer referral and help to mitigate reluctance toward help-seeking through providing information and encouragement to seek support through campus services (Arthur, 2016, 2017).

Institutional Support for International Students

Services for international students have tended to focus on their initial cultural adjustment to the local academic environment, without taking a holistic view of their motivations, goals, and longer-term development. International students' needs for institutional support varies over time, as a result of their level of engagement in the local culture and as a result of changing conditions in either their home or host countries (Arthur, 2007). University personnel are encouraged to plan continuous orientation or workshops over time strategically placed, rather than a single orientation during the first week of classes, to address the developmental needs of students throughout their studies. Many international students in some of our research projects report that they struggled to understand the English-speaking guests at their orientations (e.g., student services, international office, counseling) who usually spoke too quickly and provided too much information. Instead of having a lengthy orientation (e.g., a full day or more) of information at the beginning of the academic year when students are already overwhelmed, a "rolling orientation" or a workshop per month could provide students with specific information that meets their developmental and academic needs at that time in their studies (e.g., mid-term, finals, winter blues). Thus, institutions need to strategically consider the most effective ways to orient and provide ongoing support to international students to address academic, adjustment, and developmental issues across time.

Service providers including medical services, allied health professionals, chaplaincy, and career services are encouraged to work together to design and deliver culturally informed educational, preventative, and remedial services. Counselors who build a profile in the international student center on campus are soon regarded as allies for referral and consultation from international student advisors. Counselors are also encouraged to work closely with academic departments and gain the trust of faculty members, who can help to identify and students who may need additional supports to manage their cross-cultural transitions (Arthur, 2016).

Given the emphasis placed by many students on international education as an avenue towards increasing employment options post-graduation, an obvious area of growth for supporting international students is in the domain of career services (Arthur, 2007). International students can be supported to build critical employability skills while they are a student, such as part-time work, internships, and building employer contacts, and also be supported for job-search assistance in the transition from university to work. Regardless of where international students plan to locate post-graduation (e.g., home, destination country, or other countries), career services can help students to build knowledge and skills about their emerging identities as workers and contributing members of the labor force.

Finally, it is important for institutions to be aware of how students from different backgrounds may interact with institutional supports that may not meet their needs. In a study by Jensen and Jetten (2015), students from higher SESs in Sweden and the United States made external institutional attributions about academic problems that they experienced. For example, more affluent students from both countries suggested that the professor was not giving them enough individualized attention (it was the professor's fault), and that is why they were struggling. However, students from lower SESs tended to make negative internal attributions about their academic challenges. For example, students thought they should know how to do things (it was their own fault), so they did not want to bother the professor (Jensen & Jetton, 2015). These researchers found that students from a higher SES were more likely to push for structural and institutional change, while students from a lower SES were more likely to remain quiet about their needs.

Although this study did not focus specifically on international students, the findings highlight that the most obvious social identity (e.g., ethnicity, country of origin, international student status) is not always the most salient social identity that needs to be considered and addressed. In sum, Jensen and Jetten (2015) suggest that institutional support for students from high and low SES needs to be differentiated. Specifically, low SES students benefit more from a focus on academic activities, rather than bonding activities. This focus was found to facilitate academic and professional identity development through building bridging social capital with educators and professionals, rather than bonding activities with other students. Thus, students from a lower SES background were given the opportunity to develop bridging social capital that students from higher social classes did not require. The results of this research underscore a previous point raised that international students are not a homogenous group, and research can inform the design and delivery of support services to help build and bridge sources of social capital.

Future Directions and Concluding Comments

The experiences of international students are strongly influenced by their motivations for seeking education in another country, the degree to which they are equipped to manage cross-cultural transitions, their access to social capital in their home counties, and their ability to build new sources of social capital in destination countries. The university-to-work transition for international students is pivotal for developing a personal sense of belonging in the local context and for developing the skills and experience that help international students achieve their career goals. The perception of belonging is tied to current and future identities as workers and citizens in their home countries or in the countries where they elect to study and to the enhancement of their mobility to other countries tied to a global economy. Although the majority of international students return home or pursue education or employment in other countries, the link between their motivations to pursue international studies, future employability, and career goals need to be underscored in academic planning and service delivery.

In our examination of the school-to-work transition, we have primarily focused on the time period while students are studying internationally, yet the experience of development and identity growth does not end upon graduation. Research is needed that follows international students postgraduation to explore their experiences of navigating the university-to-work transition. In destination countries, such as Canada, researchers might consider the influence shifting economic conditions and how well the experiences of international students match the growing rhetoric about international students as preferred immigrants (Arthur & Nunes, 2014; Ziguras & Law, 2006). Policies and programs can be built to encourage international student recruitment, but their actual success in navigating conditions in the labor market needs to be documented to provide insights, directions, and their voices in determining what resources are needed.

Although many international students report that they want to stay in Canada (CBIE, 2016), the majority return home. Greater attention is needed to research about the university-to-work transition when the employment context is the home country. Such research might go beyond accounts of reverse culture shock, a concept that might need updating and revising based on new and exciting developments in the field. Instead, researchers need to focus on structural and systemic aspects of employment, the perceived value of international education, and the transition from international student to worker in their home countries (Arthur, 2003; Leung, 2007). Lastly, the increasing mobility and opportunities of the global labor market offer unprecedented opportunities for students to plan and implement multiple career pathways during their adulthood. Researchers might consider ways to cultivate the attributes, skills, and identities of students as global careerists (Reichrath-Smith & Neault, 2013). After all, international students are individuals who already have a lot of experience living and learning across cultural contexts and their future identities as workers transcend international borders.

References

Altbach, P., & Knight, J. (2007). The internationalization of higher education: Motivations and realities. *Journal of Studies in International Education*, *11*, 290–305. doi:10.1177/1028315307303542

Arnett, J. J. (2000). Emerging adulthood: A theory of development from the late teens through twenties. *American Psychologist*, *55*, 469–480. doi:10.1037/0003-066X.55.5.469

Arnett, J. J. (2008). The neglected 95%: Why American psychology needs to become less American. *American Psychologist*, 63, 602. doi:10.1037/0003-066X.63.7.602

Arthur, N. (2003). Preparing international students for the re-entry transition. *Canadian Journal of Counselling*, *37*(3), 173–185.

Arthur, N. (2007). Career planning and decision-making needs of international students. In M. Pope & H. Singaravelu (Eds.), *A handbook for counselling international students in the United States* (pp. 37–56). Alexandria, VA: American Counseling Association.

Arthur, N. (2013). International students and career development: Human capital in the global skills race. *Journal of the National Institute for Career Education and Counselling*, *31*, 43–50. doi:10.1080/03075079.2017.1293876

Arthur, N. (2014). Social justice in the Age of Talent. *International Journal of Educational and Vocational Guidance*, *14*(1), 47–60. doi:10.1007/s10775-013-9255-x

Arthur, N. (2016). Counselling international students in the context of cross-cultural transitions. In J. Draguns, W. Lonner, P. Pedersen, J. Trimble, & M. Scharrón del Río (Eds.), *Counselling across cultures* (7th ed., 301–322). Thousand Oaks, CA: SAGE.

Arthur, N. (2017). Supporting international students through strengthening their social resources. *Studies in Higher Education*, *5*, 887–894. doi:10.1080/03075079.2017.1293876

Arthur, N., & Nunes, S. (2014). Should I stay or should I go home? Career guidance with international students. In G. Arulmani, A. Bakshi, F. Leong, & T. Watts (Eds.), *Handbook of career development: International perspectives* (pp. 587–606). New York, NY: Springer.

Arthur, N., & Popadiuk, N. E. (2010). A cultural formulation approach to career counseling with international students. *Journal of Career Development*, *37*, 423–440. doi:10.1177/0894845309345845

Beech, S. (2014). International student mobility: The role of social networks. *Social & Cultural Geography*, *16*, 332–350. doi:10.1080/14649365.2014.983961

Blustein, D. L. (2006). *The psychology of working: A new perspective for career development, counseling, and public policy*. Mahwah, NJ: Erlbaum.

Bohman, E. (2014). Attracting the world: Institutional initiatives' effects on international students' decision to enroll. *Community College Journal of Research and Practice*, *38*(8), 710–720. doi:10.1080/10668926.2014.897081

Bordieu, P. (1986). The forms of capital. In J. Richardson (Ed.), *Handbook of theory and research for the sociology of education* (pp. 241–258). Westport, CT: Greenwood.

Brennan, M., & Dellow, D. A. (2013). International students as a resource for achieving comprehensive internationalization. *New Directions for Community Colleges*, *161*, 27–37. doi:10.1002/cc.20046

Bowlby, J. (1988). *A secure base: Parent–child attachments and healthy human relationships*: New York, NY: Basic Books.

Campbell, A. (2010). Developing generic skills and attributes of international students: The (ir)relevance of the Australian university experience. *Journal of Higher Education Policy & Management*, *32*, 487–497. doi:10.1080/1360080X.2010.511121

Canadian Bureau for International Education. (2016). Facts and figures. Retrieved from https://cbie.ca/media/facts-and-figures/

Chittooran, M., & Sankar-Gomes, A. (2007). The families of international students in U.S. universities: Adjustment issues and implications for counselors. In M. Pope & H. Singaravelu (Eds.), *A handbook for counselling international students in the United States* (pp. 113–136). Alexandria, VA: American Counseling Association.

Cote, J. E. (2014). The dangerous myth of emerging adulthood: An evidence-based critique of a flawed developmental theory. *Applied Developmental Science*, *18*, 177–188.

Crenshaw, K. (1991). Mapping the margins: intersectionality, identity politics, and violence against women of color. *Stanford Law Review*, *43*, 1241–1299. doi:10.2307/1229039

Cui, D., Arthur, N., & Domene, J. (2017). What is missing from the literature on accompanying spouses of international students? Reflections on three issues. *Canadian Journal of Higher Education, 47*(1), 171–190.

Curtin, N., Stewart, A. J., & Ostrove, J. M. (2013). Fostering academic self-concept: Advisor support and sense of belonging among international and domestic graduate students. *American Educational Research Journal, 50*, 108–137. doi:10.3102/000283121244662

Engbers, T. A., Thompson, M. F., & Slaper, T. F. (2017). Theory and measurement in social capital research. *Sociology Indices Research, 132*, 537–555. doi:10.1007/s11205-016-1299-0

Flores, L. (2009). Empowering life choices: Career counseling in the contexts of race and class. In N. Gysbers, M. Heppner, & J. Johnston (Eds.), *Career counseling: Contexts, processes, and techniques* (pp. 49–74). Alexandria, VA: American Counseling Association.

Gaertner, S. L., Rust, M. C., Dovidio, J. F., Bachman, B. A., & Anastasio, P. A. (1994). The contact hypothesis: The role a common ingroup identity on reducing intergroup bias. *Small Group Research, 25*, 224–249. doi:10.1177/1046496494252005

Glass, C., Kociolek, E., Wongtrirat, R., Lynch, J., & Cong, S. (2015). Uneven experiences: The impact of student-faculty interactions on international students' sense of belonging. *Journal of International Students*, 5(4), 353–367.

Gopal, A. (2016). Academic experiences of international graduate students: The Canadian perspective in the context of internationalization. In K. Bista & C. Foster (Eds.), *Exploring the social and academic experiences of international students in higher education institutions* (pp. 21–37). Hershey, PA: IGI Global.

Helms, J. E. (1993). Introduction: Review of racial identity terminology. In J. E. Helms (Ed.), *Black and White racial identity: Theory, research, and practice* (pp. 3–8). Westport, CT: Praeger.

Imamura, M., & Zhang, Y. B. (2014). Functions of the common ingroup identity model and acculturation strategies in intercultural communication: American host nationals' communication with Chinese international students. *International Journal of Intercultural Relations, 43*(Pt B), 227–238.

Jensen, D. H., & Jetten, J. (2015). Bridging and bonding interactions in higher education: social capital and students' academic and professional identity formation. *Frontiers in Psychology, 6*(126), 1–11. doi:10.3389/fpsyg.2015.0012610.1016/j.ijintrel.2014.08.018

Johnson, L., & Sandhu, D. (2007). Isolation, adjustment, and acculturation issues of international students: Intervention strategies for counselors. In M. Pope & H. Singaravelu (Eds.), *A handbook for counselling international students in the United States* (pp. 13–36). Alexandria, VA: American Counseling Association.

Kuo, B. C. H., & Roysircar, G. (2006). An exploratory study of cross-cultural adaptation of adolescent Taiwanese unaccompanied sojourners in Canada. *International Journal of Intercultural Relations, 30*(2), 159–183. doi:10.1016/j.ijintrel.2005.07.007

Lee, K., & Chen, S. (2015). Brief report: Interpersonal conflicts between Chinese and Taiwanese international students. *Journal of Psychology and Behavioral Science, 3*(2), 54–60. doi:10.15640/jpbs.v3n2a7

Leung, A. (2007). Returning home and issues related to reverse culture shock. In M. Pope & H. Singaravelu (Eds.), *A handbook for counselling international students in the United States* (pp. 37–56). Alexandria, VA: American Counseling Association.

Li, J, Marbley, A. F., Bradley, L. J., & Lan, W. (2016). Attitudes toward seeking professional counseling services among Chinese international students: acculturation, ethnic identity, and English proficiency. *Journal of Multicultural Counseling and Development, 44*, 65–76. doi:10.1002/jmcd.12037

Lin, Y. J., & Flores, L. Y. (2013). Job search self-efficacy of East Asian international graduate students. *Journal of Career Development, 40*, 186–202. doi:10.1177/0894845311418655

Markus, H. R., & Kitayama, S. (1991). Culture and the self: implications for cognition, emotion, and motivation. *Psychological Review, 98*, 224–253. doi:10.1037/0033-295X.98.2.224

Martinez, C. (2006). Abusive family experiences and object relations disturbances: a case study. *Clinical Case Studies, 5*, 209–219. doi:10.1177/1534650104264922

Mazzarol, T., & Soutar, G. N. (2002). "Push-pull" factors influencing international student destination choice. *International Journal of Educational Management, 16*(2), 82–90. doi:10.1108/09513540210418403

Phinney, J. S. (1996). Understanding ethnic diversity: The role of ethnic identity. *American Behavioral Scientist, 40*, 143–152. doi:10.1177/0002764296040002005

Nelson, L. J., Badger, S., & Wu, B. (2004). The influence of culture in emerging adulthood: perspectives of Chinese college students. *International Journal of Behavioural Development, 28*, 26–36. doi:10.1080/01650250344000244

Nelson, L. J., & Chen, X. (2007). Emerging adulthood in China: The role of social and cultural factors. *Child Development Perspectives, 1*, 86–91. doi:10.1111/j.1750-8606.2007.00020.x

Nunes, S., & Arthur, N. (2013). International students' experiences of integrating into the workforce. *Journal of Employment Counseling, 50*, 34–45. doi:10.1002/j.2161-1920.2013.00023.x

Oyserman, D., Coon, H., & Kemmelmeier, M. (2002). Rethinking individualism and collectivism: Evaluation of theoretical assumptions and meta-analyses. *Psychological Bulletin, 128*(1), 3–72. doi:10.1037//0033-2909.128.1.3

Pedersen, P. (1991). Counseling international students. *The Counseling Psychologist, 19*(1), 10–58. doi:10.1177/0011000091191002

Perna, L.W., & Titus, M.A. (2005). The relationship between parental involvement as social capital and college enrollment: an examination of racial/ethnic group differences. *Journal of Higher Education, 76*, 485–518. doi:10.1353/jhe.2005.0036

Popadiuk, N. E. (2009). Unaccompanied Asian secondary students in Canada. *International Journal for the Advancement of Counselling, 31*(4), 229–243.

Popadiuk, N. E. (2010). Asian international student transition to high school in Canada. *The Qualitative Report, 15*(6), 1523–1548.

Popadiuk, N., & Arthur, N. (2014). Key relationships for international student university-to-work transitions. *Journal of Career Development, 41*(2), 122–140. doi:10.1177/0894845313481851

Popadiuk, N. E., & Marshall, S. (2011). East Asian international student experiences as learners of English as an additional language: Implications for school counsellors. *Canadian Journal of Counselling and Psychotherapy, 45*(3), 220–239. doi:10.1037/h0042025

Prilleltensky, I., & Stead, G. B. (2012). Critical psychology and career development: Unpacking the adjustment-challenge dilemma. *Journal of Career Development, 39*, 321–340. doi:10.1177/0894845310384403

Putnam, R. D. (2000). *Bowling along: The collapse and revival of American community*. New York, NY: Simon & Schuster.

Reichrath-Smith, C., & Neault, R. A. (2013). The global careerist: Internal and external supports needed for success. *Journal of the National Institute for Career Education and Counselling, 31*, 51–58.

Richardson, M. S. (2012). Counseling for work and relationship. *The Counseling Psychologist, 40*(2), 190–242. doi:10.1177/0011000011406452

Sakurai, T., McCall-Wolf, F., & Kashima, E. S. (2010). Building intercultural links: the impact of a multicultural intervention programme on social ties of international students in Australia. *International Journal of Intercultural Relations, 34*, 176–185. doi:10.1016/j.ijintrel.2009.11.002

Schmitt, M. T., Spears, R., & Branscombe, N. R. (2003). Constructing a minority group identity out of shared rejection: The case of international students. *European Journal of Social Psychology, 33*, 1–12. doi:10.1002/ejsp.131

Schoon, I., Chen, M., Kneale, D., & Jager, J. (2012). Becoming adults in Britain: Lifestyles and well-being in times of social change. *Longitudinal and Life Course Studies*, *3*, 173–189. doi:10.14301/llcs.v3i2.181

Schultheiss, D. E. P. (2007). The emergence of a relational cultural paradigm for vocational psychology. *International Journal of Educational and Vocational Guidance*, *7*, 191–201. doi:10.1007/s10775-007-9123-7

Schwartz, S. J. (2016). Turning point for a turning point: Advancing emerging adulthood theory and research. *Emerging Adulthood*, *4*(5), 307–317. doi:10.1177/2167696815624640

Seiter, L. N., & Nelson, L. J. (2011). An examination of emerging adulthood in college students and nonstudents in India. *Journal of Adolescent Research*, *20*, 1–31. doi:10.1177/0743558410391262

She, Q., & Wotherspoon, T. (2013). International student mobility and highly skilled migration: A comparative study of Canada, the United States, and the United Kingdom. *Sociology, Social Work and Family Studies*, *2*(1), 132–146. doi:10.1186/2193-1801-2-132

Simmons, O. S. (2011). Lost in transition: the implications of social capital for higher education access. *Notre Dame Law Review*, *87*, 205–252.

Tajfel, H., & Turner, J. (1979). An integrative theory of intergroup conflict. In W.G. Austin & S. Worchel (Eds.). *The social psychology of intergroup relations* (pp. 33–47). Monterey, CA: Brooks/Cole.

Tierney, W. (2000). Power, identity, and the dilemma of college student departure. In J. Braxton (Ed.), *Reworking the student departure puzzle* (pp. 213–234). Nashville, TN: Vanderbilt University Press.

Tinto, V. (1993). *Leaving college: Rethinking the causes and cures of student attrition* (2nd ed.). Chicago, IL: University of Chicago Press.

Triandis, H. C. (1995). *Individualism and collectivism*. Boulder, CO: Westview Press.

Vignoles, V. L., Owe, E., Smith, P. B., Easterbrook, M. J., Brown, R., . . . Bond, M. H. (2016). Beyond the "East–West" dichotomy: Global variation in cultural models of selfhood. *American Psychological Association*, *8*, 966–1000. doi:10.1037/xge0000175

Wintre, M. G., Kandasamy, A. R., Chavoshi, S., & Wright, L. (2015). Are international undergraduate students emerging adults? Motivations for studying abroad. *Emerging Adulthood*, 3(4), 225–264. doi:10.1177/2167696815571665

Yan, K. (2017). *Chinese international students' stressors and coping strategies in the United States*. New York, NY: Springer.

Ziguras, C., & Law, S. (2006). Recruiting international students as skilled immigrants: the global "skills race" as viewed from Australia and Malaysia. *Globalisation, Societies, and Education*, 4(1), 59–76. doi:10.1080/14767720600555087

19

Young Adult Transnational School-to-Work Transitions in the Context of Work Migration in Europe

Oana Negru-Subtirica

Introduction

> *Oh the passenger / He rides and he rides / He sees things from under glass / He looks through his window side.*
>
> **Iggy Pop, "The Passenger"**

The transition to adulthood integrates an exploration of and commitment to diverse occupational paths, leading to an active construction of work identities. Nowadays, emerging adults' work exploration experiences increasingly go beyond the boundaries of their own countries, leading to transnational transitions to work. Work migration in the past decades indicates that more and more young adults choose or are forced to live their first work experiences beyond the borders of their homeland, often engaged in jobs that are not compatible with their academic qualifications (Schneider, Saw, & Broda, 2015). Analyses of labor migration patterns in central and eastern Europe show an increase in youth migration in the last decade, especially in educated young adults who had little to no work experiences prior to migration (Horváth, 2008, 2012). These trends can make them passengers, who ride through the global landscape, as in the previously cited Iggy Pop song. Their journeys need to be better understood, and the present chapter explores such transnational transitions to work among emerging adults in Europe.

Oana Negru-Subtirica, *Young Adult Transnational School-to-Work Transitions in the Context of Work Migration in Europe* In: *Young Adult Development at the School-to-Work Transition.* E. Anne Marshall and Jennifer E. Symonds, Oxford University Press (2021). © Oxford University Press. DOI: 10.1093/oso/9780190941512.003.0019.

The Wanderer and the Passenger: A Developmental View of Transnational School-to-Work Transitions

Emerging adult workers who enter the workplace in another country, after graduation from their academic studies, have their first encounter with a full-time job in another work system than the one they are familiar with in their homeland. While their conceptualizations of work and their work identities are developed and crafted in their countries of origin, their first real work experiences occur in a country of settlement. This pattern, depicting a *transnational school-to-work transition,* needs to be more thoroughly researched. Existing studies on contemporary transitions to adulthood show that most normative developmental tasks of adulthood (e.g., marriage, children, financial independence) are postponed longer, as emerging adults spend increasingly more time in educational settings (Arnett, 2011). Finding a job is one core developmental task that many emerging adults enrolled in postsecondary education postpone until after they graduate.

Extensive schooling, such as tertiary or university education, maintains emerging adults in a state of increased identity exploration and experimentation with different life roles (e.g., student, lover). In terms of the worker role, research indicates that young adults in North America and western Europe have diverse, often short-term and transitory work experiences during their university studies (Quintini & Manfredi, 2009). This group mainly opts for temporary or project-based employment that is not necessarily linked to their educational paths. For instance, a qualitative study conducted on South Korean youth working during their holidays in Canada pointed out that these work experiences are perceived "as a way of exploring their "true selves" and enhancing social mobility, both of which constitute stories of self-development" (Yoon, 2014, p. 1025). The benefits of this type of work include financial independence from parents, a broadened outlook on the world of work, and the development of a more complex and personally relevant understanding of work. Also, young people who work during schooling tend to develop employment and work goals congruent with their vocational interests and educational background and are more flexible in adjusting goals to changing employment trends (Koepke & Denissen, 2012). However, these findings mainly refer to youth from privileged socioeconomic backgrounds in countries with stable economies such as the United States, Finland, Belgium, and the Netherlands.

A different trend emerges from studies of youth in countries with more unstable socioeconomic contexts and high rates of youth unemployment (e.g., Spain, Greece). In these countries, work experiences during school are more rare and families financially support young people throughout their academic studies and into their 20s (Eichhorst, Hinte, & Rinne, 2013). In Mediterranean countries such as Italy (Buhl & Lanz, 2007; Scabini, 2000) and in formerly communist countries such as Romania (Damian, Negru-Subtirica, Pop, & Baban, 2016; Negru, 2012), families usually socialize their offspring to focus mainly on education and encourage them to postpone employment until after graduation. Increasingly, however, many young adults' families can no longer financially support them after their academic studies are finished, and some graduates do not find work in their countries of origin. Demographic data indicate that more and more of these young adults, especially in the former communist bloc, express migration intentions (e.g., Romania; Williams, Jephcote, Janta, & Li, 2018) and then emigrate to find stable well-paid employment after they complete their education (Horváth, 2008, 2012).

Work migration is an increasing phenomenon that has been legitimized in recent decades by stronger political and economic collaborations among countries and by the rise of the Internet as a universal tool of communication. This phenomenon is also linked to educational and occupational dynamics in immigrants' countries of origin and in their countries of settlement. Contemporary perspectives on transnational careers praise the rise of *boundaryless careers* (Arthur & Rousseau, 1996) in light of increasing globalization and the expansion of multinational companies. A boundaryless career transcends the classical organizational boundaries of space, type of work, organizational position, or sociocognitive personal capital and empowers individuals to construct and reconstruct their careers in a global world as free and self-determined people (Sullivan & Arthur, 2006). Although it appears attractive, this concept paints a rather romanticized picture of work migration, suggesting a *planned* stance regarding migration to another country. While some young adults do plan for a boundaryless career, they tend to be white-collar, highly qualified individuals, usually employed by multinational companies (Inkson, Gunz, Ganesh, & Roper, 2012). Many emerging adults who enter a work migration process are pushed into this trajectory by complex social inequalities in their country of origin that greatly constrain their social mobility (e.g., the European core–periphery system, King, 2018). The next section analyzes factors related to inequalities that push young adults in entering transnational school-to-work transitions.

Why Do Emerging Adults Pursue Transnational School-to-Work Transitions?

Transnational school-to-work transitions are often an outcome of social inequality (differential access to resources as a function of personal characteristics such as gender, immigrant status, socioeconomic status, or educational status) and low social mobility (changes in social position, social class, financial affluence, or occupational prestige) in young adults' homelands. High levels of social inequality tend to be associated with reduced social mobility (Corak, 2013; Heckhausen & Shane, 2015), increasing the vulnerability of already marginalized individuals and groups. This pattern makes those embarking on transnational school-to-work transitions very vulnerable to underemployment and work-related discrimination (Blustein, 2011; Duffy, Blustein, Diemer, & Autin, 2016). Some social inequalities have a distinct impact on social mobility and may push university graduates to search for jobs in another country; these include incompatibility between university curricula and labor market requirements and limited work prospects in one's homeland after graduation.

The *compatibility between university curricula and labor market requirements* has come under great scrutiny. Labor markets are more dynamic in the 21st century, with job descriptions changing frequently and employers requiring new skills in their young employees. Changes in the labor market are linked to the rise of the Internet, the automatization of work, and the outsourcing of lower status jobs (Dicken, 2003). Universities seem to have difficulties in keeping up with employers' expectations of increased flexibility and adaptability. Specific organizational projects need even more precise and specialized sets of skills. This situation requires universities to perpetually develop flexible and customized educational curricula. However, with increasing volumes of students enrolling in higher education, this goal becomes very difficult to achieve; universities are not often able to prepare the fully fledged and immediately employable graduates that employers prefer (Tynjälä, Välimaa, & Sarja, 2003). Moreover, academic programs and qualifications are less dynamic than job descriptions; university curricula may include knowledge and skill development that are insufficient for the future job markets.

Labor markets do not have as many job openings as there are graduates in some occupational fields, creating a gap between supply and demand. Therefore, many new graduates face poor employment prospects; they must find a job in any field available or go through a new cycle of professional training. This may lead a graduate from an economics program to, for example, enter training to become a beta tester for an IT company. There is a third option: Graduates can move to a more economically stable country, where they may be able to find employment that matches their academic qualifications. Not all graduates who migrate are able to find work within their field, however. The work migration option is an opportunity to use the skills and knowledge acquired during education, either in a domain-specific manner or as transferable or soft skills.

Some wonder why emerging adults choose to migrate, rather than simply look for work in their own country. This brings us to the second source of social inequalities for this group. In many European countries the *rate of youth unemployment* has increased in the past decade, especially in the years following the 2008–2009 economic recession (International Labour Organization, 2012). European Commission (2016) data indicated that from 2008 to 2011 the employment rate of Romanian university graduates has decreased from 84.8% to 70.1%. A similar trend was depicted also for Italy, with a decrease from a 65% employment rate of university graduates in 2008 to 57.5% in 2011.This downward trend has diminished in recent years, but it is still linked to unstable socioeconomic contexts (such as the closing of major employment organizations) that reduce the number and availability of new jobs in a country or a specific area of that country. Furthermore, existing jobs may be of a lower status or lower-paying than expected for the academic qualifications young people have obtained. Such underemployment is very unattractive to these young people; lower-paying work cannot ensure the financial independence desirable at this age, and lower status jobs reduce the social mobility these well-educated emerging adults desire at the beginning of their career. The high employment expectations university graduates hold may not reflect occupational prospects in their homelands. Therefore, many young adults search for employment in more affluent and economically stable countries.

In Romania, an eastern European country from the former communist bloc, the positive social perception of university education (mainly due to limited access to higher education during the communist regime) has led to a sharp increase in the number of university graduates, beginning in 2000 (Karaś, Cieciuch, Negru, & Crocetti, 2015). Parents value education above financial independence for their children; most university students have few or no work experiences during university and continue to be financially supported by their families (European Commission, 2010). Most entry-level wages in Romania (except in the IT sector) do not provide even partial financial independence, even if the employment is in one's field of study (Vasile, Prelipcean, & Şandru, 2010). The prospects are even more grim for graduates who come from small urban or rural communities, where employment opportunities are almost nonexistent (Horváth, 2008).

Many young adults are pushed by the previously mentioned social inequalities and by reduced social mobility to emigrate to successfully complete the school-to-work transition. They arrive in the country of settlement as educated adults who already hold certain views of work and of themselves as workers. The experience of migration involves a dual transition; the school-to-work transition occurs simultaneously with their transition to a new culture. Thus, the meaning of work and the vocational identities of these young people are further impacted by their transition to a new culture.

Dimensions of Work in Transnational School-to-Work Transitions

Work, as a human action and a life role, encompasses a myriad of personal, relational, economic, and cultural dimensions. The next section explores the meaning of work and work identity, with a focus on the particularities of transnational school-to-work transitions.

The Meaning of Work

Duffy and colleagues (2016) proposed a unified theory of the psychology of work, shifting the focus from the concept of career development to the idea of *decent work*. This definition aims to include individuals exposed to greater levels of social inequality and reduced social mobility. In the psychology of work literature, decent work includes "(a) physical and interpersonally safe working conditions (e.g., absence of physical, mental, or emotional abuse), (b) hours that allow for free time and adequate rest, (c) organizational values that complement family and social values; (d) adequate compensation, and (e) access to adequate health care" (Duffy et al., 2016, p. 130). This definition moves away from the classical career development discourse that defines work as self-determined, value-driven, and self-organizing to embrace a conceptualization centered on socioeconomic benefits and constraints. According to this perspective, need satisfaction is an outcome of decent work.

Particularly in migration and transnational school-to-work transitions, it is important to consider that work can satisfy multiple human needs, including needs for survival, power, social connection, and self-determination. Although these needs may be valued equally in society, they are valued differently by different individuals (Blustein, 2001, 2006, 2011). Thus, in analyzing how young adult immigrants perceive the meaning of their work, we should acknowledge that the need for survival may be their most powerful motivator, outweighing the need for self-determination. For these youth, the need to buy food and pay their rent prevent a focus on finding a job that matches their professional interests and allows creativity. This stance on the meaning of work somewhat contradicts the tenets of classical career development discourse but fits neatly in the psychology of work framework.

To date, few studies have addressed the meaning of work and individual work identity in young adults involved in their first migration cycle. To our knowledge, no studies have yet analyzed these constructs in young adults who have made transnational school-to-work transitions. In light of the grim outlook for youth employment in Europe (Eichhorst et al., 2013), more youth may see work migration as the only solution to access decent work. Socioeconomic and social mobility constraints reduce the attractiveness of school-to-work transitions in young adults' homelands. When approaching graduation, students may start (re)constructing their employment expectations by expanding their search for decent work to a country of settlement.

(Re)constructing the personal meaning of work to include the prospect of work migration is positively viewed in the European context, where the creation and then enlargement of the European Union (EU) has encouraged greater labor mobility. A European identity, in which EU citizens would perceive themselves as Europeans (i.e., European identity), in addition to their national identity (i.e., French, Romanian) was a cornerstone in the creation and then enlargement of the EU (Bruter, 2005). Additionally, the European Qualifications Framework (Young, 2008), a core project of the European Commission introduced occupational qualifications that are valid across European countries. This initiative contributes to an emerging European identity narrative of free access to work and jobs for citizens in the EU, a narrative that may influence the construction of meaning regarding work for many European young adults who are preparing for school-to-work transitions (Young, 2008).

Wages differ substantially across employment sectors and levels, as well as between western European countries or "old Europe" (e.g., Italy, Germany) and central and eastern European countries (e.g., Romania, Bulgaria). The result is an influx of young people migrating for work postgraduation (Holland, Fic, Rincon-Aznar, Stokes, & Paluchowsk, 2011; Horváth, 2012; Prelipceanu, 2008). Initially, EU occupational policies were predicated on the idea that people would be able to find employment in a country of settlement according to their educational and occupational qualifications from their homeland (Young, 2008); for instance, a clinical psychologist from Romania could also find employment as a clinical psychologist in France. This plan proved to be very ambitious, in light of the differential economic, occupational, and professional advancement conditions throughout the EU. The European identity narrative was very successful in countries where the occupational dynamics and compatibility education—labor market were low (e.g., Romania), in that youth from these countries were very open in embracing their European identity and hence eager to search for employment in other European countries. Nevertheless, transnational work mobility from old Europe countries remains limited, despite sustained policy efforts, with youth being rather reluctant to move to another European country in search of employment (Eichhorst et al., 2013).

Work Identity

Previous research underscores that work identity encompasses personal factors, such as awareness of self as an employee in the context of a job, and social facets, such as one's identification with the organization (Skorikov & Vondracek, 2011). The personal side of work identity focuses on the way individuals integrate the worker role into their coherent sense of self. Erikson's (1950, 1968) identity model, developed further by Marcia (1966), views the interplay between identity exploration, or the analysis and investigation of existing alternatives, and identity commitment, or selection and adherence to one alternative, as the core of identity formation across the life span. As work becomes a salient life domain in the transition to adulthood, work identity grows more complex with processes of work exploration and commitment becoming central to identity development (Super, Savickas, & Super, 1996).

The interplay between work exploration and commitment is the cornerstone of a coherent work identity. Research shows that young employees with high levels of both work commitment and exploration (i.e., achievement status) are more engaged in work and less susceptible to job burnout (Crocetti, Avanzi, Hawk, Fraccaroli, & Meeus, 2014; Luyckx, Duriez, Klimstra, & De Witte, 2010). These employees also show higher life satisfaction and positive views of their past (Crocetti, Palmonari, & Pojaghi, 2011). How, then, do young adults who have their first work experiences in a country of settlement balance work commitments with work exploration? The vocational self and the meaning attached to work are constructed in different cultures and socioeconomic contexts. Therefore, it is useful to depict how they integrate possibly contradictory beliefs about the self as a worker into their daily work goals and long-term work strivings.

Work identities are the product of socialization (Blustein, 2011) that begins in early childhood. Research shows that the processes of circumscription, referring to selection of a desirable occupation, and compromise, meaning the choice of an accessible occupation, occur until adolescence (see Gottfredson, 2005 for a review). The processes of work socialization are closely determined by the cultural context (Whiston & Keller, 2004) and the socioeconomic status of one's family of origin and community (Hill, Ramirez, & Dumka, 2003). In transnational school-to-work transitions, work socialization from the country of origin may influence meaning construction related to work and work identity. More specifically, predefined conceptualizations influence work exploration and work commitment. Although these assumptions are backed up by theoretical (e.g., Blustein, 2001, 2006, 2011; Gottfredson, 2005) and empirical findings (Skorikov & Vondracek, 2011; Whiston & Keller, 2004), more research is needed on how these factors play out in individual transitions.

How do immigrant young adults integrate their country of origin work identity with their work identity in a country of settlement? Let's consider the example of Maya, a young adult who plans to become a kindergarten teacher and undergoes lengthy training to prepare for this occupation. When she cannot find decent work in her field in her homeland and her parents can no longer support her financially, she decides to move to another country. There, she cannot find a job in her field but finds a decent job as a florist's assistant. This job has advantages: It enables her to pay her rent, save money, and obtain health insurance. There are some disadvantages: the florist's assistant job is not one she envisioned for herself through occupational circumscription and compromise; it is not the job that she explored and committed to during her studies; and it is not a job her parents, friends, and peers view as suitable for her. Yet, this job qualifies as decent work, according to the psychology of work framework proposed by Blustein and colleagues (Blustein, 2001, 2006, 2011; Duffy et al., 2016) and according to International Labor Organization standards (2008, 2012). This hypothetical case matches the real-life experience of many young adult migrants whose work identities constructed in their homelands are challenged and changed by the migration experience and work experiences in their country of settlement.

Adapting to Work in a Country of Settlement

The concept of "new beginnings" is relevant to consider for young adults who undergo transnational school-to-work transitions. Do these individuals start work with a clean slate in a country of settlement? Or does their cognitive, emotional, and behavioral work-relevant history from their homelands influence how they view and commit to work in the new country? According to the psychology of work theory (Blustein, 2001, 2006, 2011; Duffy et al., 2016) and the social cognitive model of career development (Lent, Brown, & Hackett, 1994), our work-relevant orientation and history follows us, even in the absence of meaningful previous work experiences. Research on the meaning of work and the work identities of adult migrants has identified several external factors that contribute to a successful transition to work in a country of settlement. I will next focus on two categories of factors: work design characteristics and social relations.

First, I will analyze the role of *work design characteristics* in developing immigrants' work identities in a country of settlement. Work design characteristics refer to "the attributes of the task, job, and social and organizational environment" (Humphrey, Nahrgang, & Morgeson, 2007, p. 1333). Young adult migrants may differently adapt to jobs and organizations in countries of settlement depending on work designs that accommodate their conceptualizations of work, developed in their homelands. In a study that analyzed occupational commitment among immigrant accountants (Yu, Kim, & Restubog, 2015), the authors found that that immigrant adults' work identity was supported by a work design focused on job autonomy, especially when the immigrant employees were not in managerial positions. Participants in this study valued work environments that respected their cultural diversity more than workplaces that offered training. These findings may be particularly relevant to skilled immigrant workers whose work identity is stable enough to support a strong commitment to a specific occupation; results could be different for those without a committed work identity. On the other hand, a lack of work exploration and commitment upon arrival in the country of settlement may be a benefit for potential employers. Organizations who respect immigrants' cultural and ethnic backgrounds can integrate these values into the work design of immigrant employees' jobs. For instance, anthropological studies on central and eastern European migrants in low-skilled but high-demand jobs show that these workers value respect and honesty in an employer, regardless of the physical challenge involved in their work (e.g., Brinkmeier, 2011). Interpreting these findings considering Blustein and colleagues' psychology of work theory suggests that decent work that satisfies survival and social connection needs can bring work fulfillment and well-being among immigrants. This pattern may not apply to young immigrant workers who hold rigid views of work; they may have foreclosed work identities, unrealistic expectations related to their professional interests, limited prior work exploration, or little awareness of job requirements and organizational demands. Such migrants will likely have difficulty in finding work opportunities or organizations that can "live up" to these high expectations.

Second, in terms of *social relations*, studies on immigrants underscore that the level of acculturative stress decreases and positive adaptation in the country of settlement increases when there is access to a supportive community that eases the initial adjustment to a new context and work world (Anghel, 2011; Birman, Trickett, & Buchanan, 2005; Sandu, Toth, & Tudor, 2018). This community may consist of family, friends or peers from their homeland, or even formal and informal groups of immigrants from culturally similar countries. Shanahan (2000) found that family and community role models offer both scaffolding (i.e., provision of guided support for approaching new tasks; this support is gradually removed, as people learn how to approach the new tasks, to increase autonomy) and vicarious learning opportunities for adaptive behaviors, cognitions, and emotions in life role transitions for young adults. Demographic trends for east to west migration in Europe suggest that migration routes are selected by many immigrants in part to ensure access to a strong national community in the country of settlement and/or the presence of family members and friends there, with an already established social network (Favell, 2008; Sandu et al., 2018). To support those making transnational school-to-work transitions, a familiar community can offer modeling experiences and coherent work narratives that can help newcomers. Role models in the country of settlement, whether co-ethnics or perhaps natives when there are no language barriers, are of the utmost importance to adult work socialization, work exploration, and commitment. Community members in a new country can serve as a major agent of work socialization, facilitating the acculturation and integration processes linked to worker roles.

Implications for Research

More in-depth research is needed to understand how young people prepare for and view their transitions to work in a country of settlement and how they juxtapose their transition experiences with conceptualizations of a work self "imported" from their homeland. To date, few studies have analyzed how the meaning of work is (re)constructed in educated emerging adults experiencing transnational school-to-work transitions. In-depth qualitative analyses will yield valuable information about how the meaning of work as promoted and internalized in the homeland is adapted and integrated into one's life as a worker in the country of settlement. Quantitative analyses could focus on work migration destinations and patterns that can assist workers, employers, educators, and policy makers.

The way young adults who migrate for work construct their vocational identities is central to understanding work migration in the 21st century. An immigrant's work identity is embedded in the way he or she makes sense of the immigration. By investigating young migrants' vocational identity in a country of settlement through qualitative and participative methodologies, researchers can identify potential personal resources and barriers to their adaptation. Schneider and colleagues (2015) pointed out that more research on migration patterns of young adults is needed as "despite the numbers of young adults who migrate, little is known about the characteristics of this population" (p. 564). The authors attribute this shortcoming to the limited accessibility of data on continuous migration and the lack of statistics on young migrants' "participation in education and the labor market, including the types of jobs they might be seeking" (p. 565).

Work is embedded in complex social, cultural, and economic contexts that shape access to work and the meaning of work (International Labor Organization, 2008, 2012). The personal significance attached to one's work contributes to work identity development, and vice versa. Studying these factors from an interdisciplinary perspective could illuminate how, for instance, economic constraints in young adults' homelands may prompt the channeling of personal resources to "make it" in a country of settlement. One question that could be explored is whether those who know returning home is not a viable alternative (i.e., those who must remain in the country of settlement) develop more adaptive work identities than those who know they have the option to return home.

Implications for Educational and Occupational Policies

The previous discussion holds important implications for educational and occupational policies targeting immigrant young adults. Many European countries (e.g., Spain, Greece, Portugal) had a considerable increase in youth unemployment over the last decade, mainly due to the 2008–2009 economic recession (Eichhorst, et al., 2013; Eichhorst & Neder, 2014). Analyzing the EU situation for 2012, Eichhorst and colleagues observed that

> only three out of 27 countries exhibit youth unemployment rates of less than 10%. The average rate in the EU was nearly 23% in 2012. Significantly higher rates can be

> observed in Ireland (30%), Slovakia (34%), Italy (more than 35%), Portugal (nearly 38%) and, above all, in Croatia (43%), the former Yugoslavia (already for years 54% and higher) as well as in the widely discussed crisis countries Spain (53%) and Greece (more than 55%). (2013, p. 2)

Eurostat (2018) data for May 2018 indicate that 3.377 million young people (under the age of 25) are unemployed in the EU, with Greece (43.2%), Spain (33.8%), and Italy (31.9%) having the highest levels of youth unemployment. This vulnerability strongly impacts these young peoples' financial, physical, and psychological well-being, and it also negatively influences their future chances of accessing decent work (Schmillen & Umkehrer, 2013). As Eichhorst and colleagues (2013) assert, even temporary work migration can be a possible solution to the crisis of youth unemployment and underemployment. However, more information is needed about the potential immediate, middle, and long-term implications of this and other proposed solutions.

From an educational policy perspective, the overeducation of many emerging adults leads to an oversupply of graduates in occupational fields that cannot provide enough jobs (Dolton & Vignoles, 2000). Keeping young adults in education as a protective system to avoid (or at least delay) unemployment is viewed as both a positive and a negative social reality (Rubb, 2003). The reality of employment availability in the country of settlement will likely require significant adaptation for educated young adult immigrants, as demographic data indicates that most young people who migrate are underemployed in their countries of settlement (Chiswick & Miller, 2009; Fernández & Ortega, 2008). In light of these somewhat bleak prospects, educational curricula could integrate applied activities to help students understand how knowledge and skills developed through education can apply to different types of work that may appear unrelated to their educational field. Thus, throughout university, young adults could develop more fluid expectations for the work they will do and increase their cognitive flexibility in dealing with unexpected work prospects. By actively reflecting on diverse and creative applications of their knowledge and skills, they can construct alternative work selves and be more prepared for a challenging transnational school-to-work transition as immigrants.

From a national and regional occupational policy perspective, it would be helpful to focus more closely on the way those who experience transnational school-to-work transitions envision their migration. Occupational policies must differentiate between labor migration and welfare migration; the former refers to migration in search of decent work opportunities, while the latter refers to migration prompted by the welfare benefits offered by a country of settlement (De Giorgi & Pellizzari, 2009; Zimmermann, 2013). Examining how young adult immigrants describe their work identity could shed light on the goals that guide their behavior. Developing support programs that facilitate work transitions for new immigrants could benefit both employers and local communities in countries of settlement (Bimrose & McNair, 2011). Such programs could include concise and easily understandable descriptions of immigrants' legal obligations and rights in a specific country and how they could use their academic qualifications from their homeland. This could help reframe the meaning of work to be consistent with work prospects in the country of settlement and could prompt work exploration behaviors that might help migrants form an adaptive work identity.

Conclusions

In this chapter I analyzed transnational school-to-work transitions in the European context, focusing primarily on young adults who graduated from university. Existing demographic data indicate that the number of young adults who enter work migration has increased in the past decades (e.g., Schneider et al., 2015). Nevertheless, little is known about their work migration patterns or about how they develop their work identities and their meaning of work while adapting to life in a country of settlement. As work is embedded in complex social, cultural, and economic contexts, future multidisciplinary studies could focus on depicting the interaction between personal work identities and organizational and relational factors that facilitate or inhibit work adaptation in a country of settlement. This complex process is an integral part of the acculturative tasks that emerging adult migrants undertake. Additionally, from a demographic analysis perspective, in line with Schneider and colleagues' (2015) recommendations, large-scale surveys depicting work migration patterns could integrate more in-depth investigations of young adults' job search and employment patterns in their countries of settlement.

References

Anghel, R. G. (2011). From irregular migrants to fellow Europeans: Changes in Romanian migratory flows. In M. Bommes, & G. Sciortino (Eds.), *Foggy social structures: Irregular migration, European labour markets and the welfare state* (pp. 23–43). Amsterdam, The Netherlands: Amsterdam University Press.

Arnett, J. J. (2011). Emerging adulthood(s): The cultural psychology of a new life stage. In L. J. Arnett (Ed.), *Bridging cultural and developmental approaches to psychology: New syntheses in theory, research, and policy* (pp. 255–275). New York, NY: Oxford University Press.

Arthur, M. B., & Rousseau, D. M. (1996). Introduction: The boundaryless career as a new employment principle. In M. B. Arthur & D. M. Rousseau (Eds.), *The boundaryless career: A new employment principle for a new organizational era* (pp. 1–20). New York, NY: Oxford University Press.

Bimrose, J., & McNair, S. (2011). Career support for migrants: Transformation or adaptation? *Journal of Vocational Behavior, 78*, 325–333.

Birman, D., Trickett, E., & Buchanan, R. M. (2005). A tale of two cities: Replication of a study on the acculturation and adaptation of immigrant adolescents from the former Soviet Union in a different community context. *American Journal of Community Psychology, 35*, 83–101.

Blustein, D. L. (2001). Extending the reach of vocational psychology: Toward an inclusive and integrated psychology of working. *Journal of Vocational Behavior, 59*, 171–182.

Blustein, D. L. (2006). *The psychology of working: A new perspective for career development, counseling, and public policy*. New York, NY: Routledge.

Blustein, D. L. (2011). A relational theory of working. *Journal of Vocational Behavior, 79*, 1–17.

Brinkmeier, E. (2011). Illegality in everyday life: Polish workers in Dutch agriculture. In M. Bommes, & G. Sciortino (Eds.), *Foggy social structures: Irregular migration, European labour markets and the welfare state* (pp. 45–65). Amsterdam, The Netherlands: Amsterdam University Press.

Bruter, M. (2005). *Citizens of Europe?: The emergence of a mass European identity*. Houndmills, NY: Palgrave Macmillan.

Buhl, H. M., & Lanz, M. (2007). Emerging adulthood in Europe: Common traits and variability across five European countries. *Journal of Adolescent Research, 22*, 439–443.

Chiswick, B. R., & Miller, P. W. (2009). The international transferability of immigrants' human capital. *Economics of Education Review, 28*, 162–169.

Corak, M. (2013). Income inequality, equality of opportunity, and intergenerational mobility. *Journal of Economic Perspectives, 27*, 79–102.

Crocetti, E., Avanzi, L., Hawk, S. T., Fraccaroli, F., & Meeus, W. (2014). Personal and social facets of job identity: A person-centered approach. *Journal of Business and Psychology, 29*, 281–300.

Crocetti, E., Palmonari, A., & Pojaghi, B. (2011). Work identity, wellbeing, and time perspective of typical and atypical young workers. In M. Cortini, G. Tanucci, & E. Morin (Eds.), *Boundaryless careers and occupational well-being. An interdisciplinary approach* (pp. 181–190). London, England: Palgrave MacMillan.

Damian, L. E., Negru-Subtirica, O., Pop, E. I., & Baban, A. (2016). The costs of being the best: Consequences of academic achievement on students' identity, perfectionism, and vocational development. In A. Montgomery, & I. Kehoe (Eds.), *Reimagining the purpose of schools and educational organisations,* (pp. 173–188). Cham, Switzerland: Springer.

De Giorgi, G., & Pellizzari, M. (2009). Welfare migration in Europe. *Labour Economics, 16*, 353–363.

Dicken, P. (2003). *Global shift: Reshaping the global economic map in the 21st century*. London, England: SAGE.

Dolton, P., & Vignoles, A. (2000). The incidence and effects of overeducation in the UK graduate labour market. *Economics of Education Review, 19*, 179–198.

Duffy, R. D., Blustein, D. L., Diemer, M. A., & Autin, K. L. (2016). The psychology of working theory. *Journal of Counseling Psychology, 63*, 127–148.

Eichhorst, W., & Neder, F. (2014, March). Youth unemployment in Mediterranean countries (IZA policy paper 80). *IZA*. Retrieved from http://ftp.iza.org/pp80.pdf

Eichhorst, W., Hinte, H., & Rinne, U. (2013, July). Youth unemployment in Europe: What to do about it (IZA policy paper 65). *IZA*. Retrieved from http://ftp.iza.org/pp65.pdf

Erikson, E. H. (1950). *Childhood and society*. New York, NY: Norton.

Erikson, E. H. (1968). *Identity: Youth and crisis*. New York, NY: Norton.

European Commission. (2010). Efficiency and effectiveness of public expenditure on tertiary education in the EU. Retrieved from http://ec.europa.eu/economy_finance/publications/occasional_paper/2010/op70_en.htm

European Commission. (2016). *Education and training monitor 2016: Country analysis.* Retrieved from: europski-fondovi.eu › monitor2016-country-reports_en

Eurostat. (2018, July 2). Euro area unemployment at 8.4%. Retrieved from http://ec.europa.eu/eurostat/documents/2995521/9034240/3-02072018-AP-EN.pdf/bfcf5c1a-fca8-4541-aa0a-2d5dc2e090da

Favell, A. (2008). The new face of East–West migration in Europe. *Journal of Ethnic and Migration Studies*, *34*, 701–716.

Fernández, C., & Ortega, C. (2008). Labor market assimilation of immigrants in Spain: employment at the expense of bad job-matches?. *Spanish Economic Review*, *10*, 83–107.

Gottfredson, L. S. (2005). Applying Gottfredson's theory of circumscription and compromise in career guidance and counseling. In D. Brown, & R. Lent (Eds.), *Career development and counseling: Putting theory and research to work* (1st ed., pp. 71–100). Hoboken, NJ: Wiley.

Heckhausen, J., & Shane, J. (2015). Social mobility in the transition to adulthood: Educational systems, career entry, and individual agency. In L. A. Jensen (Ed.), *The Oxford handbook of human development and culture* (pp. 535–553). New York, NY: Oxford University Press.

Hill, N. E., Ramirez, C., & Dumka, L. E. (2003). Early adolescents' career aspirations: A qualitative study of perceived barriers and family support among low-income, ethnically diverse adolescents. *Journal of Family Issues*, *24*, 934–959.

Holland, D., Fic, T., Rincon-Aznar, A., Stokes, L., & Paluchowski, P. (2011) *Labour mobility within the EU – The impact of enlargement and the functioning of the transitional arrangements*. London, England: National Institute of Economic and Social Research.

Horváth, I. (2008). The culture of migration of Romanian youth. *Journal of Ethnic and Migration Studies*, *34*, 771–786.

Horváth, I. (2012). Migrația internațională a cetățenilor români după 1989 [International migration of Romanian citizens after 1989]. In V. Rotariu, & V. Voineagu (Eds.), *Inerție și schimbare: Dimensiuni sociale ale tranziției în România* [Inertia and change: Social dimensions of transition in Romania] (pp. 199–222). Iași, Romania: Polirom.

Humphrey, S. E., Nahrgang, J. D., & Morgeson, F. P. (2007). Integrating motivational, social, and contextual work design features: A meta-analytic summary and theoretical extension of the work design literature. *Journal of Applied Psychology*, *92*, 1332–1356.

Inkson, K., Gunz, H., Ganesh, S., & Roper, J. (2012). Boundaryless careers: Bringing back boundaries. *Organization Studies*, *33*, 323–340.

International Labor Organization. (2008). Work of work report 2008: Income inequalities in the age of financial globalization. Retrieved from http://www.ilo.org/wcmsp5/groups/public/@dgreports/@dcomm/@publ/documents/publication/wcms_100354.pdf

International Labor Organization. (2012). Decent work indicators: Concepts and definitions. Retrieved from http://www.ilo.org/wcmsp5/groups/public/---dgreports/---integration/documents/publication/wcms_229374.pdf

Karaś, D., Cieciuch, J., Negru, O., & Crocetti, E. (2015). Relationships between identity and well-being in Italian, Polish, and Romanian emerging adults. *Social Indicators Research*, *121*, 727–743.

King, R. (2018). Theorising new European youth mobilities. *Population, Space and Place*, *24*, e2117.

Koepke, S., & Denissen, J. J. (2012). Dynamics of identity development and separation: Individuation in parent–child relationships during adolescence and emerging adulthood: A conceptual integration. *Developmental Review, 32*, 67–88.

Lent, R. W., Brown, S. D., & Hackett, G. (1994). Toward a unifying social cognitive theory of career and academic interest, choice, and performance. *Journal of Vocational Behavior, 45*, 79–122.

Luyckx, K., Duriez, B., Klimstra, T., & De Witte, H. (2010). Identity statuses in young adult employees: Prospective relations with work engagement and burnout. *Journal of Vocational Behavior, 77*, 339–349.

Marcia, J. E. (1966). Development and validation of ego-identity status. *Journal of Personality and Social Psychology, 3*, 551–558.

Negru, O. (2012). The time of your life: Emerging adulthood characteristics in a sample of Romanian high-school and university students. *Cognition, Brain, Behavior, Behavior. An Interdisciplinary Journal, 16*, 357–367.

Prelipceanu, R. (2008). The new migration patterns of educated Romanians to the EU: What challenge for the individuals and for the nation-state? *Romanian Journal of European Affairs, 8*, 75–87.

Quintini, G., & Manfredi, T. (2009). *Going separate ways? School-to-work transitions in the United States and Europe* (OECD social, employment and migration working papers no. 90). Paris, France: OECD.

Rubb, S. (2003). Overeducation in the labor market: A comment and re-analysis of a meta-analysis. *Economics of Education Review, 22*, 621–629.

Sandu, D., Toth, G., & Tudor, E. (2018). The nexus of motivation–experience in the migration process of young Romanians. *Population, Space and Place, 24*, e2114.

Scabini, E. (2000). Parent–child relationships in Italian families: Connectedness and autonomy in the transition to adulthood. *Psicologia: Teoria e Pesquisa, 16*, 23–30.

Schmillen, A., & Umkehrer, M. (2013, June). The scars of youth: Effects of early-career unemployment on future unemployment experiences (IAB discussion paper 65). *IAB.* Retrieved from http://doku.iab.de/discussionpapers/2013/dp0613.pdf

Schneider, B., Saw, G. K., & Broda, M. (2015). Work and work migration within and across countries in emerging and young adulthood. In L. A. Jensen (Ed.), *The Oxford handbook of human development and culture. An interdisciplinary perspective* (pp. 554–569). New York, NY: Oxford University Press.

Shanahan, M. J. (2000). Pathways to adulthood in changing societies: Variability and mechanisms in life course perspective. *Annual review of Sociology, 26*, 667–692.

Skorikov, V. B., & Vondracek, F. W. (2011). Occupational identity. In S. J. Schwartz, K. Luyckx, & V. L. Vignoles (Eds.), *Handbook of identity theory and research* (pp. 693–714). New York, NY: Springer.

Sullivan, S. E., & Arthur, M. B. (2006). The evolution of the boundaryless career concept: Examining physical and psychological mobility. *Journal of Vocational Behavior, 69*, 19–29.

Super, D. E., Savickas, M. L., & Super C. M. (1996). The life-span, life-space approach to careers. In D. Brown, & L. Brooks (Eds), *Career choice and development* (3rd ed., pp. 121–178). San Francisco, CA: Jossey-Bass.

Tynjälä, P., Välimaa, J., & Sarja, A. (2003). Pedagogical perspectives on the relationships between higher education and working life. *Higher Education, 46*, 147–166.

Vasile, V., Prelipcean, G., & Şandru, D. M. (2010). *Îmbunătăţirea competenţelor profesionale în rândul absolvenţilor şi tinerilor: O şansă pentru viitor* [Improving vocational competences among graduates and youths: A chance for the future]. Bucharest, Romania: Institutul European din România.

Williams, A. M., Jephcote, C., Janta, H., & Li, G. (2018). The migration intentions of young adults in Europe: A comparative, multilevel analysis. *Population, Space and Place, 24,* e2123.

Whiston, S. C., & Keller, B. K. (2004). The influences of the family of origin on career development: A review and analysis. *The Counseling Psychologist, 32,* 493–568.

Yoon, K. (2014). Transnational youth mobility in the neoliberal economy of experience. *Journal of Youth Studies, 17,* 1014–1028.

Young, M. (2008). Towards a European qualifications framework: Some cautionary observations. *Journal of European Industrial Training, 32,* 128–137.

Yu, K. H., Kim, S., & Restubog, S. (2015). Transnational contexts for professional identity development in accounting. *Organization Studies, 36,* 1577–1597.

Zimmermann, K. F. (2013, September). The mobility challenge for growth and integration in Europe (IZA policy paper 69). *IZA.* Retrieved from http://ftp.iza.org/pp69.pdf

SECTION 6
THE NATURE OF THE SCHOOL-TO-WORK TRANSITION—TWO CONCEPTUALIZATIONS

20

Requisite Metamorphoses

College Graduates Transitioning from School to Work

Tammy J. Halstead

Introduction

The age at which young people reach adulthood is increasing, a reality that led Jeffrey Jensen Arnett to recognize a new developmental stage that he called *emerging adulthood* (Arnett, 2000). Emerging adulthood, occurring between the ages of 18 and 29 (Arnett, 2004), is a time characterized by change and exploration. During this stage, young people are neither completely adult nor completely adolescent, "lacking the anchor of the relatively clear social roles of either adolescence or adulthood" (Sharon, 2016, p. 162). It is a time of transition, a time of development and growth, and a time to build self-awareness (Arnett, 2004).

Looking back to the 1970s, young adults typically settled into a career, became financially independent, and married in their early 20s; however, over the last 50 years, there has been a significant trend toward delaying adult life decisions about love, work, and identity (Arnett, 2004). Today's young people are waiting longer to incorporate key aspects of adulthood into their lives, including taking responsibility for themselves, achieving financial independence, and making long-term career decisions. With these commitments taking place later in life, the late teens and 20s have become a time of exploration and change, and a time of preparation for adulthood (Arnett, 2000; European Group for Integrated Social Research, 2001; Shulman, Blatt, & Feldman, 2006). This transition period has been described as being "in training" for adulthood, with young people often feeling that they are both adults and adolescents simultaneously (European Group for Integrated Social Research, 2001, p. 103), or feeling in-between adulthood and adolescence (Sharon, 2016).

Tammy J. Halstead, *Requisite Metamorphoses* In: *Young Adult Development at the School-to-Work Transition.*
E. Anne Marshall and Jennifer E. Symonds, Oxford University Press (2021). © Oxford University Press.
DOI: 10.1093/oso/9780190941512.003.0020.

At the same time, an increasing number of emerging adults are attending college. In 1960, 45% of 16- to 24-year-old high school graduates were enrolled in college; in 1970, that proportion was 52% (National Center for Education Statistics, 1999) and in 2015, the rate rose to 69% (Bureau of Labor Statistics, 2016). During college, students often experience an unprecedented amount of freedom combined with few role requirements. They may not be living completely independently and often still receive financial support from parents. In some cases, parents may be very involved in their children's college life. Because they are not required during this time to take on full adult responsibilities, college students are able to explore life without being constrained by role expectations (Arnett, 2000).

This freedom to explore and to delay major adult decisions results in a moratorium on adulthood (Arnett, 2004), during which time emerging adults try on and explore various life choices (Arnett, 2000; European Group for Integrated Social research, 2001; Shulman et al., 2006), including careers. There is a cost to this delay in adulthood, as emerging adults may experience stress related to this unsettled period and may miss out on the developmental progress that can be gained from the experiences that are indicators of adulthood (Sharon, 2016).

Exploration and greater understanding of personal and vocational identity are key to development in emerging adulthood and these usually become clearer toward the end of this developmental period (Arnett, 2000). In the early stages of emerging adulthood, a high school graduate's ideas and plans for their transition to the world of work may be very different than their ideas and plans in later stages. Postsecondary graduates may not commit to a long-term career until many years later. For four or five years following graduation, the length of time emerging adults stay at any one job may be very short (Arnett, 2012). During this time of shorter-term, intermediary career steps, emerging adults consider various possibilities and discern the career that best fits their personal interests, values, and styles. "A key feature of emerging adulthood is that it is the period of life that offers the most opportunity for identity exploration in the areas of love, work, and worldviews" (Arnett, 2000, p. 473). These emerging adulthood exploratory experiences play a significant role in school-to-work transitions.

This chapter focuses on the transition from college to career for emerging adults and explores some of the ways the transition requires graduates to develop, grow, and change. For example, at graduation emerging adults who plan to enter the workforce embark on a full-time job search, which may be a new experience requiring learning and new skills. In addition, once they are in their first postgraduate job, they must learn the culture and mores of the professional environment, which can be very different from the college environment (Rosemond & Owens, 2018). In the midst of these new experiences, emerging adults are also growing in self-knowledge, learning the types of work activities and roles that are fulfilling to them, and developing a new social network. In ways, each of these experiences represents an opportunity for metamorphosis for the graduate. The following sections look more closely at the idea of metamorphosis and at the ways job search, vocational identity, adapting to workplace culture, and the development of a social network are metamorphoses that emerging adults face when transitioning from college to career.

A Time of Transition: Metamorphoses Required

Any life change or move to a new environment requires some learning and adaptability. One particular aspect of the current school-to-work transition process, however, is that recent college graduates are facing the necessity of simultaneous adaptations: moving from being a student to being a worker, adapting to the culture of the workplace, and growing through emerging adulthood. Rosemond and Owens (2018) write, "The transformation of a new identity would require a level of maturity to anticipate roles and tasks leading to transition from school to work" (p. 346–347). The multifaceted nature of this particular time in their lives makes for a "perfect storm" of change and challenge (Halstead, 2014, p. 3). College graduation carries with it unique expectations and possibilities and the search for a career is "one of the most important tasks that graduating college students face" (Yang & Gysbers, 2007, p. 157).

College graduates end their time at four-year institutions with the goal of leaving behind their role as student and moving into a long-term career (McDow & Zabrucky, 2015). The career search process is particularly important for recent graduate emerging adults because one's first job is an important factor affecting future career status, earnings, and career path over time (Saks & Ashforth, 1999). Families, graduates, faculty, and administrators all have expectations that graduates will move onto a chosen career path. Further, they expect that the career chosen will demonstrate the value of the graduates' new college degree.

Self-efficacy in the college to work transition processes may impact a graduate's ability to move through the various metamorphoses effectively. Halstead and Lare (2018) investigated college graduates' college to career transition self-efficacy in their first five years after graduating with a bachelor's degree. Participants were emerging adults aged 21 to 29 who had graduated within the last four years from a public or private college. The guiding question for this mixed-methods study was, What is the relationship between emerging adulthood and career transition self-efficacy of recent college graduates? Participants completed self-efficacy and perceived adulthood self-report assessments and 10 participants were interviewed about their experiences during the school-to-work transition. The findings indicated that a more fully developed sense of adulthood was a predictor of career transition self-efficacy. In contrast, young people in the early stages of emerging adulthood (i.e. a less developed sense of adulthood) demonstrated lower levels of self-efficacy about their school-to-work transition. This group may face particular challenges during the simultaneous transition into adulthood and into the workforce (Halstead & Lare, 2018).

The confluence of graduating from college and embarking on a career search during the already tumultuous time that is emerging adulthood makes this a vitally important and significant time—and one that is often difficult to navigate (Halstead & Lare, 2018; Wood & Kaczynski, 2007). "In a few short years, the college experience must help them learn to take personal responsibility for their beliefs and actions, which amounts to asking them to literally 'change their minds'—to go from depending on authority to becoming the authors of their own lives" (Magolda, 2012, p. 33). Fouad and Bynner (2008) argue that emerging adults must be "emotionally, cognitively, and socially ready for a transition and must marshal their resources to make the transition" (p. 244). A successful transition requires graduates to adapt, adjust, and make changes to who they are, how they behave and think, and how they see themselves during a brief slice of time (Rosemond & Owens, 2018); in short, a successful transition requires a metamorphosis.

Both the transition from college to work and the transition through emerging adulthood have been identified as significant and challenging times of life (Arnett, 2000; Blustein, Kenna, Murphy, DeVoy, & DeWine, 2005), yet, research has not fully explored the role of work and career development in emerging adults (Murphy, Blustein, Bohlig, & Platt, 2010). Fouad and Bynner (2008) argue that preparation for the transition to work requires a level of emotional, cognitive, and social development that enables a young adult to pull together all the resources they need to be successful (p. 244).

In their study "The College-to-Career Transition: An Exploration of Emerging Adulthood," Murphy et al. (2010) used a qualitative research method to explore the experience of 10 college graduates who received bachelors' degrees and began their transition to the world of work within the three years prior to the study. Half of the participants were males and half were females; their ages ranged from 22 to 25 years. All were employed full-time, and none were enrolled in or had attended graduate school at the time of the study. The interview questions focused on participants' experiences of their career development. The researchers found that the postgraduation experience of their emerging adult participants was "multifaceted and often very challenging psychologically and vocationally" (Murphy et al., 2010, p. 175). During this time of "negotiating uncertain work environments," "seeming endless possibilities," and "limited opportunities," delaying or avoiding career decisions can seem like a plausible response for emerging adults (Murphy et al., 2010, p. 175). Delays in deciding on a long-term career path may stem from needing more time for exploration or may also be due to feelings of uncertainty in their new role as a working professional.

Setting goals is a common practice that can be valuable to making progress during transitions. In their 2006 study of goal setting, Shulman, Blatt, and Feldman (2006) asked why some emerging adults are effective in setting and achieving goals while others are not. In this qualitative study 70 emerging adults in Israel, aged 21 to 26, were interviewed. Questions focused on their descriptions of themselves, their personal and professional dreams, and the changes they have experienced in the past and expect to experience in the future. Data themes indicated that these young adults had either a "doing" orientation or a "reflective" orientation that impacted the extent to which they were effective in moving toward goals. Further, each of these two orientations viewed the idea of *change* in different ways, which further impacted their effectiveness. Participants with a "doing" orientation were in constant action—doing more and more—but often not understanding the significance or importance of what they were doing. This group had a tendency to view change as needing constant attention to be maintained. In contrast, participants with a "reflective" orientation viewed making changes as an ongoing developmental process. This group also had high levels of self-awareness and could see how their actions fit into longer-term dreams and plans (Shulman et al., 2006). While there were differences in the goal-setting effectiveness among individuals, based on their orientation, all participants—regardless of their orientation—recognized the importance of their transitions and felt *compelled* to move forward to bring those transitions to fruition. This experience of compulsion is important; emerging adults know that any moratorium or delay is temporary. They realize they will have to move forward and that will mean transforming themselves if they wish to excel in their new worlds. In the next sections, we will consider various components of the requisite metamorphosis.

Metamorphosis: Finding Work

Young adults' recognition of the significance of their series of transitions and their urge to bring these changes to fruition are important aspects in the process of metamorphosis. This process is often initiated with the search for a first job immediately preceding, or after, graduation. For some, securing a job after graduation can be the foundational step on which other possible transitions will rest. Prior experience in the world of work has been shown to be helpful; in Wood and Kaczynski's (2007) case study of 18 college graduates, participants reported that the best preparation they received for transitioning to the world of work came from part-time work experiences. Age or other life experience can also influence the process; King (2011) found that emerging adults who delayed college by one year to work or travel had a higher level of confidence. Other factors that have been found to contribute to successful work search include higher levels of self-efficacy related to job search activities (Eden & Aviram, 1993; Halstead & Lare, 2018; Saks & Ashforth, 1999) and participating in job search interventions focused on improving self-presentation, setting goals, and receiving social support (Liu, Huang, & Wang, 2014).

Although important, a job can be difficult to secure. Changes in the economy and the labor market in recent history has made the transition into the world of work more challenging for emerging adults (Rosemond & Owens, 2018). In addition, both unemployment and underemployment rates for recent college graduates are higher than rates for all college graduates (Abel, Deitz, & Su, 2014). For 40% of job seekers, it takes longer than 15 weeks to secure employment; the search process takes more than 26 weeks for 26% of job seekers (Ilg, 2011). In interviews with recent college graduates, Halstead (2014) found the initial search process to be a significant point of frustration, a frustration that sometimes overshadowed longer-term planning or higher-level reflection. One participant searched for 10 months before she "accepted that [she was] not going to find a job" relevant to her bachelor's degree (Halstead, 2014, p. 145). For these young adults, the job search itself was the most difficult component of their transition.

Metamorphosis: Vocational Identity and Growth

Although finding a first job after graduation is an important early step, attainment of that first postgraduate role does not conclude the metamorphosis. Vocational identity and career growth are additional components in the transformation. Arnett (2000) describes vocational identity as knowing the type of work that will be of interest long-term and understanding the likelihood of securing that type of work. Emerging adults seek to answer the questions: "What kind of work am I good at? What kind of work would I find satisfying for the long-term? What are my chances of getting a job in the field that seems to suit me best?" (Arnett, 2000, p. 474). Or, as Konstam and Lehmann (2010) observe, "experimentation in the work place is partially motivated by a search for purpose, meaning, and satisfaction with respect to one's career " (p. 152).

Fouad and Bynner (2008) state that vocational identity and career decisions evolve over time, moving through four stages: (a) *diffusion*, where vocational identity is completely unknown; (b) *foreclosure*, where decisions are made to quickly eliminate some career options; (c) *moratorium*, where the remaining options can be explored and imagined; and, eventually (d) *commitment*, where a clear vocational identity becomes realized (p. 243). One pathway toward commitment is the process of seeking out diverse life experiences that ultimately lead to a deeper understanding of their own values and interests (Arnett, 2000). That deeper understanding of values and interests ultimately results in the actualization of vocational identity (Arnett, 2004).

Vocational identity is tentative at first and emerging adults may not consider the longer-term implications of working in a certain job. At this stage, they may think of their work life as a way to earn an income, without attributing any significance to the decision about the type of work they would find fulfilling, long-term (Arnett, 2000). As they develop, however, their aim in securing employment becomes more purposeful and begins to be recognized as the first step on a pathway to longer-term goals they are beginning to set for themselves (Arnett, 2000). Gradually, vocational identity is further explored and eventually internalized. While many recent graduates may have a career plan, the plan is subject to revision throughout the emerging adulthood years, with each revision incorporating a deeper understanding of their own values, interests, and goals (Arnett, 2004). They are learning what they want from both life and work, and they are creating and transforming their own identity.

In a longitudinal study by Staff, Harris, Sabates, and Briddell (2010), occupational certainty and wages were examined in adolescents and emerging adults over the course of a10-year period from ages 16 to 26. Their research used data from the National Education Longitudinal Study, a study that gathered information at 8th grade, 10th grade, 12th grade, and at age 26. Participants in this study reached age 26 in the year 2000, the last year of data collection for the group. At age 26, participants reported wages earned from their primary job and responded to questions to discern their occupational certainty. Specifically, they were asked to select the career they planned to have when they were 30 years old from a list of 16 broad occupational categories (e.g. protective service, sales, manager, administrator); they also could select the option *don't know* (Staff et al., 2010, p. 666). Results showed that the 26-year-olds who were uncertain about next steps in their career paths earned significantly less income than their peers who had clear vocational identities. These results held true even when controlling for differences in education, type of work, and level of experience. Staff et al. (2010) argue that a clearer sense of vocational identity helps young people make successful career decisions and also eases the college to work transition. This study supports the importance of vocational identity as emerging adults transition from college to work.

An interesting study by Konstam and Lehmann (2010) explored the roles of leisure and work engagement as related to career indecision in college graduate emerging adults. These authors identify the period of emerging adulthood as the most significant period of life for identity exploration, which impacts career choice and satisfaction. They posit that leisure activities represent an important way emerging adults "express and learn about themselves" (Konstam & Lehmann, 2010, p. 153) and that understanding leisure activities and preferences can complement an understanding of career choice and satisfaction. Further, they suggest that emerging adults who have clear preferences for leisure activities may be better able to make decisions about longer-term career preferences. Specifically, Konstam and Lehmann sought to answer the question of whether high levels of competence, control, and enjoyment related to leisure activities was an indicator for determining career decisiveness.

The study's 64 participants ranged in age from 25 to 30; each participant held either an associate's, bachelor's, or master's degree. Participants were surveyed using three different assessment instruments: the Career Decision-Making Difficulties Questionnaire, the Leisure Diagnostic Battery, and the Utrecht Work Engagement Scale. The results showed that emerging adults who were indecisive about their careers were significantly less likely to report freedom in leisure activities and less likely to be engaged at work (Konstam & Lehmann, 2010). The findings suggest that career decision challenges can have a broad impact on life experiences, including leisure activities. Thus, the metamorphosis or transformation involved in learning one's vocational identity is not only vital to the school-to-work transition process but also can impact other areas of life such as leisure activities and engagement at work.

Metamorphosis: Workplace Culture and Expectations

Understanding workplace culture can be defined as "demonstrating socially acceptable workplace behavior, understanding the organizational hierarchy and expectations of a workplace, interacting with colleagues in a way that aligns with organizational and departmental expectations, and being aware of social mores of a specific work environment" (Halstead, 2014, p. 10). The cultural metamorphosis required to move successfully from college to career also involves employers, many of whom deem recent college graduates deficient in important workplace competencies such as communication skills, problem-solving, and professionalism (Casner-Lotto, & Barrington, 2006). Part of this culture difference may stem from the difference in focus "between learning at university, where the emphasis is on the student's needs, and learning in the workplace, where the emphasis is on the organization's and the client's needs" (Crebert, Bates, Bell, Patrick & Cragnolini, 2004, p. 157).

A metamorphosis is required because the culture of the workplace is different from the culture of college. This difference can be seen in tasks and roles (Rosemond & Owens, 2018), the ways people interact with each other, the expectations held by leaders, and the way learning occurs; adaptation requires effort, development, and practice. Rosemond and Owens (2018) argue that emerging adults entering the workforce are "challenged by the lack of recognition of the shifts needed within tasks and an awareness of career socialization and development" (p. 346). Wood and Kaczynski (2007) found that graduates were "unprepared for the office environment, in particular dealing with colleagues and managers" (p. 100) and were "unaware of language choices and how to communicate at different levels" (p. 101).

One example of the difference between college and workplace cultures is the way people are expected to learn their roles. In classrooms, students are given clear expectations of what success looks like, receive direct feedback on submitted work in a short time frame, and may have the opportunity to modify their work and resubmit for additional feedback or higher grades. This loop of feedback and improvement may be different from the situation in the workplace and, in fact, may not be beneficial in a work environment. In the workplace, employees may have vague job descriptions, nontangible success measures, and little feedback. Employers may expect that new workers figure things out on their own, become highly adaptable to changing expectations and circumstances (Fouad & Bynner, 2008), and improve themselves without the benefit of direct and frequent feedback (Olson, 2014). Different ways of learning and expectations make transitions more challenging for new workers, who must change the way they are accustomed to growing, developing, and learning.

Murphy et al. (2010) emphasizes adaptability as key to a successful college to work transition; van Vianen, De Pater, and Preenen (2009) argue that the ideal time to develop this important competency is when graduates are first entering the workforce. Similarly, happenstance theory holds that unplanned events are an important part of career development (Kim, Rhee, Ha, Yang, & Lee, 2016). The structured college experience does not generally allow for enough unplanned experiences through which students could become prepared for the relatively less structured workplace environment. In fact, Casner-Lotto and Barrington (2006) report an incongruity between what young workers expect in the workplace and what really occurs, writing that "much of what they've learned in school is not applicable" (p. 21). Mastering common workplace demands, such as adaptability, are part of the metamorphosis required for successful transitions from college. Adaptability is not only a workplace expectation, but also an asset in preparing for the workplace such that adaptable individuals will display confidence, curiosity, and a sense of control over their vocational futures (Fouad et al., 2016).

In addition to adaptability, the level of initiative and self-motivation required in the workplace may exceed that which is commonly expected in a college setting. Recent graduates will need to be adept at applying knowledge in new ways, evaluating outcomes, and making adjustments independently (Campana & Peterson, 2013; Polach, 2004). When new workers initially experience the requirements of the workplace, they are often surprised by the unexpected differences and may not be prepared to excel (Olson, 2014). Taken together, the difficulty making cultural and environmental adjustments to the workplace, in combination with emerging adults' perception of unpreparedness for the work place, turns what many people assume will be a natural progression into a difficult and tumultuous transition that requires a metamorphosis in growth, understanding, and behavior.

Metamorphosis: Social Network

In addition to adapting to the culture and expectations of the workplace, college graduate emerging adults who are entering the workforce often must build a new social network. Having a strong social support system is an important to a successful workplace transition (Murphy et al., 2010; Polach, 2004). In fact, Murphy et al. (2010) found that "social support or lack thereof related to [participants'] sense of well-being, their experience of the transition, and how, and how their expectations of the transitions were met or unfulfilled" (p. 177). In Halstead's (2014) study, several participants named the social transition as one of their most significant challenges in their transition from student to worker. Specifically, they complained of not having friends close by and of missing the environment of college where they were surrounded by peers and had ample opportunities, often facilitated by their colleges, to connect and establish relationships with peers.

In the new work environment, it may be necessary for emerging adults to transform their expectations and practices regarding where and how socialization takes place and how they establish friendships and acquaintances (Polach, 2004). For example, in the college environment, students were often surrounded by peers their age and may have had more free time to foster and build connections. In a workplace with less facilitated interaction among employees who also have less free time outside of work and fewer peers of the same age, developing a social network requires a metamorphosis. In adapting to this new environment, emerging adults may need to be more "deliberate and focused" in trying to meet new people (Polach, 2004, p. 15), recognizing that co-workers may interact with one another differently than fellow students interacted at school.

This difficulty may be particularly challenging for some graduates whose entry into the world of work includes a move to a different geographic area. However, if graduates are purposeful in researching neighborhoods and housing options before relocating, they may be able to find places to live that enable them to meet friends more easily. For example, sharing a house with others, living in an area with plenty of after work activities, or seeking out neighborhoods populated by fellow young professionals (Polach, 2004) can all aid the socialization process.

Polach (2004) writes that, in addition to learning the rules of a new workplace, the transition from college to work also includes "myriad social steps . . . such as moving to a new city, making friends, managing expenses against a real income, finding a place of worship, and fitting into a social group" (p. 5). These realities are part of the demand placed on new workers to grow and change rapidly in the initial period following graduation. Creating a new social network requires time and, often, different strategies than previously used. The ability to navigate the new social rules comprises an important metamorphosis for the emerging adult who is new to the workplace.

How the Transition Feels

The previously described challenges and experiences demonstrate that the transition from college to work requires adaptation, evolution, and transformation. As graduates go through this process of remaking themselves in a new environment and culture, it is helpful to understand and gain insight about how the metamorphoses feel to them. To investigate the extent to which graduates feel prepared, Landrum, Hettich, and Wilner (2010) surveyed alumni who held bachelor's degrees in psychology about their perceptions of workforce readiness; they were asked to rank their own readiness at the time of graduation *and* the level of readiness they felt had been expected in the workforce. In 36 out of 37 competency areas, alumni responded that the level of preparedness they felt following graduation was lower than the level of preparedness expected in the workplace. Competency areas included handling conflict, managing multiple tasks, receiving feedback, self-discipline, and decision-making. The sense of unpreparedness for required changes may represent a common feeling in the very early stages of the transition from college to work.

In a phenomenological study, Polach (2004) posed the question, "What is it like working in a large corporate environment as your first job following college graduation?" (p. 9). Polach interviewed eight recent college graduates about their first-year experience in the workforce. Data themes identified included (a) frustration at the lack of structure in the work environment, (b) the critical nature of developing friendships for their overall well-being and feeling successful, and (c) a wish for more feedback than was provided and a simultaneous recognition that feedback is important due to lack of confidence about their own performance. Participants in this study experienced the move from college to work as one that required transformations, or metamorphoses, and also one that was, overall, a positive experience where they were able to grow, learn, and contribute. This positive feeling about the transition experience is echoed in the Murphy et al.'s (2010) study where a key theme was an overarching sense of optimism about the future.

Hope and optimism were also present as one of the most compelling and overarching themes in Halstead's (2014) study. This optimism was present whether they were currently satisfied with their transition or not. They shared, "I think I am heading towards a successful transition—I just haven't gotten there yet—It will happen"; "I have a couple of offers and so I am going somewhere . . . so I feel I am ready for that. . . . I am really well prepared for it"; and "My transition was a lesson (laughs). It taught me a lot. I would rather have the experience . . . than to not have it. At the end of the day it helped me grow"

(Halstead, 2014, p. 130). It seems that many recent graduates have a strong sense of optimism about eventually getting where they want to go, regardless of whether they know what they need to do to attain those goals (Halstead & Lare, 2018; Johnson & Monserud, 2010).

Halstead's (2014) study also, however, found frustration and lack of readiness in emerging adults experience of their transition; several participants expressed a sense of surprise at learning, after graduation, what it would actually take to progress in their chosen career path. One participant shared, "I wish my department would have told me [more about what to expect]" (p. 143). Later in the interview she talked about the "reality check" of getting rejection emails, which helped her realize she needed a master's degree to get where she wanted in her profession. Surprise was echoed in another participant's interview—he wished that professors had talked about "the reality of life after college" and expressed that "professors were not open in talking about what was required to move into the profession" (p. 143).

Frustration at the inability to find a job in a chosen profession was another theme. One participant shared, "I don't really have the ability to plan long-term right now. . . . I don't really have the freedom to choose beyond this moment [because I have bills to pay]" (Halstead, 2014, p. 156). The experience of taking a job they do not want, out of financial necessity, is one faced by many graduates (Sharon, 2016). In cases where securing a job after graduation is really a foundational step to a successful transition, without which a graduate cannot afford to move forward, it adds intensity to the transition and the expectations that accompany it. Other participants who felt unfulfilled with the progress of their transition or who were frustrated with the state of their transition used phrases such as "I was stressed out" or describing feelings of being "worn out" or "mentally drained" (Halstead, 2014, p. 128). In essence, when young adults seek to explore life options and gain confidence in their own identity and values, they face complex and conflicting expectations and experiences, while still maintaining hope about what is to come.

What to Do: Supporting Transition to the Workforce

In transitioning to life after college, graduates need a career plan, a strategic approach or route to help guide them through emerging adulthood, vocational choice, and identity formation (Arnett, 2004; Rosemond & Owens, 2018). One of the most important thing colleges can do today is to address the developmental needs of students and alumni who are in the midst of emerging adulthood and choosing career paths (Arnett, 2012; Fouad et al.,

2016; Rosemond & Owens, 2018), and the college environment is uniquely equipped to support students' identity development (Arnett, 2016; Rosemond & Owens, 2018). The process of exploring and developing personal and vocational identity prepares graduates for making career decisions that are right for them and facilitate the transition from college to career (Staff et al., 2010). In the metamorphoses required to grow into one's personal and professional identities and to transition from college to career, there are specific things that students and recent graduates can do—and also things that colleges and universities can do to facilitate this developmental process. For example, internships and other experiences that mimic real-life situations and provide hands-on learning experiences are valuable and enjoyable ways to support the school-to-work transition (Halstead & Lare, 2018). Different individuals value and gain benefit different aspects of these experiences; for example, the experiences can help one choose a career, confirm an already chosen path, prepare for work after graduation, get to know people before entering a profession in a full-time capacity, or experience fulfillment when a permanent full-time job in their chosen field is not available.

Travel may be another way students and graduates can support the required metamorphoses they face. To examine the impact of travel or working for a year, King (2011) interviewed 23 college students about their experiences in a *gap year*. The results showed that emerging adults who took a gap year before college described themselves as having more confidence, maturity, and independence than those who did not. Further, these emerging adults described themselves as being different selves than they were before the travel and work exploration of their gap year. Further, a study of backpackers under the age of 30 found that skills including effective communication, self-confidence, decision making, feeling comfortable around all types of people, and adaptability were all enhanced through their travel experiences (Pearce & Foster, 2007). Travel and other experiences can aid in understanding workplaces or settings that may be of interest; moreover, interacting and making decisions in diverse environments that are unfamiliar provide broadened perspectives and promote maturity, in conjunction with skill development to help individuals succeed in the workplace (Oddou, Mendenhall, & Ritchie, 2000).

Injecting "learning partnerships" (Magolda, 2012, p. 34) into college and postcollege experiences can support the metamorphosis from school to work. Learning partnerships are experiences facilitated by educators to "promote the kind of development that will enable graduates to navigate life's challenges" (p. 34) and can occur in a school or a work environment. Results of a longitudinal study of college graduates over the course of more than 20 years provided the foundation for Magolda's learning partnerships model, in which educators specifically seek to incorporate approaches to help students become more adept at "self-authorship" (p. 34) to gain a clearer concept of their own identities and belief systems. Some of the techniques used to foster this development in students include using an interdisciplinary approach that adds real-life complexity and nuance to issues and topics encountered in the classroom, teaching as a facilitator rather than an authority figure, and encouraging students to solve problems on their own, thereby increasing their confidence and personal authority.

Another study focused on skill development was conducted in 2013 by Campana and Peterson, who created a college course intended to mimic a work environment by adopting policies similar to those found in the workplace (such as consequences for tardiness and absences) and work assignments that demanded problem-solving and application of knowledge. The goal was to see if workplace competencies could be injected into a college environment and how this would be experienced by educators and students. Surveys were administered to students in the first week of class and after the completion of the course; instructors also captured their own thoughts and observations about the process. At the end of the course, students were found to have a higher level of professionalism and paid more attention to the details of their work. Instructors also found that developing the course led them to pay more attention to their goals for their students and to be deliberate about the natural ways coursework can develop skills that are necessary for the transition from college to career (Campana & Peterson, 2013). By encouraging educators to be more mindful of goals and by educating students while purposefully aiming to increase important workplace competencies, instructors can help facilitate a successful school-to-work transition.

In addition to these strategies, which colleges and universities can implement to help facilitate student and graduate vocational identity, students may also take ownership of the process themselves by purposefully seeking out the support of career services offices and other campus departments. Most colleges offer career development workshops designed to help develop vocational acumen including resume writing, articulating value to potential employers, interviewing success, recognizing professional strengths, exploring career paths, and effective job search strategies. Participating in these existing campus programs can be highly beneficial to students' ability to grow their vocational identity. Purposefully seeking out mentors is another way students and recent graduates can significantly impact their own growth; mentorship has a positive influence on a student's career planning initiatives, and decreases students' self-defeating job search behaviors (Renna, Steinbauer, Taylor, & Detwiler, 2014). In short, colleges and universities often offer a variety of workshops and support to aid student career development; when students and recent graduates purposefully seek out resources, programs, and guidance to build their own personal and vocational identity, they can take control of their own metamorphosis.

Conclusion

The transition from postsecondary school to work is a tumultuous time for many emerging adults and requires that young people behave, interact, and think differently than they did as students. The metamorphoses required to transition successfully include making adaptations related to finding employment, navigating new cultures, building a social network, acquiring new definitions of success and learning, and changing the way they see their own identities. Gaining a sense of vocational identity is an important purpose for the exploration that occurs during this time.

The catalyst for these requisite metamorphoses is each young person's particular convergence of transitions from school to work and from adolescent to adult. The transformative experience of this life stage is multifaceted and complex. Emerging adults may feel unprepared, yet optimistic; like an adult, yet not like an adult; excited to be entering the world of work, yet frustrated by unfulfilled ideals. The research presented in this chapter shows that successful transition experiences can have a long-term impact on future work and life success and happiness.

Given the importance of these simultaneous transitions and the demands of the metamorphosis, it is important to explore ways to support young people in undertaking this transformational identity work. Encouraging them to create a plan, providing opportunities to gain real-world experience outside of school, having classrooms that inject skill development, and fostering learning partnerships to develop self-authorship are all vehicles that ultimately promote a successful school-to-work transition for emerging adults.

References

Abel, J. R., Deitz, R., & Su, Y. (2014). Are recent college graduates finding good jobs? *Current Issues in Economics and Finance, 20*(1), 1–8.

Arnett, J. J. (2000). Emerging adulthood. A theory of development from the late teens through the twenties. *American Psychologist, 55*(5), 469–480.

Arnett, J. J. (2004). *Emerging adulthood: The winding road from late teens through the twenties.* New York, NY: Oxford University Press.

Arnett, J. J. (2012, December). *Emerging adulthood on campus: The new life stage and college students today.* Invited address, Franklin & Marshall College, Lancaster, PA.

Arnett, J. J. (2016). College students as emerging adults: The developmental implications of the college context. *Emerging Adulthood, 4*(3), 219–222.

Blustein, D. L., Kenna, A. C., Murphy, K. A., DeVoy, J. E., & DeWine, D. B. (2005). Qualitative research in career development: Exploring the center and margins of discourse about careers and working. *Journal of Career Assessment, 13*, 351–370.

Bureau of Labor Statistics. (2016). Economic news release: College enrollment and work activity of 2015 high school graduates. Retrieved from http://www.bls.gov/news.release/hsgec.nr0.htm

Campana, K. L., & Peterson, J. J. (2013). Do bosses give extra-credit? Using the classroom to model real-world work experiences. *College Teaching, 61*(2), 60–66.

Casner-Lotto, J., & Barrington, L. (2006). Are they really ready to work? Employers' perspectives on the basic knowledge and applied skills of new entrants to the 21st century U.S. workforce. *Partnership for 21st Century Skills.* Retrieved from https://files.eric.ed.gov/fulltext/ED519465.pdf

Crebert, G., Bates, M., Bell, B., Patrick, C., & Cragnolini, V. (2004). Developing generic skills at university, during work placement and in employment: Graduates' perceptions. *Higher Education Research & Development, 23*(2), 147–165.

Eden, D., & Aviram, A. (1993). Self-efficacy training to speed reemployment: Helping people to help themselves. Journal of Applied Psychology, 78(3), 352–360.

European Group for Integrated Social Research. (2001). Misleading trajectories: Transition dilemmas of young adults in Europe. *Journal of Youth Studies, 4*(1), 101–118.

Fouad, N. A., & Bynner, J. (2008). Work transitions. *American Psychologist, 63*(4), 241–251.

Fouad, N. A., Ghosh, A., Chang, W., Figueiredo, C., & Bachhuber, T. (2016). Career exploration among college students. *Journal of College Student Development, 57*(4), 460–464.

Halstead, T. J. (2014). *An exploration of career transition self-efficacy in emerging adult college graduates* (Doctoral dissertation, East Stroudsburg University, PA). Retrieved from http://hdl.handle.net/2069/2297

Halstead, T. J., & Lare, D. (2018). An exploration of career transition self-efficacy in emerging adult college graduates. *Journal of College Student Development, 59*(2), 177–191.

Ilg, R. (2011, May). How long before the unemployed find jobs or quit looking? (Issues in labor statistics, summary 11-01). *U.S. Bureau of Labor Statistics.* Retrieved from https://www.bls.gov/opub/btn/archive/how-long-before-the-unemployed-find-jobs-or-quit-looking.pdf

Johnson, M. K., & Monserud, M. A. (2010). Judgments about work and the features of young adults' jobs. *Work and Occupations, 37*(2), 194–224.

Kim, B., Rhee, E., Ha, G., Yang, J., & Lee, S. M. (2016). Tolerance of uncertainty: Links to happenstance, career decision self-efficacy, and career satisfaction. *Career Development Quarterly, 64*, 140–152.

King, A. (2011). Minding the gap? Young people's accounts of taking a gap year as a form of identity work in higher education. *Journal of Youth Studies, 14*(3), 341–357.

Konstam, V., & Lehmann, I. S. (2010). Emerging adults at work and at play: Leisure, work engagement, and career indecision. *Journal of Career Assessment, 19*(2), 151–164.

Landrum, R. E., Hettich, P. I., & Wilner, A. (2010). Alumni perceptions of workforce readiness. *Teaching of Psychology, 37*(2), 97–106.

Liu, S., Huang, J. L., & Wang, M. (2014). Effectiveness of Job Search Interventions: A Meta-Analytic Review. *Psychological Bulletin, 140*(4), 1009–1041.

Magolda, M. B. B. (2012). Building learning partnerships. *Change: The Magazine of Higher Education, 44*(1), 32–38. doi:10.10080/00091383.2012.636002

McDow, L. W., & Zabrucky, K. M. (2015). Effectiveness or a career development course on students' job search skills and self-efficacy. *Journal of College Student Development, 56*(6), 632–636.

Murphy, K. A., Blustein, D. L., Bohlig, A. J., & Platt, M. G. (2010). The college-to-career transition: An exploration of emerging adulthood. *Journal of Counseling & Development, 88*(2), 174–181.

National Center for Education Statistics. (1999). Table 187: College enrollment rates of high school graduates, by sex: 1960 to 1998. *Digest of Education Statistics.* Retrieved from https://nces.ed.gov/programs/digest/d99/d99t187.asp

Oddou, G., Mendenhall, M. E., & Ritchie, J. B. (2000). Leveraging travel as a tool for global leadership development. *Human Resource Management, 39*(2–3), 159–172.

Olson, J. S. (2014). Transitions from formal education to the workplace. *New Directions for Adult and Continuing Education, 143*, 73–82.

Pearce, P. L., & Foster, F. (2007). A "university of travel": Backpacker learning. *Tourism Management, 28*(5), 1285–1298.

Polach, J. L. (2004). Understanding the experience of college graduates during their first year of employment. *Human Resource Development Quarterly, 15*(1), 5–23.

Renna, R. W., Steinbauer, R., Taylor, R., & Detwiler, D. (2014). School-to-work transition: Mentor career support and student career planning, job search intentions, and self-defeating job search behavior. *Journal of Vocational Behavior, 85*(3), 422–432.

Rosemond, M. M., & Owens, D. (2018). Exploring career development in emerging adult collegians. *Education, 138*(4), 337–352.

Saks, A. M., & Ashforth, B. E. (1999). Effects of individual differences and job search behaviors on the employment status of recent university graduates. *Journal of Vocational Behavior, 54*, 335–349.

Sharon, T. (2016). Constructing adulthood: Markers of adulthood and well-being among emerging adults. *Emerging Adulthood, 4*(3), 161–167.

Shulman, S., Blatt, S. J., & Feldman, B. (2006). Vicissitudes of the impetus for growth and change among emerging adults. *Psychoanalytic Psychology, 23*(1), 159–180.

Staff, J., Harris, A., Sabates, R., & Briddell, L. (2010). Uncertainty in early occupational aspirations: Role exploration or aimlessness? *Social Forces, 89*(2), 659–684.

van Vianen, E. M., De Pater, I. E., & Preenen, P. T. Y. (2009). Adaptable careers: Maximizing less and exploring more. *Career Development Quarterly, 57*, 298–309.

Wood, L., & Kaczynski, D. (2007). University students in USA and Australia: Anticipation and reflection on the transition to work. *International Journal of Employment Studies, 15*(2), 91–106.

Yang, E., & Gysbers, N. C. (2007). Career transitions of college seniors. *Career Development Quarterly, 56*, 157–169.

21

A New Adulthood

Conceptualizing Transition Using a Generational Framework

Johanna Wyn and Dan Woodman

Introduction

It makes common sense to think of youth as a period of transition, a phase of the life cycle in which people move into their adult identities and social positions. This chapter holds this idea up to scrutiny. We argue that, as it has come to be used in youth studies and youth policy, a youth transitions framework is a weak tool for understanding young people's lives. It oversimplifies the significant problems of the failing nexus between education and work, insecure and precarious work, and the challenges faced by young people in achieving stability. For this reason, it is a poor basis for informing programs that aim to address these problems.

McLeod and Wright (2016) have argued that within youth studies there has been a tendency for "keywords" to become naturalized within discourses on young people, claiming as "truths" what are essentially assumptions. They argue that it is important to ask "What keywords do, what they open up and shut down, what they discipline and productively bring into view" (McLeod & Wright, 2016, p. 789). While increasingly critiqued, the notion of youth as a transition, and the transitions approaches in youth studies, have long had this sense of taken-for-grantedness.

Furlong and colleagues (2017) argue that the concept of transition focuses almost exclusively on the transitions that people make (and almost always the focus is on the young). Instead, Furlong and colleagues, drawing on the established sociological tools of Norbert Elias and C. Wright Mills, highlight the need to see shifting youth transitions as one way to study long-running changes in society (such as the collapse in the youth labor market that started

Johanna Wyn and Dan Woodman, *A New Adulthood* In: *Young Adult Development at the School-to-Work Transition.* E. Anne Marshall and Jennifer E. Symonds, Oxford University Press (2021). © Oxford University Press.
DOI: 10.1093/oso/9780190941512.003.0021.

in the late 1970s). Their "long view" offers a new insight into the normalization of precarious work and provides a perspective on the shallowness of neoliberal policies that for too long have blamed young people for labor markets that no longer offer enough people jobs that can sustain a good life.

Our approach resonates with this one. We use concepts from the sociology of generations to understand the intersections between individual lives and societal transitions, arguing that a "new adulthood" has emerged (Woodman & Wyn 2015). Recognizing that the idea of social generation has for over a decade provoked quite heated debate in the youth studies community (France & Roberts, 2015), we offer an approach that we hope "productively brings into view" (McLeod & Wright, 2016, p. 789) the kinds of pressures and constraints, as well as the new opportunities, that this generation of young people must contend with. By understanding the dynamics that both make young people's lives possible and constrain them, we can do more than simply document problems—we can understand and thereby address them.

Youth Transitions

The concept of transition has become almost synonymous with youth studies. Talbut and Lesko (2012, p. 2) highlight that the concept of youth invokes a universal category of transitional beings on their way to productive, responsible, and legal adulthood. Transition as a metaphor is attractive to youth researchers because it draws attention to patterns of trajectories. An example is research showing how patterns of achieving independent living and forming life partnerships and responsibilities (including marriage and becoming parents) are occurring at a later age for young people in Australia and other countries (Australian Bureau of Statistics, 2013; International Labour Organisation [ILO], 2013). This kind of research leads intuitively to the identification of normative and nonnormative patterns. Perhaps for this reason, the idea of transition has been especially popular with researchers who have a policy focus (Woodman & Wyn 2013). Measures of the correlations between educational credentials and full-time employment, for example, have informed the idea that there are smooth and risky transitions. Young people who achieve postsecondary qualifications tend to have better outcomes in the labor market (or experience "smooth" transitions) than their peers who are less qualified (Lamb, Jackson, Walstab, & Huo, 2015) and are therefore "at risk" (and experience blemished transitions).

This kind of evidence has been a key source of information for government policies that aim to reduce the proportions of young people who are at risk (of making flawed transitions of various types), and especially those who are not in employment, education or training (known as NEETs). Informed by the assumption of a causal relationship between level of education and employment, these policies are popular in policy circles in large part because they put the onus on young people to gain educational credentials so that they are more competitive in the labor marketplace.

However, as many commentators and researchers point out, this market-based approach (often referred to as neoliberalism) is proving to be hollow. Insecure work has been heralded as the "new normal" for young people, who are making up a substantial segment of a new "precariat" (Standing, 2011). There is little evidence that youth unemployment can be addressed solely through personal investment in education and faith in labor markets. Finding a secure, full-time job has become increasingly difficult, despite increased levels of education and training. The ILO (2013) reports that globally youth unemployment is estimated to be 13%, which is very close to its historic peak in the aftermath of the 2008–2009 global recession (p. vii). The emergence of underemployment and insecure work across the globe is further undermining the value of educational credentials (Yeung & Alipio, 2013; Anagnost, Arai & Ren, 2013).

The idea of transition, with its focus on young people's progress and its measurement of normative patterns has limited capacity to guide analysis beyond identifying problematic types of transition, and the problematic youth attached to them. It provides little insight into dynamics of new labor markets that are denying more young people a livelihood. We argue that an alternative framework is needed to understand and address the problematic situation for young people that transitions research has highlighted. Before turning to outline what such a framework might look like, as the purpose of this chapter is to provide a critical perspective on the way in which the metaphor of transition is used in youth studies, it is worth a closer look at the historical legacy of the concept of transition.

Transition Draws on a Developmental Legacy

The idea of youth transition as a problematic and deficit phase of life owes a significant debt to the work of G. Stanley Hall. In 1904, Hall coined the term *adolescence* to describe a distinctive phase of psychological development, characterized by stormy and stressful relationships and risky behavior (G. S. Hall, 1904). It is easy to see how this psychological approach has been easily translated into the contemporary focus on problematic youth transitions (from education to work). The assumption of a close relationship between problematic youthful transitions that infuses current thinking also bears the legacy of developmental theorists such as Piaget, (1954) and Erikson (1965). These theorists drew on Freud's thinking about the developmental and transitional stages of the psyche from infancy through to maturity to propose that youth represented a distinctive, universal, and essential stage of life during which developmental tasks must be mastered to ensure the transition to healthy, rational adulthood. In other words, positing youth as a problematic transition.

The metaphor of transitions achieved prominence in youth studies in the United Kingdom in the 1980s, as full-time employment in what was called the teenage labor market in many Western countries became increasingly scarce. Young people (many of whom would rather have been employed) sought refuge in education, hoping to gain the credentials to compete for jobs in new knowledge, service, and high-skill economies (Furlong, 2013; ILO, 2013). In this way, the economic developments of the 1980s and 1990s created the conditions for a new youth. The focus on their changing patterns of life readily suggested an extended period of youth, a key and enduring feature of which was the complex relationship between the spheres of education and work. While this complex and relatively loose relationship has been documented in studies such as Andres and Wyn's (2010) international analysis of youth transitions, it has not received much attention until recently. Instead, the idea of extended transitions has been widely employed to refer to the gap between young people completing postsecondary education and finding a secure job, directing attention to a raft of deficits in young people (such as studying the wrong courses, being underprepared for work, or having poor attitudes).

This ancestry in developmental psychology of many ideas central to youth transitions frameworks needs to be highlighted, because it underpins the often-implicit assumption that youth is a deficit phase—incomplete and risky—compared to adulthood. It is reflected in the idea of emerging adulthood, proposed by Arnett (2000), which seeks to insert a phase of psychological development between adolescence and adulthood. As Cohen and Ainley (2000) have argued, achieving employment and becoming a "mature adult" are often conflated within transitions research. This reflected in the category NEET, a widely used category in policy frameworks that highlights the deficits of young people who have failed to conform to institutionally sanctioned transition markers. A similar point is made by Kelly (2006) when he argues that young people are compelled to perform the "entrepreneurial self," demonstrating their maturity through entrepreneurial performances of the transition from education to the labor market. While transition from education to work is arguably a focus for young people and researchers alike, it is important that researchers do not unwittingly reinforce the view that development/transition are a form of progression toward maturity or completion and by implication that children and young people are faulty, or lesser, relative to adults.

A Transition Metaphor Misses Important Relationships

The developmental/transition legacy also deserves scrutiny because the developmental/transitional conflation emphasizes young people's progress and downplays societal change. Young people are living at a time of rapid societal transitions, particularly in the Global South but also across the North. This tendency for youth researchers to give insufficient attention to the intersections between individual biography and history is pivotal to a new analysis of young people and labor markets by Furlong and colleagues (2017). Taking issue with Standing's (2011) analysis of the emergence of precarious work as a new phenomenon for young people, this work takes the long view of the relationship between young people and work, going back to the mid-1980s. Adopting the sociogenesis approach developed by Norbert Elias (2012), they ask, How did precarious work come about and what is it related to?

Sociogenesis is the tracing of social transformation over the long-run, looking at the events that shift social relations (the web of human interdependencies and power relations) and how these link to shifts in personality and dispositions. Furlong and colleagues (2017) use this approach to provide a necessarily rough outline of how precarious work as it is experienced today emerged, allowing them to not only understand the past, but shed light on contemporary problems and where society may be heading in the future. Furlong and colleagues point out that a focus on the current situation alone is the analytical equivalent to studying a photograph or a series of photographs that capture single moments in time. They argue that a snap-shot approach, especially one that only provides a lens on the present is a poor analytical device compared to the complexity that is visible watching a movie of connected images over time. This point is also made by T. Hall, Coffey, and Lashua (2009) who argue that much transitions research misses the relationships and events that occur between measured transitional points, and reiterated by Cuervo and Wyn (2014) in their discussion of the metaphor of transition in youth studies. Transition is not a poor word per se; rather, it is a poor term when used to denote a transfer.

Taking this sociogenetic approach enables Furlong and colleagues (2017) to shift away from a linear, normative transitions approach to focus on the interrelationships of history and biography. They find that precarious youth employment is related to longer term processes of change in the way people work, that first became visible in the 1980s (Furlong et al., 2017). This is consistent with our understanding that a new adulthood has been forged during this time (Dwyer & Wyn, 2001; Wyn & Woodman, 2006; Woodman & Wyn, 2015). Furlong and colleagues (2017) argue that investments in education have not been able to halt the steady erosion of employment opportunities, creating underemployment. In turn, increasing investments in education by young people and their families, alongside the deterioration of the labor market, have made life management more complex for all age groups. Rather than simply creating an extended youth, these gradual and historic changes have fundamentally altered the life course, creating what we call a "new adulthood."

As Furlong and colleagues (2017) point out, an approach (enabled by simplistic transitions frameworks) that aims to measure successful and risky patterns facilitates an individualizing policy focus that easily slips into punitive policies, which have inflicted considerable suffering on young people. Policy frameworks based on this understanding of transition make it relatively simple to assume that it is young people who are the problem, ignoring the long-term shifts in demand for labor and instead focusing on remediating those with risky patterns. Policies have forced young people into institutionally condoned stages of transition, including poorly conceived training schemes and dead-end qualifications, regardless of young people's aspirations. This is exemplified in the neat and simplified concept of NEETs as the problem that needs fixing (Roberts, 2011).

A New Adulthood

The concept of a new adulthood emerged from analysis of the Life Patterns longitudinal research program, which began in the mid-1990s and continues today. It tracks the lives of two cohorts of young Australians, one that left secondary school in 1991 and the other that left secondary school in 2006. The 1991 cohort entered the labor market at a time when it was being restructured through deregulation and decentralization of industrial relations, responding to pressure to lower the cost of labor to compete in globalized markets, resulting in the rise of casual and flexible jobs (Cuervo & Wyn, 2016; Crofts et al., 2015). The onus on young people was entrenched in policies such as

Young People's Participation in Post-Compulsory Education and Training (Finn, 1991) and *Putting General Education to Work* (Mayer, 1992) that strongly encouraged young people to undertake postcompulsory education on the understanding that tertiary education would future-proof young people against rising unemployment and underemployment levels. It did not.

The effect of these changes on young people's opportunities and attitudes has gradually become better understood. For example, partly because of the delay in achieving secure employment, at the age of 29, only 12% of participants in the Life Patterns research program were in a parenting role, 34% were married, and 25% more were on an ongoing or de facto relationship. This is significantly different from their parents' generation, for whom a majority of women were married at age 23 and of men at age 25. The majority of women in this previous generation who became parents also did so before the age of 30 (see Australian Bureau of Statistics, 2009). Andres and Wyn (2010) argue that despite the modest goals and hopes of this generation (e.g., job security, building their own family), the Life Patterns participants were affected by the twin trends of extended study and insecure work, which signified putting these goals on hold until they reached greater financial stability. For a significant minority, this stability never arrived. Young people now faced an adulthood characterized by changes in the field of employment with rising unstable employment, multiple job and occupation changes, and re-entry into education to gain skills and qualifications as needed. While the statistical data on transitions points to a simple extension of the phase of youth, the qualitative data reveals the emergence of distinctive attitudes and subjectivities, linked to these new realities, which have informed young people's decision-making.

These circumstances created the conditions for a new adulthood, heralding a shift in the life course from the traditional notion of clear life phases (childhood, youth, and adulthood) to a more nuanced understanding of changing life patterns. The idea of a new adulthood is in contrast with the popular notion that youth has been extended (compared with the baby boomer generation, which are often the explicit or implicit benchmark and norm). The notion that there is an extended youth or a new phase called *emerging adulthood* clings to the idea of developmental stages. By contrast, the idea of a new adulthood draws on the understanding that all life stages are a product of social conditions, and there is no longer any prospect of young people transitioning into the adulthood of a bygone era (Wyn & Woodman, 2007). It destabilizes the presumption that childhood, youth, and adulthood are universal and essential phases of life, independent of social conditions. Research on the nature of adulthood by Blatterer (2007) and Silva (2013) supports the view that adulthood itself has been redefined, and the delayed adulthood thesis is based on an anachronistic model of adulthood based on a simplified version the conditions that prevailed in the late 1950s and 1960s.

The relational nature of the new adulthood as a concept is highlighted by its synergies with Bourdieu's (1993) concepts of habitus and field, which he proposed as thinking tools to explore how social patterns emerge and endure across time. To elaborate briefly, habitus is defined as a system of durable and transposable dispositions that are structured by an individual's social practices (Bourdieu, 1990, p. 53). These dispositions, which influence decisions about education, employment, and lifestyle, respond to changing circumstances as individuals engage in new fields. Bourdieu (1990) defines *field* as a structured space with its own logic, rules, practices, and history, shaped over time by individuals and institutions. Framed in this way, the use of the term *new adulthood* signals a shift in the dispositions and practices experienced by young people in the post-1970 generation as they have sought to manage the emerging new complexity of life (Furlong et al., 2017). There has been a generational accommodation to, and partial active shaping of, the changing rules of the game of transition from education to work (Wyn et. al., 2017). In expanding the analysis of this relational approach to understanding the relationship between individual biographies and social conditions, we have found developing the social generations approach to be useful.

Social Generation

The sociology of generations emerged in the 1920s through the work of Karl Mannheim, Francois Mentre, and Jose Ortega y Gassett, among others, who were interested in the way in which the intersections of sociohistorical milieu and individual biographies might create distinctive generational consciousnesses and political cleavages (Woodman, 2011). New collective forms of subjectivity can emerge among young people in the face of changing historical conditions that make reliance on previous ways of acting and thinking difficult (Mannheim, 1952). Their primary point of reference was the suffering wrought by the Great War (now usually called World War 1), which meant that the new generation could not and would not live the same types of adult lives as their parents.

The central sociological dynamic in a social generational framework is the weight given to cultural, individual, and structural processes in shaping the meaning and experience of youth and adulthood. This means that rather than simply mapping institutional markers of the life course as a transitions approach invites us to do, a social generations approach gives significance to the institutionalized possibilities for youth and adulthood posed by social and economic conditions and government policies and how these are reshaped over time. A social generation is not simply created by broad-scale economic and social change, but by policy decisions and the at times unavoidable work of reshaping what it means to be an adult or a young person (Woodman, 2013: para. 3.3)

Thus a generations approach offers a reflexive framework for tracing the way generational change is made, through the work that young people do to manage changing circumstances and policy frameworks. To illustrate what this might mean for analysis, we have used the concept of transition regime as an alternative to the notion of youth transitions. The concept of *transition regimes* was originally put forward by du Bois-Reymond and Stauber (2005, p. 63) to acknowledge young people's patterns of life, but at the same time to recognize that these patterns are a response to economic and social realities and policy frameworks. Du Bois-Reymond and Stauber used the concept of transition regime to refer to the institutional processes, practices, and discourses of education systems, labor markets, and welfare systems that create imperatives, possibilities, and risks for young people through the implementation of institutional transition points and statuses, which are embedded in policies that both encourage and coerce.

It is reasonable to think of these transition regimes as in the process of becoming global (Woodman & Wyn, 2015, p. 22). Increases in rates of educational participation across many countries are a central component in global transition regimes for young people. The increase in participation by young people, extending the time spent in education through to their early to mid-20s has significantly altered the shape of so-called youth transitions—to an extent that is generation-making. For example, at a population level, increases in educational participation have created new patterns of internal migration, as young people move from rural to urban and regional centers where secondary educational institutions are located. The sheer numbers of young people seeking educational opportunities in global education markets has resulted in a mass movement of internationally mobile students (increasing more than threefold from 1.3 million in 1990 to nearly 4.3 million in 2011; OECD, 2013). While not all young people in this generation are mobile in this way, nonetheless the mass nature of engagement in education (and mobility) creates a generational disposition or outlook. At a cultural level, transition regimes have created new aspirations for young people and their families that distinguish them from earlier generations.

The institutionalized nature of transition regimes extends far beyond educational policies that encourage greater educational participation. They also encompass the impact of policies on young people. Mizen (2002) provides an example of how the state in the United Kingdom, through policies that withhold income support to young people who do not conform to requirements to be engaged in education or training, has redefined the meaning of youth, creating new categories of deserving and undeserving young people. The same analysis can be used to analyze Australian youth policies that demonize young people who are unemployed by withholding income support for a period of weeks or months if young people leave a job.

Young people around the world are increasingly engaged in these global transition regimes as youth labor markets and the demand for skills are reshaped by globalization (ILO, 2013; Brown et al., 2011). Broad patterns recur across different localities as young people struggle to manage the complex work of life management (Furlong et al., 2017). For example, Feixa and Cangas (2005), who analyze the changing meaning of youth in Mexico and Chile, reveal the ways in which young people mobilize the resources available to them to navigate the pressures and uncertainties created by transition regimes. This reinforces the conclusions drawn by Farrugia and Watson (2011): Those who are most disadvantaged are positioned to work the hardest to manage fragmenting, isolating, and individualizing processes, reshaping the lives for young people around the world. This struggle to find stability and security in the face of increasing employment precarity marks a generation and suggests that it is no longer appropriate to see their patterns of life during their 20s as simply an experimental stage that precedes stable adult lives. Instead, the struggle to manage complexity that is apparent in their 20s can be seen as a step into the new adulthood that itself is increasingly defined by precariousness and insecurity (Woodman & Wyn, 2015).

Shifting from a descriptive, linear framework such as transitions to the relational framework of social generations offers researchers, professionals working with young people, and policymakers the insights they will need to address the widening gap between haves and have-nots in our young population—and the increasing reality that despite their enormous investment in education, this generation and likely the next one will be finding ways to make do with insecure and often unsustaining work. Focusing on young people's patterns of transition alone helps to foster the belief that it is the young people who need to change something about their attitudes or actions—and not labor markets that are failing (Woodman and Wyn, 2013). The focus on smooth transition as a goal assumes that the stable adulthood that was available in the 1960s (for a large proportion of the population) shows a blindness to the changing nature of adulthood itself. Transitions research in Australia has identified the same groups of young people (young people who are poor, those in rural and isolated areas, and young Indigenous people) as disadvantaged and at risk for over 30 years, but this information has provided little in the way of insight into how to address these problems. A social generations approach at least offers the potential to understand how transition is two-sided: Young people (as all humans do) are moving through a life course; society is also changing, and it is the interaction between the two that defines the new youth and new adulthood of today.

The Generation Debate

The idea that a focus on social generations provides new insights has stimulated discussion within the youth studies community. At the heart of this discussion and debate is the question of what has changed and what has stayed the same. While some of this discussion has been promoted by researchers advocating for the continuing value of transitions approaches, much has reflected a distrust of the concept of social generation. From 2006 on, the *Journal of Youth Studies* has hosted an ongoing debate about the value of social generations as a framework, in which researchers debated the conclusion that there was "considerable convergence of evidence both within Australia and across other western countries of similarities in new life patterns that could be considered to constitute a generational shift in contrast to an extended transition to adulthood" (Wyn & Woodman, 2006, p. 497).

Ken Roberts (2006) defended the use of a transitions approach, saying that Wyn and Woodman's diagnosis—of overdomination by a transition paradigm and attention to education and work and neglect of generation shifts—was mistaken, and therefore the use of a social generations approach was a remedy for a nonexistent illness (p. 264). Roberts argued that transitions approaches do not assume linearity in the direction of transitions and that they are not inherently based on a developmental model. However, he upheld a normative and somewhat essentialist notion of adulthood, because "eventually most young people reach adult destinations. . . . They marry, become parents, and achieve employment that will support an adult lifestyle." Roberts, 2006, p. 264). He referred to the new complexities in finding secure and stable work as "disorderly" transitions that were mainly experienced by the disadvantaged and felt that "even if disorderliness had become the new rule, this would not render the transition paradigm obsolete" (p. 264). In other words, things have stayed much the same, despite some hiccups for the disadvantaged. In retrospect, it is clear that there is agreement that some things may have changed but that the researchers are drawing on different kinds of evidence. Whereas Ken Roberts was drawing on statistical data interpreted through long-standing frameworks, which showed young people eventually reaching predetermined markers of progress, Wyn, Woodman, and their colleagues, drawing on the rich data set of the Life Patterns research program that includes both quantitative and qualitative evidence, were searching for a conceptual framework that enabled them to give voice to the distinctive, subjective views of the young people and found this in a social generations framework that acknowledges the intersecting forces of subjective dispositions and social conditions.

More recently, Alan France and Steven Roberts (2015) took issue with the concept of social generation because of the belief that a social generation is homogeneous, with a collective identity—thereby meaning that a scholar using the concept was at least implicitly demoting the relevance of class (and presumably gender and other social divisions). In their view, the concept of social generation was in danger of becoming a new orthodoxy with the threatening prospect of implying that class analysis would become redundant. The question of what has changed and what has stayed the same in young people's lives is important, because inequalities (not just class-based ones) are on the rise. However, while surveys show that inequality is enduring, interviews with young people show that the ways in which this is experienced, and by whom, changes. New inequalities are emerging and the ways in which young people experience them is distinctive to their generation (e.g., inequalities in housing, homelessness, precarious work, gender-based violence). We have argued (Woodman & Wyn, 2015) that social change and new risks are not facades behind which more real, and long-standing, forms of inequality are hidden but are central to the way inequalities—including but not limited to, class, gender, and race—are made in the conditions facing emerging generations of young people. A generations approach provides a robust framework for asking how class, gender, and race, among others, are being made an remade in young lives in the context of a rapidly changing social world.

Conclusion

This chapter has taken up how we theorize—and, hence, see—young people's lives. Theoretical frameworks (such as, social generation, transitions, class, and gender) direct researchers to "see" particular social dynamics and hence to draw on particular kinds of evidence. Patterns of transition and of inequality generally tell a story of a mainstream and an at-risk group. It is true that these broad patterns can be found across time and in different places as revealed by statistical patterns. However, explorations of young people's subjective interpretations of their lives tell a story of differentiation (from and with a generation) and of the diverse ways in which lives are built. We have subjected the idea of youth transitions—a "key word" in youth studies—to critique. Our aim has been to invite those interested in the lives of young people to consider the ways in which changing social conditions also change what it means to be young—and what it may mean to be an adult. If nothing else, thinking twice about using the word *transition* may encourage youth researchers and policymakers to reflect on what young people are supposed to be transferring in to—and how all of our lives are subject to increasingly global changes. A generations approach leads us to the same conclusion that Furlong et al. (2017) come to—that it is time to shift the focus from the supposed deficits in young people and explore instead the conditions that young people contend with, including the policy arrangements that enable insecure work, unaffordable housing, and education debts.

References

Anagnost, A., Arai, A., & Ren, H. (Eds). (2013). *Global futures in East Asia: Youth, nation and the new economy in uncertain times*, Stanford, CA: Stanford University Press.

Andres, L., & Wyn, J. (2010). *The making of a generation: The children of the 1970's in adulthood.* Toronto, ON: University of Toronto Press.

Arnett, J. (2000). Emerging Adulthood. A theory of development from the late teens through the twenties, *American Psychologist, 55*(5), 469–480.

Australian Bureau of Statistics. (2009, December). Patterns in work. *4102.0: Australian Social Trends.* Retrieved from https://www.abs.gov.au/AUSSTATS/abs@.nsf/Lookup/4102.0Main+Features50Dec+2009

Australian Bureau of Statistics. (2013, April). Young adults then and now. *4102.0: Australian Social Trends.* Retrieved from https://www.abs.gov.au/AUSSTATS/abs@.nsf/Lookup/4102.0Main+Features40April+2013

Blatterer, H. (2007). *Coming of age in times of uncertainty*. New York, NY: Berghahn Books.

Bourdieu, P. (1990). *The logic of practice*. Cambridge, England: Polity.

Bourdieu, P. (1993). *Sociology in question*. London, England: SAGE.

Brown, P., Lauder, H., & Ashton, D. (2011). *The global auction: The broken promises of education, jobs and incomes*. New York, NY: Oxford University Press.

Cohen, P., & Ainley, P. (2000). "In the country of the blind?" Youth studies and cultural studies in Britain. *Journal of Youth Studies, 3*(1), 79–95.

Crofts, J., Cuervo, H., Wyn, J., Smith, G., & Woodman, D. (2015). *Life patterns: Ten years following generation Y.* Melbourne, Australia: Youth Research Centre.

Cuervo, H., & Wyn J. (2014). Reflections on the use of spatial and relational metaphors in youth studies. *Journal of Youth Studies, 17*(7), 901–915.

Cuervo, H., & Wyn, J. (2016). An unspoken crisis: The "scarring effects" of the complex nexus between education and work on two generations of young Australians. *International Journal of Lifelong Education, 35*(2), 122–135.

du Bois-Reymond, M., & Stauber, B. (2005). Biographical turning points in young people's transitions to work across Europe. In H. Helve & G. Holm (Eds.), *Contemporary youth research: Local expressions and global connections* (pp. 63–75). Aldershot, England: Ashgate.

Dwyer, P., & Wyn, J. (2001). *Youth, education and risk: Facing the future.* London, England: Routledge Falmer.

Elias, N. (2012). *On the process of civilisation: Sociogenetic and psychogenetic investigations.* (translated by E. Jephcott). Dublin, Ireland: University College Dublin Press.

Erikson, E. H. (1965). *Childhood and society.* Harmondsworth, England: Penguin Books.

Farrugia D., & Watson J. (2011). If anyone helps you then you're a failure": Youth homelessness, identity, and relationships in late modernity. In S. Beadle, R. Holdsworth, & J. Wyn (Eds.), *For we are young and . . . ? Young people in a time of uncertainty* (pp. 142–57). Carlton, Australia: Melbourne University Press.

Feixa, C., & Cangas, Y. G. (2005). The socio-cultural construction of youth in Latin America: achievements and failures. In H. Helve & G. Holm (Eds.), *Contemporary youth research: Local expressions and global connections* (pp. 39–48). Aldershot, England: Ashgate.

Finn, B. C. (1991). *Young people's participation in post-compulsory education and training: Report of the AEC Review Committee.* Canberra, Australia: Australian Government Publishing Service.

Furlong, A. (2013). *Youth studies: An introduction.* New York, NY: Routledge.

Furlong, A., Goodwin, J. H., Hadfield, S., Hall, S., Lowden, K., & O'Connor, H. (2017). *Young people in the labour market: Past and present.* London, England: Routledge.

France, A., & Roberts, S. (2015). The problem of social generations: A critique of the new emerging orthodoxy in youth studies. *Journal of Youth Studies, 18*(2), 215–230.

Hall, G. S. (1904). *Adolescence.* Englewood Cliffs, NJ: Prentice-Hall.

Hall, T., Coffey, A., & Lashua, B. (2009). Steps and stages: Rethinking transitions in youth and place. *Journal of Youth Studies, 12*(5), 547–561.

International Labour Organisation. (2013). *Global employment trends for youth 2013: A generation at risk.* Geneva, Switzerland: International Institute for Labour Studies.

McLeod, J., & Wright, K. (2016). What does wellbeing do? An approach to defamiliarize keywords in youth studies. *Journal of Youth Studies, 19*(6), 766–792.

Kelly, P. (2006). The entrepreneurial self and "youth at-risk": Exploring the horizons of identity in the twenty-first century. *Journal of Youth Studies, 9*(1), 17–32.

Lamb, S., Jackson, J., Walstab, A., & Huo, S. (2015) *Educational opportunity in Australia 2015: Who succeeds and who misses out.* Melbourne, Australia: Centre for International Research on Education Systems, for the Mitchell Institute.

Mannheim, K. (1952). The problem of generations. In P. Kecskemeti (Ed.), *Essays on the sociology of knowledge* (pp. 276–322). London, England: Routledge. (Original work published 1923)

Mayer, E. C. (1992). *Putting general education to work: The key competencies report* (Report of the Committee to Advise the Australian Education Council and Ministers for Vocational Employment, Education and Training). Canberra, Australia: Australian Government Publishing Service.

Mizen, P. (2002). Putting the politics back into youth studies: Keynesianism, monetarism and the changing state. *Journal of Youth Studies, 5*(1), 5–20.

OECD. (2013). *OECD employment outlook 2013.* Paris: Author.

Piaget, J. (1954). *The construction of reality in the child.* New York, NY: Basic Books.

Roberts, S. (2011). Beyond "NEET" and "tidy" pathways: considering the "missing middle" of youth transition studies. *Journal of Youth Studies, 14*(1), 21–39.

Silva, J. M. (2013). *Coming up short: Working-class adulthood in an age of uncertainty.* New York, NY: Oxford University Press.

Standing, G. (2011). *The precariat: The new dangerous class.* London, England: Bloomsbury Academic.

Talburt, S., & Lesko, N. (2012) An introduction to seven technologies of youth studies. In N. Lesko & S. Talburt (Eds.), *Youth Studies: Keywords and Movements* (pp. 1–10). New York, NY: Routledge.

Woodman, D. (2011). A generations approach to youth research. In S. Beadle, R. Holdsworth, & J. Wyn (Eds.), *For we are young and . . . ? Young people in a time of uncertainty: possibilities and challenges* (pp. 29–48). Melbourne, Australia: Melbourne University Press.

Woodman, D. (2013). Researching "ordinary" young people in a changing world: The sociology of generations and the "missing middle" in youth research. *Sociological Research Online, 18*(1), 179–190.

Woodman, D., & Wyn, J. (2013). Youth policy and generations: Why youth policy needs to "rethink youth." *Social Policy and Society, 12*(2), 265–275.

Woodman, D., & Wyn, J. (2015). *Youth and generation: Rethinking change and inequality in young people's lives.* London, England: SAGE.

Wyn, J., Cuervo, H., Crofts, J., & Woodman, D. (2017). Gendered transitions from education to work: The mysterious relationship between the fields of education and work. *Journal of Sociology, 53*(2), 492–506. doi:1440783317700736

Wyn, J., & Woodman, D. (2006). Generation, youth and social change in Australia. *Journal of Youth Studies, 9*(5), 495–514.

Wyn, J., & Woodman, D (2007). Researching youth in a context of social change: A reply to Roberts. *Journal of Youth Studies, 10*(3), 373–381.

Yeung, W., & Alipio, C. (2013). Transitioning to adulthood in Asia: School, work, and family life. *Annals of the American Academy of Political and Social Science, 646*, 6–27.

Index

For the benefit of digital users, indexed terms that span two pages (e.g., 52–53) may, on occasion, appear on only one of those pages.

Tables and figures are indicated by *t* and *f* following the page number